CONCISE ENCYCLOPEDIA

BLOOMSBURY
BOOKS

First published in this edition 1994 by Bloomsbury Books,
an imprint of the Godfrey Cave Group, 42 Bloomsbury Street,
London, WC1B 3QJ.

© 1994 Geddes & Grosset Ltd,
David Dale House, New Lanark, Scotland.

ISBN 1 85471 288 8

Printed and bound in France.
by Maury Eurolivres

Contents

SPACE AND ASTRONOMY

For many centuries observing space and questioning the origins and evolution of the universe has provided mankind with one of its great challenges. Observational records exist which date from the ancient civilizations of China, Babylonia and Egypt, yet even with the modern development of deep-space probes and powerful radio-telescopes, there are still many questions which remain unanswered.

This section provides an up-to-date dictionary of terms commonly used in the study of space and astronomy. The entries are arranged A to Z with cross-references given in SMALL CAPITALS.

*

antimatter is matter that is made up of antiparticles, that is particles that have the same mass as ordinary matter but have opposite values for other properties (e.g. charge). So if matter is made up of electrons, neutrons and protons, antimatter is composed of *positrons*, anti-neutrons and anti-protons. The coming together of matter and antimatter results in the destruction of both particles and the production of energy.

asteroid alternatively called a *meteorite*, is actually a *planetoid*; a rocky or metallic body that is one of many orbiting the Sun between the orbits of Mars and Jupiter. Most of these tiny planets are very small, some reaching a few hundred kilometres across but the largest, *Ceres*, has a diameter of about 1000 kilometres. Collisions between asteroids sometimes produce smaller pieces that occasionally fall to Earth and these fragments are also called meteorites. The many craters seen on the surfaces of some planets are probably due to asteroid impact.

Meteors, or *shooting stars*, are the remnants of comet debris, which should they fall into the Earth's atmosphere, burn up as they are destroyed by friction (*see also* COMET).

astronaut is someone who has undergone very special and rigorous training to prepare for space travel.

an astronaut

The first astronaut was Yuri Gagarin who orbited the Earth in 1961 and his spacecraft *Vostok I* took 98 minutes for one orbit. Valentina Tereshkova was the first woman in space. Both these astronauts were from the former Soviet Union now the CIS.

July, 1969 saw an American team actually landing on the Moon and since then there have been numerous missions by the CIS to an orbiting SPACE STATION, and America has launched several SPACE SHUTTLES, the first reusable vehicle capable of space flight.

When a rocket is launched from Earth there are tremendous forces pushing down on the astronaut, due to the enormously high acceleration required to reach orbit. An astronaut must therefore be very fit, and highly skilled in science and technology so that he or she can operate the equipment in the spacecraft and carry out numerous experiments in space. The early astronauts were test pilots from the armed forces but today more scientists and doctors are involved. Over 400 people have now flown in space although only a small proportion are women. To help train astronauts for the weightlessness of space, special aeroplanes are used. These dive at high speed from a great height to produce a weightless effect for a short time. When actually in space it is necessary to wear a space suit which is specially designed to cater for the astronaut's safety. The suit is made up of layers of special material with tubular networks: it provides protection from radiation, the cold of space and supplies air from a portable pack (or life support system). The helmet has a visor to cut out harmful rays from the Sun and a microphone with headphones to allow communication with other astronauts on the spacecraft.

astronomy is the scientific study of the various bodies in the 'heavens' and has been in existence for thousands of years. From the earliest times, people have plotted the positions of the stars and planets, devising a yearly calendar governed by the movements of the Earth and Moon relative to the Sun. When making a journey, people in former times always used the positions of the various heavenly bodies to guide the direction which they took. Hence some knowledge of astronomy was very important to early travellers and explorers. Early astronomers gained a great deal of knowledge from their studies and were able to predict the appearance of COMETS and ECLIPSES. It became possible to make many more discoveries in astronomy following the invention of the lens telescope, in 1608. This was devised by a Dutchman, Hans Lippershey, who was a maker of spectacles by profession rather than an astronomer!

Up until the Middle Ages, it was thought that the Earth was at the centre of the universe and that other heavenly bodies revolved around it. Nicolaus Copernicus, during the 1540s, put forward the idea (which had first been taught, in 170 BC, by Aristarchus) that the Earth travelled around the Sun. The idea of the Sun being the centre of the SOLAR SYSTEM, gradually gained acceptance.

In the latter half of the 20th century, SATELLITES and space probes have given us much new and exciting information about the farthest regions of space. For example, modern astronomers have spent (and continue to spend) many years studying the wealth of data sent back to Earth by such space probes as *Viking* 1 and 2 and *Voyager* 1 and 2.

aurora this is the luminous and often highly coloured streaks or sheets of light in the sky, formed by high-speed, electrically charged solar particles entering the upper atmosphere of the Earth. Here, the particles give up electrons and molecules are created associated with the release of light. These effects are related to SUNSPOT activity and are called the *Northern Lights* (aurora borealis) in the northern hemisphere, and the *Southern Lights* (aurora australis) in the southern hemisphere.

big bang is a theory which has been put forward by some scientists to explain the origins of the universe. It proposes that about 15,000 million years ago there was a vast explosion which sent all the material spinning rapidly outwards as a mass of atoms. Physicists think that in a matter of minutes, a huge cloud of hydrogen atoms had formed and continued to spread outwards, dispersing into separate clouds as it did so. These hydrogen atoms make up about 90% of the universe, and the clouds formed GALAXIES of stars including the MILKY WAY. The outward expansion is still continuing but it is thought that this may one day cease. All the material may eventually collapse and collide together (the BIG CRUNCH) but it is thought that before this occurs, the Sun will burn hotter and the Earth will be consumed in about 5000 million years from the present.

There is much speculation about the origin of the dust and gases which were scattered at the time of the big bang, and also the possible cause of the huge explosion.

big crunch gravity attracts the galaxies in the Universe together, and the force it exerts depends on their mass, but it is over-ridden by the expansion and moving apart which is still continuing, possibly as a result of the BIG BANG. The Big Crunch theory proposes that there may be hidden material (consisting of single atomic particles) between the galaxies which, if present in sufficient quantities, could add to the gravitational pull. This extra gravity might be enough to slow down and halt the expansion and indeed put it into reverse. If this occurred the galaxies would be pulled together, collide and be destroyed in the Big Crunch.

binary star a pair of stars held together by the force of gravity which orbit around each other. These double stars may be so close to one another that each goes round the other in a few hours. In this instance they are so close as to be almost touching and travel very fast. Others are vast distances apart and travel around each other in thousands or even millions of years. Many stars in the MILKY WAY are binary stars and each member of the pair may differ in shape, size and brightness.

black hole it is thought that there are black holes in space which are collapsed stars, and the proposal for these was first put forward by Karl Schwarzschild, a German astronomer, in 1916. It is believed that when a star (which may be many times larger than our Sun), comes to the end of its 'life,' it collapses so quickly that no material, not even light, can be emitted. This type of event is known as an *implosion* and because of the enormous gravitational force of the collapsed material, it is seen as a hole from which no light escapes. The space around the black hole is curved into a complete circle. It is thought that many apparent single stars are in fact BINARY STARS with a black hole as a partner. Much recent work on black holes has been carried out by Stephen Hawking, a British physicist (*see also* NEUTRON STAR).

calendar calendars were devised by Man to mark the passage of time, and were devised by early astronomers according to the phases of the Moon or on the orbit of the Earth around the Sun. The 365 day year was based on the *Julian* calendar introduced by the Roman Emperor, Julius Caesar, in 46BC. In fact, the Earth takes 365¼ days to go once around the Sun (a solar year) so on this system, every fourth or *leap* year, an extra day has to be added. In fact, the calendar year is still inaccurate and several proposals have been put forward for its reform.

comet is composed of rock, ice, dust and frozen gases and usually cannot be seen. A comet becomes visible when it approaches closer to the Sun because it appears to flare up and look bright. It has a *head*, consisting of a solid core or nucleus of rock surrounded by a layer of gas, the *corona*. The nucleus is irregular in shape and just a few kilometres in diameter (In fact Halley's comet is elongated and is roughly 15 x 4km). A comet moves in a long, eccentric orbit around the Sun and one complete cycle is called a *period*. The orbit may take the comet a long distance from the Sun when it cannot be seen. Near to the Sun, particles of dust and gas are knocked away from the head of the comet and trail out to form a brightly glowing *tail*. When the orbit takes the comet away from the Sun it leaves tail first. Comets are believed to be left over remnants of the BIG BANG explosion and each time they approach the Sun, some of the ice melts. Eventually, it is thought that a comet loses its ice, dust and gas and becomes a piece of orbiting rock. The shortest period belongs to Ericke's comet and is only $3^1/_2$ years. Others have much longer periods lasting hundreds or even thousands of years (e.g. Ikeya-Seki, 880 years).

The most familiar comet, which has excited interest for a long time, is Halley's comet which appears every 76 years and is next due in 2062. In 1986 the spacecraft, *Giotto*, belonging to the European Space Agency, flew to within 539 km of the comet, gaining valuable information and photographs, until its cameras were obscured by dust.

constellation a group of stars which are placed together and given a name, although there is no scientific basis for the grouping. Many were named by astronomers of the Babylonian empire some 2000 years before the birth of Christ and the most ancient form the twelve signs of the zodiac. Thirty nine constellations are visible in the northern hemisphere and forty six in the southern. Familiar examples in the northern hemisphere include the Great Bear (*Ursa Major*), the Bull (*Taurus*), the Hunter (*Orion*) and the Pole or North Star.

corona the coloured rings (seen through thin cloud) around the Sun or Moon, caused by DIFFRACTION of light by water droplets.

cosmic rays these are 'rays' composed of ionizing radiation from space and consisting mainly of protons (*see* ATOM) and alpha particles (helium nuclei) (*see* RADIOACTIVITY), and a small proportion of heavier atomic nuclei. When these particles interact with the Earth's atmosphere, secondary radiation is created, including mesons, neutrons (*see* ELEMENTARY PARTICLES), positrons (*see* ANTIMATTER) and electrons (*see* ATOM). Cosmic rays seem to come from three sources: galactic rays, possibly formed from SUPERNOVA explosions; solar cosmic rays and the SOLAR WIND.

daylength the length of daylight changes throughout the year except on the equator where there are approximately 12 hours of light and 12 hours of darkness. The changes occur because the

Earth is tilted on its axis, and it alters on a daily basis as the Earth proceeds on its orbit around the Sun. At any point in the year, while countries in the northern hemisphere are tilted more towards the Sun, those in the south are further away and vice versa. This governs the onset of the four different seasons of the year. Latitude also affects daylength, and those countries at latitudes greater than 67° north or south experience the midnight sun during midsummer when it does not become dark at all. The lengths of day and night are the same throughout the world on the two equinoxes (21th March and 23rd September).

Earth the Earth is one of a group of nine planets which orbit a star that we call the SUN. It occurs in one small part of the GALAXY (also called the MILKY WAY) which is referred to as the SOLAR SYSTEM. The Earth is the fifth largest of the planets and the third nearest to the Sun. Most of the Earth's surface is covered by the oceans – about two-thirds compared to one third which is land. A layer of air, the ATMOSPHERE, surrounds the Earth which is sub-divided into a number of different regions according to height above the surface. The Earth, as viewed from space, is like a blue ball or sphere which is flattened at both the poles. At the equator, the radius of the Earth is 6378 km or 3963 miles.

The Earth itself is composed of four main layers; an outer *crust* overlying a *mantle*, followed by an *outer core* and *inner core*. The rocky crust varies in thickness, being about 40 km thick under the continents and 8 km under the oceans. It 'floats' on the mantle which is made up of extremely hot rock and is about 2900 km thick (*see* PLATE TECTONICS). The core is so hot that it is part liquid, with a temperature in the region of 6500 K. The outer core is believed to be about 2250 km thick and is thought to be more liquid than the inner core which is solid and composed mainly of iron and nickel. The Earth is the only one of the nine planets able to support life which exists entirely in a narrow band on or near the crust. The Earth's weight increases every day by about 25 tonnes because fine space dust finds its way down to the surface.

eclipse the name given to a total or partial disappearance of a planet or moon by passing into the shadow of another. A *solar eclipse* occurs when a new moon passes between the Earth and the Sun. A *lunar eclipse* happens when the Sun, Earth and Moon are in a line and the Earth is situated between the Moon and the Sun and its shadow falls on the Moon. Different types of eclipse happen each year but a solar eclipse usually appears as partial when viewed from Earth. Even during a complete solar eclipse, the Moon is only just large enough to cover the Sun, and the shadow which it throws onto one part of the Earth is only a few kilometres wide so few people are able to see it. It is generally the case that the Moon is not completely in line and so the eclipse is only partial.

a solar eclipse

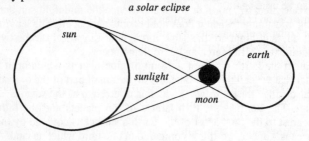

escape velocity this is the velocity necessary for a rocket or space probe to escape from the pull exerted by the gravity of a planet. The velocity varies according to the mass and diameter of the planet. For the Earth it is 25,000 mph and for the Moon, 5350 mph. No light escapes from a black hole because the escape velocity is greater than the speed of light.

expansion theory the theory that the galaxies of space are still rapidly moving apart which may have been caused by the BIG BANG explosion. The speed at which the galaxies are travelling is calculated by studying a property of light known as the *red shift*. For every extra million light years of distance (one light year is around 9.5 million million kilometres), the speed the galaxies are travelling increases by about 15 km per second. The relationship between speed and distance is called *Hubble's law*.

galaxy the name given to a huge group or band of stars. Our galaxy, which includes the Sun, is also called the MILKY WAY and it contains about 100,000 million stars. It is thought that there are many million more galaxies as well as the Milky Way, and the nearest large one to us is called *Andromeda*. Galaxies have different shapes, the Milky Way and Andromeda being spiral-shaped, others appearing as saucers. The Milky Way is approximately 10^5 light years across.

heat shield a spacecraft encounters extreme and intense heat especially when it re-enters the Earth's atmosphere from space.

The heat is caused by friction because the space ship is travelling so fast. A heat shield is a special heat resistant layer which prevents the spacecraft from burning up. In earlier space ships the shields were constructed from materials that could not be re-used, as they burned but only very slowly. The space shuttle has special heat-resistant tiles composed of silicon and carbon which can be used again.

implosion is the opposite of an explosion. It is a rapid inrushing or collapse of materials inwards instead of outwards. Stars may *implode*, the gravitational force pulling all materials inwards. These collapsed stars are very dense in the centre and form a BLACK HOLE or NEUTRON STAR.

infrared astronomy the study of infrared radiation (*see* ELECTROMAGNETIC WAVES) given off from heavenly bodies such as the stars and planets. Infrared radiation has a wavelength of 0.8 to 1000μm which is shorter than that of radio waves and longer than that of visible light. Infrared radiation passes through parts of the galaxy obscured by dust, highlighting otherwise invisible structures. More infrared radiation is emitted by hotter structures than by colder ones, and it penetrates the Earth's atmosphere more readily than visible light. The radiation tends to be obscured by water vapour in the Earth's atmosphere but this problem can be partially overcome by siting observatories at high altitudes. Hence infrared astronomers are able to gain valuable information about distant space bodies and have discovered 'young' stars which have not begun to glow brightly.

interstellar medium the matter found throughout space and comprising gas and dust – mainly hydrogen, helium and interstellar molecules. In all it amounts to about 10% of the mass of the galaxy.

Jupiter is the giant planet of our SOLAR SYSTEM, more than one thousand times larger than Earth. It is one of the 'gas giants' being composed mainly of hydrogen. Its atmosphere is made up of hydrogen with approximately 15% helium and traces of water, ammonia and methane. This forms a liquid 'shell' surrounding a zone of metallic hydrogen (that is the hydrogen is compressed so much that it behaves like metal), which itself surrounds a core made partly of rock and ice. This core has a mass ten times greater than that of the Earth. Violent storms and winds rage around Jupiter whipping up bands of frozen chemicals such as ammonia. One such storm is the *Great Red Spot,* visible on the surface as an enormous cyclone that has probably lasted for hundreds of years. Jupiter spins very rapidly so that one of its days lasts for only nine hours and fifty minutes. This rapid spin drags the whirling gases into bands which appear dark and light. A year on Jupiter lasts for nearly 12 Earth years because the planet is farther from the Sun and has a greater orbit. Jupiter is the fifth planet from the Sun and because of its rapid rate of spin, it bulges outwards at its equator. Hence the diameter at the equator is 142,800 km compared to 134,000 km at the poles. The outermost layers of Jupiter are very cold, in the region of -150°C, but the very centre of the planet is extremely hot probably exceeding the temperature of the Sun. Jupiter's great mass means that it exerts a strong gravitational pull and is able to hold down the molecules of gas which swirl around its bulk. A person on Jupiter would be twice as heavy compared to his or her weight on Earth.

Jupiter has its own satellites or moons orbiting around it and some of these are as large as Earth's moon. The *Voyager* spacecraft passed close to Jupiter in 1979 and sent fascinating information about the planet and its moons back to Earth. This revealed that two of the moons, called *Ganymede* and *Callisto*, have craters pitting their surface like Earth's moon. Another moon, *Europa*, was shown to be a ball of yellow ice. The closest moon to Jupiter, *Io*, has several erupting volcanoes and a surface of yellow sulphur. Enormous electrical energy exists between Io and Jupiter estimated to be equivalent, in any one second, to all the electrical power generated in the United States.

light year a measure of the distance travelled by light in one year, which is in the region of 9.467×10^{12} kilometres. Light travels at 299,792 kilometres per second and it takes 8 minutes for it to reach Earth from the Sun. The great distances between the various galaxies and heavenly bodies can be measured in light years. The nearest star to Earth (after the Sun), is more than four light years distant and is called *Proxima Centauri* (*see also* PARSEC).

magellanic clouds are two separate GALAXIES, detached from the MILKY WAY which appear, when viewed from the southern hemisphere, as diffuse patches of light. The largest is approximately 180,000 LIGHT YEARS away and the smallest is 230,000 light years distant. Both contain several thousand million stars. They are the nearest galaxies and part of a larger group which includes the Milky Way. They were first discovered by a Portuguese sailor called Magellan in 1520 and can only be viewed from near the equator or in the southern hemisphere.

NEBULAe are present in both clouds indicating the formation of new stars.

Mars is the fourth planet in the SOLAR SYSTEM and the one nearest to the Earth. Its orbit lies between that of the EARTH and JUPITER, and it is about half the size of Earth. It has a thin atmosphere, exerting a pressure less than one hundredth of that of the Earth. It also has a small mass about one tenth of that of the Earth so that a person on Mars would weigh about 60% less than Earth weight. Mars is often called the *Red Planet* as it has a dusty, reddish surface strewn with rocks. It is much colder than the Earth with an atmosphere mainly of carbon dioxide which is frozen at the two poles. The polar ice caps melt and re-form as the seasons change. Minimum surface temperatures are in the region of -100°C with the maximum only about -30°C. A year on Mars lasts for 687 Earth days and the length of one day is almost the same, 24 hours and 37 minutes. The diameter of Mars is 6794 km and the crust in the northern part of the planet is composed of basalt (volcanic rock, *see* IGNEOUS ROCKS). There are many extinct volcanoes, canyons and impact craters and evidence of water erosion at some stage in the planet's history. The mountains are much higher, and the valleys deeper than those which exist on Earth, hence there must have been violent movements of the crust during the past. The deepest valley called *Valles Marineris*, is 4000 km long, 75 km wide and up to 7 km deep. The highest mountain, *Olympus Mons*, rises 23 km from the surface of Mars, and is three times taller than Mount Everest.

There are two small, irregularly shaped SATELLITES or moons orbiting Mars, called *Phobos* and *Deimos*. Phobos, the larger, is only 27 km from one end to the other and just 6000 km above the planet's surface. Its orbit is a gradually descending spiral and it is estimated that in 40 million years' time it will collide with Mars. The *Viking* space probe landed on Mars in 1976 and many valuable photographs were taken and soil samples obtained. There had been speculation for many years about the possibility of the existence of life on Mars but the space probe failed to discover any evidence for this.

matter any substance that occupies space and has mass, the material of which the UNIVERSE is made.

megaparsec a unit for defining distance of objects outside the galaxy, equal to 10^6 PARSECS (or 3.26×10^6 light years).

Mercury the first planet of the SOLAR SYSTEM and nearest to the

SUN. It has no atmosphere, and so during the day the surface temperature reaches 425°C (enough to melt lead), but at night the heat all escapes and it becomes intensely cold, -170°C. A day on Mercury lasts for 59 Earth days but the planet travels its orbit so fast that a year is only 88 days. Mercury is a very dense planet for, although it is only slightly bigger than the Moon, it has an enormous mass which is almost the same as that of the Earth. It is thought that this is accounted for by Mercury having a huge metallic core. Very little was known about the surface of the planet until it was visited by the *Mariner 10* spacecraft which passed to within 800 km of it in 1974. It revealed that Mercury has a wrinkled surface with thousands of craters which have been caused by the impact of meteors and other larger space bodies. The largest crater, 1300 km across and known as the *Caloris Basin*, must have been caused by the collision of an enormous space body. Mercury has very little gravity and an elliptical orbit, which takes it to within 46 million kilometres of the Sun at its nearest point and 70 million kilometres when farthest away.

Milky Way the galaxy, which includes the SOLAR SYSTEM, and consists of millions of STARS and NEBULAE. It stretches for about 100,000 light years and our solar system is in the region of 30,000 light years from the centre. It has a spiral shape with trailing *arms* which slowly revolve around the centre. The solar system is one tiny part occurring a long way out on one of the trailing spiral arms. There are probably millions of galaxies, including others with the same spiral shape. The Milky Way appears as a glowing cloud of light thrown out by the many millions of stars it contains.

Moon the Earth's one satellite, which orbits the Earth at an average distance of 384,000 kilometres (238,600 miles). It has no atmosphere, water or magnetic field, and surface temperatures reach extremes of 127°C and -173°C. It takes nearly 28 days to complete its orbit around the Earth, and always presents the same face towards Earth. As it orbits around the Earth each 28 days, the Moon passes through *phases* from new to first quarter to full to last quarter and back to new again. One half of the moon is always in sunlight and the phases depend upon the amount of the lit half which can be seen from Earth. A *new moon* occurs when the Earth, Moon and Sun are approximately in line with one another, and none of the lit half can be seen at all; it appears that there is no Moon. About a week later a small *sliver* of the lit half can be seen from Earth and this grows throughout the month until the whole of the lit half is visible at *full moon*. In the second half of the cycle, the amount of the lit half of the Moon which can be seen from Earth gradually declines once more. When the Moon is apparently growing in size, it is called *waxing* and when it is declining it is called *waning*.

The diameter of the Moon is 3476 kilometres and its mass is 0.0123 of that of the Earth. Its density is 0.61 of that of the Earth and it has a thick crust (up to 125 kilometres or 75 miles) made up of volcanic rocks. There is probably a small core of iron, with a radius of approximately 300 kilometres (186 miles).

The surface of the Moon is heavily cratered, probably due to meteorite impact, and the largest (viewed from Earth), is 300 kilometres (186 miles) across and surrounded by gigantic cliffs, (up to 4250 metres or 14,000 feet high). The dark side of the Moon was a mystery until 1959 when *Luna 3*, a Russian space rocket took photographs of it as it flew round. The surface is dry and rocky and in 1969, the American astronauts Neil Armstrong and Edwin Aldrin made the first human footprints on its dusty surface. Other spacecraft have since landed and brought back samples of lunar rock and soil, and analysis of these has revealed that the Moon must be at least 4000 million years old. A distinctive feature of the Moon is its *maria* (sing. *mare*) which were once thought to be seas. The name was coined before modern study found them to be dry, but their origin is not yet established although it is thought that they date from 3300 million years ago. The tendency now is to dispense with the Latin, e.g. *Sea of Showers* instead of *Mare Imbrium*.

nebula (pl. *nebulae*) a cloud of interstellar matter, consisting of gases and dust, in which stars originate and also die. When stars die, their gases and dust are poured back out into space forming *planetary nebulae*. Dark patches in the Milky Way galaxy are nebulae which obliterate the light from the stars behind them. Sometimes surrounding stars throw their light onto a nebula making it glow brightly. The *Orion Nebula* has a cluster of stars being formed within its cloud. It is 1300 LIGHT YEARS away and about 15 light years from one side to the other.

Neptune is normally the eighth planet of the SOLAR SYSTEM with its orbit between that of URANUS and PLUTO. However, for about twenty years in every 248 years, Pluto's orbit approaches closer to the Sun than Neptune's. At the time of writing, the two planets are within this period and Neptune will be the outermost one until 1999. Neptune is a vast planet, one of the *gas giants*, and is around 4497 million kilometres from the Sun. It is extremely cold with surface temperatures of approximately -200°C, and the atmosphere consists mainly of methane, hydrogen and helium. The diameter at the poles is 48,700 kilometres and at the equator it is 48,400 km which is about four times that of the Earth. The mass of the planet is 17 times greater than that of Earth and it takes 165 years to circle once around the Sun. Neptune is such a long way from the Earth that it can only be viewed using the most powerful telescopes, and even then it appears to be minute. Two astronomers, John Couch Adams in 1845 in Britain, and Urbain Leverrier in France in 1846, worked out the existence and position of Neptune before it could actually be seen. They noticed that the path of the orbit of nearby URANUS was not as expected, and worked out that it was being affected by the gravitational pull of another planet. A year later, Neptune was viewed for the first time. Neptune spins once on its axis every 18 to 20 hours and probably has a core of frozen rock and ice.

Most information about Neptune has been obtained from the *Voyager 2* space probe in August, 1989. It took 9000 photographs which shows that Neptune is surrounded by a faint series of rings. There is a large dark cloud, the size of the Earth, called the *Dark Spot* which has a spinning oval shape. Winds whip through the atmosphere at velocities of 2000 kilometres per hour and there are white methane clouds which constantly change shape. Neptune has 8 SATELLITES or moons, two of which are large and are called *Triton* and *Nereid.* Triton is the largest moon and is about the same size as MERCURY; its orbit is in the opposite direction to that of the other moons. It has a frozen surface with icy volcanic mountains and appears to have lakes of frozen gas and methane. The thin atmosphere of Neptune is composed mainly of nitrogen gas.

neutron star a small body with a seemingly impossibly high density. A star that has exhausted its fuel supply collapses under gravitational forces so intense that its electrons and protons are crushed together and form neutrons. This produces a star ten million times more dense than a WHITE DWARF – equivalent to a cupful of matter weighing many million tons on Earth. Although no neutron stars have definitely been identified, it is thought that PULSARS may belong to this group.

nova (plural *novae*) in the literal sense this is a new star, (nova being Latin for *new*), but it may also be a star that suddenly burns brighter by a factor of five to ten thousand. It seems that a nova is one partner in a BINARY STAR. The smaller star burns much hotter than the sun while the other partner is a vast expanse of hot red mist called a RED GIANT. An explosion results if cooler gas from the red cloud reaches the hot star, causing it to burn up more brightly – a nova. A red giant may eventually become a WHITE DWARF.

orbit the path of one heavenly body moving around another which results from the gravitational force attracting them together. The lighter body moves around the heavier one which is itself also in motion. The speed at which a heavenly body travels depends upon the size of its orbit. This is itself determined by the distance between the two heavenly bodies.

parallax the apparent movement in the position of a heavenly body due in fact to a change in the position of the observer. It is therefore caused, in reality, by the Earth moving through space on its orbit. The distance of a heavenly body from Earth can be calculated by astronomers using parallax. The direction of the body from Earth is measured at two six month intervals when the Earth is at either side of its orbit. From the apparent change in position, the distance of the body from Earth can be deduced.

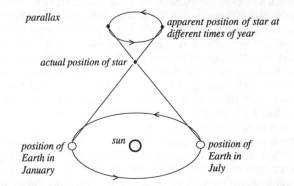

parallax

apparent position of star at different times of year

actual position of star

position of Earth in January

sun

position of Earth in July

parsec an astronomical unit of distance which is used for measurements beyond the SOLAR SYSTEM, and which corresponds to a PARALLAX of one second of arc. (There are 3600 arc seconds in one degree). A parsec is 30,857,000,000,000 kilometres or

3.2616 LIGHT YEARS. The nearest star to Earth has been calculated as being 1.3 parsecs distant.

planet the name given originally to seven heavenly bodies that were thought to move among the stars, which were themselves thought to be stationary. It is derived from the Greek word for *wanderer*. The term is now used to describe those heavenly bodies moving in definite orbits around the SUN which, in order of distance are: MERCURY, VENUS, EARTH, MARS, JUPITER, SATURN, URANUS, NEPTUNE and PLUTO. Mercury and Venus are termed the *inferior planets* and Mars to Pluto the *superior planets*, the latter because they revolve outside the Earth's orbit. The planets travel their own particular orbit but are all moving in the same direction.

Pluto the ninth and smallest planet in the SOLAR SYSTEM and the one that lies farthest away from the SUN. The existence of Pluto was predicted by an American astronomer called Percival Lowell from the behaviour of the orbits of its closest neighbours, NEPTUNE and URANUS. Pluto was finally spotted in 1930, fourteen years after Lowell died. Pluto appears as a tiny speck when viewed from Earth and little is known about it, but it probably has an iron core and a rocky surface with a covering of methane ice. Since it is so far from the Sun (a maximum of 7,338 million kilometres), it must be extremely cold, in the region of -230°C. A day on Pluto lasts for almost seven Earth days and a year is 248.4 Earth years. At the equator, the planet has a diameter in the region of 3,500 kilometres. Pluto has a wide elliptical orbit which sometimes brings it closer to the Sun. In 1989, it was at its closest point to the Sun (called its *perihelion*), but this only occurs every 248 years. During this phase of its orbit, Pluto apparently has a thin atmosphere composed of methane gas. However, when it moves away from the Sun again it is possible that this becomes frozen once again. In 1979 it was discovered that Pluto has one small satellite (which was named *Charon*), and is about a quarter the size of Pluto. The two bodies effectively form a double planet system.

Proxima Centauri a small, faint red star which is the closest one to the SOLAR SYSTEM (some 4.3 light years away) yet to be discovered. It occurs in the constellation of *Centaurus* and is the third and smallest member of a series of three stars called *Alpha Centauri*. It takes about a million years for it to orbit the other two stars which are larger and brighter. Proxima Centauri occasionally burns more brightly for short periods of time but is usually quite dim.

pulsar pulsars are thought to be collapsed, rotating NEUTRON STARS which are left after a SUPERNOVA explosion. A pulsar is a source of radio frequency radiation which is given out in regular short bursts. The radiation is in the form of a beam which sweeps through space as the pulsar rotates, and is detected on Earth if Earth happens to lie in its path. The first pulsar was found to emanate from the *Crab Nebula* which is a supernova.

quasar any of the quasi-stellar objects (i.e. like stars) which are extremely compact, give out light and yet are enormously distant bodies – up to 10^{10} LIGHT YEARS away.

radio astronomy the detection of a large range of radio waves (especially radiation given off by hydrogen atoms in space) which are emitted by numerous sources. These include the SUN, PULSARS, remnants of SUPERNOVAE and QUASARS.

radiotelescope the instrument used to detect and analyse extraterrestrial electromagnetic radiation (light and radio waves). There are two types – the *parabolic reflector*, which focuses the radiation on to an aerial, and the *interferometer*, where an interference pattern (*see* DIFFRACTION) of 'fringes' is formed and precise wave length measurements can be made. The latter is more accurate while the former is easier to move. The parabolic reflector is in the form of a large metal dish which can be pointed in different directions, used in conjunction with others and mounted on a rail so that it can be moved. The largest system in the world is built across a valley at Arecibo in Puerto Rico, and is 305 metres across.

red giant an ageing star that is extremely hot and has used up about 10% of its hydrogen. The outer layers are cooler than the intensely hot centre. As the name implies, these are very large stars. The red giant, *Aldebaran*, is 35 times larger than the SUN with a diameter of 50,100,000 kilometres. Some red giants go on to become WHITE DWARFS, using up their hydrogen at an increased rate. The Sun will eventually become a red giant in about 5000 million years time.

satellite any body, whether natural or manmade, that orbits a much larger body under the force of gravitation. Hence the MOON is a *natural satellite* of the Earth. All the planets, except for MERCURY and VENUS, have at least one natural satellite. *Artificial satellites* are manmade spacecraft launched into orbit from Earth. The first satellite to be launched was the Russian *Sputnik I* in 1957, but many hundreds have followed since then. Some satellites, especially those used for communications, are placed in a special *geostationary* orbit. This orbit is about 36,000 km above the Earth's surface. The satellite orbits the Earth in the same period of time as Earth rotates on its axis (24 hours). Hence the satellite maintains the same position relative to the Earth and appears to be stationary. Equipment on Earth therefore does not need to be adjusted to follow the satellite.

Many other satellites are used for other purposes such as meteorological recordings and weather forecasting. Each satellite has a dish aerial facing towards Earth and *thruster* motors to help maintain its position. When the fuel supply for the thrusters is exhausted, the satellite drifts out of its orbit and can no longer be used. The equipment on board a satellite or spaceship requires electricity which is usually derived from solar powered cells (*see* PHOTOELECTRIC CELL). (However, spacecraft travelling long distances away from the Sun have electricity generated by small nuclear reactors).

Saturn one of the four *gas giants*, the second largest planet and sixth in the SOLAR SYSTEM, with an orbit between that of JUPITER and URANUS. Saturn has a diameter at the equator of about 120,800 kilometres and is a maximum distance of 1,507,000,000 kilometres from the SUN. Saturn rotates very fast and this causes it to flatten at its poles and bulge at the equator. A day on Saturn lasts for $10^{1}/_{4}$ hours and a year, (or one complete orbit of the Sun) for 29.45 Earth years. Saturn is a cold planet of frozen gases and ice and has a surface temperature in the region of -170°C. It is mainly gaseous with an outer zone of hydrogen and helium over a metallic hydrogen layer and a core of ice silicate. The atmosphere is rich in methane and ethane. Saturn is well-known for its *rings* which are, in fact, ice particles and other debris thought to be the remains of a SATELLITE which broke up close to the planet. The rings are wide, in the region of 267,876 kilometres across, but they are extremely thin (only a few kilometres). The *Voyager* space probes approached close to Saturn in 1980 and 1981 and photographs taken revealed that there were many more rings than had previously been detected. They are brighter than those of any other planet.

Saturn has 24 satellites or moons, some of which were discovered by the *Voyager* spacecraft, including *Atlas, Prometheus* and *Calypso. Titan* is the largest moon and, at 5200 kilometres diameter, is larger than mercury. It is the only moon known to

SPACE AND ASTRONOMY

have a detectable atmosphere, a layer of gases above its surface.
Sirius also known as the *Dog Star* because it occurs in the constellation called the *Greater Dog, Canus Major*, this is the
brightest star in the night sky. It is a BINARY STAR with a *white
dwarf* as its partner and shines brightly because it lies quite close
to Earth, only 0.5 light years distant.
solar energy is energy which reaches Earth from the sun in the
form of heat and light. 85% of solar energy is reflected back into
space and only 15% reaches the Earth's surface, but it is this energy which sustains all life.
solar system the system comprising the sun (a star of spectral
type G), around which revolve the nine planets in elliptical orbits.
Nearest the SUN is MERCURY, then VENUS, EARTH, MARS, JUPITER,
SATURN, URANUS, NEPTUNE AND PLUTO. In addition, there are numerous SATELLITES, a few thousand ASTEROIDS (so far discovered)
and millions of COMETS. The age of the solar system is put at 4.5 to
4.6 billion years, a figure determined by the *radiometric dating*
(uranium-lead content) of iron meteorites (*see* DATING METHODS).
They are thought to be fragments or cores from early planets and
thus representative of the early stages of the solar system.

the solar system

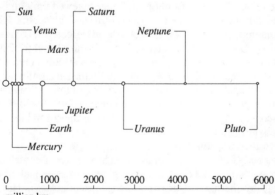

solar wind the term for the stream of charged, high-energy particles (mainly electrons, protons and alpha particles) given out by
the SUN. The particles travel at hundreds of kilometres per second,
and the wind is greatest during flare and SUNSPOT activity. Around

25

the Earth, the particles have velocities of 300 – 500 kilometres per second, and some become trapped in the magnetic field to form the VAN ALLAN RADIATION BELT. However, some reach the upper atmosphere and move to the poles, producing AURORA.

space probe is an unmanned spacecraft, such as *Voyager* 1 and 2, launched to travel through the SOLAR SYSTEM and beyond and programmed to send back data and photographs. Space probes eventually move so far away that contact with them is lost forever but they continue to travel for thousands of years. Vehicles from space probes have landed on Venus and Mars, obtaining valuable information.

space station a manned space research centre, including living accommodation, in which astronauts live and work for several months at a time. The manned space station, *Mir*, of the former Soviet Union was launched in 1986. At the end of the 1990s a new space station designed for eight people will be launched. It is called *Freedom* and is a joint American, Canadian, European and Japanese venture and all the materials for its construction are being carried out by SPACE SHUTTLE and assembled in space. It will be 500km (310 miles) above the surface of the Earth.

space telescope is a telescope launched into orbit in order to obtain images of stars and other heavenly bodies which are much clearer than if viewed from Earth. Images viewed through Earth-based telescopes are subject to distortion due to atmospheric factors, but such problems do not affect telescopes that are sited in space. Space telescopes have a special mirror and the images are radioed back to Earth where they can be studied on a screen and photographs obtained. In April 1990, the SPACE SHUTTLE *Discovery* launched the *Hubble* space telescope to undertake observations of the stars. After the launch it was found that the telescope's huge mirror was not working properly and it was repaired during a latter shuttle flight.

space time *see* **relativity**

star a body of fiery gas, similar to the SUN, which is contained by its own gravitational field. Stars are glowing masses that produce energy by thermonuclear reactions (NUCLEAR FUSION). The core acts as a natural NUCLEAR REACTOR, where hydrogen is consumed and forms helium with the production of electromagnetic radiation. A classification system for stars, based upon the spectrum of light they emit, groups stars as various *spectral types*. The sequence is, in order of descending temperature: O – hottest blue stars; B – hot blue stars; A – blue-white stars; F – white stars; G – yellow stars; K – orange stars; M – coolest red stars. Stellar evolution is the various stages in the life of a star, beginning with its creation from the condensation of gas, primarily hydrogen. The growth of the gas cloud pulls in more gas, and the increase in gravity compresses the molecules together, attracting more material and creating a denser mass. The heat normally produced by molecules due to their vibratory motion is increased greatly and the temperature is raised to millions of degrees, which enables nuclear fusion to take place. The supply of hydrogen continues to be consumed (and the star occupies the main sequence of the Hertzsprung-Russell diagram) until about 10% has gone. (The Hertzsprung-Russell diagram is a graph of star types from hot to cooler, depending upon the stage each has reached in its evolution.) When 10% of the hydrogen has been consumed the rate of combustion increases. This is accompanied by collapses in the core and an expansion of the hydrogen-burning surface layers, forming a RED GIANT. Progressive gravitational collapses and burning of the helium (which is generated by the consumption of the hydrogen) results in a WHITE DWARF, which is a sphere of enormously dense gas. The white dwarf cools over many millions of years and forms a *black dwarf* – an invisible ball of gases in space. Other sequences of events may occur, depending upon the size of the star formed. BLACK HOLES and NEUTRON STARS may form red (super) giants via a SUPERNOVA stage.

Sun is the star nearest to Earth around which Earth and the other planets move in elliptical orbits. It is one of millions of stars in the MILKY WAY but is the centre of the SOLAR SYSTEM. It was formed around five thousand million years ago and is about half way through its life cycle. It has a diameter of 1,392,000 kilometres and a mass of 2×10^{30} kilograms. The interior reaches a temperature of 13 million degrees centigrade while the visible surface is about 6000°C. The internal temperature is such that thermonuclear reactions occur, converting hydrogen to helium with the release of vast quantities of energy. The Sun is approximately 90% hydrogen and 8% helium and will one day become a RED GIANT.

sunspots the appearance of dark areas on the surface of the SUN. The occurrence reaches a maximum approximately every eleven years in a phase known as the sunspot cycle. They are usually short-lived (less than one month) and are caused by magnetism drawing away heat to leave a cooler area which is the sunspot. The black appearance is due to a lowering of the temperature to about 4000K. Sunspots have intense magnetic fields and are associated with magnetic storms and effects such as the *aurora borealis* (*see* AURORA). They may send out solar flares which are explosions occurring in the vicinity of the sunspots.

supernova (*plural* **supernovae**) a large star that explodes, it is thought, because of the exhaustion of its hydrogen (*see* SUN), whereupon it collapses, generating high temperatures and triggering thermonuclear reactions. A large part of its matter is thrown out into space, leaving a residue that is termed a WHITE DWARF star. Such events are very rare, but at the time of the explosion the stars become one hundred million times brighter than the Sun. A supernova was sighted in 1987 in the large MAGELLANIC CLOUD, 170,000 light years distant.

telescope is an instrument for magnifying an image of a distant object, the main types of astronomical telescopes being *refractors* and *reflectors*. The refracting type have lenses to produce an enlarged, upside-down image. In the reflecting type there are large mirrors with a curved profile which collect the light and direct it onto a second mirror and into the eyepiece (*see also* RADIOTELESCOPE).

universe all matter, energy and space that exists which is continuing to expand since its formation (*see* BIG BANG).

Uranus is the seventh planet in the SOLAR SYSTEM and one of the four *gas giants* with an orbit between those of Saturn and Neptune. Uranus has a diameter at the equator of 50,080 kilometres and lies an average distance of 2,869,600,000 kilometres from the Sun. The surface temperatures are in the region of -240°C. It is composed mainly of gases with a thick atmosphere of methane, helium and hydrogen. Uranus was the first planet to be observed with a telescope and was discovered by William Herschel, a German astronomer in 1781. Uranus remained a mystery until quite recently but in 1986, *Voyager 2* approached close to the planet and obtained valuable information and photographs. The planet appeared blue, due to its thick atmosphere of gases and a faint ring system consisting of 13 main rings. Uranus was known to have five moons but a further ten, some less than 50 kilometres in diameter, were discovered by Voyager 2. A day on Uranus lasts for about $17\frac{1}{2}$ hours and a year is equivalent to 84 Earth years. Its largest moon is *Titania* with a diameter of 1600 km. All five moons are very cold and icy with a surface covered in craters and cracks. *Ariel* has deep wide valleys and *Miranda*, the smallest moon, is a mass of canyons and cracks with cliffs reaching up to 20km. Uranus has a greatly tilted axis so that some parts of the planet's surface are exposed to the Sun for half of the planet's orbit (about 40 years) and are then in continuous darkness for the rest of the time. Due to the tilt of the axis, the Sun is sometimes shining almost directly onto each of Uranus' poles during parts of its orbit.

Van Allen belts are two belts of radiation consisting of charged particles (electrons and protons) trapped in the Earth's magnetic field. The result is the formation of two belts around the Earth. They were discovered in 1958 by an American physicist called James Van Allen. The lower belt occurs between 2000 and 5000km above the equator and its particles are derived from the Earth's atmosphere. The particles in the upper belt, at around 20,000km, are derived from the solar wind. The Van Allen belts are part of the Earth's magnetosphere, an area of space in which charged particles are affected by the Earth's magnetic field rather than that of the Sun.

Venus is the second planet in the solar system with its orbit between those of Mercury and Earth and it is also the brightest. It is known as the Morning or Evening star. Venus is about 108.2 million km (67 million miles) from the Sun and is extremely hot with a surface temperature in the region of 470°C. It has a thick atmosphere of mainly carbon dioxide, sulphuric acid and other poisonous substances which obscure its surface. The size of Venus is similar to Earth with a diameter at the equator of 12,300 km. The atmosphere of carbon dioxide traps heat from the Sun (the greenhouse effect) allowing none to escape. Hence the surface rocks are boiling hot and winds whip through the atmosphere at speeds in excess of 320 km/hr. Venus is unusual in being the only planet to spin on its axis in the opposite direction to the path of its orbit. Also it spins very slowly so that a 'day' on Venus is very long, equivalent to 243 Earth days. A year is 225 days. Venus has no satellites and because its surface is hidden, much of the known information about the planet has been obtained from SPACE PROBES. The *Magellan* space probe launched by the USA in 1989 visited Venus, sending back valuable photographs. *Venera 13*, a Russian probe landed on Venus in 1982, and obtained a rock sample and other information. The surface of the obtained a rock sample and other information. The surface of the planet has been shown to be mountainous with peaks 12 kilometres high. It is covered with craters and also a rift vally. It is possible that there are active volcanoes.

white dwarf a type of star that is very dense with a low luminosity. White dwarfs result from the explosion of stars that have used up their available hydrogen (*see* STAR). Due to their small size, their surface temperatures are high, and they appear white (*see also* SUPERNOVA).

X-ray astronomy stars emit a variety of electromagnetic radiation including X-rays (*see* ELECTROMAGNETIC WAVES), but this is unable to penetrate the Earth's atmosphere to be detected. Very hot stars send out large amounts of X-rays which can be detected by equipment contained on space satellites. The satellite ROSAT launched in 1990 has equipment to undertake X-ray astronomy and obtain information about distant bodies in space (e.g. WHITE DWARFS and SUPERNOVAE) that are emitting X-rays.

GEOGRAPHY AND GEOLOGY

The study of the Earth's surface, climate and natural resources is of great importance to mankind because only by learning more about the planet's past is it possible to prepare for the future.

This section explains the terms commonly used in the study of the Earths' geography and geology. The entries are in A to Z order and cross-references are given in SMALL CAPITALS.

*

alluvium deposits produced as a result of the action of streams or RIVERS. Moving water carries sediment, particles of sand, mud and silt, and the faster it moves the greater the load it can carry. When the velocity of the water is checked due to it meeting a stationary or slower moving body of water, then much or all of the sediment is dropped forming alluvium. In mountainous regions where streams descend to lowlands, a fan or cone of sediment may build up. Rivers in areas of less extreme geography deposit alluvium on the flood plain where the water changes velocity along the curving course of the river, or when rivers overflow their banks during floods.

aquifer a layer of rock, sand or gravel that is porous and therefore allows the passage and collection of water. If the layer has sufficient porosity and permeability it may provide enough GROUNDWATER to produce springs or wells. If the layers above and below the aquifer are impermeable, the water is under pressure (*hydrostatic pressure*) and can be extracted in an *Artesian Well* whilst the level of the well is lower than that of the WATER TABLE. A significant proportion of London's water supply comes from the London Basin (an Artesian basin), although the supply is diminishing because the water table and pressure have fallen due to prolonged extraction of water. In many cases pumps may be required to raise the water to the surface.

an artesian basin

artesian well

water table

---

porosity– the spaces within a rock or sediment referring to the pores that are able to release their contained water.
permeability– the ability of a material to allow the passage of water, air, etc.
impermeable– any material that does not allow passage of fluids.

---

atmosphere the layer of gases and dust surrounding the Earth which can be divided into shells, the lowermost being the TROPOSPHERE which is overlain by the STRATOSPHERE. The density falls with height and because it is thinner, breathing is more difficult at high altitudes. Almost 75% of the total mass is contained within the troposphere. The main gases found in the atmosphere are nitrogen (78%), oxygen (21%), the inert gas argon (0.9%), carbon dioxide (0.03%) and then very small amounts of other inert gases, with methane, hydrogen, water vapour and ozone. The ozone exists mainly in a layer (*see* OZONE LAYER) at a height of about 25 to 30 km although it is found elsewhere within the stratosphere.

Atmospheric pressure is the downward force of the atmosphere on the surface of the Earth and is roughly equivalent to a force of 1kg/cm^2 and originally defined as the pressure that will support a column of mercury 760mm high at 0°C, sea level and a latitude of 45° (*see* **S** - BAROMETER).

Beaufort scale a system for indicating wind strength, developed in 1805 by Admiral F.B. Beaufort. Measurements are taken 10m above the ground and each of 12 levels is characterized by particular features on the landscape or certain effects upon people or objects. Wind speed is measured in metres per second.

Scale	Wind speed	Weather condtion	Identifying features on land
0	< 0.3	calm	smoke rises vertically
1	0.3 – 1.5	light air	smoke indiates wind direction
2	1.6 – 3.3	light breeze	wind vane moves; wind felt on face
3	3.4 – 5.4	gentle breeze	twigs move; light flag extended
4	5.5 – 7.9	moderate breeze	small branches moved; dust raised
5	8.0 – 10.7	fresh breeze	small trees sway; wavelets on inland water
6	10.8 – 13.8	strong breeze	large branches move
7	13.9 – 17.1	near gale	whole trees in motion; some resistance when walking
8	17.2 – 20.7	gale/fresh gale	twigs broken off trees; resistance slows walking
9	20.8 – 24.4	strong gale	chimney pots and slates may be removed
10	24.5 – 28.4	storm	considerable structural damage; trees uprooted
11	28.5 – 32.7	violent storm	widespread damage; lives endangered
12	> 32.7	hurricane	catastrophic damage; loss of life

boulder clay a deposit that is glacial in origin and made up of boulders of varying sizes in finer-grained material, mainly clay. It is laid down beneath a glacier or ice sheet and shows little or no structure. Large blocks plucked from the terrain over which the ice has moved may be found in a matrix of finer material which has been ground down by the glacier. An alternative and more frequently used term is *till*, of which several types have been defined depending upon their specific mode of formation and position within the ice body. *Moraine* is an associated term referring to ridges of rock debris carried and deposited by ice sheets or glaciers of the various types; lateral moraine accumulates at the edge of a glacier and terminal moraine at the leading edge. Ground moraine is the same as boulder clay.

chalk a soft, fine-grained SEDIMENTARY ROCK made of calcium carbonate formed mainly from the skeletons and shells of very small marine organisms. It is formed primarily as deposits of calcareous mud in shallow seas, but it can also be formed by chemical precipitation. Chalk deposited in the Upper Cretaceous approximately 100 million years ago now covers much of northwest Europe, and can be seen in the White Cliffs of Dover and the cliffs near Calais. Chalk produces a particular scenery, with low rolling hills, dry valleys and steep scarps (an escarpment or steep slope which ends a flat or gently sloping area).

Chalk is an important AQUIFER and is used in the manufacture of CEMENT and FERTILIZERS.

climate characteristic weather conditions produced by a combination of factors, such as rainfall and temperature. Whether taken singly or jointly these factors, together with influencing features such as altitude and latitude, produce a distinctive arrangement of zones around the Earth each with a generally consistent climate when studied over a period of time. The major climatic zones are, from the equator:

> *humid tropical* —hot and wet
> *subtropical, arid and semi-arid* —desert conditions, extremes of
> daily temperature
> *humid temperate* —warm and moist with mild winters
> *boreal (N. hemisphere)* —long, cold, winters and short summers
> *sub-arctic (or sub-antarctic)* —generally cold with low rainfall
> *polar* —always cold

Climatic patterns are very dependent upon heat received from the Sun and at the poles the rays have had to travel further and in so doing have lost much of their heat, producing the coldest regions on the Earth. Conversely, air near the equator is very warm and can therefore hold a great deal of water vapour resulting in hot and wet conditions - humid tropical. There are more complex systems of climate classification, e.g. Köppen and Thornthwaite which are based upon precipitation and evaporation, characteristic vegetation and temperature. In each system, the Earth can be split into numerous provinces and smaller areas producing quite a detailed overall picture.

cloud clouds are droplets of water or ice formed by the condensation of moisture in a mass of rising air. Water vapour formed by evaporation from seas, lakes and rivers is ordinarily contained in air and only becomes visible when it condenses to form water droplets. Warm air can hold more water vapour than cold air thus when air rises, becoming cooler, it becomes saturated ("full") of water and eventually droplets form, as cloud, each droplet forming around a central nucleus such as dust, pollen or a smoke particle.

Clouds are classified firstly upon their shape, and also by their height. There are three major groups: *cumulus* ("heap" clouds), *stratus* (sheetlike) and *cirrus* (resembling fibres) which are divided further as cloud forms show a mix of shape, e.g. *cirrocumulus*.

cirrus *cirro-cumulus*

stratus *cumulus*

coal a mineral deposit that contains a very high carbon content and occurs in banded layers (seams) resembling rock. It is formed from ancient forest vegetation that has accumulated and been transformed into PEAT. With time, increasing pressure from

35

sediments above and some heating, the peat becomes coal of various types, each type (or *rank*) being marked by the carbon content which increases with pressure and temperature, and the volatiles content, which decreases at the same time. Volatiles are substances that readily become gas, specifically in this case, a mixture of hydrogen, methane and carbon dioxide which are released when coal is heated.

The coal of highest rank is anthracite which is 95% carbon with a little moisture and volatile matter. Bituminous coals contain from about 45% to 75% carbon while lignite has 70% moisture and volatiles.

Coal beds occur in sequences of sandstone and shale called, collectively, *coal measures*. Most of the world's anthracite and bituminous coals accumulated in the Carboniferous period (*see* GEOLOGICAL TIMETABLE) and the coal measures reach thousands of metres in thickness in many countries. The countries with the greatest reserves of coal include USA, CIS, China, Australia and Germany.

Although coal is used less than it was as a primary energy source, its byproducts are still used in the chemicals industry, for the manufacture of dyes, drugs, pesticides and other compounds.

continent one of several large landmasses covering 29% of the Earth's surface of which 65% is in the northern hemisphere. Where the continent edge meets the sea is a continental shelf and slope which is often cut by submarine canyons. Further oceanward lies the deepest parts of the ocean, the abyssal plain. There are seven continents making up the Earth:

	highest point (metres)	area (sq km)
Asia	8848	43,608,000
Africa	5895	30,335,000
North and Central America	6194	25,349,000
South America	6960	17,611,000
Antarctica	5140	14,000,000
Europe	5642	10,498,000
Oceania	4205	8,900,000

crystal a solid that has a particular, ordered, structure and shape with usually flat faces and a chemical composition that varies little. The arrangement of the atoms in the crystal in a specific framework give it a characteristic shape and if conditions permit when the crystal is growing, the crystal faces are arranged in a constant geometric relationship. Many solids have a crystalline structure, from household items such as sugar and salt to chemicals, metals and the minerals within rocks. If a solution of a chemical or a magma (molten rock) is allowed to cool slowly, crystals will develop. Similarly, if a crystal is placed in a saturated solution of the same compound *crystallization* will occur. If, however, the solution or magma is cooled suddenly, either the crystals formed are microscopic or the resulting solid exhibits no crystalline form (is *amorphous*).

The regular formation of crystal faces is part of a crystal's *symmetry* which is described for each crystal system, by three properties: planes, axes and a centre of symmetry. These properties together create six crystal systems. These are:

Cubic	common salt
Tetragonal	zircon
Hexagonal	calcite; quartz
Orthorhombic	topaz; barytes; sulphur
Monoclinic	gypsum
Triclinic	feldspars

Crystallography is the scientific study of crystals, their form and structure.

cyclone an area of low atmospheric pressure with closely packed isobars producing a steep pressure gradient and therefore very strong winds. Due to the Earth's rotation, the winds circulate clockwise in the southern hemisphere and anticlockwise in the northern hemisphere. In tropical regions, cyclones (tropical hurricanes) combine very high rainfall with destructive winds which results in widespread damage and possible loss of life.

Outside the tropics, in more temperate climates, the term cyclone is being replaced by *depression* (or *low*) in which the pressure may fall to 940 or 950 mb (millibars). Compare this with the average pressure at sea-level which is 1013 mb.

An *anticyclone* is a high pressure area (around 1030 - 1050 mb) and usually results in stable weather.

dating methods are used in a number of scientific subjects, whether geography, geology or archaeology, where it is often necessary to date a sample and there are several ways in which this can be achieved. In many instances, a relative age can be determined quite readily, for example in geology one rock cutting across another can provide clues as to the order of formation of rock sequences, or the order in which rocks were folded or deformed (*see* folds and faults). However, to obtain an *absolute* or true age (bearing in mind any experimental errors), the radioactive decay of ISOTOPES can be employed -*radiometric dating*.

Radiocarbon dating is one such method. This relies upon the uptake by plants and animals of small quantities of naturally-occurring radioactive ^{14}C in the atmosphere. When the organism dies, the uptake stops and the ^{14}C decays with a half-life (see S-RADIOACTIVITY) of 5730 years, and the age of a sample can be calculated from the remaining radioactivity. This method is useful for dating organic material within the last 70,000 years but the accuracy of the methods falls between 40,000 and 70,000 years.

Rocks can be dated by one of several methods each of which relies upon the radioactive decay of one element to another. In these cases the half-life is very long enabling the dating of very old rocks. Uranium-lead was an early method in which uranium-238 (^{238}U) decays to lead-206 with a half-life of 4.5 billion years.

Other systems are:

Rb/Sr	rubidium-87 decays to strontium-87 half-life of 50 billion years.
K/Ar	potassium-40 decays to argon-40 half-life of 1.5 billion years.
Th/Pb	thorium-232 decays to lead-208 half-life of 14 billion years.
Sm/Nd	samarium-147 decays to neodymium-143 half-life of 2.5 billion years.

The long half-lives make these systems useful in dating Lower Palaeozoic and Precambrian rocks (*see* GEOLOGICAL TIMESCALE). Sm/Nd is resistant to metamorphism and can be used on extraterrestrial materials: Th/Pb is often used with other methods because it is not an accurate method alone; Rb/Sr is useful for dating metamorphic rocks and in general the best results for dating are obtained from igneous or metamorphic rocks.

desert an arid or semi-arid (that is, dry and parched with under 25cm (10 in.) of rainfall annually) region in which there is little or no vegetation. The term was always applied to hot tropical and subtropical deserts, but is equally applicable to areas within continents where there is low rainfall and perennial ice-cold deserts.

The vegetation is controlled by the rainfall and varies from sparse, drought-resistant shrubs and cacti to sudden blooms of annual plants in response to a short period of torrential rain. If the groundwater conditions permit, e.g. if the water table is near to the surface creating a spring, or the geology is such that an artesian well (*see* AQUIFER) is created, then an oasis may develop within a hot desert, providing an island of green.

Hot deserts are found in Africa, Australia, United States, Chile and cold deserts in the Arctic, eastern Argentina and mountainous regions.

Hot desert extremes:

extreme of shade temperature: Death Valley, California
maximum 28°C;
maximum daily range 41°C
maximum ground surface temperature: Sahara 78°C
extreme of rainfall: Chicama, Peru, 4mm per year

The process whereby desert conditions and processes extend to new areas adjacent to existing deserts is called *desertification*.

drainage is the movement of water derived from rain, snowfall and melting of ice and snow, over the land (and through it in subterranean waterways) which results eventually in its discharge into the sea. The flow of streams and rivers is influenced by the underlying rocks, how they are arranged and whether there are any structural features that the water may follow. Further factors affecting drainage include soil type, climate and the influence of man.

There are a number of recognizable patterns which can be related to the geology:

1. Dendritic   a random branching unaffected by surface rocks
2. Trellis   streams aligned with the trend of underlying rocks.
3. Parallel   streams running parallel to each other due to folded rocks, or steep slopes with little vegetation.
4. Rectangular controlled by faults and joints, the latter often in igneous rocks.
5. Annular   formation of streams in circular patterns around a structure of the same shape (e.g. an igneous intrusion).
6. Barbed   a drainage pattern where the tributaries imply a direction of flow contrary to what actually happens.
7. Radial   streams flowing outwards from a higher area.
8. Centripetal the flow of streams into a central depression where there may be a lake or river.

When a drainage pattern is a direct result of the underlying geology, it is said to be *accordant* (the opposite case being *discordant*).

earthquake movement of the earth, which is often violent, and caused by the sudden release of stress that may have accumulated over a long period. Waves of disturbance -*seismic* waves - spread out from the origin or *focus*, of the earthquake which is most likely to be movement along a FAULT, although some are associated with volcanic activity.

Earthquakes are classified by their depth of focus: shallow (less than 70km); intermediate (70 to 300km); deep (more than 300km).

areas of earthquake activity

Over three quarters of earthquake energy is concentrated in a belt around the Pacific and this is because most seismic activity occurs at the margins of tectonic plates (*see* PLATE TECTONICS). This means that certain regions of the world are more likely to suffer earthquakes, for example the west coast of N. & S. America, Japan, the Philippines, S.E. Asia and New Zealand.

The effects of earthquakes are naturally very alarming and can be quite catastrophic. Near the focus, ground waves actually throw about the land surface. Surface effects may include opening of fissures (large cracks), the breaking of roads and pipes, buckling and twisting of railway lines and the collapse of bridges and buildings. Secondary effects can be equally destructive if the ground vibrations initiate landslides, avalanches and TSUNAMI or cause fires.

There are several systems of measuring the intensity of earthquakes, the one in common use being that devised by Richter, an American seismologist. The Richter Scale is:

Rating	Identifying features
1 Instrumental	detected only by seismographs
2 Feeble	noticed by sensitive people
3 Slight	similar to a passing lorry
4 Moderate	loose objects are rocked
5 Rather strong	felt generally
6 Strong	trees sway; loose objects fall
7 Very strong	walls crack
8 Destructive	chimneys fall; masonry cracks
9 Ruinous	houses collapse where ground starts to crack
10 Disastrous	ground badly cracked; buildings destroyed
11 Very disastrous	bridges and most buildings destroyed; landslides
12 Catastrophic	ground moves in waves; total destruction

Because this is a logarithmic scale, the magnitude of one level is very much more than the previous level. Over the last ninety years not many earthquakes have registered over 8 on the Richter scale. Some earlier ones include San Francisco (1906), Kansu in China (1920), Japanese trench (1933), Chile (1960) and offshore Japan (1968). *See also* SEISMOGRAPH.

erosion the destructive breakdown of rock and soil by a variety of *agents* that, together with weathering, forms *denudation*, or a wearing away of the land surface. Erosion occurs because of the mechanical action of material carried by agents: water (rivers, currents, waves), ice (glaciers) and wind. Wind laden with sand can scour rock, rocks embedded in glaciers grind down the rocks over which they pass and gravel and pebbles in streams and rivers excavate their own course and may create pot holes, undercut banks, etc. Water can also carry material in solution. There are six different kinds of erosion processes, each with a different effect:

process	effect
abrasion	wearing away through grinding, rubbing and polishing.
attrition	the reduction in size of particles by friction and impact.
cavitation	characteristic of high energy river waters (e.g. waterfalls, cataracts) where air bubbles collapse sending out shock waves that impact on the walls of the river bed (a very localized occurrence).
corrasion	the use of boulders, pebbles, sand etc. carried by a river, to wear away the floor and sides of the river bed.
corrosion	all erosion achieved through solution and chemical reaction with materials encountered in the water.
deflation	the removal of loose sand and silt by the wind.

The effect of these processes can be very marked, with time, and can combine to deepen gorges, create and enlarge waterfalls and result in the movement of a waterfall upstream. The latter occurs through undercutting of lower, softer rocks which then cause the collapse of overhanging ledges.

waterfall erosion

soft rock

evaporite a sedimentary rock formed by the evaporation of water containing various salts, resulting in their deposition. The particular sediment created depends upon the concentration of ions (*see* **C**-ION) in solution, and the solubility (*see* SOLUTIONS) of each salt formed. The least soluble - calcium carbonate and magnesium carbonate - precipitate first, followed by sodium sulphate, then sodium chloride, potassium chloride and magnesium sulphate. A typical sequence of evaporite deposits could show calcite, possibly dolomite, gypsum (or anhydrite), rock salt, and finally potassium and magnesium salts (e.g. carnallite, $KCl.MgCl.6H_2O$).

There are several major deposits of evaporites in the world, e.g. the Stassfurt deposits in Germany, the Wieliczka salt mines in Poland, Texas and New Mexico, Chile and Cheshire in Britain. Some of these deposits are over 3500m thick, and since about 5m of evaporites would require the evaporation of 300m of seawater, it is clear that very special conditions existed in the past. To accumulate such vast thicknesses, there must be a shallow area of water from which evaporation and precipitation proceeds; which is periodically refilled with salt water, *and* there must be a gradual subsidence of the land to permit continued build up of the salts.

Modern evaporites are being formed in places such as the Caspian Sea, the Arabian Gulf and deposits have been formed recently in Eritrea.

faults *see* FOLDS.

floods a flood is where land not normally covered by water is temporarily underwater and can occur for several reasons and the scale of the flood may vary enormously. An increase in rainfall, particularly if prolonged may lead to flooding as may a sudden thaw of lying snow. Flooding of coastal areas by the sea may be caused by the combination of a very high tide and stormy conditions generating high waves. Perhaps most devastating of all are the TSUNAMI caused by earthquakes. Large areas of, for example, S.E. Asia, continually face the threat of floods.

When a river is in flood it carries a far greater load of rocks, boulders, sand and silt and its destructive power is therefore increased. In some cases, flood waters have been so powerful as to carve new channels for the river and in so doing demolish houses, roads, bridges, wash away trees and soil and transport vast piles of boulders and masonry seemingly impossible distances.

floodplain is the area in a river valley which may be covered by water when a river is in flood, and which is built up of ALLUVIUM. The floodplain is developed by a river's movement with time and the deposition and transport of sediment. Whether it is due to existing features along a river's course, or simply due to turbulence of flow and subsequent deposition of material where a river slows, the course of a river will include numerous bends. Subsequent erosion and deposition of sediment results in a meandering (*see* RIVERS) of the river with deposition of alluvium and a progressive movement along of the river bends, forming a floodplain.

development of a floodplain

alluvium deposits

folds and *faults* are both geological features developed through tectonic activity. Folds are produced when rock layers undergo compression resulting in a buckling and folding of the rocks - a *ductile* or flowing deformation. There is an almost infinite variety in the shape, size and orientation of folds and an earlier generation of folds may be refolded by subsequent periods of deformation. Their size may range from microscopic to folds occupying hillsides or even whole mountains.

The way folds are formed will depend upon the amount of compression, the rock types involved and the thicknesses of the layers, because different rocks respond in different ways, but each fold possesses certain common features. The zone of greatest curvature is the *hinge* and the *limbs* lie between hinges or on either side of the hinge. The *axial plane* is an imaginary feature bisecting the angle between limbs and the *fold axis* is where the axial plane meets the hinge zone.

Faults are generally planar features, and are caused by *brittle* deformation. Rocks are moved, or *displaced*, across faults by as little as a few millimetres or as much as several kilometres (although possibly not all in the same event). There are several types of faults, depending upon the movement across the fault, and the orientation of the fault plane. The measurement of movement uses a horizontal and vertical component, the heave and throw respectively. If the movement is up or down the fault plane it is a dip-slip fault; if it is sideways, the term is strike-slip.

two examples of vertical dip-slip fault movement

two examples of horizontal strike-slip fault movement

Many faults produce associated features such as zones of crushed rock, or striations (grooves) known as *slickensides*, on adjacent rock surfaces, where minerals such as quartz or calcite may grow.

Major faults today account for many surface features and are an important part of the *plate tectonic* structure and development of the Earth.

fossils are the remains of once-living plants and animals, or evidence of their existence, that have been preserved (usually) in the rock layers of the Earth. The term may include the preservation in ice of woolly mammoths that lived 20,000 years, although anything younger than about 10,000 years is not generally considered a fossil.

Fossils may be bones, shells, borings, trails, casts and the fossilized remains of something associated with or caused by an organism, e.g. tracks or a worm burrow, are called *trace fossils*. Although many rock sequences contain a large number of fossils, conditions prevailing at the time have to be just right to ensure preservation. Vital to the process is that the organism be covered quickly with sediment, something that will happen more readily in marine rather than terrestrial conditions. Even then, significant changes may occur - soft parts usually decay and shells may be replaced chemically, or dissolved away leaving a mould to be filled by a different material. Occasionally, a whole insect may be preserved in amber.

The scientific study of fossils is called *palaeontology*.

fossil fuels include PETROLEUM (oil), COAL and NATURAL GAS - fuels created by the fossilization of plant and animal remains. Oil and gas are often found together with the gas lying over the oil and beneath the impermeable layer which seals the reservoir.

geochemistry a part of GEOLOGY that deals with the chemical make-up of the Earth, including the distribution of elements (and ISOTOPES) and their movement within the various natural systems (ATMOSPHERE, LITHOSPHERE, etc.). Recently, it has also been taken to include other planets and moons within the solar system. The geochemical cycle, in broad terms, illustrates the way in which elements from MAGMA (the 'starting point') move through different processes and geochemical environments.

geochronology the study of time on a geological scale using *absolute* or *relative* dating methods. Absolute methods (*see* DATING METHODS) provide an age for a rock and involve the use of radioactive elements with known rates of decay. Relative ages are determined by putting rock sequences in order through study of their sequence of deposition or folding. Fossils can also be used in relative age dating.

geography the study of the Earth's surface, including all the land forms (*see* GEOMORPHOLOGY), their formation and associated processes, which comprise *physical* geography. Such aspects as climate, topography and oceanography are covered. *Human* geography deals with the social and political perspectives of the subject including populations and their distribution. In addition, geography may cover the distribution and exploitation of natural resources, map-making and REMOTE SENSING.

geological timescale a division of time since the formation of the Earth (4600 million years ago) into units, during which rock sequences were deposited, deformed and eroded and life of diverse types emerged, flourished and, often, ceased.

The table below shows the various subdivisions, and many of the names owe their derivation to particular locations, rock sequences and so on.

Cenozoic	Recent	Modern Man
	Pleistocene	Stone Age Man
	Pliocene	many mammals, elephants
	Oligocene	pig and ape ancestors
	Eocene	
	Palaeocene	horse and cattle ancestors
Mezozoic	Cretateous	end of the dinosaus and the ammonites
	Jurassic	appearance of birds and ammmals
	Triassic	dinosaurs appear; corals of modern type
Palaeozoic	Permian	amphibians and reptiles more common; conifer trees appear
	Carboniferous	coal forests; reptiles appear, winged insects
	Devonian	amphibians appear; fishes more common ammonites appear; early trees; spiders
	Silurian	first coral reefs; appearance of spore-bearing land plants
	Ordovician	trilobites and graptolites common; first fish-like vertebrates
	Cambrian	first fossils period; trilobites, grapolites, molluscs, crinoids, radiolaria, etc.
	Precambrian	sponges, worms, algae, bacteria; all primitive forms

Derivation of some geological names:

Cenozoic—recent life   *Palaeonzoic*—ancient life
Mesozoic—mediaeval life   *Archaen*—primaeval

The Roman name for Wales (*Cambria*) led to Cambrian, while the names of two Celtic tribes, the *Silures* and *Ordovices* provided the remaining lower Palaeonzoic names. Carboniferous is related to the proliferation of coal (i.e. carbon) and Cretaceous comes from *creta*, meaning chalk. The Triassic is a threefold division in Germany, while the *Jura* mountains lent their name to the Jurassic

geology the scientific study of the Earth, including its origins, structure, processes and composition. It includes a number of topics which have developed into subjects in their own right: GEOCHEMISTRY, MINERALOGY, petrology (study of rocks), structural geology, GEOPHYSICS, PALAEONTOLOGY, STRATIGRAPHY, economic and physical geology. Charles Lyell (1797 - 1875) was an influential figure in the early years of geological study and wrote *Principles of Geology*.

geomagnetism the study of the Earth's magnetic (*geomagnetic*) field which has varied with time. At mid-oceanic ridges (*see* PLATE TECTONICS) where new crust is created, measurement of the geomagnetic field shows stripes relating to reversals of the Earth's magnetic field which is taken up in the newly-formed rocks. This provides a tool in determining the age of much of the oceanic crust and is a vital piece of evidence in supporting the theory of plate tectonics.

geomagnetic fields of the mid-atlantic ridge

geomorphology a subject that grew out of geology around the middle of last century, and is the study of *landforms*, their origin and change, i.e. the study of the Earth's surface. Landforms are composed of various rock types and formed from the surface materials of the Earth by geomorphological processes which originate from tectonic movements and the climate. Landforms can be arranged into certain categories based upon factors such as the underlying structural geology, the nature of the topography, i.e. the surface features, and the terrain (soil, vegetation etc.), and the type of geomorphological processes dominant.

geophysics is the study of all processes *within* the Earth (i.e. the crust and the interior) and is concerned with the physical properties of the Earth. Included are seismology (*see* SEISMOGRAPH), GEOMAGNETISM, gravity, HYDROLOGY, oceanography (the study of the oceans, currents, tides, sea-floor and so on), heat flow within the Earth and related topics. As with many other subject areas, the component topics often develop to the point of becoming a subject in their own right, and boundaries between subjects merge.

geothermal energy the temperature within the Earth increases with depth (this is called the *geothermal gradient*), although not uniformly, and the average gradient is in the range 20 to 40°C per kilometre. At the edges of some tectonic plates (*see* PLATE TECTONICS) the gradient increases dramatically and it is sometimes possible to harness this heat as geothermal energy.

The high heat flow may be caused by magmatic activity (*see* MAGMA) or by the radioactive decay of certain elements. When water or brine (water containing dissolved salts) circulates through these rocks, it becomes heated and may appear at the surface as a warm spring, or if it is temporarily contained and heated further, it may force out a body of steam and water as a *geyser* (derived from geysir, the Icelandic for gusher or roarer).

Geothermal energy is 'tapped' all over the world, including Iceland, New Zealand, California and Italy. Iceland, New Zealand and Kenya have geothermal power stations.

glacier an enormous mass of ice, on land, that moves very slowly. About 10% of the Earth's land is covered by glaciers although during the last glaciation this was nearer 30%. Glaciers that cover vast areas of land, e.g. Greenland, Antarctic are called ice sheets (or ice caps if smaller) and these hide the underlying land features. The more typical glaciers are either those that flow in valleys or those filling hollows in mountains. Glaciers can be classified further into polar (e.g. Greenland), sub-polar (e.g. Spitzbergen) and temperate (e.g. the Alps) depending upon the temperature of the ice.

Although glaciers move slowly, they act as powerful agents of erosion on the underlying rocks. Large blocks may be dragged off the underlying rock, become embedded in the ice and then scratch and scour the surface as the glacier moves. This produces smaller particles of rock debris and the blocks themselves may be broken. Debris is also gathered from valley sides and carried along. Ridges or piles of this rock debris are called moraine and depending upon position relative to the glacier, may mark present or former edges of the ice. In addition to the formation of moraine and associated, characteristic formations, glaciers produce some typical large scale features such as U-shaped valleys and *truncated spurs*.

truncated spur

U-shaped valley

Glaciation is the term meaning an ice age or a part of an ice age when glaciers and ice sheets are enlarged significantly.

grasslands form one of the four major types of vegetation, the others being forest, savanna and DESERT. Grasslands are characterized by seasonal drought, limited precipitation and occasional fires and these all, with grazing by animals, restrict the growth of trees and shrubs. Typical grasslands include the pampas of Argentina, the veldts of South Africa, the Steppes in the CIS and the prairies of central N. America.

The coverage of grasslands expanded after the last glaciation when climates became generally hotter and drier and there was an increase in the number of large grazing mammals.

Savanna is similar to grassland, but with scattered trees and is found extensively in S. America, southern Africa and parts of Australia. There are usually well-defined seasons: cool and dry, hot and dry followed by warm and wet and during the latter there is a rich growth of grasses and small plants. Although savanna soils may be fertile they are highly porous and water therefore drains away rapidly.

groundwater water that is contained in the voids within rocks, i.e. in pores, cracks and other cavities and spaces. It often excludes *vadose* water which occurs between the water-table and the surface. Most groundwater originates from the surface, percolating through the soil (*meteoric* water). Other sources are *juvenile* water, generated during and coming from deep magmatic processes, and *connate* water which is water trapped in a sedimentary rock since its formation.

Groundwater is a necessary component of most weathering processes and of course its relationship to the geology, water-table and surface may lead to the occurrence of AQUIFERS and artesian wells.

hardness of minerals minerals differ in their physical hardness and a test introduced in 1822 is still in use today to aid mineral classification. Moh's scale lists 10 minerals ranked by hardness and each mineral will scratch those lower on the scale where talc is the softest and diamond the hardest. In addition it is common to use the finger nail (equivalent to 2.5) or a pen-knife (5.5) to assist in the determination.

Moh's scale of hardness:

1	talc	6	orthoclase (feldspar)
2	gypsum	7	quartz
3	calcite	8	topaz
4	fluorite	9	corundum
5	apatite	10	diamond

humidity the amount of moisture in the Earth's atmosphere. *Absolute* humidity is the actual mass of water vapour in each cubic metre of air while *relative* humidity is

$$\frac{\text{water vapour content of air at a given temperature}}{\text{water vapour content required for saturation at that temperature}} \times 100\%$$

The relative humidity of air therefore varies with temperature, cold air holds little moisture, warm air much more. A *hygrometer* is the instrument used to measure relative humidity.

hurricane a wind which on the BEAUFORT SCALE exceeds 75 mph (121 km/h). Also an intense, tropical cyclonic storm that has a central calm area – the *eye* – around which move winds of very high velocity (over 160 km/h). There is usually very heavy rain, with thunderstorms and the whole system may be several hundred kilometres across.

Such storms occur mainly in the Caribbean and the Gulf of Mexico and often affect the southern states of the USA, creating considerable destruction.

hydrology the study of water and its cycle, which covers bodies of water and how they change. All physical forms of water - rain, snow, surface water - are included as are such aspects as distribution and use. The way in which water circulates between bodies of water such as seas, the atmosphere and the Earth forms the *hydrological cycle*.

The cycle consists of various stages: water falls as rain or snow of which some runs off into streams and then into lakes or rivers, while some percolates into the ground. Plants and trees take up water and lose it by transpiration to the atmosphere, while evaporation occurs from bodies of water. The water vapour in the air then condenses to cloud which eventually repeats the cycle.

the hydrological cycle

the vertical arrows show moisture returning to the atmosphere where it will condense as cloud

Of the 1.5 billion cubic kilometres of water on earth, the oceans hold 93.9%, groundwater 4.4%, polar ice 1.0%, with rivers, lakes, the atmosphere and soil holding the remainder.

ice age a period in the history of the Earth when ice sheets expanded over areas that were normally ice-free. The term is usually applied to the most recent episode in the Pleistocene (*see* GEOLOGICAL TIMESCALE), but the rock record indicates that there have been ice ages as far back as the Precambrian. Within ice ages there are fluctuations in temperature producing interglacial stages when the temperatures increase.

igneous rocks one of the three main rock types. Igneous rocks crystallize from MAGMA and are formed at the surface as LAVA flows (*extrusive*) or beneath the surface as *intrusions*, pushing their way into existing rocks. There are numerous ways of classifying igneous rocks, from mineral content to crystal size and mode of origin and emplacement. Typical rocks are basalt, granite and dolerite.

Rocks erupted at the surface as lava are called *volcanic*, while *plutonic* rocks are those large bodies solidifying at some depth; *hypabyssal* rocks are smaller and form at shallow depths. When a body of magma has time to crystallize slowly, large mineral crystals can develop while extrusion at the surface leads to a rapid cooling and formation of very small crystals (or none, if molten rock contacts water, as in a glass). A further division into acid, intermediate, basic and ultrabasic rocks is based upon silica (SiO_2) content, this being greatest in acid rocks.

Igneous intrusions may occur in several forms either parallel to or cutting through the existing rocks, and the commonest are *sills* (concordant) and *dykes* (discordant). *Plugs* commonly represent the neck of a former volcano, while *batholiths* are massive, elongate bodies that may be hundreds of kilometres long.

examples of igneous intrusions

batholiths

plugs

irrigation is when water is taken to dry land to encourage or facilitate plant growth. The water may be applied by means of canals, ditches, sprinklers or the flooding of the whole area. Flood irrigation is not always a good idea because the water evaporates from the flooded field leaving behind any salts that were dissolved in the water. If this is done repeatedly, the build up of salts may harm the soil and make it infertile. Water may be conserved and used more effectively by means of a pipe with small holes being laid around a plant, and the water drips from the holes onto the soil. Irrigation can transform arid regions but rivers from which water is diverted will inevitably be much reduced.

isobar a line on a weather map that joins points of equal pressure corrected for the varying heights of recording. Over a large area, isobars produce a map of pressure lines, similar to contours on a topographic map, which identify the high and low centres, i.e. the anticyclones and depressions.

jet stream westerly winds at high altitudes (above 12 km) found mainly between the poles and the TROPICS, that form narrow jet-like streams. The air streams move north and south of their general trend, in surges, which are probably the cause of depressions and anticyclones. There are a number of separate jet streams but the most constant is that of the subtropics. Jet stream speed and location is of importance to high-flying aircraft.

latitude and **longitude** latitude is the angular distance, north or south from the equator, of a point on the Earth's surface. The equator is 0° and points can therefore be measured in degrees south or north of this line. The imaginary lines drawn on a map or globe are the lines of latitude.

Longitude is a similar concept. It is the angular distance of a point measured on the Earth's surface to the east or west of a 'central' reference point. The referent point in this case is the plane created by a *meridian* (an imaginary circle that cuts the poles and goes over the Earth's surface and the point in question) going through Greenwich in England. A point may be 0° longitude if it sits on this line or a number of degrees east or west. The Greenwich Meridian, based upon the Greenwich Observatory, was established by an international agreement in 1884. There is a time difference of one hour when travelling 15° of longitude at the equator (*see also* TROPICS).

lava molten rock at about 1100 or 1200°C erupted from a VOL-CANO or a similar fissure. It may flow onto the ground (subaerial) or onto the sea floor (submarine). Due to rapid cooling in air or water, most lavas show a fine-grained or glassy structure. The way lava is erupted, flows, and its shape as a flow is determined by its viscosity. *Pahoehoe* lava is a fluid basaltic type which forms rope-like flows due to molten lava in the centre of the flow dragging the solidifying crust into folds. A more viscous lava, *Aa* (both terms are Hawaiian words) flows more slowly and forms jagged, pointed blocks. Often a stream of lava will be contained by craggy sides of partly solidified lava. *Pillow lavas* are formed on the sea floor and as their name suggests, consists of pillow-like shapes built up and out from the source with one pillow rupturing at some point to allow more lava out to form another pillow. *Pumice* is lava filled with small air bubbles, creating a light, rough stone.

There are roughly 10,000 active volcanoes occurring in belts coinciding with the margins between tectonic plates. Lavas may cover vast areas, e.g. 250,000 square kilometres of the Deccan Plain of India, and 130,000 square kilometres in the Columbia River plateau region of the western USA. Such eruptions have occurred throughout geological time.

lightning and **thunder** lightning is the discharge of high voltage electricity between a CLOUD and its base and between the base of the cloud and the Earth. (It has been shown that in a cumulonimbus cloud, positive charge collects at the top, and negative at the base). Lightning occurs when the increasing charge (of electricity) in the cloud overcomes the resistance of the air, leading to a *discharge*, seen as a flash. The discharge to ground is actually followed by a return discharge up to the cloud and this is the visible sign of lightning. There are various forms of lightning including sheet, fork and ball and it may carry a charge of around 10,000 amps.

The *thunder* is the rumbling noise that accompanies lightning and it is due to the sudden heating and expansion of the air by the discharge, causing sound waves. The sound often continues for some time because sound is generated at various points along the discharge - the latter can be several kilometres long. The thunder comes after the lightning because sound travels more slowly than light and this allows an approximate measure of distance from the flash to be made. For every 5 seconds between the flash and the thunder, the lightning will be roughly one mile away.

limestone a sedimentary rock that is made up mainly of calcite (calcium carbonate, $CaCO_3$) with dolomite ($CaMg(CO_3)_2$). There are essentially three groups of limestone: chemical, organic and detrital. These groups reflect the enormous variety of limestones which may contain the broken remains of marine organisms - shells, coral etc.(detrital); minute organic remains of, for example, algae, foraminifera as in chalk, make an *organic* limestone; and grains formed as concentrically layered pellets (ooliths and pisoliths) in shallow marine waters which with EVAPORITES are examples of chemical limestones.

Limestones are important economically and have many uses. They form AQUIFERS and reservoirs for oil and gas and are used in the manufacture of cement, in agriculture, as roadstone and when cut and finished slabs are used to face buildings. Where limestone outcrops ('appears') at the surface, the process of water flow and dissolution of the rock may lead to a *karst* topography where there is a virtual absence of surface drainage and groundwater moves along joints into holes, enlarging them over time to form potholes and caves which, in a well-developed and extensive case, may result in collapses of rock over caves and voids to produce towering rock pinnacles (as in China).

magma the fluid, molten rock beneath the surface of the Earth. Magma may undergo many stages of change and movement before being extruded at the surface as *lava*, or intruded at some depth as an intrusion (*see* IGNEOUS ROCKS). The composition varies because in moving upwards through the crust, volatiles (gases and liquids) may be lost and some minerals may crystallize out, thus changing the nature of the remaining melt. Magma reaches the surface through pipes into volcanoes, or through fissures but at depth it may form bodies many kilometres across.

Magmas are formed by the partial melting of mantle (the layer between the Earth's crust and core) in areas of *subduction*, where tectonic plates are destroyed (*see* PLATE TECTONICS) as one plate descends beneath another. Magmas usually undergo many changes in composition as they move towards the surface.

maps are flat, two-dimensional representations of three-dimensional subjects, e.g. an area of land, which contain a variety of data, which will differ depending upon the type of map. Differing scales, that is the ratio of a distance on the map to the actual distance on the ground, enable smaller or larger areas of land to be represented.

A standard topographical map indicates the shape of the land by means of *contours* (lines joining points of equal height) and on it the road, rivers, rail lines, towns, forests and parkland may be marked. Maps can be drawn up to illustrate land usage, relief (i.e.

the shape of the land surface), superficial deposits (river and glacial deposits on top of the underlying rocks) or solid geology (the rocks shown with all things above stripped away).

A *map projection* is the representation of the complete surface of the Earth on a plane. There is a large number of such projections and each presents the globe in a different way and thus finds different uses.

Projection	Types	used for
Mercator	cylindrical	navigation
Conical	conic	maps of a small continent
Gnomonic	azimuthal	seismic survey; navigational
Peter's	modified cylindrical	depicts the Earth's densely populated areas in
proportion		to each other
Stereographic	azimuthal	used widely in structural geology and crystallography

One of the commonest is the Mercator projection named after the Flemish geographer who used it for his world map of 1569.

a mercator projection

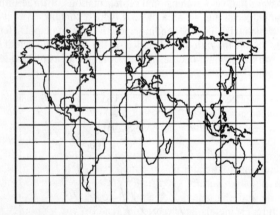

metamorphic rocks are rocks formed by the alteration or recrystallization of existing rocks by the application of heat, pressure, change in volatiles (gases and liquids), or a combination of these factors. There are several categories of *metamorphism* based upon the conditions of origin: *regional* - high pressure and temperature as found in *orogenic* (mountain-building) areas; *contact* - where the rocks are adjacent to an igneous body and have been altered by the heat (with little or no pressure); *dynamic* – very high, confined pressure with some heat, as generated in an area of faulting or thrusting, i.e. where rock masses slide against each other; *burial* – which involves high pressure and low temperature as found, for example, at great depth in sequences of sedimentary rocks.

The key feature of all metamorphic rocks is that the existing *assemblage* (group) of minerals is changed by the pressure and/or heat and the presence of fluids or other volatiles. New minerals grow that are characteristic of the new conditions. Some typical metamorphic rocks are schist, slate, gneiss, marble, quartzite and hornfels. Depending upon the type of metamorphism, there are systems of classification into *zones* or *grades* where specific minerals appear in response to increasing pressure and/or temperature.

meteorology is the scientific study of the conditions and processes within the Earth's atmosphere. This includes the pressure, temperature, wind speed, cloud formations, etc. which, over a period of time, enable meteorologists to predict likely future WEATHER patterns. Information is generated by weather stations, and also by satellites in orbit around the Earth.

mineralogy the scientific study of MINERALS, i.e. any chemical element or compound extracted from the Earth. It involves the following properties: colour, CRYSTAL form and cleavage, HARDNESS, specific gravity, lustre (how the mineral reflects light) and streak (the colour created by scratching the mineral on a special porcelain plate). Together, these properties help identify and classify minerals and one of the most important features is the *cleavage*.

Cleavage is the tendency for minerals to split along particular, characteristic planes which reflect and are controlled by the internal structure of the crystal. The plane of splitting is that which is weakest, due to the atomic structure of the crystal.

minerals are naturally-occurring inorganic substances that have definite and characteristic chemical compositions and CRYSTAL structures. Minerals have particular features and properties (*see, for example* HARDNESS *and also* MINERALOGY). Some elements occur as minerals, such as gold, diamond and copper but most minerals are made up of several elements (*see* **ST**- ELEMENT). Rocks are composed of minerals. There are about 2000 minerals, although the commonest rocks contain combinations from about 30 minerals, which in addition to quartz and calcite come from five or six main groups, all silicates. Silicate minerals are the most abundant rock-forming minerals and comprise about 95% of the Earth's crust, reflecting the fact that oxygen and silicon are the two commonest elements in rocks. The average make up of rocks in the crust is as follows:

silicia	SiO_2	59.3%
alumina	Al_2O_3	15.3%
iron	FeO	3.7%
oxides	Fe_2O_3	3.1%
lime	CaO	5.1%
soda	Na_2O	3.8%
potash	K_2O	3.1%
magnesia	MgO	3.5%
titania	TiO_2	0.7%
water	H_2O	1.3%
phosporus pentoxide	P_2O_5	0.3%

Silicate minerals are based upon a tetrahedral arrangement of four oxygen ions with one silicon ion, and these tetrahedral units are joined in various ways to each other and differing metal ions.

typical tetrahedral arrangement of a silicate mineral with the silicon ion shown at the centre

Some of the mineral groups:

group	example	structure
Feldspars	orthoclase	framework (tectosilicate)
Pyroxenes	augite	single-chain (inosilicate)
Amphiboles	horneblende	double-chain (inosilicate)
Micas	biotite	flat sheets (phyllosilicate)
Clays	kaolinite	flat sheets (phyllosilicate)
Garnet	pyrope	linked tetrahedra (neosilicate)

Minerals are mined and extracted for diverse purposes, e.g. ornamental stone (in the form of rocks), to generate metals for further use (gold, copper, iron, etc.) or as valuable items in their own right, e.g. diamonds.

monsoon generally refers to winds that blow in opposite directions during different seasons. Monsoons are related to temperature changes in the subtropics and pressure alterations associated with changing JET STREAMS. The word is derived from the Arabic *mausim* which means season, and its meaning has been extended to include the rains that accompany the wind. The Indian subcontinent has a rainy season in its southwesterly monsoon and other areas where monsoons are seen to strongest effect are S.E. Asia, China and Pakistan. However, monsoons also occur in N. Australia, E. & W. Africa.

mountains the formation of mountain chains clearly involves phenomenal movements of the Earth's crust and unimaginable forces, even though the process takes place over many millions of years. The process of mountain building (OROGENY or orogenesis) involves the accumulation of enormous thicknesses of sediments which are subsequently folded, faulted and thrusted, with igneous intrusions at depth (plutons of granite), producing rock complexes involving sedimentary, igneous and metamorphic rocks. A massive linear area that has been compressed in this way is called an orogenic belt and the formation of such belts is interpreted by means of PLATE TECTONICS. Different mechanisms are postulated for the formation of mountain chains, e.g the Andes by subduction of oceanic lithosphere; the collision of continents for the Himalayas and the addition of vast basins of sedimentary rocks and *island arcs* onto an existing plate in the case of the North American Cordillera (*see* PLATE TECTONICS *for definition of terms*).

The result of these global crustal movements is the mountain ranges as we see them today where the higher peaks belong to the younger ranges. The highest points on the seven continents are as follows:

peak	height	continent	country
Everest	8848m	Asia	Nepal/China
Acongagura	6960m	South America	Argentina
McKinley	6194m	N. & Central America	Alaska
Kilimanjaro	5895m	Africa	Tanzania
Elbrus	5642m	Europe	CIS
Vinson Massif	5140m	Antarctica	Antarctica
Mauna Kea	4205m	Oceania	Hawaii

Mountains have a considerable effect on local weather conditions and south-facing slopes in the northern hemisphere are warmer and drier than north-facing slopes because they receive more sun. When warm, moist air reaches a mountain, it cools as it rises, releasing moisture so on the leeward side the air descends and absorbs moisture. In many instances, deserts occur on the leeward side of a mountain range, e.g. the Gobi Desert (Asia), and the Mojave Desert of western North America. It is well-known that the temperature falls with height on a mountain – approximately 6°C for each 100m. Mountains thus show a variety of plants that vary with altitude.

natural gas hydrocarbons in a gaseous state which when found are often associated with liquid petroleum. The gas is a mixture of methane and ethane, with propane and small quantities of butane, nitrogen, carbon dioxide and sulphur compounds.

As with petroleum, gas owes its origin to the deposition of sediments that contain a lot of organic matter. After deposition and burial and through the action of heat, with time, oil and gas are produced. These migrate to a suitable reservoir rock where it resides until it is extracted by drilling. World gas reserves:

gas-producing country	%world share	reserves	%world share
CIS	37	CIS	38
USA	25	Iran	14
Canada	5	Adu Dhabi	4.25
Netherlands	3	Saudi Arabia	4.25
Algeria	2.5	USA	4
UK	2.3	Quatar	4
Indonesia	2.3	Algeria	2.7
Norway	1.4	Venezuela	2.5

The massive gas reserves of western Canada were first discovered towards the end of the last century when drilling for water for construction of the Canadian Pacific Railway.

oceans technically, those bodies of water that occupy the ocean basins, the latter beginning at the edge of the continental shelf. Marginal seas such as the Mediterranean, Caribbean and Baltic are not classed as oceans. A more general definition is all the water on the Earth's surface, excluding lakes and inland seas. The oceans are the North and South Atlantic; North and South Pacific; Indian and Arctic. Together with all the seas the salt water covers almost 71% of the Earth's surface.

From the shore the land dips away gently in most cases - the continental shelf - after which the gradient increases on the continental slope leading to the deep sea platform (at about 4 km depth). There are many areas of shallow seas on the continental shelf (*epicontinental seas*) e.g. North Sea, Baltic and Hudson Bay. In the ice age, much of the shelf would have been land and conversely should much ice melt, the continents would be submerged further. The floors of the oceans display both mountains, in the form of the mid-oceanic ridges, and deep trenches. The ridges rise 2-3 km from the floor and extend for thousands of kilometres while the trenches reach over 11 km below sea level, at their deepest (Mariana Trench, south-east of Japan).

The six ocean zones are:

littoral zone		between low and high water spring tides
pelagic zone	0-180 m	floating *plankton* and swimming *nekton*
neretic zone	low tide-180 m	*benthic* organisms
bathyal zone	180-1800 m	beyond light penetration, but much benthic life (crawling, burrowing or fixed plants and animals)
abyssal zone	>1800 m	
abyssal plain	~4000 m	ooze of calcareous and siliceous skeletal remains; red clay only below 5000 m

The oceans contain *currents*, i.e. faster-moving large-scale flows (the slower movements are called *drifts*). Several factors contribute to the formation of currents, namely the rotation of the Earth, prevailing winds, differences in temperature and sea water densities. Major currents move clockwise in the northern hemisphere and anticlockwise in the southern hemisphere. Well-known currents include the Gulf Stream and the Humboldt current.

the major currents

Oceanography is the study of all aspects of the oceans from their structure and composition to the life within and the movements of the water.

ore a naturally-occurring substance that contains metals or other compounds that are commercially useful and which it is economically feasible to mine for profit. *Native ores*, such as gold and copper, occur as the metallic element itself and not in a compound but most metals have to be extracted from compounds, commonly the oxide or sulphide. Minerals containing metallic elements are called ore minerals and ore deposits are aggregates of these minerals.

Extraction of an ore commonly involves removal from a pit (open cast mine) or shaft (in a deep mine). The ore rock is then crushed and possibly washed and sorted before being treated with heat or mixed with chemicals. A furnace may then be used to smelt the ore to produce the metal which separates off from the waste or slag.

Ores are produced geologically in several ways. Some mineral concentrations are associated with magmas, e.g. nickel, cobalt, chromium, platinum or tungsten compounds. Ore minerals are usually found in veins with no obvious connection to igneous activity and in this case may be formed by percolation of hot water laden with metals. Weathering and erosion can also lead to the concentration of certain ore minerals (bauxite or gold and zircon respectively).

orogony *see* MOUNTAINS.

ozone layer (*see also* S – OZONE) a part of the Earth's atmosphere, at approximately 15 -30 km height, that contains ozone. Ozone is present in very small amounts (one to ten parts per million) but it fulfils a very important role by absorbing much of the Sun's ultraviolet radiation, which has harmful effects in excess, causing skin cancer and cataracts and unpredictable consequences to crops, and plankton.

Recent scientific studies have shown a thinning of the ozone layer over the last 20 years, with the appearance of a hole over Antarctica in 1985. This depletion has been caused mainly by the build-up of CFCs (chlorofluorocarbons) from aerosol can propellants, refrigerants and chemicals used in some manufacturing processes. The chlorine in CFCs reacts with ozone to form ordinary oxygen, lessening the effectiveness of the layer. CFCs are now being phased out but the effects of their past use will affect the ozone layer for some time to come.

peat an organic deposit formed from plant debris which is laid down with little or no alteration or decomposition (break down) in a water-logged environment. Bogs, fens, swamps, moors and wetlands are all sites of peat production with some variation in peat structure depending upon the acidity of the conditions.

The conditions are vital so that oxygen is not available for the decay of plant material. As peat accumulates over the years, water is squeezed out and the lower peat layers shrink. However, air drying is essential when peat is cut for fuel. Acid conditions are commonest and *sphagnum moss* is the dominant peat vegetation. However, peat may form in shallow lakes through the gradual takeover by marsh vegetation, or it may develop in shallow lagoons, flood plains or deltas. Conditions for peat formation are currently found all over the world, and in addition to Ireland and Scotland, also on the coastal plains of Virginia and North Carolina, in the Everglades of Florida, Indonesia, India and Malaysia. After the last ice age there were lengthy periods of peat formation. The preserving properties of peat bogs have been seen to great effect over recent years when whole baby woolly mammoths and humans have been found.

permafrost is ground that is permanently frozen, save for surface melting in the summer. It is technically defined as being when the temperature is below 0°C for two consecutive years, and it can extend to depths of several hundred metres. The top layer that thaws in the summer is called the *active layer* and there may be unfrozen ground between this and the permafrost, a zone which is called *talik*. Depths of 1500 metres in Siberia and 650 metres in North America have been recorded and today permafrost underlies 20 – 25% of the Earth's land area – a figure that was much greater during parts of the Pleistocene.

The ground in areas of permafrost shows distinctive features including patterns of circles, polygonal cracks; mounds and pingos. Polygonal cracks are due to the contraction caused by cooling in winter and in Spitzbergen the polygons may reach 200 metres across. Mounds are caused simply by the increase in volume that accompanies freezing of water which pushes up surface layers of soil. Large mounds, up to 40 to 50 metres high are called *pingos*.

petroleum (or *crude oil*) is a mixture of naturally-occurring hydrocarbons formed by the decay of organic matter which, under pressure and increased temperatures, form oil. The often mentioned '*reservoir*' is the rock in which oil (and gas) is found and common types of reservoir rock are sandstone, limestone or dolomite. The oil migrates, after formation from the source rocks to the reservoir (because such vast quantities could not have been formed in place) where it must be contained by a *trap*. A trap is a particular geological configuration where the oil is confined by impermeable rocks.

typical geological traps

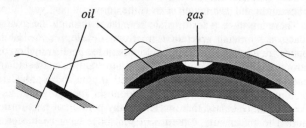

Most of the world's petroleum reserves are in the Middle East although the CIS and USA currently produce a significant proportion of the world's oil.

The modern oil industry began over a century ago when a well was bored for water in Pennsylvania, and oil appeared. Petroleum also occurs in the form of *asphalt* or *bitumen*, syrupy liquids or near solid in form, and there are significant deposits today. The Pitch Lake of Trinidad, over 500 metres across and about 40 metres deep, is fed from beneath as the asphalt is removed. There are similar occurrences in Venezuela and California and in Alberta, Canada are the famous Athabasca Oil Sands, where the sandstone is full of tar, an oil of asphalt.

Petroleum consists of many hydrocarbons (*see* S-HYDROCAR-BONS) of differingä composition with small amounts of sulphur, oxygen and nitrogen. The components areä separated and treated chemically to provide the basic building blocks and products forä the vast petrochemicals industry (*see* S-PETROCHEMICALS).

plate tectonics a concept that brings together the variety of features and processes of the Earth's crust and accounts for continental drift, sea-floor spreading, volcanic and earthquake activity, and crustal structure.

It has long been noticed how coastlines on opposite sides of oceans, e.g. the Atlantic, seemed to fit together. Other geological features led to the theory that continents were joined together millions of years ago. This theory was supported by a reconstruction of fossil magnetic poles and in 1962 by the idea of sea-floor spreading where ocean ridges were the site of new crust formation, with slabs of crust moving away from these central sites. All this was brought together with the idea that the *lithosphere* (the crust and uppermost part of the mantle) is made up of seven large and twelve smaller plates composed of oceanic or continental crust. The plates move relative to each other with linear regions of creation and destruction of the lithosphere.

There are three types of plate boundary; *ocean ridges* where plates are moving apart (constructive); *ocean trenches* where plates are moving together (also for young mountain ranges) (destructive); *transform faults* where plates move sideways past each other (conservative). At destructive plate boundaries one tectonic plate dips beneath the other at an oceanic trench in a process called *subduction* and in so doing old lithosphere is returned to the mantle. *Island arcs* are an example of volcanic activity associated with subduction at an ocean trench, where there is very often also earthquakes. Where two continental plates converge, the continents collide to produce mountains as seen in the Alps and Himalayas today. The transform faults of conservative plate boundaries are generated by the relative motion of two plates alongside each other and the best known example is the San Andreas fault in California, a region which suffers earthquakes along this major fracture.

plate boundaries

San Andreas fault indicated by broken line

rain one form of precipitation in which drops of water condense from the water vapour in the atmosphere to form rain drops. Other types of precipitation, all water in some liquid or solid form, include snow, hail, sleet, drizzle and also dew. Snow forms below 0°C and depending upon the temperature, occurs in different shapes. When the temperature is well below freezing, it forms ice *spicules* which are small and needle-like. Nearer to 0°C, the characteristic snowflakes grow, but at extremely low temperatures snow becomes powdery. Because snow can vary in its form and accumulation, accurate measurement of falls is difficult, but 25mm of water will be produced by about 300 mm of newly-fallen snow.

Hail is a small pellet of frozen water that forms by rain drops being taken higher into colder parts of the atmosphere. As it then falls, the hailstone grows by adding layers of ice, due to condensation of moisture upon the cold nucleus. *Dew* is the condensation of water vapour in the air caused by a cooling of the air.

remote sensing is the collection of a variety of information without contact with the object of study. This includes aerial photography from both aircraft and satellites and the use of infrared, ultraviolet and microwave radiation emitted from the object, e.g. an individual site, part of a town, crop and forest patterns. Another type of remote sensing involves the production of an impulse of light, or radar, which is reflected by the object and the image is then captured on film or tape.

Using these various techniques, large areas of the ground can be studied and surprisingly sharp pictures obtained which can be used in many ways. Remote sensing is used in agriculture and forestry, civil engineering, geology, geography and archaeology, amongst others. In addition, it is possible to create pictures with a remarkable amount of detail which would otherwise take a very long time to collect.

rivers streams of water that flow into the sea or in some cases into lakes or swamps. Rivers form part of the cyclical nature of water, comprising water falling from the atmosphere as some form of precipitation (*see* RAIN) and being partly fed by groundwaters or run-off from the melting of glaciers (both of which in any case are derived from atmospheric water).

Rivers develop their own immediate scenery and a river valley will owe its form to the original slope of the land, the underlying rocks and the climate. A river with its tributaries is called a *river system*, and the area from which its water is derived is the *drainage basin* (*see also* DRAINAGE). As rivers grow in size and velocity, rock and soil debris washed into them is carried downstream, eroding the river bed and sides as it goes. As a river continues to flow and carry debris, depositing much material in times of FLOOD, it widens its valley floor, forming a FLOODPLAIN. As it does, the river swings from side to side forming wide loops, called *meanders*. Eventually as meanders develop into ever more contorted loops, a narrow neck of land may be left which is eventually breached. Thus the river alters and shortens its course, leaving a horseshoe-shaped remnant, or *ox-bow* lake.

*development of river meander leading
to the formation of an Ox-bow lake*

rocks are aggregates of MINERALS or organic matter, and can be divided into three types, based upon the way they are formed: IGNEOUS, SEDIMENTARY and METAMORPHIC.

sedimentary rocks are rocks formed from existing rock sources through the processes of erosion, weathering and include rocks of organic or chemical origin. They can be divided into *clastic* rocks, that is made of fragments, *organic* or *chemical*.

The clastic rocks are further divided on grain size into coarse (or *rudaceous*, grains of 1-2 mm), medium (or *arenaceous*, eg sandstone) and fine (or *argillaceous* up to 0.06 mm). When the grains comprising clastic rocks are deposited (usually in water) compaction of the soft sediment and subsequent *lithification* (that is, turning into rock) produces the layered effect, or *bedding*, that is often visible in cliffs and outcrops in rivers. It is also common for original features to be preserved, for example ripples, small or large dune structures, which in an exposed rock face appear as inclined beds called *current bedding*. *Graded bedding* shows a gradual change in grain size from the base, where it is coarse, to the top of a bed, where it is fine and this is due to the settling of material onto the sea floor from a current caused by some earth movement.

Many sedimentary rocks, particularly shale, limestone and

finer sandstone contain FOSSILS of animals and plants from millions of years ago, and with the original features mentioned above, these are useful in working out the sequence of events in an area where the rocks have been strongly folded.

seismograph in the study of earthquakes (*seismology*), seismographs are used to record the shock waves (*seismic* waves) as they spread out from the source. The seismograph has some means of conducting the ground vibrations through a device to turn movement into a signal that can be recorded. There are numerous seismic stations around the world that record ground movements, each containing several seismographs with numerous *seismometers* (the actual detector linked to a seismograph).

soil is the thin layer of uncompacted material comprising organic matter and minute mineral grains that overlies rock and provides the means by which plants can grow. Soil is formed by the breakdown of rock, in a number of ways. Rock is initially fractured and broken up by weathering: the action of water, ice and wind, and any acids dissolved in water moving over, or percolating through the rock. This allows in various organisms that speed up the breakdown process and mosses, lichens, fungi then take hold and after a while there forms a mixture of organisms including bacteria, decayed organic material, weathered rock and *humus* which is called *topsoil*. Humus is decomposing (breaking down) organic material produced from dead organisms, leaves and other organic material by the action of bacteria and fungi.

The texture of the soil affects its ability to support plants and the most fertile soils are *loams* which contain mixtures of sand, silt and clay with organic material. This ensures there is sufficient water and minerals (which 'stick' to the finer particles) while the coarser sand grains provide air spaces, vital to roots. In addition to plant roots, soil contains an enormous number of organisms including fungi, algae, insects, earthworms, nematodes (roundworms) and several billion bacteria. Earthworms are useful in that they aerate the soil, and the bacteria alter the mineral composition of the soil.

The parent rock is the primary factor in determining the nature of a soil. While sand, silt and clay produce a loam, sand alone is too porous and clay too compacted and impervious (doesn't allow water through). A clay soil can be improved by adding lime, hence a *marl* (a lime rich clay) forms a good soil. Limestone itself does not produce a soil. The rate of breakdown of the rock is also important. Granites decompose slowly but basaltic rocks are the opposite and therefore yield their soil components quickly. This is seen particularly in volcanic areas where lava flows and volcanic ash quickly lead to very productive soils.It can take hundreds of years for soils to become fertile, but to be productive agriculturally, the soil has to be cared for with irrigation, fertilization and prevention of erosion all being important factors. This is apparent when you consider that the soil provides approximately 18 kg of nitrogen, 4 kg of potassium and 3 kg of phosphorus to grow one ton of wheat grain.

stalactites and stalagmites in areas of LIMESTONE where caves form and streams trickle through the rocks and caves, calcium-rich waters tend to drop from cave roofs. As there is a little evaporation from these drops of water, some of the dissolved calcium is deposited, as calcite (calcium carbonate, $CaCO_3$). This deposit builds up very slowly into a stalactite projecting down from the roof. If water continues to drop to the floor, a complementary upward growth develops into a stalagmite - and often the two meet to form a column, or pillar.

Many limestone caves exhibit spectacular developments e.g. White Scar at Ingleton in Yorkshire; La Cave in the Dordogne; Wookey Hole in the Mendips and many other places.

stratigraphy is the branch of geology concerned with the study of stratified rocks, i.e. rocks that were originally laid down in layers. It deals with the position of rocks in geological time and space, their classification and correlation between different areas. Rock units can be identified and differentiated by several means.

Stratigraphy began about two hundred years ago when it was first realized that in a normal sequence of rocks, relatively unaffected by any tectonic movements, younger rocks will lie above older rocks. This was known as the 'law' of superposition, but it soon became apparent that all sorts of geological events could upset this simplistic theory.

stratosphere one of the layers of the atmosphere, lying above the TROPOSPHERE. It lies at a height of between 10 and 50 km and shows an increase in temperature from bottom to top where it is 0°C. (The average temperature above is -60°C). A very large part of the ozone (*see* OZONE LAYER) in the atmosphere is found in the stratosphere and the absorption of ultraviolet radiation contributes to the higher temperature in the upper reaches. This inversion of temperature creates a stability which limits the vertical extent of cloud and produces the sideways extension of a cumulonimbus cloud into the characteristic shape.

thunder *see* LIGHTNING.

tides the regular rise and fall of the water levels in the world's oceans and seas which is due to the gravitational effect of the Moon and Sun. The Moon exerts a stronger pull than the Sun (roughly twice the effect) and variation in tides is caused by the relative positions of the three bodies and the distribution of water on the Earth. When the Sun, Moon and Earth are aligned, the effects are combined and result in a maximum, the high *spring tide* (when the Moon is new or full), conversely when the Sun is at right angles to the Moon, the effect is minimised resulting in a low *Neap tide*.

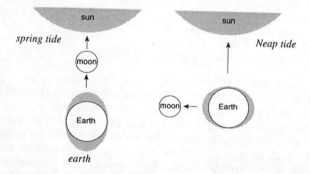

The effect of tides in the open oceans is negligible, perhaps one metre, and enclosed areas of water such as the Black Sea exhibit differences in the order of centimetres. However, in shallow seas where the tide may be channelled by the shores, tides of six to nine metres may be created.

The tides around Britain's coasts vary markedly due in part to the effect of the *Coriolis force*. This is when air or water is pushed to the side because of the Earth's rotation. Hence in the northern hemisphere, water moving across the surface is pushed to the right (and conversely in the southern hemisphere). Hence the tidal wave which passes northwards up the Irish Sea creates higher tides on the Welsh and English coasts than on the Irish side, and as the tidal wave moves into the North Sea, the Coriolis force pushes the water to the right giving higher tides on the British coastline than on the coasts of Norway and Denmark. The potential for generating energy from tides has long been realized and the first tidal power station was built in France and made operational in 1966.

time zones zones which run north-south, with some variations across the Earth, and which represent different times. Each zone is one hour earlier or later than the adjacent zone, and is 15° of *longitude*. The zones were devised for convenience, but to compensate for the accumulated time change, the *International Date-Line* was introduced. The line runs roughly on the 180° meridian, although it does detour around land areas in the Pacific Ocean, and to cross it going east means repeating a day, while in the opposite direction losing a day.

tornado a narrow column of air that rotates rapidly and leaves total devastation in its path. It develops around a centre of very low pressure with high velocity winds (well over 300 km/hour) blowing anticlockwise and with a violent downdraught. The typical appearance is of a funnel or snake-like column filled with cloud and usually no more than 150 metres across.

a tornado column

The precise way in which tornadoes form is not known although it involves the interface of warm moist air with dry cooler air and an inversion of temperatures with some event acting as a trigger, possibly an intense cold front. These conditions are found in many countries at mid to low latitudes but particularly so in the mid-west of the USA. The destruction created by tornadoes is due partly to the violent winds and partly to the very low pressure. This has the effect of causing buildings to explode outwards because the pressure outside exceeds that inside and although a tornado may affect an area only 100-150 metres across, the destruction is total. Tornadoes are often unpredictable in their behaviour and can lose contact with the ground or retrace its route. When it moves out over the sea, and once the tunnel has joined with the waves, a *waterspout* is formed.

tropics are two lines of LATITUDE that lie 23.5° north and south of the equator. The northern line is the *Tropic of Cancer* and the southern one the *Tropic of Capricorn*, and the region between them is called the tropics.

The term tropical is often used to describe climate, vegetation etc but it is not an accurate usage of the word. In general a tropical climate does not have a cool season and the mean temperature never falls below 20°C. Rainfall can be very high indeed and in many countries these conditions produce a dense, lush vegetation e.g. tropical rain forests.

troposphere the part of the Earth's atmosphere between the surface and the *tropopause* (the boundary with the STRATOSPHERE). The tropopause is the point at which the change in temperature with height (the lapse-rate) stops and the temperature remains constant for several kilometres. Within the troposphere itself, the temperature decreases approximately 6.5°C for each kilometre of height. The troposphere is also the layer that contains most of the water vapour and about 75% of the weight of gas in the atmosphere and it is the zone where turbulence is greatest and most weather features occur.

The level of the tropopause, and therefore the top of the troposphere, varies from about 17 km at the equator falling to 9 km or lower at the poles. The height variation relates to temperature and pressure at sea-level.

tsunami (plural is also tsunami) an enormous sea wave caused by the sudden large-scale movement of the sea floor resulting in the displacement of large volumes of water. The cause may be an EARTHQUAKE, volcanic eruption, a submarine, slide or slump of sediment which may itself have been started by an earthquake or tremor. The slipping of thousands of tonnes of rock from the sides of fjords may also cause tsunami.

The effect of this sea floor movement in the open ocean may not be seen at all, as the resulting wave may only be one metre or less in height. However, because the whole depth of water is affected, there is a vast amount of energy involved, so when the waves reach shallow water or small bays, the effects can be catastrophic. The waves may travel at several hundred kilometres per hour (600-900) and reach heights of 15-30 metres. The devastation caused is clearly going to be terrible and there are many such instances in the record.

The word originates from the Japanese (*tsu*: harbour and *nami*: waves) where there have been many instances of destructive tsunami. In 1933, an earthquake triggered tsunami with waves up to 27 metres high and thousands of people were drowned along the Japanese coast. The waves were actually recorded about 10 hours later in San Francisco, having crossed the Pacific. It seems that tsunami are generated by submarine earthquakes registering 8 or over on the Richter scale.

tundra is the treeless region between the snow and ice of the arctic and the northern extent of tree growth. Large treeless plains can be found in northern Canada, Alaska, northern Siberia and northern Scandinavia. The ground is subject to PERMAFROST but the surface layer melts in the summer, so soil conditions are very poor, being waterlogged and marshy. The surface therefore can support little plant life. Cold temperatures and high winds also limit the diversity of plants, restricting the *flora* to grasses, mosses, lichens, sedges and dwarf shrubs. Some areas of tundra receive the same low level of precipitation as deserts yet the soil remains saturated due to the partial thaw of the permafrost. Most growth occurs in rapid bursts during the almost continuous daylight of the very short summers.

Due to the inhospitable conditions, animal life is also limited, although more numerous in summer. In addition to insects (midges, mosquitoes, etc.) and migratory birds, there are wolves, arctic foxes, lemmings, hares, snowy owls and the herbivorous reindeer in Europe and caribou in northern America. Polar bears occur at the coast.

In addition to this arctic tundra, there is also *alpine tundra* which is found on the highest mountain tops and is therefore widely spread. However, conditions differ because of daylight throughout the year and plant growth in the tropical alpine tundra also occurs all year round.

unconformity is a break in the deposition of SEDIMENTARY ROCKS representing a gap in the geological record. The unconformity is the junction between younger rocks (above) and older and is formed by a succession of rocks being pushed and possibly folded, eroded and then submerged again so that new sediments is deposited on the older rocks. Usually the rocks above and beneath the unconformity lie at different angles.

However it is possible for an unconformity to be represented by differing beds with the same orientation (*disconformity*), or simply by a surface which indicates non-deposition but shows no other apparent breaks, or by sediments being deposited on an igneous intrusion which has been eroded.

volcano a natural vent or opening in the Earth's crust which is connected by a pipe, or *conduit*, to a chamber at a depth that contains MAGMA. Through this pipe (usually called a *vent*) may be ejected LAVA, volcanic gases, steam and ash and it is the amount of gas held in the lava, and the way in which it is released on reaching the surface that determines the type of *eruption*.

Volcanoes may be *active* i.e. actually erupting whether just clouds of ash and steam or lava; *extinct* that is the activity ceased a long time ago; or *dormant*. Dormant volcanoes have often in the past been thought to be extinct, only to erupt again with startling ferocity.

Volcanoes can be described by the type of eruption which is named after a particular volcano which exhibits a specific eruption pattern. These are:

Hawaiian	violent eruptions with viscous lava and *nuées ardentes**
Peléean	moderate eruptions, small explosions and lava of average viscosity
Strombolian	very explosive after a dormant period with ash/gas clouds and gas filled lava
Vesuvian	very explosive with *pyroclastics*** ejected in a column up to 50 kg high producing thick airfall deposits
Plinian	outpouring of fluid lava and little explosive activity

*nuées ardentes - an old term meaning an incandescent ash flow that moves rapidly

**pyroclastics - volcanic rocks formed from broken fragments e.g. bombs, pumice, ash, cinders

Volcanoes of the Hawaiian type are also called *shield* volcanoes. The sides of the volcanoes are almost flat due to the rapid flow of the lava. *Composite* volcanoes show greater angles of slope due to a build up of lava and pyroclastic material. Both shield and composite types are also called central type because the supply comes from a central vent, as opposed to *fissure* volcanoes which erupt through splits where the crust is under tension.

shield volcano with a central vent

Active volcanoes occur in belts associated with the tectonic plates (*see* PLATE TECTONICS) with about 80% of the active subaerial volcanoes at destructive plate margins, 15% at constructive plate margins and the remainder within plates. Most submarine volcanism is at constructive plate margins.

The environmental effect of volcanoes can be very significant, whether it be the enormous amounts of ash ejected into the atmosphere or the consequences of lava flows consuming the countryside. At the time of eruption, volcanic materials are often over 1000°C, hence flows either burn, push over or cover whatever they meet.

Over 500 volcanoes have been active in historic times but only about 50 erupt each year, often on a very small scale.

water table the level below which water saturates the spaces in the ground; the top of the zone where groundwater saturates permeable rocks. It is where atmospheric pressure is equalled by the pressure in the groundwater. The position (*elevation*) of the water table varies with the amount of rainfall etc, loss through evaporation and transpiration from vegetation, percolations through the soil. A spring or seepage occurs when, due to geological conditions, the water table rises above ground level (*see also* AQUIFER).

weather the combined effect of atmospheric pressure, temperature, sunshine, cloud, humidity, wind and the amount of precipitation which together make up the weather for a certain place over a particular (usually short) time period. The weather varies enormously around the Earth but some countries have a stable weather pattern while Britain has a changeable one because it is at a location where many different air masses meet. The surface at which two air masses with different meteorological properties meet is called a *front*.

a cold front   *a warm front*

A *warm front* occurs in a depression, between warm air moving over cold air, and it heralds drizzle followed by heavy rain which then gives way to rising temperatures. A *cold front* is the leading edge of a cold air mass which moves under warm air, forcing the latter to rise. The result is a fall in temperature, with rainfall passing behind the front.

weathering is a combination of chemical and physical processes on the surface of the Earth, or very near to it, which breaks down rocks and minerals. Weathering takes various forms and can be divided into mechanical, chemical and organic:

mechanical	*freeze-thaw action* (alternate freezing and thawing of water in cracks producing widening or break up) *exfoliation* peeling off in thin rock layers (like onion skin) *disintegration* into grains
chemical	*carbonation* the reaction of weak carbonic acid (H_2CO_3) with the rock *hydrolysis* combination of water with minerals to form insoluble residues (e.g. clay, minerals) *oxidation* and *reduction*
organic	*breakdown* by flora and fauna e.g. burrowing animals, tree roots, and the release of *organic acids* from decomposed plants which react with minerals

These weathering processes together produce a layer of material which may then be moved by processes of EROSION.

wind a generally horizontal or near-horizontal movement of air caused by changes in atmospheric pressure in which air normally moves from areas of high to low pressure. Wind speed is greater when the ISOBARS (lines joining points at the same pressure) are closely packed on weather maps and the *Beaufort scale* provides a systematic guide to windspeed. Due to the Earth's rotation and the effect of the Coriolis force (*see* TIDES), air in the northern hemisphere flows clockwise around a high pressure area and anticlockwise around a low.

The *Trade Winds* play an important part in the atmospheric circulation of the Earth and they are mainly easterly winds that blow from the subtropics to the equator. The *Westerlies* flow from the high pressure of the subtropics to the low pressure of the temperate zone. The Westerlies form one of the strongest wind flows and their strength increases with height (*see* JET STREAM) and depressions are most common in this wind system. The *Doldrums* is a zone of calms or light winds around the equator applied particularly to the oceans, with obvious links to the time when sailing ships were becalmed. Also linked to sailing are the *Roaring Forties*, which are Westerlies in the southern hemisphere where they tend to be stronger. However, the supposed link of Trade wind with early travel on the sea is incorrect–their origin is from the latin word meaning constant.

the trade winds

In addition to its destructive power, wind provides an additional hazard when combined with cold. *Wind-chill* is the effect wind has in lowering apparent temperatures through increasing heat loss from the body. For example in calm conditions at 10°F there is little danger for someone properly clothed, but if the wind speed in 25 mph, then the wind-chill creates an equivalent temperature of -29°F which is potentially harmful.

NATURAL HISTORY

The animal and plant kingdoms contain so many millions of species that it would be impossible to cover them all in one volume. All living things can be classified, however, according to their stucture and anatomy. This section of the *Concise Encylopedia* lists the different classes and groups found in nature and explains their common characteristics. There are also explanations of more general terms commonly used to describe features of the natural world. The entries are in A to Z order, and there are cross-references, indicated in SMALL CAPITALS, to enable you to relate specific animals or plants to their parent group.

*

acid rain contains a high concentration of dissolved chemical pollutants such as sulphur and nitrogen oxides. The pollutants arise as gases, given off mainly by the burning of fossil fuels (coal and oil) by industries, vehicles and power stations. The wind may carry the acid gases a long way from their source, but eventually they dissolve in water and fall elsewhere as acid rain. Both the gases and the acid rain cause damage to plant and animal life and lead to an increase in the acidity of water sources such as lakes and rivers. This may cause long-term deterioration in the natural environment affecting numerous plants, animals and micro-organisms.

adaptation a feature or characteristic of an organism that has evolved under the processes of natural selection. It enables the organism to exploit a particular aspect of its environment more efficiently. All organisms have adaptations enabling them to survive in their habitat.

Familiar adaptations include the shape and size of birds' beaks and animals' teeth (according to what they eat); the powerful, digging front legs and claws in such burrowing animals as moles and flippers in swimming animals such as seals. However, if they become too specialized, they may not be able to survive a sudden change (e.g. in climate) and may become extinct. There are fears for the survival of the panda, which is highly specialized and adapted in terms of its habitat and diet (because it consists solely of bamboo shoots).

The illustration below shows how the human foot has adapted for an upright stance whereas the chimpanzee foot has adapted for gripping and climbing.

chimpanzee foot   *human foot*

adaptive radiation the separation of species through evolutionary process and natural selection (*see* DARWIN and NATURAL SELECTION) into many descendant species which are able to exploit a variety of different habitats. An example is the vast numbers of different amphibians which have evolved since their early ancestors moved on to land.

agnathan lampreys and hagfishes (order Cyclostomata) belong to the vertebrate class called Agnatha. These are aquatic, eel-like animals belonging to a very ancient group. Their characteristic feature is a lack of jaws and they have a sucking mouth with horny teeth. They are scavengers or parasites on larger fish.

alga the common name for a simple water plant which lacks roots, stems and leaves but is able to PHOTOSYNTHESIZE. *Algae* range in size from single cells to plants many metres in length.

amoeba *see* PROTOZOAN.

amphibian salamanders, newts, frogs and toads, are members of the vertebrate class called the Amphibia which were the first vertebrates to colonize the land about 370 million years ago. The modern ones tend to be highly specialized and not typical of their fossil ancestors, and many of their characteristics are adaptations for life on land. However, most have to return to water to breed and the young (larvae – *see* **ST** – LARVA and METAMORPHOSIS) are aquatic and breathe through gills. In order to become adults they undergo METAMORPHOSIS. Adult amphibians respire through nostrils that are linked by a passage to the roof of the mouth, and also through their skin which is kept moist.

anaconda *see* SQUAMA.

angiosperm one of the class Angiospermae, the flowering plants. These are the most complex and highly developed plants and this enables them to live in a great many different habitats as they have evolved various specializations. The female reproductive cell or gamete is formed within a structure called an *ovule*, itself protected by a closed sheath known as the *carpel*. After fertilization, the ovule develops into a seed and seeds may be contained by fruits, (*see* also FLOWERS and PLANTS).

annelid ragworms (class Polychaeta), earthworms (class Oligochaeta) and leeches (class Hirudinea) belong to the invertebrate phylum Annelida. These familiar animals have an outer layer or cuticle usually composed of *collagen*-like proteins. The body is cylindrical in shape and divided into segments each bearing stiff bristles (*chaetae*) made of chitin (a hydrocarbon with nitrogen). The body cavity is called the *coelom* and is fluid filled. It provides a firm base (*hydrostatic skeleton*), against which muscles present in the body wall can contract to cause movement. A simple nervous system (*see* **ST**) consisting of a pair of *nerve cords* with *ganglia* (swellings) is present. Some worms live in the soil and leaf litter whereas others inhabit marine or freshwater habitats. Earthworms are a vital part of the cycle of decay, eating soil which passes through the gut, food substances being absorbed along the way. Waste material passes out of the body as *castings*. The activity of earthworms helps to till and aerate the soil and the castings improve the texture. Hence they are of great value to farmers, gardeners and horticulturists.

an earthworm

anthozoan or **actinozoan** one belonging to the class Anthozoa or Actinozoa which includes sea pens, sea pansies, sea feathers, sea fans, sea anemones and corals. This class of small marine animals belongs to the phylum Coelenterata (*see* CNIDARIAN) which also includes jellyfish and hydras. They are very simple animals with a circular body plan (known as *radial symmetry*) in the form of a structure called a *polyp*. A polyp is a small cylinder attached to an underlying surface such as a rock, the free end usually having a ring of tentacles for feeding.

a sea anemone

The polyps may exist alone or in colonies, as with many of the corals. Corals have hard external skeletons (exoskeletons) made of calcium carbonate, which are often delicately shaped and coloured. Other animals in this group have structures forming a simple internal skeleton.

apes *see* **primates**

arachnid spiders, scorpions, mites, ticks, king crabs, harvestmen, etc. all belong to this class of INVERTEBRATES called Arachnida.

Some animals in this group, especially the spiders, are very familiar to, and hold a special fascination for man. Most arachnids are terrestrial animals and, unlike insects, they have a head and thorax (middle region of the body) which are not divided from one another. These are formed from eight segments and make up a structure called the *prosoma*. The rest of the body is made up of 13 segments and is called the *opithosoma*. In the head region there are two pairs of projections or *appendages*. The first are called *chelicerae* and are adapted for piercing and grasping prey as most arachnids are carnivorous. The second pair are called the *pedipalps* and these can be specialized to perform a variety of different functions as sense organs, for copulation or noise production. Behind these are four pairs of walking legs and on the *opithosoma*, there may be other specialized appendages, e.g. for silk spinning (spinnerets in spiders) or for injecting poison (as with scorpions). Ticks and mites are parasites on other animals but most arachnids are free-living.

an arachnid

chelicerae

pedipalps

opithosoma

arthropod one belonging to the largest phylum of INVERTEBRATE animals called Arthropoda which contains over one million known species occupying many different habitats. They are often highly specialized and include such classes as the Crustacea (lobsters, crabs, shrimps), Insecta (insects), Arachnida (spiders, mites, scorpions) and Myriapoda (millipedes and centipedes).

artiodactyl one of the mammalian order Artiodactyla that includes cattle, camels, hippopotamuses, pigs, deer, antelope, goats, sheep and llamas. These animals are even-toed with the third and fourth toes equally developed to support the whole weight of the body. They are one order of mammals which make up the group commonly called the Ungulates, the other being the Perissodactyla (horses, tapirs, rhinoceros and zebra).

avian (bird) belonging to Aves, a *class* of VERTEBRATES which evolved from flying reptiles and still show some features of their ancestry. The most notable of these is the production of reptilian-like eggs and the presence of scales on the legs. Typically, the body of a bird is highly modified for flight with a lighter skeleton than that of other vertebrates. Some organs may even be absent to reduce weight, e.g. females possess only one ovary. The front limbs are developed as wings which are aerodynamically special-ized for flight. Birds are covered with feathers and those of the wings are modified for flight while others provide insulation. The breastbone of the skeleton is well developed and has a structure called a *keel* to which the large flight muscles are attached. Birds lack teeth but grind up food in a special part of the gut called the *gizzard*. The jaws are developed to form a beak or bill and a great many different sizes and shapes occur enabling birds to exploit numerous different habitats and types of food.

class Aves

subclass Archaeornithes extinct early birds, e.g. *Archaeopteryx*	subclass Neornithes all modern birds
super order Palaeognathae (the walking birds or ratites) usually flightless and large, e.g. ostrich, emu, cassowary kiwi, elephant bird, moa, rhea.	super order Neognathae (the flying birds) contains numerous orders, e.g. perching, (Passeriformes) including all the song birds, parrots, (Psittaciformes) and eagles, hawks, vultures, etc. (Falconiformes)

Bacillariophyta is the division to which *diatoms*, a type of ALGAE, belong. They are simple, single-celled plants, which sometimes form chains or colonies, and live in both marine and fresh water environments. They are vital ORGANISMS in the PLANKTON and, since they PHOTOSYNTHESIZE, form the basis of FOOD CHAINS. They have beautiful and unique glassy cell walls made of silica and are important fossils. Enormous accumulations of their cell walls are mined as *diatomaceous earth* (or kieselguhr) which has various uses in industry. Planktonic diatoms store food as oil and this has contributed to the petroleum reserves that are extracted and used today.

barrier reef a reef of coral built up in a line running parallel to the shore but at some distance from it, so as to create a lagoon. A good example is the Great Barrier Reef, Australia which is almost 2000 km (1250 miles) long. A barrier reef usually provides a rich and varied habitat and is home to many different kinds of plants and animals.

beaver *see* RODENT.

benthos the benthos consists of all the plants and animals living in or on the bottom of the sea, lake or a river. The organisms are described as *benthic* and they may burrow, crawl or remain attached.

biome a geographical area that is characterized by particular ECOSYSTEMS of plants, animals and micro-organisms. It is created by and related to climate and is usually mainly distinguished by the form of vegetation it supports. Examples of biomes are desert, savanna, tropical forest, chaparral (scrubland), temperate grassland, temperate deciduous forest, taiga (coniferous or boreal forest) and tundra.

biosphere the region of the Earth's surface (both land and water) and its immediate atmosphere, which can support any living organism.

birds *see* AVIAN.

bivalve many species of shellfish, e.g. mussels, oysters, scallops, clams and razorshells, are called bivalves (class Bivalvia) of the phylum Mollusca.

These animals are characterized by having a body enclosed within a shell divided into two halves (bivalve shell) which is flattened and hinged along the mid-line. They have a smaller head than that of most other molluscs and usually do not move around, living on the bottom of lakes or the sea. However, more mobile kinds such as scallops occur and also burrowing ones such as the shipworm and razorshell.

boa *see* SQUAMA.

bony fishes most fish have a bony skeleton containing calcium phosphate and a body covered with overlapping scales. These are the bony fishes or class Osteichthyes and include many familiar freshwater and marine species. They have jaws (compare AGNATHA), gills covered by a protective flap called the *operculum* and often possess an air sac called a *swim bladder* for buoyancy. They usually lay large numbers of eggs which are fertilized externally and examples include cod, haddock, salmon, trout and sticklebacks.

a bony fish

gills

swim bladder

brachiopod lampshells are an ancient group of marine animals belonging to the phylum Brachiopoda. Along with two other phyla, they possess a special structure called a lophophore which is used for feeding and RESPIRATION. They have a bivalve shell and a stalk, known as a peduncle, which attaches the animal to the surface on which it lives. Brachiopods are very important INDEX FOSSILS and one kind, *Lingula* has survived to the present day little changed from the Ordovician geological period, 500 – 440 million years ago.

Lingula

brackish water occurs in estuaries (*see* ESTUARY) and is intermediate in saltiness between sea and fresh water.

bryophyte these simple plants belong to the class Bryophyta. They are mosses which commonly thrive in shady, wet conditions and have a waxy, outer layer (*cuticle*) which helps to prevent them from drying out. Mosses lack true roots but may be attached to a surface by hairs (*rhizoids*) or use other plants for support. The hornworts and liverworts are other simple plants which are commonly included in the Bryophyta, although this is now considered to be scientifically incorrect. The three types, although sharing several common features, are probably not closely related.

butterflies *see* LEPIDOPTERAN.

camels *see* ARTIODACTYL.

camouflage a kind of colour pattern or body shape which helps to disguise an animal and enable it to blend into its background. This is useful for both predators and prey animals and can be seen in many different species from invertebrates to large MAMMALS. Patterns of camouflage have evolved through the processes of natural selection (*see* DARWIN) and may be quite intricate and complex.

Examples include moths patterned to look like bark or possessing false eye spots, preying mantis, many fishes and animals such as tiger and zebra.

capybara *see* RODENT.

carnivore belonging to an order of mammals called Carnivora. They are largely flesh-eaters, including both predators and carrion eaters and those which combine the two. Many of these animals show adaptations of the jaws and teeth. They possess a powerful bite and large piercing and shearing teeth. They often have retractile claws and two sub-orders are recognized, the toe-footed carnivores (*Fissipedia*) such as wolves, dogs, cats, raccoons, weasels and badgers, and the fin-footed carnivores (*Pinnepedia*), e.g. walruses, sea lions and seals.

carnivorous plants there are about 400 different species of carnivorous plants that are usually insectivorous. They often grow in poor conditions which would not normally supply enough minerals and nourishment. Hence they are specially adapted to attract, trap and digest mainly insect prey in ingenious and highly effective ways. For example, *Sundews* secrete a sticky substance on the leaves which holds insects fast. *Pitcher plants* have modified leaves forming a water-filled trap with smooth sides into which an insect falls and drowns. *Venus fly traps* have hinged leaves with spines at the edges which snap shut over an insect. Once an insect (or other small prey) is caught, these carnivorous plants release digestive ENZYMES and eventually dissolved food substances are absorbed.

the pitcher plant

cartilaginous fishes a class of fishes called the Chondrichthyes which are highly specialized, having a skeleton composed entirely of CARTILAGE. The most familiar examples are the *rays*, *sharks* and *skates* (belonging to the sub-class Elasmobranchii) and also the ratfish, sub-class Holocephali (Chimeras).

cats *see* CARNIVORE.

caterpillars *see* LEPIDOPTERAN.

cattle *see* ARTIODACTYL.

centipede *see* MYRIAPOD.

cephalopod belonging to the class Cephalopoda and including nautilus, squids, cuttlefish, octopuses and the (extinct) fossil ammonites. The most advanced group in the phylum Mollusca.

The ammonites had well-developed spiral shells with the animal living inside the last chamber, but *Nautilus* is the only living species that has this structure. In the modern species the shell is much reduced as in the squids, or is inside the body as in cuttlefish or absent altogether as in octopuses. Cephalopods are mainly marine predators, with a well-developed head surrounded by a ring of tentacles used to seize their prey. They swim by jet propulsion – expelling water from the body using muscular action. They have complicated eyes and excellent vision and a well-developed nervous system which makes them the most intelligent invertebrate animals. Cuttlefish are able to show remarkable colour changes possibly as a means of communication.

a squid

cestode belonging to the class Cestoda of the phylum Platyhelminthes. These are the parasitic *tapeworms* of man and animals. Tapeworms live inside the gut of a vertebrate having a head with suckers and hooks which attaches the animal to the intestinal lining of its host. Behind the head there is a series of sacs (called *proglottids*) which give the appearance of segments. Each of these has male and female sex organs and these animals are *hermaphrodite*. The outer surface is protected from the digestive juices of the host's gut by a tough, outer CUTICLE. Tapeworms do not have a gut but dissolved food substances are absorbed over the whole body surface. The life cycle requires both a primary and secondary host. In one tapeworm that affects humans *Taenia saginata*, the beef tapeworm, the primary host containing the adult animal is man and the secondary hosts are cattle. Human beings are infected by eating poorly cooked meat containing cysts (immature worms with a protective shell) which develop into adults once they have been eaten.

the sucker-head of the tapeworm (right) and a cross-section of the body (left)

cetacean belonging to the order Cetacea, these are dolphins and whales. They are characterized by having forelimbs developed as *flippers*, and a powerful, flattened tail with two *flukes*, and a dorsal fin. These animals are excellent swimmers and have a thick layer of blubber (fat) beneath a nearly hairless skin serving as insulation and a food store. Air is drawn into the lungs through a blowhole on the upper surface and can be shut off when the animal dives. Dolphins, killer whales and toothed whales are predators belonging to the sub-order *Odontocetti*. Many of the great whales, e.g. the blue whale, are plankton-feeders belonging to the sub-order *Mysticetti*. They filter vast quantities of sea water through whalebone plates in order to extract their food. The blue whale is the largest known living animal, in excess of 150 tonnes in weight and 30 metres (100 feet) in length.

chameleon *see* SQUAMA.

chelonian belonging to the order Chelonia of the class Reptilia (see REPTILE) turtles and including terrapins and tortoises. The body of these animals is encased in a bony shell covered by horny plates. Both marine and land-dwelling species occur and they have jaws developed as horny beaks without teeth. These are a very ancient group of reptiles apparently little changed throughout their evolutionary history.

chimera *see* CARTILAGINOUS FISHES.

chiropteran the bat belongs to the mammalian order Chiroptera, the main characteristic of which is flight. They have membrane-like wings spread between elongated forelimbs and fingers and the hind limbs and, occasionally, the tail. Most bats are nocturnal insect-eaters, catching their prey on the wing. They have large ears adapted for *echo-location* by means of which they locate prey and sense their surroundings. Some are nectar-feeders, others eat fruit and *vampire* bats suck blood.

Chlorophyta green algae, belonging to the division Chlorophyta are the largest and most varied group of algae, possessing chlorophyll and able to photosynthesize. They are mainly aquatic in both marine and freshwater although are able to live on land in damp conditions. A well-known type is *Spirogyra*.

cnidarian hydras, jellyfish and sea anemones and corals belong to the phylum Cnidaria (or *Coelenterata*). These simple aquatic invertebrates have two body forms, an attached stalk called a *polyp* and a free-swimming bell called a *medusa*. Depending upon the species, one or other body form may predominate or one may succeed another in what is known as an 'alternation of generations.' These animals are carnivorous, with stinging cells which immobilize their prey, and tentacles around the 'mouth.' (*see* ACTINOZOA and HYDROZOA).

cobra *see* SQUAMA.

cockroach *see* ORTHOPTERAN.

coelacanth a type of bony fish, belonging to the order Coelacanthiformes, sub-order Crossypterygii, the flesh-finned fishes. All were thought to be extinct but a living representative was discovered in 1938. Living coelacanths are members of the genus *Latimeria* and have a characteristic three-lobed tail fin. They are large fish living at great depths on the floor of the Indian Ocean and 'walk' on their crutch-like pectoral fins. Coelacanths give birth to live young and do not possess lungs. They are a remnant of numerous kinds of lobe-finned fishes that were present in the *Devonian* geological period (408 – 360 million years ago). However, these extinct forms were freshwater animals with lungs and some were the ancestors of the amphibians.

coleopteran beetles and weevils belong to a vast order, Coleoptera, (the largest in the animal kingdom), of the class Insecta, and there are about 500,000 known species. They are found in a great number of different habitats, some feeding on vegetation, others on decaying material and the rest are predatory and carnivorous. They have two pairs of wings but the first are protective sheaths (called *elytra*) which are hard and, when folded, meet precisely in a line along the middle of the back. They protect the delicate, membranous hindwings which are used for flying (but are reduced or not present in other species). The mouth parts are often enlarged for biting, and both young (larvae) and adult beetles of certain species can be serious economic pests of crops, timber and stored food. Many beetles are beautifully coloured and patterned.

colony a group of individuals of the same species, living together and to some extent dependent on one another. In some cases the individuals may actually be joined, as in corals, and function as one unit. In others, e.g. social insets such as bees and ants, they are separate individuals but have a complex organization with specialized functions.

commensalism *see* SYMBIOSIS.

conservation means managing the environment in such a way as to preserve the natural resources of plants, animals and minerals etc. and to minimize the impact of man. The natural environment is in a constant state of change, and species become extinct and landscapes and climate alters, but this is usually over a long period of time. Man's activities are often devastating and whole ECOSYSTEMS can be lost very rapidly (e.g. clearance of the tropical rainforest). The environment which is left after such activities is usually significantly poorer and man's gains tend to be short-lived. Hence conservation involves planning ahead, preservation, restoration and reconstruction all the while minimizing damage. This may be on a small scale or global, and conservation is now recognized to be of vital importance to the survival and quality of life of human beings as well as other plants and animals.

copepod tiny marine and freshwater invertebrate animals which belong to the large sub-class called Copepoda of the class Crustacea. They are all between 0.5 – 2mm long and do not have a shell (carapace) or compound eyes. They have five or six pairs of swimming legs and are very important species in the PLANKTON. Some may be free-living filter feeders while others (e.g. the fish louse) are parasitic. A well-known freshwater type has one simple eye (ocellus) in the mid-line and is called *Cyclops*.

corals *see* ANTHOZOAN.

cricket *see* ORTHOPTERAN.

crustacean lobsters, crayfish, crabs, shrimps, pill bugs, prawns, barnacles, water fleas and COPEPODS belong to the class Crustacea of the phylum Arthropoda. They have a well-defined head and the body (thorax and abdomen) is divided into segments although these may not be obvious. Various projections called appendages are used for a variety of different purposes, e.g. swimming, feeding and as gills for RESPIRATION.

cyanobacteria the commonly-named blue-green algae which are now regarded as bacteria. They are *procaryotic* organisms and may be single-celled or occur in colonies or as filaments. They are found in all aquatic environments and are often very specialized, growing, for example in hot springs. They possess the ability to photosynthesize and some are able to trap nitrogen and are important in soil fertility. Some kinds occur in the PLANKTON, others form *symbiotic* (SYMBIOSIS) relationships with other organisms (e.g. lichens). Blooms of some species in freshwater lakes which have been enriched with agricultural fertilizers can be a problem, as toxins are produced that are lethal to fish and other animals.

cyclostomata *see* AGNATHAN.

decapod prawns, shrimps, lobsters and crabs belong to the order Decapoda of the class Crustacea (*see* CRUSTACIAN). These animals characteristically possess five pairs of walking legs, the first pair of which (in the crawling varieties) are modified to form powerful pincers. The others are used for feeding or swimming.

decomposer an organism that break down dead organic matter such as plants, animals and animal waste in order to obtain energy, leaving behind simple organic or inorganic waste. Carbon dioxide is produced and heat is released during decomposition and the main organisms involved are bacteria and fungi but also earthworms (*see* ANNELID) and other INVERTEBRATES.

deforestation the felling and removal of trees from an area of natural forest which usually has a devastating effect on the environment. It is carried out to provide wood for fuel (for local people) or for the timber trade, or to clear land for agriculture. Often the soil is very low in minerals and its fertility is soon exhausted. On slopes the soil can be washed away by water gushing down, leading to erosion and landslides. The end result of deforestation can be the creation of near-desert conditions.

deer *see* ARTIODACTYLA.

diatoms *see* BACILLARIOPHYTA.

dinosaurs were a large group of reptiles that flourished some 190 to 65 million years ago during the *Jurassic* and *Cretaceous* geological periods (*see* GEOLOGICAL TIMESCALE). They showed a tremendous variety of body shape and size included flying species. It was once thought that they were all slow, cold-blooded creatures but now scientists believe that many were fast-moving and able to keep their bodies warm by metabolic activities.

The climate in the Cretaceous period changed considerably. For reasons that are still not absolutely clear, the vast majority of the dinosaurs disappeared in a mass extinction occurring over 5 to 10 million years at the end of the Cretaceous.

a dinosaur

dipteran flies belong to a large insect order Diptera which containins about 80,000 species. These are called the true or two-winged flies but the back pair are modified to form knobs (*halteres*) used for balance. The mouth of a fly is adapted to pierce, lap or suck and they feed on sap, nectar and rotting organic matter. Some, e.g. mosquitoes, feed on blood. The LARVA (maggot) eventually forms a pupa and becomes an adult through metamorphosis.

the common house fly

dog *see* CARNIVORE.
dolphin *see* CETACEAN.
earthworms *see* ANNELID.
echinoderm starfish, brittle stars, sea urchins, sea cucumbers, sea lilies and sea daisies belong to the phylum Echinodermata. These marine invertebrates have existed for a very long time as fossil forms have been found in rocks 500 million years old. They commonly have five arms radiating from a central disc which is the body. The arms bear many tiny tube feet which act like suction pads and are used for movement, feeding and respiration. They have an external shell of plates containing calcium often with bumps or spines and some are able to regenerate lost arms.
echo location the use by animals of high-pitched pulses of

sound which bounce off surrounding objects allowing the location of these to be determined. Nocturnal animals such as bats and aquatic mammals like dolphins produce these sounds and echo location enables them to make sense of their environment and to locate prey.

the bat has large ears adapted for echo location

ecology this is the study of the relationship between plants and animals and their environment. Ecology (also known as *bionomics*) is concerned with, for example, predator-prey relationships, population changes (in the species present) and competition between species.

ecosystem all the biological life and non-biological components (e.g. minerals in the soil) within an area and the inter-reactions and relationships between them all. Thus an ecosystem includes all the organisms in a community and the geology, chemistry and climate and it may be a lake, forest, region of tundra, etc. Various cycles operate within an ecosystem. Energy, in the form of sunlight, is converted to chemical energy by green plants and is then consumed by animals and released as heat. Food substances, or nutrients, are returned to the cycle as wastes.

ectoproct *see* MOSS ANIMAL.

elasmobranch *see* CARTILAGINOUS FISHES.

elephant *see* PROBOSCIDEAN.

environment the area which surrounds and supports an organism, including all the other living creatures which share the area as well as all the inorganic elements (e.g. minerals contained in the soil).

epiphyte a plant that grows up on another plant purely for support and which is not rooted in the ground. The commonest examples are *mosses*, *lichens* and some tropical orchids.

estuary a coastal inlet that is affected by marine tides and freshwater in the form of a river draining from the land. An estuary is usually a drowned valley created by a rise in sea level after the last ICE AGE. Estuaries usually contain a lot of sediment (sand, silt, etc.) washed from the land and the tidal currents may produce channels, sandbanks and sand waves. Organisms which inhabit an estuary are adapted to cope with the changes in the *salinity* (saltiness) of the water. They often provide rich feeding grounds especially for many birds, e.g. waders, ducks and geese.

eutherian mammals which have a placenta with which to nourish their embryos within the womb of the mother, belong to the sub-class Eutheria.

eutrophic a body of water, usually a lake or slow-moving river, which is over-rich in nitrogen and phosphorus due to contamination by agricultural fertilizers or sewage. This leads to rapid growth of algae (*algal blooms*) which uses up the oxygen available to other species due to bacteria decomposing dead algae. The final outcome is the death of fish and other organisms and the process is known as *eutrophication*.

fanworm *see* POLYCHAETE.

foraminifer belonging to a phylum of small marine animals (Protozoans) called Foraminifera which have hard shells made of calcium carbonate or silica and are important in the fossil record. Sedimentary rocks such as chalk may contain many foraminiferan fossils and modern ones are often found in deep sea oozes.

fossil *see* **GG**.

frog *see* AMPHIBIAN.

fungus any one of a number of kinds of simple plants without the photosynthetic pigment CHLOROPHYLL. Fungi cause decay in fabrics, timber and food and diseases in some plants and animals. They may be single-celled or form strands called filaments and are used in BIOTECHNOLOGY in baking, brewing and to make antibiotics.

gastropod an invertebrate animal, typically (but not always) with a shell such as the limpet, whelk, conch, snail and slug belonging to the class Gastropoda of the phylum Mollusca. They have a large muscular foot used for movement (hence *gastropod*), a distinct head with eyes and a coiled or twisted shell. Most are marine but some live in freshwater and others are adapted for life on land.

a snail

gila monster *see* SQUAMA.

goats *see* ARTIODACTYL.

grasshopper *see* ORTHOPTERAN.

greenhouse effect and global warming normally the solar radiation from the sun is absorbed by the Earth's surface and re-emitted as INFRARED radiation. However, this radiation can become trapped in the Earth's atmosphere by carbon dioxide, water vapour, clouds and ozone causing a heating up and consequent rise in the global temperature. Due to the activities of man, the amount of CO_2 in the atmosphere is rising caused, for example, by the clearance of forests (trees trap CO_2) and the burning of fossil fuels. It has been estimated that the global temperature could rise by between 1.5°C and 4.5°C over the next 50 years. This would cause significant melting of the polar ice caps and a consequent rise in sea level causing widespread flooding of coastal areas throughout the world.

growth rings the rings seen if you cut through the woody stem of a plant, for example, the trunk of a tree. Each ring represents one year's growth and by counting the number of rings, the age of the tree can be discovered. Also, each ring is different and comparison of dead and living trees provides a dating method (and information about past climates) for periods within the past eight thousand years. This is known as DENDROCHRONOLOGY.

gymnosperm conifers, cycads and ginkgos are seed plants belonging to the class (or subdivision) Gymnospermae of the division Spermatophyta. They have an ancient history as fossils and are found in rocks dating back to the Devonian geological period (408 – 360 million years ago). They produce *naked seeds* (hence *gymnosperm*) which are not enclosed by a protective sheath (*carpel*). *Compare* ANGIOSPERM.

habitat the place where a plant or animal normally lives, e.g. river, pond, seashore.

hagfish *see* AGNATHAN.

halophyte a plant that can tolerate a high level of salt in the soil. Such conditions occur in salt marshes, tidal river estuaries (and on motorway verges and central reservations) and a typical species is rice grass (*Spartina*).

hedgehogs *see* INSECTIVORE.

hemipteran bugs belong to the order Hemiptera of the class Insecta. This is a very large group and includes leaf hoppers, scale insects, bed bugs, aphids, cicadas and water boatmen. The typical body shape is a flattened oval with two pairs of wings folded flat down on the back of the resting insect. Their mouths are tubes adapted for piercing and sucking; some are herbivorous, others carnivorous and yet others parasitic. Some are serious agricultural pests transmitting plant diseases through feeding on sap.

a land bug

herbaceous (*herb-like*) describing a plant with little or no woody stem in which all the green parts die back at the end of each season. Either the whole plant dies (having produced and dispersed seeds) as in *annuals*, or parts of the plant (roots) survive beneath the ground and grow up again the following year, as in *perennials*.

hibernation an adaptation seen in some animals in which a sleep-like state occurs that enables them to survive the cold winter months when food is scarce. Some marked changes occur, notably a drop in body temperature to about 1°C above the surrounding air, and a slowing of the pulse and metabolic rate to about 1% of normal. In this state the animal's energy requirements are reduced and it uses up stored body fat. Bears, bats, hedgehogs, some fish, amphibians and reptiles are examples of animals which hibernate.

hippopotamus *see* ARTIODACTYL.

holocephali *see* CARTILAGINOUS FISHES.

homeothermy (homiothermy) means warm-bloodedness and is the ability of an animal to keep up a constant body temperature, independent of the heat or cold of its environment. It is a typical feature of birds and mammals and various metabolic processes are involved (*see also* POIKILOTHERMY).

homing the ability of animals to find their way home, especially referring to birds. Many bird species fly thousands of miles over land and sea during annual migrations to return to the same area year by year. It is thought that they navigate by means of the sun and stars and by using magnetic fields.

hominid a member of the primate family Hominidae, which includes modern man as well as fossil hominids that may have evolved around 3.5 million years ago. All belong to the genus Homo. Their main physical characteristic is the ability to walk upright (known as *bipedalism*), and there are also changes in the shape of the skull and teeth compared to those of other primates. They have (or had) complex social and cultural behaviour patterns.

horse *see* PERISSODACTYL.

human *see* HOMINID.

humus material that makes up the organic part of soil being formed from decayed plant and animal remains. It has a characteristic dark colour and its composition varies according to the amount and type of material present. It holds water (and it forms a physical state known as a COLLOID), which can then be used by growing plants and helps to prevent the loss of minerals from the soil by leaching. Hence it is very important in determining soil fertility. Humus may be more ACIDIC (*mor*), as in the soil of coniferous forests, or ALKALINE (*mull*), as found in the soil of deciduous woodlands and grasslands. Humus contains numerous MICRO-ORGANISMS and INVERTEBRATE animals, and its presence is of obvious economic importance in the cultivation of food crops.

hydrozoan corals known as millepore corals, hydras and such animals as the Portuguese man-of-war (*Physalia*) and *Vellela* belong to the class Hydrozoa of the phylum Cnidaria. These are mostly marine invertebrates although freshwater types (e.g. *Hydra*) do occur. Many are colonial so that what appears to be a single animal is, in reality, made up of numerous small individuals as with *Physalia* and *Vellela*.

Physalia is a colony of dozens or perhaps hundreds of individuals. Some form the gas-filled float, others are for feeding having tentacles and a mouth, yet others are protective, possessing stinging cells and some are for reproduction.

hymenopteran bees (*see below*), wasps, ants, sawflies and ichneumon flies belong to the order Hymenoptera of the class Insecta.

worker bee

queen bee

drone

These insects have a narrow 'wasp waist' and usually possess wings. The mouthparts are adapted in a variety of ways, i.e. for biting, sucking or lapping. A structure called an *ovipositor* at the hind end of the body is used for egg laying. It may be adapted for piercing, sawing or stinging and is often long and looped forward.

Some are social insects living in colonies, notably the ants and some bees and wasps. Honey bees have always been an important species to man.

ichneumon fly *see* HYMENOPTERAN.

iguana *see* SQUAMA.

insecta a very important class of invertebrate animals belonging to the phylum Arthropoda, with over three quarters of a million species known to Man. They inhabit a wide variety of habitats, both on land and in water, and there are 26 orders including beetles (Coleoptera), flies (Diptera), bees and ants (Hymenoptera), butterflies (Lepidoptera), grasshoppers (Orthoptera) and dragonflies (Odonata). The body of an insect is divided into three regions known as the head, thorax and abdomen. The head often bears projections called *antennae* which are sense organs, and eyes and mouthparts adapted to feed on various food substances. The thorax bears three pairs of legs and also possibly wings and is composed of three segments. The abdomen or rear part of the body is made up of 11 segments.

insectivore moles, shrews and hedgehogs are small mammals belonging to the order Insectivora. They are mainly nocturnal, with long snouts bearing sensitive hairs which respond to touch, and tweezer-like (incisor) teeth. Their diet is mainly insects although other foods are taken and they are quite a primitive group which seem to have changed very little since their emergence in the *Cretaceous* geological period about 130 million years ago.

the mole has well-developed feet which help it to dig and shovel earth

isopod woodlice, fishlice and pill bugs belong to the order Isopoda of the class Crustacea. These familiar invertebrates inhabit marine, freshwater and terrestrial environments and many are parasites. Woodlice are important DECOMPOSERS living in damp places under stones and near the soil surface.

kangaroo *see* METATHERIAN.

killer whale *see* CETACEAN.

king crab *see* ARACHNID.

koala bear *see* METATHERIAN.

lamprey *see* AGNATHAN.

leaf hopper *see* HEMIPTERAN.

leech *see* ANNELID.

lepidopteran moths and butterflies belong to the order Lepidoptera of the class Insecta. The body, wings and legs of the adult insects are covered with numerous, minute scales and the mouth parts are in the form of a long tube (called a *proboscis*) which is often held coiled beneath the head. This is uncoiled and extended to enable the insect to feed on nectar. Two large pairs of fine wings, often brightly coloured, are characteristic of this group and are held vertically in resting butterflies whereas moths hold their wings in various positions. The immature insects are called caterpillars and they have a well-defined head with chewing mouthparts and a segmented body, usually with each segment bearing a pair of legs. Many caterpillars are serious economic pests of food crops and trees and may transmit plant diseases. The caterpillar becomes an adult by undergoing METAMORPHOSIS via a *pupa* (or *chrysalis*). The pupa may be surrounded by a silk cocoon which the caterpillar produces from special silk glands. Others use leaves or similar material to construct a cocoon.

lichen a plant-like growth formed from two organisms which live together in a symbiotic relationship (*see* SYMBIOSIS). The two organisms involved are a FUNGUS and an ALGA. A lichen forms a distinct structure which is not similar to either partner on its own. Usually most of the plant body is made up of the fungus with the algal cells distributed within. The fungus protects the algal cells and the alga provides the fungus with food through PHOTOSYNTHESIS. A lichen is typically very slow growing and varies in size from a few millimetres to several metres across. It may form a thin flat crust, be leaf-like or upright and branching. Often, lichens are found in conditions that are too cold or exposed for other plants such as Arctic and mountainous regions. Reindeer moss and Iceland moss are lichens that provide an important food source in Arctic regions. Other lichens contain substances that are used in dyes, perfumes, cosmetics and medicines, as well as poisons.

limpet *see* GASTROPOD.

littoral a term for the shallow water environment of a lake or the sea that lies close to the shore. In the sea, the littoral zone includes the tidal area between the high and low water marks. Sunlight is able to penetrate so that rooted aquatic plants can grow and usually there is a wide variety and abundance of organisms.

llama *see* ARTIODACTYL.

lobster *see* DECAPOD.

locust *see* ORTHOPTERAN.

lugworm *see* POLYCHAETE.

malacostracan prawns, and other similar marine and freshwater animals belong to the subclass Malacostraca of the class Crustacea. They typically have compound eyes on stalks and numerous legs or appendages used for a number of different functions including swimming, and a hard shell or carapace.

mamba *see* SQUAMA.

mammal belonging to the vertebrate class Mammalia which contains approximately 4500 species. Mammals have a number of distinguishing characteristics. They have hair; four different types of teeth (*heterodont*); small bones in the middle ear which conduct sound waves; they are warm-blooded and able to regulate their body temperature and produce sweat as a cooling mechanism. The heart is four-chambered and keeps oxygenated and deoxygenated blood separate and a layer of muscle called the diaphragm is used to fill the lungs with air. The young of mammals develop within the body of the mother and fertilization of the egg is internal. Mammary glands produce milk with which to feed the young once they are born. Mammals possess very complex sense organs and larger brains than other vertebrates of a similar size. They are adaptable and are found in almost all habitats.

mammoth *see* PROBOSCIDEAN.

metatherian a marsupial mammal belonging to the subclass Metatheria of the class Mammalia. The distinctive feature is that the female has a pouch on the lower part of the body (abdomen) which is called the *marsupium*. Marsupials are born at a very early stage of development and crawl into the pouch and fix on to a teat. Here they complete their development until they are able to leave their mother's pouch. Familiar marsupials include kangaroos, koala bears and opossums, and these mammals are only found in Australia and America. The group evolved about 80 million years ago during the late *Cretaceous* geological period. The break up of early land masses meant that the spread of marsupials was restricted. As a result, and especially in Australia, the marsupials have adapted to occupy habits and lifestyles which might otherwise have been filled by placental mammals.

an opossum

mice *see* RODENT.

migration the seasonal movement of animals especially birds, fish and some mammals (e.g. porpoises). Climatic conditions usually trigger off migration where perhaps lower temperatures result in less food being available. Some animals, particularly birds, travel vast distances, e.g. golden plovers, fly 8000 miles from the Arctic to South America. Migrating animals seem to use three mechanisms for finding their way. Over short distances an animal moves to successive familiar landmarks (*piloting*). In *orientation*, a straight line path is taken, based upon the animal adopting a particular compass direction. *Navigation* is the most complex process because the animal must first determine its present position before taking a direction relative to that. It seems that some birds use the sun, stars (often the North star which moves very little), and an 'internal clock' which makes allowances for the relative positions of these heavenly bodies. Even when the sun is hidden by cloud, many birds are able to continue their migration quite accurately by plotting their direction with respect to the Earth's magnetic field.

millipede *see* MYRIAPOD.

millipore coral *see* HYDROZOAN.

mimicry a resemblance in which one species has evolved to look like another species. Mimicry occurs in both the plant and animal kingdoms but is mainly found in insects. There are two main types of mimicry. The first is called *Batesian mimicry*, (named after the British naturalist H.W. Bates, 1825 – 1892). In this, one harmless species mimics the appearance of another, usually poisonous, species. A good example of this is the non-poisonous Viceroy butterfly mimicking the orange and black colour of the poisonous Monarch butterfly. Predators learn to avoid the harmful butterfly and leave the mimic alone as well because of the close resemblance. The second type is *Mullerian mimicry* (named after the German zoologist J.F.T. Müller, 1821 – 1897). In this, different species which are either poisonous or just distasteful to the predator, have evolved to resemble each other. The resemblance ensures that the predator avoids all the similar looking species so all achieve protection.

mites *see* ARACHNID.

mole *see* INSECTIVORE.

mollusc invertebrate animals, many with shells, such as slugs and snails (class Gastropoda), mussels and oysters (class Bivalvia) and cuttlefish, squids and octopuses (class Cephalopoda) all belong to the phylum Mollusca. Most molluscs are marine but there are freshwater and land-living varieties and it is a large group of animals including over 50,000 species.

monitor lizard *see* SQUAMA.

monkey *see* PRIMATE.

mosquito *see* DIPTERN.

moss animala and sea mats (phylum Ectoprocta or Bryozoa). These are a group of marine invertebrate animals, many of which are important reef builders. Individual animals are tiny, (only about 1mm across) and resemble the polyps of the phylum Cnidaria. However, they form colonies which may extend for over half a metre. There are around 5000 species and many have a hard external skeleton containing calcium into which the body can be withdrawn. They have a mouth surrounded by tentacles which waft in the water and trap particles of food.

moths *see* LEPIDOPTERAN.

myriapod centipedes (subclass Chilopoda) and millipedes (subclass Diplopoda) belong to the class Myriapoda of the phylum Arthropoda. These familiar invertebrate animals have a distinct head with antennae and a long segmented body. Centipedes have one pair of legs per segment and are carnivorous. Millipedes have two pairs of legs on each segment and are herbivorous.

nautilus *see* CEPHALOPOD.

nekton animals which swim in the PELAGIC (*see also* OCEANS) zone of the sea or a lake such as jellyfish, fish, turtles and whales.

nematode roundworms are invertebrate animals belonging to the phylum Nematoda. They have a characteristically rounded body which tapers at either end and some are only about 1mm in length while others may reach 1 metre. There are numerous species and they may inhabit water, leaf litter and damp soil and also occur in plant tissues and as PARASITES in animals. They only have muscles running lengthways (longitudinally) down the body and this is unique to the roundworms. Some free living species are of vital importance as DECOMPOSERS in the soil but others are serious economic pests attacking the roots of crop plants. Yet others are serious parasites of man and animals. Humans can be affected by over 50 nematode species, e.g. threadworms.

neritic zone the shallow water marine zone near the shore, which extends from low tide to a depth of approximately 200 metres. Most *benthic* organisms (*see* BENTHOS) live in this zone because sunlight can penetrate to these depths. Sediments deposited here are sand and clays, and those laid down in ancient seas (now sandstones and mudstones), preserve features such as ripple marks and fossils of marine organisms.

newt *see* AMPHIBIAN.

niche all the environmental factors that affect an organism within its community. These factors include living space, available food, climate and all the conditions necessary for the survival and reproduction of the species. Although many species co-exist side by side, each occupies a specific niche within a community with circumstances which apply uniquely to them.

octopus *see* CEPHALOPOD.

odonate dragonflies and damselflies belong to the order Odonata of the class Insecta. These familiar large insects are carnivorous both as adults and *nymphs* (LARVAE). Eggs are laid in or near water and the aquatic nymphs which hatch out have gills for breathing. They are skilful and voracious hunters with biting mouthparts that are on a plate or *mask* held beneath the head. This is shot out suddenly to seize the prey, which includes invertebrates and even small fish. The nymph crawls up a stalk of a reed, or other plant, right out of the water just before its final moult. The adult which emerges has a pair of large compound eyes and two pairs of large wings with conspicuous veins. In dragonflies the wings are always held out horizontally at right angles to the body in the resting insect. In damselflies, the resting insect holds its wings folded over its back. These insects have very good eyesight and are excellent hunters catching insect prey in flight with their legs. They are often brightly and beautifully coloured and are a very ancient group. Some fossil species found in rocks from the Carboniferous era had wingspans of over half a metre.

a dragonfly

oligochaete earthworms and some other worm species belong to the class Oligochaeta of the phylum Annelida. They are distinguished by having very few bristles (chaetae) which are not borne on special structures called *parapodia* (*see* ANNELID).

opossum *see* METATHERIAN.

orthopteran grasshoppers, crickets, locusts, preying mantis and cockroaches belong to the order Orthopteran of the class Insecta. This is a large order of insects containing many species familiar to Man. They are usually large and mainly herbivorous with biting mouthparts. Two pairs of wings may be present but some species are wingless. The hind pair of legs are often large and modified for jumping. Many produce sounds by rubbing one part of the body against another (often wings and hind legs), using special *stridulatory* organs to produce noise which is called *stridulation*. Some species, especially locusts and cockroaches are pests of crops or buildings.

a cricket

osteichthye *see* BONY FISHES.

paramecium *see* PROTOZOAN.

pelagic any organisms swimming and living in the sea between the surface and middle depths including many fish, marine mammals and plankton. Pelagic sediments (called *ooze*) are deep water deposits made up of the shells of minute organisms and small quantities of fine debris.

perissodactyl herbivorous grazing mammals such as horses, zebra, rhinoceros and tapir belong to the order Perissodactyla of the class Mammalia. These animals characteristically have hoofed feet and an odd number of toes. The teeth are specialized for grinding and the gut adapted for the digestion of cellulose. This was a distinct mammalian line 60 million years ago in the EOCENE geological period (see MAMMAL).

photic zone the uppermost, surface layer of a lake or sea where sufficient light penetrates to allow PHOTOSYNTHESIS to take place. The extent varies according to the quality of the water, (i.e. whether it is cloudy due to suspended particles), but it can extend to a depth of 200 metres.

physalia *see* HYDROZOAN.

pig *see* ARTIODACTYL.

pitcher plant *see* CARNIVOROUS PLANTS.

plankton *see* ST.

Plasmodium *see* SPOROZOAN.

platyhelminth flatworms, of which there are about 20,000 species, belong to the phylum Platyhelminthes. There are four classes in this group; the Turbellaria (free-living worms), Cestoda (tapeworms), Trematoda (parasitic flukes) and Monogenea (flukes).

platypus *see* PROTOTHERIAN.

poikilothermy means cold-bloodedness and is a feature of all animals except mammals and birds. The body temperature of these animals varies according to that of the surrounding environment, but they adjust by seeking sun or shade as required. Also, the blood flow to some body tissues is adjusted according to whether heat needs to be lost or conserved (*see also* HOMEOTHERMY).

pollution is contamination of the natural environment with harmful substances which have usually been released due to the activities of Man. The substances which cause the pollution are called *pollutants* and include chemicals from industry and agriculture, gases from the burning of fossil fuels, industrial and domestic waste in landfill sites and sewage. Pollution is regarded as a serious problem because of the threat it poses to the health, not just of humans, but of all animals and plants. Many countries have stringent regulations in order to control pollution levels.

polychaete worms such as the ragworm (*Nereis*), lugworm (*Arenicola*) and fan worm (*Sabella*) belong to the class Polychaeta of the phylum Annelida. These characteristically possess a protruding pair of bumps or lobes on each segment, each having numerous bristles or chaetae. Most of these worms are marine animals and live in tubes constructed from pieces of shell and sand. Lugworms and ragworms make burrows in the mud or sand. Most species have a distinct head often with jaws and eyes.

population a group of individuals which belong to the same species. Populations may be genetically isolated, rarely breeding with other members of the same species outwith their particular area. Or, one dense population may merge with another. Usually, a population is affected by such factors as birth and death rates, density (numbers) and immigration and emigration.

population dynamics the study of the changes that occur in population numbers, whether plant or animal, and the factors that control or influence these changes. Distinction is made between factors that are dependent or independent of population density. For example, a natural occurrence such as a flood is an independent factor while food supply is dependent.

poriferan sponges, of which there are about 9000 species, belong to a phylum of invertebrate animals, the Porifera. Most sponges are marine and live attached to rocks or other surfaces. They have a hollow, sac-like body punctured with holes and an internal skeleton made up of tiny spines (spicules) of calcium carbonate, silica or protein. Sponges are filter feeders taking particles of food from the water and digesting them. They are very simple animals with no muscle or nerves and are able to regenerate lost parts of their body structure.

a sponge

Portuguese man-of-war *see* HYDROZOAN.

prawn *see* MALACOSTRACAN.

preying mantis *see* ORTHOPTERAN.

primate the mammalian order which includes monkeys, lemurs, apes and humans. Evidence suggests that primates evolved from tree-dwelling INSECTIVORES late in the Cretaceous geological period. Characteristic features are manual dexterity (permitted by thumbs and big toes that can touch and grasp), good binocular vision and eye-to-hand co-ordination. The brain is large and the primates are highly intelligent. There are two suborders, the Prosimii (lemurs) and Anthropoidea (monkeys, apes and humans).

proboscidean elephants belong to the order Proboscidea and are placental mammals characterized by having a trunk (proboscis) and tusks which are modified incisor teeth. The order evolved during the Eocene geological period and was much larger in numbers of species containing, for example, the extinct mammoths. There are just two modern species, the African and Indian elephant.

prototherian two groups of mammals, the platypuses and spiny anteaters (Echidnas) belong to the subclass Prototheria, the *monotremes*. These are the only living mammals that lay eggs and today they are only found in Australia and New Guinea. The monotremes resemble reptiles in the structure of their skeleton and in the laying of eggs. They are warm-blooded although the body temperature is variable and lower than that of most other mammals. It is thought that the monotremes originated about 150 million years ago early in the development of the mammals.

protozoan used to be the term for a phylum of small, single-celled (mainly) micro-organisms, but now a general word for the PROTISTA. Included are such organisms as *Amoeba* and *Paramecium* and they are very widely distributed in aquatic and damp terrestrial habitats. Some feed on decaying organic material (*saprophytes*) while others are parasites, e.g. *Trypsanosoma* which causes sleeping sickness.

pterophyte ferns belong to a division of the plant kingdom called the Pterophyta. There are about 12,000 species of ferns which emerged as far back as the Carboniferous geological period.

a fern

Ferns are just about all terrestrial and the majority are found in tropical regions. The leaves are usually called *fronds* and each is made up of numerous very small leaves. They are considered to be a fairly primitive group of plants and many of the extinct ferns grew to an enormous size and are well preserved as fossils.

quadrat a small sampling plot (usually one square metre), which is chosen at random and within which organisms found are counted and studied. This is like a 'window' into the area as a whole and the types of animals and plants to be found there. This may be done in relation to a particular species or several different types of organisms.

race a group of individuals which is different in one or more ways from other members of the same species. They may be different because they occupy another geographical area, perhaps showing a variation in colour, or they may exhibit *behavioural*, *physiological* or even genetic differences. The term is sometimes used in the same way as sub-species. Usually, animals from different races are able to interbreed.

racoon *see* CARNIVORE.

radiolarian tiny, marine protozoan animals, present in PLANKTON, belong to the order Radiolaria. These organisms have a spherical body shape and characteristically possess a beautiful intricate skeleton often composed of silica. This is perforated with holes to make a large variety of patterns, and may be in the form of a lattice of spheres, one inside the other. Often there are many spines or hooks projecting outwards. When Radiolarians die their skeletons, which are highly resistant to decay, settle on the ocean floor to accumulate as *Radiolarian ooze*. When compressed into rock it forms *flint* and *chert*. Radiolarian fossils are very important to geologists and are among the few found in the most ancient rocks from the Precambrian geological period (more than 590 million years old).

various forms of radiolarian

ragworm *see* POLYCHAETE.
rat *see* RODENT.
rattlesnake *see* SQUAMA.
ray *see* CARTILAGINOUS FISHES.
reindeer moss *see* LICHEN.

reptile belonging to the class Reptilia, a class of VERTEBRATES which were the first animals to truly colonize dry land and to exist entirely independently of water. Often they live in extremely hot conditions such as semi-desert. They have a dry skin covered with horny scales which protects them from drying out. Reptiles usually lay eggs in holes which they excavate in the sand or mud. The eggs are covered by a protective shell which is porous and allows for the passage of air. Some retain the eggs inside the body until they hatch. Reptiles are cold-blooded (*see* POIKILOTHERMY), but are able to maintain an even body temperature by behavioural means such as basking in the sun. There is evidence that some extinct reptiles (e.g. some of the DINOSAURS), were warm-blooded. Modern reptiles include snakes, lizards, turtles, tortoises and crocodiles.

rhinoceros *see* PERISSODACTYL.

rice grass *see* HALOPHYTE.

rodent belonging to the Rodentia order of mammals containing rats, mice, squirrels, capybaras and beavers. The upper and lower jaws contain a single pair of long incisor teeth which grow continuously throughout the animal's life. These are adapted for gnawing, and the absence of enamel on the back means that they wear to a chisel-like cutting edge. Rodents are herbivorous or omnivorous and tend to breed rapidly. Some, notably rats, are serious pests, spoiling food and are responsible for the spread of diseases.

roundworm *see* NEMATODE.

salamander *see* AMPHIBIAN.

sawfly *see* HYMENOPTERAN.

sea anemone *see* ANTHOZOAN.

sea cucumber, **sea daisy, sea lily, sea urchin** *see* ECHINODERM.

sea lion and **seal** *see* CARNIVORE.

sea snake *see* SQUAMA.

scale insect *see* HEMIPTERAN.

scorpion *see* ARACHNID.

shark *see* CARTILAGINOUS FISHES.

sheep *see* ARTIODACTYL.

shrimp *see* MALACOSTRACAN.

skate *see* CARTILAGINOUS FISHES.

slug and **snail** see GASTROPOD.

snake *see* SQUAMA.

spiny anteater *see* PROTOTHERIAN.

spirogyra *see* CHLOROPHYTE.

sporozoan a class of protozoan organisms which are parasites of higher animals and some cause serious diseases in Man. An example is *Plasmodium* which causes malaria and is transmitted by the mosquito.

squama lizards and snakes belong to the order Squamata of the class Reptilia. They are covered by horny scales and male animals are unique in possessing a paired penis. Lizards possess movable eyelids and most have four limbs, e.g. iguanas, monitor lizards, chameleons and gila monsters. Snakes lack movable eyelids and are able to dislocate their lower jaw in order to swallow large prey. Some are constrictor types, e.g. boas, pythons and anacondas, while others may be venomous, e.g. cobras, vipers, mambas, rattlesnakes and sea snakes.

a sea snake

squid *see* CEPHALOPOD.

squirrel *see* RODENT.

starfish *see* ECHINODERM.

sundew *see* CARNIVOROUS PLANTS.

tapeworm *see* CESTOD.

tapir *see* PERISSODACTYL.

terrapin *see* CHELONIAN.

territory a specific area that animals, whether singly or in groups, defend to exclude other members of their species. A territory may be used for feeding, mating and breeding or all these activities and the size varies greatly from the small nesting territory of sea birds to the large areas used by red squirrels. Many mammals mark their territories with scent while birds use song. Territory differs from home range, the latter being the area in which an animal roams but it is not defended.

tick *see* ARACHNID.

toad *see* AMPHIBIAN.

tortoise *see* CHELONIAN.

trypanosome *see* PROTOZOAN.

turbellarian flatworms such as *Planaria*, belong to the class Turbellaria of the phylum Platyhelminthes. These are simple, small animals, mostly marine although Planarians are common in fresh water streams and ponds. They are carnivorous and move by undulating the body in a wave-like way, or by means of small hairs called *cilia* on their underside.

a flatworm

turtle *see* CHELONIAN.

ungulate *see* ARTIODACTYL and PERISSODACTYL.

variation the differences between individuals of the same population or species.

venus fly trap *see* CARNIVOROUS PLANTS.

vertebrate belonging to the subphylum Vertebrata, a major group which includes all the animals with backbones: fishes, amphibians, reptiles, birds and mammals (*see* individual entries).

viper *see* SQUAMA.

walrus *see* CARNIVORE.

water boatman *see* HEMIPTERAN.

weevil *see* COLEOPTERAN.

whelk *see* GASTROPOD.

zebra *see* PERISSODACTYL.

SCIENCE AND TECHNOLOGY

The term *Science and Technology* covers many areas including biology, anatomy, chemistry, mathematics, engineering and physics. This section explains concepts and theories which are essential in the study of all these subjects. The entries are arranged A to Z and cross-references are given in SMALL CAPITALS.

*

acceleration *see* VELOCITY.

acids and bases *acids* are chemical compounds in a liquid form which, depending upon their strength, may occur naturally in foods as very weak acids (e.g. citric acid in lemons) or may form corrosive liquids (e.g. sulphuric acid) which has many industrial uses. Most acids have a sour taste, although it is not advisable to taste them as many are poisonous and can burn skin. Acids turn litmus paper from blue to red (*see* INDICATOR) and an acidic solution has a pH lower than 7. To aid digestion, our bodies produce acids to break down food.

Some examples of acids		
citric	$C_3H_5O(COOH)_3$	found in lemons and fizzy drinks
hydrochloric	HCl	occurs in the stomach, used a lot in the chemical, food and oil industries
sulphuric	H_2SO_4	a strong acid used to make fertilizers, dyes, explosives, iron and steel; also used in car batteries
nitric	HNO_3	used to make explosives, fertilizers, and dyes
formic	HCOOH	an organic acid found in stinging nettles

A mixture of concentrated nitric and hydrochloric acids (in the ratio 1:4) is called *aqua regia* ('royal water') because it will dissolve the 'noble' metals such as gold.

Bases are the opposite to acids and if a base is reacted with an acid in the correct proportions, the two are cancelled out (*neutralized*), producing water and a salt. Nevertheless, bases can be highly reactive and corrosive. Bases turn red litmus paper blue.

Some examples of bases		
lime/calcium hydroxide	$Ca(OH)_2$	used industrially and in cement production
caustic soda/sodium	$Na(OH)$	used to make other chemicals; also hydroxide in paper, aluminium, soap, petro-chemicals manufacture
magnesium oxide	MgO	used in antacid preparations

If a compound (usually the oxide -O, or hydroxide -OH of a metallic element) can function as an acid *or* as an alkali (a soluble base) it is said to be *amphoteric*, that is it can combine with an acid or a base to form a salt.

acoustics *see* SOUND.

adhesives are materials that will bond (stick) solids together, through initially wetting the surfaces to be joined and then solidifying to form a joint. Some adhesives, or glues can be made from natural materials such as bones, horn and hides by boiling and simple chemical treatment. Glues made in this way are a mixture of proteins.

Adhesives made from chemicals are called synthetic, and these tend to be stronger than the natural forms. There are several types of synthetic adhesive including thermosetting resins, thermoplastic resins and epoxy resins, the last being among the strongest. Synthetic adhesives have numerous uses including in the manufacture of furniture, textiles, car windscreens, electrical products and also in construction.

In recent years, 'superglues' have been introduced which, it is claimed, are capable of sticking together most surfaces. Great care has to be taken when working with these compounds as they can also stick fingers together and can be dangerous if they come into contact with eyes, etc.

aerodynamics the study of the movement and control of solid objects such as aircraft, rockets, etc. in air. As objects move through the air there is a resistance or *drag* which works against the direction of movement, and the drag increases with speed. All machines used in transport: aircraft, cars, trains, lorries, are designed with streamlined bodies to reduce drag to a minimum. This involves using smooth curved shapes rather than angular shapes.

the aerodynamics of an aircraft wing

Another important aspect of aerodynamics is *lift*, which is an upward force vital in the take off and flight of aircraft. All aircraft have wings with a curved top surface, and a flatter lower surface. This feature is based upon *Bernoulli's Theorem* (which applies to both liquid and air) which proves that when the flow of air speeds up, the air pressure is reduced. The characteristic *aerofoil* shape of a wing means that air travelling over the top, curved surface has to travel further than air beneath the wing. It therefore moves faster, causing a reduction in air pressure and the wing is lifted, or pushed upwards.

The aerofoil shape is not only used on aircraft—the same principle is applied to rudders, the vanes on a windmill, and even on racing cars, although in the latter case it is to keep the car on the racetrack!

aerosol a fine mist or fog consisting of liquid or solid particles in a gas. It also refers to a pressurized container with a spray mechanism for dispersal of a fine mist of fluid droplets. This system is used for deodorants, paints, insecticides and other chemicals. Within the can is the liquid to be sprayed, and a propellant gas which is under pressure. When the valve is opened by pressing the button, the gas forces (propels) the contents out through the nozzle. Until very recently, the propellants used were commonly CFCs or chlorofluorocarbons, but because it has been proven that these chemicals damage the ozone layer (*see* **GG**: OZONE LAYER.), alternative compounds have been sought.

An *atomizer* is another way of creating an aerosol, but does not require a propellant gas.

ageing includes all the changes which take place as an animal grows older. Animals age at different rates, from some adult insects which only live for a day (mayflies), to elephants (up to 70 years) and tortoises and parrots which may have a life span of well over 100 years. Ageing is perhaps best understood and most studied in human beings. In people, the cells which make up the different parts of the body age at different rates, and while most are renewed some are not (e.g. brain cells), so the whole process is very complicated. As ageing occurs, noticeable physical changes take place which include wrinkling of the skin, greying hair, deterioration in sight, hearing, taste, smell, memory and stiffening of limbs and joints. However, there is a great difference between individual people in the ways in which they are affected by these processes depending upon their inherited (genetic) make up and their lifestyle and environment.

alcohols organic compounds containing carbon, oxygen and hydrogen and with a particular structure where a hydroxyl group, (oxygen and hydrogen, OH), is linked to a carbon. Alcohols are mainly liquids and are used in a variety of ways:

alcohol	formula	uses
methanol	CH_3OH	solvent; manufacture of paints, varnishes, etc.
ethanol	CH_3CH_2OH	alcoholic drinks; solvent; food industry; perfumes
propanol	$CH_3CH_2CH_2OH$	solvent
butanol	$C_4H_{10}O$ (4 different forms)	solvents; artificial flavourings

The alcohols are produced by various chemical reactions, but ethanol occurs naturally by fermentation in which yeast converts sugar to alcohol with carbon dioxide being the side product.

Antifreeze is a liquid added to the water in the cooling systems of car engines. The antifreeze lowers the freezing point of the water, avoiding freezing in the winter. The main component of antifreezes is ethylene glycol, although alcohols may be used.

aldehydes (also known as *alkanals*) another group of organic compounds containing carbon, hydrogen and oxygen which have a particular group, CHO, joined to another carbon atom. The oxygen is joined to the carbon by a double bond, the hydrogen by a single bond. Aldehydes are mainly colourless liquids or solids with typical odours and wide uses:

aldehyde	formula	uses
formaldehyde (methanol)	HCHO	as a solution in water for its germicidal action; also for sterilizing instruments and storing specimens in pathology
acetaldehyde (ethanal)	CH_3CHO	as a stepping stone in the manufacture of other chemicals
propanal	CH_3CH_2CHO	a chemical intermediate

algebra is the use of symbols, usually letters, to help solve mathematical problems where the object is to find the value of an unknown quantity or to study complex theories. In its simplest form it may involve the determination of an unknown in an equation such as: $3x + 1 = 16$, where x is obviously equal to 5. Albert Einstein used a very advanced form of algebra in deriving the equations for his general theory of relativity. The formal rules of algebra were developed by al Khuwãrizmi, an Arab mathematician in the ninth century.

algorithm a set of rules that together form a mathematical procedure that allows a problem to be solved in a certain number of stages. Each rule is very carefully defined so that, theoretically, a machine can undertake the process.

An algorithm is a way of reaching the right answer to a difficult problem by breaking the problem down into simple stages. The stages allow the action to be successfully achieved without necessarily understanding fully the whole process. To be an algorithm, a list of instructions must have an end and be short enough to allow each to be completed, and the process must end at some point. Computer programs contain algorithms, but simpler more everyday examples include making a telephone call and following a recipe. Long division is another example.

alimentary canal *see* DIGESTION.

alkali a base which when dissolved in water produces a solution with a pH over 7, e.g. Na_2CO_3, $Ca(OH)_2$. These are alkaline solutions. Hydroxides of the metallic elements sodium and potassium (NaOH and KOH respectively) produce strong alkalis, as does ammonia in solution (as ammonium hydroxide, NH_4OH).

alloys a mixture or compound containing two (or more) metals, or a metal with a non-metal, e.g. iron-carbon where the metal is the larger component. Alloys tend to have properties which are described as metallic, but alloying is a means of increasing a particularly useful property such as strength, resistance to corrosion or high temperatures.

Bronze was probably the first man-made alloy, made of copper and tin, and it was used for weapons, pans, ornaments. Other common alloys are *brass*, which is copper and zinc, and *steel* which is iron and carbon. There are hundreds of alloys, each created for a particular use, from coins to aircraft parts. This is shown by the different types of brass and bronze now available: brass may also contain aluminium, iron, nickel, tin, lead or manganese while the term bronze is now applied to alloys of copper not containing tin, e.g. aluminium bronze (corrosion resistant), beryllium bronze (high hardness) and manganese bronze (high strength).

A special type of alloy is an *amalgam*—an alloy of a metal with mercury. Mercury is an unusual metal because it is a heavy, silver liquid at room temperature and most metals will mix with it to form an amalgam. For many years dentists have used such an amalgam, with silver, for fillings in teeth, although modern materials are now being used more.

aluminium is a silvery-white metallic element that in air forms a protective coating of aluminium oxide which prevents further corrosion. It is ductile and malleable (*see* DUCTILITY) and a good conductor of electricity and is used for the manufacture of a large number of things, from drinks cans and foil to pans, cars and aircraft. Aluminium is the commonest metallic element in the Earth's crust and the third most common overall (at about 8%). It is extracted from the mineral *bauxite* (aluminium hydroxides formed by weathering of aluminium-bearing rocks, in tropical conditions) by electrolysis (*see* ELECTROLYSIS). Salts of aluminium are important in the purification of waters and as catalysts (*see* CATALYSIS). The oxide is important in the production of cement, abrasives (*corundum*), refractories and ceramics.

Aluminium occurs in a number of drugs and medications but there is a body of opinion that an excess of aluminium in some form may damage the brain of old people or the very young.

ammonia is a colourless gas made up of nitrogen and hydrogen (NH_3) and it is a very useful chemical compound. It has a sharp, pungent smell, is lighter than air and very soluble in water. It is used in the manufacture of nitric acid, nylon, plastics, explosives and fertilizers. Ammonia is also used in refrigeration equipment as a coolant. Ammonia gas can be turned into a liquid by cooling to -33.5°C, and when it becomes gas again, it takes a lot of heat from the surroundings, thus producing the cooling effect.

Ammonia occurs naturally in some gases given off at hot springs, and it results from the breakdown of proteins and urea by bacteria. It is manufactured industrially by the *Haber process* which involves the reaction of nitrogen with hydrogen under very high temperature (500°C) and pressure (300 atmospheres) and in the presence of a catalyst (*see* CATALYSIS).

ampere the unit used for measuring electric current, usually abbreviated to amps, which was named after the French physicist André Ampère who did much important work in the early 19th century. Machines and appliances use differing currents and with a mains supply of 240 volts, an electric fire will use between 4 and 8 amps. The ampere has a very specific definition, created in 1948, relating to the force produced between two wires in a vacuum, when current is passed. Prior to that the unit related to the amount of silver deposited per second from a silver nitrate solution when one ampere was passed!

analogue *see* DIGITAL AND ANALOGUE.

analysis (in chemistry) involves the use of one, or a combination of several analytical techniques and pieces of equipment to identify a substance or a mixture of substances. *Qualitative* analysis is when the components are identified, and *quantitative* analysis involves the determination of the relative amount of constituents, usually elements, making up a sample.

Qualitative analysis of inorganic (*see* CHEMISTRY) substances can be done using a variety of *reagents* (a known substance or solution that produces a characteristic reaction) and/or one of several physical methods of analysis, such as spectroscopy (infra-red or ultraviolet) or X-ray analysis. Spectroscopy (infra red, ultra violet and also nuclear magnetic resonance) and mass spectrometry are used in organic qualitative analysis and in addition the compound type can be identified by specific reactions which produce known products.

Further methods are adopted for quantitative analysis including the use of certain reactions to precipitate a compound which is then weighed accurately; physical techniques such as spectroscopy and others which relate to a particular property, e.g. electrical and optical, and *volumetric analysis* which involves *titrations*. Titration is when measured amounts of a solution are added, progressively, to a known volume of a second solution until the chemical reaction between them is complete (shown by an indicator) thus enabling the unknown strength of one solution to be calculated. Chromatography is very useful in separating the components of a mixture prior to analysis.

Chemical analysis is used widely in areas such as chemistry itself, medicine, food technology, geology, environmental control, drug testing in sport, forensic science and many more.

anatomy is the scientific study of the structure of living things, which enables an understanding to be built up of how different parts of a plant or animal work. Anatomical study often involves dissection of dead specimens.

animals—*kingdom animalia* modern biologists usually group animals together in the biological kingdom called *Animalia* which contains many different *phyla* (*see* CLASSIFICATION). The simplest animals are the sponges (phylum *Porifera*) and the most complicated, including man and other mammals, belong to the phylum *Chordata*. These animals are constructed of many cells (multicellular) performing a variety of functions which, unlike those of plants, do not have outer cell walls. Animals cannot manufacture their own food but must take it in from the outside in some way. Also. animals possess nerves and muscles which vary greatly in complexity between the different groups. Most animals reproduce by means of sexual reproduction and store carbohydrates as an energy reserve in the form of glycogen (a compound made up of glucose units). In plants, carbohydrate is stored as starch.

anodizing is a process for depositing a hard, very thin layer of oxide on a metal. The metal is usually aluminium or an alloy and the oxide layer provides a non-corrosive coating of aluminium oxide (Al_2O_3) which is resistant to scratches and which protects the underlying metal. Anodizing is achieved by electrolysis and the metal made is the anode, often in a bath of sulphuric, chromic or oxalic acid. Such metals are used in many ways: for window frames, and in trains and aircraft, for example. The oxide coating may be rendered decorative by the use of a dye during electrolysis. Anodized items can be made to retain their natural brightness through the use of very high purity aluminium or an aluminium-magnesium alloy, because in these cases the oxide layer formed is transparent.

Archimedes' Principle a law of physics, named after the Greek mathematician Archimedes (287–212 BC). It states that when a body is partly or totally immersed in a liquid, the apparent loss in weight equals the weight of the displaced liquid. Archimedes was a prolific inventor and investigator. He did much scientific work with levers and pulleys and invented the Archimedean screw which is essentially a hollow screw which, with its base in water, when turned, lifts water to a higher level. The device is still used for irrigation if pumps are not available.

Archimedian screw

arithmetic the science of numbers which includes addition, subtraction, division, multiplication, fractions, decimals, roots and so on. Arithmetic was first used by the Babylonians about

4000 years ago but the system currently used is that of Arabic numerals. The Romans used a different system in which letters represent quantities:

Roman	Arabic	Roman	Arabic
I	1	X	10
II	2	L	50
III	3	C	100
IV	4	D	500
V	5	M	1000

For example, XIV = 14 and MDCCCCVC represents 1995.

asexual reproduction any form of reproduction in which a new individual is produced from a single parent without the production or fusion of sex cells (gametes). It occurs in plants, micro-organisms and some of the simpler animals, often alternating with a sexual phase. Different types of asexual reproduction occur, one of which is by division of a single cell into two, known as *fission,* as seen in Amoeba, a member of the kingdom *Protista*. Another method is *fragmentation* in which parts of the plant or animal separate off, or the whole breaks up with new individuals being formed from the portions. This is seen in some invertebrate animals, particularly earthworms.

Budding is another form of asexual reproduction which occurs in such animals as hydras, sea anemones and corals. A small bud is produced from the parent which may break off and form a new animal or remain attached. Asexual reproduction is also seen in plants, e.g. in the production of bulbs, corms and tubers known as *vegetative propagation*. Such plants as ferns and mosses may have an asexual stage, producing spores, and this is known as the *sporophyte generation*.

atom the smallest particle that makes up all matter, and yet is still chemically representative of the element. Atoms are less than microscopic in size and yet they are made up of even smaller particles. At the centre of an atom is a relatively heavy *nucleus* containing *protons* and *neutrons*. The protons are positively charged and they are offset by an equal number of electrons with negative charge that occupy *orbitals* around the nucleus. The atom is overall electrically neutral and the various elements in the periodic table each have a unique number of protons in their nucleus. The electron weighs a little more than one two thousandth part of a proton!

Orbitals provide a means of simplifying and expressing *atomic structure* and related processes, such as bonding. The theory put forward by Niels Bohr, the famous Danish physicist, proposed that electrons encircled the nucleus in definite orbits. This was discovered to be too simple and the new theory visualized a charge cloud or orbital which represents the likely distribution of the electron in space. There are various types of orbital, each with a different cloud shape around the nucleus (dependent upon atomic structure) and these orbitals interact, merge and change when chemical bonds are formed. The precursor to this picture of atomic structure began with Democritus several hundred years BC. In the 19th century Dalton put forward theories to explain the structure of matter and was the first to calculate the weights of some atoms.

Elements that have more than 83 protons are unstable and decay radioactively, while those with over 92 protons occur only in the laboratory, as a result of high energy experiments (*see also* BONDS). Atoms of an element that have differing numbers of neutrons are called isotopes.

atomic number (*symbol* Z) is the number of protons in the nucleus of an atom. All atoms of the same element have the same number of protons but may have differing numbers of neutrons (producing isotopes). *Atomic weight* or *relative atomic mass* is the ratio of the average mass of an element (i.e. the average for the mixture of isotopes in a natural element) to one twelfth of the mass of carbon -12 atom. Chemical notation places the atomic number as a subscript before the symbol for the element, e.g. chlorine has 17 protons -$_{17}$Cl.

autotrophism means 'self-feeding' and describes the situation in which an organism manufactures the materials it requires for life from inorganic (*see* CHEMISTRY) substances. Plants are *photoautotrophs*, using light as an energy source and carbon dioxide, minerals and water taken from the air and soil. Some bacteria are *chemoautotrophs* obtaining energy from chemical reactions using such substances as ammonia and sulphur.

averages in statistics, average is a general term for *mean, median* and *mode*. The arithmetic mean is the value obtained from a set of figures by adding all the values in the *data set* (collection of numbers) and dividing by the number of readings. The median is the middle reading in a set, so if there are nine readings for temperature, height, weight or a similar quantity, arranged in order, the median is the middle, or in this case, the fifth value. The mode is the value that occurs most frequently in a set of readings, hence in a range of temperatures such as 17°, 18°, 12°, 17°, 21°, 16°, 19°, 17°, the mode is 17°.

bacteria are single celled organisms belonging to the kingdom *Monera* and have a unique type of cell called procaryotic (procaryote). They were the first organisms to exist on Earth but their activities have always been extremely significant as they are important in all life processes. Bacteria may have a protective, slimy outer layer called a capsule and in some, 'hairs' known as filaments are present which cause movement. Two types of bacteria, which each have a different cell wall structure (Gram positive or Gram negative) are recognized by a test known as Gram's stain. Bacteria show a number of different shapes and forms which help to distinguish between the various types. These are *spiral* (spirilli, spirillus), *spherical* (cocci, coccus), *rod-like* (bacilli, bacillus), *comma-shaped* (vibrio) and *corkscrew-shaped* (spirochaetae). They may require an environment containing oxygen, in which case they are described as *aerobic*, or exist in conditions without oxygen, when they are known as *anaerobic*. Bacteria are vitally important in the decomposition of all organic (*see* CHEMISTRY) material and are the main agents in the chemical cycles of carbon, oxygen, nitrogen and sulphur. Most bacteria obtain their food from decaying or dead organic material (*saprotrophs*). Others are parasites and some are *autotrophs* (*see* AUTOTROPHISM), obtaining energy from chemical reactions using inorganic materials such as sulphur and ammonia. Bacteria usually reproduce asexually (*see* ASEXUAL REPRODUCTION) by simple fission but some have a form of sexual reproduction. Some are responsible for very serious diseases in animals, plants and man, e.g. typhoid, syphilis, tuberculosis, diphtheria and cholera.

ballistics is the study of the *flight path* of *projectiles* (i.e. an object that has been projected into the air) under the influence of gravity. The trajectory is the path taken by an object and is usually a particular length, distinguishing it from an orbit. A *ballistic missile* is a missile fired from the ground which follows a flight path shaped like a parabola and which is powered and guided only during the first phase of flight.

Ballistics is a term applied to bullets, rockets, missiles and similar objects.

bar code is a series of black bars printed on a white background that represent codes that can be scanned and interpreted by a reader and computer respectively. Bar codes are found on most products in supermarkets, on books and other items and they contain a product number and maker's identification number.

ISBN 1-85534-490-4

a typical barcode

9 781855 344907

As the product is dragged past an optical scanner at the checkout, or a light pen is moved over the bar code, the computer matches the product with the price list in its memory. In addition to speeding up the process of adding up items, the use of bar codes helps an accurate analysis of stock to be made, allowing restocking to be undertaken before a product line is exhausted. It also facilitates the output of a detailed, itemized receipt.

barometer is an instrument used to measure atmospheric pressure, i.e. the pressure that the atmosphere exerts on the Earth. The principle of the barometer was discovered by Torricelli, a 17th century Italian physicist. It is used to help predict forthcoming weather changes which result from changes in atmospheric pressure. A mercury barometer is a thin tube, closed at one end which is almost filled with mercury and the open end is stood in a mercury-filled container or reservoir. The vertical height of the mercury column that can be maintained by the atmospheric pressure pushing down on the reservoir is taken as the value of atmospheric pressure at the time of reading. The column is usually about 760 mm high. The mercury barometer is most accurate but a more compact device is the *aneroid barometer* (meaning 'without liquid'). This consists of a small metal box-like chamber (with a thin corrugated lid) which is evacuated (to create a vacuum). Subsequent changes of pressure move the lid and this movement is magnified and translated onto a dial.

bases *see* ACIDS

battery a device, usually portable, in which a chemical change is harnessed to produce electricity. Many batteries are to all intents and purposes non-rechargeable and these are called primary cells and the most important is the Leclanché type. One of the commonest arrangements is a positive electrode made up of a rod of carbon surrounded by a mixture of manganese dioxide and powdered carbon in a case and the whole thing stands in an *electrolyte* (*see* ELECTROLYSIS) of ammonium chloride in the form of a paste. The outer case of zinc acts as the negative electrode. When the battery is connected, a current flows due to reactions and the movement of ions between the various components, thus creating a voltage.

The other important type of battery is the secondary cell, which can be recharged, e.g. the lead *accumulator*, or car battery. In this cell, plates of lead and lead oxide are suspended in sulphuric acid and on charging there are chemical changes (because of *electrolysis*) which are complete when it is charged. When the terminals are wired up, the chemical changes are reversed and current flows until the battery is discharged. The sulphuric acid used has to be of a certain relative density and discharge should not be continued beyond a certain point because insoluble salts build up on the plates. Other types of accumulator include nickel-iron, in which the nickel oxide plate is positive and the iron is negative, in a solution of potassium hydroxide; zinc-air, sodium/sulphur and lithium/chlorine. Although the last two are higher energy cells than most accumulation, they require high operating temperatures.

behaviour (in animals) this includes all the activities which an animal (or person) carries out during its life and is a major area of scientific study. Those who study behaviour wish to find out why an animal acts in a particular way and what factors might affect this. Behaviour can be divided into three categories known as *reflex*, *instinctive* and *learned*. Reflex behaviour is totally spontaneous and does not involve any conscious act of the will, e.g. if you accidentally touch something hot your hand is immediately and rapidly withdrawn. Instinctive behaviour is inborn and does not need to be learned, being present in all members of a species. The classic example is the male three-spined stickleback fish protecting his territory. Male sticklebacks have a red belly and this acts as a trigger for the defensive behaviour. A male stickleback will attack models only vaguely resembling a rival fish provided that the red colouration is present. More realistic stickleback models without a red underside are ignored. Much of animal behaviour is *learned*, i.e. it is changed by experience, and this can be seen especially in the young of a species as they play and experiment in the environment which surrounds them. Various types of learned behaviour are recognized. It is generally agreed that all behaviour is a mix, instinct combined with learning and modification by environmental conditions.

benzene a hydrocarbon that is toxic and carcinogenic (may cause cancer). At room temperature it is a colourless liquid with a characteristic smell and it has the formula C_6H_6. The six atoms of carbon form a ring with bond angles of 120°. The ring structure is very stable because although the convention is to show benzene with three double bonds, the bonding electrons are not localized and are spread around the ring.

ring structure for benzene

Benzene was isolated by Faraday, the British physicist, in 1825. He distilled coal tar and the lightest fraction obtained was condensed to form benzene liquid. Benzene is currently manufactured from petroleum. The benzene ring forms the basis for a large branch of chemistry that deals with *aromatic* hydrocarbons, and benzene is used principally as the starting point for production of other chemicals, e.g. phenol, styrene and nylon.

bimetal strip comprises a bar with strips of two different metals welded together. Because of the different rates of expansion, each expands (or contracts) by a different amount when subjected to heat (or cold) and the bar bends (the metal on the outside being the one that expands more). The two metals used are often brass and invar (an iron-nickel alloy), the brass expanding about twenty times more than invar. This property enables bimetallic strips to be used in thermostats, thermometers and thermal switches. Also the indicator bulbs in a car flash due to a small bimetal strip.

binary numbers is a system that uses a combination of two digits, 0 and 1, expressed to the base 2, thus beginning with the value

1 in the right-hand column, each move to the left sees an increase to the power of 2:

1×2^5	1×2^4	1×2^3	1×2^2	1×2^1	1×2^0	origin of binary numbers
32	16	8	4	2	1	binary numbers
1	0	1	1	1	0	example
Hence in the example, the figure is $32 + 8 + 4 + 2 = 46$.						

The binary number system is the basis of code information in computers, as the digits 0 and 1 are used to represent the two states of on or off in an electronic switch in a circuit.

biochemistry the scientific study of the chemistry of biological processes occurring in the cells and tissues of living organisms. Chemical compounds are the building blocks of all plants and animals, and studying the ways in which these react with one another and how they contribute to life processes is the realm of biochemistry. Biochemists are involved in a wide variety of scientific studies including the search for cures of serious diseases such as cancer and AIDS.

biological control a means of controlling pests by using their natural enemies rather than chemicals which might prove harmful to the environment. The control is artificially brought about in that large numbers of the 'predators' are introduced by human beings in order to control the pests. The method can be very successful, an example being the spread of the prickly pear cactus in Australia which was successfully controlled by the introduction of the cactus moth, whose caterpillars fed on and destroyed the young plant shoots. However, all the biological implications have to be thoroughly researched in advance as sometimes the attempted control has gone very wrong. An example of this was the introduction of large Hawaiian toads into Australian sugar cane plantations with the belief that these would eat the sugar cane beetles that damaged the crop. In fact, the toads did not eat the cane beetles but proved seriously damaging to other animals and are now a great problem in themselves. Another method of biological control used with insect pests (especially some which carry disease, such as the tsetse fly) is to use natural chemicals called pheromones which attract them so that they can be caught. Sometimes the males are caught and radiation is used to make them sterile and then they are released to mate with females. No offspring are produced from these matings and hence the number of insects decreases.

biology the scientific examination of all living things, including both plants, animals and micro-organisms which is further subdivided into specialized areas of study.

bioluminescence the production of light by living organisms which is seen in many sea-dwelling animals, e.g. deep sea fish (angler fish), hydrozoans such as *Obelia*, molluscs, e.g. squids, and some crustaceans. It is also seen in some land-dwelling insects, e.g. fireflies and glow-worms and in some bacteria and fungi. Some animals have bacteria living with them (symbiosis) and it is these which actually produce the light. The light may be given out continuously as in bacteria or 'switched' on and off as in fireflies. The light may be used to attract prey or a mate, or as a warning. A special protein (called a photoprotein) known as luciferin combines with oxygen and during this chemical reaction light is produced.

biophysics a combination of biology and physics in which the physical properties of biological mechanisms are the subject of study. The laws and techniques of physics can be used, for example, in the study of how the heart and muscles work, or in the mechanisms of respiration and blood circulation.

biotechnology the use by man of living organisms to manufacture useful products or to change materials. Examples include the fermentation of yeast to produce alcohol and in bread making, and the growth of special fungi to make antibiotics. Biotechnology mainly uses micro-organisms especially bacteria and fungi. In recent times, genetic engineering (altering the genes, *see* CHROMOSOMES and GENES or 'building blocks' which determine the nature of an organism) is increasingly being used in the field of biotechnology.

biotic *see* ORGANISM.

blast furnace is a furnace comprising a large vertical tower used mainly for the smelting of iron from iron oxide ores. The tower is made of steel plates lined with refractory bricks (firebricks) to withstand the very high operating temperatures (in excess of 1600°C). After some time, about three years, the lining will wear out and the furnace is then shut down to allow the bricks to be replaced.

The furnace is fed from the top with ore, coke and limestone ($CaCO_3$). From near the base of the tower is introduced a high pressure blast of very hot air which ignites the coke, producing carbon monoxide (CO) which then reacts with the iron oxide to produce iron (molten) and at the same time the limestone breaks down to form lime (CaO) and carbon dioxide (CO_2). The lime subsequently combines with impurities from the ore to form a molten slag. As the iron is formed it collects at the base of the furnace, and the slag floats on top. Each is run off periodically, the iron to form bars of 'pig iron' (or cast iron) which contains about 4.5% carbon. The blast furnace can also be used for smelting copper.

The slag also finds a use as *ground granulated blast-furnace slag* (ggbfs) in which it is granulated, ground and then mixed with Portland cement for use in construction. Cements made with ggbfs improve workability and resistance to deleterious reactions and although it is slower to harden, it heats up less than most cements.

blood *see* CIRCULATION.

boiling point is the temperature at which a substance changes from the liquid to the gaseous state. This occurs when the vapour pressure of a liquid is equal to atmospheric pressure. This explains why at high altitudes, water boils at a lower temperature because air pressure decreases. Boiling points of liquids are therefore quoted as the value at standard atmospheric pressure (one atmosphere).

When a substance is dissolved in a solvent such as water, the boiling point of the solvent is elevated. This is called the *molecular elevation of boiling point*, and is caused by a lowering of vapour pressure (because fewer solvent molecules escape from the liquid), hence the temperature has to be higher.

bonds are forces that hold atoms together to form a molecule; or molecules and ions to form crystals or lattices. Bonds are created by the movement of electrons and the type of bond depends upon the atoms involved and their *electronegativity* (a measure of an atom's attraction for electrons, within a molecule). Three basic bond types are recognized: *ionic* (or electrovalent), where one atom loses an electron to another atom, as in NaCl which becomes Na^+ (positive ion or *cation*) and Cl (negative ion or *anion*). Such compounds dissociate (split) into ions in solution and therefore are able to conduct electricity; *covalent* bonds where electrons are shared, often one from each participating atom, although the sharing is equal only when the atoms are identical. Covalent bonding is common in organic compounds. *Metallic* bonding is where electrons are shared between many nuclei thus facilitating conduction of electricity.

bone the hard material that forms the skeleton of most vertebrate animals and contains living cells, called *oestoblasts* and *oestocysts*, responsible for the formation and repair of bones. Bone is made up of hard connective tissue, itself consisting of a tough protein called collagen and bone salts (crystals of calcium phosphate–hydroxyapatite) which both make it strong. The skeleton of an adult human being has 206 bones, some of which are fused together and others are very small.

bone marrow a soft and spongy tissue which is found in the centre of the long bones (e.g. those of the leg and arm) and also within the spaces of other bones. The bone marrow produces blood cells especially in young animals. In older animals only some bone marrow, known as red marrow and mainly found in the vertebrae, pelvis, ribs and breastbone produces blood cells. It contains special (*myeloid*) tissue in which are found cells known as erythroblasts which develop into red blood cells or *erythrocytes*. The cells of the myeloid tissue also develop into leucocytes or white blood cells which are an essential part of the body's immune system.

botany the scientific study of all aspects of the life of plants, compare ZOOLOGY.

brain *see* NERVOUS SYSTEM.

breathing *see* RESPIRATION.

breeding and **hybrid** breeding is the production of offspring and usually refers to the interference by man to produce animals or plants with particular desirable characteristics. The results of breeding are particularly noticeable in domestic farm animals such as cattle or dogs, which look very different to their wild ancestors. Selective breeding has given us animals which provide more milk, wool or meat, and crops which produce more grain or larger, juicier fruits and succulent leaves.

A hybrid animal is the offspring of parents that are of two different species (*see* CLASSIFICATION), the most familiar example of which is the mule. A mule is the offspring of a female horse and a male donkey. Hybrid animals are usually sterile. N.B. hybrid has a different meaning in genetics where the differences in the parents are at the gene (*see* CHROMOSOMES AND GENES), rather than the species level.

bud (plant) a compact and immature plant shoot made up of many folded and unexpanded leaves or flower petals. These are tightly folded or wrapped around one another and may be enclosed in a protective, sometimes sticky sheath. When the bud opens, the petals or leaves grow and expand, a process which marks the onset of spring moving into summer. *See also* ASEXUAL REPRODUCTION.

bridges a structure used in civil engineering to cover a gap, whether over road, water or railway. For short *spans* (i.e. the distance between supports) of 300 to 600 metres, steel arches, suspension or cantilever bridges are suitable. Above 600 metres, steel suspension bridges are often used. In such bridges, the bridge deck (i.e. the floor that carries the load to the beams and supports) is hung from vertical rods or wire ropes connected to cables that go over the towers and are anchored in the ground. In the UK, the Severn bridge is such a case.

A *cantilever bridge* is usually symmetrical, comprising three spans. The two outer spans are anchored at each shore and then extend beyond the supporting pier to cover one third of the remaining span. This gap is then bridged by another element which rests on the arms of the two cantilevers.

There are other types of bridge, several with particular functions, e.g. swing bridges that rotate on a pivot to allow vessels to pass (often used for canals).

bromine is a typical member of the halogen group (*see also* PERIODIC TABLE). It is a dark red liquid with noxious vapours. It occurs naturally as bromide compounds in sea water and salt deposits, and also in marine plants. When sea water is evaporated, and after sodium chloride ('salt') crystals have precipitated out, the remaining fluid (or *bittern*) contains magnesium bromide.

Bromine is very reactive and has numerous industrial uses including the manufacture of disinfectants, fumigants, anti-knock agents for petrol and in photography.

Brownian Movement is the erratic and random movement of microscopic particles when suspended in a liquid or gas. The movement is due to the continuous movement of molecules in the surrounding gas or liquid which then impact with the particles. This phenomenon accounts for the gradual dispersal of smells in the air and the mixing of fluids which will happen with time, and which will be accelerated if the gas or fluid is hot. As the particles become larger, there is a greater chance of impacts from all sides cancelling each other out and so the movement can no longer be observed. This occurs when the particles are 3-4μ (3-4 microns, or micrometres μm; equal to 3-4 millionths of a metre).

Brownian movement is named after its discoverer, Robert Brown, a Scot (1773–1858). He was a botanist and first observed this movement when studying pollen. It is taken as evidence that kinetic energy applies to all matter and exists even when it cannot be seen.

bubbles may be of a gas within a liquid, e.g. air in water, or air surrounded by a thin soap film as with soap bubbles. Detergent or soap in water creates good bubbles due to the detergent molecules forming a stable alignment. The shape of a soap bubble is due to a balance between the pressure inside trying to blow it apart and the surface tension of the liquid trying to contract the bubble. The pressure inside a bubble decreases as the size of the bubble increases, so smaller bubbles have greater pressure inside than larger ones.

building and construction is central to the development of countries and their economies, and to the operation of almost all aspects of everyone's daily life. There are many professional people; planners, surveyors, civil and structural engineers, architects, builders and more involved, and the major parts of the construction process are: planning, design, construction for new projects, maintenance and refurbishment and restoration for existing buildings.

There is a great variety of projects from railways, houses, hospitals, offices, schools, roads, harbours to dams, airports, bridges and tunnels. Each requires numerous specialists to take a project from the drawing board in a design office to completion. Large projects in particular, which may cost many millions of pounds have to be planned and organized as near to perfection as possible to ensure smooth progress and to make best use of time, people and resources. The basic constructional materials used most often are concrete and steel, but of course brick, timber, stone etc. are also very important.

Bunsen burner *see* LABORATORY.

caffeine and tannin *caffeine* is an *alkaloid* (basic organic substance found in plants) and *purine* that occurs in tea leaves, coffee beans and other plants. It acts as a *diuretic* (a substance that increases urine formation) and as a weak stimulant to the central nervous system. It is also found in cola drinks–up to 10% in some cases.

Tannins are a large group of plant substances of use in the treatment of hides. However, the term is misused in connection with tea because tannic acid is not present and tannin is simply a general collective term. Tea does contain *polyphenols* which in some mixtures may resemble tannin in their chemical structure.

calculators are not a recent invention–only the development and inclusion of integrated circuits on silicon chips has been a recent and revolutionary step. Calculators began as mechanical devices in the 17th century and were, inevitably, laboriously slow. The first electronic calculator was produced in 1963, but its scope was very limited and calculators became generally available in the early 1970s. The first calculator that could be programmed to solve mathematical problems was made by Hewlett-Packard in 1974. Now there is an enormous variety of calculators available, some as small as credit cards.

calculus a large branch of mathematics that enables the manipulation of and working with quantities that vary continuously. The techniques of calculus were developed by two scientists at the same time, the German Gottfried Leibniz and Isaac Newton in Britain. It had its origin in the study of falling objects. *Differential calculus* concerns the rate of change of a dependent variable and involves the gradient, maxima and minima of the curve of a given function. *Integral calculus* deals with areas and volumes, and methods of summation and many of its applications developed from the study of the gradients of tangents to curves.

calcium a soft silver-white metal at room temperature which tarnishes very quickly in air, and reacts violently with water. Calcium compounds are very widely distributed; as calcium carbonate ($CaCO_3$) in limestone and chalk; as calcium sulphate ($CaSO_4$) in gypsum; within silicates occurring in minerals and there are many other occurrences. In biological systems, Calcium ions (Ca^{2+}) are vital to life as constituents of bone and teeth.

Calcium is also important industrially as lime (CaO), as $CaCO_3$ in the production of iron from its ores, and in the preparation of certain transition element metals, (*see* PERIODIC TABLE).

camera *see* PHOTOGRAPHY.

camouflage *see* **NH** CAMOUFLAGE.

cancer a disease of animal cells in which there is a rapid and uncontrolled rate of growth and reproduction. A collection of cancer cells is known as a *tumour* which is termed *benign* if it remains localized in one place. A *malignant* tumour spreads, invades and destroys surrounding healthy tissue. It spreads via the bloodstream and produces secondary cancers in other parts of the body by a process known as *metastasis*. These malignant cancers can often prove fatal as they disrupt the normal functioning of cells in the affected tissues. The search for the cure and causes of various kinds of cancer is a vast area of scientific and medical research. The treatment and life expectancy of people affected by most kinds of cancer has greatly improved in recent years. Some substances and environmental factors (known as *carcinogens*) are known to increase the risk of cancer developing and the best known of these is cigarette smoke. Cancer treatment involves surgery, radiotherapy (the use of radiation to destroy tumours), chemotherapy (the administration of drugs to destroy tumours) and the giving of more specialized drugs (cytotoxic) which attack the malignant cells in a special way.

capacitor a device for storing electric charge comprising two plates separated, in its simplest form, by air but usually by an insulating material called a *dielectric*. Commercial capacitors have foil plates separated by a dielectric such as Mylar, forming a sandwich which is rolled up into a cylindrical shape. This gives a large area of plate in a small device. Other dielectrics include mica, certain plastics and aluminium oxide. Capacitors are used a great deal in electrical circuits in televisions, radios and other electronic equipment. The capacitor works by a charge on one plate inducing an equal charge on the opposite plate and a change in the charge is mirrored between plates.

capillary *see* CIRCULATION.

capillary action a phenomenon related to surface tension in liquids in which there is an attraction between the sides of a glass tube and water molecules. The result is that water is pulled up a very thin glass tube (a *capillary tube*), and it will move further the thinner the tube. This action happens with other liquids including alcohol, but mercury moves in the opposite way. Many occurrences involving the movement of water involve capillary action, e.g. tissues soaking up water, walls taking in water producing damp.

capsule a widely used term in biology which describes a structure found in flowering plants, mosses and liverworts, bacteria and animals.

1. In flowering plants, a capsule is a dry fruit containing seeds which splits when ripe. The splitting and releasing of the seeds occurs in different ways, e.g. splitting into different parts, known as valves, in the iris, through holes or pores as in the snapdragon, or through a lid as in the scarlet pimpernel.

2. In plants called bryophotes (*see* **NH**: BRYOPHOTES), which includes liverworts and mosses, a capsule contains spores and is produced on the end of a thick stalk (seta). It is known as a sporophyte.

3. Some bacteria produce an outer sheath of gelatinous material surrounding the cell wall which is protective and is called a capsule.

4. In vertebrate animals a connective tissue sheath known as a capsule surrounds some of the joints in the skeleton. Also, a membrane or fibrous connective tissue sheath called a capsule encloses and protects some vertebrate organs such as the kidney.

carbides are compounds of metals with carbon which in many instances result in hard, refractory materials with very high melting points. Tungsten or tantalum carbide are used for tools as are mixtures with cobalt and nickel. Other uses include:

metal	property of resulting carbide	use
titanium	resists molten metals; high melting point, hardness and heat resistance	parts in fast reactors; gas turbine blades; coatings on rocket components
chromium	inert chemically	electrodes, parts for use with corrosive chemicals
tantalum	high melting point; metallic conduction	elements in electric furnaces

carbohydrates are chemical compounds made up of carbon, hydrogen and oxygen forming a very large and important group of substances. The most familiar ones are sugars, starch and cellulose and carbohydrates are manufactured by green plants during the process of photosynthesis. Carbohydrates are a vital food source for animals as they are broken down within the body to provide the energy required for all the various life processes.

carbon a non-metallic element that occurs as the element in two forms, graphite and diamond, and in numerous compounds. Carbon is unique in the enormous number of compounds it can form both in inorganic form, e.g. carbon dioxide, carbonates, and in being the basis of organic chemistry. Carbon is *allotropic*, i.e. it exists in several elemental forms–carbon black, in addition to graphite and diamonds, each differing in their crystalline structure and thus their properties.

Carbon is used extensively; in steelmaking, for motor brushes, cathode ray tubes and *active carbon* is used as a purifying agent in removal of air pollutants, water treatment and purification of chemicals, and as carbon fibres. Carbon is the standard for measuring atomic masses (*see* ATOMIC NUMBER) and the radioactive carbon -14 is used in radio carbon dating (*see* **GG**: DATING METHODS).

carbon dioxide is a colourless gas at room temperature that *sublimes* at -78.5°C. It occurs naturally in the atmosphere and is the source of carbon for plants, playing a vital role in plant and animal respiration and metabolism (since it is exhaled by animals and absorbed by plants during photosynthesis). Carbon dioxide forms when coal, wood etc. are burned and it is a byproduct of fermentation. It is produced industrially from *synthesis gas* (a mixture of hydrogen and carbon monoxide) used in the production of ammonia. Its physical properties make it a useful refrigerant and it is dissolved in mineral waters and fizzy drinks, creating bubbles. Also, since it is heavier than air and does not support combustion it is used in fire extinguishers.

Sublimation is when a solid substance changes to the vapour phase *without* first becoming liquid.

carbon fibres fibres consisting of oriented carbon chains which produce a material that is very strong for its weight. Carbon (or graphite) fibres are manufactured by heating polyacrylonitrile $(CH_2.CHCN)_n$) fibres initially at low temperatures to stabilize the fibres and then at high temperatures (2500°C) and under tension to orientate the graphite along the fibres. The resulting fibres are usually 8–11µm in diameter and are not generally totally crystalline, with graphite crystals in amorphous carbon. The fibres are used as a reinforcing material in resins and ceramics producing strong materials able to withstand high temperatures and with a higher strength to weight ratio than metals.

Comparative strength of carbon fibres and selected materials			
Material	Density	Tensile strength	Temp. of use (°C)
aluminium	2.7	0.06	600
steel	7.9	2.0	1200
aluminium oxide fibre	4.0	2.0	800
carbon fibre	1.9	2.3	2500
glass	2.5	0.07	700
silicon fibre	2.2	5.8	750
magnesium	1.74	0.04	200

carbon monoxide a colourless gas with no smell that is formed when coke and similar fuels are burnt in a limited supply of air, i.e. incomplete combustion. It also occurs in the exhaust emissions of car engines. It is used industrially because of its reducing properties (*see* OXIDATION AND REDUCTION), for example in metallurgy.

One of its most important properties is its toxicity. It is poisonous when breathed in because it combines with haemoglobin in the blood which reduces the capacity of the blood to carry oxygen (*see* CIRCULATION).

carnivores any animal that eats the flesh of other animals, often referring to mammals belonging to the order *Carnivora* (*see* **NH**). Some highly specialized plants are carnivorous and these usually trap insects or small frogs, etc. and secrete enzymes which break them down enabling the products of digestion to be absorbed.

cartilage a special type of connective tissue which, together with bone, forms the skeleton of vertebrate animals. It is composed of proteins and carbohydrates, especially collagen which is a fibrous substance that makes cartilage tough and elastic. Cartilage is found in various parts of the skeleton, e.g. between the vertebrae of the backbone and around joints. It is also present in rings around the windpipe (trachea) and in the ears and nose.

cast iron or *pig iron* is the impure form of iron produced in a blast furnace. It contains 2–4.5% carbon in a form called *cementite* (Fe_3C) and other elements such as silicon, phosphorus, sulphur and manganese. Cast irons are often too brittle to use but additions of other metals can improve its workability. Wrought iron is made by melting cast iron and scrap iron in a special furnace, removing most of the impurities. Cast iron melts at 1200°C, whereas wrought iron softens at 1000°C and melts at 1500°C (*see also* STEEL).

catalysis the use of a catalyst to alter the rate of a chemical reaction. A catalyst usually increases the speed at which a chemical reaction proceeds, but is itself unchanged at the end of the reaction. In practice the catalyst may be changed physically, if not chemically. Catalysts are used a great deal in the chemical industry, iron and platinum being common examples. Metal oxides are also used (copper, zinc, aluminium, titanium) and *zeolites* have become more important over recent years. In biological systems, enzymes are the natural organic equivalent of catalysts.

A *catalytic converter* is fitted to new cars to reduce the volume of exhaust gases produced. The gases pass over a honeycomb structure (which greatly increases the surface area) that is coated with a catalyst such as platinum or palladium and reactions produce water vapour and carbon dioxide.

Zeolites are natural or synthetic alumina silicates of sodium, potassium calcium and barium that contain cavities with water.

The water can be removed by heating and then occupied by other molecules. With small amounts of platinum or palladium they are used in the catalytic cracking of hydrocarbons.

cathode ray tube is an evacuated tube in which *cathode rays* are produced and strike a fluorescent screen; it forms the basis of a television and a *cathode ray oscilloscope* which is used in laboratories and radar systems. At one end of the tube is an assembly (*electron gun*) that produces a beam of electrons which can be focused. The beam passes between two sets of plates, each of which can deflect the electron beam when a voltage is applied to the plates. The resulting beam then impinges upon the screen which is coated with zinc sulphide and fluoresces where the electrons strike.

cathode ray tube

electron beam

electron gun   *charged plates*

screen

caustic soda chemically is sodium hydroxide (NaOH), a whitish substance that gives a strongly alkaline (*see* ALKALIS) solution in water and will burn skin. It is *deliquescent*, that is it picks up moisture from the air and may eventually liquefy. It is used a great deal in the laboratory and is a very important industrial chemical, being used in the manufacture of pulp and paper, soap and detergents, petrochemicals, textiles and other chemicals. Sodium hydroxide is itself manufactured by the electrolysis of sodium chloride solution, chlorine being the other product, or by the addition of hot sodium carbonate solution to quicklime (calcium oxide, CaO).

cell the smallest and most basic unit of all living organisms. A cell is able to perform the main functions of life which are metabolism, growth and reproduction and there are two main types, procaryote and eucaryote. Bacteria and blue-green algae are procaryotes and all other animals and plants are eucaryotes. The simple organisms consist of a single cell and are termed unicellular, e.g bacteria. However, most living creatures are formed of vast numbers of cells which congregate together to form highly specialized tissues and organs. A typical cell has an outer layer or membrane surrounding a jelly-like substance called *cytoplasm*. Various structures called organelles (*see* ORGAN) are contained within the cytoplasm which are responsible for a number of different activities. The largest structure present is the nucleus surrounded by a (nuclear) membrane which contains the chromosomes and genes. Plant cells differ from animal ones in having an outer wall composed of a carbohydrate substance called cellulose. These walls may be thick giving strength and shape to the structure of the plant. Substances pass into and out of cells across the cell membranes e.g. food materials and oxygen and carbon dioxide.

a typical cell

nucleus

organelles

cytoplasm

membrane

cell division the formation of two daughter cells from one parent cell, with the nucleus dividing first by a process known as *mitosis*. The end result is that the nucleus of each daughter cell contains the same number of chromosomes (carrying the genes) as the original parent cell. The chromosomes are in the form of strands of material which come together in pairs. These eventually arrange themselves across the centre of the nucleus and the nuclear membrane disappears. Each member of a pair is now composed of two strands, known as *chromatids,* which are joined at a single point called a centromere. As mitosis progresses, the centromeres split and one chromatid from each of the pairs moves to opposite ends. A nuclear membrane forms around each group of chromatids, now the new chromosomes and then the cytoplasm itself divides to form two daughter cells each with its own nucleus. Another type of cell division occurs in the formation of sex cells (sperm and eggs), and this is known as *meiosis*. In meiosis, the stages of mitosis are repeated again after a resting phase. The end result is that four daughter cells are produced, each with half the number of chromosomes of the parent cell, a condition known as *haploid*. At fertilization, two haploid cells (a sperm and an egg) fuse together so that the new individual has the full number of chromosomes, half from each parent, and this condition is known as *diploid*. Most cells are diploid with only the sex cells (gametes) being haploid. *See also* FERTILIZATION, REPRODUCTION (diagram of mitosis) CHROMOSOME AND GENE.

cellular communications are radios, but particularly telephones that can be used almost anywhere (car phones, portable telephone) and linked to exchanges and standard telephone lines by means of an almost countrywide network. The network is divided into cells and when a user with a portable or car phone makes a call, it is transmitted to a base station and then to a telephone exchange. From the exchange the signal is then directed to the recipient either via a landline or through a similar route of cells.

Each cell has a relay station to deal with all calls in that cell and when a user moves to another cell another station takes over.

cellulose a type of carbohydrate (known as a *polysaccharide*) which is composed of chains of glucose (sugar) units. It makes up the cells walls of many plants and has a fibrous structure which gives strength. Cellulose is not easily digested and some herbivores have evolved a strategy for dealing with this in that they possess a four-chambered stomach containing bacteria which are able to break down cellulose. These are known as *ruminant* animals. In humans, cellulose is important as dietary fibre.

cement is any compound or mix that binds materials together, but generally refers to Portland cement used in building and construction. Cement is manufactured from chalk or limestone, with clay which provides the necessary lime, silica and alumina. The mix is crushed and heated in a kiln to form a *clinker* (a partly melted, dense ash) which contains calcium silicates and aluminates. The clinker is finely ground and gypsum (calcium sulphate, $CaSO_4$) added. The cement product then goes through complex *hydration* (combination with water) reactions which eventually result in a hard stone-like material.

There are now many different cements which have particular properties depending upon their composition. These include: ordinary Portland cement, rapid-hardening cement, Portland blast-furnace cement, sulphate-resistant cement and micro-silica cement.

Enormous quantities of cement are used in construction for mortars or in concrete.

centre of gravity of a body is the point through which the total effect of gravity acting upon all parts of the body are effectively concentrated. This usually coincides with the *centre of mass* and is the point at which the weight or downward force due to gravity acts. When applied to everyday objects, this means that some will fall over more easily than others. The stability of an object can be increased by lowering its centre of gravity, perhaps by enlarging its base. A good example is in transport where large tall loads are unstable (due to a high centre of gravity) whereas racing cars are designed to have a low centre of gravity to allow them to move at high speeds.

centrifuge a machine for separating out particles suspended in a liquid. It comprises two arms about a central pivot, each arm holding a tube. When the arms are rotated rapidly about the central point the suspended particles are forced outwards to the bottom of the tubes and different particles will separate at different speeds, depending upon their size and mass. An *ultracentrifuge* rotates at very high speeds (up to 60,000 rpm) and is used for determining the masses of polymers and proteins. In industry, centrifuges are used for separating mixtures and in the production of cream and sugar.

centripetal force is the force necessary to move an object in a circular path, such as a ball on the end of a rope. The ball follows a circular route because there is a force in towards the centre of the circle–the centripetal force. If the rope is released, the ball continues in the direction at the time and moves off at a tangent. The force can be felt easily when some weighty object is swung around and the person holding the rope stays in the same place, and an object will only move in a circle if the centripetal force is provided. Centripetal force applies when a car corners, the friction between tyres and road providing the force and in some fairground rides. The same applies to a satellite orbiting the Earth where gravitational attraction between the bodies supplies the centripetal force.

ceramics is the term generally applied to items manufactured from clays and includes pottery and *porcelain* where a moist clay is moulded to shape and fired in a kiln until it hardens. Decorative glazes can be added and many domestic and commercial items are produced in this way. These are *traditional ceramics* made of 50–60% clay to which animal bone is added (to control the porosity) producing a non-porous *china*. The mineral *feldspar* can be added in place of bone, producing porcelain goods, e.g. insulators. Clay minerals with no additions are used to produce bricks, tiles, pipes and similar construction materials.

Considerable advances have been made in recent years in the field of materials technology and many ceramics or *composites* (a mix of materials, often as fibres of one material in a different matrix) have been developed.

Light ceramics	carbon fibres; carbides and nitrides; silicon dioxide; aluminium dioxide
Glasses (see GLASS)	there are three major commercial systems: a) soda-lime-silica (Na_2O–CaO–SiO_2) b) lead crystal (PbO–SiO_2) c) low expansion borosilicate (B_2O_3-SiO_2 -Na_2O -CaO)
Glass ceramics	glass containing very small crystals
Refractory oxides	able to withstand the action of corrosive solids, liquids and gases at high temperatures e.g. alumina (Al_2O_3) in lasers, zirconia (ZrO_2) in developing ceramic steels, magnesia (MgO) in pollution control, titania (TiO_2) in enamelling and catalysis
Refractory metals	metal carbides, nitrides, borides and silicides, for use in cutting tools, electrodes, heating elements and protective coatings

cereals are important food crops derived from wild grasses which have been grown by man for thousands of years. Cereals are grown for their seeds, which are usually ground to produce flour and contain important nutrients such as carbohydrates, proteins, vitamins and calcium. Over the centuries farmers have selectively cultivated cereal crops only sowing the seeds from the best and biggest plants and those that produced the most grain. This is an example of plant breeding and the end result is that cultivated cereals now look very different from the wild grasses that are their 'ancestors.'

chemical reaction the interaction between substances (reactants) producing different or altered substances (products) in which bond elements are broken and reformed. Reactions may proceed at normal pressure and temperature, or special conditions may be necessary, e.g. high pressure, or the presence of a catalyst (*see* CATALYSIS). Some terms refer to typical reactions, e.g. *hydrolysis* is the breakdown of a substance by water. The *heat or reaction* is the heat given out or required when certain amounts of substances react under constant pressure. Other heat quantities of a similar nature include:

heat of combustion	the heat evolved when one mole (*see* MOLECULE) of a substance is burned in oxygen.
heat of dissociation	the heat required to dissociate (splitting a molecule into simpler fragments) one mole of a compound.
heat of formation	the heat given out or required when one mole of a substance is formed from its constituent elements at standard pressure and temperature.

chemistry is the study of the composition of substances, their reactions and effects upon one another and the resulting changes. There are three main branches: physical, inorganic and organic. *Physical chemistry* deals with the link between chemical composition and physical properties and the physical changes due to reactions. *Inorganic chemistry* is the study of the elements and their compounds (excluding the organic compounds of carbon), and the group and period characteristics as arranged in the periodic table. *Organic chemistry* is the study of carbon compounds, of which there are an enormous number and many are compounds with hydrogen, the hydrocarbons. Organic chemistry also deals with compounds of significant benefit to man–drugs, vitamins, antibiotics, polymers and plastics, and many more.

The study of chemistry really began in the 17th century when Boyle, an Irish scientist introduced the idea of elements. Since then many scientists have become famous for diverse discoveries–from the discovery of hydrogen by Cavendish (1766) and the synthesis of an organic compound from inorganic substances by Wöhler (1828) to the determination of the structure of DNA by Watson and Crick in 1953.

chlorine the second element in the halogens group which is a yellow-green choking gas which is harmful if inhaled. It occurs as the chloride, mainly sodium chloride (NaCl), but also magnesium chloride and others. It is manufactured by the electrolysis of brine (which also produces sodium hydroxide, NaOH) and stored as a liquid. It is a very important material in the chemicals industry and its powerful oxidizing properties are utilized in bleaches and disinfectants. It is also used in the production of hydrochloric acid and numerous organic chemicals. Compounds derived from chlorine are used in water sterilization, paper manufacture, solvents, PVC and other polymers, refrigerants and more.

Hydrocarbons containing chlorine account for a very large proportion of chlorine derivatives.

chlorofluorocarbons or CFCs are organic compounds that contain chlorine and fluorine (both halogens). Although CFCs have in the past had numerous industrial uses, as aerosol propellants, in refrigerants and are produced when manufacturing foam plastics, their use is now being curbed and much reduced because of their harmful environmental effect.

Although CFCs are stable for a long time, they eventually break down and release their chlorine which reacts with ozone in the atmospheric ozone layer (*see* GG: OZONE LAYER) producing oxygen and chlorine oxide. This reduction in ozone then has direct detrimental effects upon plants and animals on Earth.

chloroplast and chlorophyll chloroplasts are the organelles (*see* CELL) present within the cells of green plants and algae, e.g. *Spirogyra*, which are the site of photosynthesis. They contain chlorophyll which is the pigment that gives the plant its green colour. Chlorophyll is essential in photosynthesis as it traps energy from sunlight and helps the plant to manufacture its food from carbon dioxide and water. The chloroplasts (and chlorophyll) are mainly found in the leaves but also in the stems of green plants.

cholesterol a type of fatty substance which occurs naturally and is produced within animal bodies. In mammals such as man it is made mainly in the liver, carried in the bloodstream and stored within cell membranes. Cholesterol is used to make some hormones and also a substance known as bile which is important in digestion. Cholesterol can cause a problem in some people when too much is present in the blood. It may build up on the inner walls of arteries (*see* CIRCULATION), (*arteriosclerosis*) causing them to become narrow and more easily blocked by a blood clot which can lead to a heart attack (*see* CIRCULATION).

chromatography is a technique used in chemical and biological analysis in which the constituents of a mixture can be separated. There are numerous closely-related techniques but each depends upon one principle–the differing rate at which components of a mixture move through a stationary phase due to the presence of a mobile phase. The simplest case is that of a piece of blotting paper dipped into water. A drop of ink placed on the blotting paper will move up as the water ascends the paper, and in so doing will be separated into its component pigments. In this case the water is the mobile phase and the paper is the stationary phase, and this is essentially a form of paper chromatography. Other chromatographic techniques include:

gas chromatography where a gas is the mobile phase. Used for complex mixtures of organic materials.

high performance liquid chromatography passage of the sample through a column by means of a liquid mobile phase under pressure.

thin layer chromatography separation by solvent movement across a flat surface of special paper, powdered cellulose, silica gel, alumina (aluminium oxide) or other stationary phase. It is used widely in qualitative analysis.

ion-exchange chromatography separation of ionic materials by a solution passing over the surface of a resin which contains ions that can be exchanged. It is used in inorganic chemistry to separate metal mixtures or to separate amino acids.

gel permeation chromatography is where materials are separated by molecular size by a solution passing through a porous polymer gel, in which small molecules are trapped, while larger molecules move.

chromosomes and **genes** chromosomes are threads of material that are found within the nucleus of each living cell. They consist mainly of chains of dna (composed of a substance called nucleic acid) and parts of these are called genes which are the "blueprints" or plans that determine everything about the organism. Each living organism has a particular number of chromosomes which contain very many genes. Human beings have 23 pairs of chromosomes, 22 of which look the same in males and females. The 23rd pair are the sex chromosomes, which in males look like an XY and in females an XX. Although the chromosomes look similar in all individuals belonging to a species, the genes that they carry are all slightly different hence each one is unique. *See also* heredity and mutation.

circuit an electrically-conducting path that when complete allows a current to flow through it. A circuit may be very simple consisting merely of a battery connected by copper wire to a bulb and then back to the opposite terminal of the battery. When cells and batteries were first made (in the early 1800s by the Italian scientist Volta), how charge moved around a circuit remained a mystery. The convention became that current flowed as a positive charge from the positive terminal around to the negative terminal. This is contrary to what actually happens since electrons flow in the opposite direction, but the convention remains (*see also* ELECTRICITY).

a simple circuit diagram

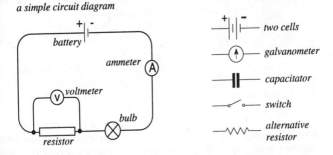

circulation (of the blood) is the process by which blood is moved around an animal's body by the pumping action of the heart.

The blood carries oxygen and food to all the cells of the body and also takes carbon dioxide from them to the lungs where it is eliminated. Blood which contains oxygen (oxygenated blood), is pumped through blood vessels called *arteries* by the left side of the heart. As the arteries reach the tissues and organs they become very tiny (arterioles and capillaries). Here blood releases its oxygen (becoming deoxygenated), and this is picked up and used by cells. Cells release carbon dioxide into the deoxygenated blood as it passes through more capillaries. The blood is now transported through tiny vessels (venules) which become larger *veins* and then it passes back to the right side of the heart. From here it passes to the lungs where carbon dioxide is released and oxygen is picked up before it returns to the left side of the heart once again. This type of blood circulation is described as 'double'. The heart is divided into two sides which each act as an independent pump with no communication between them. Each side is further divided into two chambers, the upper one is called the *atrium* and collects incoming blood passing it to the lower *ventricle*. This is a strong, muscular pump which contracts and pumps blood out either to the body or to the lungs. Arteries always carry oxygenated blood except for the pulmonary artery which takes blood from the heart to the lungs. Veins always transport deoxygenated blood except for the pulmonary artery which takes oxygenated blood from the lungs to the heart.

the human heart

atrium

aorta

pulmonary artery

ventricle

classification a means of grouping living organisms according to how similar they are to each other. For the early biologists, the physical similarities between organisms were the most important feature. However, increasingly in modern times the similarities between organisms at a genetic level have become more important in understanding their relationships. One main method of classification is most commonly recognized and this was originally devised by a Swedish naturalist, Carolus Linnaeus (1707–88) and is known as the *Linnaean system*. In this, all living things belong to a particular species and very similar species are grouped together in a *genus* (*pl.* genera), (*see* CLASSIFICATION). Hence in biology, each living organism has a double-barrelled name, first its generic (genus) and then its specific (species) 'label' and these are given in Latin. Examples are *Lumbricus terrestris* (the earthworm), *Rana temporaria* (the common frog), *Homo sapiens* (human beings) and, among plants, *Quercus robur* (the common oak), *Primula vulgaris* (primrose) and *Taraxacum officinale* (the dandelion). Genera which show similar features are grouped into families and these in turn into orders. Numbers of orders are put into classes which are grouped into a phylum (*pl.* phyla). Finally, phyla are placed together in a kingdom. In plants, the grouping division usually replaces phylum but otherwise the classification is the same.

clone a living organism which is an exact genetic copy of another individual and is produced from a single cell by an asexual process (*see* ASEXUAL REPRODUCTION).

cloning is an artificial process engineered by man and much used in the breeding of plants (e.g. cuttings). However, some animal clones have also been produced in the laboratory under strictly controlled conditions.

colloids were defined originally as substances in solution that could not get through a dialysis (semi-permeable) membrane. The definition of a colloid now is one of particle size–when the size range is 10^{-4} to 10^{-6}mm and it therefore falls between a coarse suspension and a true solution. Most substances can now be prepared to exist in this state and many exist naturally as colloids. Common examples of colloidal solutions include starch and albumen, butter and cell cytoplasm.

An *emulsion* is a colloidal solution of one liquid in another; generally one is water or a solution in water and the other is an oil or a similar liquid that does not mix with water. Emulsions are used widely in industry in food and pharmaceuticals, cosmetics, paints and lubricants.

combustion or burning, is actually a chemical reaction that occurs quickly and involves the high temperature oxidation of a substance, i.e. it combines with oxygen, to produce heat, light and flame, and of course ashes (oxides). Combustion of fossil fuels is the source of most energy used in homes, factories and offices. When coal or a similar fuel is burned, the carbon is converted to carbon dioxide or carbon monoxide and the hydrogen to water vapour. Combustion is a vital industrial process and although it generally refers to burning in oxygen, it is used on other occasions when, for example, a substance is burnt in hydrogen.

compact disc is a disc used to hold music, graphics or data for replaying. The disc has a layer of aluminium and music is recorded as very small pits etched into the surface. The pits are tiny–about half a micrometre (μm) wide and one to three wide. Each track is about 1.5μm from the next. The music is replayed by focusing a laser beam on the disc. The beam is partially reflected, depending upon whether or not it strikes a pit, and the reflected beam is detected as a series of pulses which is changed back into a copy of the original recording. Because there is no physical contact between the disc and the playing medium, compact discs should last much longer than their earlier counterparts: magnetic tapes and vinyl records.

compound is when two or more elements combine chemically in a substance and in definite proportions to produce molecules held together by chemical bonds. The formation of a compound necessitates a chemical reaction and the elements cannot be separated physically. Also, the same compound is formed irrespective of its origin so one molecule of water is two atoms of hydrogen and one of oxygen no matter how it is made.

The above can be regarded as the specific definition of compound but there are instances when the boundaries are blurred. For example, many silicate minerals, e.g. the feldspars, have varying compositions, as do many polymers although all are chemically combined. Indeed materials such as glass and steel are not mixtures and yet they do not fall readily into the definition of compound.

concentration *see* SOLUTIONS.

concrete a building material comprising a mixture of sand, cement, stone and water, which after it is set becomes very hard. Concrete is used in vast quantities for all types of building and construction and often steel rods or meshes are set into the concrete to increase its strength–*reinforced* concrete. *Prestressed concrete* is when the concrete is under compression, achieved by stretching the reinforcing rods and keeping them in tension after the concrete has set. Prestressed concrete is useful for large spans or where beams have to be as light as possible.

There is a whole technology surrounding concrete, with a variety of types and numerous compounds and materials that can be added to a mix to confer particular properties. *Aerated concrete* made up solely of cement, water and gas bubbles is used for its insulating properties; *lightweight concrete* utilizes lightweight aggregates (synthetic or natural) to form an insulating and lighter concrete; *high strength concrete* has obvious benefits while a denser concrete for protective shields can be made by using barytes, iron or lead shot in place of stone. Additives to concrete (known as *admixtures*) are used to alter the properties of the mix or the hardened material and include water reducers, accelerators, plasticizers, corrosion inhibitors and many others. This variety of concrete type renders it one of, if not the most versatile building material.

condensation is the process by which a substance changes from the gaseous state to the liquid state. In so doing energy is lost, i.e. it is cooled. There are many everyday examples of condensation–water forming on a pan lid when vegetables are cooking; water droplets on a cold tap in the bathroom; the steam from a kettle which is actually the hot water vapour condensing as tiny water droplets in the cooler air. *Cloud* (*see* **G**: CLOUD) is another example which is due to warm air saturated with water vapour being cooled.

The physical process of condensation is used in the chemicals industry when substances are purified by distillation. In chemistry a *condensation reaction* is the reaction of one molecule with another and the elimination of a simple molecule such as water.

conduction and convection *conduction* of heat is a process of heat moving through a material and is due to molecular vibrations. When a material is heated, the molecules vibrate rapidly and knock into neighbouring molecules which transfers the heat (or thermal energy) along the material. Metals e.g. copper and aluminium are the best conductors of heat while liquids and gases are progressively poor conductors.

In a gas or liquid that is free to move, *convection* is the process that moves heat from one part to another. As water in a tank is heated, the hot water rises and cooler water sinks. This establishes a convection current. Convection is used to great effect in the hot water systems in houses. A similar effect is seen with gases and when air is warmed, this sets up currents which on a large scale create onshore and offshore winds at the coast. On a smaller scale, radiators warm the air in a room by convection.

conductor and insulator electric conductors are materials that allow a flow of electrons, producing an electric current. As with conduction of heat, metals form the best electrical conductors because electrons around the outside of the atoms are loosely held and can move freely. Poor conductors include water, glass and air, indeed most non-metals.

A material that does not conduct electric charge is called an *insulator*. Plastics, rubber, glass and air form insulators because their electrons are not usually free to move.

connective tissue a type of tissue which is commonly found in the bodies of animals. It is further divided into a variety of different sorts depending upon the materials from which it is composed. It is usually composed of a non-living core containing various fibres in which are spread a number of cells.

construction *see* BUILDING AND CONSTRUCTION.

contraction and expansion when a solid is heated and its molecules vibrate more due to the input of thermal energy, the result is that the molecules move apart a little and the solid *expands*, almost imperceptibly. When the reverse happens, the solid *contracts*. Although the expansion in a solid may be negligible, the resulting force can be very large. In construction particularly, account has to be taken for the expansion of steel and concrete and all bridges have expansion joints to avoid damage which would otherwise be caused. Railways lines have a similar feature but in this case, line ends have overlapping joints.

The property of expansion also has its useful aspects and it can be applied to numerous devices which contain a bimetal strip.

Liquids generally expand more than solids, producing an increase in volume. Water is a notable exception to this statement and its behaviour is quite complex. As water cools from boiling it contracts a very small amount until it reaches 4°C at which point it expands a little. As we all know, at 0°C it forms ice and expands a great deal but on further cooling it contracts more. At 4°C water has its least volume and therefore its greatest density and it will sink beneath colder or warmer water. This is the reason for ponds freezing on the surface while fish can survive in the slightly warmer water at depth.

copper is a red-brown metal which is very malleable and ductile (*see* DUCTILITY) and has numerous uses. It occurs as native copper (as the metal itself, often with silver, lead and other metals) and in a variety of mineral forms, e.g. malachite ($CuCO_3.Cu(OH)_2$), bornite ($CuFeS_3$) and chalcopyrite ($CuFeS_2$). The ores are concentrated and copper is extracted by smelting and refining by electrolysis. Copper has been an important metal for thousands of years in its alloys, brass and bronze, and it is now used in coins as an alloy (with nickel).

convection *see* CONDUCTION AND CONVECTION.

Pure copper is an excellent electrical conductor and is used in wiring and a significant proportion of copper production is taken in electrical applications. It is also used for pipes in plumbing although plastics are being used increasingly in this context. Copper is also employed in fungicides, paints, pigments and printing.

corrosion is the process of metals and alloys being attacked chemically by moisture, air, acids or alkalis. If left to continue, the metal will be gradually worn away. Corrosion may occur uniformly or it may be concentrated at weak points or joints. It may also produce an oxide layer, as on aluminium which protects against further attack. The more serious effects are seen with corrosion where some moisture is present because this sets up an electrolytic process and with underground corrosion the soil acts as the electrolyte (*see* ELECTROLYSIS).

Corrosion can be prevented or slowed by applying protective layers (paint, anodizing, or plating with zinc, nickel, chromium etc.). *Cathodic protection* is also used in the protection of underground structures (e.g. pipelines) by making the object/structure in question the cathode in a circuit which has a voltage higher than the estimated voltage of corrosion. The anode in this circuit may dissolve away and be replaced when necessary. Steel reinforcement (*see* CONCRETE) can be cathodically protected providing it is continuous electrically.

coulomb is the unit of electrical charge and is defined as the charge passing a point in a circuit when a current of one ampère flows for one second, thus a charge of 8 coulombs passes if a current of 2 ampères flows for 4 seconds. One coulomb is equal to the charge on approximately 6.25×10^{18} electrons!

cracking *see* PETROCHEMICALS.

cytology the branch of biology devoted to the scientific study of cells, including both their structure and function, that depends very much on the use of the light and electron microscope.

Darwin and natural selection. Charles Darwin (1809–1882) was one of the most famous naturalists ever to have lived and he devised the theory of evolution (known as *Darwinism*) to explain the great variety of plants and animals which he saw around him. He arrived at his theories during a five year voyage around the world (the voyage of the Beagle) and when he returned to England in 1859 he published a scientific paper (with the title *Origin of Species*). He proposed that some individuals in a species are more successful than others (they have a greater degree of 'fitness"). In the competition for food or for a mate they are more likely to be successful and these characteristics are inherited by their offspring which means that eventually these features become more widespread. He called this 'survival of the fittest.' Following from this, plants and animals were gradually able to change and adapt to new conditions and environments. Hence new species eventually evolved from an original, ancestral stock. Darwin's theories were not accepted at the time and caused outrage because they questioned the Biblical version of God's Creation as a one-off event. However, now they are largely accepted and have been expanded by the modern study of genes and inheritance. Darwin's theory can be summarized as follows: from organisms which have the ability to change, new species can emerge that will adapt to new environments. Old species which are no longer suited to the surrounding environment will eventually die out.

decibel *see* SOUND.

deciduous and evergreen deciduous plants shed their leaves at the end of the growing season, which is the Autumn in temperate regions such as Britain. Examples include familiar trees such as the oak and sycamore. Evergreen plants on the other hand, keep their leaves all through the year and these include the cone-bearing coniferous trees (conifers) such as Sitka spruce.

decimal numbers is the most commonly used number system based on powers of ten. The *decimal point* is the dot that divides the number's whole part from the fractional part (i.e. that which is less than one). However, numbers need not contain a decimal point : 789 is also a decimal number. A decimal is itself less than one and is written after the decimal point e.g. 0.789 and 0.00987. Decimal numbers are written within the place value system, that is, the value given to a digit depends upon its position in the number and with the decimal system each column has ten times the value of the column to the right thus:

The number 7891 is really:

seven 1000s	eight 100s	nine 10s	and one 1
(10^3)	(10^2)	(10^1)	(10^0)
7	8	9	1

A common fraction such as $1/4$ can be changed into decimal form by dividing the 1 by 4 to give 0.25.

dehydration in a chemical reaction or process is the removal by heat of water held in a molecule or compound. Sometimes a catalyst is used, or a dehydrating agent such as sulphuric acid (H_2SO_4). Dehydration is used a great deal in the food industry in the production of coffee, soups, sauces, mashed potato, milk and so on. It arrests the processes of natural decay because there is no moisture available for micro-organisms to survive and chemical reactions are slowed or stopped. Of course, dehydration produces a reduction in volume and particularly weight which is useful for storage and transport.

In medicine, dehydration is the excessive, often dangerous, loss of water from body tissues, accompanied by loss of vital salts. The average daily intake of water is about 2 litres but lack of water for just a few days can be dangerous because the heart can be affected.

dendrochronology a technique of dating past events using the growth rings of trees. Each year a new ring of wood is added to the trunk just beneath the bark and this is called an annual ring. It is possible to date the rings in living trees by working back year by year. Then this pattern of rings can be used to date fossil trees or specimens of wood found at archaeological, or other sites. The longest living trees are the most useful and the standard one is the bristle cone pine, which can live for up to 5000 years and be used to date specimens older than this.

density is the mass of a substance, per unit volume, given by the following equation:

$$\text{density (d)} = \frac{\text{mass (M)}}{\text{volume (V)}}$$

It is measured in kilograms per cubic metre (kg/m^3), although it may be more convenient on occasion to use grams per cubic centimetre (g/cm^3). Density varies with temperature; only a little in the case of solids and liquids which usually expand and therefore become less dense, with gases the density varies a great deal depending upon its container and the surrounding pressure.

Relative density is the density of a material compared to that of water, given by the following equation:

$$\text{relative density} = \frac{\text{density of a substance}}{\text{density of water}}$$

Relative density used to be called *specific gravity*.

It has no units, but is the same value as the density when measured in g/cm^3. Some typical densities:

	kg/m^3	g/cm^3		kg/m^3	g/cm^3
air	1.3	0.0013	aluminium	2700	2.7
soft wood	450	0.45	diamond	3500	3.5
hard wood	800	0.80	steel	7700	7.7
petrol	800	0.80	lead	11400	11.4
water	1000	1.00	mercury	13600	13.6
hardened cement	2200	2.2	gold	19300	19.3
granite	2600	2.6			

detergents and soaps are both cleaning agents that remove grease and dirt and hold it in suspension for washing away. Soap acts as a detergent but there are now many synthetic detergents derived from petroleum. The detergent molecules contain two distinct groups; one which gives the molecule solubility in water, e.g. a sulphate, and long hydrocarbon chains which enable it to dissolve oily materials. When detergent molecules come into contact with grease, the hydrocarbon chains which are *hydrophobic* (water-hating) attach to the grease, and the other end of the molecule which is *hydrophilic* (water-loving) is in the water. The grease is then enclosed and can be removed from the garment. Detergents are made in many forms: washing-up liquids, powders, shampoo, etc.

Soaps are sodium and potassium salts of *fatty acids* (a type of organic acid of animal or vegetable origin) which are heated in large vats with dilute sodium hydroxide (caustic soda) to effect *hydrolysis* (*see* CHEMICAL REACTION). Sodium chloride is then added to precipitate the soap from the solution. The soap may then be treated with perfumes before being made into bars or flakes.

Metallic soaps are a very different group of compounds, being insoluble in water. They are metal salts (metals such as lithium, aluminium, calcium, and zinc) of long carboxylic acid chains (organic acids with one or more carboxyl, -COOH, groups) and are used in cosmetics, pharmaceuticals, fungicides and lubricating oils.

differentiation a mathematical operation used in calculus for finding the derivative of a function. Depending upon the complexity of the function there are different methods of differentiation. The simplest relates to the common function;

$$f(x) \text{ or } y = x^n$$

This has the derivative (or differential coefficient);

$$f^1(x) \text{ or } \frac{dy}{dx} = nx^{n-1}$$

Thus, for example, if $y = 4x^3$, $\frac{dy}{dx} = 12x^2$

and for $y = 3x^3 + 4x^2$, $\frac{dy}{dx} = 9x^2 + 8x$

diffraction is the bending of waves around an obstacle and as they pass through a narrow gap. This applies to all waves; water, sound, light and electromagnetic, and can be detected by a change in the shape of the wavefront and by *interference* patterns. When a beam of light passes through a narrow slit it is diffracted but the slit has to be very narrow indeed (less than 0.01mm) to have any effect. If *monochromatic* (one wavelength) light is used, and the diffracted light is passed through two further slits, then an interference pattern of light and dark fringes is created. In 1801, Thomas Young the physicist used an experimental procedure such as this to measure the wavelength of light. The fact that sound can be diffracted is easily shown because it is possible to hear round corners.

diffusion is the process that occurs in gases and liquids whereby one liquid is spread throughout the body of another, e.g. an ink drop in water, due to the molecular motion of the water (*see* BROWNIAN MOTION), producing a more uniform concentration. The same process occurs with gases and accounts, for example, for the smell of a gas leak filling a room. The molecular movement of gases is more vigorous than liquids and the molecules distribute themselves equally within the volume in which they are enclosed.

Diffusion also occurs across cell membranes and a similar mechanism is used in dialysis as a means of separating certain molecules.

digestion the process by which organisms break down solid food into small particles which can be used by the body.

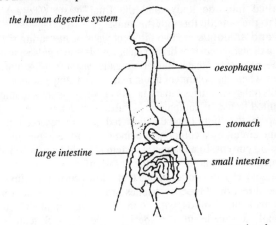

the human digestive system

oesophagus

stomach

large intestine

small intestine

In human beings, the digestive process starts in the mouth where food is cut up into smaller particles by the teeth. The food is mixed with saliva containing an enzyme which breaks down starch into sugar. The food is then swallowed and passes via a tube called the *oesophagus* into the stomach. In the stomach a fluid, the gastric juice, is released which contains hydrochloric acid and enzymes. The stomach has muscular walls and is able to expand and contract and further manipulate the food. Proteins are broken down and eventually a semi-solid acidic mass (known as *chyme*), is passed into the small intestine. Alkaline fluid from an organ called the *pancreas* (pancreatic juice) is added here and this contains more enzymes which further break down the food. Also, *bile*, a thick fluid produced by the liver and stored in the *gall bladder* located nearby, is added to the food in the intestine. This contains bile salts, bile pigments and cholesterol and aids in the digestion of fatty substances. As the food passes along the highly coiled length of the small intestine it continues to be broken down into minute particles (molecules) which can be absorbed into fine blood vessels present in the intestinal wall. The blood circulation carries the food to all parts of the body where it is used by cells to perform all the functions of life and to provide energy. Any food substances that cannot be digested, such as fibre, are passed to the large intestine which is the final part of the alimentary canal or digestive system. Here water is removed and reabsorbed into the body, and the final waste (*faeces*) is passed to the outside through the anus.

digital and analogue are two different ways of measuring some value—a digital system uses distinct units, e.g. electrical pulses, while analogue is a quantity that is similar to another quantity, (e.g. a thermometer where the column of liquid represents a temperature).

The digital system uses binary numbers which renders it admirably suited to use in computers. Numbers and letters are coded by groups of the digits 1 and 0 and each digit is represented in an electronic circuit by a component being on or off, e.g. passing or not passing current. In a magnetic system it could be magnetized or not magnetized that produces the on/off effect.

diode a device with two terminals that allows current to flow in only one direction. Modern varieties are *solid state* (electronic devices made up of solids, with no moving parts, filaments, etc.) and usually are made up of a special *silicon chip*. Silicon is a semiconductor used to make diodes. A crystal of silicon with phosphorus and boron added to opposite halves (a process called *doping*) has a poorly-conducting junction called the *depletion layer* between the two halves. The phosphorus increases the number of electrons available to move through the material and the boron makes holes into which electrons can move. Depending upon the current flow in the circuit, the diode passes current easily when the depletion layer is thin but when the current is reversed, the depletion layer thickens and no current is passed.

This property of diodes means they can be used to turn alternating current into a direct current, a process called rectification. Then the diode is called a *rectifier*. The diode may be used for *half-wave rectification* in which it simply blocks the backward half of the current, or with a more complex arrangement of diodes, *full-wave rectification* can be achieved in which the blocked half of the alternating current is reversed and flows through as direct current. This is the principle employed in radios and tape recorders that can use a mains adaptor, or batteries.

diploid *see* CELL DIVISION.

disease any illness that affects an organism which, in man, is caused in two main ways. Often diseases are caused by infectious micro-organisms e.g. bacteria, viruses and fungi (*see* FUNGUS). Bacteria can be killed with antibiotic drugs such as penicillin and examples of bacterial diseases are cholera, tuberculosis and typhoid. Viruses are not susceptible to antibiotics and the illnesses they cause have to be fought off by the body's immune system, although protection can be given against some of these by means of vaccination. The common cold is a viral disease, and those which can be prevented by vaccination include mumps and measles. The second group of diseases are caused by the failure of a body system to work properly. This may be an inherited disorder, e.g. cystic fibrosis, or occur at some stage in a person's life for an unknown reason. A common example is *Diabetes mellitus* which occurs when an organ called the pancreas fails to produce enough of the hormone insulin, itself responsible for the breakdown of sugars in food.

distillation is the separation of a liquid mixture into its components. The liquid is first heated to vapour which is then cooled so that it condenses and can be collected as a liquid. The mixture can then be separated if the components liquids have different boiling points, each one vaporizing at a different temperature.

Distillation is one of the most common separation processes in industry and it permits a high degree of separation. It is performed in a large column within which there are a number of trays (or plates) at different levels. The liquid is fed in through a heater and a constant flow is maintained between the ascending vapour and descending liquid. The vapour is then taken out at the top of the column through a condenser. *Fractional distillation* is the term applied to this process and the column is the fractionating column. Whisky is distilled in this manner and crude oil is refined by the same means. *Flash distillation* involves the rapid removal of solvent by moving the liquid from high to low pressure so that part turns immediately to vapour and is condensed. This technique is used in the desalination of sea water, i.e. the removal of salts from sea water to provide fresh water.

DNA stands for deoxyribonucleic acid and this is the material of which the chromosomes and genes are composed. It occurs as strands in the nucleus of each cell and contains all the instructions which determine the structure and function of that cell. One of the most exciting discoveries of this century occurred in 1953 when two scientists, James Watson and Francis Crick, worked out and demonstrated the structure of DNA. They found that it occurs as two spiral threads coiling round each other (a double helix) with 'bridges' across at intervals connecting the two, as in a ladder. Four types of molecules (known as bases) occur on the 'rungs' of the ladder and these pair up in particular ways (*base pairing*). These four molecules store all the genetic information by being built up in different combinations. In cell division, the two DNA threads split apart and each reproduces the missing half to rebuild the double helix. Sometimes the copying does not occur properly and can result in a mutation. Many mutations are lethal but minute changes can occur in this way and this is the genetic basis for evolution and species change.

DNA structure   rung   bridge

Doppler effect is the change in the observed frequency or wavelength of a wave when the source producing the wave is moving. If the source, e.g. a vehicle, is moving towards the listener, the frequency increases (and the wavelength decreases) and the opposite happens as it moves away. The result is the pitch of the sound changes as the vehicle approaches, passes and moves away. The principle applies to all electromagnetic radiation including light. The light from a moving object appears more red when it is moving away from the observer. This is taken to mean that stars in distant galaxies are moving away from us when they exhibit the *red shift*.

drugs and pharmacology *drugs* are substances which, when introduced into an animal's body, produce some kind of effect or response. Most drugs are given to help cure illnesses or other medical conditions and there are a great number of different kinds. **Pharmacology** is the name of the scientific study of all aspects of drugs and medicines including their preparation, uses, properties and effects. Drugs may be given in a variety of different ways: 1. by mouth (orally) as capsules, tablets or in liquid form, by injection; 2. as a cream or ointment applied to the skin; 3. by inhalation (sometimes using an inhaler); 4. by means of skin patches or insertion just beneath the skin and 5. suppositories which are placed via the anus into the end of the digestive tract (the rectum). New drugs are rigorously tested before their use is allowed but many occur naturally in plants. caffeine (in coffee and tea) and alcohol are examples of drugs which are in widespread use.

ductility and malleability ductility is the property of metals or alloys that allows them to be drawn out into a thin wire and although their shape is permanently changed they retain their strength and do not crack. *Malleability* is similar but is the property that allows metals and alloys to have their shape altered by hammering, rolling or similar process, into thin sheets.

Most metals are ductile, notable examples being copper and gold. The same metals are very malleable and gold can be produced as very thin gold leaf which is $2\mu m$ (micrometres) thick. The high ductility and malleability of metals is due to their molecular structure, in which the lattice can be greatly altered before the atoms are torn apart and the metal breaks.

dyes (or dyestuffs) are substances with a strong colour that can be fixed to material to be dyed, such as fabrics and fibres, plastics, etc. The synthetic dye manufacturing industry began in 1857 when Perkin & Sons set up a factory to produce mauveine. At that time the wool and cotton trade was undergoing vast expansion and demand for dyes was heavy. In the past dyes had been made mainly from plants but mauveine was soon followed by the production of other synthetic dyes. Alizarin appeared in 1869, Congo Red in 1884 and indigo in 1897. Now dye production is a vast industry undertaken in complex chemical plants.

In some cases when a dye does not fix to the material, a *mordant* may be necessary. This is a compound (aluminium, chromium and iron hydroxides) that impregnates the fabric and then the dye reacts with the mordant to ensure stability. There are many types of dye, which are categorized according to application.

ear *see* HEARING.

ecdysis and moulting *ecdysis* is the process of shedding skin. It is undergone by a group of invertebrate animals and it enables them to grow. It is a characteristic of arthropods such as insects, spiders and crabs which possess a tough, outer shell. At the start of ecdysis a hormone is released under the influence of which the new shell (or *exoskeleton*) begins to form beneath the old one. In addition some materials are reabsorbed from the old exoskeleton and these can then be used again. Eventually, the old exoskeleton splits and the animal extracts itself from its former covering. To begin with the new exoskeleton is very soft and the animal is often rather vulnerable at this stage. The new exoskeleton expands, often involving the animal taking in air or water to increase its body size and it hardens by the incorporation of a special substance called *chitin* (or *calcium* salts in crabs). The animal is thus larger than it was before and may undergo this process several times during the course of its life (*see also* METAMORPHOSIS).

moulting is a term which is sometimes used to describe ecdysis. However, more familiarly, it is applied to the loss of fur or hair or feathers which often takes place in vertebrate animals, especially in the spring.

echo is when a reflected sound is heard a short time after the original sound was made. There is a delay between making a sound and hearing its echo because it takes the sound waves a little time to travel the distance (light travels so quickly that it does not exhibit this phenomenon). The time delay can be used in echo-sounding machines to locate the sea bed or submerged objects. SONAR (Sound Navigation Ranging) is such a device that operates with high frequency sound, collecting the returning waves that have been reflected from submerged objects. In all such cases, the distance can be calculated from the time taken for the sound to return. Echo-sounding equipment is used in ships and boats and *radar* is a similar principle but uses microwaves.

In small spaces, particularly rooms and halls, the echo time may be very short and the echo is not heard but becomes mixed up with the original sound, and the whole sound seems to be extended. This is called *reverberation* and may be a problem in concert halls where walls and ceilings may have to be modified to reduce the effect.

egg an egg, also known as an *ovum* (*pl.* ova), is the female reproductive cell. An egg may have a hard outer shell, as in birds and turtles, and is usually surrounded by one or more protective layers called membranes. After the egg is fertilized by a male sex cell (*sperm*), it divides into several cells which become an embryo. The embryo is nourished by a supply of food from the yolk within the egg. Some eggs contain very little yolk whereas others, such as those of birds, have a large amount which enables a chick to grow quite large before it hatches. Eggs may be extremely small, as in female mammals, which keep the developing embryos inside their bodies. The young of mammals are supplied with all that they need from the body of the mother and grow until they are ready to be born. There are two exceptions to this, the duck-billed platypus and spiny anteater, which are unique among mammals in that they lay eggs (*see* REPRODUCTION).

elasticity is the property of any material such that it stretches when forces are applied and recovers its original form when the forces are removed. To stretch a spring or other elastic material a stretching force must be applied to both ends. As the stretching force is increased, the extension becomes greater and up to a certain point the extension is proportional to the force. However, there is a limit to this proportional response and beyond a material's *elastic limit*, it is permanently stretched and will not return to its original length. *Hooke's Law* records this physical relationship but applies only to materials if the elastic limit is not exceeded. All materials are elastic to some extent but in many cases the extension is a very small amount.

electricity is a general term to cover the energy associated with electric charges, whether static or dynamic. In a simple circuit the *potential difference* between the battery terminals (i.e. the difference in potential) causes a current to flow. Current is measured in ampères and potential difference in volts. Batteries supply *direct current* but the electricity supply to homes and offices is *alternating current*. Power stations generate electricity by means of massive alternators (*see* GENERATOR) driven by turbines which are themselves driven by steam from coal, gas or oil-fired boilers (or heat from a nuclear reactor). The alternators generate a current of 20, 000 amps at a voltage of 25, 000 volts, which passes through a transformer and then into overhead power cables at a reduced current but a higher voltage–up to 400, 000 or 400 kilovolts. The current is reduced to minimize the power losses due to heating in the long cables. The cables feed the nationwide network (the *Grid*) and power from the Grid is distributed by substations where transformers reduce the voltage to 240 volts for ordinary consumption. Heavy industry uses supply at 33, 000 volts and light industry 11, 000 volts. *See also* STATIC ELECTRICITY.

electrocardiogram (ECG) and electroencephalogram (EEG) are both records of the electrical activity in the heart and brain respectively. The ECG is recorded on an electrocardiograph connected through leads to pads on the chest and legs or arms. It often indicates abnormal heart activity and is therefore a useful diagnostic tool.

The EEG records the brain's electrical activity on an electroencephalograph. Electrodes placed on the scalp record activity, or brain waves, of which there are four types associated with particular phases of activity or rest.

electrolysis is the chemical decomposition (breaking down) of a substance in solution or molten state when an electric current is passed. The solution is called an *electrolyte* and it permits the passage of a current because it forms ions in solution. A strong electrolyte, e.g. sulphuric acid, undergoes complete ionization. When the current passes through the solutions the ions move to the electrodes of opposite charge; the *cathode* being negatively-charged and attracting positively-charged ions (*cation*); the *anode* being positively-charged and attracting *anions* which are negatively-charged ions. At the electrodes the ions give up their charges to form atoms or groups. Gases are liberated, and solids deposited.

Electrolysis is used a great deal in industry to extract and purify metals and also to electroplate objects. *Electroplating* consists of metal salts dissolved in a solution into which are put the electrodes. The cathode has the metal plated onto it and the anode dissolves into the solution replacing the metal ions. This technique is used to plate with chrome, nickel, gold, silver and other metals and also to anodize (*see* ANODIZING).

electromagnet is a magnet created by passing a current through a coil of wire which is wound around a soft iron core; the core becomes a magnet whilst the current is on. The coil of wire is called a *solenoid*. This magnetic effect of electric current was discovered by Oersted, a Danish scientist. There is a cumulative magnetic effect because in producing a magnetic field, the coil magnetizes the core which produces a magnetic field that can be about a thousand times stronger than the field from the core alone.

Electromagnets are clearly useful because the magnetic field generated can be controlled easily. They are used in televisions to control the electron beams in the cathode ray tube, and also in devices such as switches, electric bells, loudspeakers and in the earpiece of the telephone.

An associated phenomenon is that of *electromagnetic induction* in which an electric current is produced in a conductor when it is moved through a magnetic field (*see also* GENERATOR).

electromagnetic waves come from a number of sources and are the effect of oscillating electric and magnetic fields. The wavelength of these waves varies but all travel through free space (a vacuum) at approximately $3 \times 10^8 ms^{-1}$ (300, 000 kilometres per second), which is the speed of light. The *electromagnetic spectrum* contains waves from low frequency/long wavelength radio waves (long wave) through microwave, infrared and the visible spectrum to ultraviolet x-rays and the short wavelength/high frequency gamma rays.

Approximate wavelengths and frequencies for electromagnetic waves		
	wavelength (m)	*frequency* (Hz)
gamma rays	$10^{-13}–10^{10}$	$10^{19}-10^{21}$
X-rays	$10^{-10}-10^{-8}$	$10^{17}–10^{19}$
ultraviolet radiation	$10^{-8}–10^{-7}$	$10^{15}–10^{17}$
visible light	$10^{-7}–10^{-6}$	$10^{14}–10^{15}$
infrared radiation	$10^{-6}–10^{-2}$	$10^{11}–10^{14}$
microwaves	$10^{-2}–10^{-1}$	$10^{10}–10^{11}$
radio waves	$10^{-1}–10^{4}$	$10^{5}–10^{10}$

Electromagnetic waves are generated when particles with an electrical charge change their energy, e.g. when an electron changes orbit around a nucleus. It also happens when electrons or nuclei oscillate and their kinetic energy changes. A large change in energy produces high frequency/short wavelength radiation.

Radio waves are the longest in the spectrum and are used to transmit sound and pictures. Microwaves have wavelengths of a few centimetres and have numerous uses. *Infrared* (IR) waves are generated by the continuous motion of molecules in materials, and hot objects give out most. When an electric fire is switched on the infrared radiation is felt in the heat. As objects become hotter and hotter, their molecules vibrate more rapidly and the wavelength of the radiation becomes shorter. Eventually it impinges on the visible spectrum and the object appears 'red-hot'. *Ultraviolet* (UV) radiation occurs beyond the violet end of the visible light spectrum, is a component of sunlight and is emitted by white-hot objects. Ultraviolet light from the sun converts steroids in the skin to essential vitamin D but an excess of UV light can be harmful. However, much of the sun's ultraviolet radiation is stopped by the Earth's ozone layer (*see* **GG**: OZONE LAYER). *Gamma rays* are very short wavelength radiation released during radioactive decay and are the most penetrating of all radiations.

electronics is an important area of science and technology that deals with electrical circuits using semiconductors, diodes, transistors, etc. and other devices in which the movement of electrons is controlled to create switches and other components. Technology has advanced so much in recent years that electronic circuits can fit onto a single *silicon chip* and highly complex circuits are constructed on *printed circuit boards* where individual components are linked by metal traces printed on the board and through which the current flows.

The use of such boards and microelectronic components is widespread and they are found in computers, cars, watches, televisions, space craft and many other machines and pieces of equipment.

electroscope is an instrument used in physics for the detection of small electrical charges. It consists of a metal cap joined to a rod which projects down into a case. At the bottom of the rod is a gold leaf. When a charged object touches the cap, some charge is transferred to the rod and gold leaf and because like charges repel each other, the gold leaf rises. When it is charged, the electroscope can be used to determine whether the charge on an object is positive or negative.

element a pure substance that comprises atoms of the same kind and which cannot be broken down into simpler substances in ordinary chemical reactions (nuclear reactions can, however, alter elements). There are 103 elements known to us, of which 92 occur naturally and the rest have been created in the laboratory. Indeed scientists continue to experiment and occasionally claim the existence of another element.

Elements combine together to form compounds and under normal conditions all but two elements (bromine and mercury) are either a solid or a gas. The elements are classified by their atomic number into the periodic table (*see* PERIODIC TABLE) which comprises groups and periods with similar properties and behaviour.

elementary particles (or *fundamental particles* or *subatomic particles*) are the basic particles and building blocks of which all matter is made. The three key particles in all atoms–electrons, neutron and protons–have now been supplemented by new particles. Essentially two types are thought to exist, *leptons* and *hadrons* and these are identified by the different ways in which they interact with other particles. Leptons include the electron and the *neutrino*, the latter having no charge and virtually no mass. The neutrino was originally proposed on the basis of theory, to preserve the physical laws of mass, energy and momentum and it has since been established experimentally. The proton and neutron are called hadrons although they are not truly elementary particles and it is now thought that these are composed of real elementary particles called *quarks*. Quarks have become part of a highly elaborate theory of hadron structure in which hadrons occur in two forms, *baryons* and *mesons*, the first comprising three quarks and the latter two plus a quark and its antiquark (*see* **SA**: ANTIMATTER). In addition quarks have properties termed 'flavour' and 'colour charge' producing a highly complex character for each particle. Although this theory seems to be generally accepted by physicists, quarks have yet to be confirmed experimentally.

embryo the stage in the development of a new plant or animal which follows on from the fertilization of an egg by a sperm. It is most often used to describe the young of a mammal before birth, while they are developing within the mother, and in birds, to the growing chick while it is still inside the egg. Doctors define an 'embryo'as the stage in the development of a human being, from two weeks after fertilization until two months, and after this the word 'foetus' is used (*see* REPRODUCTION).

embryology the branch of biological or medical study which is concerned with all aspects of the growth and development of embryos.

emulsion *see* COLLOID.

endocrine system this is the name given to a network of small organs (known as *glands*), within the body of an animal which are responsible for the production of chemical signalling substances called hormones. A hormone is released into the bloodstream and travels in the body until it reaches its target cells or organ somewhere else, where it causes a response to occur. There are several endocrine glands in the body of a human being including the *pituitary* gland (at the base of the brain), the *thyroid* gland (in the neck), and the paired *adrenal* glands (one above each kidney). The male and female sex organs (the *testes* and *ovaries*), are also endocrine glands which produce hormones that are responsible for the changes which occur at puberty and control fertility. (*See* HORMONE, REPRODUCTION.)

energy is the capacity to do work, and there are many different forms of energy: light, heat, sound, electrical, kinetic, potential and more, and all are measured in joules (J). *Kinetic energy* is possessed by moving objects and for a mass m, with a constant speed v, the kinetic energy is $\frac{1}{2}mv^2$. So a ball kicked by a footballer has kinetic energy which it loses when it hits the net of the goal, pushing the net outwards. Objects have *potential energy* by virtue of their position, that is, they have been moved and when released can do work. Hence a stretched spring, a car at the top of a hill, or a weight on a shelf all have potential energy. The energy is defined as mgh where m is the mass which is raised through a height h and g is the acceleration of free fall. *Thermal energy* (sometimes called heat energy) is that kinetic and potential energy possessed by an object's molecules and it rises with an increase in temperature. *Electrical energy* is that stored in batteries, and *electromagnetic waves* and sound waves also possess energy.

The law of conservation of energy states that energy cannot be created, nor can it be destroyed, however it can be changed from one form to another. This means that in any action all energy can be accounted for. This may be a simple procedure such as throwing a ball where chemical energy in the arm launches the ball which then has kinetic energy. Depending upon the throw it may have potential energy if the ball stops momentarily before falling, again with kinetic energy. Then when it hits the ground the kinetic energy becomes sound and thermal energy.

Society today requires vast amounts of energy to survive and this is supplied as electricity, oil, gas, coal, etc. However, the primary source of energy is the sun which is stored in plants which in turn provide energy either as food or as fuels. In addition to burning fuels for energy, alternative and renewable sources are being exploited such as tidal, wind, solar and hydroelectric.

engines are machines that convert energy into work, and fuel undergoes combustion to supply the energy. Petrol and diesel engines use the chemical energy from their fuels and electric motors use electrical energy stored in a battery or from a generator. The human body is also an engine, and food is the fuel. There are essentially two types of engine: those in which the combustion is internal as in the internal combustion engine (*see* TRANSPORT), and those where the fuel is burned outside the engine itself—external combustion.

Engines are used to power all sorts of vehicles such as boats, aeroplanes and cars and although the internal combustion engine is not particularly efficient, it does provide a means of rapidly turning fuel into mechanical work. In the 1940s a British engineer, Frank Whittle, invented the gas turbine or *jet engine*. Air enters the front of the engine, is compressed and then enters a combustion chamber where liquid fuel is burnt. The energy produced expands the gas and shoots it out where it provides both thrust for motion and energy to drive the turbine which operates the compressor.

The *efficiency* of an engine is a ratio of the work provided for the energy put in. In general, most systems that burn fuels are very inefficient because so much energy is lost as heat. As a percentage, the efficiency of petrol and diesel engines is 25% and 35% respectively, while power stations are only around 30% efficient in producing electrical energy. Although electric motors are in themselves about 75% efficient, the process supplying the electrical input energy is only around 30% efficient.

entomology the specialized branch of biology which is concerned with the study of insects. A person who studies insects is known as an entomologist.

entropy is a measure of the disorder or randomness of a system which tends always to increase. The increase is because at every stage of energy transfer, some energy is wasted and the greater the disorder, the higher is the entropy. One result of entropy is that heat always flows from a hot to a cold body and this is the basis of the second law of thermodynamics which can be rewritten as: any system will always undergo change so as to increase the entropy.

enzyme enzymes are naturally-occurring protein molecules that are found in all living things, and which act as catalysts (i.e. they speed up and activate chemical reactions, *see* CATALYSIS) within cells. Enzymes are very specialized and each only acts on a certain substance. Also, conditions of temperature and acidity or alkalinity have to be just right or the reaction will not take place. This is one of the reasons why a stable body temperature is maintained in mammals. Some enzymes are involved in breaking down processes, e.g. digestive enzymes such as *ptyalin* which is present in saliva and breaks down starch to sugar. Others are involved in reactions to build up more complex molecules from simpler ones such as in tissue growth.

equilibrium is when a system, whether chemical or physical, remains the same over time. In physics an object is in equilibrium if all the forces acting on it are equal and opposite. However, there are three equilibrium states. If a system returns to equilibrium position after being moved slightly, then it is in stable equilibrium, e.g. tipping slightly a box with a wide base. Unstable equilibrium is when the system moves from equilibrium when moved slightly, e.g. a pencil 'stood' on its point, and neutral equilibrium is when a movement results in a new equilibrium position, as with a ball. In chemistry equilibrium is reached in a chemical reaction when the proportion of reactants and products is constant, as the rate of the forward and reverse reactions is the same. Equilibrium is affected by changes in temperature, pressure or concentration of the reactants.

eucaryote the type of cell found in all plants and animals (but not bacteria or blue-green algae (cyanobacteria) in which the nucleus is bound within a membrane. *See also* PROCARYOTE.

evaporation is the process that occurs when a liquid turns into a vapour. Heat accelerates the process, which happens because some molecules near the surface of the liquid gain sufficient kinetic energy (*see* ENERGY) to overcome the attractive forces of the liquid's molecules and escape into the surrounding atmosphere. During the process of evaporation from a container, the temperature of the liquid falls until heat is replaced from heat in the surroundings. This is the reason why swimmers feel cold when leaving the water–because heat energy is taken from the body, converted into kinetic energy enabling some water molecules to escape.

Evaporation is occurring all around us as rainwater puddles dry in the sun or as moisture evaporates from lakes, rivers, etc. eventually to form cloud and then rain. The principle is also used in industry where solutions are made more concentrated by evaporating off the solvent, and also in cooling and refrigeration systems. In a refrigerator, a volatile liquid evaporates and its vapour is pumped away. As it evaporates, it draws heat from the stored food. The pump then compresses the vapour back to liquid and heat is given off via the cooling fins at the back of the refrigerator.

evolution the gradual change, over a long period of time, of one species of animal or plant. The organisms eventually acquire characteristics which are different from those of the ancestral species. This is able to occur firstly, if there has been genetic mutation which allows for different information to be passed on from a parent to its offspring. Secondly, if the offspring (one or several) which received the different characteristic proves better suited to its environment than other member of the species, then it is more likely to survive and reproduce. In this way the new characteristic tends to be preserved while those individuals not possessing it are more likely to die out. These changes are very small and take place slowly over many thousands of years, but it is thought that all living organisms have evolved from different ancestors in this way. The study of fossils (*see* **G** FOSSILS) has helped in the understanding of how this may have taken place in particular species. *See also* DARWINISM, CHROMOSOME AND DNA.

Homonid evolution

excretion the name give to the process by which an organism gets rid of the waste products of metabolism and eliminates them from its body. It differs from the process of getting rid of food waste, which is called egestion and is concerned with eliminating material that has been taken in. Excretion gets rid of waste products manufactured within the organism itself. The main waste products are carbon dioxide, water and nitrogen-containing substances from the breakdown of protein.

One way that these are disposed of is by diffusion of leakage to the outside (in plants and simple animals) either from a single cell or through the body. Higher animals have developed specialized organs for excretion of waste products and these include gills, lungs and kidneys.

expansion *see* CONTRACTION AND EXPANSION.

explosives are substances or mixtures that, when heated or subjected to a shock or a blow, release a very large amount of energy very violently. The chemicals are actually undergoing rapid decomposition, producing large volumes of gas and quantities of heat. Explosives have numerous uses both military and civil. In construction they are used for clearing land and blasting new cuttings through rock, in mining, quarrying and tunnelling and also to demolish large structures, e.g. old cooling towers or multi-storey buildings.

There are basically three groups of explosives. *Propellants* are compound that burn at a steady speed and can be detonated (set off) only under very specific conditions, e.g. as used in rockets. *Initiators* (or primary explosives) are extremely sensitive to heat and shock and are used in very small quantities to initiate explosions in large masses of less sensitive explosive. Compounds such as mercury fulminate ($Hg(ONC)_2$) and some metallic azides, e.g. lead azide, $Pb(N3)_2$, are initiators. *High explosives* are very powerful yet more stable and are used in bombs and shells.

Dynamite is a mixture of nitroglycerine with other compounds while tnt (trinitrotoluene) is a very violent explosive made from toluene with nitric and sulphuric acids. Plastic explosives can be moulded by hand and are made of a high explosive such as cyclonite mixed with an oil binder.

extinction when a plant or animal species dies out completely this is called extinction and it has occurred many times to thousands of plant and animal species in the course of the Earth's history. There have been times of mass extinctions, e.g. at the end of the Palaeozoic geological era (*see* **GG**: GEOLOGICAL TIMESCALE) about 248 million years ago when it is thought around 90% of species ceased to exist. A further similar event took place some 65 million years ago in the early Tertiary period, when the dinosaurs became extinct. Until the appearance of modern man, which was very recent in terms of geological time (about 100,000 years ago) extinctions could be described as 'natural' occurring due to the processes of evolution. Mass extinctions were probably brought about by climatic (especially temperature) changes, volcanic activity and possibly collision of asteroids with the Earth. Man's impact upon the Earth has been enormous as whole environments have been changed by tree felling, development of modern agriculture and industry and by pollution. Sadly, the extinction of many species which used to inhabit the Earth has been brought about by the destructive activities of human beings.

extrusion is a manufacturing process used in the production of shaped metal but particularly plastic goods. It is the most economical of plastic shaping methods and the products are simple in shape and have features in just two dimensions so that they can be extruded in the third, continuous, dimension. Pipes and gutters, strips, tubes, fibres can all be produced in this way. The essence of the process is a large screw which receives grains or pellets of plastic which have been heated and compressed and the melt is then forced out through a die which gives the section its shape. PVC foam can also be produced by extrusion.

In the extrusion of metal a block is forced by a ram out through a die. Some metals are extruded while cold but most are heated to increase the malleability (*see* DUCTILITY and MALLEABILITY).

eye *see* SIGHT.

fats are a group of naturally-existing compounds known as *lipids*. They are composed of combinations of one molecule of a substance called glycerol and three of fatty acids. They are found widely in plants and animals and are very important as long term energy stores having twice the number of calories as carbohydrates. In mammals there is a layer of fat deposited beneath the skin which provides insulation, preventing heat loss from the body. This is an absolutely vital provision for many animals, enabling some to inhabit the coldest regions of the Earth, e.g. seals, polar bears and penguins. These fat reserves enable some animals, e.g. bears and hedgehogs, to hibernate through the cold winter months and when they emerge in the spring they must immediately replenish their fat stores. The layer of fat beneath the skin helps to cushion the body against injury and at deeper levels it is stored as fatty (adipose) tissue.

fermentation is a process carried out by certain micro-organisms, e.g. yeast, bacteria and moulds which break down organic substances (those containing carbon, hydrogen and oxygen) into simpler molecules, producing energy. Alcoholic fermentation is a process which has been harnessed by man for centuries, and in this yeast converts sugar to alcohol and carbon dioxide, and it is used to produce such drinks as wine, beer and cider. Fermentation is one of the processes now used in biotechnology and is important in the manufacture of cheese, yoghurt and bread. Also, and most importantly, it is used in the production of drugs such as antibiotics and in genetic engineering.

fertilization is the fusion or joining together of the male (sperm) and female (egg or ovum) sex cells which is the essential part of sexual reproduction. Fertilization describes the process in which the two cells come together to become one and it sets in motion a chain of events, (involving further cell division and growth) which eventually gives rise to a new individual. It is a common event in both plants and animals and enables genetic 'mixing' to occur as the new organism receives its characteristics from each parent. In many animals, e.g. most fish, fertilization is described as *external* as the eggs are laid outside the body and sperm are shed over them. In many other animals, e.g. mammals, fertilization is *internal* as the male sex cells are released inside the body of the female.

fertilizers are chemicals added to the soil to improve crops and their yield and the growth of plants and flowers. Fertilizers replace the nutrients in the soil that are extracted by growing plants. Modern farming is very intensive and natural processes are unable to provide all the necessary nutrients required. In addition to carbon, hydrogen, oxygen there are other *essential elements* such as nitrogen, phosphorus, potassium, calcium, magnesium and sulphur; plants require *trace elements* (perhaps in parts per million quantities) such as iron, boron, manganese, zinc, copper, molybdenum and chlorine. Artificial fertilizers make up a lot of the deficits in these elements.

Ammonium sulphate is an important nitrogenous fertilizer (i.e. nitrogen supplying) and other chemicals used include sodium nitrate, urea and ammonia. *Superphosphates* contain phosphorus, the chemical used being calcium hydrogen phosphate, $Ca(H_2PO_4)_2$.

It is essential that fertilizers are used correctly and that they are not overused as the excess nutrients can have detrimental effects on the land, and particularly on streams and rivers. As the nutrients drain into water they encourage the growth of algae and surface plants which choke the stream and results in a lack of oxygen in the water which eventually kills animal and plant life beneath the surface.

filters and filtration a filter is a device for separating solids or particles suspended in solution from the liquid, and filtration is the separation process. It may also involve removing particles from a gas. There are numerous materials which are used as filters; filter paper–a pure cellulose paper used in laboratories; cloth and paper filters are used in engines to clean oil and air; crushed charcoal and sand are used in industry and in the medical field dialysis machines use membranes as filters to cleanse the blood of patients with defective kidneys.

The *filtrate* is the clear liquid that results from filtration while the solid particles left are called the *residue*.

flash point is the lowest temperature at which certain liquids give off sufficient inflammable vapour to produce a brief flash when a small flame is applied. The term is used particularly for products such as petrol which vaporize very easily, because it is for all practical purposes the temperature at which petrol burns. It is important to be aware of this when petrol is used, transported or stored.

The same applies to industrial solvents such as toluene, benzene, ethanol, etc. which have flash points up to 13°C. Benzene has a melting point of about 5°C but will generate an explosive vapour while solid.

flight a few specialized groups of animals possess particular features which enable them to fly and these include insects such as beetles, flies, dragonflies and butterflies and birds and bats. In beetles, the forewings are hardened and form protective covers for the rear pair of flying wings which are moved in co-ordination and these are the most ancient group known to have possessed flight. Bees and wasps also have two pairs of flying wings which are hooked together and move as one. Similarly, in butterflies, the two pairs of wings are overlapped and move as a single pair and are covered with numerous minute scales. Insect wings are extensions of the outer covering (*cuticle*) of the middle part of the body (*thorax*) behind the head. They are membranes with veins running through them, and are moved by large flight muscles which bend the thorax out of shape. As they move up and down the angle of the wings in relation to the body alters which allows for lift on both the up and down strokes of the beat.

In birds and bats the wings are modified forelimbs or arms. In bats the membranous wings are a layer of skin spread between the long forelimbs and fingers and the body and hindlimbs. Birds possess several adaptations for flight including a lighter skeleton than other vertebrate animals, fewer organs to reduce weight and aerodynamic wings with modified flight feathers.

a bird wing

flotation and buoyancy buoyancy is the upward thrust felt by an object in a fluid and is equal to the weight of the fluid displaced (*see* ARCHIMEDES' PRINCIPLE). An object in water experiences this upthrust because although the object is under pressure on all sides from the liquid, the pressure is greatest where the water is deepest, i.e. underneath the object. Hence an object will float if the upthrust is more than its weight and the *law of flotation* states that a floating object will displace its own weight of the fluid in which it floats. Thus if a block is floated in water and then in a less dense fluid, it will float lower in the less dense fluid to displace a greater volume.

This principle applies to ships, and because salt water is denser than fresh water a ship floats lower in fresh water. Water temperature also affects density and therefore affects flotation. All ships have a line marked on their side (the *Plimsoll line*) which indicates the point beyond which the ship cannot be loaded. This is particularly important for a ship sailing from cold salt water to warm, less salty water.

flowers are the reproductive organs of a group of plants called *Angiospermae* (or *Anthophyta*) which are the flowering plants. They vary greatly in size from the very small and insignificant to the large and magnificent, showing an enormous range of colours and patterns of petals. Before the flower bud opens it is usually tightly folded and enclosed by green, leaf-like structures called *sepals*. These together make up an outer supporting structure for the flower called the *calyx*.When the flower bud opens the coloured petals expand and the sepals may wither and fall off. Petals may attract insects to the flower for pollination, but the actual reproductive parts are contained inside them. These are the *stamens* which are the male organs and the *carpels* which are female and contain egg cells or *ovules*. These structures are supported at the base by a portion of the flower called the *receptacle*. Following fertilization, the ovules eventually form seeds.

a flower

petal —— stamen

—— carpel

receptacle ——

food chain in simple terms, a food chain is the route by which energy is transferred through a number of organisms by one eating another from a lower level (called a *trophic* level). At the base of the chain are the primary producers which are the green plants. These are able to use energy from the sun to manufacture food substances from carbon dioxide and water. These food substances (glucose, cellulose and starch) are made use of by animals at the next level in the chain. The herbivores which eat the green plants are known as primary consumers. These in turn are eaten by carnivores (flesh-eating animals) which are called secondary consumers. There may be more than one level of secondary consumer (a flesh-eater may itself be eaten by a larger carnivore) ending up with animals at the end of the chain, e.g. lions, which are not preyed upon and are called the top predators. However, when these and all organisms die, they are eaten by scavenging animals and the remains eventually broken down by micro-organisms so none of the energy is lost but is used again. Food chains are often highly complicated and all of those that exist in a given environment are inter-linked and form a food web. A food chain should be perfectly balanced with many more organisms at the lower levels than at the higher ones. Sometimes the natural balances are upset and this may be due to human interference. For example, in Britain there are no large carnivores such as wolves because they were hunted and killed off during the Middle Ages. In Scotland red deer numbers are too high and (although the situation is complicated) these would, at one time, have been hunted by wolves.

fluids are substances that flow easily and readily alter their shape in response to outside forces. Liquids and gases are both fluids. Liquids have freely-moving particles which tend to be restricted to the one mass, but gases expand to fill their containing space and do not maintain the same volume. These properties of fluids are very useful in many ways, particularly in industry where machines utilize fluid or gas-filled chambers or cylinders to operate mechanisms, e.g. the braking system on a car.

Hydrostatic is the term applied to a machine using fluid pressure, and *pneumatic* is a system that uses compressed air, e.g. air-brakes, pneumatic drills and other tools.

food additives are chemicals added to foods by manufacturers to improve a particular property whether it is colour, shelf-life, taste or appearance. In addition to colourings and preservatives there are anti-oxidants to stop reaction of the food with oxygen, sweeteners, flavour enhancers (e.g. sodium glutamate), emulsifiers, pH adjusters and many more.

There is now a regulatory system in Europe whereby each additive that can be used in food is given a number and it is then listed on the packaging. Although the vast proportion of these compounds cause no problems, some do create side effects in some people. *Tartrazine* is a well-known example. It is a yellow colouring agent but can cause hyperactivity in children and also skin complaints and breathing problems. Other *E factors* may cause dizziness, vomiting or muscular weakness.

food preservation is the prevention of food spoilage through chemical decomposition and action of micro-organisms. It is generally achieved by the sterilization of the food which destroys any bacteria by heating in sealed containers (canning), or by pickling, drying, freezing, smoking, etc. Pickling, drying and salting are methods that were used over history and these kept foods through the use of agents (acid, i.e. vinegar, and smoke) in which bacteria would not survive, or by the removal of water (essential to the growth of bacteria) as in drying.

These established methods have been supplemented by more modern techniques such as canning and freezing and also *freeze-drying*. Freeze-drying is used for numerous foods, notably coffee (and has been used for some time in the medical, veterinary and pharmaceutical fields) and perishable foods. The process involves freezing, producing ice from the liquid content of the material and then *sublimation*, i.e. the ice is extracted as vapour at low pressure and temperature. Foods preserved in this way can be kept for very long periods.

Another recent innovation is that of *irradiation* in which food is subjected to ionizing radiations (radioactivity) to kill micro-organisms. The technique is still under scrutiny and not everyone is fully convinced that it is suitable.

force is the push or pull upon a body which may cause it to move, stop moving or alter direction of motion. Force is defined as the mass of a body multiplied by its acceleration. If the mass is in kilograms and the acceleration in metres per second (m/s^2) then the force is in *newtons*. An object will continue to move at a constant speed and in a straight line unless another force acts upon it. For example, a craft in space under the influence of no forces will maintain the same speed in the same direction and would need a force to change its direction. This is the basis of *Newton's first law of motion* which states that an object will continue in a state of rest or uniform motion in a straight line unless an external force acts upon it. This second law of motion relates to momentum and the third law can be given concisely as–to every action there is an equal, opposite reaction.

On Earth, we have to contend with friction and gravity but objects can move at a constant velocity or be at rest if forces acting on them are balanced. So an aeroplane can maintain a constant air speed because lift and weight are balanced, as are thrust and air resistance. However, should any of these constituent forces change then the velocity of the aeroplane would change.

formula (*plural* **formulae**) in mathematics or physics is a law or relationship denoted by symbols and figures and possibly expressed in algebraic (*see* ALGEBRA) form.

In chemistry it is a type of shorthand notation that enables a substance to be written in terms of elements and molecules using letters to represent the elements (*see* SYMBOLS). There are three types of chemical formula: an *empirical formula* shows the simplest ratio of atoms present in a compound, e.g. butane has the empirical formula C_2H_5, although it is really C_4H_{10}. The number and type of atoms present is shown in the *molecular formula,* in the case of butane, C_4H_{10}, which means there are four carbon and ten hydrogen atoms in every molecule. The *structural formula* indicates the structure of a molecule and shows the bonds between atoms.

fossils *see* **GG**: FOSSILS

freezing is the change in a material's state from liquid to solid brought about by reducing its temperature. The temperature at which this change occurs is called the *freezing point*. For pure substances the freezing point is the same as the *melting point*. The freezing point varies enormously between materials as the following table shows:

hydrogen	-259°C	water	0°C
oxygen	-218°C	sodium	98°C
nitrogen	-210°C	silicon	1410°C
argon	-189°C	carbon	3550°C
mercury	-39°C		

Impurities reduce the freezing point, e.g. salt reduces the freezing point of water and this property is exploited in car engines by adding *antifreeze* to the coolant to avoid freezing in winter.

frequency represented by the symbol f is the number of complete wavelengths (*see* WAVE) of a wave motion, per second. Frequency is measured in hertz (Hz) and is calculated from the formula; $c = f \lambda$, where c is the speed of the wave, and λ (lambda) is the wavelength. In the *electromagnetic* spectrum there is a large range of frequencies from low frequency radio waves to very high frequency gamma rays.

Sound waves are very different from light waves, and the human ear can hear sounds with frequencies between 20 Hz and 20, 000 Hz (or 20 KHz). A different frequency is heard as a different sound with high frequencies being sounds of high pitch. The scientific pitch of middle C on the piano has a frequency of 256 Hz and the Cs below and above are 128 Hz and 512 Hz, although when a piano is tuned these frequencies are changed slightly.

friction is the force that acts against motion, trying to stop materials and objects sliding across each other. A moving object will tend to slow down due to friction, and a force has to be exerted to keep it moving. The force required will differ depending upon the surface and the nature of the material moving across it. Friction is higher between solids (or a solid and liquid) than between solids and air.

The reason for friction is that rough surfaces have minute projections which restrict movement, and also there is a tendency for molecules to stick together under pressure. Friction in solids can be divided into *static friction* and *dynamic friction*. If an object is being pushed across a surface, the static friction is the maximum force, applied just before the object moves while the dynamic friction is that in action when the object is moving and it is much less than the static friction. There is also *fluid friction* when an object moves through a liquid or a gas. The effects of friction can be seen all around us the difficulty of pushing a heavy box across the floor; being able to walk and run because of the friction between our shoes and the ground; a car's tyres gripping the road and a train's wheels gripping the rails. In all these cases, friction causes the loss of energy as heat, something that applies to all machines.

fruit a fruit develops from the ovary of a flower and is given the name when it is mature and ripe. It contains the seeds and there are two main kinds, dry, e.g. an acorn and succulent or juicy, e.g. a tomato. The fruit is the means by which the seeds, which will become new plants, are protected until they are ready to be dispersed. Most juicy fruits are eaten by animals and the seeds pass through the digestive system without harm and are scattered in the droppings to grow elsewhere. Dry fruits often split open to release the seeds which may be shot out explosively, be carried away by wind or water, or cling to the fur of animals to drop off elsewhere. There are several different kinds of juicy fruit including a berry (e.g. blackberry) which is an *aggregate* fruit formed from one flower, but with lots of seeds) a pineapple which is a *multiple fruit* formed from a cluster of flowers and a cherry, a *simple fruit* also known as a drupe containing a stone surrounding the seed. Many of the food plants that we think of as vegetables are actually fruits, e.g. peas, beans and marrows. Pears and apples are known as *pomes* and they and some other kinds of fruit such as strawberries are also called *false fruits*. This is because the fruit does not just develop from the ovary of the flower but also from the receptacle (*see* FLOWERS).

fuel is a material that stores energy and upon combustion will release that energy. Fossil fuels (*see* **GG** FOSSIL FUELS) are the most widely used and account for most of the world's energy supply, with petroleum being the largest contributor. When these fuels are burnt (oil, gas, coal) energy is released and the other products are carbon dioxide, water and a variety of other gases and solids that depend upon the original composition or purity of the fuel. Nuclear fuels such as plutonium and uranium are unstable and release large amount of energy in nuclear reactions.

fuel cell is a cell that generates electricity directly by the conversion through electrochemical reactions, of fuels (gas or liquid) fed into the cell. The two components required are a fuel and an oxidant which are supplied to the electrodes and invariably a catalyst is used (*see* CATALYSIS). Fuels used include hydrogen (H_2), hydrazine (N_2H_4), ammonia (NH_3), and methanol (CH_3OH) and the oxidant is usually oxygen (O_2) or air. The electrolyte (*see* ELECTROLYSIS) in the cell can be a solution or solid, or special ion-exchange resins which, as the name suggests, contain ions that can be replaced by other ions.

Fuel cells have been used on spacecraft. In these, hydrogen and oxygen are combined to produce electricity and water is formed as a very useful byproduct. However, the efficient fuel cells have failed to gain a foothold for use in industry.

fungus (Kingdom Fungi) all fungi are simple organisms which may be one cell or exist as threads (or *filaments*) of many cells. They were once classified as simple plants but as they contain no chlorophyll and cannot photosynthesize, they are now placed in their own kingdom–fungi. Fungi absorb their food from other organic material and are vital in the breakdown and recycling of organic substances. They are essential in that they make minerals available to the roots of growing plants. Fungi are vital organisms for man, being used in the processes of biotechnology and fermentation. Some are harmful causing diseases in plants and animals, others are parasites and a few are edible, e.g. mushrooms. The scientific study of fungi is called *mycology*.

fuse is a very useful, protective device for electrical circuits. Most electrical appliances have their own fuse in the plug and in addition circuits, whether domestic or industrial, have fuses.

In all circuits there is the possibility of a fault developing and too much current flowing, which could damage the circuit or cause a fire. The fuse is placed in the circuit to avoid this possibility. The commonest form of fuse is a short piece of thin wire encased in a small glass tube with metal ends which overheats, melts and breaks if too high a current flows through it. It is placed in the live wire of the circuit so that if a fault develops, the current is switched off. The fuse value is greater than, but as close as possible to the current that usually goes through the appliance; 3 amp and 13 amp fuses are commonest.

More recently, *circuit breakers* have replaced fuses. These are switches which automatically break the circuit in the event of an overload and they can be reset when the fault has been eliminated.

galvanizing is a process whereby one metal is coated with a thin layer of another, more reactive metal. It is performed to offer protection to the coated metal and iron and steel are often treated in this way. Galvanizing is done in two ways, by dipping into molten zinc or by electrodeposition, i.e. electrolysis. When iron or steel is dipped into zinc, a little aluminium or magnesium is added to prevent a zinc iron alloy forming, because this is very brittle.

With electrodeposition, the object to be coated is connected to the cathode (*see* ELECTROLYSIS) and zinc ions from the electrolyte coat the object while current flows. The layer of zinc then protects the underlying metal because corrosion affects it before the iron or steel.

galvanometer is an instrument used to measure small currents and is often called a *milliammeter* if its scale is calibrated accordingly. It uses the physical property that a wire in a magnetic field experiences a force when a current passes through the wire. The current to be measured passes through a coil in a magnetic field and as a result the coil turns, and in turn it moves a pointer across the scale. Not surprisingly, this is called the *moving coil galvanometer*. The movement of the coil is resisted by springs and it comes to rest when the force generated by the coil in the magnetic field is balanced by the springs. The higher the current, the greater the force generated and the further the pointer moves across the scale. The sensitivity of the meter (i.e. giving more pointer movement for a particular current) can be increased in several ways and some galvanometers use a light indicator in place of the pointer. A beam of light is shone onto a mirror positioned on the coil and any movement deflects the beam along the scale.

Although galvanometers are used a lot and can be converted for use as an ammeter or voltmeter, many modern versions are digital instruments.

gas is the fluid state of matter (solid and liquid being the others). Gases are capable of continuing expansion in every direction because the molecules are held together only very loosely. A gas will therefore fill whatever contains it and because the molecules move around rapidly and at random, they bump into each other and the walls of the container which results in a PRESSURE being exerted on the walls. If a certain amount of gas in a container is put into another container half the size, the pressure doubles (if the temperature is constant). Also, heating a gas in a container increases the pressure. It can be seen therefore that the temperature, pressure and volume of a *fixed mass* of gas are all related and many years ago, early experimentation with gases resulted in three *gas laws*, which when combined can be stated as:

For a fixed mass of gas, $\dfrac{pv}{T}$ is constant

Where p is pressure, v is volume and T is temperature. The three laws individually are

$\dfrac{p}{T}$ = constant if v is unchanged   the Pressure law

$\dfrac{v}{T}$ = constant if p is unchanged   Charles' law

pv = constant if T is unchanged   Boyle's law

Only an *ideal gas* obeys these laws exactly and no gas can be considered ideal in this sense, although many approach this point at medium pressures and temperatures.

gas turbine is a type of internal combustion engine used in aircraft and ships, which is often called the *jet engine* because it involves the production of a jet of hot gas which provides the propulsion. The engine was invented by Frank Whittle, a British engineer, in the 1940s (*see* ENGINES).

The jet engine produces a forward force by thrusting out gas behind and it takes in large quantities of air for this purpose. The air also supplies the oxygen needed for combustion of the fuel. The air intake is therefore at the front of the engine, and behind is the compressor which consists of a number of blade-like fans. The compressor forces air under high pressure into the combustion chamber where the fuel (kerosene) burns to produce a hot gas which expands and is thrust out of the rear of the engine, creating a forward thrust on the engine. This gas passes through the turbine before being expelled providing the rotational force to turn the compressor.

Geiger counter (**Geiger tube** *or* **Geiger-Müller tube**) is an instrument that can detect and measure ionizing radiations, mainly alpha, beta and gamma rays. It was named after the German physicist Hans Geiger. It is made of a sealed and enclosed tube with a fine wire down the centre of the tube. The tube is filled with argon gas at low pressure and the wire is the anode and the tube forms the cathode. The end of the tube is covered by a mica window through which the radiations pass. When a particle with a charge (or gamma rays) enters the tube, the argon is ionized into electrons and positive *ions* which move to their respective and opposingly charged electrodes and for a moment the gas conducts and a small current flows in the circuit. This is registered by a *ratemeter* (or *scaler*) and can be converted to a series of clicks.

generator is a machine that produces an electric current from mechanical motion. It is based upon the principle of electromagnetic induction (*see also* ELECTROMAGNET). If a coil in a magnetic field is rotated, a current is generated (induced) as the coil cuts through the magnetic field. As the coil completes its rotation, it cuts the field in the opposite direction and an induced current flows in the opposite direction. This is the basis of an alternating current generator, or *alternator*. To enable the coil to continue turning, carbon brushes form the connection between the coil and the outside circuit by rubbing against slip rings fixed to the ends of the coil. To generate direct current from a generator, the device is fitted with a *commutator* and instead of having two slip rings the generator has one ring which is split (i.e. the split ring, or commutator) and the coil ends connect to each half. Then every time the coil passes the split the connections are reversed and current flows in a constant direction to the outside circuit.

Cars have alternators for charging the battery (after the supply has been turned into direct current) and enormous versions are used in power stations for generating mains electricity.

genes *see* CHROMOSOMES AND GENES.

genetics and genetic engineering genetics is the name given to the branch of science which deals with the study of *genes* and *chromosomes* and the way in which characteristics are passed on from parents to offspring (called heredity). It is one of the most important areas of modern scientific study especially in helping us to gain an understanding of how certain hereditary diseases and disorders are passed on. Also, it enables new strains of organisms with useful characteristics to be bred more easily. Genetic engineering is the term given to the modification by human beings of an organism's genetic make-up and this is done in two main ways. Firstly, DNA from one organism might be transferred to another where it would not normally occur. This has been carried out in the fight against various diseases and is a technique within *biotechnology*. An example is the gene that codes for the *hormone* insulin in human beings which has been inserted into the cells of certain bacteria. The bacteria have been harnessed to produce insulin which is then used to treat diabetes. Secondly, DNA from two different organisms has been combined to produce an entirely new species. It is this second area of research which has caused a great deal of concern and fears that harmful organisms might be produced. Hence it is subject to extremely strict regulation and controls so that all the organisms involved remain securely within the laboratory.

geometry is a branch of mathematics that deals with the properties of lines, curves and surfaces. It includes the study of planar (flat) figures such as the circle and triangle and also three-dimensional figures such as the sphere and cube. Geometry (meaning measurement of the Earth) was first used in the measurement of land areas and today it is the basis of much calculation undertaken by engineers, builders and architects.

Co-ordinate geometry is where points, lines and shapes are represented by algebraic (*see* ALGEBRA) expressions. In two dimensions the plane containing a point is represented by x and y axes at right angles to each other which meet at the origin, O. The position of a point can then be defined by two distances, one along the x and one along the y axis, which intersect at the point in question. Lines are represented by equations, whether straight or curved. The values given to the particular position of a point are its *Cartesian co-ordinates*.

A well-known *theorem* (a rule proven by reasoning) in geometry is *Pythagoras' theorem* which states that in a right-angled triangle, the (area of the) square on the hypotenuse (the longest side opposite the right angle) equals the sum (of the areas) of the squares on the other two sides.

gestation and birth is the period of time in a mammal between fertilization of the egg and birth of the young which, in human beings, is also called *pregnancy*. The gestation period is characteristic of the species concerned and varies from 18 days in the mouse to 9 months in human beings and 18 to 23 months in the Indian elephant. Usually, larger mammals have longer gestation periods and their offspring require care for a greater length of time before they can live independently. Following fertilization of the egg in a mammal such as man, cells divide rapidly to become an embryo which becomes attached, by means of a special organ called the *placenta*, to the wall of the *womb* (*uterus*). The placenta allows oxygen and food to pass to the baby through a connecting cord called the *umbilical cord.*

When the gestation period is completed and the baby is ready to be born, the process of birth takes place. This is triggered off by hormones which cause the womb to contract by means of the powerful muscles which are present in its wall. The baby is gradually forced through the birth canal (*vagina*) to the outside and afterwards the placenta is also shed. Most mammals eat through the umbilical cord (but it is cut after a human birth) and the portion which is left attached to the baby soon dries, shrivels and drops off leaving a mark called the *umbilicus* or navel.

human foetal development

Animals which give birth to live young as described above are called *viviparous*, whereas those which lay eggs that develop and hatch outside the mother's body (e.g. birds and some reptiles) are called *oviparous*. Some animals keep their eggs inside the body for protection. The young are nourished within the egg and not by the body of the mother and these animals (e.g. some fish, reptiles and insects) are called *ovoviviparous*.

gills *see* LUNGS.

gland *see* ENDOCRINE SYSTEM.

glass is the hard transparent material from which windows, bottles, jars and glasses, lenses and laboratory ware is made. There are several types of glass but the essential ingredient in all is silica (SiO_2).

Man-made glasses appeared about 4000 BC in Egypt and by 1500 BC it had developed into both an art and a technology. Glass science was then not developed until the work of numerous scientists including Faraday, then later Zeiss, Abbé and Schott. Over 30 elements had been used in experimental glasses by the turn of this century and now 70 have been tried but just three commercial systems account for nearly all glass production (*see* CERAMICS).

The raw materials are heated in a furnace forming a red-hot liquid. A blob of this molten glass on the end of a 'blow-pipe' can be blown into intricate and beautiful shapes by glass-blowers. However, most glassware is produced from moulds (for bottles, etc.) and sheet glass is made by floating molten glass on a bed of molten tin. Glass is used in many ways and its properties can be altered by the processing or by addition of other materials.

Toughened glass is manufactured by cooling glass rapidly under cold air; laminated glass has a plastic sandwiched by two layers of glass, increasing toughness and glass fibres in a resin form a useful *composite* (i.e. a mix or combination of materials) for making strong but light structures e.g. boat and car bodies. *Bullet-proof* glass is a very effective composite which consists of several sections with different properties.

glycerol (or glycerin) is a sweet-tasting, viscous (thick, syrupy) liquid with no colour or smell. It belongs to the alcohol group but has a structure similar to a sugar. Its formula is $HOCH_2CH(OH)CH_2OH$ and it is derived synthetically from propane (C_3H_6), or as a byproduct in the production of soap. It occurs naturally in plants and animals as a component of stored fats. It is an extremely useful compound and is used in the manufacture of ice cream, sweets and other foodstuffs, toilet preparations, resins and explosives. It also has the useful property that it can absorb up to 50% of its weight of water vapour which means it can be used as a moisturizing agent.

gold and the noble metals gold is a bright yellow metal and a good conductor of electricity and heat. It is soft and malleable (*see* DUCTILITY) and can be produced as very thin (even seethrough) leaf or drawn out into wire and it is very resistant to corrosion. Of course its primary use for thousands of years has been in the making of jewellery and coins, and today its value is fundamentally important to the financial stability of the world's currency markets.

Gold occurs as nuggets or veins or smaller particles in quartz or in streams after it has been weathered out of its original site. It is also found in the residue after copper has been purified by *electrolysis*. It is extracted from ore by dissolving the gold in potassium cyanide (KCN) solution (the cyanide process) or by the amalgamation process which involves treatment with mercury to form an amalgam which is processed further.

In addition to the applications mentioned above, gold is used in dentistry, photography, medicine, in electrical contacts (in microchips) and conductors. The purity or fineness of gold is measured in *carats*, which are parts of gold in 24 parts of the alloy. Thus pure gold is 24 carat. Jewellery is often made of 9 carat gold, in which the remaining 15 parts are copper.

Gold is also one of the *noble metals*, with silver, platinum etc. and all have similar properties.

graph is a drawing or picture that represents data and numerical values, or shows the mathematical relationship between two or more variables. Often this takes the form of plotting (positioning) points at a certain place, relative to two values measured along axes at right angles to each other (*see cartesian co-ordinates* in GEOMETRY). A *histogram* is a type of graph consisting of a number of blocks drawn with reference to two axes such that the area of each block is directly proportional to the value of the frequency. A *bar graph* looks similar to a histogram but the height of the block is then the relevant factor. A *pie chart* is another graphical method of representing data in which a circle is divided into different sized sectors where the angle of the sector is proportional to the size of the sample, expressed as a percentage.

gravity or gravitational force is the downward pull exerted by the material making up the Earth. A gravitational attraction exists between all objects and this will increase with their mass and with a lessening of the distance between them. Although this attraction is always present, in most instances it is so very small as to be unnoticeable and the attraction which dominates is that of the Earth, which affects objects on its surface (*see* WEIGHT). If gravity is thought of as a gravitational field exerting a force on a mass, the value of that field strength, g, can be calculated as almost 10 m/s^2 (metres per second, per second). This means that a falling object near the Earth's surface accelerates at 10 m/s^2; alternatively a mass of one kilogram near the Earth's surface has a force acting on it due to gravity, of 10 N (newtons).

Gravity on the Moon is much less than on Earth–about one sixth, hence although an astronaut's *mass* remains the same, his or her weight is much less.

growth the process by which living organisms increase in size and often in weight. It is brought about by cells dividing and often becoming more specialized to form the bulk of a particular tissue or *organ*. All organisms have a maximum size which is determined by their genetic make-up and the growth process is controlled by HORMONES. Once the individual has reached its full size there is no more growth but cell division occurs to repair and replace worn out or damaged tissues. Growth often occurs in spurts as can be seen in the development of a human child. A baby grows fastest during the first six months of life and there is a further growth spurt at the time of adolescence.

habitat *see* **NH**

hair a hair is any fine outgrowth from the surface of a plant or animal. Hairs are found on many living organisms and may be used for a variety of different purposes. The hair or fur of mammals is composed of dead cells in which a substance called *keratin* has been laid down. It is used for insulation to keep the animal warm and may occur in a variety of colours. The colour is determined by the presence and amount of a certain dye or *pigment* known as *melanin*. The base of each hair is embedded in the skin and has a tiny muscle attached to it. In cold conditions the hair is raised by these muscles to stand up straight and this traps a layer of air which has a warming effect. People notice this happening when they have "goose pimples" in response to the skin feeling cold.

epidermis   *hair*   *dermis*   *sweat gland*   *a human hair*

halogens are the elements fluorine, CHLORINE, BROMINE, iodine and astatine which form a group in the PERIODIC TABLE. They are the extreme form of the non-metals and show typical characteristics forming covalent diatomic molecules, i.e. form molecules of two atoms, e.g. Br_2. At room temperature fluorine and chlorine are gases, bromine is a volatile liquid and iodine a volatile solid. Astatine exists only as short-lived, radioactive isotopes. The reactivity increases from iodine to fluorine and the latter reacts with all elements save helium, neon and argon to form compounds. Halogens occur naturally in salt deposits and as IONS in sea water.

haploid *see* CELL DIVISION.

hard water is water that does not readily produce a lather with soap (*see* DETERGENTS AND SOAP) because of dissolved compounds (carbonates, sulphates and chlorides) of calcium, magnesium, sodium and iron. The use of soap results in the formation of a scum due to a chemical reaction between the metal IONS and fatty acids in the soap, producing salts. Water that does produce a good lather is called soft water.

Temporary hardness is one of two types and is due to water passing over carbonate-rich rocks such as chalk or limestone. This produces metal hydrogen carbonates which dissolve in the water and upon boiling these salts form insoluble carbonates which in a kettle results in kettle fur. This leaves the water soft. *Permanent hardness* is caused by metal sulphates (calcium or magnesium sulphates or chlorides) and cannot be removed by boiling. Special ion-exchange water softeners must be used in this case.

hearing the means by which animals are able to receive and decode sound waves which is usually closely related to balance, especially in vertebrates. Specialized small organs called RECEPTORS, which are often hair-like, vibrate in response to sound waves. This triggers off an electrical impulse in a sensory nerve (one which travels to the brain) which is in contact with the receptor (or receptors). The information is transmitted to the brain where it is decoded and interpreted as sound. In many invertebrates sound receptors may be relatively simple structures. However, in other animals such as mammals, complex and specialized organs, the ears, are used to detect sound.

the human ear   *semicircular canal*

pinna

cochlea

tympanic membrane

Fish have simpler ears than mammals and also a *lateral line system* which has sensory cells along the body, both of which are used for hearing. Amphibians (frogs and toads), reptiles and birds possess ears with a simpler structure than those found in mammals.

lateral line system

heart *see* CIRCULATION.

heat is ENERGY, and is measured in JOULES. It is stored in materials as vibrations of the molecules and the vibration increases with temperature. Heat travels by CONDUCTION, CONVECTION and by electromagnetic RADIATION and material states, i.e. whether something is liquid, solid or gas, depends upon the heat available. In a solid the molecules are attracted together and this overcomes the kinetic energy possessed by virtue of the molecules vibrating. If energy is put in and the molecules can be separated enough to become free, then the solid becomes a liquid. The work done in separating the molecules is called the *latent heat of fusion*. Similarly, the *latent heat of vaporization* is the heat required to turn a liquid into gas. When these changes are reversed, the material gives out heat.

The human body generates heat from food and the liver is a major heat-producing organ. Muscles also generate heat as a byproduct during activity.

heat exchanger is used to transfer heat from one fluid (i.e. a liquid or gas) to another without the fluids coming into contact. Heat exchangers are used a great deal to cool machines, e.g. the radiator in a car engine, or to conserve heat in an industrial (often chemical) process so that it can be used elsewhere in the process.

helium is one of the INERT GASES (or noble gases), so called because it has a stable electronic configuration and no chemical reactivity as such. It occurs naturally in very small quantities and being non-inflammable is used as an inert atmosphere for arc welding, for airships and balloons, in gas lasers and with oxygen as the atmosphere for deep sea divers. Helium liquefies below 4K (-269°C) and is used extensively in *cryogenics*–the study of materials at very low temperatures.

Helium has no colour, taste or smell and was named after *helios*, the greek for Sun. It is formed in stars such as the Sun as hydrogen nuclei are pressed together in the processes of nuclear fusion (*see* NUCLEAR FISSION AND FUSION).

herbivore any animal that feeds on plants, e.g. the familiar grazing mammals such as cows, sheep and horses.

heredity the passing on of characteristics from parents to offspring which is accomplished through the transfer of genes (*see* CHROMOSOMES AND GENES). Some of the basic laws of heredity were studied and worked out by an Austrian monk, Gregor Mendel (1822–1884) who carried out experiments with pea plants. He noticed that some characteristics were dominant over others, e.g. tallness is dominant to shortness in these plants. The study of genetics during this century has established that there are *dominant* and *recessive* genes for many characteristics and this is particularly important in some inherited diseases. A dominant gene is one which will always be seen in the offspring. A recessive gene will only be seen if it is present as a 'double dose', i.e. one from each parent. *See* also DNA, GENETICS.

Mendel's experiment with pea plants

tall plant

small plant

tall plant

hertz *see* FREQUENCY.

holography is a method of recording and then projecting a three-dimensional image using light from a LASER but without the need of a camera. A single laser beam is split into two by a special mirror, with half the beam continuing straight through the mirror onto photographic film. The other part of the beam is reflected by the mirror onto the object in question and then onto the film. The two beams produce an interference pattern, or *hologram* on the film which when illuminated with laser light recreates a three-dimensional image of the object. A screen is not required and the light forms an image in mid-air.

There are now holograms that do not need laser light to produce an image, for example, some credit cards have holograms that work with reflected daylight.

homing *see* **NH**

hominid *see* **NH**

hormone an organic substance produced in minute amounts by special cells within plants and animals, which acts as a 'chemical messenger' causing a powerful response somewhere else in the body. In mammals hormones are produced and released (secreted) by special small organs called glands (the *endocrine* glands), and travel in the bloodstream. The site at which they produce a response is called the 'target,' (*see* ENDOCRINE SYSTEM).

horsepower is a measure of power which originates from the time when steam engines began to replace horses. The name was coined by James Watt the British engineer and one horsepower is equivalent to about _ kW, or more accurately, 746 W. It has become the standard practice to measure engine power in *brake horsepower*. This is horsepower measured by means of the resistance offered by a brake and shows the useful horsepower that can be produced by an engine. A typical car develops around 90–100 brake horsepower (bhp) while an articulated lorry develops 400 or 500 bhp.

horticulture this refers to the cultivation of all kinds of garden and greenhouse plants including flowers, vegetables and fruit. Horticulture is concerned with the breeding of new varieties of plants by propagation and seed production. Many of our food plants, especially fruit and vegetables, result from the techniques of horticulture.

hybrid *see* **breeding**

hydraulics is the study of fluid flow, and the practical application of the dynamics of liquids in science and engineering. Hydraulics is thus a very important subject as it is relevant to the design of harbours, canals, dams or the study of the flow of water in pipes. *Hydraulic machinery* is operated, and the power transmitted using the pressure of a liquid. Such machines use the properties of liquids that they cannot, for all practical purposes, be squashed and when pressure is applied to a confined liquid, the pressure applies to all parts of the liquid. The transference of a force through the liquid is arranged in such a way as to produce a greater force in the machine, e.g. in a hydraulic car jack.

Most car braking systems use this hydraulic principle. When the brake pedal is pushed, a piston in a cylinder forces brake fluid through narrow pipes which go to the wheels. At the wheels, the fluid pressure pushes pistons in cylinders which then move the brakes which are in the form of pads or shoes which move against the drum or disc attached to the wheel.

hydrocarbons are *organic* compounds (*see* CHEMISTRY) that contain only CARBON and HYDROGEN. There are many different hydrocarbon types and they form one of the most important groups of organic compounds. There is a fundamental division into two groups based on structure: *aliphatic* hydrocarbons comprise carbon atoms in open chains and in addition to the main groups such as alkanes (the paraffins), this term includes all compounds made by the replacement of atoms in a molecule. *Aromatic* hydrocarbons are characterized by a ring structure made up of six carbon atoms as found in BENZENE (C_6H_6). These are also called closed-chain or cyclic compounds.

Aliphatic hydrocarbon groups include the *alkanes*, with a general formula C_nH_{2n+2}, e.g. ethane C_2H_6. The first four compounds in the series are gases, then liquids and the higher members (above $C_{16}H_{34}$) are waxy solids. Alkanes are the main components of petroleum and in general they are quite resistant to chemical action. The *alkenes* have the formula C_nH_{2n} and resemble the alkanes, but are more reactive. They are used as fuels and in the manufacture of other substances, e.g. alcohols and glycerols. The *alkynes* (or acetylenes) have triple bonds between two carbons, and a general formula of C_nH_n. Acetylene is a well-known member of this series.

hydroelectricity is ELECTRICITY that is generated from water moving from a high to a low level. If a river or lake is dammed to form a large reservoir then the water is held back, high above the original river level, and the body of water has enormous *potential*

ENERGY. To turn this into electrical energy the vast concrete dam contains a tunnel down which water can be directed and at the foot of the tunnel, before the water rejoins the river, the force of the flow is used to turn the blades of a large turbine linked to a generator, thus creating electricity.

Some power plants of this nature are called *pumped storage schemes* in which water flows through the day from a high level to a low level reservoir to generate electricity and at night when demand for electricity is low, water is pumped back up to the higher level ready for supply the next day.

Hydroelectric schemes are an alternative, or 'green' energy source because they do not cause pollution. However, they can change the local environment very considerably because they alter the balance of plant and animal life around the dam, and particularly when the valley is flooded to create the reservoir.

hydrogen and the hydrides hydrogen is the lightest element and forms molecules comprising two atoms, H_2. It occurs free and is widely distributed in water (H_2O), organic matter (HYDROCARBONS and CARBOHYDRATES) and minerals. The ordinary hydrogen atom has a nucleus of one proton, with one electron. There are other ISOTOPES and in addition to *protium*, there is *deuterium* which contains one neutron and tritium, containing two neutrons.

Hydrogen is manufactured by the ELECTROLYSIS of water and is produced in the treatment of petroleum with catalysts (*see* CATALYSIS). It is explosive over a wide range of mixtures with oxygen and because of this is no longer used in ballooning (where it has been replaced by HELIUM). It is used in numerous industrial processes including the production of methanol and ammonia and in metallurgy.

Hydrogen reacts with most elements to form **hydrides** of which there are several different types. Some are ionic and salt-like while most of the non-metals form covalent compounds (*see* BONDS), e.g. methane, CH_4. There are then many more complex compounds. Hydrides are often used as catalysts in hydrogenation reactions, i.e. the addition of hydrogen to a substance, frequently used in the refining of petroleum.

hydrometer is an instrument used for measuring the relative DENSITY of a liquid. It is a quick and convenient tool, although not as accurate as some other methods. The hydrometer consists of a tubular stem with a weighted bulbous base. It floats in the liquid to be measured and the density can be read from the graduated scale on the stem. The narrow stem ensures that small changes in density create readily visible changes in the reading. Hydrometers are used in checking the quality of beer and also in testing the level of charge in a car battery, because the relative density of the acid in a battery varies with the available charge.

hydroxides are compounds that contain the OH group which is present as the hydroxyl ion OH⁻. ALKALIS are the hydroxides of metals and are strongly basic. Hydroxides such as caustic soda (NaOH), potassium hydroxide (KOH) and ammonium hydroxide (NH₄OH) are commonly used in industry in the production of soap, detergents, bleaches, paper and many other items.

hypertonic and hypotonic a hypertonic solution is one which has a higher *osmotic* pressure (*see* OSMOSIS) than another, or a standard, with which it is being compared. Hypotonic is the opposite, i.e. it has a lower osmotic pressure than the solution to which it is compared. *Isotonic* solutions are those with the same concentration.

These concentration differences are important in cells (*see* OSMOREGULATION).

immune system the natural defence system which operates within a vertebrate animal to protect it from infections, caused mainly by such micro-organisms as BACTERIA and VIRUSES. The cells which operate the immune system are the white blood cells or *leucocytes* of which there are a number of different types. The immune system is provoked into action by the presence of 'foreign' PROTEIN substances which are called *antigens*. Many substances are antigens but they are commonly found on the surface of bacteria and viruses. When the white blood cells encounter antigens in the body, they produce special proteins called *antibodies* which trap the foreign material. The antibody and antigen are locked together like two pieces of a jigsaw puzzle and are eventually 'eaten up' by other cells of the immune system called *macrophages*. More antibodies are rapidly produced by the cells and will always recognize, and be ready to bind to, the antigens. In this way, the animal becomes *resistant* to a particular disease and this is the basis of vaccination.

Vaccination A preparation of a virus or bacteria which causes a particular disease is treated to kill it or make it harmless, but it still provokes the production of antibodies (an immune response) when it is injected into the bloodstream. These antibodies are then always available to attack any live micro-organisms of that type which the animal might encounter in the future.

Particular antibodies are produced to each kind of antigen and the immune system operates in two ways. Firstly, there is the inborn or *natural immunity* present from birth which is not specialized and operates against almost any substance that threatens the body. Secondly, there is *acquired immunity* which is the situation described above and brought about by an encounter with a particular foreign substance.

indicators are substances used to detect the presence of other chemicals. Most often an indicator is used in the laboratory to show the pH of a liquid, i.e. its acidity or alkalinity. Indicators are used in *titrimetry* which is the fast reaction of two solutions to an end point determined by a visual indicator and the two solutions are commonly an acid and a base.

The simplest indicator is *litmus paper* which shows red in acid and blue in alkali. *Universal indicator* is a mix which shows a gradual series of colour changes over a range of pH. However, most such indicators operate over a narrower pH range, e.g. methyl orange is red below pH 3.1 and changes to orange and then yellow as the pH reaches 4.4 Other indicators in acid-base reactions include:

Indicator	Low pH colour	High pH colour	Range
thymol blue	red	yellow	1.2–2.8
methyl red	red	yellow	4.2–6.3
bromothymol blue	yellow	blue	6.0–7.6
phenol red	yellow	red	6.8–8.4
phenolphthalin	colourless	red	8.3–10.0
alizarin yellow	yellow	orange	10.1–12.0

Indicators tend to be complex organic molecules and, for example, phenolphthalin comprises three benzene rings arranged thus:

Another group, called *redox indicators*, show different colours depending upon whether they are oxidized or reduced (*see* OXIDA-

TION AND REDUCTION). The change occurs over a narrow range of electric potential within the system under study.

inductance is when a circuit carrying an electric current is characterized by the formation of a magnetic field. Similarly a current can be made to flow when the position of the magnetic field moves relative to the circuit (*see* ELECTROMAGNET, GENERATOR). The unit of inductance is the henry (H), named after the American physicist Joseph Henry who was a pioneer in this field. Due to inductance a change in the current within one circuit can cause a current to flow in a nearby circuit. This is because if current flows through a circuit containing a coil, a magnetic field is created and an adjacent coil, in a separate circuit but within the magnetic field, experiences an *induced current*.

inert gases are the gases in group 0 of the PERIODIC TABLE, known also as the *noble gases*. These are helium, neon, argon, krypton, xenon and radon and they make up approximately 1% of air, by volume, with argon the most abundant. As their name suggests, these elements are chemically unreactive, due to their stable electronic configuration. They can be extracted from liquid air by fractional DISTILLATION and helium occurs in natural gas deposits. Their stability makes them useful in many applications, e.g. helium and argon are used as inert atmospheres for welding, in light bulbs and fluorescent lamps. Helium in its liquid form is important in low temperature research.

inertia the property of a body that causes it to oppose any change in its velocity, even if the velocity is zero. An object at rest requires a FORCE to make it move, and a moving object requires a force to make it slow down or accelerate or change direction. Newton called this resistance to a change of velocity inertia. The greater the mass of a body, the higher is its inertia.

infection and toxin an infection is a disease or illness which is caused by the invasion of a micro-organism which, because it is able to do this, is called a PATHOGEN. In animals and man most pathogens are bacteria or viruses but in plants a wide range of fungi are pathogenic. A high standard of hygiene is the best means of preventing infections from occurring, and sometimes people who are sick with an infectious disease require special isolation, nursing and care.

There are a number of ways in which a pathogen can enter an animal's body. 1. It might be breathed in; 2, it may enter the bloodstream through a cut or wound; 3, it might be carried by a blood-sucking insect such as a mosquito which passes the pathogen on when it bites or stings; 4, it may be present on food (called contaminated) which is then eaten; 5, in drinking water, particularly that which is contaminated by sewage and 6, through sexual intercourse–a sexually transmitted disease.

Often the illness is caused not by the micro-organism itself but by a poison, known as a *toxin*, which it produces and this is especially true of bacteria.

infinity is the term used to describe a number or quantity which has a value that is too large to be measured. For example, outer space is regarded as infinite since it has no limits. By convention, infinity (designated by the symbol ∞) is the result of dividing any number by zero. If a value is so small as to be incalculable, it can be written as negative infinity (-∞) and it is called infinitesimal.

infrared and **ultraviolet** *see* ELECTROMAGNETIC WAVES.

injection moulding is an industrial process, similar to EXTRUSION, used for the production of plastic mouldings. Granular or powdered plastic is fed into a hopper which feeds into a screw mechanism. The heat generated by the screw and outside heaters produces a plastic melt by the time it reaches the end of the screw. The melt is then injected or forced through a nozzle into a cool mould and pressure is maintained while the entrance to the mould is blocked by solidified melt. The moulding is then released and the process is repeated. Most injection moulding machines run automatically and large quantities can be produced at low cost. There is a large range of products which can be manufactured in this way including small boats, buckets and bowls, crates, telephone hand-sets and small gears.

instinct *see* BEHAVIOUR.

insulation is the means of preventing the passage of heat or heat loss by conduction, convection or radiation (it also applies when an electric current is prevented from passing). There are many ways of providing thermal insulation, the commonest example being the insulating materials used in houses to reduce heat loss. Cavity walls can be filled with foam, roof spaces lined with fibreglass or polystyrene beads and windows can be double glazed.

A vacuum prevents conduction and convection and this property is utilized in a vacuum flask to retain heat in hot drinks. There are several examples of natural insulation, notably the fur and feathers of mammals and birds respectively.

insulator *see* CONDUCTOR.

intelligence the ability of animals to learn and understand and so to be able to live effectively in their surroundings. Human beings are considered to be the most intelligent of animals and this ability depends upon GENETIC make-up and environment. The potential for developing a person's intelligence is considered to be at its greatest during childhood, especially in the early years. Also, it is thought to be important to use intellectual abilities throughout life in order to exercise our intelligence to its full power.

invertebrate animals are those 'without a backbone' or rather which lack an internal skeleton. They make up 95% of animal species and show many different kinds of specializations which allow them to adopt all sorts of lifestyles and habitats.

ion is an atom or molecule that is charged due to the loss or gain of an electron or electrons. A *cation* is positively charged and an *anion* negatively charged. *Ionization* is the process that results in ions and it can occur in a number of ways including a molecule breaking down into ions in solution, or the production of ions due to the bombardment of atoms by radiation. During electrolysis, ions are attracted to the electrode with an opposite charge.

iron is a metallic element in group 8 of the PERIODIC TABLE, which in its pure form is silver-white. It is a common component of minerals in clays, granites and sandstones and is a dominant element in meteorites. It occurs naturally as several minerals: magnetite (Fe_3O_4), haematite (Fe_2O_3), limonite ($FeO(OH)_nH_2O$), siderite ($FeCO_3$) and pyrite (FeS_2). In combination with copper it occurs as chalcopyrite, $CuFeS_2$. Pure iron melts at 1535°C and is extracted from its ores by the BLAST FURNACE process.

Iron is a widely used metal, in combination with other metals. Cast and wrought iron (*see* CAST IRON) are both used extensively but most iron goes into the production of STEEL.

Iron is also of biological significance because it is essential to the red blood cells. These cells contain the pigment *haemoglobin* which is made up of the iron-containing pigment haem and the protein globin. Haemoglobin is responsible for the transport of oxygen around the body, hence if there is insufficient iron in the diet anaemia may result.

irradiation is the exposure of an object to radiation which may be electromagnetic radiation such as X-rays or gamma rays. The radiation may also come from a radioactive source. Above a certain level radiation harms organisms and this principle is adopted when using irradiation as a technique for food preservation. Very specific irradiation is used in medicine when obtaining an X-ray or in the use of ionizing radiations to treat cancer.

isomers are chemical compounds with the same molecular formula, i.e. same composition and molecular weight, but which differ in their chemical structure. This property is called *isomerism*, of which there are two types. *Structural isomers* differ in the way that their atoms are joined together whether it be changes in the arrangement of carbon atoms in the chain or the position of a group or atom on the chain or ring. *Tautomerism* is a special case of structural isomerism which is termed dynamic. This is because a compound exists as a mixture of two isomers in equilibrium and removal of one isomer results in conversion of the other to restore the equilibrium. The other type of isomerism is *stereoisomerism* in which isomeric compounds have atoms bonded in the same way but arranged differently in space. One type of stereoisomerism is *optical isomerism* due to asymmetry of the molecules and in this case the isomers differ in the direction in which they rotate a plane of polarized light (*see* POLARIZATION OF LIGHT).

isotope is one of several atoms of the same element that have the same ATOMIC NUMBER (i.e. same number of protons) but differing numbers of neutrons in the nucleus (affecting their atomic mass). The chemical properties of isotopes are therefore the same, only physical properties affected by mass differ. Most elements exist naturally as a mixture of isotopes but can be separated upon their slightly different physical properties. For laboratory purposes MASS SPECTROMETRY is often used. *Radioisotopes* are isotopes which emit RADIOACTIVITY and decay at a particular rate, e.g. carbon -14.

Chemical symbols can be used to show the different configurations of isotopes, thus for hydrogen there are three isotopes:

	Protium	Deuterium	Tritium
	ordinary hydrogen		
protons	1	1	1
neutrons	0	1	2
electrons	1	1	1
symbol	$_1^1H$	$_1^2H$	$_1^3H$

When deuterium replaces hydrogen in a water molecule, the resulting compound is called *heavy water*.

joule (J) is the unit for measurements of ENERGY and WORK. It is equal to a force of one newton moving one metre (one newton is the force required to give a mass of one kilogram an acceleration of one metre per second, per second). The unit is named after the British physicist James Prescott Joule who investigated the link between mechanical, electrical and heat energy.

One thousand joules is called a kilojoule. Energy used to be measured in *calories*, one calorie being 4.1868 joules.

kidney *see* OSMOREGULATION.

kiln is a furnace or large oven that has many uses. The most obvious is its use for drying, baking and hardening clay objects such as plates, cups and similar domestic items, but also bricks and other building components. Kilns vary greatly in size depending upon their use and modern versions are heated by gas or electricity.

The minerals extraction industry also uses kilns for drying ore, driving off carbon dioxide from limestone or roasting sulphide ores to remove sulphur as sulphur dioxide, prior to further processing.

laboratory any room or building that is especially built or equipped for undertaking scientific experiments, research or chemicals manufacture. The study of physics, chemistry, biology, medicine, geology and other subjects usually involves some work in a laboratory and each is equipped with special instruments.

A chemical laboratory typically contains balances for weighing samples, bottles of chemicals including dangerous acids, a vast array of glassware (test tubes, flasks etc.) and bunsen burners. The *bunsen burner* is a gas burner consisting of a small vertical tube with an adjustable air inlet at the base to control the flame. The flame produced by burning the hydrocarbon gas/air mix has an inner cone where carbon monoxide is formed and an outer fringe where it is burnt. When the gas is burnt completely the flame temperature is very high, around 1450°C. The burner was invented by Robert Wilhelm Bunsen, a German scientist.

laminates are materials produced by bonding together under pressure two or more different materials. Plastics are commonly used in this way, bonded to chipboard or another building board, to make kitchen units and worktops and other items of furniture. Wood, such as *plywood*, is made of veneers bonded together which is in effect a laminate. Laminated plastics are composites made up of plastics and reinforcing or strengthening materials, e.g. carbon fibres, glass fibres. Glass sheet can also be made in laminated form with layers of glass joined by tough plastic and these are used for security glass, sound insulation, fire resistance, etc. The overriding feature of laminates is that the combination of materials albeit in thin sheets produces a composite material which is much stronger than the individual components alone.

larva and metamorphosis a larva is a young or immature form of an animal which looks and often behaves differently to the adult. There may be several larval stages and this is a common feature of invertebrate animals. Familiar larvae are those of butterflies and moths (caterpillars), those of flies (maggots) and those of many marine animals, huge numbers of which make up PLANKTON. Larvae can feed and lead an independent life but, (with one or two exceptions), are not able to reproduce. Usually an animal passes through several larval stages before undergoing a process known as *metamorphosis* to become an adult. In insects, the final larval stage is a *pupa* or *chrysalis* during which all activities such as feeding and walking cease. The body is enclosed within an outer case and, under the influence of HORMONES, it gradually changes to become an adult. Usually, there is a breakdown of some of the larval tissues which are then re-used, and some of the cells which were inactive in the larva divide to form the body of the adult. When the process is complete, the pupal case splits and the adult emerges.

larvae   *pupa*   *adult*

laser is an acronym for *L*ight *A*mplification by *S*timulated *E*mission of *R*adiation and is a device that produces an intense beam of light of one wavelength (*monochromatic*) in which the waves are all in step with each other (*coherent* light). In its simplest form a ruby crystal shaped like a cylinder is subjected to flashes of white light from an external source. The chromium atoms in the ruby become excited through absorbing photons of LIGHT and when struck by more photons, light energy is released. One end of the cylinder is mirrored to reflect light back into the crystal and the other end is partially reflecting, allowing the escape of the coherent light. The ruby laser produces pulses of laser light and is called a *pulse laser*.

Lasers have also been constructed using INERT GASES (helium and neon mixed; argon alone) and carbon dioxide. These are called *gas lasers*, and produce a continuous beam of laser light. Lasers are being used for an increasing number of tasks including printing, communications, compact disc players (*see* CD TECHNOLOGY), cutting metals, HOLOGRAPHY and for an ever-widening range of surgical techniques in medicine. Lasers are also used in shops at the checkout, to read BAR CODES.

learning *see* BEHAVIOUR.

lens is a device that makes a beam of rays passing through it either converge (meet at a point) or diverge. Optical lenses are made of a uniform transparent medium such as glass or a plastic and they refract the light (*see* REFRACTION). They are either convex (thickest in the middle) or concave (thickest at the edges) in shape and lenses can be made with combinations of these profiles or one side may be flat (plane). Light rays that pass through a convex lens are bent towards the *principal axis* (or optical axis– the line joining the centre of curvature of the two lens surfaces), and away from the axis with a concave lens. The *focus* is where the light rays are brought together at a point and the focal length is the distance of the focus from the centre of the lens.

A convex lens forms a small image of the object which is inverted (upside down) and on the opposite side of the lens. This is called a *real image* and can be seen on a screen. As an object in the distance is brought nearer to a convex lens the image moves away from the lens and becomes larger. The image formed by a concave lens is always upright, smaller than the object and it is a *virtual image*, that is it cannot be projected because although the rays of light appear to come to the observer from the image, they do not actually do so.

Lenses can be found in many optical instruments including the camera and the telescope and also in the human eye (*see* SIGHT).

lever a simple machine which at its simplest consists of a rigid beam which pivots at a point called the *fulcrum*. A load applied at one end can be balanced by an *effort* (a force) applied at the opposite end. There are three classes of lever depending upon the position of fulcrum, load and effort. The fulcrum may be between the effort and load (sometimes called a first-class lever); if the load is between the fulcrum and effort it is second class; and a third class lever has the effort between the fulcrum and load. Examples of these are pliers, a wheelbarrow and the shovel on a mechanical digger.

Although the work done by both effort and load must be equal, it is possible by moving a small effort through a large distance to move a very large load, albeit through a small distance.

light is ELECTROMAGNETIC WAVES of a particular wavelength which are visible to the human eye. Objects can only be seen if light reflected from them or given off by them reaches the eye. Light is given out by hot objects and the hotter the object the nearer to the blue end of the spectrum is the light emitted. The Sun is our primary source of light and the light travels at almost 3×10^5 (300, 000) km/s through space. The light waves are made up of packets or quanta (singular, quantum) of energy, called *photons*. Every photon can be considered to be a particle of light energy, the energy increasing as the wavelength shortens.

White light is actually made up of a range of colours. This can be shown by passing a very narrow beam of light through a prism. Because the individual colours have different wavelengths they are refracted by differing amounts and the resulting *dispersion* produces the characteristic *spectrum*.

A beam of light can often be seen particularly if a torch is shone on a misty night or in a dark room where there is smoke, or if sunlight highlights dust particles. In each case the edge of the beam indicates that light travels in straight lines and because of this a shadow forms when an object is placed between a light source and a flat surface.

light bulbs consist of a glass bulb within which is a filament of tungsten. When a current is passed, the tungsten glows white hot, giving out light. Tungsten is used because it has a very high melting point (3410°C) and because the thin wire of the filament would burn up quickly in air, the bulb contains argon and/or nitrogen to provide an inert atmosphere. Only a small proportion of the energy of a light bulb is given out in the form of visible light. Fluorescent lights are often used because to achieve the same illumination, they use only a third of the power. Fluorescent lamps, or strips, contain a vapour, e.g. mercury, under low pressure. Electrons from an electrode bombard the mercury atoms making electrons move into a higher orbit around the mercury nuclei. When the electrons move back into their normal orbit, ultraviolet light is given off which causes a coating on the tube to glow. Neon and other INERT GASES are used for this purpose, as is sodium.

lightning conductor was invented by the American Benjamin Franklin. It is made of a metal rod (often copper) attached to the top of a building and which is then connected by cable to a metal plate buried in the ground. If and when lightning strikes, the lightning conductor provides a suitable path for electrons to move to the ground, without causing damage to the building. The ground, or as it is known, the *earth*, has an unlimited capacity to accept electrons. A lightning conductor may also help reduce the possibility of lightning striking. This is because there is a flow of IONS from the point of the conductor which lowers the charge induced on the roof by the thundercloud. The result is that some of the charge on the cloud is cancelled out, lowering the risk of a strike.

linear equation is an equation in which the variables in the equation are not raised to any power (squared, etc.) but may have a coefficient. Thus $y = mx + c$ is a linear equation and the slope of the line plotted has a gradient m and c is the value where the line crosses the y-axis. This is known as the *intercept*. Sets of linear equations are used in engineering to describe the behaviour of structures.

linear motor otherwise known as a *linear induction motor*, relies essentially upon the principle of ELECTROMAGNETIC induction, that is when current flows through a coil, magnetic forces cause the coil to spin. In the linear motor, electromagnets are laid flat and when a current is passed, a metal bar skims across them, i.e. it becomes a method of propulsion. Linear motors are now used in trains that do not run on conventional rails, but 'float' over a guiding rail due to the magnetic fields generated.

liquid is a fluid state of matter that has no definite shape and will take on the shape of its container. A liquid has more kinetic energy than a solid but less than a gas, and although it flows freely the molecules stick together to form drops, unlike gases which continue to spread out whenever possible. Liquids can form solids or gases if cooled or heated but many substances such as oxygen, nitrogen and other gases will only form liquids if cooled a great deal or put under pressure.

liquid crystals are substances that are liquids which on heating become cloudy and in this state they show alignment of mol-

207

ecules in an ordered structure, as in a crystal. At higher temperatures still there is a transition to a clear liquid. The application of a current disrupts the molecules, causing realignment and optical effects, darkening the liquid and this property has been exploited for use in displays. *Liquid crystal displays* are used in calculators and watches and also in thin thermometers which work by laying a strip containing the liquid crystals on a child's forehead and the temperature is shown by the segments of crystal changing colour.

liver the liver is a large and very important organ present in the body of vertebrate animals, just below the ribs in the region called the ABDOMEN. It is composed of many groups of liver cells (called lobules) which are richly supplied with blood vessels. The liver plays a critical role in the regulation of many of the processes of METABOLISM. A vein called the hepatic portal vein carries the products of digestion to the liver. Here any extra glucose (sugar) which is not immediately needed is converted to a form in which it can be stored known as glycogen. This is then available as a source of energy for MUSCLES. PROTEINS are broken down in the liver and the excess building blocks, (amino acids), of which they are composed, are changed to ammonia and then to urea, a waste product which is excreted by the kidneys. Lipids, which are the products of the digestion of fat, are broken down in the liver and CHOLESTEROL, an essential part of cell membranes, some hormones and the nervous system, is produced. Bile, which is stored in the gall bladder and then passed to the intestine, is produced in the liver. In addition, poisonous substances (toxins) such as alcohol are broken down (detoxified) by liver cells. Important blood proteins are produced and also substances which are essential in blood clotting. Vitamin A is both produced and stored in the liver and it is a storage site for vitamins D, E and K. Iron is also stored and some hormones and damaged red blood cells are processed and removed.

logarithm abbreviated to log, is a mathematical function first introduced to render multiplication and division with large numbers more simple. However, the advent of calculators and computers has reduced the former dependency on logs. The basic definition is that if a number x is expressed as a *power* (i.e. the number of times a quantity is multiplied by itself) of another number, y, that is $x = y^n$, then n is the logarithm of x to the base y, written as $\log_y x$.

There are two types of log in use; *common* (or Briggs') and

Napierian or *natural.* Common logs have base 10, $\log_{10}x$. Addition of the logs of two numbers gives their *product,* while subtraction of two numbers' logs is the means of division. Natural logs are to the base e where e is a constant with the value 2.71828. The two logs can be related by the function:

$$\log_e x = 2.303 \log_{10}x$$

loudspeaker is a device for turning an electric current into sound and is found in radios, televisions, and many other pieces of equipment that output sound. The commonest design is the *moving-coil loudspeaker.* This consists of a cylindrical magnet with a central south pole surrounded by a circular north pole producing a strong radial magnetic field. There is also a coil sandwiched between the two poles of the magnet which is free to move forwards and backwards and a stiff paper cone that is fastened to the coil. Because the wire of the coil is positioned at right angles to the magnetic field, when current flows through the coil, it moves.

When an alternating current passes through the coil it moves forwards and backwards and the paper cone vibrates resulting in sound waves.

lubricants are a vital group of materials used in modern industry to make surfaces slide more easily over each other, by reducing FRICTION. Without *lubrication* surfaces grind against each other, producing wear and this can shorten the working life of a machine or engine. In the main, lubricants are liquid in form and are made from oil. However, there are other liquid lubricants (vegetable and mineral oils), some plastic lubricants (fatty acids, soaps) and also some solids, such as graphite and talc. Vehicle engines use oil as a lubricant and turbines for aircraft use synthetic fluids. The main synthetic lubricants are silicones, polyglycols, esters and halogenated (*see* HALOGENS) HYDROCARBONS.

Greases made from a liquid lubricant with a thickening agent are also used to combat wear where temperature and shearing forces apply. A petroleum oil forms the base, and a soap mixture the thickener, often with additives such as graphite, glycerine or fatty acids.

luminescence is when a body gives out light due to a cause other than a high temperature. It is due to a temporary change in the electronic structure of an atom, and involves an electron taking in energy and moving to a higher orbit in the atom which is then re-emitted as light when the electron falls back to its original orbit. The energy required to promote the electron to a higher orbit may come from light (*photoluminescence*) or from collisions of the atoms with fast particles (*fluorescence*). When materials continue to give out light after the primary energy source has been removed, this is called *phosphorescence*.

This phenomenon of luminescence is put to use in the CATHODE RAY TUBE of TELEVISIONS. It also occurs in nature and is called BIOLUMINESCENCE.

lungs and gills lungs are the sac-like organs which are used for RESPIRATION in air-breathing vertebrate animals. In mammals a pair of lungs are situated within the rib cage in the region of the body behind the head known as the thorax. Each lung is made of a thin, moist membrane which is highly folded, and it is here that oxygen is taken in to the body and carbon dioxide is given up. The lungs do not have muscles of their own but are filled and emptied by the muscular movement of a sheet-like layer dividing the thorax from the abdomen, known as the DIAPHRAGM. The diaphragm flattens, which reduces the pressure in the thoracic cavity enabling the lungs to expand and fill with air (inhalation). When the diaphragm muscles relax it arches upwards forcing air out of the lungs (exhalation). This is accompanied (and the effect made greater) by outward and inward movement of the ribs which are controlled by other (intercostal) muscles. Gills, which are present in many invertebrate animals and also in fish, are organs which fulfil the same function as lungs.

the human lungs

In mammals such as man, air enters through the nose (and mouth) and passes into the windpipe or TRACHEA which itself branches into two smaller tubes called bronchi (*singular* bronchus). Each bronchus goes to one lung and further divides into smaller, finer tubes known as bronchioles. Each bronchiole is surrounded by a tiny sac called an alveolus (*plural* alveoli) formed from one minute fold of the lung membrane. On one side of the membrane there is air and on the other there are numerous tiny blood vessels called capillaries. Blood which contains little oxygen (deoxygenated) is brought via a branch of the pulmonary artery to each lung. The artery divides many times eventually forming capillaries surrounding the alveoli. In the same way, other capillaries unite and become larger eventually forming the pulmonary veins which take oxygenated blood back to the heart. The heart pumps it around the body. Carbon dioxide passes out from the capillaries across the alveoli into the lungs and oxygen passes into the blood in the opposite direction, this process being known as gaseous exchange. The numerous folds of the membrane forming the alveoli increase the surface area over which this is able to take place.

lymph system is a network of fine tubules occurring throughout the body of a vertebrate animal. In places the tubules are swollen to form lumps of tissue known as *lymph nodes* or glands.

the lymph system

heart

liver

kidneys

This network transports the lymph–a colourless, watery fluid which is mainly water but also contains white blood cells (called *leucocytes* and *lymphocytes*) PROTEIN and digested fats. The lymphocytes are an essential part of the body's IMMUNE SYSTEM and collect in the lymph glands and nodes. In the event of an infection these cells multiply rapidly and this often causes a swelling which can be felt through the skin. (An example of this is the adenoids and tonsils which often become enlarged in the case of an infection of the nose or throat.) Lymph, which contains waste matter from cells, drains into the tubules from all the tissues of the body. It is filtered when it reaches the lymph nodes, where bacteria and other foreign and waste material are destroyed. The lymph tubules finally drain into two major lymphatic vessels that empty into veins at the base of the neck. The circulation of lymph is by muscular action rather than by the beating of the heart and it is essential in the transport of digested fats as well as in the immune system.

In children, white blood cells are produced in the thymus gland but this shrinks as adulthood is reached. In adults, white blood cells are produced in the bone marrow, spleen and lymph nodes.

machine is basically a means of overcoming resistance at a point by applying a FORCE at another point. Although a machine does not reduce the amount of work to be done to achieve a task, it does allow the work to be done more conveniently.

There are six *simple machines* in the study of physics. These are the wheel and axle, wedge, LEVER, PULLEY, screw and the inclined plane. Each in its own way can be used for a particular task–the lever or pulley to raise a load, the wheel to transport a load and so on. More complex machines usually involve the input of energy either for modification or for driving a mechanism to achieve a task.

The *mechanical advantage* of a machine is the ratio of the load moved to the effort put in to achieve the movement. The *velocity ratio* is the distance moved by the effort divided by the distance moved by the load. An inclined plane, or *ramp*, doesn't appear very much like a machine but it is because it enables a load to be taken gradually to a height to which the load could not have been lifted vertically. In this case the velocity ratio is essentially the length of the ramp over the height of the ramp.

Mach number is the speed of a body expressed as a ratio with the speed of sound. It was named after an Austrian physicist Ernst Mach. If the Mach number is below 1 then the speed is *subsonic*; above 1 is *supersonic* and as an aircraft increases its speed to go over Mach 1 it is said to *break the sound barrier*. *Hypersonic* is when speeds are in excess of Mach 5. Most passenger airliners travel subsonically but Concorde flies at Mach 2. Certain military planes reach over Mach 3.

The noise associated with breaking the sound barrier is a *sonic boom*. A subsonic aircraft produces pressure waves in front of itself and these waves travel at the speed of sound. A supersonic aircraft overtakes the pressure waves creating a shock wave like a cone with the point of the cone at the nose of the aircraft. The shock wave creates a typical double bang which can be strong enough to damage buildings.

magnetism is the effective force which originates within the Earth and which behaves as if there were a powerful magnet at the centre of the Earth, producing a magnetic field. The magnetic field has its north and south poles pointing approximately to the geographic north and south poles and a compass needle or freely swinging magnet will align itself along the line of the magnetic field. With the correct instrument it can also be seen that the magnetic field dips into the Earth, increasing towards the poles.

A *bar magnet* has a north and south pole, so named because the pole at that end pointing to the north is called a north-seeking pole, and similarly with the south pole. When dipped in a material that can be magnetized, such as iron filings, the metal grains align themselves along the magnetic field between the poles of the magnet. Some materials can be magnetized in the presence of a magnet, e.g. iron and steel. Iron does not retain its magnetism, but steel does. These are called *temporary* and *permanent magnets*. A more effective way to produce a magnet is to slide a steel bar into a solenoid (coil) through which current is passed and magnetism is *induced* in the steel (*see* ELECTROMAGNET).

In addition to iron, cobalt and nickel can also be magnetized strongly and these materials are called ferro-magnetic. Non-metals and other metals such as copper, seem to be unaffected by magnetism, but very strong magnets do show some effect.

The origin of magnetism is actually unknown, although it is attributed to the flow of electric current. On the electronic scale within magnetic materials it is thought that electrons act as minute magnets (because electrons carry a charge) as they spin around their nuclei in atoms. In some elements, this electron spin is cancelled out but in others it is not and each atom or molecule acts as a magnet contributing to the overall magnetic nature of the material.

a bar magnet

magnetometer is an instrument for measuring the strength of a magnetic field. The *deflection magnetometer* consists of a long magnetic pointer pivoted on a short magnet. The pointer swings along a scale, allowing small deflections of the magnet to be measured. Other versions have a small coil which generates a voltage on moving through a magnetic field. More complex and sensitive magnetometers are used for special purposes, for example, it is possible to tow a magnetometer behind an aircraft to detect changes in the Earth's magnetic field that may be due to mineral deposits, including oil.

magnification is the ratio of the size of the image to the object in an optical magnifying system. Magnification of an object can be achieved by simple means, e.g. a hand lens or *magnifying glass* which is merely a convex LENS. A far greater magnification can be achieved by using a *compound microscope* which consists essentially of two convex lenses with a short focus, called the objective and the eyepiece. The two lenses are at opposite ends of a tube beneath which is a stage upon which the sample (object) is placed. Magnifications of several hundred can be obtained with this microscope. For greater magnification still (above 1500) an electron microscope is used.

The *electron microscope* uses a beam of electrons striking the object. In the *transmission electron microscope* (*tem*) the electron beam passes through a thin slice of the sample and the resulting image is formed by the scattering of the beam which is enlarged and focused on a fluorescent screen. The *scanning electron microscope* (*sem*) actually scans the surface of the sample and the image is created by secondary electrons which are emitted from the sample. Scanning does not magnify the object as much as transmission electron microscopy, but the image is three-dimensional. Magnifications up to 200, 000 can be achieved with *tem*.

Microscopes are used throughout science and engineering often with modifications to fulfil a particular role. They are used for studying samples of plant and animal tissue, rock samples to determine the minerals and structures present, metals and non-metals to determine structure and much more.

malleability *see* DUCTILITY.

mammals *see* NH

maser stands for *M*icrowave *A*mplification by *S*timulated *E*mission of *R*adiation and is a microwave amplifier/oscillator that works in a similar way to the LASER and after it was discovered prompted the research which resulted in the laser. An atom already in an excited state, due to absorption of energy, gives out a photon due to absorption of further energy. The 'active' material of the maser is therefore built up to an excited state and enclosed to generate a wave of just one frequency. The microwaves produced can also be used in a clock, because of their very precise frequency.

mass *see* WEIGHT.

mass number is the total number of *protons* and *neutrons* in the nucleus of an ATOM. Atoms of a particular element may have differing mass numbers because of different numbers of neutrons in the nucleus, i.e. they are ISOTOPES.

mass spectrometry is a technique to analyse samples to determine the elements in a compound or the various isotopes in an element. The *mass spectrometer* bombards the sample with high energy electrons, producing charged IONS, and fragments which are neutral. The ions are then deflected in a magnetic field that separates them according to their mass, and then pass through a slit to a collector. The output is a printed chart (a *mass spectrum*) containing a series of lines or peaks where each peak corresponds to a particular ion and its mass. If isotopes are being identified, the mass spectrometer provides the mass and relative amount of each isotope.

Mass spectrometry is used for the identification and structural analysis of organic compounds and the determination of elemental traces in inorganic materials.

mathematical symbols in addition to the well-known symbols of arithmetic, such as = (equals), – (minus), + (plus), x (multiplied by) and ÷ or / (divided by), there are many other useful symbols which permit the shorthand writing of scientific formulae, equations and statements. These are used in mathematics, physics, chemistry, astronomy, geology and others scientific and engineering disciplines. A sample is shown below:

± plus or minus	Σ the sum of
> greater than	α proportional to
< less than	≈ similar or equal to
≥ greater than or equal to	≡ equivalent to
≤ less than or equal to	∴ therefore
= equal by definition	∵ because

mathematics is the science of relationships that involve numbers and shapes and has been around for thousands of years since the ancient Egyptians used geometry in construction. It is divided into two main categories–*pure* and *applied mathematics*. Pure mathematics includes algebra, arithmetic, geometry, trigonometry and calculus (*see individual entries*). Applied mathematics verges onto other subject or parts of subjects and includes statistics, mechanics, computing and mathematical aspects of topics such as thermodynamics, astronomy and optics.

matrix (*plural* **matrices**) is an array of elements, that is, numbers or algebraic symbols, set out in rows and columns. It may be a square or a rectangle of elements. Matrices are very useful for condensing information and are used in many ways, for example in solving simultaneous LINEAR EQUATIONS (simultaneous equations are two or more equations with two or more unknowns which may have a unique solution). The order of a matrix refers to the number of rows and columns, thus;

$$A = \{2\ 1\ 3\}$$ has one row and three columns while
$$B = \begin{Bmatrix} 2 & 6 \\ 1 & 4 \end{Bmatrix}$$ has two rows and two columns

Matrices with one row are called *row vectors* and similarly *column vectors* have just one column.

Only matrices of the same order can be added or subtracted and to be multiplied the second matrix must have the same number of columns as the first has rows. The multiplication is carried out by combining the rows and columns of each matrix to form a new matrix where the various elements are the products of the rows of the first and the columns of the second matrices. Thus if

$$A = \begin{Bmatrix} a & b \\ c & d \end{Bmatrix} \quad \text{and} \quad B = \begin{Bmatrix} w & x \\ y & z \end{Bmatrix}$$

then
$$AB = \begin{Bmatrix} aw + by & ax + bz \\ cw + dy & cx + dz \end{Bmatrix}$$

matter is any substance that occupies space and has mass and is the material of which the universe is made. Matter exists normally in three states: gas, liquid and solid. Most substances can be made to exist in all three states at different temperatures, thus by cooling a gas it eventually becomes liquid and then a solid. *Plasma* is considered a fourth state and consists of a high temperature gas of charged particles (electrons and ions). Although it contains charged particles, a plasma is neutral overall but it can support an electric current. Stars are made of plasma, but it finds applications in the study of controlled nuclear fusion (*see* NUCLEAR FISSION AND FUSION).

mechanics is the part of physics that deals with the way matter behaves under the influence of forces. It involves:

dynamics the study of objects that are subjected to forces which result in changes of motion.

statics the study of objects subjected to forces but where no motion is produced.

kinematics the study of motion without reference to mass or force but which deals with velocity and acceleration of parts of a moving system.

Newton's law of motion (*see* FORCE) forms the basics of mechanics save at the atomic level, when behaviour is explained by QUANTUM MECHANICS.

meiosis and mitosis *see* CELL DIVISION.

melting point *see* FREEZING.

membrane a membrane is a thin sheet of tissue widely found in living organisms. It covers, lines or joins cells, organelles (small organs), organs and tissues and consists of a double layer of lipids (fats) in which protein molecules are suspended. Water and fat soluble substances are able to pass across a membrane but sugars cannot. Other substances or ions are actively carried across a membrane by a complex system known as *active transport.*

memory a function of the brain in animals which enables information to be stored and brought back for use later. Several areas of the brain (such as the temporal lobes) are involved in memory and although, in man, this function has been widely studied it is not entirely understood. Placing information in the memory involves three stages-registration, storage and recall. The information is committed either to the *short term memory* or the *long term memory*. It tends to quickly fade from the short term memory if not needed but if used often, is transferred to the long term memory. Information is usually lost (forgetfulness) during the process of retrieval or recollection. Sometimes this can be helped if the circumstances in which the information was registered can be recreated. This is a technique which is used by the police when they are trying to gain information (which might have been only fleetingly seen) from witnesses at the scene of a crime.

metabolism is the name given to all the chemical and physical processes which occur in living organisms. These are of two kinds, *catabolic* (or breaking down) as in the digestion of food, and *anabolic* (or building up) as in the production of more complicated MOLECULES from simple ones. All these processes require energy and ENZYMES in order to take place. Plants trap energy from the sun during PHOTOSYNTHESIS and animals gain energy from the consumption of food. The metabolic rate is the speed at which food is used or broken down to produce energy, and this varies greatly between different species of animals. In people, children have a higher metabolic rate than adults and more energy is required by someone during hard work than by someone who is at rest.

metal fatigue is the structural failure of metals due to repeated application of stress, which results in a change to the crystalline nature of the metal. *Stress* is force per unit area and when it is applied to a material, a *strain* is developed, that is a distortion. Minor defects in the surface of a metal may provide points where stress can build up and a crack may form. This is particularly important in the design and construction of aircraft, bridges, machinery and buildings to ensure that there is not a sudden, catastrophic failure.

metallurgy is the scientific study of metals and their alloys. It includes the extraction of metals from their ores and their processing for use. *Extractive metallurgy* deals with production of the metals from their ores and *physical metallurgy* is the study of the structure of metals and their properties.

Metals are studied in the laboratory using a microscope to allow small flaws and cracks to be seen. Such studies are important in designing to avoid or minimize METAL FATIGUE.

metals are materials that are generally ductile, malleable (*see* DUCTILITY), dense with a metallic lustre (or sheen) and usually good conductors of heat and electricity. There are about 80 metals in all, some of which occur as the pure metal, but most are found as compounds in rocks and deposits. Pure metals are used for certain applications (e.g. GOLD in jewellery and copper in electrical goods) but it is usually the case that mixtures of metals (ALLOYS) provide the properties required for specific applications.

Metallic elements are generally electropositive, that is they give up electrons to produce a cation (e.g. Na^+) in reactions. When reacting with water, bases are produced. Elements that show some features of both metals and non-metals are called METALLOIDS or semimetals, e.g. arsenic, bismuth and antimony.

metamorphosis *see* LARVA.

methane is the first member of the alkane (*see* HYDROCARBONS) series, and has the formula CH_4. It is a colourless, odourless gas and the main component of coal gas and a byproduct of decaying vegetable matter. It is the primary component of natural gas and occurs in coal mines where mixed with air it forms highly explosive *firedamp*. It is highly flammable and is used in the manufacture of hydrogen, ammonia, carbon monoxide and other chemicals.

metric system is a system of measurement of weights and measures based upon the principle that levels of units are related by the factor 10, i.e. it is a decimal system that began with the metre. There are now seven basic units of measurement: metre, second, kilogram, ampere, kelvin, candela (light) and mole and each has a standard value and is defined very precisely. *See also* SI UNITS.

microbiology and micro-organism microbiology is the scientific study of all aspects of the life of micro-organisms or microbes. These organisms are so called because they can only be seen with a microscope. They include bacteria, viruses, yeasts and moulds, many of the (largely single-celled) organisms called protozoa (*see* PROTISTA) and some algae and fungi. Many of these organisms are highly significant for man because of their use in BIOTECHNOLOGY and GENETIC ENGINEERING and also because some cause diseases of various kinds. The study of microbiology has advanced significantly along with the technological development of microscopes, particularly the electron microscope and also with more advanced laboratory facilities.

microphone is a device for changing sound into electric current. It is essentially the reverse process to that which happens in a LOUDSPEAKER. In a moving coil microphone, sound waves cause vibration in a diaphragm made of paper or plastic and this moves a small coil which rests in the field of a cylindrical magnet. A small current is *induced* in the coil due to it moving through the magnetic field and this can be amplified and output through a loudspeaker. A variety of microphones are now in use: *carbon microphone* where the diaphragm changes the resistance in a carbon contact; *condenser microphone* and a crystal microphone which relies upon the PIEZOELECTRIC EFFECT in crystals.

microwaves are electromagnetic waves with wavelengths of a few centimetres or less. Microwaves are used for communications, e.g. via satellites, and intense beams are produced in a MASER. Microwaves are easily deflected and as they have a shorter wavelength than radiowaves, they are suitable for use in radar systems because they can detect small objects. Heat is produced when microwaves are absorbed and this effect is utilized in microwave ovens. A unit called the MAGNETRON generates the microwaves and these impart their energy to the water in the food, producing heat and the cooking effect.

mirror an object or surface that reflects light. Mirrors are made from glass coated with a thin metallic layer but polished metal surfaces have the same effect. When light strikes a mirrored surface, it is reflected in a particular way, according to the laws of REFLECTION. A plane mirror has a flat surface which bounces back light, creating an image 'behind' the mirror. Curved mirrors are convex or concave. Concave mirrors produce a magnifying effect if the object is sufficiently near to the mirror, but distant objects are smaller and inverted. Convex mirrors produce upright images that are smaller than the object. Concave mirrors are used in car headlights while convex mirrors are often used for driving mirrors because they produce a wide angle of view.

mitochondrion (*pl.* mitochondria) a type of rod-shaped organelle found in the cytoplasm (cell contents except for the nucleus) of EUCARYOTIC cells which is surrounded by a double membrane. Mitochondria have been called the 'power houses' of the cell as they are very important in the generation of energy in a form called ATP. ATP production is the end result of cellular respiration and provides energy for all metabolic processes. As mitochondria are the sites where this takes place, they are especially abundant in cells which require lots of energy such as those of muscles. Mitochondria contain a form of DNA, structures called ribosomes in which proteins are manufactured with numerous enzymes, each specific to a particular metabolic process.

molecule and mole a *molecule* is the smallest chemical unit of an element or compound that can exist independently. It consists of atoms bonded together in a particular combination, e.g. oxygen, O_2, is two oxygen atoms and carbon dioxide, CO_2, is on carbon and two oxygen atoms. Molecules may contain thousands of atoms. Gases, organic compounds, liquid and many solids consists of molecules but some materials, e.g. metals and ionic substances are different and comprise changed atoms or IONS.

The *mole* is the unit of substance that contains the same number of elementary particles as there are in 12 grams of carbon. One mole of a substance contains 6.023×10^{23} molecular atoms, or ions, or electrons.

momentum is the property of an object defined as the product of its velocity and mass and it is measured in kgm/s. Momentum is related to force as follows:

force = the rate of change of momentum.

Changes in momentum occur mainly due to the interaction between two bodies. During any interaction the total momentum of the bodies involved remains the same, providing no external force, such as FRICTION, is acting. Newton's second law of motion states that the rate of change of momentum of a body is directly proportional to the force acting and occurs in the direction in which the force ends.

If a body is rotating around an axis then it has *angular momentum* which is the product of its momentum and its perpendicular distance from the fixed axis.

Momentum can be seen around us all the time, but one of the most obvious examples is the collision of balls on the snooker table.

monera the biological kingdom in which all the organisms have PROCARYOTIC cells and are the bacteria and cyanobacteria (formerly called blue-green algae). *See* PROCARYOTE.

motors (electric) the basic principle behind most common electric motors is that when current is passed through a coil in a magnetic field, a turning effect is produced. In a d.c. (direct current) motor a coil rotates between the poles of a permanent magnet and is connected to a battery via carbon brushes which contact a split ring or *commutator*. The commutator reverses the current direction every half-turn of the coil ensuring that the coil continues to rotate (*see also* GENERATOR). Motors are used in many different devices and pieces of equipment, such as hair-dryers, mixers and food processors, drills and so on. Such motors operate from an a.c. (alternating current) supply and in this case an electromagnet is used because it can match the change in current and yet maintain a constant turning effect. In addition, the smooth and reliable running of these motors is ensured by: the incorporation of several coils at different angles each connected to a set of commutator pieces; several hundred turns of wire in each coil, on a soft iron core (as *armature*) which becomes magnetized, increasing the strength of the magnetic field; the poles of the magnet are shaped into a curve creating a magnetic field that is almost radial, giving a constant turning force (*see also* INDUCTANCE).

muscle a special type of tissue which is responsible for movements in the body of an animal and which often works by pulling against the hard SKELETON. Muscle cells are elongated and arranged as bundles (called fibres) and in mammals there are three types controlled by different parts of the nervous system. *Voluntary* or striated muscle operates limbs and joints and is under the conscious control of the will. Each muscle fibre consists of smaller elongated *fibrils* (myofibrils) and these either lengthen and become thinner, or shorten and become fatter, as they slide over one another, depending upon whether the muscle is contracting or relaxing. *Involuntary* or smooth muscle is not under conscious control but is regulated by a special part of the nervous system (called the *autonomic nervous system*). These muscles work automatically and are responsible for the contractions of the gut, and of the womb at the time of birth. This type of muscle also occurs at various other sites within the body. *Cardiac muscle* is the third specialized kind and is responsible for the beating of the heart which continues throughout life. This muscle is involuntary but the rate of beat is affected by activity of an important nerve called the vagus nerve. The *pacemaker* is a collection of specialized cardiac muscle cells situated in the wall of the right atrium (one of the upper chambers of the heart). These cells are under the control of the autonomic nervous system and produce the contractions which stimulate the rest of the heart to contract.

mutation any change which occurs in the DNA in the chromosomes of cells. Mutation is one way in which genetic variation occurs and allows natural selection to operate (*see* GENETICS). This is because any alteration in the sex cells may produce an inherited change (mutation) in the characteristics of later generations of the organism. Mutations occur naturally during the time when DNA is copying itself, as in cell division although they are relatively rare and most are harmful or lethal. They can occur much more frequently following exposure to certain chemicals and radiation (X-rays), and these agents are known as *mutagens*. A *mutant* is an organism which shows the effects of a mutation.

natural selection *see* DARWINISM.

mycology the name given to the scientific study of all aspects of the life of FUNGI.

nervous system a network of specialized cells and tissues which is present in all multicellular animals to a greater or lesser degree (with the exception of sponges). The activity of the nervous system consists of electrical impulses which are caused by the movement of chemical (sodium and potassium) IONS. The nervous system includes RECEPTORS, which receive information from the surrounding environment and are called *sensory*. These are concerned with the senses such as sight, sound, touch and pressure and they transmit the information which they detect along nerves (called sensory nerves) and these travel to the central nervous system. In the simpler animals such as invertebrates, this often consists of a paired nerve cord with swellings along its length called *ganglia* (*sing.* ganglion). In vertebrate animals, the central nervous system is highly complex and consists of the brain and spinal cord. Within the central nervous system all the information is decoded and, if appropriate, a response is initiated. This often consists of a signal being sent outwards along a nerve (called a motor nerve) which travels to a muscle causing a contraction to occur. In vertebrates, a part of the nervous system is concerned with the control of the involuntary or smooth MUSCLE of the body. This is called the autonomic nervous system and consists of two divisions, the *sympathetic* and *parasympathetic* which act in opposite ways (antagonistic). It is sometimes called *involuntary* because its activity regulates the internal environment of the body and it supplies the smooth muscle (heart, gut, etc.) and glands with their motor nerve supply.

A nerve is made up of numerous nerve cells or 'neurons'. some nerves are sensory, others are motor and yet others are mixed carrying both types of neurons. Each neuron has a cell body (containing the neucleus) and many fine projections called 'dendrites'. Dendrites from surrounding neurons are able to communicate with one another across a gap called a 'synapse'. A long, fine projection runs out from the neuron cell body and this is called an 'axon'. It may be surrounded by a fatty sheath (called a 'myelin sheath') which is restricted at intervals at sites which are known as 'nodes of Ranvier'.

nitrides are very similar compounds to CARBIDES and form hard materials with high melting points. Metals such as titanium, chromium, vanadium, zirconium and hafnium are used and these result in nitrides with high hardness, resistance to molten metals and a high corrosion resistance. As such they are used in crucibles for melting metal, protective coatings for moving surfaces and cutting tools.

nitrogen is a colourless gas existing as a diatomic molecule, N_2. It occurs in air (75% by weight), and as nitrates, ammonia and in PROTEINS. It is relatively unreactive at room temperature but reacts with some elements on heating. It is used extensively in the production of ammonia in liquid form as a refrigerant (its melting point is -210°C) and as an inert atmosphere. It is obtained industrially by the fractionation of liquid air.

Nitrogen is a vital element in the life cycle of both plants and animals and there is a regular circulation, called the *nitrogen cycle*. Bacteria take nitrogen from the atmosphere (*nitrogen fixation*) and plants use nitrate ions (NO_3^-) from the soil. The nitrogen is incorporated into plant tissue, which is then eaten by animals. The nitrogen is returned to the soil by the decomposition of dead plants and animals and by excretion.

noise is a random mixture of changing frequencies of sound as produced, for example, by an electric drill. It is also the term describing the background disturbance registered when a signal of some description is being measured. The effect occurs in electrical circuits and is due to interference arising from other sources, e.g. lightning, electric motors, random motion of electrons making up the current. This often happens with a radio receiver and electronic filtering is often undertaken to improve the signal and reduce the noise.

nose *see* SMELL.

nuclear energy is the energy produced by the controlled decay of radioactive elements. Upon decay, an element such as uranium releases energy as heat which can be harnessed. During radioactive decay the energy given off per atom is thousands and thousands times more than during burning. However, the decay often has to be accelerated by bombarding the material with neutrons.

NUCLEAR FISSION is the splitting of such atoms and is the way in which electricity is generated for nuclear power. In a *nuclear re-*

actor heat from the nuclear reactions heats water into steam which drives the turbines. The core of a reactor contains the nuclear fuel which may be uranium dioxide with uranium-235. Neutrons produced by the fission reactions are slowed down by a graphite core to ensure the *chain reaction* continues. The graphite core is called the *moderator*. *Control rods* of boron-steel are lowered into or taken out of the reactor to control the rate of fission. Boron absorbs neutrons and so if rods are lowered there are fewer neutrons available for the nuclear fission and the reactor core temperature will fall. This is a *thermal reactor*. In a *fast breeder reactor* low grade uranium surrounds the core and impact from neutrons creates some uranium-239 which forms plutonium, which itself can be used as a reactor fuel. *Nuclear fusion* (*see* NUCLEAR FISSION AND FUSION) has not yet been harnessed for commercial power production.

Nuclear energy has the benefit of producing a lot of energy from a small amount of fuel and it doesn't produce gases that contribute to the *greenhouse effect* (*see* NH: GREENHOUSE EFFECT). However, the waste produced is very dangerous and must be stored or treated very carefully. The waste products are from the reprocessing of used fuel in which unused uranium is separated from the waste and small quantities of plutonium-239 (as produced and used in fast breeder reactors). Plutonium-239 is very hazardous indeed and is used in the production of nuclear weapons.

nuclear fission and fusion nuclear fission is the splitting process which results when a neutron strikes a nucleus of, for example, uranium-235. The nucleus splits into two and releases more neutrons and a lot of energy. A *chain reaction* develops when the neutrons go on to split further nuclei and the energy released becomes enormous. The splitting of the uranium creates two other nuclei, both radioactive:

Uranium-235 + neutron → Krypton-90 + Barium-144 + neutrons + energy

This chain reaction occurs when there is a certain mass of uranium-235, known as the *critical mass*. This was the principle employed in the first *atom bomb*, when two pieces of uranium-235 were brought together to exceed the critical mass and produce a destructive force of unimaginable proportions.

Nuclear fusion is where two nuclei are combined to form a single nucleus with an accompanying release of energy. Ordinarily nuclei would repel each other due to the like electrical charge and so very high collision speeds have to be used, which in practice means the use of incredibly high temperatures. A fusion reaction may be:

Deuterium + Tritium → Helium + neutron + energy

$$_1^2H + _1^3H \rightarrow _2^4He + _0^1n$$

It is necessary to raise the temperature of the hydrogen gas to around 100 million K. Because thermal energy has to be supplied before the nuclear reactions occur, fusion is often called *thermonuclear fusion*. Fusion occurs in the Sun, and in an uncontrolled way in the *hydrogen bomb*, but it is technically very difficult to control in the way that nuclear fission is managed. Research into this subject involves the use of a *tokamak* which employs a magnetic field shaped like a doughnut to trap the hot gas. Thermonuclear reactors could be a solution to energy supply problems because the fuel is readily available and the waste product is not radioactive and it is also inert (unreactive).

nuclear reactor *see* NUCLEAR ENERGY.

numbers our numbers are based on Arabic numerals which in turn were based on a Hindu system, and the system is constructed upon powers of ten, i.e. the decimal system (*see* DECIMAL NUMBERS). BINARY NUMBERS use the base two and are used extensively in computer programs. *Real numbers* include all *rational numbers* (whole numbers, or integers, and fractions) and *irrational numbers*, that is those that cannot be expressed as an exact fraction , e.g. some square roots such as 2, 5 and values such as the constant π. *Complex numbers* are those written in the form $a + ib$ where a and b are real numbers and i is the square root of -1.

A *prime number* is a number that can be divided only by itself and 1, such as 2, 3, 5, 7, 11, 13, 17, 19, 23. There is an infinite number of prime numbers and over the years mathematicians have spent much time trying to find a general method for calculating primes. A *surd* is an expression that contains the root of an irrational number and which can never be expressed exactly (e.g. 3 = 1.7320508 ...).

oestrous cycle *see* REPRODUCTION.

oils are greasy liquid substances obtained from animal or vegetable matter or mineral sources, and they are complex organic compounds. There are also many synthetic oils. There are basically three groups of oils: the *fatty oils* from animal and vegetable sources; *mineral oils* from petroleum and coal; and *essential oils* derived from certain plants. Typical vegetable oils are extracted from soya beans, olives, nuts and maize. The essential oils are volatile (evaporate quickly) and are used in *aromatherapy* and in making perfumes and flavourings. Examples are peppermint oil, clove oil, oil of wintergreen and rose oil.

Mineral oils are actually fossil fuels and come under the general term of petroleum.

omnivore any animal which eats both plant and animal material, e.g. human being (*compare* carnivore and herbivore).

optical fibres are made of very thin glass rods which are flexible. When light rays enter one end of the fibre it is reflected completely within the fibres, being reflected from side to side until it emerges at the other end. Bundles of fibres are called *light pipes* and they have several very important uses. Surgeons use them to see inside the body of a patient, often without the need for an incision. Also the pipes can carry an enormous number of telephone calls, where the calls are coded and sent along the fibres as pulses of LASER light. Another remarkable feature of optical fibres is that the light exits almost as strong as it entered even if the path is several kilometres and this eliminates the need for numerous stations to boost the signal as required with ordinary telephone cables.

organ and tissue a tissue is a collection of cells within an ORGANISM, which are specialized to perform a particular function. An *organ* is a distinct and recognizable site or unit within the body of an organism which consists of two or more types of tissue. It is specialized in terms of its structure and function and, in animals, examples include the kidneys, liver, skin and eyes. In plants, flowers, stems, roots, leaves and flowers are all organs. An *organelle* is a structure within a cell which performs a particular function and is surrounded by a membrane to separate it from other cell contents, e.g. the nucleus and MITOCHONDRIA.

organism any living creature including micro-organisms, plants and animals. There are very many different kinds of organism with new species being discovered all the time. At the other end of the scale, over the course of the Earth's history, numerous types of organism have become extinct. *Biotic* is an adjective relating to life or living things (hence *biota*, the plant and animal life of a region). Thus for any organism, the other organisms around it make up the biotic environment.

osmoregulation this describes any process or mechanism in animals that regulates the concentration of salts (e.g. sodium chloride) and water in the body. Depending upon the environment it inhabits, there is a tendency for water to pass into or out of an animal's body by *osmosis*. Water tends to pass into the body of an animal which inhabits fresh water as the concentration of salts within its body is higher than that outside. Animals have a variety of structures to rid the body of excess water. In simple organisms (e.g. single-celled ones) an organelle called a *contractile vacuole* fills with water and expels it to the outside through a pore in the cell membrane. In marine animals there is a tendency to lose water from the body to the surrounding environment where the concentration of salts is higher. In vertebrate animals, whether the problem is one of water gain or loss, the kidneys are the main osmoregulatory organs. In land-dwelling animals, the outer covering of skin or cuticle forms a barrier to excess water gain or loss but many other mechanisms are also at work (including kidneys, sweating, panting, behavioural responses) so that a correct water/salt balance is maintained.

In humans, there is a pair of kidneys situated at the back of the abdomen and these are responsible for cleaning the blood and removing waste products which are then excreted. The kidney contains numerous tubules called *nephrons*, each with an expanded cup-shaped portion at one end called the Bowman's capsule. Behind this there is a folded length of tubule, known as the proximal convoluted tubule then a straight hairpin-shaped loop, the loop of Henle, and finally another looped portion called the distal convoluted tubule. Blood enters the Bowman's capsules from tiny capillaries which form a knot, called the glomerulus, inside the cup. This blood is brought to the kidney by the renal artery. Water and waste substances, such as urea, a breakdown product of protein digestion, pass along the length of the nephrons and this is known as filtrate. Useful substances, including water and salts are reabsorbed. Many capillaries surround the nephrons and cleaned or filtered blood eventually leaves the kidney in the renal vein. The distal convoluted tubules, containing the waste products which have not been re-absorbed, empty into a collecting duct and final processing takes place. The liquid which is left, known as *urine* enters the ureter which is a narrow tube leading to the *bladder*. From the bladder another tube called the urethra leads to the outside. The two kidneys daily receive between 1000 and 2000 litres of blood and process about

180 litres of filtrate. 1.5 litres of urine is produced and the rest of the filtrate is reabsorbed. If the kidneys fail, their function has to be carried out by a machine and this is known as dialysis.

a human kidney

nephrons

Bowman's capsule

osmosis is the process whereby molecules of solvent (usually water) move through a semi-permeable membrane to the more concentrated solution. This is due to the size of the molecules compared to the holes in the membrane. The holes permit the small water molecules through but not the larger solvent molecules so there is a tendency for the molecular concentrations to approach equality. *Osmotic pressure* is the pressure that must be applied to prevent osmotic flow.

Osmosis is an important mechanism in living organisms in the movement of water across cell membranes and particularly in the uptake of water by plant roots. Certain mechanisms have also evolved to prevent too much water entering cells causing rupture, or leaving cells, causing shrinkage.

oxidation and reduction are processes that occur during chemical reactions. *Oxidation* is the gain of oxygen or loss of electrons from the reactant. Oxidation can occur in the absence of oxygen as it can also be represented by the loss of hydrogen. Similarly, *reduction* is the loss of oxygen or gain of electrons from one of the reactants, and also the gain of hydrogen.

oxygen is a colourless, odourless gas vital for the respiration of most life forms. It is the most abundant of all the elements forming 21% by volume in air, almost 90% by weight of water and nearly 50% by weight of rocks in the crust. It is manufactured by the fractional DISTILLATION of liquid air and on heating reacts with most elements to form oxides. It is used extensively in industry for steel making, welding, rocket fuels and in chemical synthesis (forming other chemicals).

paint is a liquid made up of the pigment (the coloured material) in SUSPENSION within a non-volatile and a volatile part. The non-volatile oil or resin holds the pigment in place, while the volatile part enables the paint to be applied easily and it eventually evaporates (and may be water or a HYDROCARBON solvent). When applied to a surface the liquid evaporates leaving the pigment as an adhesive skin. Many paints are oil-based and are waterproof when dry and may contain additives to speed drying or improve coverage. Linseed oil was used with a thinner and a drier but synthetic compounds are now commonly used. Paints based on water are emulsions (*see* COLLOID), hence emulsion paint. These are often acrylic resins or polyvinyl acetate in water.

Of course, the earliest examples of paint were obtained from natural materials. Now there are special paints for particular purposes, e.g. anti-fouling paint to stop the growth of barnacles on a ship's hull.

pancreas an important gland present in VERTEBRATE animals situated behind and just below the stomach. It has two functions as it produces both digestive ENZYMES and the hormones insulin and glucagon which regulate the amount of sugar present in the blood. The digestive enzymes produced include trypsin, which breaks down protein; amylase which digests starch and lipase which aids in the digestion of fats. These are produced in an alkaline fluid which counteracts the acid effect of the stomach's gastric juice. The pancreatic juice, with its enzymes, passes through a tube or duct into the first part of the small intestine below the stomach which is called the *duodenum*.

paper consists of sheets of hydrated cellulose fibres derived from wood pulp. Pulp is made from timber mechanically or chemically. The mechanical method is simpler and more economical but produces weaker, poorer quality papers (e.g. newsprint). Pulp from chemical processes is stronger and brighter but more expensive. The pulp is washed, bleached and broken down and delivered to the paper mill where any fillers, size (a glue) and dyes are added. *China clay* is a common filler, providing bulk and opacity. The pulp is then watered down to make a slurry, treated further and then output onto a moving wire mesh and through presses which remove most of the water. Heated rollers then dry the paper which is then smoothed and finished (which involves pressing the surface fibres–a process known as *calendering*). The paper is then taken onto rolls for use or for cutting into sheets.

The whole process from pulp to paper can be a continuous process requiring machinery occupying hundreds of feet but it can produce sheets of paper in minutes.

parasite and symbiosis a *parasite* is an organism which obtains its food by living in or on the body of another living organism, without giving anything in return. The organism on which the parasite feeds is known as the *host*. Usually, the parasite does not kill the host as its future depends upon their mutual survival. However, sometimes a host species can become so seriously ill or weakened by the presence of the parasite that it dies. Parasites are of two kinds: *ectoparasites* attach themselves to the host's surface or skin and examples include the blood-sucking headlice, ticks and fleas. *Endoparasites* live inside the host's body, often within the gut or muscle, and examples are tapeworms, roundworms and liver flukes. Parasitic plants usually twine themselves around their host. They send projections, called haustoria (*sing.* haustorium) into the sap of the host to draw up water and food substances. A parasitic plant of this type is the dodder which lacks leaves and CHLOROPHYLL and cannot PHOTOSYNTHESIZE. Others, such as the mistletoe, are partial parasites, able to photosynthesize but obtaining minerals and water from the host.

Some other organisms live together in a way which brings mutual benefit rather than harm, and this type of relationship is called *mutualism*. Sometimes one organism benefits while the other remains unharmed and this is termed *commensalism*. These three types of relationship between organisms–parasitism, mutualism and commensalism usually of two different species–are grouped together and called *symbiosis*.

particle accelerator is a machine for increasing the speed (and therefore the kinetic energy) of charged particles such as protons, electrons and helium nuclei by accelerating them in an electric field.

Accelerators are used in the study of subatomic particles. To split an atom, particles travelling close to the speed of light are required. There are two types of accelerator *linear* and *cyclic*. Linear acceleration, or *linacs*, have to be very long, up to several kilometres, and consist of rows of electrodes separated by gaps. The ions in the beam accelerate across each gap due to a high frequency potential between alternate electrodes. *Cyclic accelerators* use a magnetic field to bend the path of the charged particles. The *cyclotron* is an example in which energies of several million electron volts are imparted to the particles as they travel along a spiral path between D-shaped electrodes. The *synchrotron* is another example. In the cyclic accelerators the stream of charged particles is accelerated to the required level and then deflected out of the ring.

The first accelerator was built by Cockcroft and Walton in 1932, and with it they split the atom for the first time. The energies of modern machines are measured in GeV (gigaelectron-volts, i.e. billions) and at the Fermi Laboratory in the USA, 800 GeV has been reached. Higher energies can be achieved using a *storage ring* which is a toroidal (doughnut-shaped) component in some accelerators. Particles enter the ring and can stay there for many weeks or months. A ring 300 metres in diameter in Geneva produces energies up to 1700 GeV.

pasteurization is the process named after the French chemist and biologist, Louis Pasteur. It involves the partial sterilization of food and kills potentially harmful bacteria. Milk is an obvious example. If it is heated to 62°C for 30 minutes, it kills bacteria that could cause tuberculosis and it increases the shelf life by delaying fermentation because other bacteria have also been killed or damaged. An alternative treatment involves heating milk to 72°C for 15 seconds. Higher temperatures still are used to produce 'long-life' milk. Pasteurization is also used with beer and wine, to eliminate any yeast which would create cloudiness in the drink.

pathogen and pathology a *pathogen* is any organism that causes disease in another organism. Most pathogens that affect humans and other animals are BACTERIA or VIRUSES, but in plants a wide range of fungi also act as pathogens. *Pathology* is the medical science and speciality in which the area of study is the causes of diseases and the ways in which these affect the body. Pathology relies on the use of powerful MICROSCOPES to study samples, and also on the techniques of MICROBIOLOGY.

periodic table is an ordered table of all the ELEMENTS arranged by their ATOMIC NUMBERS, i.e. the number of protons and electrons in an atom. The arrangement means that elements with similar properties are grouped near to each other. The horizontal rows are called *periods* and the vertical rows are *groups*. Elements with the same number of electrons in their outer shell behave in a similar way and this is the basis of the vertical group. Moving from left to right along the periods corresponds to the gradual filling of successive electron shells and an increase in the size of the atom.

The elements and their symbols are listed on page 234.

Periodic table

Group																
1A	2A	3B	4B	5B	6B	7B	8		1B	2B	3A	4A	5A	6A	7A	0
H 1																He 2
Li 3	Be 4										B 5	C 6	N 7	O 8	F 9	Ne 10
Na 11	Mg 12										Al 13	Si 14	P 15	S 16	Cl 17	Ar 18
K 19	Ca 20	Sc 21	Ti 22	V 23	Cr 24	Mn 25	Fe 26 Co 27 Ni 28		Cu 29	Zn 30	Ga 31	Ge 32	As 33	Se 34	Br 35	Kr 36
Rb 37	Sr 38	Y 39	Zr 40	Nb 41	Mo 42	Tc 43	Ru 44 Rh 45 Pd 46		Ag 47	Cd 48	In 49	Sn 50	Sb 51	Te 52	I 53	Xe 54
Cs 55	Ba 56	La* 57	Hf 72	Ta 73	W 74	Re 75	Os 76 Ir 77 Pt 78		Au 79	Hg 80	Tl 81	Pb 82	Bi 83	Po 84	At 85	Rn 86
Fr 87	Ra 88	Ac° 89														

Transition Elements

* Lanthanides	La 57	Ce 58	Pr 59	Nd 60	Pm 61	Sm 62	Eu 63	Gd 64	Tb 65	Dy 66	Ho 67	Er 68	Tm 69	Yb 70	Lu 71
° Actinades	Ac 89	Th 90	Pa 91	U 92	Np 93	Pu 94	Am 95	Cm 96	Bk 97	Cf 98	Es 99	Fm 100	Md 101	No 102	Lr 103

Element	Symbol	Atomic Number	Element	Symbol	Atomic Number
Actinium	Ac	89	Mercury	Hg	80
Aluminium	Al	13	Molybdenum	Mo	42
Americium	Am	95	Neodymium	Nd	60
Antimony	Sb	51	Neon	Ne	10
Argon	Ar	18	Neptunium	Np	93
Arsenic	As	33	Nickel	Ni	28
Astatine	At	85	Niobium	Nb	41
Barium	Ba	56	Nitrogen	N	7
Berkelium	Bk	97	Nobelium	No	102
Beryllium	Be	4	Osmium	Os	76
Bismuth	Bi	83	Oxygen	O	8
Boron	B	5	Palladium	Pd	46
Bromine	Br	35	Phosphorus	P	15
Cadmium	Cd	48	Platinum	Pt	78
Caesium	Cs	55	Plutonium	Pu	94
Calcium	Ca	20	Polonium	Po	84
Californium	Cf	98	Potassium	K	19
Carbon	C	6	Praseodymium	Pr	59
Cerium	Ce	58	Promethium	Pm	61
Chlorine	cl	17	Protactinium	Pa	91
Chromium	Cr	24	Radium	Ra	88
Cobalt	Co	27	Radon	Rn	86
Copper	Cu	29	Rhenium	Re	75
Curium	Cm	96	Rhodium	Rh	45
Dysprosium	Dy	66	Rubidium	Rb	37
Einsteinium	Es	99	Ruthenium	Ru	44
Erbium	Er	68	Samarium	Sm	62
Europium	Eu	63	Scandium	Sc	21
Fermium	Fm	100	Selenium	Se	34
Fluorine	F	9	Silicon	Si	14
Francium	Fr	87	Silver	Ag	47
Gadolinium	Gd	64	Sodium	Na	11
Gallium	Ga	31	Strontium	Sr	38
Germanium	Ge	32	Sulphur	S	16
Gold	Au	79	Tantalum	Ta	73
Hafnium	Hf	72	Technetium	Tc	43
Helium	He	2	Tellurium	Te	52
Holmium	Ho	67	Terbium	Tb	65
Hydrogen	H	1	Thallium	Tl	81
Indium	In	49	Thorium	Th	90
Iodine	I	53	Thulium	Tm	69
Iridium	Ir	77	Tin	Sn	50
Iron	Fe	26	Titanium	Ti	22
Krypton	Kr	36	Tungsten	W	74
Lanthanum	La	57	Uranium	U	92
Lawrencium	Lr	103	Vanadium	V	23
Lead	Pb	82	Xenon	Xe	54
Lithium	Li	3	Ytterbium	Yb	70
Lutetium	Lu	71	Yttrium	Y	39
Magnesium	Mg	12	Zinc	Zn	30
Manganese	Mn	25	Zirconium	Zr	40
Mendelevium	Md	101			

There are various sections within the periodic table as follows:

alkali metals	Li, Na, K, Rb, Cs, Fr
alkaline earth metals	Ca, Sr, Ba, Ra
chalcogens	O, S, Se, Te, Po
halogens	F, Cl, Br, I, At
inert gases	He, Ne, Ar, Kr, Xe, Rn
rare earth elements	Sc, Y, La to Lu
lanthanides	Ce to Lu inclusive
actinium series	Ac onwards
transuranium elements	elements after U
platinum metals	Ru, Os, Rh, Ir, Pd, Pt

Mendeléef was a Russian chemist who constructed the first periodic table, but based upon atomic weights. This basic principle, modified to use atomic numbers rather than atomic weights formed the basis of the modern table and even then, in 1869, allowed Mendeléef to predict the existence of undiscovered elements.

pesticides are chemical poisons designed to kill insects (*insecticides*), weeds (*herbicides*), fungi (*fungicides*) and other pests. Until the advent of organic pesticides in the 1930s the compounds used were inorganic mixtures such as Bordeaux mixture (copper sulphate and lime) and calcium arsenate. Some naturally-occurring organic insecticides were also used, such as pyrethrum produced from the flowers of the chrysanthemum. Now most are organic, save for some well-known examples such as DDT.

Fungicides traditionally contained sulphur, or copper or mercury although the toxicity of mercury has led to a decline in its use. Now there are a number of organic compounds and many are *systemic* i.e. they actually enter the plant. *Herbicides* are the single most important group of pesticides, as they kill weeds which compete with crops for light and nutrients and which may be sources of other pests and diseases. Herbicides may be selective (killing only certain plants) or total (non-selective) and in the main are complex organic chemicals. *Insecticides* are very important in controlling insects that consume or destroy crops, and also in limiting diseases spread by insects, such as malaria and sleeping sickness. There are naturally-occurring insecticides, e.g. nicotine, derris and pyrethrum, and synthetic compounds which form the greater proportion. Synthetic varieties include organochlorines, organophosphates and carbamates.

Pesticides do not achieve 100% success and some individuals, e.g. insects, survive to reproduce. It is possible that successive generations have a greater resistance to a particular pesticide which is overcome only by using higher concentrations of the pesticide. However, the pest may eventually become resistant to the pesticide, as happened with DDT.

petrochemicals are chemicals derived from crude oil (petroleum) and natural gas which are used to manufacture an enormous range of compounds and materials including plastics, drugs, fertilizers, solvents and detergents. Over 90% of synthetic organic materials come from these sources. A major factor in the development of petrochemicals was the dramatic rise of the motor car in the early part of this century, and the discovery of oil in large quantities. The hydrocarbons left from petroleum after the removal of the gasoline meant that producers and government sought ways of using these chemicals and consequently production of organic chemicals from these sources grew dramatically.

Petroleum is a complex mixture and *distillation* produces a number of *fractions* (see table). The operations undertaken in a *refinery*, to produce lighter fractions, are *cracking* and *reforming*. Catalytic cracking, which has replaced the old thermal process is an accelerated decomposition of middle to higher fractions over a solid catalyst usually consisting of zeolites. Catalytic reforming, which uses a platinum or platinum/rhenium catalyst, is undertaken at about 500°C and 7 to 30 atmospheres pressure. Various reactions occur simultaneously with straight-chain alkanes being converted to isomers and gasoline of a higher octane number being produced. There are other processes, including hydrocracking, steam cracking and steam reforming, which are implemented to act on a particular feedstock to produce certain chemicals.

Petroleum fractions	
methane and ethane	natural gas
propane and butanes	liquefied petroleum gases
light naphtha	
naphtha	motor spirit (gasoline)
kerosine	jet fuel
gas oil	diesel fuel
heavy distillates	feedstocks for lubricants, waxes etc.
bitumen/asphalt	

pH of a solution is a measure of that solution's acidity or alkalinity. It shows the concentration of hydrogen IONS (H^+) in an aqueous solution and is the negative logarithm (to base 10) of H^+ concentration calculated with the formula:

$$pH = \log_{10}(1/H^+)$$

The scale ranges from 1 (very acidic, e.g. concentrated hydrochloric acid) through the neutral point of 7 (pure water) to 14 (very alkaline, e.g. CAUSTIC SODA). Since pH is a logarithmic value, one unit of change is equivalent to a tenfold change in the H^+ ion concentration. The pH of solutions is checked by means of INDICATORS.

pharmacology *see* DRUGS AND PHARMACOLOGY.

pheromones a pheromone is a chemical substance that acts as a communication signal between individuals of the same species. Pheromones are found widely throughout the animal kingdom and have a number of different functions, e.g. sexual attraction (common in insects) and marking of territory (used by many mammals either by urine spraying as in dogs and members of the cat family, or by means of special scent glands often on the head or bottom). Pheromones act as *external hormones* and have been shown to be effective at very low concentrations. They are often organic acids or alcohols which are usually termed *volatile* because their effect is short-lived. Pheromones are important in techniques of biological control.

Pheromones are much rarer in plants but one of the most important economically and environmentally is produced by a plant called the 'Scary Hairy Wild Potato' (*Solanum berthaultii*). The leaves produce a pheromone which is chemically identical to the warning signal produced by aphids (small insect pests of many garden and crop plants). Breeding this aphid-repellent character into cultivated crops will hopefully lead to a reduction in aphid damage and less need for chemical insecticides.

phosphorus is a non-metal which occurs naturally as compounds and mainly as calcium phosphate ($Ca_3(PO_4)_2$), but also the mineral apatite. Phosphorus has several forms: red, white and black (a property called *allotropy*) and the white form is the most reactive. It is obtained by heating calcium phosphate with sand and carbon in an electric furnace.

Phosphorus is essential to life because calcium phosphate is a vital component of animal bones. It is also important in the compounds that it forms, e.g. phosphates are widely used in fertilizers. Phosphorus compounds are also used in the manufacture of glass and china ware, matches, detergents, special steels and foods and drinks.

photochemistry is the study of chemical reactions brought about by light. Only light that is actually absorbed will produce any effects and it is necessary to determine which parts of the spectrum are appropriate. The essential step in a photochemical reaction is the raising of an atom or molecule to an excited state by the absorbed light. Ultraviolet light is often the vehicle for such reactions and radiation from the far ultraviolet can break chemical bonds. However, the light may not actually produce a reaction directly. The excited molecule may emit the energy absorbed, affecting a neighbouring molecule which then undergoes a reaction.

Absorbed light may act as a catalyst or supply energy which renders a reaction possible. PHOTOSYNTHESIS is an example of a photochemical reaction.

photoelectric cell (or *photocell*) is a device used for the detection of light and other radiations. One type of cell, the *photoemissive cell*, makes use of the *photoelectric effect*. This is when light energy striking a substance causes energy to be transferred to electrons in the substance. When light above a certain (threshold) frequency is used, photoelectrons are generated and can create a current in a circuit. The photoemissive cell is in effect a light-powered electric cell and comprises a metal base and a transparently thin metal layer coated with selenium. Light entering the cell causes electrons to be released from the selenium and they move across a barrer to the metal layer, setting up a potential difference which can be used to drive a current. Cells of this nature can be used on solar cells and in camera light meters.

The other types of photoelectric cell are *photovoltaic* and *photoconductive* and are used to detect ultraviolet and infrared radiation, respectively.

photography is the process of capturing an image on photographic film (or plates) by means of LENSES in a *camera*. The earliest cameras produced images on metal or glass plates. Cameras consist essentially of a box with a variable aperture and a timed shutter through which light enters after which it is focused by lenses onto the light-sensitive film. The film is coated with an emulsion containing a silver halide (chloride or bromide) and on exposure to light the silver becomes easily reduced and when the film is developed a black deposit of fine silver gives a negative image. By further exposure of the negative and an underlying sensitive paper to light, a positive image is produced which is fixed and washed, producing a photograph.

A *polaroid camera* is different in that the photograph develops immediately after exposure to light. The technique of photography is based upon the incidental discovery by a German doctor, Schulze, who noticed that a silver nitrate solution on chalk turned black in sunlight. Daguerre then took the first photographs of a living person over one hundred years later, in 1839. The modern face of photography owes much to William Fox-Talbot, a British scientist who invented the negative to positive process and the American George Eastman who developed the rolls of film for cameras and who in 1892 founded Kodak.

The first moving photographs were made in 1893 by Edison (US) and Dickson (UK) in America, although only one person could view at a time. The Lumière brothers made the first practical projector–the start of the movies.

photon *see* LIGHT.

photosynthesis and transpiration *photosynthesis* is the complicated process by which green plants use the energy from the sun to make carbohydrates from carbon dioxide and water, releasing oxygen as a result. There are two stages known as the *Calvin Cycle* and the *Light Reactions* of photosynthesis which are very complex but result in the production of sugars and starch. Photosynthesis can only occur if light trapping pigments are present, and the main one of these is CHLOROPHYLL which is green-coloured and occurs in stems and leaves. Chlorophyll captures light energy and this initiates a series of energy transfer reactions which enable simple organic compounds to be made from the splitting of carbon dioxide and water. Photosynthesis is the basis of all life on Earth and regulates the atmosphere as it increases oxygen concentration while reducing the carbon dioxide concentration. *Transpiration* is the loss of water in the form of vapour through pores known as *stomata* in the leaves of plants. As much as one sixth of the water taken up by the roots can be lost in this way. The transpiration rate is affected by many environmental factors such as temperature, light and carbon dioxide levels (i.e. whether photosynthesis is taking place), humidity, air currents and water uptake from the roots. Transpiration is greatest when a plant is photosynthesizing in warm, dry, windy conditions.

phototropism the response by plants in the form of growth movement to the presence of light. Plant shoots show *positive phototropism* as they grow towards the light but roots tend to display *negative phototropism* because they grow away from the light source. Phototropism is caused by *auxin* (a plant growth HORMONE). The hormone is more abundant on the dark side of the plant and this side is induced to grow more by elongation of cells resulting in a curving towards the light.

physics is the study of matter and energy, and changes in energy without chemical alteration. Physics includes a number of topics such as magnetism, electricity, heat, light and sound (*see individual entries*). The study of modern physics also encompasses QUANTUM THEORY, atomic and nuclear physics (i.e. subatomic particles and their behaviour (*see* ELEMENTARY PARTICLES) and physics of NUCLEAR FISSION AND FUSION). As the research into topics has expanded over recent years, so new subjects begin to develop often on the boundaries of two major disciplines. This has happened in geophysics (geology and physics), biophysics (biology and physics) and astrophysics, which combines astronomy with physics.

physiology the study of all the METABOLIC functions of animals and plants including the processes of RESPIRATION, REPRODUCTION, EXCRETION, working of the NERVOUS SYSTEM, PHOTOSYNTHESIS, etc. It covers all aspects of the life of organisms and may be one specialized area of research or broadly based.

piezoelectric effect is the effect within certain crystals whereby positive and negative charges are generated on opposite faces when the crystal is subjected to pressure. The charges are reversed if the crystal is put under tension and the whole effect is reversible, i.e. the application of an electric potential produces an alteration in size of the crystal. Quartz is the commonest piezoelectric crystal and very pure crystals grown in the laboratory can be cut to vibrate at one frequency when a voltage is applied. The vibrations are used in watches and enable near perfect time to be kept. The piezoelectric effect is also used in crystal microphones and pickups. Other crystals that show the effect are Rochelle salt (sodium potassium tartrate) and barium titanate.

pig iron *see* CAST IRON.

pigments are compounds that produce colour and occur naturally in both plants and animals. In plants, *chlorophyll* imparts a green colour and animals contain *melanin* which produces the black or brown colour of hair or skin. *Carotenoids* are plant pigments, coloured orange, red and yellow, that occur in carrots and ripe tomatoes.

Synthetic pigments are used to colour plastics, textiles, inks, etc. Pigments are different from dyes and tend to be insoluble and occur as particles and many are inorganic:

Colour	Pigment
white	titanium dioxide
	lead carbonate and sulphate
	zinc oxide and sulphide
red/brown	iron oxides
	red lead
	cadmium red, orange, scarlet
yellow	iron oxides
	lead, zinc and cadmium chromates
blue	ultramarine (an aluminosilicate with sulphur)
black	carbon

pitchblende is an important ore of uranium, a mineral called Uraninite, made up primarily of uranium oxide. It is also the principal source of radium, an element discovered by Marie and Pierre Curie in 1898 (they also discovered polonium from the same source).

Pitchblende occurs as a black mass, resembling tar and the uranium in it decays to form radioactive radium and radon gas. Deposits occur in Canada, East Africa, Saxony and Colorado.

plankton very small organisms, often microscopic and including both plants and animals, which drift in the currents of oceans and lakes. The plants (or *phytoplankton*) consist mainly of single-celled algae (*Bacillariophyta*) called *diatoms* which photosynthesize and form the basis of food chains. The animals (or *zooplankton*) include the *larval* stages of larger organisms, some protozoans (Kingdom PROTISTA) and small creatures called copepods which are related to crabs (*see* **NH:** CRUSTACEA). Plankton provide food for many larger animals, e.g. whales, and are of vital importance in the FOOD CHAIN.

plants Kingdom Plantae forms one of the major kingdoms of life. Plants are distinguished from animals by their ability to manufacture food by PHOTOSYNTHESIS. This type of nutrition is termed *autotrophic* whereas that of animals, relying on taking in food from outside, is called *heterotrophic*. The photosynthetic cells of plants contain organelles (*see* ORGAN) called *chloroplasts* which contain the pigment CHLOROPHYLL and this traps light energy from the sun. Plant cells have walls (absent in animal cells), and the main substance of which these are composed is a carbodyhydrate called CELLULOSE. Plant cells store carbohydrate in the form of *starch* whereas animal cells store it as glycogen.

There are twelve divisions of the plant kingdom (the same as phyla in animals). In three of these divisions, there is no true system of structures or tubes to transport water and food. These are called *non-vascular* plants and include mosses, liverworts and hornworts. In the other divisions this *vascular tissue* is present but they are further divided into those which produce *seeds* and those which do not. The *seedless plants* are the horsetails, ferns, club mosses and whiskferns. The seed plants are divided into two groups, the *Gymnosperms* which produce 'naked' unprotected seeds, e.g. the conifers, and the *Angiosperms* (or *Anthophyta*), the flowering plants. These are the ones most familiar to us and are the most complex among plants, producing seeds within special protective coverings.

Most plants have sexual REPRODUCTION and many are also able to reproduce asexually. In the plant life cycle an *alternation of generations* occurs with a *sporophyte* generation which is *diploid* (i.e. has the full number of CHROMOSOMES) producing the *gametophyte generation* which is *haploid* (half the number of chromosomes). The sporophyte generation is nearly always the most prominent form, and in most plants the gametophyte is represented by very small structures.

Flowering plants are either *monocotyledons*, with one seed leaf or *dicotyledons*, with two. Some flowering plants are called *annuals* as they grow from seed, produce flowers and die. Others are *perennials* which grow up from the same root stock year after year even though the leafy parts die back during the winter.

plastics is a group name for mainly synthetic organic compounds which are mostly POLYMERS, formed by polymerization that can be moulded when subjected to heat and pressure. There are two types: *thermoplastics* (e.g. PVC or polyvinyl chloride) which become plastic when heated and can be heated repeatedly without changing their properties; *thermosetting plastics* such as phenol/formaldehyde resins lose their plasticity after being subjected to heat and/or pressure. Plastics are moulded and shaped while in their softened state and then cured by further heat (thermosetting e.g. epoxy resins, silicones) or cooling (thermoplastics e.g. perspex and polythene).

The first synthetic plastic was *Bakelite*, invented in 1908. Since then the plastics industry has become vast and an enormous range of domestic, leisure, industrial and commercial items are now produced. Plastics can be shaped by blow moulding, vacuum forming, EXTRUSION and INJECTION MOULDING and they are used extensively in composite materials and LAMINATES.

plutonium *see* NUCLEAR ENERGY.

pneumatics refers to the use of compressed air, usually to power machines. A supply of air is piped to the pneumatic motor which commonly features a piston within a cylinder. Compressed air pushes the piston one way and a spring or air pressure pushes it back, producing a hammer action used in drills for mixing or construction.

The greatest benefit of pneumatic tools over electrically-powered tools is that there is no chance of electric shocks or sparks which could cause a fire or explosion in certain circumstances.

polarization of light is when light is made to vibrate in one particular plane. Light normally consists of waves vibrating in many directions and because it is electromagnetic radiation there is an electric and a magnetic field vibrating at right angles to each other. If light is polarized, the electric field vibrations are confined to one plane (*plane polarized light*) called the plane of vibration and the magnetic vibrations are in one plane at right angles, the plane of polarization.

Polarization occurs when light passes through certain crystals (quartz, calcite) or is reflected from some surfaces (e.g. the sea). A polarizer produces polarized light and a polaroid filter is one such material used in sunglasses. Polarized light also has uses in mechanical engineering to reveal stress patterns in materials. Only transverse waves such as light can be polarized; longitudinal waves such as sound cannot.

pollen pollen grains are the male sex cells (*gametes*) of flowering PLANTS. They occur in small pollen sacs contained within a structure called the *anther*, which is part of the male reproductive organ of the flower. The anther occurs on the end of a thin stalk called the stamen. Pollen grains and their female equivalents, the *embryo sacs*, are the *gametophyte generation* (*see* PLANTS) in flowering plants.

pollination is the transfer of pollen from an anther to a stigma. This is part of the female reproductive organ of the flower, the other portions being the *style* and *ovary* which together make up a *carpel*. The ovary contains one or more *ovules* which develop into seeds. Pollen may be transferred by means of the wind, insects, birds, water, etc. and the grains vary in shape according to the method of pollination used by the plant. Wind-pollinated plants have light, smooth grains while insect-pollinated ones have grains which are rough or spiny. This is called *cross-pollination* as the pollen is transferred from one flower to another the same species. *Self-pollination* is where pollen is transferred from an anther to a stigma in the same flower.

polygon is a term used in GEOMETRY to describe a closed plane (i.e. two-dimensional) figure with three or more straight line sides. Common polygons are figures such as the triangle, quadrilateral and hexagon. A square is a regular polygon where the sides and all angles are equal.

For a polygon with n sides, the sum of the interior angles = $180°$ $(n-2)$. Except for the triangle and square, polygons are named after their number of sides so a ten-sided figure is called a *decagon*. Polygons are common around us, whether in a natural form as in honeycomb, or the faces of crystals or man-made as with tiles and nuts and bolts.

polymer a large, usually linear molecule that is formed from many simple molecules called *monomers*. Synthetic polymers include PVC, Teflon, polythene and nylon while naturally-occurring polymers include starch, cellulose (found in the cell walls of plants) and rubber (*see individual entries*). Early versions of polymers were modified natural compounds, e.g. the vulcanization of rubber by heating with sulphur. The first fully synthetic polymer to be developed was *Bakelite* (*see* PLASTICS) followed by urea-formaldehyde and alkyd resins in the late 1920s. Polyethylene (that is polythene) was first produced by ICI on a commercial basis in 1938 and the Dupont company in America produced the first nylon in 1941. Many synthetic polymers are produced from alkenes (*see* HYDROCARBONS) in reactions called addition polymerizations which are rapid and require only relatively low temperatures. Condensation polymerization is another means of producing polymers e.g. the nylons (polyamides) and the silicones (polysiloxanes) in which some molecule (often water) is removed at each successive reaction stage.

potassium is an alkali metal that is silver white and highly reactive. In fact, it reacts violently with water and therefore in nature occurs only as compounds. It occurs widely in silicate rocks as alkali feldspar, in blood and milk and in salt beds and as potassium chloride in sea water. Potassium is an essential element for plants and it is added to the soil by farmers, as fertilizers (such as potash). Fertilizers are the primary use of potassium but it is also used in making batteries, ceramics and glass.

power is the rate at which WORK is done. It is also regarded as the rate at which energy is converted. The unit of power is the *watt* (W) which is measured in joules per second. Thus if a machine does 10 joules of work every second, it has a power output of 10W. Electrical power can be calculated from the product of the voltage and the current.

Power is very important because many routine processes and functions require energy to do work, whether it concerns an engine, light bulbs or our bodies. In most cases, when energy is expended it is not all turned into the useful work required but some escapes or is lost, e.g. engines lose energy in vibrations and heat.

pressure is the force exerted per unit area of a surface. The pressure of a gas equals the force that its molecules exert on the walls of its container, divided by the surface area of the vessel. The pressure of a gas varies with temperature and volume (*see* GAS) and the pressure in a liquid or in air equals the weight of liquid or air above the area in question and therefore as the depth increases, the pressure also increases. This explains why air pressure decreases with height (*see* ATMOSPHERE). If force is measured in N (newtons) and area in m^2 (square metres), pressure is N/m^2 or *pascals* (Pa).

primates an order of mammals which includes monkeys, lemurs, apes and humans. Primates have highly mobile hands and feet due to the presence of thumbs and big toes which can grasp. They also have a large brain (especially the part called the *cerebrum*) and are very intelligent.

prism is a solid figure that is essentially triangular in shape (resembling a wedge) and made of a transparent material. It is used in physics to deviate or disperse a ray in optical instruments or laboratory experiments. If a narrow beam of white light passes through a prism it is split into a range of colours–the *spectrum*. The light is split because each of the colours is refracted by a different amount, because each is light of a different *wavelength* (*see* WAVE).

probability is the chance of something happening, or the likelihood that an event will occur, expressed as a fraction or decimal between 0 and 1 (or as odds). If something is absolutely certain, the probability is 1; if it is impossible, then the probability is 0, and all probabilities lie within these two figures. Thus if a coin is flipped, there is an equal chance of gaining 'heads' and 'tails', i.e. one chance out of two for heads or tails giving a probability of _ or 0.5. The probability of a particular number coming up on rolling a dice is one in six, i.e. 1/6 or 0.1666, and it is 0.5 for rolling an even number (3 possibilities out of the 6 numbers).

procaryote any *organism* which has a nucleus that is <u>not</u> surrounded by a true membrane. These organisms all belong to the Kingdom MONERA and are the BACTERIA and blue-green *algae* (*cyanobacteria*). They have a single chromosome and do not undergo meiosis or mitosis (*see* CELL DIVISION) but reproduce ASEXUALLY by a method called *binary fission*. In this, the whole cell divides and each 'daughter' cell receives a copy of the single parental chromosome. Procaryotes are very important organisms, vitally involved in all life-sustaining processes. A few are disease-causing organisms, but others are used in BIOTECHNOLOGY. They were the first organisms to evolve being the only life forms on Earth for about 2 billion years.

protein and amino acid a protein is a type of organic (*see* CHEMISTRY) compound of which there are many different kinds, and it usually contains nitrogen and sulphur. The individual MOLECULES are made up of building blocks called *amino acids* arranged in long chains (known as *polypeptide* chains). There are 20 different amino acids but a huge number of possible arrangements in a polypeptide or protein. Most proteins consist of more than one polypeptide.

protista a biological kingdom containing numerous different kinds of simple organisms, most of which are single cells. They are the simplest eucaryotic (*see* EUCARYOTE) organisms because they are usually unicellular (single-celled). However, since each protist is able to carry out lots of different functions within its one cell, and many are highly complex, some have the most elaborate of all cells. Most protists have extensions or projections out from the *cytoplasm* of the cell, called cilia, (*sing.* cilium) or flagella (*sing.* flagellum), which are used for movement. These may not be present at all stages of the life cycle but usually occur at some time or other. All protists can reproduce asexually and some also have sexual reproduction. They are important organisms in the PLANKTON and hence significant in food chains. Most require oxygen for RESPIRATION and so are called *aerobic*. Some are PHOTOSYNTHETIC (i.e. they are *autotrophic* and make their own food), others are *heterotrophic* (i.e. they absorb or ingest food) and yet others combine the two, a condition known as *mixotrophic*. Protists inhabit a wide range of environments. Many are free-living but others live inside cells and tissues of other organisms as PARASITES or in other relationships (known as *symbiosis*).

pulley is one of the six varieties of simple MACHINE. It is a wheel with a groove around the edge around which a rope can be passed. An individual pulley, suspended on an axle may make lifting a load a little easier but in general several pulleys are combined in a *block-and-tackle* system to enable the lifting of larger loads that would not normally be feasible. A rope wound around the pulleys in such a system can be pulled a long way to raise a heavy load a short distance.

pumps are machines that move gases and liquids. A basic pump is the force, or reciprocating pump in which a piston moves in and out of a cylinder. Fluid or gas is taken into the cylinder on one stroke and pushed out through a valve when the piston moves in the opposite direction. A bicycle pump or a water pump are examples of this type. Another type is the rotary pump which uses some form of spinning blade assembly to push liquid along a pipe.

Pythagoras' Theorem *see* GEOMETRY.

quantum mechanics is the system of mechanics that facilitates an explanation of the structure of the atom and the behaviour of small particles within atoms (*see* ATOM). The electronic structure of the atom comprises a nucleus around which electrons orbit at various levels. Putting energy into an atom causes electrons to move temporarily into a higher orbit, through absorption of the energy. When the electron returns to its original orbit, light energy is given off as a *quantum* or PHOTON. This principle was discovered by Max Planck (and called *quantum theory*) and it was realized that all electromagnetic radiations can be thought of in this way, i.e. a photon is a quantum of electromagnetic radiation.

Further developments were made in the subject by Heisenberg who used quantum mechanics to explain atomic structure and behaviour of subatomic particles. Essentially he stated that it is not possible to know both the position and momentum of a particle such as the electron, *at the same time* (this is called *Heisenberg's uncertainty principle*). Quantum mechanics was gradually superseded by *wave mechanics* and in the mid-1920s Schrödinger evolved his wave equation which describes the behaviour of a particle in a force field. It permitted the description of the electrons in an atom in terms of waves.

quantum numbers a set of four numbers used to describe atomic structures (*see* ATOM and QUANTUM MECHANICS). The principal quantum number (n) defines the shells (or orbits) which are visualized as orbitals (that is, a charge cloud which represents the probability distribution of an electron). The orbit nearest the nucleus has 2 electrons and $n = 1$. The second shell contains 8 electrons (and $n = 2$) and so on, the maximum number of electrons in each shell being defined by the formula $2n^2$. The orbital quantum number (l) defines the shape of the orbits and these are designated s, p, d and f, the letters arising purely for historical reasons. The magnetic orbital quantum number (m) sets the position of the orbit within a magnetic field and s is the spin quantum number. The latter is based upon the assumption that no two electrons may be exactly alike and pairs of electrons are considered to have opposite spin.

The quantum numbers n, l and m are related and allowed the electronic structure of any atom to be determined.

quantum theory *see* QUANTUM MECHANICS.

radiation (thermal) is a process by which heat is transferred from one place to another. Objects give out infrared waves and hot objects may also emit light into the ultraviolet region. Some surfaces are better emitters and absorbers of thermal radiation. Dull black surfaces are better at absorbing and emitting thermal radiation than white or silver surfaces. The nearer to a silver, mirror-like finish is a surface, the greater will be the reflection and lower the absorption of radiation.

Vacuum flasks, silver body blankets and greenhouses all make use of this property. In the case of the greenhouse, the glass permits light and short wavelength infrared radiation through from the Sun, which warms the air and the plants. The plants re-emit radiation, but of a longer wavelength and this does not pass through the glass, but is reflected back into the greenhouse, helping to maintain the higher temperature.

radio uses electromagnetic waves to send and receive information without wires (hence the former term wireless, for the radio). It includes, in its widest sense, radio, television and radar. Radiowaves are created in an antenna or aerial by making electrons oscillate. Long and medium waves are sent around the world by bouncing them off the *ionosphere* (a layer of charged particles in the upper atmosphere) but VHF (very high frequency) and UHF (ultra-high frequency waves for television) waves require a straighter path between the receiver and the transmitting aerial because these waves are not reflected by the ionosphere. Similarly, the longer wavelengths can diffract around hills and other obstacles, unlike the short wavelength VHF and UHF waves.

When a receiver is tuned to the frequency of the appropriate wave sent from the transmitter, it can amplify and rectify the signal to produce a varying current which matches the frequency of the sound wave at the microphone. This current is then used to work a loudspeaker, thus reproducing the original sound.

radioactivity means that a material naturally gives out radiations while undergoing spontaneous disintegration. The (nuclear) radiation given out by a radioactive material is one of three types: α–particles (alpha), ß–particles (beta) or gamma (γ) rays and each is a different entity with varying effects.

Radioactivity was discovered in 1896 by Henri Becquerel who found that uranium salts emitted some form of radiation capable of ionizing the air and also capable of affecting a photographic plate, through its wrapping. Further work determined the properties of the three types of radiation.

An *alpha particle* is a helium nucleus (2 protons and 2 neutrons, He^{2+}) and it has a strong ionizing effect but little penetration, having a range in air of a few centimetres. *Beta particles* are electrons moving at different speeds, in some cases almost at the speed of light. They have a negative charge and although their ionizing effect is very weak, they are more penetrating, with a range in air of about one metre. Beta particles can be stopped by a few millimetres of aluminium. *Gamma rays* are short wavelength electromagnetic waves with little ionizing effect but greatest penetration. They are never completely absorbed but lead 25mm thick reduces their intensity to half. Radioactive materials can give one or a combination of radiation types.

Radioactive decay is the emission of particles by an unstable nucleus which in so doing becomes another atom. The decaying nucleus is the parent, the resulting nucleus is the daughter which together with particles emitted are called the decay products. During decay, nuclei disintegrate randomly but at a different set rate for different atoms. The *half-life* of a radioactive *nuclide* (i.e. the radioactive form of an element) is the time taken for half the atom to decay, i.e. for the activity to fall by half. For example, uranium-238 has a half-life of 4.51×10^9 years; radium-226, 1620 years; and sodium-24, 15 hours; and radon-220 just 52 seconds.

Artificial nuclides are used in many ways, e.g. in medicine cobalt-60 in the treatment of cancer. On industrial plants radioisotopes are used to check the flow of fluids and gases, leaks, residence times in chemical processes, and a variety of isotopes are used. (*See also* DATING METHODS).

rainbow is the characteristic display of the colours of the spectrum which may form a large arc of a circle. The Sun must be behind the viewer for the rainbow to be seen. Light enters droplets of water in the sky and is refracted and internally reflected. Because the raindrop acts like a prism, the light is split up into the constituent colours.

receptor a special type of animal cell which is called *excitable* because it is sensitive to a particular type of stimulus. When the receptor cell is *excited* electrical impulses are sent along a (sensory) nerve to the central nervous system. Some receptors respond to factors or stimuli outside the animal's body and others are present internally. Receptors are sensitive to a variety of different stimuli and are often called after the *sense* which they detect. Examples are *chemoreceptor* (chemicals), *photoreceptor* (light), *mechanoreceptor* (touch) and *proprioreceptor* (pressure, movement or stretching within the body). Receptors may be grouped together within a special organ such as the ear which detects sound waves and also controls balance and posture.

recording media there are many ways in which sounds and pictures can be recorded. One medium which is fast being replaced by new technologies is the vinyl record. These are plastic discs upon which the sound is recorded in a groove cut in the disc. The sound to be recorded is fed via microphones to cutters operated by electromagnets. Thus, when a stylus is placed on the record, it vibrates along the groove and the vibrations are turned into electric currents to operate loudspeakers.

Magnetic tape can be used for recording sound (audio tape) or pictures (video tape) and consists of a plastic tape coated with magnetic particles, often iron oxide, or chromium dioxide for higher quality. Recordings are made by magnetizing the tape in a specific way. It is a very flexible medium in that tape can be re-used and edited.

More recent media include the compact disc which is a form of laser disc, and which has a very large capacity, often used in the storage of computer data.

rectifier *see* DIODE.

reflection light striking a surface may be reflected but in most cases the reflections are in all directions. When the surface is smooth, e.g. a mirror, an image is produced. When light is reflected from a surface it follows certain laws. The incoming (*incident*) ray makes an angle (angle of incidence) with the line drawn at 90° to the surface (the normal) equal to the angle of reflection which is the angle between the normal and the *reflected* ray. This encompasses the *laws of reflection*. A *reflector* is any surface that reflects electromagnetic radiation.

refraction is the bending of, most commonly, a light ray when it travels from one medium to another, e.g. air to water. The refraction occurs at the point where the light passes from one material to another and is caused by the light travelling at different velocities in the different media. The incident (*see* REFLECTION) ray passing into a material becomes the refracted ray and in an optically more dense medium is bent towards the normal to the interface. The two angles – of incidence and refraction – are related by *Snell's Law* which states that the ratio of the sines (*see* TRIGONOMETRY) of the two angles is constant for light passing from one given medium to another. The value of the ratio of the sines of the angles is called the *refractive index*, measured when light is refracted from a vacuum into the medium.

refrigeration *see* EVAPORATION.

relativity is the theory developed by Einstein and which is made up of two parts. The *special theory* states that the speed of light is the same for all observers, whatever their speed, that is light from an object travels at the same velocity whether the object is moving or stationary. Nothing may move faster than the speed of light. Further important implications of this theory are that the mass of a body is a function of its speed, and Einstein derived the *mass-energy equation*, $E = mc^2$ where c is the speed of light. As a result of this theory the concept of *time dilation* was proposed which essentially means that for someone travelling at very great speed, time passes much more slowly for them that it does for a stationary observer.

The *general theory of relativity* relates to gravity. Matter in space is said to cause space to curve so as to set up a gravitational field and gravitation becomes a property of space. The validity of Einstein's theories has been tested with experiments in modern atomic physics.

reproduction the production of new individuals of the same species either by *asexual* or *sexual* means. The term usually refers to sexual reproduction which involves the joining together (called *fusion*) of special sex cells, one of which is female (the egg or *ovum*) and the other is male (e.g. *sperm* in animals and pollen in flowering plants). The sex cells of any organism are known as *gametes*. Many organisms produce gametes within special reproductive organs. In the flower of a seed plant, the male sex organs are the stamens which produce pollen. The *carpels* are female and produce *ovules* which later develop into seeds after *fertilization*. Gametes are special cells which contain half the number of chromosomes (called haploid, *see* CELL DIVISION) of the parent. When a male and female gamete join together (*fusion*), fertilization takes place and a single cell (now called a zygote) is produced which contains the full number of chromosomes (diploid). This goes on to produce a new individual, usually by a process of many cell divisions. In mammals (and many other animals), the male sex organs are the *testes* and the female ones are the *ovaries*. These reproductive organs (also called *gonads*), are specialized structures, the cells of which produce the sperm and ova under the influence of hormones. Most adult female mammals have a reproductive cycle, called an *oestrous cycle*, during which time the eggs develop and the animal becomes ready to mate (a period known as *heat* or *oestrus*). Mating occurs at the time when the animal is most likely to become pregnant. Some mammals have a definite *breeding season* and only one oestrous cycle in a year (*monoestrous*). Others have several cycles and are *polyoestrous*. In female humans, the *menstrual cycle* replaces the oestrous cycle. Mating usually results in the fertilization of one or more egg. The cells rapidly divide and become embryos which grow and develop inside a muscular, bag-like organ called the *uterus* or womb. The animal is now said to be *pregnant*. A special organ of pregnancy, called the *placenta*, develops and this attaches the embryos to the uterus by a cord called the *umbilical cord*. This provides for the passage of food, oxygen and some other substances (e.g. vitamins and antibodies) to the embryos while waste products, (mainly carbon dioxide and urea), pass in the opposite direction and are removed by the mother's blood circulation. When the young are fully developed they are *born*, which means that they are pushed to the outside through a passage leading from the womb called the *vagina*. This is brought about by contractions of the muscles in the wall of the uterus under the influence of hormones. Immediately after birth, the placenta is also pushed out.

resistance (R) is measured in *ohms* and is the potential difference between the ends of a conductor divided by the current flowing. Superconductors apart, materials resist the flow of current to varying degrees, and some of the electrical energy is thereby converted to heat. The resistance of a wire depends on the ability of the material to conduct electricity, and the dimensions of the wire. In general, a short wire has less resistance than a long one and a thick wire less resistance than a thin one.

Resistors are devices made to produce resistance and they control the current in a circuit. They are found in radios, televisions and similar pieces of equipment. A variable resistor is called a *rheostat* and by means of a sliding contact can alter the current flowing. Wires used in circuits have a low resistance to minimize heat loss, but in some cases thermal energy is required, as in heating elements for electric kettles, fires, immersion heaters and cookers. Nichrome wire is commonly used for such applications.

resonance is the creation of vibrations in a system, such that it is vibrating at its natural frequency, due to vibrations of the same frequency being received from another source. Resonance occurs in many instances; the strings of an instrument, columns of air in a wind instrument and even an engine causing vibrations in a bus or van.

respiration and ventilation *respiration* is often used to mean *breathing* but more correctly it is a metabolic (*see* METABOLISM) process which occurs in the cells of an organism. It is the process by which living cells release energy by breaking down complicated organic substances (food molecules) into simpler ones using enzymes. In most organisms, respiration occurs in the presence of oxygen and is called *aerobic*, with water and carbon dioxide produced as waste products and energy released. Some organisms (e.g. a number of species of bacteria and yeasts) do not require oxygen but use alternative chemical reactions. This is known as *anaerobic respiration* and it is possible for it to occur for a short time in the muscles of mammals when these are being very hard worked. However, it is short-lived and results in the build up of a substance called *lactic acid* which causes muscular *cramps*. *Ventilation* is the actual process of breathing or drawing air in and out of an animal's body. Various mechanisms and structures are involved in different animals, using muscles to pump air in and out (*see also* LUNGS AND GILLS).

rubber is a high molecular weight polymer which occurs naturally, being obtained from the tree *Hevea braziliensis*. It is an elastic solid from the latex (a colloid of rubber particles in a watery base) of the tree which contains about 35% rubber. After straining, the latex is coagulated and the raw rubber is 'compounded' and other substances are added to increase strength and it is then *vulcanized* (heated with sulphur) to increase the crosslinking in its structure. This provides more elasticity and the rubber becomes less sticky. Natural rubber is a form of polyisoprene $-(CH_2.CH : C(CH_3) : (H_2)_n$.

Synthetic rubbers are polymers of simple molecules and include butyl rubber, neoprene, styrene-butadiene rubber and silicone rubber. Butyl rubber is used for the inner tubes of tyres; styrene-butadiene for car tyres; and silicone rubbers for applications requiring temperature stability, water repellence and chemical resistance.

salt is the common name for sodium chloride, NaCl. It occurs in sea water and in hot climates shallow ponds of sea water are left to evaporate to dryness, providing deposits of salt. Significant salt deposits were formed in the geological past and are now mined (*see* evaporite). In chemistry, a salt is produced by the reaction of equivalent amounts of an acid and a base, with the production of water. Salt molecules contain metal atoms with one or more non-metal atoms and are named from the acid and base from which the salt is formed, e.g. hydrochloric acid and sodium hydroxide produce sodium chloride.

saturated solution is a solution of a substance (solute) that exists in equilibrium when there is excess solute present (*see* SOLUTIONS). Heating a saturated solution allows more to dissolve producing a *supersaturated solution*. Cooling or loss of solvent will cause some of the solute to come out of solution, i.e. it will crystallize.

screw is one of the six varieties of simple *machine*. It is an extremely effective device and is used extensively for fastening things together. Screws or screw threads are also used in instruments to enable controlled movement, e.g. on a microscope stage, or in a micrometer when making accurate measurements. A screw jack is one type of jack for lifting a car to allow a wheel to be changed. This means that a heavy object like a car can be raised relatively easily.

seed *see* FLOWERS *and* PLANT.

semiconductors materials, such as silicon, that can act as a conductor of electricity or an insulator. Pure semiconductors are insulators when cold and allow current to pass when heated although at room temperature they conduct only poorly. However, by *doping* them, with small amounts of other substances, semiconductors can be made to conduct. Depending upon the material used for doping, a p- or n-type semiconductor is created (*see* DIODE).

Semiconductors may be compounds or elements. In addition to silicon, germanium selenium and lead telluride are used. Diodes, rectifiers and transistors all utilise semiconductors, as do silicon chips used in microprocessors.

sense organ *see* RECEPTOR.

sight the sense of sight is possessed by many animals. Some simple, single-celled (unicellular) organisms have cells which are sensitive to light, but cannot be said to 'see' in the way we understand it. They have *eyespots* which contain pigments (called *carotenoids*) and these are sensitive to light. They cause the cell or organism to move in a particular way in response to light. Other invertebrate animals have more complicated eyes, ranging from a fairly simple type called ocelli (*sing*. ocellus) to a more advanced kind known as a *compound* eye. Compound eyes are a feature of many Arthropod invertebrates (spiders, insects, beetles, etc.) and give very good vision especially in some insects, e.g. dragonflies and flies. Squids and octopuses (which are molluscs), have eyes that are similar to those of vertebrate animals and have excellent powers of vision.

The eyes of vertebrates are almost spherical balls filled with fluid, and contained within bony sockets in the skull. Light enters the eye through the transparent *cornea* and is bent (or refracted) as it passes through a small space filled with a fluid, the *aqueous humour*. The light passes through the *pupil* which is a hole in the centre of the coloured *iris*. The light rays pass through the lens and on through a larger cavity filled with fluid called the *vitreous humour*. The lens bends the light rays and focuses them so that they form an *image* on the layer at the back of the eye which is called the *retina*. The retina contains the actual light receptors (photoreceptors). These are pigment-containing cells of two types, *rods* and *cones*. The pigments undergo chemical changes (*bleaching*) in light of different wavelengths and this generates electrical impulses which travel to the brain along a special sensory *optic nerve*. Cones contain pigments which allow for colours to be detected and there are about 6 million in a human retina. Rods are sensitive in very dim light and allow for night vision but do not detect colour. The human retina contains about 125 million of these. Most mammals are nocturnal and have poor colour vision, but keen night sight is allowed for by the large number of rods that are present.

the human eye

suspensory ligaments

choroid

iris
lens
pupil

optic nerve

vitreous humor

cornea

silicon is a non-metallic element and the second most abundant in the Earth's crust. It does not occur as free silicon, but is found in abundance as numerous silicate minerals including quartz (SiO_2). Silicon is manufactured by reducing SiO_2 in an electric furnace but further processing is necessary to obtain pure silicon. When doped with boron or phosphorus it is used in semiconductors, (*see also* DIODE). Quartz and some silicates are used industrially to produce glass and building materials. Silicon melts at 1410_C. *Silicones* are polymers built on SiR_2O groups (where R is a hydrocarbon). Simpler substances are lower melting point oils, which are used as lubricants. More complex varieties are solid and very stable and are used as electrical insulators.

siphon is a bent tube, shaped like an upside-down U, and it can be used for transferring liquid from a higher to a lower level. One end of the tube is placed in the higher container, and the other end is primed by sucking. When the liquid flows through the tube, the end is placed in the lower container and the flow continues even though the suction is no longer there. The liquid flows due to a pressure difference between the two ends of the tube.

SI Units (Système International d'Unités) is a system of units agreed internationally. It comprises seven basic units and some supplementary units with a larger number of derived units. It also established the prefixes used for decimal multiples where the practice is to raise to 10 by a power that is a multiple of three.

basic units		derived units		
m	metre	Bq	becquerel	(radioactivity)
kg	kilogram	C	coulomb	(electric charge)
s	second	F	farad	(capacitance)
A	ampere	Gy	gray	(ionizing radiation)
K	kelvin	H	henry	(inductance)
mol	mole	Hz	hertz	(frequency)
cd	candela (light)	J	joule	(work or energy)
supplementary		lm	lumen	(luminous flux)
rad	radian (angular measurement)	lx	lux	(illuminance–one lumen/m^2)
sr	steradian (solid angle)	N	newton	(force)
		Ω	ohm	(resistance)
		Pa	pascal	(pressure)
		S	siemens	(conductance)
		Sv	sievert	(dose equivalent)
		T	tesla	(magnetic flux density)
		V	volt	(electric potential)
		W	watt	(power)
		Wb	weber	(magnetic flux)

decimal multiples					
10^{-18}	atto	a	10	deca	da
10^{-15}	femto	f	10^2	hecto	h
10^{-12}	pico	p	10^3	kilo	k
10^{-9}	nano	n	10^6	mega	M
10^{-6}	micro	μ	10^9	giga	G
10^{-3}	milli	m	10^{12}	tera	T
10^{-2}	centi	c	10^{15}	peta	P
10^{-1}	deci	d	10^{18}	exa	E

skeleton the whole structure that provides a framework and protection for an animal's body and within which organs are protected and muscles are attached. In many invertebrates there is an *exoskeleton* which may have to be shed to allow for growth (*see* ECDYSIS AND MOULTING).

Other invertebrates add to the outer edge of their exoskeleton to allow for growth, e.g. molluscs such as snails. Other animals have an *endoskeleton* which lies inside the body. Vertebrate animals have a skeleton made up of numerous bones and cartilage. In mammals over 200 bones are present, some of which are joined by *ligaments* while others are fused together. Both types of skeleton are flexible due to the presence of joints which allow for the movement of limbs, etc.

the human skeleton

Snails have a shell hardened by calcium (*calcareous*), in arthropods the skeleton is hardened by the presence of a substance called *chitin* and in crabs and lobsters the shell (carapace) is hardened with chitin and calcium salts.

skin an important organ which forms the outer covering of a vertebrate animal. There may be a variety of structures protruding from the surface of the skin (i.e. hair, fur, feathers or scales) depending upon the type of animal. The skin provides a protective layer for the body, helping to cushion it in the event of accidental knocks and preventing drying out. Also, skin helps to maintain the correct body temperature. When the body is hot the many blood *capillaries* in the skin widen allowing more blood to flow through them, and heat is lost to the outside by radiation. Sweat *glands* present in the skin secrete a salty fluid which evaporates from the surface and forms another cooling mechanism. If the body is cold, the capillaries contract to decrease blood flow and conserve heat. The layer of fat in the skin has a warming effect and small muscles attached to hair roots contract to raise the hair. The hairs trap a layer of air which helps to warm the body. Skin is a physical barrier to harmful substances or organisms which might otherwise enter more easily. It contains many receptors sensitive to pain, touch, pressure and temperature and these connect with sensory nerves (*see* NERVOUS SYSTEM) relaying messages to the brain. Hence skin is very important in enabling an animal to live within its environment. The outer layer is dead and is continually being shed and replaced by cells from underneath. In amphibians (frogs, toads, etc.) the skin has to be kept moist and there is some exchange of gases (oxygen in and carbon dioxide out) through the surface.

sleep a period of deep rest shown by many animals during which the metabolic rate (*see* METABOLISM) is lowered, awareness is reduced and the body is relaxed. Most animals sleep but some need more than others. Adult humans require about eight hours sleep each night. Other animals, (e.g. some grazing mammals), need only a few minutes sleep at any one time. Many animals are easily and rapidly awakened from sleep and this is more likely in those which are hunted as prey. There is a change in the electrical activity of the brain of a person entering into sleep and this can be recorded, producing a trace called an *electroencephalogram* (EEG). *Alpha* brainwaves are produced when an adult person is awake and *delta* waves during sleep. At the onset of sleep, low frequency waves of high amplitude are produced (known as *slow wave sleep*). These are interrupted by short periods of high frequency, low amplitude waves, during which time the person may be restless and show rapid eye movements behind closed eyelids. This is known as Rapid Eye Movement (REM) sleep and it is the time when dreaming occurs. A person who wakens during REM sleep remembers dreams but otherwise these are usually forgotten. The part of the brain especially involved in the control of sleep is called the *reticular formation.*

smell a keen sense of smell or *olfaction* is characteristic of many animals. This is achieved by special receptors (*chemoreceptors*) which are able to detect chemicals carried in the air or dissolved in water. They may be grouped together within *olfactory organs* such as the *nose* of vertebrates. The lining or *epithelium* of the *nasal cavity* contains *olfactory cells* which respond to chemical molecules dissolved in the moisture of the surface mucous membranes. These cells are neurones (*see* NERVOUS SYSTEM) which connect with branches of the *olfactory nerve* within a special area of the brain called the *olfactory bulb*. The olfactory nerve transmits the information to the *cerebral cortex* of the *brain* where it is decoded and detected as a particular smell.

sodium is an alkali metal which occurs widely—its principal source being sodium chloride (salt) in sea water and salt deposits. It is obtained by electrolysis of fused sodium chloride, but does not exist in its elemental form because it is highly reactive. When prepared, the metal is sufficiently soft to be cut with a knife and it is a silvery white colour. However, it reacts violently with water and rapidly with oxygen and the halogens. It is essential to life, particularly in the biological mechanism involved in the transmission of nerve impulses.

It forms numerous compounds with diverse uses and is itself used as a heat-transfer fluid in reactors. Compounds and their uses include: hydroxide, numerous uses: benzoate, antiseptic; carbonate, glass, soap and other manufacturing processes; chlorate, herbicide; citrate, medicinal; hypochlorite, bleaches; nitrite, in dyes, and many more.

The other alkali metals are lithium (Li), potassium (K), rubidium (Rb), caesium (Cs) and francium (Fr). Francium is radioactive and caesium is extremely reactive.

sodium hydroxide *see* CAUSTIC SODA.

solar cell is an electric cell that produces electrical energy from light. It is based upon a semiconductor device called a photoelectric cell which creates a small current due to the movement of electrons. Solar cells are ideal for use in spacecraft to power electronic equipment, but to produce an appreciable output cells have to be put into panels. In this way they are used to complement domestic heating systems.

solid a state of matter in which the component atoms, ions or molecules maintain a constant position relative to each other. Some solids are *crystalline* with a regular and repetitive arrangement of atoms while others are totally disordered (amorphous–no shape). When solids are heated, their atoms absorb the energy and vibrate more. Eventually the energy intake is sufficient to break down the structure and it melts to form a liquid. A few solids go directly from solid to gas, they *sublime*, for example solid carbon dioxide.

solution a mixture of two or more components producing a single, homogeneous phase from which there is no settling out. The term usually applies to a solution of a solid in a liquid and often the liquid is water (producing an *aqueous* solution). However, it is possible to have solutions of gases in liquids, gases in solids, liquids in liquids and solids in solids (a solid solution).

The *solute* is the substance that dissolves to make a solution, and the *solvent* is the substance in which the solute dissolves. The solvent is usually a liquid and water is the commonest. *Solubility* is the concentration of a saturated solution, i.e. the maximum amount of one substance dissolved in another.

A *solid solution* is when two or more elements share a common crystalline framework. The composition can vary, although within limits, and two types of solid solution are found. A substitional solid solution is when atoms of one element are replaced by another, e.g. nickel and copper; an interstitial solid solution is when small atoms rest in lattice spaces of the structure, as with carbon in metals. Minerals commonly exhibit solid solutions.

sonar *see* ECHO.

sound the effect upon the ear created by air vibrations with a frequency between 20 Hz (hertz) and 20 kKz (20,000 Hz). More generally, sound waves are caused by vibrations through a medium (whether gas, liquid or solid). One of the commonest sources of sound is a loudspeaker. When it produces sound, the cone vibrates, producing a series of compressions in the air. These are called longitudinal progressive waves, that is the oscillations occur in the same direction that the wave is travelling. The sound waves so produced enter the ear causing pressure changes on the ear drum, causing the brain to register the sound. Most items produce sound when they vibrate or are moved or banged together, but sound can only be transmitted through a medium and it cannot travel through a vacuum.

The speed of sound varies with the material it is travelling through, moving most quickly through solids, then liquids and gases. In air, sound travels at approximately 350 m/s. The speed increases with temperature, but is unaffected by pressure. Frequency of sound waves relates to *pitch*; high frequencies produce a sound of high pitch, e.g. a whistle at 10 kHz, while low pitch is caused by low frequencies, e.g. a bass voice at 100 Hz. Sound intensity is measured in *decibels* (db) and it is a logarithmic scale. Ordinary conversation might register 40–50 decibels, traffic 80 and thunder 100 while jet aircraft can exceed 125 dB.

specific gravity *see* DENSITY.

specific heat or specific heat capacity is the heat required by unit mass to raise its temperature by one degree, that is the gain in thermal energy divided by mass and temperature. The units are joules per kgK. The specific heat capacity varies with the material and metals have a much lower value than, for example, water. This means that much more energy is required to create a 1K (1°C) rise in 1kg of water than in 1kg of copper:

water		4200 joules required per kgK		
ice	2100	"	"	"
aluminium	900	"	"	"
glass	700	"	"	"
copper	400	"	"	

If the specific heat capacity of a substance is known, and its mass, it is possible to work out the thermal energy (heat) required to give a certain temperature rise.

spectroscopy the study of spectra using *spectroscopes* (this includes spectrometers, spectrographs, etc.). Light emitted from a hot object, or given out by a substance upon excitation can be analysed. The light or radiation passes through an analyser or *monochromator* which usually incorporates a prism to split the light into its components. This enables monochromatic light (light of a specific wavelength) to be studied. An alternative is to use a filter which absorbs unwanted frequencies. The light then passes into a detector, and there are numerous types, some employing a photoelectric cell.

Spectrometry is used to study light from the stars and also extensively in chemistry. There are numerous techniques, some of which are listed below:

type of spectrometry	applications
X-ray fluorescence	determination of most elements in e.g. rock sample
atomic absorption	determination of metals, whether in trace or minor amounts
infrared	identification of organic compounds
mass spectrometry	organic compound identification and structural analysis

Others include -spectrometry, ultraviolet, plasma emission and flame photometry.

spore and sporophyte a small reproductive structure, usually consisting of one cell only, which detaches from the parent and is dispersed. If environmental conditions are favourable it grows into a new individual. Spores are commonly produced by fungi and bacteria, but also occur in all groups of green land plants especially *ferns, horsetails* and *mosses.* The sporophyte is the phase in the life cycle of a plant that produces spores. The sporophyte is *diploid* but it produces haploid spores (*see* CELL DIVISION). It may be the dominant stage in the life cycle of a plant (as in the seed plants) or be mainly dependent upon the gametophyte structure for water and nourishment as in mosses (*Bryophyta*). (*See also* GAMETE AND GAMETOPHYTE).

starch is a *polysaccharide* found in all green plants. Polysaccharides are a large group of natural carbohydrates in which the molecules are made from simple sugars (*monosaccharides*) of the form $C_6H_{12}O_6$ (hexoses) or $C_5H_{10}O_5$

(pentoses). Starch is built up from chains of glucose ($C_6H_{12}O_6$) units arranged in two ways, as amylose (long unbranched chains) and amylopectin (long cross-linked chains). Potato and some cereal starches contain 20–30% amylose and 70–80% amylopectin. Amylose contains 200–1000 glucose units while amylopectin numbers about 20. Starch is formed and broken down in plant cells and is stored as granules and it occurs in seeds. It is insoluble in cold water and is obtained from corn, wheat, potatoes, rice and other cereals by various physical processes. It is used as an adhesive for sizing paper and has many uses in the food industry.

static electricity is electricity or electric charges, at rest. The structure of the atom is visualized as having electrons 'orbiting' a central nucleus and this means that in some materials, electrons can be removed by rubbing with a cloth. When, for example, a Perspex rod is rubbed with a woollen cloth, the cloth pulls electrons away from the rod, becoming negatively charged and leaving the rod positively charged. The reverse happens when the cloth is rubbed on a polythene rod, the rod becoming negatively charged. No charge is created, it is just that charges are separated. Charges on materials can be registered using the gold-leaf electroscope and, as with other phenomena involving charges, unlike charges attract while like charges repel (*see also* VAN DER GRAAFF GENERATOR).

statistics is the part of mathematics that deals with the collection, analysis, interpretation and presentation of quantitative data. It involves processing data with a view to predicting future outcomes, based upon the information available. Probability plays an important role in statistics. The figures can be presented in numerous graphical ways but it is important to select relevant features to illustrate a point, i.e. statistics can be very misleading, depending upon how they are presented. Statistics are used extensively by manufacturers, in medical research, insurance and, of course, in politics.

steel is iron that contains up to 1.5% carbon in the form of *cementite* (Fe_3C). The properties of steel vary with iron content and also depend upon the presence of other metals and the production method. *Alloy steels* contain alloying elements while *austenitic steel* is a solid solution of carbon in a form of iron and is normally stable only at high temperatures but can be produced by rapid cooling. *Stainless steel* is a group of chromium/nickel steels which have a high resistance to corrosion and chemical attack. A high proportion of chromium is necessary (12–25%) to provide the resistance and a low carbon content, typically 0.1%. Stainless steel has many uses: cutlery, equipment in chemical plants; ball bearings and many other items of machinery.

stroboscope is an instrument that is used to view rapidly moving objects. By shining a flashing light onto a revolving or vibrating object, the object can be made to appear stationary providing the frequency of the flashes of light match the revolutions or vibrations of the object in question. This technique is used in engineering to examine, for example, the blades of a propeller, or an engine part. It is also used to set the ignition timing in a car engine.

sulphur is a yellow, non-metallic element that exhibits *allotropy*, i.e. exhibits several physical forms. It is widely distributed in both the free state and in compounds (*see* SULPHUR COMPOUNDS), forming sulphates, sulphides and oxides, amongst others. It is manufactured by heating pyrite or purification of the naturally-occurring material. The primary use of sulphur is in the manufacture of sulphuric acid (H_2SO_4), but it is also used in the preparation of matches, dyes, fireworks, fertilizers, fungicides and the photographic industry.

sulphur compounds are very common, and include sulphates such as gypsum ($CaSO_4.2H_2O$) and anhydrite ($CaSO_4$). Metal sulphides often form minerals e.g. FeS_2 iron pyrite (also chalcopyrite, $CuFeS_2$) from which the elements can be separated. Sulphur forms several oxides including sulphur dioxide (SO_2), one of the primary gases causing acid rain. Sulphuric acid is the commonest product of sulphur and is a very strong and corrosive acid that is used very widely in the manufacture of dyestuffs, explosives and many other products.

superconductor is a material which shows practically no resistance to electric current when maintained at temperatures approaching absolute zero (which is -273°C). Each material has a critical temperature above which its behaviour is normal, resistance decreasing with falling temperature. At the critical temperature, the resistance disappears almost to nothing. If a current is induced in superconducting material by a changing magnetic field, then the current will continue to flow long after its source has been removed. Metals such as aluminium, lead, and tin become superconducting as do some ceramics, and the phenomenon has been applied to electromagnets because large currents can flow without the supply of large amounts of energy.

Other potential uses of superconductors include larger and faster computers, and the transmission of electricity without heat loss.

surface tension is the 'tension' created by forces of attraction between molecules in a liquid resulting in an apparent elastic membrane over the surface of the liquid. This attraction between molecules of the same substance is called *cohesion* and the result is that it tries to pull liquids into the smallest possible shapes. This can plainly be seen in water which forms round droplets and also supports the feet of insects on ponds and puddles. The same phenomenon is demonstrated by a needle on a piece of blotting paper which is then placed gently on water. When the paper absorbs sufficient water to sink, the needle remains afloat, because of the surface tension of the water. Droplets of mercury show the same effect, forming compact globules on a surface.

Adhesion is when molecules of two different substances are attracted to each other, as shown by water wetting glass. This attraction is also responsible for the *meniscus* formed where water meets glass. The meniscus is the upward-curving surface of the water upon meeting the glass. Mercury forms a meniscus curving down because its cohesion is greater than its adhesion with glass (*see also* CAPILLARY ACTION).

suspension is a two-phase system with denser particles distributed in a less dense liquid or gas. Settling of the particles is prevented or slowed down by the viscosity of the fluid or impacts between the particles and the molecules of the fluid. Fog is a suspension of liquid particles and smoke a suspension of solid particles.

symbiosis describes various relationships between organisms, usually two different species, which co-exist to the benefit of at least one of the parties involved. In *mutualism* both parties benefit and neither is harmed. In *commensalism* one party benefits and the other is unharmed but in *parasitism*, one organism thrives at the expense of the other (*see also* PARASITE).

symbols in chemistry are used to represent elements, atoms, molecules, etc. Each element has its own symbol of one or two letters (*see* PERIODIC TABLE), thus fluorine is F, and chlorine is Cl. Symbols are used further in formulae, i.e. the shorthand representation of a compound, for example NaCl is sodium chloride. The formulae can then be used in equations to represent chemical reactions and processes, e.g.

$$-NaOH + HCl \ \text{Æ} \ NaCl + H_2O$$

This formulae states that caustic soda and hydrochloric acid, when combined, will react to form sodium chloride and water.

Symbols are used elsewhere, particularly in the sciences, to provide a convenient shorthand, e.g. prefixes in decimal numbers (*see* SI UNITS), concepts in physics such as *m* for mass and *I* for electric current and in mathematics where a letter or figure represents a word or sentence.

symmetry is the property of a geometrical figure whose points have corresponding points reflected in a given line (axis of symmetry), point (centre of symmetry) or plane. Symmetry is closely related to balance in nature and many forms exhibit bilateral symmetry, humans included. Symmetry is very evident in crystals that have grown in ideal conditions because then the crystals faces are apparent and most crystals exhibit several symmetrical features (*see also* CRYSTALLOGRAPHY).

synthetic fibres are used widely in producing cloth and for reinforcements in composite materials. They are manufactured from polymers or modified natural materials and the first synthetic fibres, e.g. *rayon*, were made from cellulose. Rayon is produced from wood fibre treated with alkali and carbon disulphide and it is then extruded into a bath of sulphuric acid to harden the fibres. Completely synthetic fibres include: *nylons* which are polyamides, and are used in textiles, insulation and cables; *polyesters*, used in textiles and film and also for reinforcement in boats etc; *acrylics* and *glass fibres* which are incorporated in resins to increase strength.

There are inorganic fibres such as alumina (Al_2O_3) and glass wool many of which are used in insulation and packing. Asbestos was used for the production of fire resistant textiles but it is being replaced because it is hazardous to health.

tannin *see* CAFFEINE AND TANNIN.

taste and taste bud *taste* is one of the senses and is enhanced by that of smell. Hence if a person has a cold, he or she is not able to taste things properly.

The organs of taste are called *taste buds* and are situated on the tongue and sides of the mouth. They consist of groups of cells which are able to detect four different tastes—salt, sweet, bitter and sour. All the flavours which we detect are combinations of these in different proportions and the taste buds for each are grouped together in various parts of the tongue. Substances can only be tasted if they start to dissolve in the saliva

of the mouth, hence certain hard materials have no taste at all.
teeth are hard structures used by animals for biting and chewing
food and also for attacking, grooming and other activities such as
behavioural displays. In the more advanced vertebrate animals
the teeth are collected in the *jaws* but fish and amphibians (frogs
and toads) have teeth all over the *palate* (roof of the mouth).
Teeth evolved from the scales of cartilaginous fish and are adapted
according to the lifestyle of the animal. In mammals a tooth consists of a central *pulp cavity* supplied with nerves and blood vessels,
surrounded by a layer of *dentine* and an outer thickness of
enamel. Enamel is extremely hard to resist wear and decay. The
root of the tooth is embedded in a socket in the jaw bone. Four
different types of teeth are present—molar, premolar, canine and
incisor—but the numbers and arrangement differ between animals. This is known as *dentition*. Also, *jaw of carnivore*—
carnivores have well-developed canine teeth for biting and the last
premolars (upper jaw) and first molars (lower jaw) have cusps
with sharp, cutting edges for shearing through flesh. These are
called *carnassial teeth*.

Jaw of herbivore–herbivores have large, ridged premolars and
molars for grinding vegetation and incisors for cutting through
stems.

Rodent jaw–in rodents the upper and lower jaws contain a single pair of long incisors which grow continuously throughout the
animal's life. These are adapted for gnawing and there is an absence of enamel on the back which means that they wear to a
chisel-like cutting edge.

the molar tooth

enamel

gum

root

telegraph an early device for transmitting messages first developed in the late 1700s. By the mid 19th century the technique had

been refined so that information was sent along a wire as electrical pulses. Morse introduced his code in which each letter of the alphabet was represented by a different set of pulses. Telegraph messages were also used to control train movements and eventually the Post Office formed a network. The telegraph gradually faded into history when it became possible to use the telephone on an international basis.

telephone is an instrument that enables speech to be transmitted by means of electric currents or radio waves. It was invented by Alexander Graham Bell in 1876 and a public service was begun three years later after Bell brought his invention to the UK. The modern telephone consists of a mouthpiece containing a thin diaphragm of aluminium which moves with the sound of speech. This movement presses carbon granules which produces a surge of current and in the earpiece of the receiving set, these surges are changed back into sound. An electromagnet reacts to the current charges and vibrates a diaphragm, thus reproducing the voice of the speaker.

Advances in technology have improved the transmission of telephone calls and satellites are used for international calls and recently optical fibres have been introduced as a new medium of transmission.

television is the transmission of moving image by electrical means and the television set is essentially a complex cathode ray tube. The tube consists of an electron gun and a screen that fluoresces and the beam of electrons is deflected by magnetic coils. On a black and white screen, the picture is composed of lines as the spot moves across the screen and the spot is also moved down the screen, although at a slower rate. The result is that 25 images per second are shown on the screen, which to the human eye appears to be a moving picture.

Producing colour pictures is much more complex. There are three electron guns for red, green and blue and the screen is coated with thousands of tiny strips of the same colours which, when struck by electrons, glow in combination to produce a colour picture. Accurate targetting of the strips is achieved by a *shadow mask* through which the electron beams are fired.

The pictures and sounds are converted by cameras and microphones into electrical signals which are sent to transmitting aerials. Receiving aerials then pick up the signal, pass them to the television set where they form pictures and sound.

temperature is a measure of an object's overall kinetic energy.

When an object is cold, its molecules, atoms or ions have less kinetic energy–its temperature is lower. Although molecules do not stop moving altogether, at–273°C they possess the minimum possible energy. This is *absolute zero* and this temperature cannot be exceeded. The temperature scale which has -273°C (actually -273.15°C) as its zero is called the *Kelvin* scale. The degrees are the same size as centigrade degrees, but the temperatures are stated as figures without the degree. In addition to the centigrade (or *Celsius*) scale which has water freezing at 0° and boiling at 100°, there is the *Fahrenheit* scale where the respective temperatures are 32°F and 212°F. Fahrenheit can be converted to Celsius using the equation:

$$F = 1.8C + 32 \quad \text{and the reverse is} \quad C = \frac{5(F - 32)}{9}$$

tempering is the process whereby (usually) steel is heated to a particular temperature and then cooled quickly in oil or water. The heating permits stresses in the metal to be relieved and results in a toughened, less brittle material.

tensile strength of a material is the force that is required to stretch it until it breaks. It is measured using a special machine upon which the 'breaking' force can be read from a dial. Since tensile strength is the force per unit area, the breaking force is divided by the material's cross-sectional area. The units are newtons per square metre.

thermocouple is a device for measuring temperatures and consists of two different types of metallic wire joined at both ends. The temperature is measured at one join and the other join is kept at a fixed temperature. A temperature difference between the two joins causes the metals to produce a small electric current which can be metered. Thermocouples are used in furnaces because they have a range up to about 1600_C. The two metals used are often copper and *constantan*, the latter being a copper/nickel alloy which has a constant resistance irrespective of the temperature.

thermodynamics is the study of laws affecting processes that involve heat changes and energy transfer. Heat transfer from one body to another, the link between heat and work and changes of state in a fluid all come within the field of thermodynamics, it is the prerequisite to analysis of work by machinery. There are essentially three *laws of thermodynamics*. The first law says that heat is a form of energy and is conserved and any work energy produced in a closed system must arise from the conversion of existing energy, i.e. energy cannot be created or destroyed. The second law states that the entropy of any closed system cannot decrease and if the system undergoes a reversible process it remains constant, otherwise it increases. The result of this is that heat always flows from a hot body to a cooler one. The third law states that absolute zero (*see* TEMPERATURE) can never be attained.

thermometer an instrument used to measure temperature. The basis of a thermometer is a property of a substance that varies reliably with temperature, e.g. expansion. Thermometers that utilise a liquid in glass are based upon the property that liquids expand slightly when they are heated. Both mercury and alcohol are used and when the bulb at the base of the thermometer's stem is heated, the liquid expands up the stem to create a reading. More sensitivity is gained by using a narrower tube. This is the case with *clinical thermometers* where the scale covers just a few degrees on either side of the normal body temperature of 37°C.

In industry, thermocouples are used for temperature measurement in furnaces and other instruments that provide an electrical measurement are used in preference to liquid in glass thermometers which have a limited range. *Resistance thermometers* are based on the property that the electrical resistance of a conductor normally increases with heat and so it becomes more difficult to pass an electric current. A spiral of platinum wires is used in this case. A *thermistor thermometer* works on the same principle, but consists of a semiconductor in which the resistance decreases with a temperature increase, e.g. 100,000 ohms at 20°C and just 10 ohms at 100°C.

thermostat *see* BIMETAL STRIP.

tissue *see* ORGAN.

titanium is a malleable and ductile silvery-white metal that melts at 1660°C. It occurs as the minerals rutile (TiO_2) and ilmenite ($FeTiO_3$) and is obtained by reducing titanium chloride ($TiCl_4$) with magnesium. It is characterized by its lightness, strength and high resistance to corrosion and is used in alloy form (with aluminium, manganese, chromium and iron) in the aircraft industry. It is also used in missile manufacture, engines and chemical plant.

Titanium compounds have many important uses. Titanium carbide (TiC) is very resistant to chemical attack and is used in tool tips. Titanium dioxide (TiO_2) is used as a white pigment in the production of paints and printing inks and as a filler in paper, rubber, fabrics and plastics.

touch the sense of touch is made possible by specialized sets of receptors which are located in the skin and also in muscles and other internal areas of an animal's body. Touch has different elements including pressure, pain and temperature. The receptor cells which detect pain and pressure tend to be concentrated in certain areas (e.g. fingertips) and distributed less thickly elsewhere. Sensory receptor cells are associated with the hairs covering an animal's body so that the slightest movement of air can be detected. The sense organs involved in touch are specially adapted to respond to a particular sensation. Different nerve pathways are used to transmit the information to the brain where it is decoded and detected.

trace elements is a term used both in biology and geology. In biology it refers to an element that an organism requires in very small quantities. These elements may be necessary for the formation or action of vitamins, enzymes and hormones.

In geology, trace elements occur in small quantities in rocks but can be detected by geochemical analysis. Most elements except the few commonly occurring ones are present as trace elements, if at all, and in quantities of 1% or less. Often the concentrations are just a few parts per million.

transformer is a device for changing the voltage of an alternating current. It is based upon the principle of mutual induction whereby an alternating current passing through a coil (the primary) on a soft iron core induces current flow in another (secondary) coil on the core. The primary and secondary coils form a transformer. Transformers can be made to step-up or step-down a voltage by varying the number of turns in the coils. For example, if the primary coil has ten times the number of turns compared to the secondary, then the voltage in the secondary is one tenth that of the supply, and the associated current increases tenfold.

Transformers have many uses but practical versions are not 100% efficient and some energy is lost as heat. Huge transformers are used in the mains power supply between the power station and the domestic supply. Current generated at a power station goes through a step-up transformer, creating voltages of up to 400,000 volts, at much reduced currents (thus minimizing heat loss) for transmission through the power lines of the grid. Power from the *grid* then goes to substations where transformers step the voltage down by a series of transformers to 132,000 volts, then 33,000v (for heavy industry), then 11,000v for light industry and finally 240v for offices and homes.

transistor is a semiconductor that can be used for three functions: as a switch, a rectifier and as an amplifier. A transistor consists essentially of a semi-conductor chip of silicon which is doped (*see* DIODE *and* SEMICONDUCTOR) to form two p-n junction diodes back to back (p-type diode is silicon doped with boron; n-type is doped with phosphorus). Current cannot flow through a transistor unless a small current is applied to the p-type region of the semiconductor called the *base* circuit, but when this current is applied an enlarged current flows in the output or *collector* circuit. A transistor can be used to amplify current changes and practical amplifiers contain several transistors, as used in radio, to increase currents to output a signal through the loudspeaker.

Because a current must flow in the base circuit to allow current to flow in the collector circuit, a transistor can be used as a switch and is turned on and off by a change in the base current.

trigonometry is the branch of mathematics that involves the study of right-angled triangles including problem-solving involving the calculation of unknown sides and angles from known values. It involves the use of the *trigonometrical ratios*, sine, cosine and tangent. In the right-angled triangle below the ratios are:

$$\sin \theta = \frac{\text{opposite}}{\text{hypothenuse}} = \frac{yz}{xy}$$

$$\tan \theta = \frac{\text{opposite}}{\text{adjacent}} = \frac{yz}{xz}$$

$$\cos \theta = \frac{\text{adjacent}}{\text{hypotenuse}} = \frac{xz}{xy}$$

Trigonometry is used in surveying and navigation.

ultrasound (or ultrasonic waves) is sound with a frequency beyond the range of human hearing, i.e. around 20,000 Hz. Ultrasound is used extensively in industry and medicine. It is used to detect faults and cracks in metals and to test pipes; it can clean surfaces due to the rapid, small vibrations; in ultrasonic welding, soldering and machining; and in medicine ultrasound is used to scan a growing foetus and also to destroy kidney stones or gall stones. A recent development is the use of ultrasound in chemical processes, to initiate reactions in the production of food, plastics and antibiotics. Ultrasound can make chemical processes safer and cheaper as it eliminates the need for high operating temperatures and expensive catalysts.

vaccination *see* IMMUNE SYSTEM.

vacuum is defined as a space in which there is no matter. In practice a perfect vacuum cannot be achieved although interstellar space comes very close indeed. Also, special equipment in the laboratory can reach very low pressures, but in general vacuum is taken to be air or gas at very low pressure, 10^{-4} mm Hg or lower.

The *vacuum flask* uses a vacuum to help keep liquids or gases cold or hot. It was invented by the Scot, James Dewar at the end of the 19th century and it consists of a double-walled glass bottle. A vacuum is created between the glass walls, and the surfaces are silvered so that together, transfer of heat by convection and radiation is reduced to a minimum.

valency is the bonding potential or combining power of an atom or group, measured by the number of hydrogen ions (H^+, or equivalent) that the atom could combine with or replace. In an ionic compound, the charge on each ion represents the valency e.g. in NaCl, both Na^+ and Cl^- have a valency of one. In covalent compounds (*see* BONDS), the valency is represented by the number of bonds formed. In carbon dioxide, CO_2, carbon has a valency of 4 and oxygen 2. The *valency electrons* of an atom are those in the outermost shell that are involved in forming bonds and are shared, lost or gained when a compound or ion is formed, i.e. they determine the chemical reactivity.

The *electronic theory of valency* explains bonds through the assumption that specific arrangements of outer electrons in atoms (outer shells of eight electrons) confers stability (as with the inert gases, which have such a structure) through the transfer or sharing of electrons. Thus with the combination of sodium with chlorine, sodium has one electron in the outer shell, which it loses (to form the Neon stable structure) to chlorine, giving it also a stable structure, in this case, that of Argon.

Van der Graaff generator is a machine that provides a continuous supply of electrostatic charge (*see* STATIC ELECTRICITY) and which can build up a very high voltage. It consists essentially of a hollow metal sphere supported on an insulating tube. A motor-driven belt of rubber or silk carries charge (positive or negative) from the driving roller up the moving belt to the sphere, where the charge collects. Very high voltages (up to 13 million volts) can be produced and in conjunction with high voltage X-ray tubes and other equipment, these voltages are used in research to split atoms. The apparatus was named after the American physicist R.J. Van der Graaff.

velocity is the rate of change of an object's position, i.e. the speed at which an object travels. Velocity provides both the magnitude (size) and direction of travel (per unit time) and and such is called a *vector quantity*. The units are metres per second (ms^{-1} or m/s). On plotting a graph of distance moved, against time, a straight line would represent an object moving at constant velocity. However, it is usually the case that velocity changes with time, in which case an object is said to be accelerating (or decelerating). *Acceleration* is the gain in velocity of an object divided by the time taken to achieve the gain and the units are metres per second, per second. As with velocity, it is a vector quantity. Graphical plots of velocity against time are useful because the gradient of the line plotted is equal numerically to the acceleration and the area under the graph represents the distance moved.

The *terminal velocity* of an object falling through air, for example, is the constant velocity reached when the object's weight is matched by the air resistance.

vertebrate any animal with a backbone including fish, amphibians, reptiles, birds and mammals.

virus the smallest kind of micro-organism which is completely parasitic (*see* PARASITE) and exists and reproduces within the cells of a host organism. Most, but not all viruses cause diseases in plants, animals and even bacterial cells. Viruses operate by invading and taking over the metabolism of the cells which they inhabit and using the metabolic processes to reproduce. Diseases caused by viruses include influenza, herpes, AIDS, mumps, chicken pox and polio, and possibly some cancers.

viscosity is a property of fluids that indicates their resistance to flow. Oil is more viscous than water and an object will take much longer when falling through oil than when it falls through water. All fluids show this resistance to shear forces but a perfect fluid would be non-viscous. Viscosity measurements can be used to find the molecular weight of polymers.

vitamins a group of organic substances that are required in very small amounts in the human diet to maintain good health. A lack of a particular vitamin results in a *deficiency* disease. There are two groups of vitamins; those which are fat-soluble including A,D, E and K and those which are water-soluble, C (ascorbic acid) and B (Thiamine).

The six vitamin groups are as follows;

A or *Retinol*
Source; green vegetables, dairy produce, liver, fish oils
Needed for; the manufacture of rhodopsin–a pigment needed by the rod cells of the eye for night vision. Also for the maintenance of the skin and tissues
Deficiency; night blindness and possible total blindness

B complex including Thiamine, Riboflavin, Nicotinic acid, Pantothenic acid, Biotin, Folic acid, B_6, Pyroxidine, B_{12} (cyanocobalamin), Lipoic acid
Source; green vegetables, dairy produce, cereal, grains, eggs, liver, meat, nuts, potatoes, fish
Needed for; the manufacture of red blood cells, for enzyme activity and for amino acid production. Also for maintaining the fatty sheath (myelin) around nerves
Deficiency; Beri beri (B_1 deficiency) anaemia and deterioration of the nervous system (B_{12} deficiency)

C (ascorbic acid)
Source; citrus fruit, green vegetables.
Needed for; maintaining cell walls and connective tissue. Aiding the absorption of iron by the body
Deficiency; scurvy–affects skin, blood vessels and tendons

D
Source; fish oils, eggs, dairy produce
Needed for; controls calcium levels required for bone growth and repair
Deficiency; Rickets in children–deformation of the bones. Osteomalacia in adults–softening of bones

E
Source; cereal grains, eggs, green vegetables
Needed for; maintenance of cell membranes
Deficiency; unusual as common in the diet

K

Source; leafy green vegetables, especially spinach, liver
Needed for; clotting of blood
Deficiency; rare as it is also manufactured by bacteria in the gut

volt (V) i the SI unit of potential difference. It is defined formally as the difference of potential between two points on a conducting wire that is carrying a current of one ampere when the power given out between these points is one watt. The voltage across battery terminals is a measure of the potential energy given to each coulomb of charge and a potential difference of one volt exists if each coulomb has one joule of potential energy, so there is a potential difference of 6 volts if each coulomb is given 6 joules of potential energy.

water is the normal oxide of hydrogen, H_2O, and is found in one form or another in most places on Earth. It can occur in solid, liquid or gas phases, forms a large part of the Earth's surface, and is vital to life. Natural water is never absolutely pure, but contains dissolved salts, organic material, etc. Pure water freezes at 0°C and boils at 100°C and has its maximum density of 1gm/cm³ at 4°C. It occurs in all living organisms and has a remarkable combination of properties in its solvent capacity (i.e. its ability to dissolve so many substances), chemical stability, thermal properties and abundance. Water has an almost unlimited range of uses and can provide power through hydroelectric schemes.

watt *see* POWER.

wave is a periodic displacement that repeats itself and a mechanism of transferring energy through a medium. In the simple waveform shown the *amplitude* is the maximum distance moved by a point from its rest position as the wave passes. The *wavelength* is the length of one complete wave.

a waveform

wavelength

amplitude

The origin of a wave is vibrating particles which store and release energy while their average position remains constant, as it is only the wave that travels. Waves are either *longitudinal* with oscillations occurring in the direction of wave travel (e.g. sound), or *transverse* because the oscillations are from side to side, at 90° to the direction of travel (e.g. light).

The *wave equation* relates frequency (f) and wavelength (λ):

$$c - f l \quad \text{where c is the speed of the wave}$$

All forms of wave show the properties of reflection, refraction, interference and diffraction. Electromagnetic waves have these properties but have one additional feature in that they can travel through a vacuum.

weight is the gravitational force of attraction exerted on an object by the Earth and although such an attraction exists between all objects, it is so infinitesimally small as to be non-existent and the Earth is so massive that its attraction dominates. Weight is a force, measured in newtons (N), and is the force that makes an object accelerate downwards when falling to the Earth's surface. The weight of an object is therefore dependent upon its distance from the Earth, and the further away it is, the smaller the pull of the Earth and the less is the object's weight.

Mass is a measure of the quantity of matter that a substance possesses and it remains constant, but the weight of an object varies. A constant mass will therefore have different weights depending upon the gravitational effect of nearby bodies. The weight of a constant mass on Earth will be approximately six times greater than its weight on the Moon and in space the weight of that same mass would be zero. Because weight on Earth is directly proportional to mass; any instrument that measures one property also measures the other.

work is done when something is moved by a force. It is also a transfer of energy, i.e. energy is changed into a different form when work is done. Work is measured in the unit of energy, the joule and is calculated as the force, multiplied by the distance moved in the direction of the force. One joule of work is done when a force of one newton is moved through one metre, *in the direction of the force.*

X-rays are electromagnetic waves with a short wavelength (approximately 10^{-10}–10^{-8}m) and are produced when electrons moving at high speed strike a target, are stopped very quickly and X-rays are emitted. They were discovered in 1895 by Röntgen. He found that wrapped photographic plates left near a working cathode ray tube became fogged as if they had been exposed to light and he called this unknown radiation X-rays. In fact X-rays were being emitted as electrons hit the anode and walls of the cathode ray tube.

Atoms of all elements give out characteristic X-rays when hit by electrons. The stream of electrons colliding with the atom displaces electrons from inner orbitals and vacant places are then filled by electrons from the outer orbital, which give out energy as they move down. X-rays have the properties of electromagnetic radiation and also penetrate solid matter, cause ionization (by removal of electrons from atoms), make some materials fluoresce and, as mentioned, they affect photographic film. These properties render X-rays both useful and hazardous. Their ionization effect damages living tissue, but by using very small doses, they can be used in medicine to take X-ray photographs of the body. The extent to which the rays are absorbed depends upon the density and the atomic weight (or relative atomic mass, *see* ATOMIC NUMBER) of the material; the lower these factors, the more easily will the rays penetrate. The greater density of bone means it is possible to take an X-ray photograph because the flesh appears transparent while the bones are opaque.

X-rays are also used in industry for checking joints in metal and examining flaws. They are also used in *X-ray diffraction* (or X-ray crystallography) which is an analytical tool in geology, crystallography, and biophysics. X-rays directed at the sample are diffracted off the planes of atoms in the crystal. By repeating the procedure and then calculating the spacing between atomic planes, a representation of the crystal's structure can be determined. In this way the structure of some proteins and nucleic acids has been analysed.

yeast *see* FERMENTATION.

zoology the scientific study of animals.

zygote *see* REPRODUCTION.

TRANSPORT

The development of transport has enabled man to move out of his own environment and is now essential to the maintenance of modern life. This section provides definitions for a wide variety transport devices from early animal-powered vehicles through to highly sophisticated machines capable of space travel. The entries are in A to Z order with cross-references given in SMALL CAPITALS.

*

aeroplanes throughout human history there have always been people fascinated by the thought of being able to fly and several attempts are recorded, all of which were unsuccessful. These early efforts were made by constructing models of birds wings and attempting flapping flight, but it proved impossible for the weight of a person to become airborne in this way. Successful flights were first made by means of a HOT AIR BALLOON in 1783, and it was not until the early part of this century that flying by means of aeroplanes became possible. The first flight in a pow-ered 'aircraft' was made by Orville Wright at Kitty Hawk, North Carolina, USA in 1903. In 1908 he made a flight in an aircraft which lasted for one hour to be followed by a 100 mile flight by Farman in 1909. Modern aeroplanes have powerful JET ENGINES on the wings. These burn fuel (kerosene) carried in large tanks within the wings themselves. Aeroplanes have specially de-signed wings, with differences in air flow above and below them, which create an upward force called *lift* when the machine is be-ing driven forwards. Hence the fast forward motion caused by the jet engines creates enough lift to keep the heavy aeroplane in the sky.

a jumbo jet

There are many different types and sizes of modern aeroplane. Examples include the *Jumbo Jet* and the *Boeing 747*. This is one of the largest types of aeroplane and it is able to carry over 500 people as well as heavy loads of cargo. It travels at speeds of over 900 km per hour and is an extremely popular commercial aircraft, especially on long distance flights.

Supersonic aeroplanes. Supersonic means faster than the speed of sound, and a flight of this kind was first achieved in 1947 in the USA. Today the passenger aeroplane *Concorde* is able to fly at supersonic speed and completes a journey between

London and New York in three hours. It has a distinctive pointed profile at the front and triangular shaped wings and is perhaps more reminiscent of a bird than other types of aircraft.

Military fighter jet aircraft also fly at supersonic speeds. The pilots of these aircraft need to perfect low-flying skills following the contours of the land beneath.

a fighter jet

Vertical take-off aircraft is a type of military aircraft carried on a special ship called an *aircraft carrier*. It is designed for vertical take-off and landing on a small area of the deck of a ship and does not require a runway. The *SR-71A Blackbird* is a highly advanced military aircraft which flies very high and at great speed, about 3500 km/hour.

Airship is a type of cigar-shaped hot air balloon which has engines and propellers and passenger compartments. In the earlier years of the twentieth century, airships were quite frequently used to carry passengers and during the First World War they were used on bombing missions. They were filled with hydrogen gas which made the craft airborne because it is much lighter than air. A famous German airship, the *Graf Zeppelin*, made a round-the-world flight in 1929. However, the popularity of airships declined sharply due to a series of horrifying accidents in the 1920s and 1930s. Several airships caught fire when the gas ignited and many lives were lost, most notably the loss of the *Hindenburg* in 1937. It seems incredible that in spite of the risk of fire, passenger cabins on these airships had a smoking area!

In modern airships helium gas is used because it is not flammable. Small ones which do not carry passengers (called *blimps*) are sometimes seen tethered and are used for advertising purposes.
animals throughout human history people have used animals for transport, either for riding or for pulling carts, carriages and sleighs, or both. The horse is one of the most familiar animals used for transport, but also various kinds of cattle (oxen and water buffaloes) are commonly used throughout the world. In desert

areas people have always used camels as a means of transport and in polar regions, teams of husky dogs pulling a sledge have proved to be invaluable.

a horse-drawn tram

bicycle the bicycle has been a popular form of transport since the 1800s, and is a two-wheeled vehicle with pedals turned by the rider. Hence the speed at which it travels depends upon the muscular power of its rider, although on modern racing bikes, with their light frames and numerous gears, great speeds can be obtained. The earliest form of bicycle, called a *dandy horse*, was invented in the 1700s. It consisted of two wheels joined by a pole with a seat. The rider sat astride and pushed himself along the ground with his feet. This was followed by the *boneshaker*, the first bicycle with pedals which appeared in 1865. It gained its name because it had no springs and so provided its rider with a rather bumpy ride. One of the most well-known bicycles dating from Victorian times, was called the *penny farthing*. It had a huge front wheel (the *penny*) and a tiny rear wheel (the *farthing*), and a built-in step was incorporated onto the frame to enable the rider to get on and off. Bicycles with air-filled tyres and a rear wheel driven by the pedals and a chain made their appearance in the 1880s. Although bicycle styles have changed considerably over the intervening years, the basic design has remained the same.

The penny-farthing

boats smaller floating craft are usually described as boats whereas larger vessels are normally called *ships*. People have made use of boats for transport for many thousands of years, using great skill to construct their craft often from wood and animal skins. One such early boat was the *coracle*, which had a circular shape and was constructed of wickerwork covered with water-proof skins. A paddle was used to drive it along and it was used in Wales and Ireland.

Another type of boat powered by means of paddles is the *canoe* which has been traditionally used by tribal peoples throughout many parts of the world. An example is the *kayak* used by Es-kimo people and constructed from wood and sealskins.

canoe

Other early boats were powered by the wind catching an elabo-rate system of sails. Some of these were large and carried people and cargo over long distances enabling different parts of the world to be explored and colonized.

an early sailing boat

Modern sailing boats vary greatly in size from large yachts to very much smaller craft. Often two sails are present, the *jib* and the *mainsail*. The sail is triangular in shape with a curved leading edge designed to catch the wind. A *catamaran* is a very light sail-ing boat designed for going fast. It has twin hulls, the two halves of which run parallel with one another and it skims rapidly across the surface of the water.

a catamaran

a yacht

Another kind of boat, formerly much in use for the transport of freight along the canals and waterways of Britain, was the *barge*. This was a long, narrow flat-bottomed boat which was drawn by a horse walking along the tow path beside the water.

Modern small boats often have an outboard motor and a tiller and rudder for steerage. There are many different styles and sizes, some are used for fishing and others for leisure activities.

cars modern cars are constructed from thousands of components assembled on a factory production line. The car is powered by an INTERNAL COMBUSTION ENGINE which uses petrol or diesel as fuel. Racing cars, e.g. *Formula One* vehicles used in Grand Prix races are designed exclusively for speed. They are low, streamlined and lightweight and can achieve speeds in excess of 290 km per hour. The fastest car in the world is called *Thrust 2* and it has reached a speed of 1000 km per hour. Four-wheel drive cars, such as jeeps and Land Rovers, have power going to all four wheel instead of just two. This gives them better road-holding ability which is invaluable when driving over rough ground or in ice and snow.

a vintage car

a modern saloon car

carts and carriages two and four wheel carts and carriages pulled by horses or oxen have long been used as a means of transport. In Britain during earlier centuries, they were mainly used for essential work on farms; people did not travel much and when they did it was on foot or on horseback. However, by the 1700s and 1800s travel was more commonplace and a number of different styles of carriages and coaches were devised.

electric cars powered by batteries provide a useful means of transport in restricted areas such as crowded towns and cities. They are attractive because, unlike petrol and diesel engine vehicles, they are non-polluting. However, their use is restricted because their batteries soon become flat and need to be recharged. Small electric vehicles provide an invaluable means of transport and mobility for many disabled people.

helicopters were invented in the 1930s and, unlike other aircraft which have fixed wings, they have moving rotor blades which rotate very rapidly to provide *lift*. These blades can be tilted forwards to provide forward flight and to either the left or right for movement sideways. If the helicopter is to fly backwards, the blades are tilted back and rotate in the opposite direction. If they are kept at a straight angle in the horizontal plane, the helicopter lifts vertically upwards. At the tail end of the aircraft, a smaller rotor blade prevents spinning and aids turning. Some helicopters have rotor blades at either end such as the American *Boeing Vertol 107-11*. Helicopters are very versatile due to their landing and take-off capabilities and ability to hover, which means that they can be used in situations in which it would be impossible to use aeroplanes. They have many military uses in the transport of people and freight, are used in search and rescue operations, often in dangerous conditions such as over rough seas or in icy mountains, in crop spraying and control of forest fires and to bring rapid emergency medical aid to the scene of accidents.

a helicopter

hot air balloons were first launched successfully in the 1700s, the Montgolfier brothers achieving manned flight in 1783. Their balloon was a huge open-ended bag underneath which a fire burned to keep it filled with hot air. In order to cut down the serious risk of fire, the balloon had to be continuously drenched with water. However, that same year, a balloon filled with hydrogen gas was successfully launched and during the 1800s manned balloons were used for military reconnaissance operations.

Modern balloons are made of synthetic, light fabrics which are very strong, and are made to rise by bursts of flame from gas burners which heat up the air inside. Ballooning is a popular sport and balloons are also used to record and study weather conditions. Some balloons are filled with helium or hydrogen gas.

hovercraft and **hydrofoil** a hovercraft is a type of boat that skims across the top of the water on a cushion of air trapped inside a rubber skirt. Ideas for building hovercraft were first devised in the 1870s but the practical problems proved to be too great. The main problem was how to prevent the air from escaping and this was solved by Christopher Cockerell, a British engineer, in 1955. The first successful hovercraft, the SRNI, was built incorporating his idea of trapping blown air inside a rubber curtain, in 1958. Later models were built with a flexible rubber skirt all the way round the hull to trap the cushion of air, and this type of craft is still in use today. Large air propellers powered by gas turbine engines drive the boat across the water. These same engines power a fan which draws in surrounding air and drives it beneath the hull and the rubber skirt to form the air cushion. Most of the engine power is needed to maintain the air cushion, and relatively little to actually move the craft. The SRN4 Mark 3 carries over 60 cars and 400 passengers and can reach a speed of at least 60 knots.

a hovercraft

A **hydrofoil** is a type of boat with underwater 'wings' which lift the craft out of the water as it gains speed. The boat skims along on the surface resting on its wings and with most of its hull clear of the water.

internal combustion engine as the name suggests, fuel is burnt inside an internal combustion engine and the most usual type of fuel is petrol, diesel or gas (in a GAS TURBINE). The earliest internal combustion engines were invented in the 1860s using gas. Gas turbine (jet) engines were devised for some aircraft during Word War II and are now used in many naval ships, aircraft, speedboats and tanks. A petrol engine was devised by Gottlieb Daimler in 1885 and a diesel engine in 1897, by Rudolf Diesel, a German engineer.

The principle involved in all three types of engine is that fuel is burned to produce hot air which is put to work to produce movement. A typical petrol engine consists of a cylinder into which a mixture of fuel and air is drawn by a *piston* (the induction stroke). Then the piston compresses the fuel/air mixture inside the *cylinder*. It is ignited by a spark from a spark plug connected to the cylinder producing a small explosion and hot gases (the *power stroke*). Lastly the piston rises again and waste exhaust gases are forced out of the cylinder (the *exhaust stroke*). The whole process is continally repeated and this type of engine is known as a *four-stroke engine*. Engines generally have more than one cylinder, the pistons moving rapidly in series turning a *crankshaft* which is connected to the wheels of a vehicle or propeller of a boat. The fuel in a petrol engine is ignited by an electrical spark from spark plugs. Diesel engines are similar in that the fuel and air is mixed within a cylinder. However, diesel is a heavier oil than petrol and when it is compressed becomes very hot. This heat, produced by pressure, is great enough to ignite the fuel in an explosive manner, and the hot air produced is used to drive the moving parts.

There are no cylinders or pistons in a gas turbine engine. The popular name of *jet engine* comes from the jet of gas which is expelled once the fuel has been burnt.

lorry most freight is carried by road on large lorries constructed of strong materials such as steel. They usually have large wheels, often in pairs, which enable them to carry a great deal of weight.

a lorry

Smaller lorries consist of one flat trailer with a detachable driver's cab. Larger ones (*articulated lorries*) may consist of several sections giving flexibility to negotiate bends in the road. Specialized heavy goods vehicles, adapted in various ways are commonly used in the construction industry, road building and quarrying.

motor cycles have a long history, the first one being built by a German engineer, Gottlieb Daimler, in 1885. It consisted of an engine fitted to a wooden bicycle frame and the whole contraption had to be pushed in order to get it started. Today's motorbikes have similar engines (*see* INTERNAL COMBUSTION ENGINE) to those of cars but are smaller and the capacity is measured in cubic centimetres (cc). It may have from one to four cylinders and either a two or a four stroke engine. The engine is started by rapidly pushing down a kick-starter which causes it to fire. The engine may be air or water-cooled and speed is controlled by a throttle on the handlebars. The engine is connected by means of a chain to the back wheel and drives it round. Brakes and gears are controlled by foot pedals and the clutch is a hand-operated lever. Many earlier motorbikes had a sidecar to carry a passenger but this is less common now except in the sport of sidecar racing.

a motor cycle

ships before the invention of modern aeroplanes, people could only travel from one country to another by ship and voyages could take many months. Modern ships are mostly cargo vessels and their construction is often determined by the type of materials which they are to carry. The largest cargo ships are the *supertankers* which carry oil. Due to their size, often they can only unload at ports specially designed to receive them, or the oil may be pumped into special storage tanks outside the docks. Other *container ships* carry boxes of cargo of various kinds. Other kinds of cargo, especially materials such as grain and coal, can be placed directly into the holds of *bulk carrier ships*. Some foods are carried by ship, such as fruit and meat and because they are being transported over long distances, they require refrigeration. These are carried in specially designed *refrigerator ships* and are carefully monitored during the voyage.

a bulk carrier ship

Some large passenger ships (called *liners*), are still in use for luxury travel but they are fewer in number than in former years. The *Queen Elizabeth II* is one of the better known luxury liners, carrying passengers between Britain and America. The ship has luxurious accommodation as well as many leisure facilities including tennis courts, swimming pools, shops and restaurants. Another famous liner from earlier times was the *Titanic* which was struck by an iceberg on her maiden voyage in 1912. The ship sank and 1500 people lost their lives.

space travel and **space shuttles** unmanned space craft were first launched this century in 1957, but space travel became a reality in 1961, when a Russian astronaut, Yuri Gagarin, became the first person in space. He made an orbit of the Earth in a spaceship called *Vostok 1*. Many other space ships were launched in the following years until, in 1969, human beings finally stepped onto the moon. *Apollo II* of the American Apollo series of spacecraft, made a successful moon landing in July of that year. Astronaut Neil Armstrong emerged from the *lunar module* and became the first human being ever to set foot upon a heavenly body other than the Earth. (The lunar module was a specially designed vehicle that could be detached from the 'parent' spacecraft and used to make the actual descent onto the Moon's surface). Other voyages to the Moon have followed from this first landing. In 1971 the *Apollo 15* spacecraft carried a special vehicle which was driven around by the astronauts across the Moon's surface while they were engaged in research projects and collecting soil and rock samples.

The *space shuttle* is an American spacecraft which can be used over again. It is launched vertically by means of enormous rockets, but at the end of the voyage after re-entry into the Earth's atmosphere, it lands horizontally on a runway like a conventional aeroplane. The first successful launch of the space shuttle, *Columbia*, was made in 1981.

Several voyages followed but in January, 1986 a horrifying accident took place when the space shuttle *Challenger* exploded soon after take off. Countries involved in space travel have remained cautious about manned flights since this incident. However, unmanned craft have continued to be launched, travelling vast distances to parts of the universe far-removed from the Earth. Much exciting and new scientific information has been obtained from this exploration of space.

a space shuttle

submarine is a special boat designed to dive and operate beneath the surface of the sea. Submarines were first devised in 1620 and hand-operated ones were invented in the 1770s. A steam-operated submarine was in use in the 1870s. It had a fire which heated water to produce steam but when it dived, the chimney had to be pulled down and the fire put out!

During this century, submarines were developed and used during both World Wars by the opposing naval forces. They were powered by petrol-driven engines while on the surface but operated on batteries beneath the sea. In modern submarines of this type, diesel is used rather than petrol. *Nuclear-powered submarines* were first used in 1955 and modern ones are able to stay submerged for up to two years. All submarines operate on a similar principle as far as diving and rising to the surface is concerned. They have hollow ballast tanks beneath the outer 'skin' which are filled with air when the craft is on the surface. In order to dive, valves are opened and water enters the tanks driving out the air, so the submarine becomes heavier and sinks. Depth can be controlled by shutting the valves and the craft is driven by a large, rear propeller. To return to the surface, compressed air is pumped into the the tanks, with the valves open so that water is forced out. The submarine becomes lighter again and rises to the surface. Wing-like hydroplanes provide control as the submarine dives and rises.

trains the earliest trains or locomotives were powered by steam engines which were devised in the early 1700s. James Watt invented a steam engine, the design of which was used to power the early locomotives. A fire burning coal or wood heated up water in a boiler which generated steam. The steam was used to drive cylinders called *pistons* backwards and forwards and rods from these turned the wheels of the locomotive. One famous early steam locomotive was designed by George Stephenson in 1829 and was called the *Rocket*.

Stephenson's Rocket locomotive

During the 1800s, railway tracks were laid down and steam locomotives made travel increasingly possible for large numbers of people. Steam trains are still in routine use in some countries of the world and in Britain are popular tourist attractions. Many old locomotives have been restored, and famous ones such as the *Flying Scotsman* and the *Mallard* (which set the speed record for a steam train in 1938 of over 200 km per hour), are household names.

a steam locomotive

After World War II, locomotives powered by diesel engines rapidly replaced the old steam trains. These were faster, smoother and cleaner than the steam locomotives and, along with *electric trains*, form the basis of modern rail networks. Electric trains are run on electricity which is obtained either from an overhead cable or from a 'live' rail in the centre of the track. These trains are especially associated with the *Underground* railways system in London and many other cities, but they also run above ground. Some underground trains are entirely automatic, being operated by electronic signals generated via the track from a central control unit. One of the fastest trains in the world, which can achieve the high speed of 515 km per hour, is the electrically-operated French *TGV* (train à grande vitesse). One of British Rail's *Intercity* series, the *125*, is the fastest diesel train being able to reach a speed of 233 km per hour. The speed record is held by a Japanese locomotive, the *Bullet*, which is capable of speeds up to 260 km per hour.

Trains have always been used to move freight as well as passengers, and a variety of special trucks are used depending upon the materials being transported. A recent development affecting Britain and Europe has been the opening of the *Channel Tunnel* which provides a direct rail link between England and France.

trams from the early HORSE DRAWN TRAM, trams were developed in the mid 1900s as a form of public transport servicing urban and suburban areas. Commonly a tram car would be fuelled by electricity conducted through overhead cables and would run along rails which would act as the return.

As a result of the development of other forms of public transport and the increasing use of cars, trams have declined in use as a method of urban transportation. In some large cities, however, modern tram systems are being introduced in order to reduce the amount of pollution in built up areas, caused by vehicles which rely on petrol and diesel as an energy source.

COMPUTERS

At school or in the home many of us use computers on a daily basis and they play an increasingly important part in all our lives today. This section provides explanations of current terms used in computing as well as giving an overview of the historical development of information technology. The entries are in A to Z order and cross references are given in SMALL CAPITALS.

*

access to locate and retrieve the information, whether data or program instructions, stored on a disk or in a computer. Nowadays the term usually refers to the amount of time it takes to transfer information from one source to another, and is called the *access time*. It is measured in NANOSECONDS for memory chips, in MILLISECONDS for data transfer from the hard disc. Typical access times for hard disks on personal computers range between the fast (9ms) and the slow at around 100ms. The access time is determined by the time required for the disk heads to move to the correct track (the *seek time*), and then to settle down (the *settle time*) and the time needed for the sector to move under the head (*latency*).

ANSI is the acronym for the *A*merican *N*ational *S*tandards *I*nstitute, a non-governmental organisation founded in 1918 to approve the specification of data processing standards in the U.S.A. It is also responsible for the definition of high-level programming langauges.

APL (A Program Language) a high level programming language, designed for handling engineering and mathematical functions, and as a notation for communication between mathematicians. It is quick, efficient, and well-suited to "what if" applications.

architecture is the particular selection, design and inter-connection of the principal components of a computer system. Normally it refers to the physical structure of a computer, the manner in which its components are connected. It is also common to use the term as a logical description of the components in a system.

artificial intelligence (AI) is the ability of an artificial mechanism to exhibit intelligent behaviour by modifying its actions through reasoning and learning from experience. Artificial intelligence is also the name of the research discipline in which artificial mechanisms that exhibit intelligence are developed and studied. First discussed by British mathematician Alan Turing, he is regarded as one of the founders of the subject.

In recent years artificial intelligence has been used in the development of "Expert Systems" which use knowledge-based information to make seemingly rational decisions. However, this rationale is limited to a specific knowledge area. It is generally accepted that AI has not met its objectives and the necessary solutions are probably many, many years away.

ASCII *A*merican *S*tandard *C*ode for *I*nformation *I*nterchange. It is one of several standard sets of codes devised in 1968 which define the way information is transferred from one computer to another. It is one method of representing binary code, whereby specific binary patterns are represented by alphanumeric codes. The standard ASCII code contains 96 upper and lower case characters and 32 control characters that are not displayed.

asynchronous a commonly used mode of transmitting data over telephone lines. In this method of data transmission, the length of time between transmitted characters may vary. It is not dependent on the timing of the host processor being in synchronous operation with the sending processor, and therefore requires the use of start and stop bits to signal the beginning and end of each character. Asynchronous communication is used by people developing personal computers because normal telephone lines can be used.

auxiliary storage (or secondary storage) is storage other than the main computer memory, eg magnetic media such as hard or floppy discs and tapes that store data after the power supply is switched off.

back-up is the term given to the duplication of files which are stored on magnetic media such as disk, tape or diskette. It is considered essential practice to make back-up copies of all data in case of accidental loss.

BASIC *B*eginner's *A*ll-purpose *S*ymbolic *I*nstruction *C*ode is one of the most popular computer programming languages. It was developed at Dartmouth College in the USA in 1964 by John Kemeny and Thomas Kurtz. Basic is available on a wide range of computer platforms, and is one of the easiest languages in which to program. It is normally an interpretive language, with each statement being interpreted and executed as it is encountered. It can also be a compiled language, with all of the statements being compiled into machine code before execution. Early versions of Basic were criticised for not encouraging structured programming. New versions of Basic, i.e. Visual Basic, are very powerful indeed.

baud is a measure of telecommunications transmission speed, denoting the number of discrete signal elements that can be transmitted per second. Devised by the French telecommunications pioneer, J.M. Baudot, the baud rate is the standard way of representing information in telex and telegraph communications. It commonly refers to the changes in signal frequency per second, and not bits per second unless at low baud rates (300) where it is equal to bits per second. At higher rates, the number of bits per second transmitted is higher than the baud rate and one change in the electrical state of the circuit represents more than one bit of data. So 1200 bits per second can be sent at 600 baud.

bi-directional describes a device, usually a printer, that is capable of printing from right to left as well as from left to right. There are also bi-directional printer ports, capable of sending and receiving data. Serial cables are bi-directional, as they are capable of transmitting and recieving information.

binary the language of all computers in which all numbers, letters and special characters are represented by ones and zeroes. It is called base two notation. *See* BINARY NUMBERS.

bit is short for *bi*nary digi*t*. The smallest unit of information in a digital computer. It has a value of '0' or '1' which represent yes/no and either/or choices. A collection of eights bits is called a BYTE.

bitmap is the term given to a method of storing graphics information in memory in which a BIT is devoted to each pixel (picture element) on screen. A bitmap contains a bit for each point or dot on a video display, and can allow for fine resolution because each point on the display can be addressed. Unfortunately all bitmapped graphics require a great deal of memory, often in excess of one megabyte. A bit-mapped font is a font for screen and/or printer in which every character is made up of a pattern of dots and to allow display or printing a full record must be kept in the computer's memory. Again this leads to a memory-intensive process.

boot is the computer program routine designed to make the computer ready for use. To 'boot the system' or 'to initialize it' is to make it ready for normal use. In modern computers booting the system loads its operating system into memory, and prepares it to run application programs. Within the ROM of a computer is a program that is started when the power is switched on and this tells the computer to search for the computer's operating system. This is called a *cold boot*. A *warm boot* is achieved either by pressing the reset button on newer

IBM computers and compatibles or by pressing Ctrl/Alt/Del simultaneously. This is usually done to unlock the system.

buffer is an electronic memory storage device which is used for temporary storage of data passing in or out of the computer. A common use for a buffer is as a temporary holding area between a slow moving device and a fast moving device, i.e. between a computer and a printer. A buffer therefore allows different parts of the computer system to operate at optimum speeds.

bug is a hardware or software error. The term 'bug' was first coined in early computer days when a singed butterfly was found to have caused a malfunction in the MARK I computer. A programming error may be serious and can cause the computer to perform incorrectly or even crash.

byte A combination of BITS used by the computer to represent an alphabetical character, a numerical digit or special character. A page of text will require slightly more bytes than there are characters to store it, to include spaces, control characters etc. A large document will therefore need very many bytes and a great many computers have millions of bytes (megabytes) of memory. Units that are used most often are the kilobyte and megabyte representing 1000 and 1 million. These are however inaccurate because a kilobyte is actually 1,024 bytes and a megabyte 1,048,576 bytes.

CAD is the acronym for *C*omputer *A*ided *D*esign. This is special software which can create and manipulate complicated and detailed graphics shapes in the same manner in which an architect or designer might do. The draughtsperson using CAD can change, edit, save and reprint their drawings without the problem of re-drawing everything over again. Until quite recently CAD was within the realm of dedicated computer systems only, but the increased speed, memory and processing power of modern systems means that it can be undertaken on more ordinary machines. It is now commonly used in many disciplines including architecture, interior design, civil engineering, mechanical engineering and others.

capacity is the amount of text or data which may be stored in a computer or on magnetic media.

CD ROM (Compact Disc Read Only Memory) is a system invented by Phillips in 1983. CD ROM can store much larger amounts of data than conventional storage. Although slower than hard discs, a CD ROM will store in excess of 600Mb of data. They are very useful for the storage of archival data. Video and

sound can also be stored on a CD disc, making possible MULTIME-
DIA applications (*see also* CD TECHNOLOGY).

a CD disc

character a single letter, number, space, special character or symbol
that can be made to appear on screen by using the keyboard.

character set refers to the full set of numbers, punctuation
marks, alphabetic characters and symbols which a particular
computer system uses and which a printer is capable of producing.

chip A tiny chip or wafer of silicon which contains minute electronic circuitry and forms the core of a microprocessor or
computer. After the initial discovery of SEMICONDUCTORS, technological advance was rapid. Early INTEGRATED CIRCUITS duplicated
the functions of a number of electronic components but now it is
possible to create chips that contain unimaginable numbers of
components - in fact, 16 million on one chip smaller than the tip
of your finger. Chips can be mass produced and after their design,
which is undertaken on an enlarged circuit diagram, the circuitry
is transferred to plates called photomasks. Using a succession of
photomasks, the chip is coated with materials which result in several layers of doped silicon and it then forms the equivalent of a
highly complex electronic circuit.

COBOL *CO*mmon *B*usiness *O*riented *L*anguage. One of the most
commonly used computer programming languages for large
mainframe business applications.   It has never achieved the
popularity of BASIC on smaller computers such as PCs. However
for large businesses it became the choice for invoicing, salary
records, stock control because its programs are easy to read and
amend. Its function is to store, retrieve and process such data and
was therefore useful in automating such processes.

command is an instruction or set of instructions which will start or
stop an operation in a computer program, e.g. RUN, PRINT, EXIT.

compatibility is a characteristic of word or data processing
equipment which permits one machine to accept and process data
prepared by another machine without conversion. Commonly refers to data, but also can refer to hardware such as printers,
monitors, i.e. IBM compatible. To be really compatible, it should

be possible for a program or PERIPHERAL to run on a system with no modification and with everything running as intended.

computer is an eletronic data processing device, capable of accepting data, applying a prescribed set of instructions to the data, and displaying the result in some manner or form.

a modern computer

monitor

processor

keyboard

configuration the machines which are interconnected and programmed to operate as a computer system. Typically, this includes a CPU with keyboard, VDU, printer and some form of disk drive. It also refers to the setting up of a computer system or program to ensure that it matches the needs of the user. Configuration has to be performed at the outset and while modern applications software has automated the procedure to some extent there are certain elements that have to be done manually. Once established, the set up is saved in a configuration file which should not be erased or altered.

console is the terminal that is used to control the computer system. It is applied as a descriptive term to a control device on large mainframe systems. Console is also used to describe the keyboard and display in personal computer systems.

CPU (central processing unit) is the core of a computer system which contains the circuits needed to interpret and execute instructions and perform the basic computer functions. At one time it was used to describe the box which housed the electronics of the computer system. Its modern description is the integrated circuit which makes use of VLSI (Very Large Scale Integration - up to 100,000 transistors on one chip) to house the control transistors for the computer system.

cursor is an indicator on the screen of a VDU, used by a computer to direct a user to the starting position, to enter data. It can be a small line, a square of light on the screen, or an arrow symbol and can be controlled by use of the mouse, or the arrow keys on the numeric pad on the right-hand end of the keyboard.

daisy wheel the print wheel for a daisy wheel printer which produces 'letter quality' printing. It does this by rotating a print element resembling a wheel with spokes. Each spoke contains two characters of the alphabet. Daisy wheel printers were once the first choice but have now been overtaken by the technology of printing which has made inkjet, bubble-jet and laser printers more readily available.

data is jargon for information. Groups of facts, concepts, symbols, numbers, letters, or instructions that can be used to communicate.

database is a file of information (data) which is stored on a computer in a structured manner, and used by a computer program such as a database management system (DBMS). Information is usually subdivided into particular data FIELDS i.e. a space for a specific item of information.

DBMS (Database Management System) a software system for managing the storage, access, updating and maintenance of a database. Users can edit the database, save the data, and extract reports from the database using the DBMS.

data processing is the preparing and storing, handling or processing of data through a computer.

decollator A machine which separates the sheets of a multipart form or continuous paper, i.e. it separates the top sheet from the second sheet.

dedicated line a communications cable line which is dedicated exclusively to a particular communication function. For example, a dedicated line may be used in a building to connect up a number of computers.

density is a measure of the amount of information (in bits) that can be stored on magnetic media such as a floppy disk. Single density allows for a measured quantity, but there is also double density. Quad density or high density uses very fine-grained magnetic particles and although they are more expensive to produce than double density, they can store one megabyte or more on a single disk.

dial-up the process of locating and retrieving information over telephone lines.

dip switches a collection of small 'on' and 'off' switches used to select options on circuit boards without having to modify the hardware. They are frequently found inside printers, to control vertical spacing, and other variable functions and in computers and other electronic devices. Dip stands for *dual in-line package* and it is the complete unit of plastic that contains the circuit and leads for fitting into the device.

directory is the table of contents of a computer file system which allows convenient access to specific files. A directory is an area of disk which stores files. It is common practice to store the files from one particular application in a directory so that they do not get mixed up with other files. Files can then be recognised by their name. When a directory is called up on screen it usually provides several items of information:

volume label a name given when a disk is formatted.

file name the title given to a file, consisting of up to 8 characters with a three character file extension that often identifies the software program in which the file was created.

file size the size of a file is given in bytes.

date this is the date upon which the file was last opened and modified.

time the time when the file was last changed.

space free the number of bytes of space left on the disk.

disk drive the piece of hardware and electronics which enables information to be read from and written to a disk. The recording and erasing is performed by the READ/WRITE HEAD. The circuitry controlling the drive is called the disk drive controller.

a disc drive

diskette an alternative name for FLOPPY DISK.

DOS (Disk Operating System) the program responsible for communications between the computer and peripherals, such as the disk drive, printer or the monitor. It controls and manages all the peripherals connected to the computer system. It therefore must be the first program to be loaded when the computer is switched on. The commonest operating system is MS-DOS (produced by Microsoft Corporation in the USA) which was introduced in 1981.

dot matrix the means of printing characters employed in a dot matrix printer. It is an impact technology, and as such is comparatively noisy when compared to the non-impact printers such as ink-jet or laser. A dot matrix image is created by a number of pins striking a ribbon and forming the image on the paper. Printers with just 9 pins produce poor quality output and although there are versions with more pins which give better quality, they come second to the newer technologies for effect. However they are fast and are still much used for large volume repetitive work.

double-sided disk a type of floppy disk with both surfaces available for storage of data.

down time is the time when computer equipment is not available for use because of hardware or software malfunction.

DTP (Desktop Publishing) is the software and hardware which makes possible the composition of text and graphics as would normally have been done by a printer or in a newspaper office. Desktop publishing requires the use of a computer, laser printer, and various software programs to prepare and print documents. It is possible to produce anything from a single page of text to advertisements, pamphlets, books, and magazines. Computer-aided publishing has been possible since the early 1970s for organizations willing to invest large sums of money, traditional printers, for example, or publishing houses. Desktop publishing as a function of personal computers (PCs) became possible on a broad scale only in 1985, with the introduction of the first relatively inexpensive laser printer producing "letter quality" type and visuals.

A basic desktop publishing system allows its printer to produce print by employing a variety of fonts and type sizes, type justification, hyphenation, and other typesetting capabilities offered by publishing software programs. Page layouts, based upon a template, can be set up on the computer monitor and transferred, as is seen on the monitor, to the printer. Many types of graphics can be created, and the system may also incorporate art and photographs from sources inside the computer. The command codes for producing text and graphics are comparatively simple: some computers use symbols and a pointer controlled by the mouse; others use word and letter commands. A basic desktop publishing system includes a microcomputer, a laser printer that is able to print at 300 or more dots per inch (dpi), word processing software and a page description language; a software program that enables its user to position, size, and manipulate blocks of type and pictures.

In contrast to professionally printed matter, 300 dpi provides relatively low resolution. More complex laser printers or the use of an added phototypesetting unit produces finer quality print and illustrations. The addition of a computer-connected scanner allows the use of text and visual material from other sources.

dumb terminal is a computer terminal which has little or no memory or computing capability of its own and must rely on the computer for memory and processing.

dump is the process of transferring the contents of memory in one storage device to another storage device or item of hardware, e.g. it may be a dump from disk to printer, disk to tape or screen to printer. Dumps are often performed when programmers are debugging programs.

electronic mail is a method of sending messages from one computer to another via the telephone line or via network cabling. Common on networked computer systems, electronic mail can also be used to send information from any suitable computer to any other suitably-equipped computer anywhere in the world. The increasing use of electronic mail is seen to offer an alternative to the traditional methods of working in offices or administration centres. It is not necessary for the recipient to be there to receive a message and there are other advantages - e-mail is effective in terms of time, distance is no object, and it is very flexible. However, it is currently taking a back seat due to the rapid rise in popularity of the fax.

error message is a message displayed on a screen which indicates that the computer has detected an error or malfunction. *Error trapping* is the ability of a program to recognize and almost anticipate an error and then carry out a preset course of action in response to the error.

ESC (escape) is a non-printing character or keyboard control key which causes an interruption in the normal program sequence. Within a software program it is usually pressed to cancel a command or operation.

execution the process of carrying out the individual steps called for by the program in a computer.

fax (short for facsimile) a facsimile, or fax, machine is a device capable of transmitting or receiving an exact copy of a page of printed or pictorial matter over telephone lines in, usually, less than 60 seconds. It is currently the preferred method for the rapid transmission of printed material.

Facsimile transmission in some form has been available since the end of the last century. Fax was invented by a Scot - Alexander Bain. From the 1920s, newspapers used slow facsimile devices, equipped with photoelectric cells that scanned material placed on rotating drums, to transmit photographs. Police departments, the military, and some businesses sent printed matter via matched facsimile machines. Fax remained a relatively specialized communications device, however, until the development of sophisticated scanning and digitizing techniques in computer and communications technologies, and the establishment of standards that made it possible for all fax machines to communicate with one another over ordinary telephone lines.

Most contemporary fax machines conform to a set of standards, known as Group III, that were implemented in 1980, and that require digital image scanning and data compression. Machines built to conform to Group III standards can transmit data at a maximum 9,600 bits per second (bps). To transmit, the original document is fed into the machine, where it is scanned by a mirror-and-lens-aided device, or, in some faxes, by a series of light-emitting DIODES (LEDs). Light and dark picture elements - pixels, or pels - are described digitally and the message is shortened by compressing much of the white space. The receiving machine, which is addressed through its telephone number, translates the code it receives back into a pattern of greys, blacks, and white. The reconstituted message is printed out on heat-sensitive paper, using techniques similar to those for copying machines. Some fax machines can actually double as copiers and modern machines use ordinary paper, which eliminates the use of heat-sensitive paper which browns over a period of time.

field a defined group of characters or numbers, e.g. a customer number, a product description, a telephone number, address within a specific space in a database program.

fixed disk a HARD DISK which cannot be removed from its housing or interchanged.

floppy disk is a removable, secondary medium of storage for computers. The disks are made of a plastic which is coated with a magnetic material (of which the main component is ferric oxide) and the whole thing is protected by a rigid plastic case (3$^1/_2$" disks) or plastic envelope (5$^1/_4$" disks). The disk rotates within its cover and an access hole allows the READ/WRITE HEAD of the disk drive to record and retrieve information. There is a *write-protect notch* on the disc cover which can be set so that the disc drive cannot change the disk, it can only read the data stored there. The

5¼" disks are more susceptible to damage than the 3½" disks and are gradually being superseded. However, floppy disks are an essential part of any computing system because they are the means of installing software, backing up files and transferring data between users if no others means exists. The storage capacity of a disk varies and depends upon the size, the density of the magnetic particles coating the disk's surface and the drive used.

a 5 ¼ inch floppy disc

a 3 ½ inch floppy disk

font a complete set of letters, numbers, special characters and punctuation marks of a particular size and for one identifiable typeface whether roman or bold (the weight), italic or upright (the posture). The term is often used to refer to a family of fonts or typefaces although this is technically incorrect. Fonts come as bitmapped (*see* BIT MAP) or OUTLINE fonts.

format is the preparation of hard or floppy disks for use by laying down clearly defined recording areas (*see also* INITIALIZE). The format is the way in which the magnetic pattern is laid down on the disk.

In particular programs for example, a spreadsheet, the format is the overall arrangement of labels and values in the separate cells of the spreadsheet. This may relate to the layout of decimal numbers or the alignment of entries within columns. A similar concept applies to database management and word processing programs. In the latter the format will encompass all aspects of the typeface, the page layout (numbering, headers and footers) and paragraph styles.

function any single operation of a computer or word processor (e.g. editing). Also within certain programs such as spreadsheets, a procedure which is stored in the program and which will perform a particular sequence of operations or calculations to produce an end result.

function keys are special purpose keys on the keyboard of a word processor or computer system which enable the user to perform a particular task or execute a command which might otherwise take several keystrokes.

graphical user interface (GUI) the part of the software program that communicates and interacts with the user by means of pull-down menus (*see* MENU), *dialog boxes* (a box on screen that presents information and offers choices to the user about a particular function or process) and ICONS. The GUI makes computers easier to use because people recognize and respond to graphic representations of concepts, etc much more readily than if they have to read words. Microsoft WINDOWS utilizes this system to great effect.

hard disk A fixed disk that forms a storage medium within the computer. It was developed in 1973 by IBM and initially called the Winchester disk, but early versions were very expensive. Today they are a standard component of just about every computer and their mass production has reduced the price enormously. At the same time the capacity has risen dramatically, from the early sizes of 10, 20 and 40 megabytes to several hundred megabytes and even one gigabyte (that is one billion or 1,073,741,824 bytes or 1000 megabytes).

The hard disk includes the storage medium and the read/write head and the electronics to connect it to the computer. There are several disks or platters which revolve at 3600rpm and the head floats just above the disk surface to eliminate wear. The large capacity of hard disks means that several software programs can be installed on one machine plus innumerable data files. However, hard disks may fail and it is important to back up data regularly.

hardware the physical equipment such as a computer's CPU, disk drive(s), VDU, magnetic tape unit and printer in fact anything which can be connected to the computer.

head crash the physical impact of a disk head on the disk resulting in damage to its surface and a serious equipment malfunction that usually destroys data stored on the disk. It was relatively common on older systems, but modern high-tolerance engineering ensures that head crashes rarely occur.

icon is a symbol on screen that represents something or some process/function in the computer. Icons are used in a GRAPHICAL

USER INTERFACE and the image of an icon resembles the result of choosing that particluar option or command. Programs resident within Windows use numerous icons for tasks such as opening and closing files (which use small pictures of files), printing (a printer), discarding files (a dustbin) and so on. Icons can also represent software programs.

index hole is a hole punched in a floppy disk, and detected electro-optically, to indicate the beginning of the first sector.

information technology (IT) a jargon term used to describe all computer, telecommunications and related technology that is concerned with the handling or transfer of information. IT is a vast field incorporating the collection, handling, storage and sending/communication of information.

initialize to start-up or set-up the basic conditions. When disks or diskettes are initialized, they are formatted to accept data which will be stored later.

input the information to be entered into a computer system for subsequent processing. An input device is any peripheral that provides a means of getting data into the computer. It thus includes the keyboard, mouse, modem, scanner etc.

input/output the general term for the equipment and system that is used to communicate with the computer, commonly called I/O. It ensures that program instructions and data readily go into and come out of the central processing unit.

integrated circuit (IC) a module of electronic circuitry that consists of transistors and other electronic components, usually contained on a rigid board. A variety of boards are plugged into a computer to enable it to perform its various tasks.

integrated software a group of software packages each with a logical relationship to the other components. For example, a typical integrated package may include a word processor, a spreadsheet, a database, a graphics application and perhaps a communications application. The common link will be that all of these applications will operate in a similar manner and it will be possible to transfer data between them.

interface essentially a connection with associated electronic circuitry which permits two devices to be interconnected and to communicate.

k abbreviation for kilo as in kilometres. It actually means 1000, but in the computer world it is used rather more loosely because 1 kilobyte is actually 1024 bytes. It is commonly used to refer to the relative size of a computer's main memory. 64K is equal to approximately 64,000 characters of information.

log on and **log off** the procedure by which a user begins or ends working at a computer terminal or system. In MS-DOS logging on means the process of activating a drive. In networks a password may be necessary to log on to the system.

machine language a binary language which all computers use. Machine code uses the lowest form of coding, binary, to instruct the machine to change the numbers in memory locations. All other computer languages must be *compiled* from their high-level code into machine code before the programs can be executed.

magnetic media any of a wide variety of disks or tapes coated or impregnated with magnetic material, on which information can be recorded and stored. The magnetic coating is repositioned when influenced by a magnetic field and the READ/WRITE HEAD emits a magnetic field when writing to the disk or tape which produces a positive or negative charge corresponding to that item of data. When reading, the head senses the charges and decodes them. Disks are used universally but for very high capacity storage, magnetic tape is ideal.

mailbox within the electronic mail system, a disk file or memory area in which messages for a particular destination (or person) are placed. Modern bulletin-board communications systems uses a mailbox metaphor to store messages for electronic mail users. The *bulletin board* system is a telecommunications utility that facilitates informal communication between computer users.

main memory *see* **RAM**

mainframe refers to any large computer such as IBM and Cray. They do not use the same architecture as small desktop computers and are intended for use by many people, usually within a large organisation. To begin with it referred to the large cabinet that held the central processing unit and then referred to the large computers developed in the 1960s which could accommodate hundreds of DUMB TERMINALS. Now there is a difference in the use of the word and mainframe applies to a computing system that serves the needs of a whole organisation.

MBASIC Microsoft's original BASIC programming language. Now superseded by QBASIC and Visual Basic.

megabyte one million bytes (characters) of information. The common storage measurement for memory and hard disks, i.e. 4Mb of RAM, with a 210Mb hard disc drive.

memory the circuitry and devices that accept and hold binary numbers and are capable of storing data as well as programs. Memory must be installed in all modern computer systems. It is the computer's primary storage area e.g. RAM (random access memory) as distinguished from the secondary storage of disks. Typical memory devices are SIMMS, *Single In-line Memory Modules*, which are plugged into the *motherboard* of the computer. SIMMS are plug-in modules that contain all the necessary chips to add more RAM to a computer. The motherboard is the large circuit board that contains the central processing unit, the RAM, expansion slots and other microprocessors.

menu a list of operator action selections displayed on a VDU. A user is presented with a menu which will give a choice of commands or applications. Menus make the computer system easier to use. A *pull-down menu* is a selection of commands that appears after a command on the menu bar of a program has been selected. A command or action is selected and often another menu will appear. The term originated with the idea started by Macintosh. *Menu-driven software* contains programs that proceed to the next step only when the user responds to a menu prompt.

microcomputer is traditionally the smallest size of computer, of desk top size. The modern use of the term includes any small computer system. In many ways the term has lost its relevance and its meaning has been somewhat blurred by technological developments. Initially it referred to any computer that has certain key units on one integrated circuit called the MICROPROCESSOR. The first personal computers, designed for single users, were called microcomputers because their CPUs were microprocessors. However the distinction between a micro and a MINICOMPUTER has all but disappeared and many microcomputers are now more powerful than the mainframes of a few years ago.

microprocessor (also called the **microchip**) an electronic device (integrated circuit) which has been programmed to follow a set of logic driven rules. It is essentially the heart of any computer system.

microsecond one millionth of a second.

millisecond one thousandth of a second.

minicomputer a computer system usually smaller than a mainframe but larger than a microcomputer and designed for many users.

modem (*MO*dulator-*DEM*odulator) a device which will receive data from a computer, automatically translate it into codes which can be transmitted over normal telephone lines and then be reformatted by another modem on the receiving computer. The modem is an extremely important device, enabling communication and transfer of data all over the world. In order that modems facilitate communication between computers, both must conform to the same PROTOCOL.

module is a part of a program or set of programs capable of functioning on its own.

multimedia a system of presenting information as sound, text and graphics and based upon the computer. An essential component is interactivity and involvement of the user. Software systems provide encyclopaedic collections of graphics, pictures and text and even moving images. Inevitably the memory requirements of such a system are huge and a CD-ROM drive is a necessity.

nanosecond one billionth of a second.

network is the interconnection of a number of terminals or computer systems by data communication lines. It may consist of two or more computers which can communicate between each other. Networks for personal computers differ according to scope and size. *Local area networks* (LANs) usually connect just a few computers (although it may be more than 50) perhaps in order that they can share the use of an expensive peripheral. Large systems are called wide area networks and use telephone lines or similar media to link computers together. In general LANs cover distances of a few miles and some of the largest versions are found in universities and large companies. Each user has a workstation capable of processing data, unlike the DUMB TERMINALS of a multi-user system.

non-impact printer a printer which produces textual output on plain or special paper without contact between the printing mechanism and the paper. Typical examples are inkjet, bubble-jet or laser printers. Most are capable of high quality print.

OCR (*O*ptical *C*haracter *R*ecognition) an information processing technology that can convert readable text into computer data. A scanner is used to import the image into the computer, and the OCR software converts the image into text. No one software package provides a foolproof conversion of text but the more sophisticated ones have various means of highlighting queries and even recognising certain unclear characters once the user has responded to the first case. It is a useful tool for inputting large amounts of typewritten or already printed text for editing and changing.

off-line refers to equipment which is not under the direct control of the CPU. A printer may be in an off-line state when it is switched on but not capable of receiving data from the computer.

on-line refers to the operation of terminals and peripherals in direct communication with (and under the control of) the CPU of a computer, i.e. switched on and ready to receive data.

operating system (OS) a suite of computer programs (systems software) which control the overall operation of a computer. Operating systems perform the housekeeping tasks such as controlling the input and output between the computer and the peripherals, and accepting information from the keyboard or other input devices. Common operating systems are MS-DOS (*see* DOS), OS/2, UNIX, XENIX. OS/2 (*Operating System/2*) was developed ultimately by IBM although initially it was a joint development with Microsoft. However, when Microsoft devoted its energies to the improvement of WINDOWS, IBM took OS/2 and it has now gained more acceptance although is nowhere near rivalling Microsoft Windows. UNIX is written in language C and was developed by AT&T Bell Laboratories in the 1970s. It can be used on computers from personal computers to mainframes and it is suited to multiuser systems. XENIX was produced by Microsoft Corporation for use on IBM-compatible computers.

outline font is a font for printer and screen in which each character is generated from a mathematical formula. This produces a very much smoother outline to a character than can be obtained from a bitmapped font (*see* BITMAP). The use of mathematical formulae means that characters can be changed in size quite easily and only one font need reside in the memory.

output most computer output comes in the form of printed reports, letters and other printed data, or information sent to a mass storage device such as a hard disk drive, or a tape drive. But the most common output form is the image on the screen. *Output devices* are computer peripherals such as a printer, a magnetic tape drive or floppy disk, which will acccept information from the computer.

parameter is a step in any program sequence which will cause the program to take a specific course of action. It is a value that is added to a command to ensure the task is undertaken in the desired manner. For example, to format the disk in drive A one would type FORMAT A: and the A: is the parameter of the FORMAT command.

Pascal a computer language originally designed by Niklaus Wirth for the teaching of structured programming. It is very popular in colleges and schools and is used as a teaching language and in the development of applications. It is simlar to BASIC in that the computer is told what to do by statements in the program - it is a *procedural language*. It has some disadvantages in that it is too slow for large-scale development and commercial versions are changed sufficiently to make them individually isolated.

password a code assigned to a program or set of files, for security purposes, which allows the user to gain access to the file or program. It may have certain levels allowing some users the facility of read-only while others may also write and copy files.

path the means of pointing to the exact location of a file on a computer disk. It uses a hierarchical structure of directories in which files are stored. It is the name given to the location of the file using the directory structure, for example, a file called THISYEAR stored on the C drive in a directory called ACCOUNTS, has the path C:\ACCOUNTS\THISYEAR.

peripheral a generic term for equipment which is connected to the computer. These are external (to the CPU) and include such devices as external disk drives, printers, modems, CD-ROMS, scanners and VDUs.

personal computer (PC) a MICROCOMPUTER that can be programmed to perform a variety of tasks for home and office. They can be part of a large database, or a small NETWORK. The boundary between the PC and formerly specific computing set-ups such as workstations and minicomputers is now very blurred. *Workstation*s are powerful computers for use by designers, architects and engineers and feature computer-aided design (CAD) software. PCs are now evolving to this level of sophistication and similarly are in many instances performing the functions asked of a minicomputer.

port a plug or socket along which data may be passed into and out of the computer. Typically, each input and output device requires its own separate port. Most computers have a parallel and a serial port. The *parallel port* is a high-speed connection to printers while the *serial port* enables communication between the computer and serial printers, modems and other computers. In addition to receiving and transmitting data the serial port also guards against data loss.

printer the device that produces hard copy. Printers vary enormously in quality of output, speed, fonts available and so on. In addition to DAISYWHEEL and DOT MATRIX printers, which are called *impact* printers, which have distinct disadvantages in terms of flexibility and quality there are the NON-IMPACT PRINTERS. Ink-jet printers create text and graphics by spraying ink onto the page and there is always some risk of smudging the image. However, although their resolution and quality does not approach that of laser printers, they do tend to be less expensive. Laser printers use a process similar to that of photocopiers whereby ink powder is fused into the paper. To begin with, the major disadvantage of laser printers was their high cost but with the advent of reasonably priced machines the benefit of high quality print, quiet running and built-in fonts is more widely available. There are other types of printer available, e.g. thermal, but they do not form a significant part of the market.

processing is the normal operation of the computer acting upon the input data according to the instructions of the program in use.

program a set of instructions arranged for directing a digital computer to perform a desired operation or operations. Programmers use a variety of high level programming languages such as BASIC, C and Fortran to create programs (*see* PROGRAM LANGUAGE). At some stage the program is converted to machine language so that the computer can carry out the instructions. Computer programs fall into one of three categories:

system programs - which are the programs required for the computer to function. They include the operating system (e.g. MS-DOS).

utility programs - covers the programs which help keep the computer system functioning properly, providing facilities for checking disks, etc.

application programs - are the programs that most people use on their computers such as word processing, database management, desktop publishing, graphics and many more.

program language a language which is used by computer programmers to write computer routines, e.g. COBOL, BASIC, Fortran, Pascal, C, Visual Basic. The *high-level programming* *languages* such as BASIC, C, Pascal are so called because the programmer can use words and arrangements of words that resemble human language and this leaves the programmer free to concentrate on the program without having to think of how the computer will actually carry out the instructions. The language's *compiler* or *interpreter* then turns the programmer's instructions into machine language that the computer can follow.

programmer a person who designs, writes and tests computer programs.

protocol the conventions or rules which govern how and when messages are exchanged in a communications network or between two or more devices. There are many different protocols, but communicating devices must use the same protocols in order to exchange data.

QWERTY keyboard the standard typewriter/computer keyboard, denoted by the letters on the top line of characters. It was originally developed to slow down typists to stop the manual typewriters jamming the keys. There are now other alternatives to QWERTY keyboards which enable faster use and easier learning. One such system is the *Dvorak keyboard* which places the most frequently used letters together.

RAM (*Random Access Memory*) also known as main or internal memory, it refers to the memory which can be, and is, altered in normal computer operations. The RAM stores program instructions and data to make them available to the central processing unit and the CPU can write and read data. Application programs use a part of the RAM as a temporary place of storage allowing modification of the file in use until it is ready for storage permanently on disk. Any work in the RAM which has not been saved will be lost if the power fails.

random access the retrieval of information randomly from any part of the computer memory or from magnetic media which means that the computer can reach the information straight away.

read to retrieve information stored on magnetic media and transfer it to the memory of the computer.

read/write head the part of a disk drive which actually reads data from, and writes data onto a disk by travelling backwards and forwards over the surface of the disk.

robot an electro-mechanical device which may perform programmed tasks. Commonly used in automated factories to perform repetitive functions. The first industrial robots were developed in the early 1960s although they consisted of little more than an automated hand. Japan subsequently invested heavily in robots and other countries have now followed suit.

ROM (*Read Only Memory*) The part of a computer's internal memory which can be read but not altered. It contains the essential programs (system programs) that neither the computer nor user can alter or erase. The instructions that enable the computer to start up come from the ROM, although the tendency now is to put more of the operating system on ROM chips, rather than putting it on disk.

run is to execute a program.

sector A pie-shaped division of the magnetic surface on a disk which separates information into individual sections or zones. Data can be stored in these sectors and read by the disk drive. A unit of storage of one or more sectors is called a *cluster*.

software the series of programs which are loaded into the computer's internal memory which tell the computer what particular function to perform (*see also* PROGRAM).

speech recognition an information processing technology in which the spoken word is converted into signals which can be recognised by speech recognition software and converted into commands for the computer to follow.

stand-alone the term applied to a computer system which is self-contained with only the hardware and software required by the user.

syntax the set of rules which govern the way in which a command or statement is given to the computer so that it recognizes the command and proceeds accordingly.

system (or computer system) is all the necessary hardware and software required in an installation, all of which is interconnected and set up to work together (CPU, disk drives, monitor, printer, keyboard and so on).

track one of a number of concentric circles on a floppy or hard disk. The track is encoded on the disk during formatting and is a particular area on the disk for data storage. *Tracks per inch* (tpi) is a measure of the density of data storage on floppy disks, higher figures representing a greater capacity for data.

UNIX *see* **operating system**.

user-friendly jargon referring to a system that is easy to learn and operate. A user-friendly program often involves the use of menus rather than commands which have to be remembered; help which is available on-screen at the touch of a key; error messages with some explanation of the fault and solution; prompts when performing potentially damaging procedures e.g. questions such as "Do you really want to..." when deleting a file. Applications software also comes with numerous manuals including one presenting the basics of a program in a way which is easily understood.

VDU (*Visual Display Unit*) also called a monitor or video display terminal. It resembles a television screen and produces a visual picture of computer input or output. There is some concern that the electromagnetic radiation (*see* ELECTROMAGNETIC WAVES) given out by monitors may be hazardous. Monitors emit X-rays, ultraviolet radiation, electrostatic discharge and electromagnetic fields but it is not proven that these emissions are dangerous to users. However, some studies have indicated that at a distance of 18 inches the radiation from monitors is less than that of the background and this, and the use of low radiation monitors is being included in regulations for workers using computers.

volatile storage storage of which the contents are lost when power is removed, e.g. the RAM.

Windows (Microsoft Windows) is a comprehensive software facility that utilizes the graphical user interface features which were once the domain of the Macintosh. These include pull-down menus (*see* MENU), a variety of accessories and the powerful facility of moving text and graphics from one program to another via the clipboard (an area for temporarily storing items that have been copied from one area, and which are to be pasted elsewhere). It is possible to run several programs at once, each within a separate window, and to move from one to the other very quickly. All applications that run within the Windows system have a common way of working with windows, dialog boxes (*see* GRAPHICAL USER INTERFACE), etc.

word processing a methodology of document preparation, storage and editing, using a microcomputer/personal computer. Word processing is the most widespread computing application primarily because of the ease with which documents can be amended before printing.

workstation *see* **personal computer**

SPORT

A brief explanation of origin and development is given for each sport listed together with brief histories of the major sporting events. The entries are in A to Z order and cross references are given in SMALL CAPITALS to enable you to relate major competitions and events to the sport.

*

Admiral's Cup *see* YACHTING.

American football has its origins in the undisciplined ball games introduced by the early colonists to America. The basic rules of the modern game were established by college teams and the first professional game was played in Latrobe, Pennsylvania, on 31 August 1895. Today it is the USA's most popular spectator sport with televised league games regularly attracting record audiences.

The most important game of the American football season is the *Super Bowl,* contested by the winners of the two divisional leagues, the NFC (NFL before 1970) and the AFC (AFL). Inaugurated in 1966-7, it is now America's greatest sporting event. The winners have been:

1967	Green Bay Packers	1981	Oakland Raiders
1968	Green Bay Packers	1982	San Francisco 49ers
1969	New York Jets	1983	Washington Redskins
1970	Kansa City Chiefs	1984	Los Angeles Raiders
1971	Baltimore Colts	1985	San Francisco 49ers
1972	Dallas Cowboys	1986	Chicago Bears
1973	Miami Dolphins	1987	New York Giants
1974	Miami Dolphins	1988	Washington Redskins
1975	Pittsburgh Steelers	1989	San Francisco 49ers
1976	Pittsburgh Steelers	1990	San Francisco 49ers
1977	Oakland Raiders	1991	New York Giants
1978	Dallas Cowboys	1992	Washington Redskins
1979	Pittsburgh Steelers	1993	Dallas Cowboys
1980	Pittsburgh Steelers	1994	Dallas Cowboys

archery is an ancient skill which was first established as a competitive sport in the mid-nineteenth century. The first national meeting was held in York in 1844 and the Grand National Archery Society, which still governs the sport, was founded in 1861.

The sport was included in the OLYMPIC GAMES from 1900 to 1908 and again in 1920 and was reintroduced in 1972, with team events added in 1988. The *World Championship* takes place every two years and is contested on a knock-out basis.

association football has its origins in ancient ball games played in various parts of the world but much of the game's development came in England. Three British monarchs banned the sport at various times for its disruptive influence until it began to be organized in the 19th century. The first attempts at framing a set of rules for football were made in the mid-nineteenth century by a group of representatives of the English public schools and universities. Out of their meetings the Football Association (FA) was founded in 1863 and the eleven per side game became standard soon after.

The international governing body, the Fédération Internationale de Football Association (FIFA), was founded in Paris in 1904. By 1992 it had 179 members. International games have been played since 1872 when amateur teams representing Scotland and England first met for a friendly match in Glasgow. The first international championship was contested by the four home nations and lasted from 1883 to 1984.

The first *World Cup* was held in Uruguay in 1930 and has been held every four years since (except 1942 and 1946). The *European Championship*, instituted in 1958, is also held every four years and the African Nations Cup and the South American Championship every two years.

Association football pitch

Pitch area: 45-90 m x 90-120 m (50-100yd x 100-130yd)
Penalty area: 40.32 m x 16.5 m (44 yd x 18 yd)
Goal area: 18.32 m x 5.5 m (20 yd x 6 yd),
Goal: 7.32 m x 2.44 m (8 yd x 8 ft)
Penalty spot: 11 m (12 yd) from goal line

The first *World Cup* for the Jules Rimet Trophy was contested by 13 nations in Uruguay in 1930. Brazil kept the original trophy after their third victory in 1970 and teams now compete for the FIFA World Cup. Host nations qualify automatically for the final stages of the tournament. The results of the finals have been as follows:

	Host	*Winner*	*Runner-up*
1930	Uruguay	Uruguay	Argentina
1934	Italy	Italy	Czechoslovakia
1938	France	Italy	Hungary
1950	Brazil	Uruguay*	Brazil
1954	Switzerland	West Germany	Hungary
1958	Sweden	Brazil	Sweden
1962	Chile	Brazil	Czechoslovakia
1966	England	England	West Germany
1970	Mexico	Brazil	Italy
1974	West Germany	West Germany	Holland
1978	Argentina	Argentina	Holland
1982	Spain	Italy	West Germany
1986	Mexico	Argentina	West Germany
1990	Italy	West Germany	Argentina
1994	USA	Brazil**	Italy

* after extra time   ** after extra time and penalties

France will host the finals of the competition in 1998.

The *European Championship* was originally called the European Nations Cup; it took its present name in 1968. The teams compete for the Henri Delaunay Cup, named after the former General Secretary of UEFA. The results of the finals have been as follows:

	Host	*Winner*	*Runner-up*
1960	France	USSR*	Yugoslavia
1964	Spain	Spain	USSR
1968	Italy	Italy†	Yugoslavia
1972	Belgium	West Germany	USSR
1976	Yugoslavia	Czechoslovakia*	West Germany
1980	Italy	West Germany	Belgium
1984	France	France	Spain
1988	West Germany	Holland	USSR
1992	Sweden	Denmark	Germany

* after extra time   ** after extra time and penalties † after replay

The 1996 finals will be hosted by England.

The *European Cup* is properly known as the European Champion Clubs' Cup. It is an annual knock-out competition first held in 1955/6 for the best league champions of all UEFA-affiliated countries. Since 1991/2 a Champion's League has been included, together with a number of qualifying stages, and the structure of the competition has become more flexible. The winners of the competiton have been:

1956	Real Madrid	1976	Bayern Munich
1957	Real Madrid	1977	Liverpool*
1958	Real Madrid	1978	Liverpool
1959	Real Madrid	1979	Nottingham Forest*
1960	Real Madrid	1980	Nottingham Forest
1961	Benfica	1981	Liverpool
1962	Benfica	1982	Aston Villa*
1963	AC Milan	1983	SV Hamburg
1964	Inter Milan	1984	Liverpool
1965	Inter Milan	1985	Juventus
1966	Real Madrid	1986	Steaua Bucharest*
1967	Celtic	1987	FC Porto*
1968	Manchester United	1988	PSV Eindhoven
1969	AC Milan	1989	AC Milan*
1970	Feyenoord	1990	AC Milan*
1971	Ajax	1991	Red Star Belgrade
1972	Ajax*	1992	Barcelona
1973	Ajax*	1993	Marseilles
1974	Bayern Munich*	1994	AC Milan
1975	Bayern Munich		

European Cup-Winners Cup

Open to winners of domestic senior cup competitions in UEFA-affiliated countries. Originally the final play-off was decided over two games, but this changed in 1961 and it is now one game. The winners of the competition have been;

1961	AC Fiorentina	1969	Slovan Bratislava
1962	Athletico Madrid	1970	Manchester City
1963	Tottenham Hotspur	1971	Chelsea
1964	Sporting Club, Lisbon	1972	Rangers
1965	West Ham United	1973	AC Milan
1966	Borussia Dortmund	1974	FC Magdeburg
1967	Bayern Munich	1975	Dynamo Kiev*
1968	AC Milan	1976	Anderlecht*

1977	SV Hamburg	1986	Dynamo Kiev
1978	Anderlecht*	1987	Ajax
1979	Barcelona	1988	Mechelen*
1980	Valencia*	1989	Barcelona
1981	Dynamo Tblisi	1990	Sampdoria
1982	Barcelona	1991	Manchester United*
1983	Aberdeen*	1992	Werder Bremen
1984	Juventus*	1993	Parma
1985	Everton	1994	Arsenal

* Winner of the *European Super Cup,* a competition first suggested in 1972 (but not recognised by FIFA until 1974) contested by the winners of the European Cup and the Cup-Winners Cup on play-off basis.

The *UEFA Cup* is competed for by the teams not eligible for the other two competitions, the final is decided over two legs on a home and away basis. It was originally called the International Industries Fairs Inter-Cities Cup, or Fairs Cup, when it was established in 1955 and the first competition took three years to complete. It became the UEFA Cup in 1971. The winners of the competition since 1958 have been:

1958	Barcelona	1977	Juventus
1960	Barcelona	1978	PSV Eindhoven
1961	Roma	1979	Borussia Mönchengladbach
1962	Valencia		
1963	Valencia	1980	Eintracht
1964	Real Zaragossa	1981	Ipswich Town
1965	Ferencvaros	1982	Gothenburg
1966	Barcelona	1983	Anderlecht
1967	Dynamo Zagreb	1984	Tottenham Hotspur
1968	Leeds United	1985	Real Madrid
1969	Newcastle United	1986	Real Madrid
1970	Arsenal	1987	Gothenburg
1971	Leeds United	1988	Bayer Leverkusen
1972	Tottenham Hotspur	1989	Napoli
1973	Liverpool	1990	Juventus
1974	Feyenoord	1991	Inter Milan
1975	Borussia Mönchengladbach	1992	Ajax
		1993	Juventus
1976	Liverpool	1994	Inter Milan

The *English Football League* was established in 1988/9 by twelve clubs from the Midlands and North of England. By 1958 there were four divisions and 92 clubs and this set-up was retained until 1993 when the top 22 clubs formed the Premier League and the three divisions of the Football League succeeded the original divisions 2 to 4. The First Division/Premier League Champions have been:

1889	Preston North End	1927	Newcastle United
1890	Preston North End	1928	Everton
1891	Everton	1929	Sheffield Wednesday
1892	Sunderland	1930	Sheffield Wednesday
1893	Sunderland	1931	Arsenal
1894	Aston Villa	1932	Everton
1895	Sunderland	1933	Arsenal
1896	Aston Villa	1934	Arsenal
1897	Aston Villa	1935	Arsenal
1898	Sheffield United	1936	Sunderland
1899	Aston Villa	1937	Manchester City
1900	Aston Villa	1938	Arsenal
1901	Liverpool	1939	Everton
1902	Sunderland	1947	Liverpool
1903	Sheffield Wednesday	1948	Arsenal
1904	Sheffield Wednesday	1949	Portsmouth
1905	Newcastle United	1950	Portsmouth
1906	Liverpool	1951	Tottenham Hotspur
1907	Newcastle United	1952	Manchester United
1908	Manchester United	1953	Arsenal
1909	Newcastle United	1954	Wolverhampton
1910	Aston Villa	1955	Chelsea
1911	Manchester United	1956	Manchester United
1912	Blackburn Rovers	1957	Manchester United
1913	Sunderland	1958	Wolverhampton
1914	Blackburn Rovers	1959	Wolverhampton
1915	Everton	1960	Burnley
1920	West Bromwich Albion	1961	Tottenham Hotspur
1921	Burnley	1962	Ipswich Town
1922	Liverpool	1963	Everton
1923	Liverpool	1964	Liverpool
1924	Huddersfield Town	1965	Manchester United
1925	Huddersfield Town	1966	Liverpool
1926	Huddersfield Town	1967	Manchester United

1968 Manchester United	1982 Liverpool
1969 Leeds United	1983 Liverpool
1970 Everton	1984 Liverpool
1971 Arsenal	1985 Everton
1972 Derby County	1986 Liverpool
1973 Liverpool	1987 Everton
1974 Leeds United	1988 Liverpool
1975 Derby County	1989 Arsenal
1976 Liverpool	1990 Liverpool
1977 Liverpool	1991 Arsenal
1978 Nottingham Forest	1992 Leeds
1979 Liverpool	1993 Manchester United
1980 Liverpool	1994 Manchester United
1981 Aston Villa	

The *English FA Cup* was established in 1871/2 as the Football Association Challenge Cup with 15 teams from across Britain entering the first competition. It is contested annually on a knock-out basis and since 1923 the final has been played at Wembley Stadium. The winners have been:

1872 Wanderers	1894 Notts County
1873 Wanderers	1895 Aston Villa
1874 Oxford University	1896 Sheffield Wednesday
1875 Royal Engineers	1897 Aston Villa
1876 Wanderers	1898 Nottingham Forest
1877 Wanderers	1899 Sheffield United
1878 Wanderers	1900 Bury
1879 Old Etonians	1901 Tottenham Hotspur
1880 Clapham Rovers	1902 Sheffield United
1881 Old Carthusians	1903 Bury
1882 Old Etonians	1904 Manchester City
1883 Blackburn Olympic	1905 Aston Villa
1884 Blackburn Rovers	1906 Everton
1885 Blackburn Rovers	1907 Sheffield Wednesday
1886 Blackburn Rovers	1908 Wolverhampton
1887 Aston Villa	1909 Manchester United
1888 West Bromwich Albion	1910 Newcastle United
1889 Preston North End	1911 Bradford City
1890 Blackburn Rovers	1912 Barnsley
1891 Blackburn Rovers	1913 Aston Villa
1892 West Bromwich Albion	1914 Burnley
1893 Wolverhampton	1920 Aston Villa

1921	Tottenham Hotspur	1961	Tottenham Hotspur
1922	Huddersfield Town	1962	Tottenham Hotspur
1923	Bolton Wanderers	1963	Manchester United
1924	Newcastle United	1964	West Ham
1925	Sheffield United	1965	Liverpool
1926	Bolton Wanderers	1966	Everton
1927	Cardiff City	1967	Tottenham Hotspur
1928	Blackburn Rovers	1968	West Bromwich Albion
1929	Bolton Wanderers	1969	Manchester City
1930	Arsenal	1970	Chelsea
1931	West Bromwich Albion	1971	Arsenal
1932	Newcastle United	1972	Leeds United
1933	Everton	1973	Sunderland
1934	Manchester City	1974	Liverpool
1935	Sheffield Wednesday	1975	West Ham
1936	Arsenal	1976	Southampton
1937	Sunderland	1977	Manchester United
1938	Preston North End	1978	Ipswich
1939	Portsmouth	1979	Arsenal
1946	Derby County	1980	West Ham
1947	Charlton Athletic	1981	Tottenham Hotspur
1948	Manchester United	1982	Tottenham Hotspur
1949	Wolverhampton	1983	Manchester United
1950	Arsenal	1984	Everton
1951	Newcastle United	1985	Manchester United
1952	Newcastle United	1986	Liverpool
1953	Blackpool	1987	Coventry City
1954	West Bromwich Albion	1988	Wimbledon
1955	Newcastle United	1989	Liverpool
1956	Manchester City	1990	Manchester United
1957	Aston Villa	1991	Tottenham Hotspur
1958	Bolton Wanderers	1992	Liverpool
1959	Nottingham Forest	1993	Arsenal
1960	Wolverhampton	1994	Manchester United

The *English League Cup* was first contested in 1960, but it was not until 1970 that all 92 League teams competed. The Cup was first sponsored in 1982 by the Milk Marketing Board and became known as the Milk Cup until 1986 when Littlewoods took over. In 1992 Coca-Cola became the sponsor. The most successful League Cup teams have been Liverpool, Nottingham Forest and Aston Villa; all of whom have won the tournament four times.

The *Scottish Football League* was founded in 1890, two years after the English Football League. It was completely restructured in 1975/6 when the Premier Division, with the top ten clubs, was established with the remaining clubs divided into Divisions 1 and 2. A further restructuring in 1994 introduced a four-league system with ten teams in each. The 'Old Firm' of the two big Glasgow teams, Rangers and Celtic, have dominated since the League began. The First/Premier Division Champions have been:

1891	Dumbarton & Rangers	1923	Rangers	1963	Rangers
1892	Dumbarton	1924	Rangers	1964	Rangers
1893	Celtic	1925	Rangers	1965	Kilmarnock
1894	Celtic	1926	Celtic	1966	Celtic
1895	Hearts	1927	Rangers	1967	Celtic
1896	Celtic	1928	Rangers	1968	Celtic
1897	Hearts	1929	Rangers	1969	Celtic
1898	Celtic	1930	Rangers	1970	Celtic
1899	Rangers	1931	Rangers	1971	Celtic
1900	Rangers	1932	Motherwell	1972	Celtic
1901	Rangers	1933	Rangers	1973	Celtic
1902	Rangers	1934	Rangers	1974	Celtic
1903	Hibernian	1935	Rangers	1975	Rangers
1904	Third Lanark	1936	Celtic	1976	Rangers
1905	Celtic	1937	Rangers	1977	Celtic
1906	Celtic	1938	Celtic	1978	Rangers
1907	Celtic	1939	Rangers	1979	Celtic
1908	Celtic	1947	Rangers	1980	Aberdeen
1909	Celtic	1948	Hibernian	1981	Celtic
1910	Celtic	1949	Rangers	1982	Celtic
1911	Rangers	1950	Rangers	1983	Dundee Utd.
1912	Rangers	1951	Hibernian	1984	Aberdeen
1913	Rangers	1952	Hibernian	1985	Aberdeen
1914	Celtic	1953	Rangers	1986	Celtic
1915	Celtic	1954	Celtic	1987	Rangers
1916	Celtic	1955	Aberdeen	1988	Celtic
1917	Celtic	1956	Rangers	1989	Rangers
1918	Rangers	1957	Rangers	1990	Rangers
1919	Celtic	1958	Hearts	1991	Rangers
1920	Rangers	1959	Rangers	1992	Rangers
1921	Rangers	1960	Hearts	1993	Rangers
1922	Celtic	1961	Rangers	1994	Rangers
		1962	Dundee		

The first *Scottish FA Cup* competition was initiated at a meeting of eight clubs hosted by Queen's Park in 1873. It was their intention to establish a competition in Scotland similar to the English FA Cup. The final has traditionally been played at Hampden Park, Glasgow. The winners have been:

1874	Queen's Park	1911	Celtic	1959	St Mirren
1875	Queen's Park	1912	Celtic	1960	Rangers
1876	Queen's Park	1913	Falkirk	1961	Dunfermline
1877	Vale of Leven	1914	Celtic	1962	Rangers
1878	Vale of Leven	1920	Kilmarnock	1963	Rangers
1879	Vale of Leven	1921	Partick	1964	Rangers
1880	Queen's Park	1922	Morton	1965	Celtic
1881	Queen's Park	1923	Celtic	1966	Rangers
1882	Queen's Park	1924	Airdrie	1967	Celtic
1883	Dumbarton	1925	Celtic	1968	Dunfermline
1884	Queen's Park	1926	St Mirren	1969	Celtic
1885	Renton	1927	Celtic	1970	Aberdeen
1886	Queen's Park	1928	Rangers	1971	Celtic
1887	Hibernian	1929	Kilmarnock	1972	Celtic
1888	Renton	1930	Rangers	1973	Rangers
1889	Third Lanark	1931	Celtic	1974	Celtic
1890	Queen's Park	1932	Rangers	1975	Celtic
1891	Hearts	1933	Celtic	1976	Rangers
1892	Celtic	1934	Rangers	1977	Celtic
1893	Queen's Park	1935	Rangers	1978	Rangers
1894	Rangers	1936	Rangers	1979	Rangers
1895	St Bernard's	1937	Celtic	1980	Celtic
1896	Hearts	1938	East Fife	1981	Rangers
1897	Rangers	1939	Clyde	1982	Aberdeen
1898	Rangers	1947	Aberdeen	1983	Aberdeen
1899	Celtic	1948	Rangers	1984	Aberdeen
1900	Celtic	1949	Rangers	1985	Celtic
1901	Hearts	1950	Rangers	1986	Aberdeen
1902	Hibernian	1951	Celtic	1987	St Mirren
1903	Rangers	1952	Motherwell	1988	Celtic
1904	Celtic	1953	Rangers	1989	Celtic
1905	Third Lanark	1954	Celtic	1990	Aberdeen
1906	Hearts	1955	Clyde	1991	Motherwell
1907	Celtic	1956	Hearts	1992	Rangers
1908	Celtic	1957	Falkirk	1993	Rangers
1910	Dundee	1958	Clyde	1994	Dundee Utd

athletics are thought to have originated in the ancient Greek Olympic Games around 1370 BC. Organized events in England began in the mid-nineteenth century with the first regular competition taking place at Exeter College, Oxford, in 1850.

The most important competitions in international athletics are the OLYMPIC GAMES and the *World Championships*. There are also a number of events, such as the IAAF World Cup, the European Cup and the World Indoor Championships which attract top-class competition.

The first *World Championships* for athletics alone were held in 1983 at the Olympic Stadium in Helsinki, Finland. From 1993 they will be held biennially. The results of the men's events at Stuttgart in 1993 were as follows:

100m	L. Christie (UK)	9.87 sec**
200m	F. Fredericks (Namibia)	19.85 sec
400m	M. Johnson (USA)	43.65 sec
800m	P. Ruto (Kenya)	1 min 44.71 sec
1,500m	N. Morceli (Algeria)	3 min 34.24 sec
5,000m	I. Kirui (Kenya)	13 min 02.75 sec
10,000m	H. Gebresilassie (Ethiopia)	27 min 46.02 sec
Marathon	M. Plaatjes (USA)	2 hr 13 min 57 sec
110m hurdles	C. Jackson (UK)	12.91 sec*
400m hurdles	K. Young (USA)	47.18 sec
3,000m steeplechase	M. Kiptanui (Kenya)	8 min 06.36 sec
20 km walk	V. Masana (Spain)	1 hr 22 min 31 sec
50 km walk	J. A. Garcia (Spain)	3 hr 41 min 41 sec
4 x 100m	USA	37.48 sec
4 x 400m	USA	2 min 54.29 sec*
High jump	J. Sotomayor (Cuba)	2.40 metres
Long jump	M. Powell (USA)	8.59 metres
Triple jump	M. Conley (USA)	17.86 metres
Pole vault	S. Bubka (Ukraine)	6.00 metres
Shot putt	W. Günthör (USA)	21.97 metres
Discus	L. Riedel (Germany)	67.72 metres
Hammer	A. Abduvaleyiv (Tadjikstan)	81.64 metres
Javelin	J. Zelezny (Czech Rep.)	85.98 metres
Decathlon	D. O'Brien (USA)	8817 points

*World record ** European record*

The results of the women's events at Stuttgart in 1993 were:

100m	G. Devers (USA)	10.82 sec
200m	M. Ottey (Jamaica)	21.98 sec
400m	J. Miles (USA)	49.82 sec
800m	M. Mutola (Mozambique)	1 min 55.43 sec
1,500m	L. Dong(China)	4 min 00.50 sec
3,000m	Q. Yunxia (China)	8 min 28.71 sec
10,000m	W. Junxia (China)	30 min 39.30 sec
Marathon	J. Asari (Japan)	2 hr 30 min 03 sec
100m hurdles	G. Devers (USA)	12.46 sec
400m hurdles	S. Gunnel (UK)	52.74 sec*
10 km walk	S. Essayah (Finland)	42 min 59 sec
4 x 100m	Russia	41.49 sec
4 x 400m	USA	3 min 16.71 sec
High jump	I. Quintero (Cuba)	1.99 metres
Long jump	H. Drechsler (Germany)	7.11 metres
Shot putt	Z. Huang (China)	20.57 metres
Discus	O. Burova (Russia)	67.40 metres
Javelin	T. Hattestad (Norway)	69.18 metres
Heptathlon	J. Joyner-Kersee (USA)	6837 points

World record

World Mile Record (since 1954)

Year	Venue	Runner	Time
1954	Oxford	Roger Bannister (UK)	3 min 59.40 sec
1954	Turku	John Landy (Australia)	3 min 57.90 sec
1957	London	Doug Ibbotson (UK)	3 min 57.20 sec
1958	Dublin	Herb Elliott (Australia)	3 min 54.50 sec
1962	Wanganui	Peter Snell (New Zealand)	3 min 54.40 sec
1964	Auckland	Peter Snell (New Zealand)	3 min 54.10 sec
1965	Rennes	Michael Jazy (France)	3 min 53.60 sec
1966	Berkeley	Jim Ryun (USA)	3 min 51.30 sec
1967	Bakersfield	Jim Ryun (USA)	3 min 51.10 sec
1975	Kingston	Filbert Bayi (Tanzania)	3 min 51.00 sec
1975	Gothenburg	John Walker (New Zealand)	3 min 49.40 sec
1979	Oslo	Sebastian Coe (UK)	3 min 49.00 sec
1980	Oslo	Steve Ovett (UK)	3 min 48.80 sec
1981	Zurich	Sebastian Coe (UK)	3 min 48.53 sec
1981	Koblenz	Steve Ovett (UK)	3 min 48.40 sec
1981	Brussels	Sebastian Coe (UK)	3 min 47.43 sec
1985	Oslo	Steve Cram (UK)	3 min 46.32 sec
1993	Rieti	Noureddine Morceli (Algeria)	3 min 44.39 sec

British Open *see* GOLF.

badminton is believed to have originated either from Badminton Hall in Avon, *c*.1870, where it was played by the family and guests of the Duke of Beaufort, or from a game played in India around the same time. The modern rules of the sport were established in India, however, where it was very popular for a time among British Army officers. The Badminton Association was founded in England in 1893 and the International Badminton Federation in 1934.

The most important competitions are the Thomas Cup (Men), the Uber Cup, (Women) and the *World Championships*, all of which are held biennially. In recent years teams from Indonesia, China and Japan have dominated international competition.

baseball according to American folklore the game was invented by a West Point cadet, Abner Doubleday, in 1839. A game of the same name, however, is known to have been played in England prior to 1700, and it is more likely that baseball evolved from such popular bat and ball games as cricket and rounders.

The first rules of the modern game were established in 1845 by Alexander Cartwright Jr and the professional game developed almost entirely in North America where there are two 'major' leagues, the American (AL) and the National (NL), founded in 1901 and 1876 respectively.

The *World Series* is a best-of-seven contest held annually between the winners of the two professional baseball leagues. It was first played in 1903 and is now one of America's most popular sporting events. In 1992 the Toronto Blue Jays became the first non-American team to win the series when they defeated the Atlanta Braves. The winners since 1980 have been:

1980	Philadelphia Phillies	1987	Minnesota Twins
1981	Los Angeles Dodgers	1988	Los Angeles Dodgers
1982	St Louis Cardinals	1989	Oakland Athletics
1983	Baltimore Orioles	1990	Cincinnati Reds
1984	Detroit Tigers	1991	Minnesota Twins
1985	Kansas City Royals	1992	Toronto Blue Jays
1986	New York Mets	1993	Toronto Blue Jays

At international level South American teams dominate. The most successful country is Cuba, which has won the World Amateur Championships 20 times since it was established in 1938. Baseball has also been a demonstration sport at six OLYMPIC GAMES and became a medal sport for the first time in 1992.

basketball in its present form was invented in 1891 by Dr James Naismith, a sports instructor from Springfield, Massachussets, although games bearing a strong resemblance to basketball have been played for thousands of years. Early games in America featured large numbers of players but the five-a-side standard was agreed in 1895 and the first league established three years later.

In America there are now 23 professional basketball teams and it is one of the most popular spectator sports, with televised games attracting large audiences.

The *NBA Championship* is contested annually by the 23 professional basketball teams in the USA. The teams are divided into two conferences, Eastern and Western, which are sub-divided into the Western and Atlantic Divisions and the Midwest and Pacific Divisions respectively. A series of play-offs decide the champions. Recent NBA champions have been:

1980	Los Angeles Lakers	1988	Los Angeles Lakers
1981	Boston Celtics	1989	Detroit Pistons
1982	Los Angeles Lakers	1990	Detroit Pistons
1983	Philadelphia 76ers	1991	Chicago Bulls
1984	Boston Celtics	1992	Chicago Bulls
1985	Los Angeles Lakers	1993	Chicago Bulls
1986	Boston Celtics	1994	Houston Rockets
1987	Los Angeles Lakers		

At amateur level it is popular around the world and has been included in the OLYMPIC GAMES since 1936 (the woman's game was included in 1976). *World Championships*, first held in 1950 (Men) and 1953 (Women), are staged every four years and have been dominated in recent years by teams from the USA and Yugoslavia.

biathlon is one of the most physically demanding combination sports. Competitors ski over a prepared course carrying a small bore rifle and stop for either two or four shooting competitions, standing and prone. Men compete over 10km and 20km and women over 7.5km and 15km. There is also a relay event which is 4 x 7.5km with every member shooting once.

Men's biathlon has been included in the OLYMPIC GAMES since 1960 and the women's event since 1992. There is also a World Cup and a World Championship, both contested annually.

billiards is believed to have evolved from the game of *paille-malle*, played on grass. Popular in the 15th century, Louis XI, King of France (1461-83), is known to have had a table. Today there are World professional and amateur championships, played annually and biennially respectively.

bobsleigh and *toboggan* racing was pioneered by a group of Swiss enthusiasts who organised the first known bobsleigh races in the 1880's. The first two luge runs were built in 1879 at Davos in Switzerland.

There are now bobsleigh events in the OLYMPIC GAMES for two- and four man teams and for single man luge toboggans.

bowls the rules of the modern game were framed in 1848-9 by a Scottish solicitor, William Mitchell, although similar games were played as early as the thirteenth century. There are now two types of greens, the 'crown' and the 'level', the former almost exclusive to the North of England, the latter played mostly in the UK and Commonwealth countries.

World Outdoor Championships were established in 1966 for men and 1969 for women. They are held every four years, with singles, pairs, triples and fours events. The Leonard Trophy is presented to the overall best men's team. The 1993 champions were:

Men	Singles	T. Allcock (England)
	Pairs	R. Corsie and A. Marshall (Scotland)
	Triples	Israel
	Fours	Scotland
	Overall	Scotland
Women	Singles	M. Johnston (Ireland)
	Pairs	M. Johnston and P. Nolan (Ireland)
	Triples	Scotland
	Fours	Scotland
	Overall	Scotland

boxing is one of man's oldest physical contests. The first organized boxing match is thought to have taken place in the 17th century when the Duke of Albemarle organised a fight between his butler and his butcher. The modern rules which introduced gloves were set out in 1867 by the 8th Marquis of Queensbury (who gave his name to them). The first world championship fight took place in 1884 with Jack Dempsey beating George Fulljames in New York for the middleweight title.

In boxing today there are four different governing authorities, all with their own weight classes, titles and fight regulations This naturally leads to confusion, especially as all four governing bodies recognise world champions. The four are: the World Boxing

Association (founded 1960), the World Boxing Council (1963), the World Boxing Organisation (1988) and the International Boxing Federation (1983).

The weight categories accepted by the WBC are as follows:

Weight	Limit	Also known as
Heavy	over 190 lbs.	
Cruiser	190 lbs.	Junior Heavy (WBO)
Light Heavy	175 lbs.	
Super Middle	168 lbs.	
Middle	160 lbs.	
Super Welter	154 lbs.	Junior Middle (WBO, IBF, WBA)
Welter	147 lbs.	
Super Light	140 lbs.	Junior Welter (WBO, IBF, WBA)
Light	135 lbs.	
Super Feather	130 lbs.	Junior Light (WBO, IBF, WBA)
Feather	126 lbs.	
Super Bantam	122 lbs.	Junior Feather (WBO, IBF, WBA)
Bantam	118 lbs.	
Super Fly	115 lbs.	Junior Bantam (WBO, IBF, WBA)
Flyweight	112 lbs.	
Light Fly	108 lbs.	Junior Fly (WBO, IBF, WBA)
Straw	105 lbs.	Mini Fly (WBO, IBF, WBA)

The current *World Title Holders* are:

	WBC	WBA
Heavy	L. Lewis (UK)	R. Bowe (USA)
Cruiser	A. Wamba (France)	B. Czyz (USA)
Light Heavy	J. Harding (Austalia)	V. Hill (USA)
Super Middle	N. Benn (UK)	M. Nunn (USA)
Middle	G. McClellan (USA)	R. Johnson (USA)
Super Welter	T. Norris (USA)	J. Vasquez (Argentina)
Welter	P. Whitaker (USA)	C. Espana (Venezuela)
Super Light	J. C. Chavez (Mexico)	J. M. Coggi (Argentina)
Light	M. Gonzalez (Mexico)	D. Thobela (S. Africa)
Super Feather	A. Nelson (Ghana)	G. Hermandez (USA)
Feather	G. Vargaz (Columbia)	Y. K. Park (Korea)
Super Bantam	T. Patterson ((USA)	W. Vasquez (Peurto Rico)
Bantam	J. Byun (S. Korea)	J. E. Julio (Columbia)
Super Fly	S. Moon (S. Kórea)	K. Onizuka (Japan)
Fly	Y. Arbachakov (Russia)	D. Griman (Venezuela)
Light Fly	M. Carbajal (USA)	M. W. Yuh (Korea)
Straw	R. Lopez (Mexico)	C. Porpaoin (Thailand)

Calcutta Cup *see* RUGBY UNION.

canoeing as a sport can be attributed to an English barrister, John MacGregor, founder of the Royal Canoe Club in 1866. In the sport today there is flat and wild water competition featuring kayaks (double blade) and Canadian canoe (single blade). It has been included in the OLYMPIC GAMES, with several different categories, since 1936.

Commonwealth Games are held every four years and are contested by representatives of the British Commonwealth. The original idea for the games was suggested by the Rev. J Astley Cooper in the magazine *Greater Britain* in 1891. The first British Empire Games were held in 1930 in Canada and four sports were contested by representatives of Great Britain, Canada, Australia and New Zealand.

Known as the Commonwealth Games since 1970, recent Games have included ten sports. Athletics and swimming are obligatory, and the other eight are selected from 15 recognized sports, with two demonstration sports also chosen. The venues for the Games have been:

1930	Hamilton, Canada	1970	Edinburgh, Scotland
1934	London, England	1974	Christchurch, New Zealand
1938	Sydney, Australia	1978	Edmonton, Canada
1950	Auckland, New Zealand	1982	Brisbane, Australia
1954	Vancouver, Canada	1986	Edinburgh, Scotland
1958	Cardiff, Wales	1990	Auckland, New Zealand
1962	Perth, Australia	1994	Victoria, Canada
1966	Kingston, Jamaica		

County Championship *see* CRICKET.

cricket the precise origins of cricket are unclear although games with a bat and ball were played as long ago as the 13th century. The first match in which scores were kept was contested in 1744 by England and Kent. The Marylebone Cricket Club was founded in 1787 and remained the governing body for the sport until the formation of the Cricket council in 1968.

The Imperial (International from 1965) Cricket Conference (ICC) was formed in 1909 and now has nine Test-playing members, nineteen associate members and five affiliated members. The nine full, test-playing members are England, Australia, West Indies, India, Pakistan, New Zealand, Sri Lanka, South Africa (ceased to be a member in 1961, re-admitted in 1992) and Zimbabwe (from 1992).

Cricket fielding positions

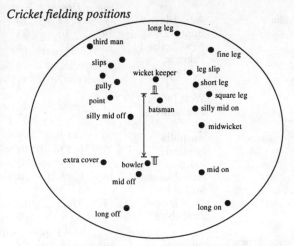

Distance wicket to wicket: 22 yards (20.1 metres)

The first Test match was played at Melbourne in 1877 between Australia and England and the first in England played by the same nations three years later, although in both these contests neither side was truly representative of their countries.

The summarized results of Test match series completed by the 1st of February 1994:

		Won	Drawn	Lost
England v	Australia	89	83	108
	India	31	36	14
	New Zealand	33	35	4
	Pakistan	14	31	7
	South Africa	46	38	18
	Sri Lanka	3	1	1
	West Indies	24	37	43
Australia v	England	108	83	89
	India	24	17	8
	New Zealand	13	12	7
	Pakistan	12	13	9
	South Africa	30	14	12
	Sri Lanka	4	3	0
	West Indies	30	20	26

		Won	Drawn	Lost
India v	Australia	8	17	24
	England	14	36	31
	New Zealand	12	13	6
	Pakistan	4	7	7
	South Africa	0	3	1
	Sri Lanka	7	6	1
	West Indies	6	30	26
	Zimbabwe	1	1	0
Pakistan v	Australia	9	13	12
	England	7	31	14
	India	7	33	4
	New Zealand	16	16	4
	Sri Lanka	6	5	1
	West Indies	7	12	12
	Zimbabwe	2	1	0
South Africa v	Australia	12	14	30
	England	18	38	46
	India	1	3	0
	New Zealand	9	6	2
	Sri Lanka	1	2	0
	West Indies	0	0	1
Sri Lanka v	Australia	0	3	4
	England	1	1	3
	India	1	6	7
	New Zealand	1	6	4
	Pakistan	1	5	6
	South Africa	0	2	1
	West Indies	0	1	0
West Indies v	Australia	26	20	30
	England	43	37	24
	India	26	30	6
	New Zealand	8	12	4
	Pakistan	12	12	7
	South Africa	1	0	0
	Sri Lanka	0	1	0
Zimbabwe v	India	0	1	1
	New Zealand	0	1	1
	Pakistan	0	1	2

		Won	Drawn	Lost
New Zealand	Australia	7	12	13
	England	4	35	33
	India	6	13	12
	Pakistan	4	16	16
	South Africa	2	6	9
	Sri Lanka	4	6	1
	West Indies	4	12	8

English *County Championship* cricket began with the first recorded match between counties contested by Kent and Surrey in 1709. The first county to be declared county champions was Surrey in 1827. From 1827 to 1889 the champions were decided on the basis of fewest matches lost and Kent, Surrey and Sussex dominated. Since 1890 the Championships have been contested on a points system. The post-war winners have been:

1946	Yorkshire	1970	Kent
1947	Middlesex	1971	Surrey
1948	Glamorgan	1972	Warwickshire
1949	Middlesex	1973	Hampshire
	and Yorkshire	1974	Worcestershire
1950	Lancaster	1975	Leicestershire
	and Surrey	1976	Middlesex
1951	Warwickshire	1977	Middlesex and Kent
1952	Surrey	1978	Kent
1953	Surrey	1979	Essex
1954	Surrey	1980	Middlesex
1955	Surrey	1981	Nottinghamshire
1956	Surrey	1982	Middlesex
1957	Surrey	1983	Essex
1958	Surrey	1984	Essex
1959	Yorkshire	1985	Middlesex
1960	Yorkshire	1986	Essex
1961	Hampshire	1987	Nottinghamshire
1962	Yorkshire	1988	Worcestershire
1963	Yorkshire	1989	Worcestershire
1964	Worcestershire	1990	Middlesex
1965	Worcestershire	1991	Essex
1966	Yorkshire	1992	Essex
1967	Yorkshire	1993	Middlesex
1968	Yorkshire	1994	Warwickshire
1969	Glamorgan		

cross-country running was first staged with an international field in 1903 at Hamilton Park Racecourse in Scotland. The World Cross-Country Championships are now held annually with the senior events being run over 5km and 12km courses for women and men respectively.

cycling the first treadle-propelled bicycle was invented by Scottish blacksmith Kirkpatrick Macmillan in 1839, but it was not until the more refined *vélocipède* was built by Pierre Michaux of Paris, in 1861, that there was any popular interest in bicycle racing. The first club was the Liverpool Velocipede Club which was formed in 1867 and the first race (over 1200 metres) took place in Paris a year later.

Included in the OLYMPIC GAMES since 1896, there are currently nine events in the programme including sprint, pursuit, time trials, and individual and team road racing events.

The *Tour De France* is the most famous cycle race in the world. First held in 1903, it is now one of the world's most popular spectator events. The course changes every year but always includes a number of mountain stages as well as time trials. It is held over a three week period. Recent overall winners have been:

1979 B. Hinault (France)	1987 S. Roche (Ireland)
1980 J. Zoetemelk (Holland)	1988 P. Delgado (Spain)
1981 B. Hinault (France)	1989 G. LeMond (USA)
1982 B. Hinault (France)	1990 G. LeMond (USA)
1983 L. Fignon (France)	1991 M. Indurain (Spain)
1984 L. Fignon (France)	1992 M. Indurain (Spain)
1985 B. Hinault (France)	1993 M. Indurain (Spain)
1986 G. LeMond (USA)	1994 M. Indurain (Spain)

Davis Cup *see* TENNIS.

English F.A Cup *see* ASSOCIATION FOOTBALL.

English Football League *see* ASSOCIATION FOOTBALL.

English League Cup *see* ASSOCIATION FOOTBALL.

European Championship *see* ARCHERY, ATHLETICS, BADMINTON, BOWLS

European Cup *see* ASSOCIATION FOOTBALL.

European Cup-Winner's Cup *see* ASSOCIATION FOOTBALL.

European Super Cup *see* ASSOCIATION FOOTBALL.

equestrianism although horse-riding is many thousands of years old, competition jumping only became popular in the late nineteenth century with the first 'Horse Show' held in Dublin in

1867. Dressage competition evolved from French and Italian horsemanship acadamies in the 16th century, while the three-day event has its origins in cavalry endurance tests.

Equestrian events have been included in the OLYMPIC GAMES since 1912, but the first competition to combine all six equestrian disciplines – show jumping, three-day eventing, dressage, carriage driving, endurance riding and vaulting – was the *World Equestrian Games*, first held in Stockholm in 1990. The second Games were staged at the Hague in 1994.

fencing has its origins in the duelling of the Middle Ages, although fighting with swords had been practised as a sport in older civilizations.

There are three types of sword used today: the *foil*, the *épée* and the *sabre*. Each is a separate discipline with a different set of rules applicable to it in competition;

weapon	weight	target
épée	770 grams	whole body
foil	500 grams (maximum)	upper body
sabre	500 grams	upper body and head

Fencing has been included in all OLYMPIC GAMES, and these tournaments count as *World Championships* in Olympic years. Women first competed in the 1924 Games.

football *see* ASSOCIATION FOOTBALL, AMERICAN FOOTBALL.

golf although the precise origins are unclear, it was in Scotland that the popular pastime was first properly organized and the first club established. The earliest rules to the game were drawn up in 1754 by enthusiasts in St Andrews who went on to form the Royal and Ancient Golf Club. In 1764 18 holes was declared as the standard round, but it was not until 1919 that the Royal and Ancient, who had decided the number, was formally recognized as the supreme authority in golfing matters.

In professional golf the most prestigious and financially rewarding competitions are the four events which make up *the majors*: the British Open, the US Open, the US Masters and US PGA. These are played annually at different courses, except the US Masters which is always played at the Augusta National course in Georgia.

Although not offering the same high levels of prize money, there is also a well-established Masters series in women's golf. These are: US Women's Open, LPGA Championships, Nabisco Dinah Shore and Du Maurier Classic.

The *British Open* was first played over three twelve-hole rounds at Prestwick, Scotland, in 1860. Prestwick hosted the first twelve Opens and all subsequent championships have been played over various seaside links courses around Britain. Prize money (totalling £10) was introduced in 1863. Since 1960 the winners of the tournament have been:

1960	K. Nagle (Australia)	1978	J. Nicklaus (USA)
1961	A. Palmer (USA)	1979	S. Ballesteros (Spain)
1962	A. Palmer (USA)	1980	T. Watson (USA)
1963	B. Charles (New Zealand)	1981	B. Rogers (USA)
		1982	T. Watson (USA)
1964	T. Lema (USA)	1983	T. Watson (USA)
1965	P. Thomson (Australia)	1984	S. Ballesteros (Spain)
1966	J. Nicklaus (USA)	1985	S. Lyle (UK)
1967	R. Vicenzo (Argentina)	1986	G. Norman (Australia)
1968	G. Player (S. Africa)	1987	N. Faldo (UK)
1969	T. Jacklin (UK)	1988	S. Ballesteros (Spain)
1970	J. Nicklaus (USA)	1989	M. Calcavecchia (USA)
1971	L. Trevino (USA)	1990	N. Faldo (UK)
1972	L. Trevino (USA)	1991	I. Baker-Finch (Australia)
1973	T. Weiskopf (USA)		
1974	G. Player (S. Africa)	1992	N. Faldo (UK)
1975	T. Watson (USA)	1993	G. Norman (Australia)
1976	J. Miller (USA)	1994	N. Price (Zimbabwe)
1977	T. Watson (USA)		

The *Ryder Cup* was launched in 1927, following a successful match between the USA and Great Britain. It is now held biennially with the teams taking it in turn to play host. The Great Britain team was succeeded by a Great Britain and Ireland team in 1973, which in turn was succeeded by a European team from 1979. The winners of the tournament have been:

1927	USA	1955	USA	1975	USA
1929	GB	1957	GB	1977	USA
1931	USA	1959	USA	1979	USA
1933	GB	1961	USA	1981	USA
1935	USA	1963	USA	1983	USA
1937	USA	1965	USA	1985	Europe
1947	USA	1967	USA	1987	Europe
1949	USA	1969	Drawn	1989	Drawn
1951	USA	1971	USA	1991	USA
1953	USA	1973	USA	1993	USA

Grand National *see* HORSE RACING.

Grand Prix *see* MOTOR RACING.

Grand Slam *see* RUGBY UNION, TENNIS.

gymnastics although the origins of gymnastics can be traced back to the ancient civilizations of Greece, Persia, China and India, as a modern competitive sport it has been developed primarily in Eastern European countries. The first national federation was formed in Germany in 1860 and gymnastics were included in the first modern OLYMPIC GAMES in 1896, although women's events were not introduced until 1928.

The apparatus used in modern gymnastics differs for men and women. Men use the parallel bars, horizontal bar, pommel horse, rings and horse vault. Women use asymmetrical bars, the beam, and the horse vault.

The *World Championships* were established in 1903 for men and 1934 for women. Both are now held biennially.

Modern rhythmic gymnastics for women use ropes, hoops, ribbons and balls in musically accompanied floor exercises, and have been included in the OLYMPIC GAMES since 1984.

handball is similar to football, only played with the hands rather than the feet. It was first played at the end of the nineteenth century in Germany and it has remained most popular in that country.

At the 1936 OLYMPIC GAMES it was played by 11-a-side teams outdoors, but when it was re-introduced in 1972 it was as a 7-a-side indoor event. *World Championships* take place every four years and a European Cup, for national champions, is contested annually.

hang gliding as a modern sport was pioneered by Otto Lilienthal in Germany in the late 19th century. The distances travelled and the duration of flights have increased dramatically in recent years with developments in technology and design. *World Championships* were first held in 1975 and are now held biennially.

hockey was played in primitive form in ancient civilizations, and tomb drawings in the Nile Valley suggest it could be as much as 4000 years old. The modern game became popular in the mid-nineteenth century when many public schools took up the sport.

The most successful teams at international level have traditionally been from India and Pakistan, although recently European teams have dominated the major competitions. The IHF World Cup and the Champion's Trophy are the premier competitions, and the sport has been included in the OLYMPIC GAMES since 1908.

horse racing has its origins in warfare, hunting, and chariot racing with the earliest reference to prize money being the purse of gold offered by Richard I in 1195. The oldest known racecourse in Britain is on the Roodee at Chester, England, which staged its first meeting in 1540.

There are two kinds of modern racing: flat racing and jumping, with the latter divided into steeplechasing and hurdle racing. The most important flat racing events in Britain are the five English Classics; the Derby, the Oaks, the St Leger and the 1000 and 2000 Guineas. Other famous races held annually include the series of Irish and French Classics, the Coronation Cup at Epsom and the Ascot Gold Cup at Royal Ascot.

In National Hunt Racing the *Grand National* and the Cheltenham Gold Cup are the two most important events in the British calendar. The Grand National is the oldest and most famous steeplechase in the world. It has been run at Aintree, Liverpool every year since 1847 with the exception of the war years and 1993, when the race was abandoned after a false start. The current course takes in 30 fences over two circuits and is four miles and four furlongs long. Recent winning horses have been:

1980	Ben Nevis	1987	Maori Venture
1981	Aldaniti	1988	Rhyme N'Reason
1982	Grittar	1989	Little Polveir
1983	Corbiere	1990	Mr Frisk
1984	Hallo Dandy	1991	Seagram
1985	Last Suspect	1992	Party Politics
1986	West Tip	1994	Minnehoma

The only horse to have ever won the Grand National three times was Red Rum (1973-74, 77).

hurling is one of Ireland's oldest competative sports, but standardized only since the foundation of the Gaelic Athletic Association in 1884. The hurl, or stick, is similar to the hockey stick only flat on both sides. The All-Ireland Championship has been held annually since 1887.

ice hockey was developed in Canada in the late nineteenth century with the first club founded in Montreal in 1880. World Championships have been held annually since 1930 with teams from North America, Scandanavia and Eastern Europe dominating in recent years. It has been included in the OLYMPIC GAMES since 1920.

ice skating is over 2000 years old and first became popular in the Netherlands, although the first known skating club was formed in Edinburgh in the mid 18th century. The first artificial ice rink was opened at the Glaciarium, London in 1876.

The modern sport can be divided in two; figure skating and speed skating. *World Championships* are contested in both disciplines. Figure skating has been included in the OLYMPIC GAMES since 1908 and speed skating was introduced in the 1924 Games (1960 for the women's event).

International Championship *see* RUGBY UNION.

judo was developed from several different schools of Japanese martial arts. The first training school was founded in Shitaya in 1882 by Dr Jigoro Kano. 'Ju' means 'soft', and the sport relies on speed and skill as opposed to brute force. Efficiency classes in judo are divided into pupil (kyu) and master (dan) grades.

*Kyu grade*s:	*Dan grades*:
1st Kyu – brown	1st to 5th Dan – black
2nd Kyu – blue	6th to 8th Dan – red and white
3rd Kyu – green	9th to 11th Dan – red
4th Kyu – orange	12th Dan – white
5th Kyu – yellow	

It has been included in the Olympics since 1964 (except 1968) and there are currently twelve weight divisions.

lacrosse was originally played by North American Indians and taken up by the French settlers, who called the game *baggataway*. The modern crosse, or playing stick, evolved from the early implement used by the Indians which was a curved stick with a net fitted at one end. The women's game evolved separately from that played by men, and they both now have *World Championships*.

lawn tennis *see* TENNIS.

modern pentathlon, as it was introduced at the 1912 OLYMPIC GAMES, consists of horse riding, fencing, shooting, swimming and cross-country running.

For many years the sport was dominated by members of the military forces, and military lore explains the origins of the modern format thus; a messenger has to ride on horseback, fight with sword and pistol, swim a river and run on foot to complete his journey. Recently the format of the sport has been amended by the Olympic Committee and instead of being competed for over three or more days it will now be staged over one day.

motor cycling the earliest motorcycle race was held in 1897 at Sheen House in Richmond over an oval course of one mile. *World Championship* races began in 1949 with classes for 50cc, 125cc, 250cc, 350cc, 500cc bikes and sidecars. In road-racing the most important series is the Isle of Man TT races which were first held in 1907. Moto-Cross, also known as *scrambling*, is a specialised branch of motorcycle racing with competitors negotiating undulating dirt tracks or circuits on specially adapted motorcycles. A *World Championship* is held annually.

motor racing was inevitable with the invention, and rapid growth in popularity, of the motor car. The first known race took place in Paris in 1887 and was won by Count Jules Felix Philippe Albert de Dion de Malfiance, riding a steam quadricycle.

The most prestigious class of racing, that of Formula One, held its first *World Championship* in 1950, although the first Grand Prix was run in France in 1906. Other notable competitions are the Le Mans circuit (for touring cars), the Indy Car World Series (16 races in North America and Australia), and the many long distance 'rally' events held around the world.

The *World Championship Grand Prix* was inaugurated in 1949. The first Grand Prix was held at Silverstone, England, and won by the Italian Guiseppe Farina. Grand Prix are now staged all over the world and points are awarded for finishing places which count towards the World Championship. Recent World Champion drivers have been:

1980	A. Jones (Australia)	1987	N. Piquet (Brazil)
1981	N. Piquet (Brazil)	1988	A. Senna (Brazil)
1982	K. Roseburg (Finland)	1989	A. Prost (France)
1983	N. Piquet (Brazil)	1990	A. Senna (Brazil)
1984	N. Lauda (Austria)	1991	A. Senna (Brazil)
1985	A. Prost (France)	1992	N. Mansell (UK)
1986	A. Prost (France)	1993	A. Prost (France)

NBA Championship *see* BASKETBALL.

netball is a seven-a-side game played primarily by women. It was developed in the USA at the end of the 19th century.

A *World Championship* has been held every four years since 1963. In recent years they have been dominated by teams from Australia and New Zealand.

Olympic Games were first staged every four years at Olympia, 120 miles west of Athens, with the earliest recorded games being held in 776 BC. The games grew in size and importance and reached the peak of their fame in the 5th and 4th centuries BC when events included running, jumping, boxing, wrestling, discus and chariot racing.

The final games of the ancient era were held in AD 393, before the Emperor of Rome, Theodosius I, decreed their prohibition because they were disapproved of by the early Christians.

The first modern Games were instigated by a Frenchman, Pierre de Fredi, Baron de Coubertin. His efforts to bring back the principle of the ancient Games and re-establish the high sporting standards of the early Greeks led to the formation of the International Olympic Committee in 1895, and thence to the staging of the 1896 Games in Athens. The venues of the summer Games have been:

I	1896	Athens, Greece
II	1900	Paris, France
III	1904	St Louis, USA
IV	1908	London, England
V	1912	Stockholm, Sweden
VI	1916	Berlin, Germany
VII	1920	Antwerp, Belgium
VIII	1924	Paris, France
IX	1928	Amsterdam, Netherlands
X	1932	Los Angeles, USA
XI	1936	Berlin, Germany
XII	1940	Not held
XIII	1944	Not held
XIV	1948	London, England
XV	1952	Helsinki, Finland
XVI	1956	Melbourne, Australia
XVII	1960	Rome, Italy
XVIII	1964	Tokyo, Japan
XIX	1968	Mexico City, Mexico
XX	1972	Munich, FR Germany
XXI	1976	Montreal, Canada
XXII	1980	Moscow, USSR
XXIII	1984	Los Angeles, USA
XXIV	1988	Seoul, South Korea
XXV	1992	Barcelona, Spain

The XXVI Games in 1996 will be held in Atlanta, USA, and the XXVII Olympic Games in the year 2000 will be held in Sydney, Australia.

rowing the earliest established sculling race, the *Dogget's Coat and Badge*, was instituted in 1715 by the Irish comedian Thomas Dogget and was rowed from London Bridge to Chelsea. The first regatta was held on the Thames at Putney in 1775.

Rowing has been a part of the OLYMPIC GAMES since 1900, and *World Championships* have been held every year since 1962.

The famous *University Boat Race* between Oxford and Cambridge Universities was first held in 1829. The Putney to Mortlake course, over a distance of 6779km (4 miles 374 yards), which is currently used has not changed since 1863. At present Cambridge lead in the series of 139 races with 70 wins to Oxford's 68. The only dead heat in the history of the race was recorded in 1877.

rugby league originated as a breakaway from Rugby Union in 1895 when the governing body refused to let northern clubs pay players who were losing their Saturday wage to play. Today it is most popular in the north of England, Australia, New Zealand and France. The most important tournaments in England are for the Premiership Trophy and the Challenge Cup. Both are contested annually.

Inaugurated in 1954, the *World Cup* was replaced by the International Championship in 1977 and revived in 1985. The winners of the competition have been:

1954	Great Britain	1972	Great Britain
1957	Australia	1975	Australia
1960	Great Britain	1977	Australia
1968	Australia	1988	Australia
1970	Australia	1992	Australia

rugby union is thought to have its origins at Rugby School, England, as the modern game can supposedly be traced back to the moment when William Webb Ellis picked up the ball and ran with it during a school football match in 1823.

The Rugby Football Union (RFU) was established in 1871 and the Federation International de Rugby Amateur (FIRA) was founded in 1934. Membership reached 49 nations in 1992.

At international level the annual *International Championship* and the recently established *World Cup* are the most important events. A home nations select team, the British Lions, has toured Australia, New Zealand and South Africa 22 times since 1888.

The first Rugby Union World Cup tournament was played in Australia and New Zealand in 1987 by 16 national teams. The second was played in Britain and France in 1991. The results of the World Cup finals played were:

1987	New Zealand	29	France	9
1991	Australia	12	England	6

The *International Championship* was first contested by the home nations in 1884, with France joining to make it the 'Five Nations' tournament in 1910. Each team plays each other once during the season, the venues alternating from year to year.

The *Grand Slam* is the beating of all four other nations in one season's games and the *Triple Crown* is awarded to the home nation team which beats the other three. The *Calcutta Cup* is played for by England and Scotland. The winners of the Championship since 1920 have been:

1920 Wales and Scotland tie
1921 England
1922 Wales
1923 England
1924 England
1925 Scotland
1926 Ireland and Scotland tie
1927 Ireland and Scotland tie
1928 England
1929 Scotland
1930 England
1931 Wales
1932 England, Wales and Scotland tie
1933 Scotland
1934 England
1935 Ireland
1936 Wales
1937 England
1938 Scotland
1939 England, Wales and Ireland tie
1947 England and Wales tie
1948 Ireland

1949 Ireland
1950 Wales
1951 Ireland
1952 Wales
1953 England
1954 England, France and Wales tie
1955 Wales and France tie
1956 Wales
1957 England
1958 England
1959 France
1960 England and France tie
1961 France
1962 France
1963 England
1964 Scotland and Wales tie
1965 Wales
1966 Wales
1967 France
1968 France
1969 Wales
1970 France and Wales tie

1971 Wales
1972 incomplete
1973 all tie
1974 Ireland
1975 Wales
1976 Wales
1977 France
1978 Wales
1979 Wales
1980 England
1981 France
1982 Ireland
1983 France and Ireland tie
1984 Scotland
1985 Ireland
1986 France and Scotland tie
1987 France
1988 Wales and France tie
1989 France
1990 Scotland
1991 England
1992 England
1993 France
1994 Ireland

Ryder Cup *see* GOLF.

Scottish FA Cup *see* ASSOCIATION FOOTBALL.

Scottish Football League *see* ASSOCIATION FOOTBALL.

shooting the first shooting club, the Lucerne Shooting Guild was formed around 1466 and the first recorded match held in Zurich in 1472. It has been a feature of the OLYMPIC GAMES since the first modern games in 1896.

skiing the home of the sport is undoubtedly Scandinavia, where the first competative slalom was held in Murren, Switzerland in 1922.

There are two kinds of competative skiing; *Nordic*, which is cross-country or jumping, and *Alpine*, which is racing on prepared slopes. Nordic skiing has been included in the OLYMPIC GAMES since 1924 and *World Championships* have been held biennially since 1939. Alpine skiing has been an Olympic sport since 1936 and *World Championships* have been held biennially since 1939.

snooker it is generally thought that Colonel Sir Neville Chamberlain concocted the game of snooker in 1875 at Madras in India. The name *snooker* is taken from the nickname given to first year cadets at the Royal Military Acadamy, Woolwich. The first rules were established by The Billiards Association in 1900.

Snooker *World Championships* were first held in 1926. The tournament was discontinued in 1952 and not restored until 1964. In 1969 it became a knock-out contest. Since 1979 all finals have been held at the Crucible Theatre in Sheffield. Recent World Champions have been:

1981 S. Davis (England)	1988 S. Davis (England)
1982 A. Higgins (N. Ireland)	1989 S. Davis (England)
1983 S. Davis (England)	1990 S. Hendry (Scotland)
1984 S. Davis (England)	1991 J. Parrot (England)
1985 D. Taylor (N. Ireland)	1992 S. Hendry (Scotland)
1986 J. Johnson (England)	1993 S. Hendry (Scotland)
1987 S. Davis (England)	1994 S. Hendry (Scotland)

squash was developed at Harrow School in England in the early nineteenth century. It was originally a game for practising rackets but substituting a softer, squashy ball. The Squash Rackets Association was formed in 1928 and this became the World Squash Federation in 1992.

The *World Open Championship* was first held in 1976. Since

1979 they have been contested annually by men (annually since 1990 for women). Recent winners of the singles events have been:

	Men	Women
1990	G. Hunt (Australia)	S. Devoy (New Zealand)
1991	R. Martin (Australia)	S. Devoy (New Zealand)
1992	J. Khan (Pakistan)	S. Devoy (New Zealand)
1993	J. Khan (Pakistan)	M. Martin (Australia)
1994	J. Khan (Pakistan)	M. Martin (Australia)

Super Bowl *see* AMERICAN FOOTBALL.

swimming competatively dates back to 36 BC in Japan when Emperor G-Yozei introduced it into schools. In Britain, organized competative swimming was only introduced in 1837 when the National Swimming Society was formed.

It has been an integral part of the OLYMPIC GAMES since 1896 and water sports now include diving, water polo, synchronized swimming and swimming using breaststroke, butterfly, front crawl and backstroke over different distances.

World Championships, separate from the Olympics, were first held in 1973 and are now staged every four years. The seventh World Championships will be held in Rome in 1994.

table tennis was originally known as *ping-pong* and was widely played in England in the early part of this century. The modern game grew in popularity when textured rubber mats were attached to the faces of the wooden bats, allowing the players to put spin on the ball. The International Table Tennis Federation was founded in 1926.

The *World Championships* have been held since 1927. The Swaythling Cup is awarded to the winning men's team and the Corbillon Cup to the winning women's team. The 1993 World Championships were held in Gothenburg, Sweden. The winners at this event were:

	Men	Women
Singles	J. P. Gatien	H. J. Hwa
Doubles	W. Tao and L. Lin	L. Wei and Q. Yunping
Team	Sweden	China

tennis evolved from the indoor game of *real tennis* and is thought to have first been played at the end of the eighteenth century. It was patented by Major Wingfield, regarded as the 'father' of the game, who claimed to have invented the game of lawn tennis at his country house in Nantcwlyd, Wales, in 1874. The Marylebone Cricket Club later revised the Major's rules and in 1877 the All-England Croquet Club added Lawn Tennis to their title.

The All-England Championships at *Wimbledon* have been held since 1877 and are regarded as the most prestigious tennis championships played on grass in the world. Since 1922 they have been contested on a knock-out basis. The Men's Singles Champions have been:

1922	G. Patterson (Australia)	1962	R. Laver (Australia)
1923	W. Johnston (USA)	1963	C. McKinley (USA)
1924	J. Borotra (France)	1964	R. Emerson (Australia)
1925	R. Lacoste (France)	1965	R. Emerson (Australia)
1926	J. Borotra (France)	1966	M. Santana (Spain)
1927	H. Cochet (France)	1967	J. Newcombe (Australia)
1928	R. Lacoste (France)	1968	R. Laver (Australia)
1929	H. Cochet (France)	1969	R. Laver (Australia)
1930	B. Tilden (USA)	1970	J. Newcombe (Australia)
1931	S. Wood (USA)	1971	J. Newcombe (Australia)
1932	E. Vines (USA)	1972	S. Smith (USA)
1933	J. Crawford (Australia)	1973	J. Kodes (Czech.)
1934	F. Perry (UK)	1974	J. Conners (USA)
1935	F. Perry (UK)	1975	A. Ashe (USA)
1936	F. Perry (UK)	1976	B. Borg (Sweden)
1937	D. Budge (USA)	1977	B. Borg (Sweden)
1938	D. Budge (USA)	1978	B. Borg (Sweden)
1939	B. Riggs (USA)	1979	B. Borg (Sweden)
1946	Y. Petra (France)	1980	B. Borg (Sweden)
1947	J. Kramer (USA)	1981	J. McEnroe (USA)
1948	B. Falkenburg (USA)	1982	J. Conners (USA)
1949	T. Schroeder (USA)	1983	J. McEnroe (USA)
1950	B. Patty (USA)	1984	J. McEnroe (USA)
1951	D. Savitt (USA)	1985	B. Becker (Germany)
1952	F. Sedgeman (Australia)	1986	B. Becker (Germany)
1953	V. Seixas (USA)	1987	P. Cash (Australia)
1954	J. Drobny (Egypt)	1988	S. Edberg (Sweden)
1955	T. Trabert (USA)	1989	B. Becker (Germany)
1956	L. Hoad (Australia)	1990	S. Edberg (Sweden)
1957	L. Hoad (Australia)	1991	M. Stich (Germany)
1958	A. Cooper (Australia)	1992	A. Agassi (USA)
1959	A. Olmedo (USA)	1993	P. Sampras (USA)
1960	N. Fraser (Australia)	1994	P. Sampras (USA)
1961	R. Laver (Australia)		

The Women's Singles Champions have been:

1922 S. Lenglen (France)	1961 A. Mortimer (UK)
1923 S. Lenglen (France)	1962 K. Susman (USA)
1924 K. McKane (UK)	1963 M. Smith (Australia)
1925 S. Lenglen (France)	1964 M. Bueno (Brazil)
1926 K. Godfree (UK)	1965 M. Smith (Australia)
1927 H. Wills (USA)	1966 B. J. King (USA)
1928 H. Wills (USA)	1967 B. J. King (USA)
1929 H. Wills (USA)	1968 B. J. King (USA)
1930 H. Moody (USA)	1969 A. Hayden-Jones (UK)
1931 C. Aussem (Germany)	1970 M. Court (Australia)
1932 H. Moody (USA)	1971 E. Goolagong (Australia)
1933 H. Moody (USA)	1972 B. J. King (USA)
1934 D. Round (UK)	1973 B. J. King (USA)
1935 H. Moody (USA)	1974 C. Evert (USA)
1936 H. Jacobs (USA)	1975 B. J. King (USA)
1937 D. Round (UK)	1976 C. Evert (USA)
1938 H. Moody (USA)	1977 V. Wade (UK)
1939 A. Marble (USA)	1978 M. Navratilova (Czech.)
1946 P. Betz (USA)	1979 M. Navratilova (Czech.)
1946 P. Betz (USA)	1980 E. Cawley (Australia)
1947 M. Osborne (USA)	1981 C. Evert Lloyd (USA)
1948 L. Brough (USA)	1982 M. Navratilova (USA)
1949 L. Brough (USA)	1983 M. Navratilova (USA)
1950 L. Brough (USA)	1984 M. Navratilova (USA)
1951 D. Hart (USA)	1985 M. Navratilova (USA)
1952 M. Connolly (USA)	1986 M. Navratilova (USA)
1953 M. Connolly (USA)	1987 M. Navratilova (USA)
1954 M. Connolly (USA)	1988 S. Graf (Germany)
1955 L. Brough (USA)	1989 S. Graf (Germany)
1956 S. Fry (USA)	1990 M. Navratilova (USA)
1957 A. Gibson (USA)	1991 S. Graf (Germany)
1958 A. Gibson (USA)	1992 S. Graf (Germany)
1959 M. Bueno (Brazil)	1993 S. Graf (Germany)
1960 M. Bueno (Brazil)	1994 C. Martinez (Spain)

To achieve the *Grand Slam* in international tennis is to hold the titles to all four major tournaments simultaneously. These tournaments are: Wimbledon, the French Open, the Australian Open and the US Open.

The *Davis Cup* was established in 1900 by American player Dwight F. Davis as an international challenge match. Since 1972 a World Group of 16 nations have played-off for the Cup. Each match is decided over two pairs of singles and a doubles. Recent winners of this event have been:

1980	Czechoslovakia	1987	Sweden
1981	USA	1988	F R Germany
1982	USA	1989	F R Germany
1983	Australia	1990	USA
1984	Sweden	1991	France
1985	Sweden	1992	USA
1986	Australia	1993	Germany

test cricket *see* CRICKET.

toboggan *see* BOBSLEIGH.

Tour De France *see* CYCLING.

UEFA Cup *see* ASSOCIATION FOOTBALL.

University Boat Race *see* ROWING.

volleyball was invented by sports instructor William Morgan in 1895 and was originally intended for those who found basketball too strenuous. The game quickly spread from North America around the world, reaching Britain in 1914. An International Federation was founded in 1948 and the sport has been included in the OLYMPIC GAMES since 1964.

A *World Championship* was first staged in 1949 and the event has been held every four years since 1952. In recent years teams from the USA, Russia and China have dominated.

walking has been included in the OLYMPIC GAMES since 1906. It is defined as 'progression by steps so that unbroken contact with the ground is maintained'. Road walking is now more common than track walking and the current Olympic distances for men are 20km and 50km.

water polo originally known as 'football in the water', the sport was developed in Britain in the late 19th century. Given official recognition in 1885 by the Amateur Swimming Association of Great Britain and included in the OLYMPIC GAMES since 1900. The *World Championship* was first held separately from the World Swimming Championships (*see* SWIMMING) in 1991.

water skiing pioneered by Ralph Samuelson on Lake Pepin, Minnesota in 1922. Competition today is divided into three events; trick skiing, slalom and jumping, the *World Championship* has been held biennially since 1949.

weightlifting competitions go back to the Chou Dynasty in China and were an integral part of the ancient OLYMPIC GAMES.

The sport has been included in the modern Games since 1896. Contests are decided by the aggregate of two forms of lifting, the snatch and the clean and jerk. In 1993 it was decided by the International Weightlifting Federation to introduce a new set of 10 weight catagories. These are:

Men: 54kg, 59kg, 64kg, 70kg, 76kg, 83kg, 91kg, 99kg, 108kg, over 108kg

Women: 46kg, 50kg, 54kg, 59kg, 64kg, 70kg, 76kg, 83kg, over 83kg

Wimbledon *see* TENNIS.

Winter Olympic Games although ice-skating was included in the 1908 Olympic Games, the first international competition to feature a variety of winter sports was not held until 1924. This event, called the International Winter Sports Week, was later ratified by the International Olympic Commitee as being the first Winter Olympic Games. The venues of the games have been:

1924	Chamonix	1964	Innsbruck
1928	St Moritz	1968	Grenoble
1932	Lake Placid	1972	Sapporo
1936	Garnisch-Partenkirchen	1976	Innsbruck
		1980	Lake Placid
1948	St Moritz	1984	Sarajevo
1952	Oslo	1988	Calgary
1956	Cortina d'Ampezzo	1992	Albertville
1960	Squaw Valley	1994	Lillehammer

From 1994 the Winter Games will be held in the middle of the four-year Olympic cycle.

World Cup *see* ASSOCIATION FOOTBALL, RUGBY LEAGUE, RUGBY UNION.

World Championship *see individual sports.*

World Equestrian Games *see* EQUESTRIANISM.

World Mile Record *see* ATHLETICS.

World Open Championship *see* SQUASH.

World Outdoor Championship see BOWLS.

World Series *see* BASEBALL.

World Title Holders see BOXING.

wrestling was one of the most important events in the ancient OLYMPIC GAMES and has been included in the modern Games since 1896. There are two styles; Greco-Roman and freestyle, with the main difference being that in Greco-Roman the use of the legs is prohibited. A *World Championship* was first staged in 1904 and it is now an annual event in non-Olympic years.

yachting as a sport is thought to have begun in the 17th century in the Netherlands, then the world's greatest maritime power. The first recorded yacht race, however, took place in 1661 when Charles II challenged the Duke of York to a race over a 23 mile stretch of the River Thames.

Included in the OLYMPIC GAMES since 1900, there have been variations in the number of different classes through the years due to changes in technology and design.

The *Admiral's Cup* was first held in 1957 and is now held biennially. National three-boat teams compete over a six-race series, combining inshore and outshore racing. The races take place in the English Channel, at Cowes and in the Solent, and culminate in the Fastnet race from Cowes to Fastnet Rock, off the Irish coast, and back. Recent winners have been:

1975	UK	1985	FR Germany
1977	UK	1987	New Zealand
1979	Australia	1989	UK
1981	UK	1991	France
1983	FR Germany	1993	Germany

FAMOUS PEOPLE

This section of the *Concise Encyclopedia* provides essential details of the lives of important people in history and the modern world. The entries are in A to Z order, and there are cross-references, indicated in SMALL CAPITALS, to enable you to relate a person to other major people, and therefore to events.

*

Achebe, Chinua (1930–) Nigerian novelist and poet whose work focuses on Ibo society and the legacy of colonialism. He won the Nobel Prize for literature in 1989.

Acheson, Dean [Gooderham] (1893–1971) American lawyer and statesman who was responsible for formulating and developing several important strands of American foreign policy, notably the MARSHALL Plan and the establishment of NATO.

Adams, Ansel [Easton] (1902–84) American photographer, noted for his detailed, deep-focus studies of American landscape.

Addison, Joseph (1672–1719) English essayist and poet. With his friend Richard STEELE he founded the influential magazine *The Spectator* in 1711.

Adenauer, Konrad (1876–1967) German statesman who was imprisoned twice by the Nazi regime (1934, 1944). As chancellor of West Germany (1949–63) he had a major role in world politics.

Adler, Alfred (1870–1937) Austrian psychiatrist. He was an associate of FREUD, whose emphasis on sexuality he rejected, founding a school of psychoanalysis based on the individual's quest to overcome feelings of inadequacy (the 'inferiority complex').

Aeschylus (524–456 BC) Greek dramatist regarded as the founder of Greek tragedy. Seven of his plays survive, including *Prometheus Bound* and the *Oresteia* trilogy.

Akihito *see* **Hirohito**.

Albee, Edward [Franklin] (1928–) American dramatist. His plays include *Who's Afraid of Virginia Woolf* (1962) and *A Delicate Balance* (1966).

Alexander VI, Pope *see* BORGIA, RODRIGO.

Alexander the Great (356–323 BC) Macedonian king. The pupil of ARISTOTLE, he inherited the kingdom of Macedon from his father **Philip II** (382–336 BC). He conquered Greece in 336, Egypt in 331, and the Persian Empire by 328. He extended his conquests to the east and defeated an Indian army in 326. He died in Babylon, and was buried in the city he founded, Alexandria.

Ali, Muhammad [Cassius Clay] (1942–) American boxer and world heavyweight champion (1964–67, 1974–78, 1978).

Allen, Woody [Allen Stewart Konigsberg] (1935–) American film director, actor and writer noted for his satirical films about the neuroses of New York intellectuals.

Allende [Gossens], Salvador (1908–73) Chilean politician. He was elected president of his country in 1970, thus becoming the first freely elected Marxist president in Latin America. He was overthrown and killed in a coup that brought PINOCHET to power.

Amin [Dada], Idi (1925–) Ugandan dictator. He ruled Uganda from 1971 to 1979 (appointing himself president for life in 1976), but was overthrown.

Amis, Sir Kingsley (1922–) English novelist and poet whose first novel *Lucky Jim* (1954), a satire on academic life, is a comic masterpiece. His later novels are darker in tone. He is the father of **Martin Amis** (1949–) who is also a novelist.

Amundsen, Roald (1872–1928) Norwegian explorer and navigator, leader of the first expedition to reach the South Pole in 1911.

Andersen, Hans Christian (1805–75) Danish writer, best known now for his fairy tales, e.g. 'The Emperor's New Clothes'.

Anderson, Carl David *see* HESS, VICTOR FRANCIS.

Andropov, Yuri [Vladimirovich] (1914–84) Soviet statesman. Former head of the KGB and president of the USSR (1983–84).

Angelou, Maya (1928–) American dramatist, poet and short-story writer. One of the leading black writers of the 20th century.

Antony, Mark [Marcus Antonius] (*c*.83–30 BC) Roman soldier who fought with Julius CAESAR in the Gallic wars, and after Caesar's assassination defeated Brutus and Cassius at the battle of Philipi (42). He deserted his wife for the Egyptian Queen **Cleopatra** (69–30 BC), their forces being defeated by AUGUSTUS at Actium. He and Cleopatra committed suicide.

Apollinaire, Guillaume [Apollinaris Kostrowitzky] (1880–1918) French art critic and writer who had great influence among avant-garde artists and poets at the beginning of the 20th century. A friend of PICASSO and champion of Cubism, he also supported Orphism and Futurism and originated the term Surrealism.

Aquinas, Thomas *see* THOMAS AQUINAS.

Aquino, [Maria] Corazon (1933–) Filipino politician. She was elected President of the Philippines in 1986, following the assassination of her husband Benigno Aquino, the most prominent opponent of MARCOS.

Arafat, Yasser (1929–) Palestinian leader, who helped found the anti-Israeli guerrilla force *Al Fatah*, and became chairman of the Palestine Liberation Organization in 1968.

Aragon, Louis (1897–1982) French poet, essayist and novelist. One of the founders of both Dadaism and Surrealism.

Arden, John (1930–) English dramatist, regarded as one of the leading left-wing playwrights of his generation.

Aristophanes (*c*.448–380 BC) Greek comic dramatist, eleven of whose comedies survive. The objects of his satire ranged from politicians to his fellow dramatists (EURIPIDES being one) and his plays are a valuable record of the intellectual debates of the day. The most popular of his plays now is *Lysistrata*.

Aristotle (384–322 BC) Greek philosopher. He taught at PLATO's Academy for 20 years, and became tutor to ALEXANDER THE GREAT, and formed his own school (the Lyceum) in Athens in 335. His works, including *Nicomachean Ethics, Poetics* and *Politics*, were re-introduced to the Western world in the Middle Ages via Arabian scholarship and had a profound influence on almost every field of intellectual inquiry until the Renaissance.

Armstrong, [Daniel] Louis 'Satchmo' (1900–1971) American jazz trumpeter, singer and leader of many popular jazz bands. He had a genius for improvisation and became one of the best-loved entertainers of the 20th century.

Armstrong, Neil [Alden] (1930–) American astronaut. He commanded the Apollo 11 moon landing mission, in which he became the first man to walk on the moon.

Arp, Jean *or* **Hans** (1887–1966) German-born French sculptor and painter. A founder of Dadaism, his work was abstract in form.

Arthur (*fl.* 6th century AD) a possibly mythical Celtic warrior-king of post-Roman Britain, who may have organized resistance against the Saxon invaders. He is credited in legend with having won a battle over the Saxons at 'Mount Badon', and is supposed to have been buried at Glastonbury.

Ashcroft, Dame Peggy (1907–91) English actress. One of the most popular stage and film actresses of her generation, she won an Oscar for her role in *A Passage to India* (1984).

Ashdown, Paddy [Jeremy John Dunham Ashdown] (1941–) English Liberal politician. He was elected leader of the Liberal and Social Democratic Party in 1988.

Ashe, Arthur (1943–93) American tennis player. The first black tennis player to win the US open (1968), the Australian open (1970), and the Wimbledon men's competition (1975).

Ashton, Sir Frederick [William Mallandaine] (1906–88) Ecuadorian-born British choreographer and co-founder of the Royal Ballet. His ballets include *A Month in the Country* (1976).

Asquith, Herbert Henry [1st Earl of Oxford and Asquith]

(1852–1928) British statesman. He was leader of the Liberal Party (1908–26) and prime minister (1908–16).

Astaire, Fred [Frederick Austerlitz] (1899–1987) American dancer, singer and actor. His partnership with **Ginger Rogers** [Virginia McMath] (1911–) resulted in a series of classic song-and-dance films, e.g. *Top Hat* (1935).

Astor, Nancy Witcher [Langhorne] [Viscountess Astor] (1879–1964) American-born British politician. She was elected to parliament as a Conservative MP, becoming the first woman to take her seat in Parliament.

Atatürk, Kemal [Mustafa Kemal Atatürk] (1881–1938) Turkish general and statesman, regarded as the creator of the modern Turkish state.

Attenborough, Sir David [Frederick] (1926–) English naturalist and broadcaster. He is Richard ATTENBOROUGH's brother.

Attenborough, Sir Richard [Samuel] (1923–) English film director, producer and actor. He was created a life peer in 1993.

Attlee, Clement [Richard] [1st Earl Attlee] (1883–1967) British statesman. Leader of the Labour Party (1939–55) and prime minister (1945–51), his 1945 administration introduced widespread nationalization and a programme of social security reforms.

Auden, W[ystan] H[ugh] (1907–73) English-born American poet. The leading left-wing poet of his generation, he later drifted away from Marxism towards a Christian and socially conservative position.

Augustine, Saint [Augustine of Hippo] (354–430) Latin Church Father. Born in what is now Tunisia, his father was a pagan and he was brought up a Christian by his mother. Reacting against the licentious life he led in Carthage, he converted to Manichaeanism for a while before returning to the Church. He was Bishop of Hippo (396–430) and wrote a spiritual autobiography, *Confessions*, and *City of God*, a major work of Christian apologetics.

Augustine, Saint (d. 604) Italian monk. He was dispatched to Britain in 597 by Pope GREGORY I to convert the Anglo-Saxons to Christianity and impose the authority of Rome on the Celtic Church. He became the first Archbishop of Canterbury in 601.

Augustus [originally Gaius Octavianus] (63 BC–14 AD) Roman emperor. After adoption by his uncle Julius CAESAR in 44 BC, he took the name Gaius Julius Caesar Octavianus. He became the first Emperor of Rome in 31 BC after defeating Mark ANTONY.

Aurelius, Marcus (121–80) Roman emperor and philosopher.

Renowned by his contemporaries for his nobility and learning, he spent much of his reign in war against the incoming 'barbarians' in the eastern part of the Empire.

Austen, Jane (1775–1817) English novelist. Her six great novels, *Sense and Sensibility* (1811), *Pride and Prejudice* (1813), *Mansfield Park* (1814), *Emma* (1816) and *Northanger Abbey* and *Persuasion* (1818) are set within the confines of the society in which she lived, the well-bred essentially rural middle class of Regency England. She is renowned for her masterly dialogue, finely tuned satire and moral sense.

Ayckbourn, Alan (1939–) English dramatist noted for satirical comedies including *The Norman Conquests* (1974).

Ayer, Sir A[lfred] J[ules] (1910–89) English philosopher, whose work is based on 'logical positivism' and the rejection of metaphysics and has been highly influential on British 'common-sense' philosophy.

Baader, Andreas *see* MEINHOFF, ULRIKE.

Babbage, Charles (1792–1871) English mathematician. His primitive 'calculating machines' are regarded as the precursors of the modern computer.

Bacall, Lauren *see* BOGART, HUMPHREY.

Bach, Johann Sebastian (1685–1750) German composer. His works include some of the greatest music in several forms, e.g. his six cello suites, choral masterpieces such as the *St Matthew Passion*, and works for harpsichord, clavichord and the organ, such as *The Well-Tempered Clavier* and *The Art of Fugue*. Four of his sons were also composers: **Wilhelm Friedemann** (1710– 84), **Karl Philipp Emanuel** (1714–88), **Johann Christoph Friedrich** (1732–95), and **Johann [John] Christian** (1735–82), who became a court musician in London, where he was known as 'the English Bach', and influenced MOZART.

Bacon, Francis (1561–1626) English philosopher and statesman. He served both ELIZABETH I and her successor JAMES VI AND I in various offices until his conviction and disgrace for bribery in 1621. His writings on philosophy and the need for rational scientific method are landmarks in the history of human thought.

Bacon, Francis (1909–92) Irish-born British painter. His works feature twisted and contorted human shapes, often in weird landscapes or spaces.

Baez, Joan (1941–) American folksinger, renowned for her 'protest songs' on civil rights and the Vietnam war in the 1960s.

Baird, John Logie (1888–1946) Scottish engineer who invented a mechanically scanned system of television in the mid–1920s.

Baker, Dame Janet [Abbott] (1933–) English mezzosoprano who became one of Britain's most popular opera singers in the 1960s and had parts created for her by composers such as BRITTEN. She was appointed a DBE in 1976.

Baldwin, James [Arthur] (1924–87) American novelist, dramatist and essayist. His main concern was with the role of blacks in American society, and, to a lesser extent, that of homosexuals. His novels include *Go Tell it on the Mountain* (1953).

Baldwin, Stanley [1st Earl Baldwin of Bewdley] (1867–1947) British statesman and Conservative prime minister (1923–24, 1924–29, 1935–37) Notable aspects of his premierships include the passing of a state of emergency during the 1926 General Strike, his refusal to accept Wallis Simpson as Edward VIII's wife (*see* WINDSOR) and his failure to deal with the rise of European totalitarianism.

Balzac, Honoré de (1799–1860) French novelist. His great collection of novels and short stories describe the lives of French men and women of every class. His works include *La Comédie humaine* ('the Human Comedy').

Bancroft, Anne *see* BROOKS, MEL.

Banda, Hastings [Kamuzu] (1905–) Malawi statesman, first president of Nyasaland from 1963 and president of Malawi (formerly Nyasaland) from 1966. One of the longest-ruling leaders in the world, he was appointed president for life in 1971.

Banks, Sir Joseph (1743–1820) English botanist and explorer. He sailed with COOK on his 1768–71 voyage round the world as a representative of the Royal Society and discovered many species of animals and plants.

Bannister, Sir Roger (1929–) British athlete and doctor who became the first man to run a mile in four minutes in 1954.

Banting, Sir Frederick [Grant] (1891–1941) Canadian physician whose research into diabetes with the American physiologist **Charles Herbert Best** (1899–1978) resulted in the isolation of the hormone insulin in a form suitable for treating diabetes.

Barber, Samuel (1910–81) American composer who worked with recognizably 19th-century harmonies and forms. His works include the popular *Adagio for Strings* (1936).

Bardeen, John (1908–91) American physicist and electrical engineer. He won two Nobel prizes, the first in 1956 for research that led to the invention of the transistor, the second in 1972 for research into the theory of superconductivity.

Bardot, Brigitte (1934–) French actress. The leading 'sex symbol' of the 1950s. Since the 1970s she has devoted herself to animal rights and welfare.

Barenboim, Daniel (1942–) Argentinian-born Israeli concert pianist and conductor. He married the cellist Jacqueline DU PRÉ in 1967 and was awarded the Legion of Honour in 1987.

Barnard, Christian [Neethling] (1922–) South African surgeon, who performed the first heart transplant in 1967.

Barrie, Sir J[ames] M[atthew] (1860–1937) Scottish dramatist and novelist, remembered principally for *Peter Pan* (1904).

Barth, Karl (1886–1968) Swiss Protestant theologian whose theology was based on an orthodox 'theocentric' conception of divine grace and is seen as a reaction against the simplifications of 19th-century liberal theology. He was a committed and courageous opponent of Nazism.

Barthes, Roland (1915–80) French literary and cultural critic, whose semiological studies were regarded as necessary reading in the 1960s and 70s. His works include *Elements of Sociology*.

Bartók, Béla (1881–1945) Hungarian composer and pianist. He was a noted collector of folk songs, upon which many of his works are based. His works include the ballet *The Miraculous Mandarin*, string quartets and *Concerto for Orchestra*.

Basie, Count [William] (1904–84) American jazz composer and bandleader. He was a jazz pianist of great ability, and his big band featured singers such as Ella FITZGERALD and Frank SINATRA.

Bates, H[erbert] E[rnest] (1905–74) English novelist and short-story writer. His works include the comic novel *The Darling Buds of May* (1958) featuring the Larkins, an unruly farming family.

Baudelaire, Charles (1821–67) French poet noted for his fascination with the macabre and alleged Satanism. He became a leading Symbolist poet and his works include *Les Fleurs du mal*.

Beadle, George Wells *see* TATUM, EDWARD LAWRIE.

Beaumont, Sir Francis *see* FLETCHER, JOHN.

Beauvoir, Simone de (1908–86) French novelist and essayist whose works explore the female predicament from the standpoint of existential feminism, e.g. *The Second Sex* (1949).

Beaverbrook, Max [William Maxwell Aitken, 1st Baron Beaverbrook] (1879–1964) Canadian-born British newspaper proprietor and Conservative politician. In World War I he served as minister of information (1918) and in World War II as minister of aircraft production (1940–41).

Bechet, Sidney (1897–1959) American jazz saxophonist and clarinettist. He never learned to read music but became one of the greatest soprano saxophone virtuosos of the 20th century.

Becket, Thomas à (1118–70) English saint. Of Norman descent, he became Chancellor of England in 1155 and Archbishop of Canterbury in 1162. Relations between Becket and Henry II deteriorated due to the former's strong allegiance to Church rather than King, and Becket was murdered by four of the King's knights. Becket was canonized in 1173.

Beckett, Samuel (1906–89) Irish dramatist and novelist. His works, generally bleak and existentialist in philosophy, include the play *Waiting for Godot* (1952) and the short novel *Malone Dies* (1951).

Becquerel, Antoine Henri *see* CURIE, MARIE.

Bede, the Venerable, Saint (*c.*673–735) Anglo-Saxon monk and historian. Prodigiously learned, he settled for life in the monastery at Jarrow in 682.

Beecham, Sir Thomas (1879–1961) English conductor, noted for his interpretations of the works of DELIUS, STRAUSS and SIBELIUS, and for his sharply witty ripostes.

Beerbohm, Sir [Henry] Max[imilian] (1872–1956) English parodist, caricaturist and essayist. The parodies of authors such as Henry JAMES and KIPLING established him as one of the greatest of all parodists. His only novel is *Zuleika Dobson*.

Beethoven, Ludwig van (1770–1827) German composer. Regarded as the greatest Romantic composer, he became famous throughout Europe in the 1790s as a brilliant pianist with a special gift for improvisation. His works include a violin concerto, nine symphonies, piano sonatas, string quartets, masses, and one of the greatest operas, *Fidelio* (1805).

Begin, Menachem (1913–92) Polish-born Israeli statesman. He was commander of the Irgun militant Zionist group (1943–48) and prime minister of Israel (1977–84). He and SADAT were awarded the Nobel Peace Prize in 1978, after Egypt and Israel signed a peace treaty.

Behan, Brendan (1923–64) Irish dramatist and poet. He was an Irish Republican Army supporter from an early age, and two of his works were directly based on his imprisonment for IRA activity, *The Quare Fellow* (1954) and *Borstal Boy* (1958).

Beiderbecke, [Leon] Bix (1903–31) American jazz cornetist, pianist and composer, who is regarded as one of the few white jazz musicians to have had any significant influence on the development of jazz.

Bell, Alexander Graham (1847–1922) Scottish-born American inventor and scientist. He succeeded in producing a device for transmitting the voice in 1875, and patented the telephone the following year. He founded the Bell Telephone Company in 1877, and patented the gramophone in 1887.

Bellini, Giovanni (*c.*1430–1516) Italian painter. The most prominent of a family of noted artists, including his father **Jacopo** (*c.*1400–*c.*1470) and his brother **Gentile** (*c.*1429–*c.*1507).

Belloc, Hilaire (1870–1953) French-born English poet, essayist, historian and Liberal MP noted for his prolific output of all kinds of books, and for his robust Roman Catholicism, anti-imperialism and nationalism.

Bellow, Saul (1915–) Canadian-born American novelist, widely regarded as one of the greatest living writers. His novels include *Dangling Man* (1944) and *More Die of Heartbreak* (1987). He was awarded the Nobel prize for literature in 1976.

Ben Bella, [Mohammed] Ahmed (1916–) Algerian statesman. A leading figure of his country's independence movement in the late 1940s and 1950s, he became prime minister in 1962 shortly after independence. He was deposed in 1965 following a military coup and was imprisoned until 1980.

Ben-Gurion, David [David Gruen] (1886–1973) Polish-born Israeli statesman. He settled in Palestine in 1906, where he was active in the socialist wing of the Zionist movement. He was the first prime minister of Israel (1948–53) and was prime minister again, 1955–63.

Benn, Tony [Anthony Neil Wedgwood Benn, formerly Viscount Stansgate] (1925–) British politician. Since the late 1970s he has been regarded as one of the leading figures of the radical left in the Labour Party.

Bennett, [Enoch] Arnold (1867–1931) English novelist, dramatist and essayist. His most popular novels centred on industrial life in the Black Country Potteries and include the Clayhanger trilogy, *Clayhanger*, *Hilda Lessways* and *These Twain*.

Bentham, Jeremy (1748–1832) English philosopher. He is famous for his proposition that the prime aim of political and philosophical inquiry should be the 'greatest happiness of the greatest number', expounded in his *Introduction to the Principles of Morals and Legislation* (1789).

Bentine, Michael *see* MILLIGAN, SPIKE.

Bentley, Edmund Clerihew (1875–1956) English journalist, noted for his classic detective novel, *Trent's Last Case* (1913), and his invention of the clerihew.

Berenson, Bernard (1865–1959) Lithuanian-born American art critic. Highly influential in the early development of art history.

Berg, Alban (1885–1935) Austrian composer. He studied under SCHOENBERG and his atonal twelve-tone technique. His works include songs, chamber works and the operas *Wozzeck* and *Lulu*.

Bergman, Ingmar (1918–) Swedish film and stage director. His films, which include *The Seventh Seal* (1956), *Wild Strawberries* (1957) and *Cries and Whispers* (1972), are claustrophobic psychological studies which have been very influential.

Bergman, Ingrid (1915–82) Swedish actress regarded as one of the most talented and beautiful actresses of her generation. Her films include *Casablanca* (1942).

Bergson, Henri Louis (1859–1941) French philosopher whose writings expound his theory of a 'vital spirit' moving in the world, bridging the apparent chasm between metaphysics and science. He was awarded the Nobel prize for literature in 1927.

Beria, Lavrenti Pavlovich (1899–1953) Georgian-born Soviet politician. He rose to power in the 1930s under STALIN, and became head of the secret police (1938–53). After Stalin's death, he was tried for treason and executed.

Berio, Luciano (1925–) Italian composer whose works are based on a system of serialism and often feature electronic components.

Berkeley, Busby [William Busby Enos] (1895–1976) American film director, noted especially for his elaborate, often surreal, dance choreography.

Berlin, Irving [Israel Baline] (1888–1989) Russian-born American songwriter. He began his career as a street singer, and eventually wrote around a thousand songs, many of which featured in highly successful shows and in several film musicals.

Berlin, Sir Isaiah (1909–) Latvian-born British philosopher and historian. His works focus on the history of ideas, with particular reference to historical determinism.

Berlioz, Hector (1803–69) French composer. Regarded as a founder of modern orchestral techniques, his works include *Symphonie Fantastique* and the opera *The Trojans*.

Bernstein, Leonard (1918–90) American composer and conductor. He was musical director of the New York Philharmonic (1958–70), and a tireless popularizer of classical music. His works include chamber and choral music and several very popular musicals, e.g. *West Side Story* (1957).

Bertolucci, Bernardo (1940–) Italian film director. His films are among the most influential in modern cinema.

Best, Charles Herbert *see* BANTING SIR FREDERICK.

Best, George (1946–) Northern Irish soccer player. One of the world's finest and most entertaining wingers, his carer slowly folded in a haze of alcohol abuse and general dissipation.

Betjeman, Sir John (1906–84) English poet and essayist whose work was popular with critics and public alike. He was appointed poet laureate in 1972 and also wrote widely on architecture.

Bevan, Aneurin (1897–1960) Welsh statesman. He was Labour MP for Ebbw Vale for 30 years (1929–60), and one of the main spokespeople for the radical socialist opposition during World War II. As minister of health (1945–51), he oversaw the formation of the welfare state (*see* BEVERIDGE).

Beveridge, William Henry [1st Baron Beveridge] (1879–1963) Indian-born English economist. His 'Beveridge Report', the *Report on Social Insurance and Allied Services* (1942), became the basis for the welfare state introduced by ATTLEE's administration.

Bevin, Ernest (1881–1951) English trade unionist and statesman. He helped found the Transport and General Workers Union (1922) and was minister of labour (1940–45) in the coalition war government and Labour's foreign secretary (1945–51).

Bhutto, Zulfikar Ali (1928–79) Pakistani statesman. He was the first civilian president of Pakistan (1971–73), then prime minister (1973–77). He was deposed in a coup and executed. His daughter, **Benazir Bhutto** (1953–), became prime minister of Pakistan in 1988, but was defeated in elections in 1990.

Biko, Steve [Bantu Stephen Biko] (1947–77) South African black radical leader who helped found the Black People's Convention in order to build confidence in South African blacks that they could defeat apartheid. His death in police custody while awaiting trial was universally regarded as murder.

Birtwhistle, Sir Harrison (1934–) English composer regarded with Maxwell DAVIES and others as a leading postwar composer. His works include *Gawain and the Green Knight* (1991)).

Bismarck, Prince Otto von (1815–98) German statesman who was prime minister of Prussia (1862–90) and defeated first Austria during the 'Seven Weeks' War' (1866) and then France (1870–71). He became the first chancellor of united Germany and was dubbed the 'Iron Chancellor'.

Bizet, Georges (1838–75) French composer who is best known for his operas, e.g. *The Pearl Fishers*, *Carmen*, but who also wrote a symphony, several songs and the *L'Arlésienne* suits.

Blake, William (1757–1827) English poet and artist. His main poetic and artistic theme was innocence crippled by cynical experience. He is one of the greatest of English Romantic poets.

Blériot, Louis (1872–1936) French aviator and aeronautical engineer. A pioneer in aircraft design, he made the first flight across the English Channel in one of his monoplanes in 1909.

Bliss, Sir Arthur [Edward Drummond] (1891–1975) English composer whose work includes a choral symphony, ballets and film music. He was Master of the Queen's Music (1953–75).

Blum, Léon (1872–1950) French statesman, the first socialist and Jewish prime minister of France (1936–37, 1938, 1946–47).

Blunt, Anthony [Frederick] (1907–83) English art historian, who was knighted in 1956, and was appointed Surveyor of the Queen's Pictures in 1945, a post he held until 1972. He was stripped of his knighthood in 1979, following the public revelation that he had been a Soviet spy.

Blyton, Enid [Mary] (1897–1968) English children's writer whose most well-known books have featured such characters as Noddy and Big Ears and, for older children, *The Famous Five*.

Boas, Franz (1858–1942) German-born American anthropologist whose emphasis on linguistic structure and scientific methodology has been very influential on anthropology.

Boccioni, Umberto (1882–1916) Italian painter and sculptor who became the leading Futurist artist of the early 20th century and one of the movement's principal theorists.

Bogarde, Sir Dirk [Derek Jules Gaspard Ulric Niven van den Bogaerde] (1920–) English actor and author whose films include *Death in Venice* (1970). He has written a highly acclaimed autobiography and two novels.

Bogart, Humphrey [De Forest] (1899–1957) American actor. He formed one of the best-known screen partnerships with his (fourth) wife **Lauren Bacall** [Betty Joan Perske] (1924–).

Bohr, Niels [Henrik David] (1885–1962) Danish physicist. He was the first to apply quantum theory to explain the stability of the nuclear model of the atom. He was awarded the 1922 Nobel prize for physics.

Bolivar, Simon (1783–1830) Venezeulan-born revolutionary. He overthrew Spanish rule in Venezuela, Ecuador, Colombia and Peru. Upper Peru was renamed Bolivia in his honour.

Bond, Edward (1934–) English dramatist and screenwriter. His work was often controversial and public debate over one his play *Saved* (1965) led to the abolition of stage censorship in Britain.

Bonhoeffer, Dietrich (1906–45) German Lutheran pastor and theologian who was active in the anti-Nazi Resistance during World War II and hanged by the Gestapo in 1945. His writings are among the key spiritual works of the 20th century.

Bonnard, Pierre (1867–1947) French painter and lithographer. His work is notable for being intensely colourful, especially in his interior work.

Booth, William (1829–1912) English religious leader who established a Christian mission in London's East End in the 1860s and founded the Salvation Army in 1878.

Borg, Bjorn (1956–) Swedish tennis player who won five consecutive Wimbledon championship titles (1976–80).

Borges, Jorge Luis (1899–1986) Argentinian short-story writer, poet and critic who had a remarkable gift for creating short fictions with a beguiling metaphysical content.

Borgia, Cesare (1476–1507) Italian soldier and politician. The son of **Rodrigo Borgia** (1431–1503), he became a cardinal in 1493 after his father became pope (as Alexander VI) in 1492. He attempted to bring Italian affairs under his control in an atmosphere of intrigue, war and assassination, and was the model for MACHIAVELLI'S *Prince*. His sister **Lucrezia** (1480–1519) was a patron of the arts and also acquired a reputation for conspiracy.

Bosch, Hieronymous [Jerome van Aeken *or* Aken] (*c.*1450–1516) Dutch painter, known for his fantastic and often grotesque allegorical paintings which use imagery drawn from folk tales and religious symbolism.

Bose, Sir Jagadis Chandra (1858–1937) Indian physicist and plant physiologist. He invented the crescograph, a device that automatically records plant movements.

Bose, Subhas Chandra (1897–1945) Indian nationalist leader. He was president of the Indian National Congress (1938–39) and, in collaboration with the Japanese during World War II, organized the Indian National Army to combat British rule in India.

Boswell, James *see* Johnson, Samuel.

Botha, Louis (1862–1919) South African general and states-man. As general of the Transvaal army, he led the Boer forces against the British during the Boer War. He supported the Allies during World War I, and became first prime minister of South Africa (1910–19).

Botha, P[ieter] W[illem] (1916–) South African politician. He was prime minister (1978–84) and introduced limited reforms of apartheid.

Botham, Ian (1955–) English cricketer. A talented all-rounder, he captained England (1980–81) and scored 5,057 runs in Test matches (including 14 centuries).

Botticelli, Sandro (1444–1510) Florentine painter, best known for his graceful and serene religious works.

Boulez, Pierre (1925–) French composer and conductor who developed a composition style based on total serialism and elec-tronic instruments.

Boycott, Geoffrey (1940–) English cricketer. He is regarded as one of England's greatest modern batsmen. He captained York-shire (1970–78) and played for England (1964–74, 1977–81).

Bradman, [Sir] Don[ald George] (1908–) Australian cricketer. A brilliant batsman, he scored 117 centuries during the 1930s and 1940s. He was Australian captain (1936–48).

Bragg, Melvyn (1939–) English novelist and broadcaster. He is best known as a television presenter of arts programmes.

Brahms, Johannes (1833–97) German composer. He regarded himself as firmly in the Classical (as opposed to Romantic) tradi-tion. His works include the great choral *German Requiem* (1869), four symphonies and chamber music.

Branagh, Kenneth (1961–) Irish-born British actor and direc-tor. He founded the Renaissance Theatre Company in 1986 and has appeared regularly in films with his wife, the actress **Emma Thompson** (1959–).

Brando, Marlon (1924–) American actor. Brando's many cel-ebrated screen performances display the highly influential method acting style.

Brandt, Willy [Herbert Ernst Karl Frahm] (1913–92) German statesman. He was active in the German Resistance during World War II and became mayor of Berlin (1957–66) and chancellor of West Germany (1969–74). He was awarded the Nobel Peace Prize in 1971.

Braque, Georges (1882–1963) French painter. The term Cubism was coined in 1909 to describe his works. He also pioneered the use of collage in modern painting.

Brattain, Walter *see* SHOCKLEY, WILLIAM BRADFORD.

Braudel, Fernand (1902–85) French historian. His influential works focused on socio-economic trends and the changing relationship between man and the environment rather than on politics or military events.

Brecht, Bertolt (1898–1956) German dramatist who devised the theatre of alienation which he used in *The Threepenny Opera* (1928), for which WEILL wrote the music, and developed in plays such as *Galileo* (1938) and *Mother Courage* (1941). He settled in the US during Nazi rule in Germany, returning to East Berlin in 1949 where he founded the Berliner Ensemble theatre.

Breughel *see* BRUEGHEL.

Brezhnev, Leonid Ilyich (1906–82) Soviet statesman. He helped organize KHRUSHCHEV's downfall in 1964, and became general secretary of the Communist Party (1977–82) and Soviet president (1977–82). The period of his rule is now described as the 'period of stagnation' in the USSR.

Brian, [William] Havergal (1876–1972) English composer, frequently described as 'post-Romantic'. His more than 30 works include the huge *Gothic Symphony* (1919–27) and five operas.

Britten, [Edward] Benjamin [1st Baron Britten] (1913–76) English composer and pianist. His works include the operas *Peter Grimes* (1945) and *A Midsummer Night's Dream* (1960, chamber music, orchestral works and song cycles. His works are noted for their romantic lyricism. He was created a peer in 1976.

Brontë, Anne (1820–49), **Charlotte** (1816–55) and **Emily** (1818–48) English novelists and poets. Charlotte's *Jane Eyre*, based on her experiences as a teacher and governess, was published in 1847, and Anne's *Agnes Grey* and Emily's *Wuthering Heights* followed in 1848. Anne's *Tenant of Wildfell Hall* was published in 1848, in which year Emily died of consumption. Charlotte wrote two more novels: *Shirley* (1849) and *Villette* (1853).

Brook, Peter [Stephen Paul] (1925–) English stage and film director based in Paris. He is regarded as one of the finest experimental directors of the modern era.

Brooke, Rupert [Chawner] (1887–1915) English poet. His war poems were very popular with the public for their idealized vision of the nobility of war.

Brooks, Mel [Melvin Kaminsky] (1926–) American comedian, film writer and director, best known for his fast-moving, irreverent comedy films. His wife is the actress **Anne Bancroft** [Anna Maria Italiano] (1931–) who is noted for her serious acting.

Brown, George MacKay *see* DAVIES, SIR PETER MAXWELL.

Browning, Robert (1812–89) English poet renowned for his innovative experiments in form and narrative skill. His wife, **Elizabeth Barrett Browning** (1806–61), whom he married in 1846, was also a major poet.

Brubeck, Dave (1920–) American jazz composer and pianist. He studied musical composition with SCHOENBERG and MILHAUD, forming his 'Dave Brubeck Quartet' in 1951.

Bruce, Lenny (1925–66) American comedian who developed an influential style of satirical and often scabrous comedy which frequently brought him into conflict with the authorities.

Bruegel *or* **Brueghel, Pieter (the Elder)** (*c*.1525–69) Flemish painter who painted peasant scenes and allegories. He is best known for his magnificent landscape painting *The Hunters in the Snow* (1565). His sons **Jan Brueghel** (1568–1625) and **Pieter Brueghel (the Younger)** (*c*.1564–1637) were also painters.

Brunel, Isambard Kingdom (1806–59) English engineer. He designed steamships and in the late 1820s planned and designed the Clifton Suspension Bridge. His father, **Sir Marc Isambard Brunel** (1769–1849), was a French engineer who designed a tunnel under the Thames in London.

Buber, Martin (1878–1965) Austrian-born Jewish theologian and existentialist philosopher. His philosophy, which centres on the relationship between man and God, has had a large impact on both Jewish and Christian theology.

Buchan, John [1st Baron Tweedsmuir] (1875–1940) Scottish novelist, statesman and historian. He wrote several best-selling adventure novels, was created a peer in 1935, and was appointed governor-general of Canada (1935–40).

Buchman, Frank [Nathan Daniel] (1878–1961) American evangelist who founded the Oxford Group and the longer-lived Moral Rearmament, which were intended to provide ideological alternatives to both capitalism and communism.

Bunche, Ralph Johnson (1904–71) American diplomat and UN official. The grandson of a slave, he became the first Black to be awarded the Nobel Peace Prize, in 1950, for his attempt at reconciling Israel and the Arab states (1948–49).

Bunyan, John (1628–88) English author. Writer of several devotional works, the most famous being the remarkable allegory *Pilgrim's Progress* (1678–84).

Buñuel, Luis (1900–1983) Spanish-born film director. His early films were made in collaboration with Salvador DALI, and he is regarded as a master of Surrealist cinema.

Burgess, Anthony [John Anthony Burgess Wilson] (1917–) English novelist, critic and composer. His novels include the controversial futuristic fantasy of juvenile crime *A Clockwork Orange* (1962, filmed by KUBRICK in 1971).

Burgess, Guy (1911–63) English diplomat and spy. Recruited by Soviet Intelligence in the 1930s, he worked for MI5 during World War II and served with PHILBY at the British Embassy in Washington DC after the war. With his fellow agent, **Donald Maclean** (1913–83), he fled to the USSR in 1951.

Burke, Edmund (1729–97) Anglo-Irish statesman and philosopher. He entered parliament for the Whig party in 1765 and was soon established as the dominant political thinker of the day. His works include the cornerstone of conservative political thought, *Reflections on the Revolution in France* (1790).

Burnet, Sir Frank Macfarlane *see* MEDAWAR, SIR PETER BRIAN.

Burns, Robert (1759–96) Scottish poet, renowned as both a lyric poet and a satirist. The son of a farmer, his identification with folk tradition and his rebellious lifestyle also contribute to the unwavering popularity of his work in Scotland.

Burroughs, William S[eward] (1914–) American novelist. A friend of GINSBERG and KEROUAC, Burroughs became a heroin addict in the 1940s. His luridly obscene fiction features the squalid, nightmarish underworld of drug addiction.

Burton, Richard [Richard Jenkins] (1925–84) Welsh actor, regarded by his peers and critics as one of the most talented actors of his generation. He formed a screen partnership with Elizabeth TAYLOR, to whom he was married twice (1964–70, 1975–76).

Busby, Sir Matt[hew] (1909–94) Scottish footballer and manager of Manchester United (1946–69). Many members of his highly regarded team of 1958 died in a plane crash at Munich. His rebuilt team of 'Busby Babes' became the first English team to win the European Cup (1968).

Bush, George [Herbert Walker] (1924–) American Republican politician and 41st president of the US. The son of a wealthy senator, he served in the US Navy (1942–45), became US ambassador to the UN (1971–73), special envoy to China (1974–75) and CIA director (1976). He served under Reagan as vice-president (1980–88) and was elected president in 1988.

Buthelezi, Chief Gatsha (1928–) South African Zulu chief and politician. He helped found the paramilitary organization Inkatha.

Butler, R[ichard] A[usten], [Baron] (1902–82) English Conservative politician. As minister of education (1941–45), he introduced the Education Act of 1944. He was also chancellor of the exchequer (1951–55), home secretary (1957–62) and foreign secretary (1963–64). He was created a life peer in 1965.

Byron, Lord George Gordon Noel [6th Baron Byron of Rochdale] (1788–1824) English poet. His works include many superb lyrics and the long satirical poem *Don Juan* (1819–21).

Cadbury, George (1839–1922) English businessman, social reformer and philanthropist. With his brother **Michael Cadbury** (1835–99) he established the model village of Bournville, near Birmingham, for the Cadbury work force.

Caesar, [Gaius] Julius (100–44 BC) Roman soldier and historian. He negotiated and formed the 'First Triumvirate' with the politician **Marcus Licinius Crassus** (c.114–53 BC) and the statesman and general **Pompey** [Gnaeus Pompeius Magnus] (106–48 BC) in 60, after which he fought in Gaul for nine years, and invaded Britain in 55 and 54. Appointed dictator by the Senate in 49, he defeated Pompey at Pharsalia in 48, and was himself assassinated by a largely aristocratic group of conspirators.

Cage, John (1912–92) American composer. His experimental music, e.g. *4 minutes 33 seconds* (1952), in which the performers remain silent, has been derided and admired in equal proportions.

Cagney, James (1899–1986) American film actor, originally a dancer but best remembered for his many portrayals of gangsters, e.g. in *The Public Enemy* (1931), *Angels with Dirty Faces* (1938).

Caligula [Gaius Caesar Augustus Germanicus] (12–41) Roman emperor (37–41) who became tyrannical and was assassinated by a conspiracy and succeeded by his uncle, CLAUDIUS.

Callaghan, [Leonard] James [Baron Callaghan of Cardiff] (1912–) British Labour statesman prime minister (1976–79). After a vote of no confidence in his premiership in the House of Commons, he called a general election, which Labour lost.

Callas, Maria (1923–77) American-born Greek operatic soprano, renowned both for her voice and acting skills, which made her one of the most revered opera singers of the 20th century.

Calvin, John (1509–64) French religious reformer who had to flee from France to Switzerland, where, in 1536, he published his *Institutes of the Christian Religion*, a summation of his Protestant faith and the founding text of Calvinism. He settled in Geneva, where he established the first Presbyterian government.

Calvino, Italo (1923–85) Cuban-Italian novelist, essayist and critic. His early novels belonged in the Italian realist tradition, while his later, highly complex explorations of fantasy and myth have been compared to Latin American 'magic realism'.

Campbell, Sir Malcolm (1885–1948) English racing driver. He was awarded a knighthood in 1931, the year he set a land speed record of 246 mph, for his achievements in setting land and water speed records. His son, **Donald [Malcolm] Campbell,** (1921–67) held the English water speed record, at a speed of 276 mph, but he died on Lake Coniston while trying to break it.

Campbell, Mrs Patrick [Beatrice Stella Tanner] (1865–1940) English actress. She was regarded as one of the finest (and wittiest) actresses of her generation.

Campbell-Bannerman, Sir Henry (1836–1908) British statesman. He was Liberal prime minister (1905–08) and played a major part in healing rifts in the Liberal party after the Boer War.

Camus, Albert (1913–60) French novelist, essayist and dramatist, and a leading Existentialist writer. He joined the French Resistance during the war, and was awarded the Nobel prize for literature in 1957. His major works include the novel *The Outsider* and *The Rebel*, a study of 20th-century totalitarianism.

Canaletto, Giovanni Antonio Canal (1697–1768) Venetian painter. An unrivalled architectural painter with an excellent sense of composition, his work includes many views of Venice.

Capa, Robert [André Friedmann] (1913–54) Hungarian photographer who became one of the best-known war photographers of the century. He was killed by a mine in Vietnam.

Capek, Karel (1890–1938) Czech dramatist, novelist and essayist. With his brother **Josef Capek** (1887–1945), he wrote *The Insect Play* (1921), a prophetic satire on totalitarianism.

Capone, Al[phonse] (1899–1947) Italian-born American gangster. Nicknamed 'Scarface', he established his powerful criminal empire, specializing in bootleg liquor, prostitution and extortion, in Chicago during the prohibition era. He was eventually jailed for tax evasion and died of syphilis.

Capote, Truman (1924–84) American novelist and socialite.

His varied works include light romances, e.g. *Breakfast at Tiffany's* (1958), as well as realist explorations of murder.

Capra, Frank (1897–1991) Italian-born American film director. His comedies, usually portraying an ultimately successful struggle by a decent, everyday American against the flawed political system, were enormously popular in the 1930s.

Caravaggio, Michelangelo Merisi da (1573–1610) Italian painter. Noted for his bold, expressive use of chiaroscuro, his religious paintings caused controversy by using everyday people as the models for his Biblical characters.

Carlyle, Thomas (1795–1881) Scottish historian and essayist. Hailed by many of his contemporaries as a great social critic and philosopher, he frequently attacked the materialism of the Industrial Age.

Carnap, Rudolf (1891–1970) German-born American philosopher. Regarded as a leading logical positivist, he attempted to develop a formal language that would remove ambiguity from scientific language.

Carné, Marcel (1909–) French film director. His films include the highly acclaimed theatrical epic *Les Enfants du paradis* (1944), filmed during the German occupation of France.

Carnegie, Andrew (1835–1919) Scottish-born American industrialist and philanthropist who believed that personal wealth should be used for the benefit of all members of society.

Carreras, José [Maria] (1946–) Spanish lyric tenor, one of the finest tenors (with DOMINGO, PAVAROTTI) of the late 20th century.

Carroll, Lewis (pseud. of Charles Lutwidge Dodgson) (1832–98) English author, clergyman and mathematician. His most famous works are the two remarkable 'Alice' books, *Alice's Adventures in Wonderland* and *Through the Looking Glass*.

Carter, Jimmy [James Earl Carter] (1924–) American Democratic statesman and 39th president of the US (1977–81). A successful peanut farmer, he became governor of Georgia (1974–77) and defeated Gerald FORD in the 1976 presidential campaign. His administration made significant attempts at linking overseas trade with human rights issues.

Cartier-Bresson, Henri (1908–) French photographer and film director. His documentary black-and-white photographs were taken without prior composition and an uncropped frame.

Caruso, Enrico (1873–1921) Italian tenor. Born in Naples, he sang most of the great tenor roles in Italian and French opera and is regarded as perhaps the most outstanding operatic tenor of all time. He was one of the first great singers to make recordings.

Casals, Pablo (1876–1973) Spanish cellist, pianist and composer. His recordings of BACH's cello suites and of the DVORAK cello concerto are particularly highly regarded.

Casement, Sir Roger [David] (1864–1916) British consular official and Irish nationalist. While working for the British colonial service, he exposed the repression of the people of the Congo by its Belgian rulers in 1904. Knighted in 1911, he adopted Irish nationalism shortly afterwards and was hanged for treason.

Castro [Ruz], Fidel (1927–) Cuban statesman, prime minister (1959–76) and president (1976–). He led a coup in 1959, and shortly afterwards announced his conversion to communism. He survived several attempts at overthrow by exiled opponents and the CIA, e.g. the Bay of Pigs invasion in 1961, but survived with Soviet subsidies which began to decrease in the late 1980s.

Catherine II ('the Great') (1729–96) Russian empress. She became Empress on the death of her husband, **Peter III** (1728–62), who was murdered by one of her lovers. She consolidated and expanded the Russian Empire by conques, and scandalized European opinion by having a supposedly legion number of paramours and heading an intrigue-raddled court, while patronizing Enlightenment philosophers such as VOLTAIRE and DIDEROT.

Cavell, Edith [Louisa] (1865–1915) English nurse. She treated both German and Allied casualties in Brussels during the German occupation, and was executed by the German authorities, who accused her of helping British soldiers to escape to Holland.

Caxton, William (c.1422–91) English printer and translator. His *Recuyell of the Historyes of Troy* (printed at Bruges, 1475), is the first book to be printed in English.

Ceausescu, Nicolae (1918–89) Romanian dictator. Secretary general of the Romanian Communist Party from 1969 and president of Romania from 1974, his regime was overthrown by dissident Communists in 1989, and he and his wife were executed.

Cecil, William, 1st Baron Burghley, (1520–98) English statesman who served, with skill and dexterity, both HENRY VIII and MARY I (converting to Roman Catholicism under Mary), and was one of the prime architects of ELIZABETH I's succession.

Cervantes [Saavedra], Miguel de (1547–1616) Spanish novelist, dramatist and poet. His most famous work was the satirical masterpiece *Don Quixote de la Mancha*.

Cézanne, Paul (1839–1906) French painter whose works include landscapes and still lifes. He was very influential on succeeding generations of painters, notably the Cubists.

Chadwick, Sir James (1891–1974) English physicist. He discovered the neutron in 1932, and was awarded the Nobel prize for physics in 1935.

Chagall, Marc (1887–1985) Russian-born French painter. His vividly coloured work features unusual compositions drawing on symbolism from Russian and Jewish folk art.

Chain, Sir Ernst Boris (1906–79) German-born British biochemist. He prepared penicillin for clinical use, and with FLOREY and Alexander FLEMING, shared the 1945 Nobel prize for physiology or medicine.

Chamberlain, [Arthur] Neville (1869–1940) British statesman and Conservative prime minister (1937–40). He pursued a policy of appeasement towards the totalitarian powers of Germany, Italy and Japan in the 1930s. He died shortly after illness forced his resignation from CHURCHILL's war cabinet.

Chandler, Raymond [Thornton] (1888–1959) American novelist and screenwriter. His detective novels, e.g. *Farewell, My Lovely* (1940) are classics of the genre.

Chanel, Coco [Gabrielle Bonheur Chanel] (1883–1971) French couturière and perfumer who originated the thin, low-waist style for women's dresses.

Chaplin, Sir Charlie [Spencer] (1889–1977) English comedian and film director. His gentleman-tramp character with a beguiling shuffle, bowler hat and cane became perhaps the most famous comic creation of the 20th century.

Charlemagne (*c*.742–814) king of the Franks and Holy Roman emperor. In 771 he became sole ruler of the Frankish kingdom and spent the early part of his reign conquering (and converting to Christianity) neighbouring kingdoms. He led an army into Spain to fight the Moors in 778. In 800 he was crowned emperor after crushing a Roman revolt against the Pope.

Charles, Prince [Charles Philip Arthur George, Prince of Wales] (1948–) heir apparent to ELIZABETH II of the United Kingdom. He married **Lady Diana Spencer** (1961–) in 1981, and they had two children. They separated in 1992.

Charles, Ray [Ray Charles Robinson] (1930–) American singer, pianist and songwriter. Originally a blues/jazz singer, he became one of the most popular singers in the world.

Charlton, Bobby [Robert Charlton] (1937–) English footballer, capped over 100 times for England. His brother **Jack Charlton** [John Charlton] (1935–), also an England player, became the manager of the Irish international team and led them to the World Cup finals in 1990 and 1994..

Chatham, William Pitt, 1st Earl of *see* **Pitt, William**.

Chaucer, Geoffrey (*c*.1340–70) English poet. His great narrative skill is displayed at its finest in *The Canterbury Tales* (*c*.1387), a masterpiece of wit and humour in which various pilgrims tell each other stories..

Chekhov, Anton Pavlovich (1860–1904) Russian dramatist and short-story writer. A physician, he became one of the greatest writers of his age, his works, notable for their wit and dramatic power, including the plays *Uncle Vanya* and *Three Sisters* and the short story 'The Lady with the Little Dog'.

Cherenkov, Pavel Alekseievich (1904–) Soviet physicist. In the mid–1930s, he discovered the form of radiation known as Cherenkhov radiation, and was awarded the 1958 Nobel prize for physics.

Cherubini, Luigi (1760–1842) Italian composer who settled in Paris. He wrote operas, e.g. *Médée*, and other works and was much admired by BEETHOVEN, whose opera, *Fidelio*, followed the story of *Médée* closely in its study of feminine psychology and stress on democratic values.

Chesterton, G[ilbert] K[eith] (1874–1936) English essayist, novelist, critic and poet. With his friend BELLOC, he became known as a gifted disputant for what they saw as the glory of old, rural Roman Catholic England.

Chiang Ch'ing *or* **Jiang Qing** (1913–) Chinese Communist politician and actress. She married MAO as his third wife in 1939 and was the main force behind the savage purges of the Cultural Revolution in the late 1960s. After Mao's death, her power waned, and she was arrested in 1976 with three confederates (the 'Gang of Four') and charged with murder and subversion. She was sentenced to death in 1981, the sentence later being suspended.

Chiang Kai-shek *or* **Jiang Jie Shi** (1887–1975) Chinese general and statesman. He was president of China (1928–38, 1943–49), then, after losing the civil war to MAO TSE-TUNG and his forces, fled the mainland to establish the nationalist republic of China in Formosa, of which he was president (1950–57).

Chirico, Giorgio de (1888–1978) Greek-born Italian painter whose dreamlike pictures of open, deserted squares were hailed by the Surrealists as precursors of their own works in the early 1920s.

Chomsky, Noam [Avram] (1928–) American linguist, philosopher and political activist. His innovative work in linguistics is based on the principles that humans are born with an innate capacity for learning grammatical structures. He was a notable opponent of the Vietnam war.

Chopin, Frédéric [François] (1810–49) Polish pianist and composer. His emotional, melancholy works, often regarded as quintessentially Polish in mood, include over 50 mazurkas, two piano concertos and 25 preludes.

Chou En-Lai *or* **Zhou En Lai** (1898–1976) Chinese Communist statesman. He was foreign minister (1949–58) and prime minister (1949–76) of the People's Republic of China and was regarded as a moderate during the chaos of China's Cultural Revolution in the late 1960s.

Christie, [Dame] Agatha [Clarissa Mary] (1890–1976) English detective story writer whose ingeniously plotted novels, e.g. The Murder of Roger Ackroyd, established her as one of the great writers in the genre.

Churchill, Sir Winston [Leonard Spencer] (1874–1965) British Conservative statesman and writer. After an adventurous early life which included escape from imprisonment by Louis BOTHA during the Boer War, he held several posts under both Liberal and Conservative governments. He opposed CHAMBERLAIN'S policy of appeasement in the 1930s and served as prime minister (1940–45) during World War II. His works include *History of the English-Speaking Peoples*. He was awarded the Nobel prize for literature (1953).

Clapton, Eric (1945–) English guitarist. Recognized as one of the most influential rock guitarists, he played with the Yardbirds (1963 –65) and Cream (1966–68).

Clark, Jim [James Clark] (1936–68) Scottish racing driver who was World Champion in 1963 and 1965 and winner of 25 Grand Prix events. He was killed in a crash in West Germany.

Claudius (10 BC–54) Roman emperor who extended the Empire, initiated the conquest of Britain in 43 and extended Roman citizenship. His fourth wife (and niece), Agrippina, was the mother of his successor NERO.

Cleese, John [Marwood] (1939–) English comedy actor and writer. He was one of the main talents involved in the highly in-fluential TV comedy series, *Monty Python's Flying Circus* (1969–74).

Clemenceau, Georges [Eugène Benjamin] (1841–1929) French statesman. A leading left-winger, he was an outspoken critic of the French government's war policy in the early days of World War I. He was prime minister (1906–19, 1917–20) and his forceful negotiation of the Versailles Treaty is believed to have led directly to World War II.

Cleopatra *see* ANTONY, MARK.

Clinton, Bill [William Jefferson Davis Clinton] (1946–) American politician and 42nd President of the United States. A lawyer, he became Arkansas attorney general (1974–79), then state governor (1979–81, 1983–). Defeated George BUSH in the 1992 presidential election. *See also* GORE.

Clive, Kitty *see* **Garrick, David**.

Clive, Sir Robert [1st Baron Clive of Plassey] (1725–74) English general and administrator in India. He worked for the East India Company (1743–46) before joining the Indian army. An MP in England (1760–62) and governor of Bengal (1764–67).

Cockcroft, Sir John Douglas (1897–1967) English nuclear physicist. With the Irish physicist **Sir Ernest [Thomas Sinton] Walton** (1903–), he produced the first laboratory splitting of an atomic nucleus, for which they shared the 1951 Nobel prize for physics.

Cockerell, Sir Christopher Sydney (1910–) English engineer. He invented the hovercraft, the prototype of which first crossed the English Channel in 1959.

Cocteau, Jean (1889–1963) French film director, novelist, dramatist, poet and critic. His experimental, surreal films were highly influential on modern film-makers. The best known of his hovels is *Les Enfants Terribles*.

Coleridge, Samuel Taylor (1772–1834) English poet and critic. With WORDSWORTH he published *Lyrical Ballads* in 1798, a land-mark in English poetry in its rejection of a special 'poetic' language and advocacy of clear everyday language.

Colette, [Sidonie Gabrielle] (1873–1954) French novelist. Her novels, e.g. *Chéri* and *Gigi*, are often erotic and display a strong sympathy for animals and the natural world.

Collins, Michael (1890–1922) Irish Republican politician. A Sinn Fein leader, he negotiated the 1922 peace treaty with Britain that resulted in the establishment of the Irish Free State. He was killed in an ambush during the civil war that followed.

Coltrane, John [William] (1926–67) American jazz saxophonist. A virtuoso on the tenor and soprano saxophones, he became an influential and popular jazz musician.

Columba, St (521–97) Irish missionary. Accused of being involved in one of Ulster's many bloody civil conflicts, as penance he fled to the Western Isles of Scotland to proselytise for Christianity. He established a monastic settlement on the island of Iona.

Columbus, Christopher (1451–1506) Italian navigator. Under the patronage of Spain, he led an expedition to seek a western route to the Far East. He discovered the New World in 1492, making landfall in the West Indies and made two subsequent voyages in 1493 and 1498, reaching South America on the third.

Compton, Arthur Holly (1892–1962) American physicist. He was a prominent researcher into X-rays, gamma rays and nuclear energy, and discovered the Compton effect. He was awarded the 1927 Nobel prize for physics.

Compton, Denis [Charles Scott] (1918–) English cricketer, who played for Middlesex and England (1937–57) and who was regarded as one of the best all-rounders ever in cricket.

Compton-Burnett, Dame Ivy (1892–1969) English novelist. Her novels were mostly in dialogue and featured the traumas of upper-middle-class Edwardian family life.

Connery, Sean [Thomas] (1930–) Scottish film actor. One of the finest film actors of his time, he initially achieved worldwide fame as Ian FLEMING's character James Bond.

Conrad, Joseph [Teodor Josef Konrad Korzeniowsky] (1857–1924) Polish-born English writer. He qualified as a master mariner in 1886 and his many works often featured isolated characters in exotic locations. His novels include *Heart of Darkness*.

Constable, John (1776–1837) English painter. Drawing inspiration from nature, he produced works such as *View on the Stour*, which were initially more influential in France than England. He and Turner are considered to be the most important English landscape painters.

Constantine I (*c*.274–337) Roman Emperor. He became the first Christian Emperor in 312, when, before a battle, he reportedly saw a cross in the sky inscribed 'In this sign conquer'. He moved the capital to Byzantium (which he renamed Constantinople) in 330. Christianity became the Empire's official religion in 324.

Cook, (Captain) James (1728–79) English explorer who charted and claimed the east coast of Australia for Britain and discovered New Caledonia. On his third and last voyage to the Pacific (1776–79), he was killed by islanders in Hawaii.

Cooper, Gary [Frank James Cooper] (1901–61) American film actor who specialized as the quiet, couragous hero in many westerns and adventure films, e.g. *High Noon*.

Cooper, James Fenimore (1789–1851) American novelist. His adventure novels, such as *The Last of the Mohicans*, established the enduring 'frontier myth' of America.

Copernicus, Nicolaus (1473–1543) Polish astronomer. His great work *De Revolutionibus* (1543) sets out his theory that the earth and planets revolve around the sun.

Copland, Aaron (1900–1990) American composer, pianist and conductor. He was influential in American music in incorporating elements from traditional American folk songs in his compositions. His works include the ballet score *Rodeo*.

Coppola, Francis Ford (1939–) American film director and screenwriter. His most successful films include the modern classics, *The Godfather* (1972) and *Apocalypse Now* (1979).

Corday, Charlotte *see* MARAT, JEAN PAUL.

Corman, Roger (1926–) American film director and producer. Known primarily in the 1950s and 1960s as a creator of cheap B movies he also fostered the careers of many prominent American directors and actors, including COPPOLA, DE NIRO and SCORSESE.

Cosgrave, W[illiam] T[homas] (1880–1965) Irish nationalist politician. He became first president of the Irish Free State (1922–32). His son **Liam Cosgrave** (1920–) became Fine Gael prime minister of the Republic of Ireland (1973–77).

Courbet, Gustave (1819–77) French painter. Considered to be the founder of Realism, his work was frequently condemned as 'socialistic' because he scorned the established classical outlook.

Cousteau, Jacques [Yves] (1910–) French oceanographer. He invented the aqualung (1943) and developed techniques of underwater cinematography that were influential in raising awareness of the world's oceans.

Coward, Sir Noel [Pierce] (1899–1973) English dramatist, actor and composer. His witty, sophisticated comedies and amusing songs were regarded as mildly shocking in their day and include *Private Lives* and *Blithe Spirit*.

Cowper, William (1731–1800) English poet. Best known in his own day as an engaging satirist and nature poet, his darker religious poems are now seen as of more lasting importance.

Cranmer, Thomas (1489–1556) English prelate. Appointed Archbishop of Canterbury in 1533 (while secretly married), he pronounced the annulment of the marriage of HENRY VIII to Catherine of Aragon in 1533. A moderate Protestant reformer, he was executed by MARY I.

Crassus *see* CAESAR, JULIUS.

Crawford, Joan [Lucille le Sueur] (1908–77) American film actress. One of the first leading women in Hollywood although many of her films were formulatic melodramas.

Crick, Francis [Harry Compton] (1916–) English molecular biologist. With James Dewey WATSON, he discovered the structure of DNA, and was awarded the 1962 Nobel prize for physiology or medicine.

Crippen, Hawley Harvey (1862–1910) American doctor who poisoned his wife in London in 1910. His dramatic capture on board ship involved the first use of radio for police purposes.

Cripps, Sir [Richard] Stafford (1889–1952) British Labour statesman. A leading left-winger, he became chancellor of the exchequer (1947-50), and introduced a programme of high taxation and wage restraint to deal with Britain's economic problems.

Cromwell, Oliver (1599–1658) English soldier and statesman. A Puritan country squire and MP, he was a noted critic of CHARLES I during the 1628–29 Parliament. He displayed a strong grasp of military skill during the opening year of the Civil War (1642), forming his 'Ironsides' regiment the following year. He led Parliament's New Model Army to victory at Naseby (1645) and crushed Welsh and Scottish rebellions before signing Charles I's death warrant in 1649. After a murderous conquest of Ireland in 1649, his victory over a second Scottish rebellion in 1651 ended the Civil War. He was nominated 'Lord Protector' of the Commonwealth in 1653, and established an authoritarian rule, dissolving parliament when it displeased him. He was succeeded as Protector (1658–59) by his son, **Richard Cromwell** (1626–72).

Cromwell, Thomas (*c.*1485–1540) English statesman. Of humble origin, he rose to power through the patronage of Cardinal WOLSEY, and became HENRY VIII's chief adviser. He fostered the passing of Reformation legislation, established the king's legal status as head of the Church in England, and oversaw the dissolution of the monasteries.

Crosby, Bing [Harry Lillis Crosby] (1904–77) American singer and actor. His relaxed, jazz-influenced style of 'crooning' made him one of the most popular and imitated singers of the century.

cummings, e[dward] e[stlin] (1894–1962) American poet, novelist and artist. His experimental free verse and distinctive use of typography influenced many other poets.

Curie, Marie (1867–1934) Polish-born French chemist. With her husband **Pierre Curie** (1859–1906), also a chemist, and the physicist **Antoine Henri Becquerel** (1852–1908), she was awarded the 1903 Nobel prize for physics for work on radioactivity, the first woman to win a Nobel prize. She subsequently became the first person to win two Nobel prizes when her discovery of radium and polonium led to her being awarded the 1911 prize for chemistry.

Cyrano de Bergerac, Savinien (1619–1655) French soldier, poet and dramatist. Most famous in the popular imagination for having an enormous nose and for having (reputedly) fought around a thousand duels. His works include several satires, and his life was dramatized by Edmond ROSTAND in a verse drama.

Dahl, Roald (1916–90) English author (of Norwegian parentage) known primarily for his entertaining children's stories, e.g. *Charlie and the Chocolate Factory*, and collections of humorous poems. Stories for adults include the collection *Kiss, Kiss*.

Daladier, Edouard (1884–1970) French socialist statesman. He was prime minister (1933, 1934, 1938–40) and signed the Munich Pact of 1938. He denounced the Vichy government in 1943, and was then imprisoned for the duration of the war.

Dalai Lama [Tenzin Gyatso] (1935–) Tibetan spiritual and temporal leader. He became the 14th Dalai Lama in 1940, and fled Tibet in 1959 following the Chinese invasion of his country. He was awarded the 1989 Nobel Peace Prize in recognition for his commitment to the non-violent liberation of his homeland.

Dale, Sir Henry Hallett (1875–1968) English physiologist. He and **Otto Lowei** (1873–1961) were awarded the 1936 Nobel prize for physiology or medicine for their work on the chemical basis of nerve impulse transmission.

Dali, Salvador (1904–89) Spanish surrealist painter. His finely executed paintings, or 'dream photographs', did much to popularise the surrealist movement. He also collaborated on surreal films with Luis BUÑUEL.

D'Annunzio, Gabriele (1863–1938) Italian poet, novelist, dramatist and political adventurer. As a writer, the sensuous imagery of much of his work has been widely admired and his oratory was credited with Italy's joining the allies in World War I. He seized the city of Fiume in 1919, which he ruled until 1920 and became a supporter of MUSSOLINI.

Dante (Alighieri) (1265-1321) Italian poet. Expelled from Florence in 1309 for political reasons, he spent 20 years in wandering exile, during which he wrote his masterpiece, the *Divine Comedy*. His literary influence was enormous, and resulted in Tuscan becoming the language of literary Italy.

Danton, Georges Jacques (1759-94) French revolutionary. After the fall of the monarchy in 1792, he became minister of justice and voted for the death of King LOUIS XVI. His efforts to moderate the Revolutionary Terror failed, despite his eloquence. He was outmanoeuvred by ROBESPIERRE and executed.

Darnley, Lord *see* MARY, QUEEN OF SCOTS.

Darwin, Charles [Robert] (1809-82) English naturalist. The grandson of the physician and poet **Erasmus Darwin** (1731-1802), he sailed as a naturalist to South America and the Pacific (1831-36) where his studies among the rich animal and plant life of the area formed the basis for his revolutionary theory of evolution by natural selection. Darwin's theory rapidly found acceptance not only amongst scientists but among society at large.

Daumier, Honoré (1808-79) French cartoonist, painter and sculptor. One of the most proficient satirists of all time, his caricatures of the king resulted in a term in jail. He was also an innovative lithographer, painter and sculptor.

David, Jacques-Louis (1748-1825) French painter. The leading artist of the French Revolution, he was imprisoned after the death of ROBESPIERRE but survived to become painter to NAPOLEON.

Davies, Sir Peter Maxwell (1934–) English composer. With BIRTWHISTLE, he founded the Pierrot Players (later called the Fires of London). Since 1970 he has been based in Orkney and has frequently collaborated with the Orcadian poet, novelist and short-story writer **George Mackay Brown** (1921–).

Davis, Bette [Ruth Elizabeth Davis] (1908–89) American actress, whose electrifying and commanding screen presence made her a highly rated film actresses. Her films include *All About Eve*.

Davis, Sir Colin [Rex] (1927–) English conductor. Noted particularly for his interpretations of BERLIOZ, he was conductor of the BBC Symphony Orchestra (1967–71).

Davis, Miles [Dewey] (1926–91) American jazz trumpeter, composer and bandleader. The leading exponent of the influential 'cool jazz' school.

Davisson, Clinton Joseph *see* THOMSON, SIR GEORGE PAGET.

Davy, Sir Humphry (1778-1829) English chemist. An ingenious experimenter, he discovered many new metals, e.g. sodium and potassium, and developed ground-breaking studies in electro-chemistry. He was knighted in 1812, and invented the 'Davy lamp' for miners in 1815.

Dawes, Charles G[ates] (1865–1951) American banker. He devised the Dawes Plan of 1924 for German reparation payments after World War I. He was US vice-president (1925–29) and was awarded the 1925 Nobel Peace Prize.

Day, Doris [Doris Kappelhoff] (1924–) American film actress, famous for her light-hearted, girl-next-door image.

Dayan, Moshe (1915–81) Israeli general and statesman. He commanded the Israeli forces during the Sinai invasion (1956) and was minister of defence during the Six Day War of 1967. He played an important part in the talks leading to the Israel-Egypt peace treaty of 1979.

Day Lewis, Cecil (1904–72) Irish-born English poet. In the 1930s he was regarded as part of the 'AUDEN generation' of left-wing poets. He became poet laureate in 1968.

Dean, Christopher *see* TORVILL, JAYNE.

Dean, James [Byron] (1931–55) American film actor. He became a cult figure in the 1950s for his portrayal of troubled, disaffected adolescence, e.g. in *East of Eden* and *Rebel Without a Cause*. He died in a car crash.

Debussy, [Achille] Claude (1862–1918) French composer. Regarded as the founder of impressionism in music and one of the strongest influences on modern music, his works include orchestral pieces, e.g. *La Mer*, and the opera *Pelléas et Mélisande*.

Defoe, Daniel (1600-1731) English novelist and pamphleteer. His works include two remarkable novels, *Robinson Crusoe* (1719) and *Moll Flanders* (1722) although he was better known in his lifetime as a skilled and prolific propagandist.

Degas, [Hilaire Germain] Edgar (1834-1917) French painter and sculptor. He met Monet in the 1860s, after which he began exhibiting with the Impressionists. He is especially noted for his paintings and pastel drawings of racehorses and ballet dancers.

de Gaulle, Charles [André Joseph Marie] (1890–1970) French general, statesman and first president (1958–69) of the Fifth Republic. An opponent of the Vichy regime led by PÉTAIN, he fled to Britain in 1940, where he led the Free French forces. Elected president of the provisional government in 1945, he resigned in 1946 after disagreement over his executive powers. He was asked to form a government in 1958, during the Algerian crisis. He granted independence to France's colonies in Africa (1959–60), oversaw increased economic prosperity, fostered France's independent nuclear deterrent policy and strongly opposed the UK's entry into the Common Market. His party won a large majority in the election following the student riots of 1968. He resigned in 1969, after being defeated on constitutional reform.

de Klerk, F[rederik] W[illem] (1936–) South African statesman who succeeded P. W. BOTHA as leader of the ruling National party and president (1989) and continued the policy of dismantling apartheid, in 1990 legalizing the African National Congress and organizing MANDELA's release from prison. He presided over South Africa's first free elections in 1994 but was defeated by Mandela.

Delacroix, Eugène (1798-1863) French painter. His early work, while Romantic in subject matter, owes much to classical composition. He studied CONSTABLE's work and in turn influenced other artists, particularly those of the Barbizon School.

de la Mare, Walter [John] (1873–1956) English poet and novelist. Much of his work was written for children and the loss of childhood innocence is a major theme in his work. His works include the poetry collection *The Listeners*.

Delaunay, Robert (1885–1941) French painter who founded the movement called 'Orphism', the name given by APOLLINAIRE to Delaunay's introduction of colour abstraction into his Cubist-style paintings. He influenced many other artists, notably KLEE.

Delius, Frederick (1862–1934) English composer. Unconnected to any traditional school, he is noted for his six operas, including *A Village Romeo and Juliet*, and large orchestral pieces.

de Mille, Cecil B[lount] (1881–1959) American film producer and director. With GOLDWYN, he is credited with creating the mass movie industry of Hollywood. His films were extravagantly produced epics that achieved enormous success throughout the world, e.g. *The Ten Commandments* (1923).

Dempsey, Jack [William Harrison Dempsey] (1895 –1983) American boxer. An ex-miner who became one of the most popular boxers of his day, he was world heavyweight champion (1919–26).

Deng Xiaoping *or* **Teng Hsiao-p'ing** (1904–) Chinese Communist statesman. Denounced in the Cultural Revolution of the late 1960s as a 'capitalist roader', he re-emerged as a powerful figure in the late 1970s. He introduced economic reforms and developed friendly relations with the West, but also sanctioned the Tiananmen Square massacre of dissident students.

De Niro, Robert (1943–) American actor, who is regarded as one of the finest modern screen actors, with a remarkable facility for submerging himself in a wide variety of roles. His films include *Taxi Driver*, *Midnight Run* and *The Godfather II*, for which he won an Oscar.

Depardieu, Gerard (1948–) French actor. Established in the 1970s as a leading man in French films, his strong performances and independent character have made him popular worldwide, notably in *Danton*, *Cyrano de Bergerac* and *Green Card*.

Derain, André (1880–1954) French painter. He was influenced by PICASSO and BRAQUE, and became one of the leading Fauvist painters.

Desai, Morarji [Ranchhodji] (1896–) Indian statesman. He held several posts under NEHRU, founded the Janata party in opposition to Indira GANDHI's Congress Party, which he defeated in the 1977 general election, and was prime minister (1977–79).

Descartes, René (1596-1650) French philosopher and mathematician. He proposed a dualistic philosophy based on the separation of soul and body, mind and matter, and sought to establish his system on mathematics and pure reason, his most famous dictum being '*Cogito ergo sum*', 'I think, therefore I am'.

De Sica, Vittorio (1902–74) Italian film director and actor. His early films, e.g. *Bicycle Thieves* (1948), are regarded as among the finest Italian neo-realist films for their compassionate insight into the lives of the poor.

De Valera, Eamon (1882–1975) American-born Irish statesman. He was sentenced to death by the British government for his part in the 1916 Easter Rising, but was reprieved after US intervention. He became president of Sinn Féin (1917–1926). He opposed the Anglo-Irish Treaty (1921), gave largely symbolic leadership to the anti-Treaty forces during the civil war (1922–23), and was imprisoned (1923–24). He became prime minister (1932–48, 1951–54, 1957–59) and president (1959–73).

Devine, George [Alexander Cassady] (1910–65) English stage director and administrator. He became one of the most prominent influences on the British stage as artistic director of the English Stage Company at the Royal Court.

De Vries, Hugo [Marie] (1848–1935) Dutch botanist and geneticist. He rediscovered the genetic principles first put forward by MENDEL, and developed the theory of evolution through the mutation of genes.

Diaghilev, Sergei [Pavlovich] (1872–1929) Russian ballet impresario. Founder of the Ballet Russe de Diaghilev in 1911, he became a very influential ballet impresario, drawing on the talents of composers such as STRAVINSKY and artists such as PICASSO.

Dickens, Charles [John Huffam] (1812–70) English novelist. His prolific output included plays, pamphlets and lectures, as well as novels and short stories. Immensely popular with both the American and British reading public, he continues to be one of the most widely read writers in the English language. His novels include *David Copperfield*, *Bleak House* and *Great Expectations*.

Dickinson, Emily (1830–86) American poet. Although only seven of her *c*.2000 poems were printed in her lifetime she became recognized as a uniquely gifted poet following the wider publication of her work in the 1890s.

Diderot, Denis (1713–84) French philosopher. With others, he edited the great *Encyclopédie*, 17 volumes of which appeared under Diderot's overall direction between 1751 and 1772.

Dietrich, Marlene [Maria Magdelene von Losch] (1902–92) German-born American singer and film actress, notable for her strong sexual presence and husky, alluring voice.

Dior, Christian (1905–57) French couturier who created the 'New Look' of the late 1940s, with a narrow waist and full pleated skirt, which was very popular in the austerity of postwar Europe.

Dirac, Paul Adrien Maurice (1902–84) English physicist. He devised a complete mathematical formulation of EINSTEIN's theory of relativity and predicted the existence of antimatter. He shared the 1933 Nobel prize for physics with SCHRÖDINGER.

Disney, Walt[er Elias] (1901–66) American cartoonist and film producer. His cartoon films of the 1930s and 40s achieved high critical and popular acclaim, Mickey Mouse and Donald Duck being two of his famous creations. He built Disneyland amusement park in California (1955), and planned Disney World in Florida (1971).

Disraeli, Benjamin [1st Earl of Beaconsfield] (1804–81) British statesman and novelist. He became a Tory member of parliament in 1837 and prime minister (1868, 1874-80). He promoted protectionism and a romantic imperialism which appealed to Queen VICTORIA and most of the British public, much to the ire of his great rival, GLADSTONE.

Dobzhansky, Theodosius (1900–75) Russian-born American geneticist. His seminal studies of genetic variation linked Darwin's evolutionary theory with MENDEL's heredity laws.

Doenitz, Karl *see* DÖNITZ, KARL.

Dolci, Danilo (1924–) Italian social reformer. Described as the 'GANDHI of Italy', he built schools and community centres in poverty-stricken Sicily in the face of fierce opposition from an unholy alliance of church, state and Mafia.

Dollfus, Engelbert (1892–1934) Austrian statesman. A devout Roman Catholic, he became leader of the Christian Socialist Party and was elected chancellor (1932–34). He opposed the German Anschluss and was assassinated by Austrian Nazis.

Domingo, Placido (1941–) Spanish tenor who studied in Mexico City. He is regarded as one of the finest modern operatic tenors for his sophisticated vocal technique and considerable acting ability.

Dominic, St (*c*.1170-1221) Spanish monk. Noted for his asceticism, he founded the Dominican Order of monks and helped the forces of the Inquisition in their barbarous treatment of the Albigensians in Southern France. He was canonized in 1234.

Donatello [Donato di Niccolò di Betto Bardi] (*c*.1386-1466) Florentine sculptor. One of the leading sculptors of the early Renaissance, his most famous work is the huge bronze statue of *David* (1430s).

Dönitz *or* **Doenitz, Karl** (1891–1980) German admiral. He was commander of the German navy (1943–45). As head of the Nazi state following HITLER's suicide, he surrendered unconditionally to the Allies, and was sentenced at Nuremberg to ten years imprisonment for war crimes.

Donleavy, J[ames] P[atrick] (1926–) American-born Irish novelist. His most popular works are comic adventures set in Dublin's undergraduate community, e.g. *The Ginger Man*.

Donne, John (1573-1631) English poet and divine. After occasional hazardous adventures, such as accompanying Sir Francis DRAKE on his raid on Cadiz, he became Dean of St Paul's in 1621 and was regarded as one of the greatest preachers of his day. His poetry is among the finest metaphysical verse.

Doré, Gustave (1832-83) French sculptor, painter and illustrator. Trained as a caricaturist, he became well known for his book illustrations and realistic drawings of London slums.

Dostoyevsky, Fyodor Mikhailovich (1821-81) Russian novelist. His novels, e.g. *Crime and Punishment*, are profound explorations of sin and redemption through suffering. With TOLSTOY he was profoundly influential on modern literature.

Douglas-Home, Sir Alec [Baron Home of the Hirsel] (1903–) Scottish Conservative politician. He became the 14th Earl of Home in 1951, renouncing his title in 1963 to contest (and win) the seat of Kinross after succeeding Harold MACMILLAN as prime minister. The furore over his unexpected emergence as party leader resulted in reform of the Tory leadership election process.

Doyle, Sir Arthur Conan (1859–1930) Scottish novelist, short-story writer and physician. His most famous creation is the amateur detective Sherlock Holmes.

Drake, Sir Francis (*c.*1540-1596) English navigator and pirate. He became a highly popular hero to the English following his successful depradations upon Spanish ships and settlements in the Caribbean in the early 1570s. He circumnavigated the world (1577-80) and was one of the leading lights in the victory over the Spanish Armada (1588).

Dreyfus, Alfred (1859-1935) French army officer. Imprisoned in 1894 on Devil's Island on a false charge of espionage, the 'Dreyfus affair' scandalized much of Europe for the anti-semitism of the prosecution case. ZOLA's magnificent pamphlet *J'accuse* (1898) was written in his defence, and Dreyfus was released in 1906.

Dryden, John (1631-1700) English poet, dramatist and critic. One of the most important literary figures of his time, he was also a highly significant contributor to the religious and political controversies of the day. He was also the first great English critic, and an outstanding poet. His works include the social comedy *Marriage à la Mode* and the verse tragedy *All for Love*. He became poet laureate in 1668 but lost the post in 1688 in the political upheaval surrounding the replacement of King JAMES II by WILLIAM III and Mary.

Dubcek, Alexander (1921–92) Czech statesman. As first secretary of the Communist Party (1968–69), he introduced political reforms which ended with the Russian invasion of 1968. Following Czechoslovakian independence, he was appointed chairman of the federal assembly (1989).

Dubuffet, Jean (1901–85) French painter. He devised the concept of 'Art Brut' in reaction against 'museum art', and made paintings assembled from bits of rubbish, broken glass, etc.

Duchamp, Marcel (1887–1968) French-born American painter and sculptor. One of the early pioneers of Dadaism, he introduced the concept of the 'found object'.

Dulles, John Foster (1888–1959) American Republican statesman and lawyer. He was secretary of state (1953–59) under EISENHOWER, and developed the confrontational foreign policy of 'brinkmanship' in the Cold War against the USSR.

Dumas, Alexandre [*Dumas père*] (1802-70) French novelist and dramatist, whose entertaining Romantic novels, e.g. *The Three Musketeers*, achieved instant and lasting popularity. His illegitimate son, also called **Alexandre Dumas** [*Dumas fils*] (1824-95) also wrote novels and plays, e.g. *Camille*.

Du Maurier, Dame Daphne (1907–89) English novelist and short-story writer. Several of her works have been made into successful films, e.g. the novels *Rebecca* and *Jamaica Inn*, and the stort story 'Don't Look Now'.

Duncan, Isadora (1878–1927) American dancer and choreographer. She developed a free, interpretative style of dancing that was very influential on the development of modern dance (e.g. on DIAGHILEV). Her ardent feminism and unconventional lifestyle alienated many of her contemporaries.

du Pré, Jacqueline (1945–87) English cellist. She became recognized as one of the world's finest cellists in the 1960s and married BARENBOIM in 1967, with whom she frequently performed. Her performing career came to an end in 1973, after she developed multiple sclerosis. Although confined to a wheelchair, she pursued an active teaching career until her death.

Dürer, Albrecht (1471-1528) German engraver and painter. A leading figure of the Northern Renaissance, his work is outstanding in its attention to detail and its emotional content. A superb draughtsman, his albums of engravings were highly influential on other artists.

Durrell, Lawrence [George] (1912–90) English poet, novelist and travel writer. His masterpiece is the series of sexual and linguistically elaborate novels comprising the 'Alexandria Quartet'.

Dvorak, Antonin (1841-1904) Czech composer. Strongly influenced by Slavonic folk music, his work was widely praised and he was made a director of the New York Conservatory in 1891. His most famous work is *Symphony No. 9 from the New World*.

Dyck, Sir Anthony van (1599-1641) Flemish painter. Renowned for his unique and influential style of portraiture, investing his sitters with character and refinement of detail, he became court painter to CHARLES I in 1632.

Dylan, Bob [Robert Allen Zimmerman] (1941–) American folk/rock singer and songwriter. He became the most prominent 'protest' folksinger in the 1960s and his lyrics are very highly regarded by some critics. *See also* BAEZ.

Earhart, Amelia (1898–1937) American aviator. She was the first woman to make a solo flight across the Atlantic (1932), after which she became a celebrity. She disappeared on a flight across the Pacific while attempting a round-the-world flight.

Eastman, George (1854–1932) American inventor of photographic equipment and philanthropist. His invention of the Kodak roll-film camera revolutionized the photographic industry, as did his development of colour photography in the late 1920s.

Eco, Umberto (1932–) Italian critic and novelist. A leading literary critic, he is also highly regarded as a writer of fiction. His best-known work is the medieval philosophical whodunit, *The Name of the Rose*.

Eddy, Mary Baker (1821–1910) American religious leader. A faith healer, she devised a system of healing based on the Bible which she called 'Christian Science', and founded the Church of Christ, Scientist, in Boston (1879).

Eden, Sir [Robert] Anthony [1st Earl of Avon] (1897–1977) British Conservative statesman. He served several terms as foreign minister and was prime minister (1955–57). He resigned following the Suez Crisis, when British and French occupation of Egypt after NASSER's nationalization of the Suez Canal received worldwide condemnation.

Edison, Thomas [Alva] (1847–1931) American inventor. One of the most prolific and successful inventors of all time, he patented over a thousand inventions, including the gramophone, the incandescent electric light bulb, and the microphone.

Edward, Prince *see* **Elizabeth II.**

Ehrlich, Paul (1854–1915) German bacteriologist. He did significant research into immunology and chemotherapy, and developed a cure for syphilis (1910). He was awarded the 1908 Nobel prize for physiology or medicine.

Eichmann, [Karl] Adolf (1906–62) Austrian Nazi leader and war criminal. He oversaw the 'Final Solution' (deportation of Jews to death camps) and escaped to Argentina at the end of the war but was captured and tried for crimes against humanity by the Israelis in 1960 and executed.

Eijkman, Christiaan (1858–1930) Dutch physician who discovered that beriberi is caused by nutritional deficiency. His research led to the discovery of 'essential food factors', i.e. vitamins. He shared the 1929 Nobel prize for physiology or medicine with Sir Frederick HOPKINS.

Einstein, Albert (1879–1955) German-born physicist and mathematician. His formulations of the special theory of relativity (1906) and general theory of relativity (1916), and research into quantum theory, mark him as one of the greatest of all thinkers. He was awarded the 1921 Nobel prize for physics. Being Jewish and a pacifist, he was forced to flee Nazi Germany in 1933, and became a US citizen in 1940.

Eisenhower, Dwight D[avid] (1890–1969) American general and Republican statesman, known as 'Ike'. He became supreme commander of the Allied forces in 1943 and 34th president of the US (1953–60).

Eisenstein, Sergei Mikhailovich (1898–1948) Soviet film director. He served with the Red Army (1918–20) during the Civil War and became one of the most influential directors of all time with films such as *Battleship Potemkin* (1925), in which he deployed his theory of film montage.

Elgar, Sir Edward [William] (1857–1934) English composer. A master of many styles, he became recognized as the leading British composer with works such as the *Enigma Variations*, the oratorio *The Dream of Gerontius* and his famous *Cello Concerto*.

El Greco [Domenikos Theotocopolous] (1541–1614) Cretan-born Spanish painter, sculptor and architect. He studied in Italy before settling in Toledo where he worked in an emotional and spiritually evocative style, using a palette of cold blues and greys at a time when the vogue was for warmer colours. His works include *The Burial of Count Orgaz*.

Eliot, George [pseud. of Mary Ann Evans] (1819–80) English novelist. Her novels, e.g. *The Mill on the Floss* and *Middlemarch*, deal with the problems of ethical choice in the rapidly changing rural environment of 19th-century England. She lived, unmarried, with her partner, the English writer **George Henry Lewes** (1817–78).

Eliot, T[homas] S[tearns] (1888–1965) American-born English poet and critic. His early poetry, e.g. *The Waste Land*, is concerned with the breakdown of civilized values in the postwar 'Jazz Era'. He also wrote verse dramas and published critical works.

Elizabeth I (1533–1603) queen of England. The daughter of Henry VIII and Anne Boleyn, she was brought up a Protestant. She was crowned queen in 1588 and instituted a cautious religious toleration. Guided by William CECIL, she established the Church of England and pursued a shrewd divide-and-rule policy in home and foreign affairs, surviving various plots and a Spanish attempt at invasion by armada in 1588. The later years of her reign saw a flourishing of literature and a great age of drama.

Elizabeth II (1926–) queen of the United Kingdom from 1952. The daughter of GEORGE VI. She married Prince PHILIP in 1947, and has four children: Prince CHARLES, Princess Anne (1950–), Prince Andrew (1960–) and Prince Edward (1964–). She is regarded as the most formal of all modern European monarchs.

Ellington, Duke [Edward Kennedy Ellington] (1899–1974) American jazz composer, pianist and band-leader. Regarded as one of the finest jazz composers, his many works include 'Mood Indigo' and 'Sophisticated Lady'.

Elton, Charles Sutherland (1900–) English ecologist. His field studies of animal communities in their environments raised awareness of the ability of animals to adapt to changing habitats.

Emerson, Ralph Waldo (1803–82) American essayist, philosopher and poet who developed a philosophy of 'transcendentalism', based upon the authenticity of the individual conscience against both church and state.

Engels, Friedrich *see* MARX, KARL.

Epicurus (341–271 BC) Greek philosopher. He founded the Epicurean school of philosophy, which teaches that the highest good and proper study of mankind is pleasure, and that this can be attained through a life of simplicity and moderation.

Erasmus, Desiderius (*c.*1466–1536) Dutch humanist. One of the leading scholars of the Renaissance, he was a strong advocate of tolerance in an intolerant age. His works include *Praise of Folly*, written partly in tribute to his friend Thomas MORE.

Ernst, Max (1891–1976) German-born French painter. He was a leading member of both the Dada and Surrealist movements and pioneered the use of collage and photomontage.

Euripides (480–406 BC) Greek dramatist. He was the youngest of the three great Greek tragedians, the others being AESCHYLUS and SOPHOCLES. Nineteen of his plays are extant, the most notable including *Medea* and *The Trojan Women*.

Evans, Sir Arthur [John] (1851–1941) English archaeologist. His excavations of the palace of Knossos in Crete resulted in the rediscovery of Minoan civilization.

Evans, Dame Edith [Mary Booth] (1888–1976) English actress, notable for her command of a wide variety of roles. She created the role of Lady Utterwood in SHAW's *Heartbreak House* and gave a definitive performance as Lady Bracknell in Wilde's *The Importance of Being Earnest*.

Eysenck, Hans [Jürgen] (1916–) German-born British psychologist. He has been a notable critic of FREUD's theory of psychoanalysis and holder of controversial views on the role of genetic factors in determining intelligence.

Fairbanks, Douglas [Douglas Elton Ullman] (1883–1939) American film actor and producer, who became one of the leading stars of silent films. His son, **Douglas Fairbanks Jr** (1909–), was also an actor. His first wife was Joan CRAWFORD.

Faraday, Michael (1791–1867) English chemist and physicist. He was an assistant to DAVY and discovered electromagnetic induction and investigated electrolysis.

Farouk, King *see* NASSER, GAMAL ABDEL.

Farquhar, George (1678–1707) Irish dramatist. His lightly satirical plays, e.g. *The Beaux' Stratagem*, mark an important transitional stage between the bawdy world of Restoration comedy and the more decorous 18th-century stage.

Fassbinder, Rainer Werner (1946–82) German film director. His films, e.g. *The Bitter Tears of Petra Von Kant*, are noted for their social comment, particularly on post-war Germany.

Faulkner, William [Harrison] (1897–1962) American novelist. Considered a master of the modern novel, his best-known work, *The Sound and the Fury*, deals with social tensions in the Old South. He was awarded the 1949 Nobel prize for literature.

Fawcett, Dame Millicent [Millicent Garrett] (1847–1929) English feminist. She became first president of the National Union of Women Suffrage Societies (1897–1919), and opposed the more militant tactics of PANKHURST.

Fellini, Federico (1920–) Italian film director. The best-known of his highly individual films is *La Dolce Vita* (1960), a cynical portrayal of Roman high society.

Fermat, Pierre de (1601–65) French mathematician. The founder of number theory, he initiated, with PASCAL, the study of probability theory.

Fermi, Enrico (1901–54) Italian-born American physicist. Awarded the Nobel prize for physics in 1938 for his work on radioactive substances and nuclear bombardment, he fled to the US. He built the first nuclear reactor at Chicago in 1942.

Ferrier, Kathleen (1912–53) English contralto. A highly regarded singer whose tragically short career ended with her death from cancer, she created the title role in BRITTEN's *Rape of Lucretia* and sang regularly with Bruno WALTER.

Feydeau, Georges (1862–1921) French dramatist, noted for his many bedroom farces, e.g. *Hotel Paradise*.

Feynman, Richard (1918–88) American physicist. He shared the 1965 Nobel prize for physics for his work in quantum electrodynamics.

Field, John (1782–1837) Irish composer and pianist who settled in Russia (1804–32) then in London. He is particularly noted for his 19 *Nocturnes*, and was an influence on CHOPIN.

Fielding, Henry (1707–54) English novelist and dramatist. His early satirical plays, e.g. *Pasquin*, provoked the British government into passing strict censorship laws and his unconventional novels which followed caused similar controversy. His greatest work, *Tom Jones*, surveys the whole of English society with masterly insight and compassion. He also wrote important tracts on social problems and worked tirelessly against legal corruption.

Fields, W. C. [William Claude Dukenfield] (1880–1946) American comedian, noted for his hard drinking, red nose, gravel voice and antipathy to children and animals.

Fischer, Bobby [Robert James Fischer] (1943–) American chess player. A grandmaster at 15 he became the first US player to win the world championship (1972) when he won against SPASSKY.

Fitzgerald, Ella (1918–) American jazz singer, whose highly praised vocal range, rhythmic subtlety and clarity of tone made her one of the most popular singers of her day.

Fitzgerald, F[rancis] Scott [Key] (1896–1940) American novelist and short-story writer. His works are moralistic fables set in

1920s 'Jazz Age' High Society and include *The Great Gatsby* and *Tender is the Night*.

Flagstad, Kirsten (1895–1962) Norwegian soprano, noted for her roles in Wagner's operas. She is regarded as one of the finest Wagnerian singers of all time.

Flaherty, Robert [Joseph] (1884–1951) American documentary film director. His films, e.g. *Nanook of the North*, set high standards for all following documentary film makers.

Flaubert, Gustave (1821–80) French novelist. His masterpiece is his first published novel, *Madame Bovary*, a study of self-deception, adultery and suicide in rural France. Flaubert is noted for his meticulously impersonal and objective narrative.

Fleming, Sir Alexander (1881–1955) Scottish bacteriologist. He discovered the antibacterial qualities of the enzyme lysozome, the substance he dubbed 'penicillin'. He shared the 1945 Nobel prize for physiology or medicine with CHAIN and FLOREY.

Fleming, Ian [Lancaster] (1908–64) English novelist. His series of novels featuring the British secret agent James Bond, e.g. *Goldfinger*, were enormous successes and have all been filmed.

Fletcher, John (1579–1625) English dramatist. One of the most popular dramatists of his day, he frequently collaborated with other dramatists, such as SHAKESPEARE, but most notably with **Sir Francis Beaumont** (1584–1616), from 1606–13). Their best-known works are tragicomedies such as *The Maid's Tragedy*.

Florey, Howard Walter, Baron (1898–1968) Australian pathologist. He shared the 1945 Nobel prize for physiology or medicine with Sir Alexander FLEMING and CHAIN for their work on penicillin.

Flynn, Errol [Leslie Thomas Flynn] (1909–59) Australian-born American film actor. His starring roles in the swashbuckling tradition, e.g. *Captain Blood*, earned him considerable popularity.

Foch, Ferdinand (1851–1929) French general and marshal of France (1918). He was given command of the Allied forces in March 1918, and led the Allies to victory following the arrival of US troops in July 1918.

Fokine, Michel (1880–1942) Russian-born American ballet dancer and choreographer. With DIAGHILEV in Paris, he created a new style of ballet, in which all the elements, dance, music, costume and *mise en scène*, formed a coherent whole.

Fonda, Henry (1905–82) American film actor, often seen as the epitome of 'decent' America, a man determined to set injustices right. His daughter, **Jane [Seymour] Fonda** (1937-) also won recognition as a fine actress, although her outspoken opposition to the Vietnam war was heavily criticised.

Fonteyn, Dame Margot [Margaret Hookham] (1919–91) English ballerina. Regarded as one of the finest classical ballerinas of the century, she partnered NUREYEV at the age of 43.

Foot, Michael [Mackintosh] (1913–) British Labour politician. A leading left-winger, pacifist and CND member, he was secretary of state of employment (1974–76) and leader of the House of Commons (1976–79), and succeeded CALLAGHAN as leader of the Labour Party (1980–83). His many books include biographies of SWIFT and BEVAN.

Ford, Ford Madox [Ford Hermann Hueffer] (1873–1939) English novelist, poet and critic. Writer of over 80 novels, e.g. *The Good Soldier*, he also founded the *Transatlantic Review* in 1924, and gave generous encouragement to many writers.

Ford, Gerald R[udolph] (1913–) American Republican statesman and 38th president of the US (1974–77). He replaced AGNEW as NIXON's vice-president in 1973, becoming president the following year, after Nixon's impeachment and resignation.

Ford, Henry (1863–1947) American car designer and manufacturer. His Model T Ford, first introduced in 1908, was enormously successful and its production line manufacture became a role model for much of industry.

Ford, John (1586–*c*.1639) English dramatist, notable for such revenge tragedies as *'Tis Pity She's a Whore*. His bleak, objective vision of human suffering and his command of blank verse were highly praised by T. S. ELIOT.

Ford, John [Sean Aloysius O'Fearna] (1895–1973) American film director. He is regarded as one of the greatest directors for his epic and poetic vision of history, particularly that of the American West, e.g. *Stagecoach* and *The Searchers*.

Forster, E[dward] M[organ] (1879–1970) English novelist and critic. His novels, e.g. *Howards End*, are mainly concerned with moral and ethical choices, and the personal relationships of educated, middle-class people.

Fox, Charles James (1749–1806) English Whig statesman. A formidable orator, he was strongly opposed to the wars against the American and French revolutionaries and was a vigorous opponent of the slave trade.

Fox, George (1624–91) English religious leader. Brought up a

Puritan, he preached opposition to established religion and advocated peace and toleration. He founded the Society of Friends (known popularly as 'Quakers') in 1647.

Fragonard, Jean-Honoré (1732–1806) French painter. One of the greatest exponents of Rococo art, his early works were historical scenes on a grand scale, but he is known for his smaller, picturesquely pretty canvases.

Francesca, Piero della *see* PIERO DELLA FRANCESCA.

Francis of Assisi, St [Giovanni Bernardone] (1181–1226) Italian monk. He abandoned a military career to care for the poor and founded a 'brotherhood' of friars in 1210, and, in 1212, an order for women, the Poor Clares. He preached poverty, chastity and obedience to the Church, and received the stigmata in 1224. He was canonized in 1228.

Franck, César [Auguste] (1822–90) Belgian-born French composer. His best works were written late in life, e.g. his string quartet, and his work only recieved public acclaim after his death.

Franck, James (1882–1964) German-born American physicist. With the German physicist **Gustav Ludwig Hertz** (1887–1975), he shared the 1925 Nobel prize for physics for work on the quantum theory, notably the effects of bombarding atoms with electrons.

Franco, Francisco (1892–1975) Spanish general and dictator. He led the right-wing rebellion against the Spanish Republican government during the Spanish Civil War (1936–39). He became leader of the Fascist Falange Party in 1937, and ruled Spain from 1939 until his death.

Frank, Anne (1929–45) German-born Dutch Jewish girl. Her journal describing her family's experiences while hiding from the Nazis is one of the most moving accounts of the terrible suffering of the Jewish people during the World War II.

Franklin, Benjamin (1706–90) American author, statesman and author. He helped draft the American Declaration of Independence, and played an active role in American political life for most of his long life. He published a highly entertaining *Autobiography* and also invented the lightning conductor.

Franklin, Rosalind Elsie (1920–58) British chemist. Her X-ray crystallography research into DNA contributed to the discovery of its structure by James WATSON and CRICK.

Frayn, Michael (1933–) English dramatist and novelist, noted for his dry, sardonic humour.

Frazer, Sir James George (1854–1941) Scottish scholar and anthropologist, whose study of religious customs and myth influenced FREUD and many 20th-century writers..

Frege, [Friedrich Ludwig] Gottlob (1848–1925) German mathematician and philosopher. He is regarded as having laid the foundations for both modern mathematical logic and the philosophy of language.

French, Sir John [Denton Pinkstone], [1st Earl of Ypres] (1852–1925) English field marshal. He commanded the British Expeditionary Force in France (1914–15) and became Lord Lieutenant of Ireland (1918–21) during the Anglo-Irish War.

Freud, Lucian (1922–) German-born British painter. The grandson of Sigmund FREUD, he is renowned for his nudes and portraits, often painted from odd angles in an extreme-realist style.

Freud, Sigmund (1856–1939) Austrian psychiatrist, who founded psychoanalysis. His writings have been enormously influential on 20th-century thought. The main tenet of Freudian theory is that neuroses and dreams are repressed manifestations of sexual desire. His stress on the importance of sex was rejected by ADLER and JUNG. His daughter **Anna Freud** (1895–1982) pioneered child psychology in the UK.

Friedman, Milton (1912–) American economist. His controversial monetarist theory of economics, stressing the need for minimal government intervention, became the dominant economic theory of the 1980s. He was awarded the 1976 Nobel prize for economics.

Friedrich, Casper David (1774–1840) German Romantic painter. Largely uninfluenced by other artists or trends, his work was highly controversial in its treatment of landscape.

Frisch, Otto Robert (1904–79) Austrian-born British nuclear physicist. He and his aunt, Lise MEITNER, discovered nuclear fission, and their work led directly to the invention of the atom bomb.

Frisch, Ragnar *see* TINBERGEN, JAN.

Frost, Robert [Lee] (1874–1963) American poet. His quiet, lyrical poems, e.g. 'Stopping by Woods on a Snow Evening', have been admired for their enigmatic use of symbolism.

Fry, C[harles] B[urgess] (1872–1956) English sportsman, regarded as one of the greatest all-round sportsmen ever, representing England in athletics, cricket and soccer.

Fry, Christopher (1907–) English dramatist, whose verse dramas, e.g. *The Lady's Not for Burning*, were popular with both critics and public.

Fry, Elizabeth (1780–1845) English prison reformer. A Quaker and preacher, she campaigned for prison reform and founded hostels for the homeless.

Fuchs, Klaus [Emil Julius] (1911–88) German-born British physicist. He began work on British atom-bomb research in 1941 and was jailed in 1950 for 14 years for passing details to the Soviet Union.

Fuchs, Sir Vivian Ernest (1908–) English explorer and scientist. He led the Commonwealth Trans-Antarctic Expedition (1955–58), which made the first overland crossing of Antarctica.

Fugard, Athol (1932–) South African dramatist, whose plays, e.g. *Boesman and Lena*, explore the tragedy of racial tension caused by apartheid in South Africa.

Fuller, [Richard] Buckminster (1895–1983) American architect and engineer. He invented the 'geodesic dome', a lightweight framework consisting of a set of polygons in the shape of a shell.

Furtwängler, Wilhelm (1886–1954) German conductor. He became one of the most popular conductors in Europe, particularly for his highly charged interpretations of WAGNER's music.

Fuseli, Henry [Johann Heinrich Füssli] (1741–1825) Swiss-born British painter. His paintings are mannered and Romantic with a sense of the grotesque and macabre.

Gable, [William] Clark (1901–60) American film actor. His rugged good looks, sardonic wit and easy-going charm made him one of the most popular film stars of his day.

Gabor, Dennis (1900–79) Hungarian-born British engineer. He was awarded the 1971 Nobel prize for physics for his invention (in 1947) of the hologram.

Gaddafi *or* **Qaddafi, Moammar al-** (1942–) Libyan statesman and military dictator. He took power in a coup in 1969 and became president in 1977. Regarded almost universally as an unpredictable and often dangerous leader, Gaddafi has openly supported terrorist groups around the world.

Gagarin, Yuri [Alekseevich] (1934–68) Soviet cosmonaut, who became, in 1961, the first man in space, when his Vostok satellite circled the earth. He died in a plane crash.

Gainsborough, Thomas (1727–88) English painter. He worked as a portrait painter, but his keen interest in landscape painting pervades most of his work, his sitters often being portrayed out of doors. He developed a light, rapid painting style based on a delicate palette.

Gaitskell, Hugh [Todd Naylor] (1906–63) British Labour politician. He was regarded as being on the right of his party, having introduced, as chancellor of the exchequer (1950–51), national health service charges. He was Labour Party leader (1955–63).

Galbraith, John Kenneth (1908–) Canadian-born American economist and diplomat. He has been notably critical of the wastefulness of capitalist society. He was American ambassador to India (1961–63). His works include *The Affluent Society*.

Galilei, Galileo (1564–1642) Italian astronomer, mathematician and natural philosopher. An innovative thinker and experimenter, he demonstrated the isochronism of the pendulum and showed that falling bodies of differing weight descend at the same rate. He also developed the refracting telescope and became convinced of the truth of COPERNICUS's theory that the earth revolved around the sun. He was unable to prove it and was forced to retract his support publicly.

Gallup, George Horace (1901–84) American statistician. He developed the opinion poll into a sophisticated device, the 'Gallup Poll', for testing public opinion, most notably on elections.

Galsworthy, John (1867–1933) English novelist and dramatist. His plays, e.g. *Strife*, attacked social injustice. His novels include the Forsyte saga triology. He was awarded the 1932 Nobel prize for literature.

Galton, Sir Francis (1822–1911) English scientist and explorer. The cousin of DARWIN, he travelled widely in Africa and made significant contributions to meteorology and to heredity. He also developed the science of fingerprinting.

Gama, Vasco da (*c*.1469–1525) Portuguese navigator. He discovered the route to India round the Cape of Good Hope (1497–99), and became Portuguese viceroy in India in 1524.

Gandhi, Indira (1917–84) Indian stateswoman and prime minister. The daughter of NEHRU, she became prime minister (1966–77) of India. Her second term of office (1980–84) saw much ethnic strife and she was assassinated by her Sikh bodyguards. Her son **Rajiv** (1944–91) became prime minister in 1984, and was killed in a suicide bomb attack.

Gandhi, Mahatma [Mohandas Karamchand Gandhi] (1869–1948) Indian nationalist statesman and spiritual leader ('Mahatma' means 'Great Soul'). A passionate advocate of non-violent resistance, Gandhi's long campaign against British rule in India, using tactics of civil disobedience through passive resistance and hunger strikes, had great influence on world public opinion. He also struggled for reconciliation between Hindus and Moslems, and championed the cause of the Hindu Harijan caste of 'untouchables'. He was assassinated by a Hindu extremist, in the wake of India's independence and partition.

Garbo, Greta [Greta Lovisa Gustafson] (1905–90) Swedish-born American film actress noted for her austere and remote beauty. Her films include *Queen Christina*.

Garibaldi, Giuseppe (1807–82) Italian patriot. Forced into exile in 1834, he returned during the year of revolutions, 1848, and took part in the defence of Rome against the French, and, in 1860, with a force a thousand strong, he took Naples and Sicily for the newly united Italy. He is regarded as the most significant figure in the struggle for Italian independence.

Garland, Judy [Frances Gumm] (1922–69) American film actress and singer. She became one of the most loved child stars of the cinema in *The Wizard of Oz* and later starred in such films as *Easter Parade* and *A Star is Born*.

Garrick, David (1717–79) English actor and dramatist. A pupil of Samuel Johnson at Lichfield, he accompanied him to London in 1737, soon making his mark as an actor. At home with tragedy, comedy or farce, he dominated the English stage for many years, and was actor-manager of Drury Lane Theatre 1747–76.

Gaskell, Mrs Elizabeth [Elizabeth Cleghorn Stevenson] (1810–65) English novelist. Her novels, e.g. *North and South*, are often concerned with the injustices of the 'two-nation' society of 19th-century England, although her most popular novel is *Cranford*, a gentle study of life in a small village.

Gauguin, Paul (1848–1903) French painter. One of the greatest exponents of Postimpressionism, his interest in primitive art led to him settling in the South Pacific islands, where he painted some of his most important masterpieces.

Gay, John (1685–1732) English dramatist and poet. His masterpiece is *The Beggars' Opera* (1728), the ballad opera on which BRECHT based his *Threepenny Opera*.

Gell-Mann, Murray (1929–) American physicist. He introduced the quark hypothesis into physics and was awarded the 1969 Nobel prize for physics for his research into particle physics.

Genet, Jean (1910–86) French dramatist and novelist. His works are often based on his experiences in the criminal underworld where he spent much of his life.

Genghis Khan [originally Temujin] (*c*.1162–1227) Mongol leader who united the Mongol tribes and conquered China, establishing an empire that stretched from the Black Sea to the Pacific.

Géricault, Théodore (1791–1824) French Romantic painter. The realism and baroque dynamism of his work had a huge influence on many painters.

Gershwin, George (1898–1937) American composer and pianist. He and his brother, the lyricist **Ira Gershwin** (1896–1983), created several very popular musicals now considered masterpieces of American music.

Getty, J[ean] Paul (1892–1976) American industrialist and art collector, renowned for his wealth, miserliness and acquisition of works of art.

Ghirlandaio, Domenico (1449–94) Florentine painter who ran a workshop with his brothers **Benedetto** (1458–97) and **Davide** (1452–1525), where he produced frescos and altarpieces for a number of churches in Florence. His son **Ridolfo** (1483–1561) was MICHELANGELO's tutor.

Giacometti, Alberto (1901–66) Swiss sculptor and painter. He became a Surrealist in 1930 and was influenced by SARTRE's existentialism.

Giap, Vo Nguyen (1912–) Vietnamese general. He led the Viet Minh army against the French and commanded the North Vietnamese army against the US during the Vietnam War.

Gibbon, Edward (1737–94) English historian. His masterpiece is his *History of the Decline and Fall of the Roman Empire* (1776–88), a work that remains a great historical study.

Gielgud, Sir [Arthur] John (1904–) English stage and film actor and producer. Regarded as one of the leading Shakespearian actors of the 20th century, he has also made appearances in several Hollywood films.

Gierek, Edward (1913–) Polish Communist statesman. He became leader of the Polish United Workers Party following GOMULKA's resignation in 1971. He presided over increasing industrial unrest and the rise of the union Solidarity.

Gilbert, Sir W(illiam) S(chwenck) (1836–1911) English dramatist and librettist. His collaboration with the composer **Sir Arthur Sullivan** (1842–1900) resulted in the popular 'Savoy Operas', e.g. *The Gondoliers* and *The Mikado*, of which there are 13 in all and which have retained their popularity.

Gill, [Arthur] Eric [Rowton] (1882–1940) English sculptor, engraver, typographer and writer. His work has been influential in several areas of art and design.

Gillespie, Dizzy [John Birks Gillespie] (1917–93) American jazz trumpeter and bandleader, renowned as a virtuoso trumpeter.

Ginsberg, Allen (1926–) American poet, regarded as the leading poet of the Beat Generation, who had much influence on the hippy culture of the 1960s.

Giorgione [Giorgio da Castelfranco] (*c.*1477–1510) Venetian painter. Little of his work has survived, although he is one of the most influential painters of his time, the importance of his work lying in his treatment of landscape, imbuing it with strong atmosphere and moods.

Giotto di Bondone (1267–1337) Florentine painter and architect who developed spatial perspective and fully rounded figures in a departure from the flat, decorative imagery of the Byzantine era.

Giscard d'Estaing, Valéry (1926–) French statesman. He served as minister of finance under DE GAULLE (1962–66) and POMPIDOU (1969–74) and was elected president (1974–81) following the latter's death.

Gladstone, William Ewart (1809–98) British statesman. He became the leader of the Liberals in 1867, and was subsequently prime minister four times: 1868–74, 1880–5, 1886, and 1892–4. He had a long rivalry with his Tory opponent, DISRAELI, whose imperialism he vehemently opposed.

Glashow, Sheldon *see* WEINBERG, STEVEN.

Glass, Philip (1937–) American composer. One of the leading avant-garde composers of the 1970s, he is noted for his deep interest in Eastern harmonies and use of repeated motifs.

Gluck, Christoph Wilibald von (1714–87) German composer. He is especially noted for his operas, e.g. *Orfeo and Eurydice*.

Godard, Jean-Luc (1930–) French film director who is regarded as one of the most influential New Wave French film directors of the 1950s with such films as *Breathless* and *Week-End*.

Gödel, Kurt (1906–78) Austrian-born American logician and mathematician. 'Godel's theorem', shows the existence of undecidable elements in arithmetic systems.

Godwin, William (1756–1836) English novelist and philosopher. He questioned the validity of established goverment and institutions, notably marriage, and had a strong influence on many radicals, including SHELLEY, who married his daughter Mary.

Goebbels, [Paul] Joseph (1897–1945) German Nazi politician.

Head of the Nazi Party propaganda section in 1929 and minister of enlightenment and propaganda (1933–45). He committed suicide after shooting his wife and children.

Goering, Hermann *see* GÖRING, HERMANN.

Goethe, Johann Wolfgang von (1749–1832) German poet, dramatist, novelist, philosopher, scientist and statesman. He was one of the most learned and influential figures of his time. His masterpiece is the verse drama *Faust*.

Gogh, Vincent Van (1853–90) Dutch painter who studied theology before taking up painting in 1880. His art was thoroughly unacademic in its realistic subject matter and bold, expressionistic style, e.g. *The Potato Eaters*, but he was later influenced by the colours of Degas and Gauguin. He spent the last two years of his life in southern France, partly in an asylum, a period of intense creativity arising out of personal anguish, e.g. *The Cornfield*, painted at the scene where he shot himself.

Gogol, Nikolai Vasilievich (1809–52) Russian short-story writer, dramatist and novelist. His two greatest works are scathing satires on Russian bureaucracy and incompetence, the play *The Government Inspector* and the novel *Dead Souls*.

Golding, William [Gerald] (1911–93) English novelist. His first novel *The Lord of the Flies* established him as a major modern novelist. He was awarded the Nobel prize for literature in 1983.

Goldoni, Carlo (1707–93) Italian dramatist. Around 150 of his 250 plays are comedies, frequently featuring satirical attacks on the aristocracy and invariably set in his native Venice.

Goldsmith, Oliver (1728–1774) Irish poet and essayist who settled in London in 1756. An entertaining essayist and one of the leading poets of his day, he did not receive acclaim until late in life. His two greatest works are the novel *The Vicar of Wakefield* and his hugely successful play *She Stoops to Conquer*.

Goldwyn, Samuel [Samuel Goldfish] (1882–1974) Polish-born American film producer. One of the founders of the Hollywood movie business, forming Metro-Goldwyn-Mayer with Louis B. MAYER in 1924, he was famous for his (mainly apocryphal) 'Goldwynisms', e.g. 'Include me out'.

Goodman, Benny [Benjamin David] (1909–86) American jazz clarinetist and bandleader. Known as the 'King of Swing', he was one of the first white jazz bandleaders to hire Black players.

Gorbachev, Mikhail Sergeevich (1931–) Soviet Communist statesman. He became general secretary of the Soviet Communist party in 1985 and soon began instituting far-reaching social and political reforms. He became 'executive president' in 1990, with wide-ranging powers, facing strong opposition from radicals such as YELTSIN and from hard-line Communists. His powers were insufficient to withstand the break-up of the USSR, and he resigned in December 1991.

Gore, Al[bert] (1948–) American politician. A former investigative reporter, tobacco and livestock farmer, and developer, he became vice-president of the USA in 1992.

Göring *or* **Goering, Hermann [Wilhelm]** (1893–1946) German Nazi politician and military leader. He served HITLER as Prussian prime minister, minister of the interior and air minister (1933–45), organizing the rebuilding of the Luftwaffe.

Gorki *or* **Gorky, Maxim** [Aleksey Maximovich Peshkov] (1868–1936) Russian novelist, dramatist and short-story writer. A firm communist, he helped formulate the doctrine of socialist realism in the USSR in the 1930s.

Gorky, Arshile [Vosdanig Manoog Adoian] (1904–48) Armenian-born American painter. Originally a surrealist, he developed an abstract approach that was influential on action painters.

Goya y Lucientes, Francisco de (1746–1828) Spanish painter and printmaker. His strong, free-flowing technique and powerful pictorial style are demonstated in early portraits of the royal family, to whom he was court painter, and in later works inspired by the behaviour of the French army in their invasion of Spain.

Grace, W[illiam] G[ilbert] (1848–1915) English cricketer and physician, one of the first English cricketers to become a national institution. He was also noted for his cunning gamesmanship.

Graham, Billy [William Franklin Graham] (1918–) American evangelist. His evangelical crusades go all over the world.

Graham, Martha (1893–1991) American dancer and choreographer who is regarded as one of the founders of modern dance.

Grahame, Kenneth (1859–1932) Scottish author. His masterpiece, *The Wind in the Willows* (1908), is a children's classic.

Grainger, Percy [Aldridge] (1882–1961) Australian-born American pianist and composer who was notable enthusiast for folk songs, on which many of his works are based.

Grant, Cary [Archibald Alexander Leach] (1904–86) English-born American film actor who became one of Hollywood's leading stars in light comedy roles and thrillers.

Grant, Ulysses S[impson] (1822–85) American soldier and

18th US President. Commander of the Union forces in the Civil War, he was elected president in 1869. He established universal suffrage for all citizens, regardless of colour.

Grappelli, Stéphane (1908–) French jazz violinist. A founder of the Quintette de Hot Club de France, which became the leading European jazz group, he is still regarded as the finest jazz violinist ever.

Grass, Günter [Wilhelm] (1927–) German novelist, dramatist and poet. His works include the novel *Die Blechtrommel* (*The Tin Drum*, 1959), a grimly comic satire on the collapse of the Third Reich as seen through the eyes of a boy.

Graves, Robert [Ranke] (1895–1985) English poet, novelist and critic. His works include his classic autobiographical account of World War I soldiering, *Goodbye to all That* (1929), several great love poems and popular historical novels.

Gray, Thomas (1716–71) English poet. His best-known poem, 'Elegy Written in a Country Churchyard' (1751), is one of the most-quoted poems in the English Language.

Greene, [Henry] Graham (1904–1991) English novelist. Regarded as one of the greatest modern novelists, he converted to Roman Catholicism in 1926 and his religious beliefs play an important part in work, e.g. *The Heart of the Matter*.

Greer, Germaine (1939–) Australian feminist, writer and broadcaster who is best known for her controversial work, *The Female Eunuch* (1970).

Grieg, Edvard [Hagerup] (1843–1907) Norwegian composer of Scottish descent. Strongly influenced by Norwegian folk music, his works include music for IBSEN's *Peer Gynt*.

Grierson, John (1898–1972) Scottish documentary film director and producer, described as the 'father of British documentary'.

Griffith, Arthur (1871–1922) Irish nationalist leader. He founded Sinn Fein in 1905, and (with Michael COLLINS) signed the Anglo-Irish Treaty of 1921. He became the first president of the Irish Free State in 1922.

Griffith, D[avid] W[ark] (1875–1948) American film director and producer. His great technical skill was highly influential on other film-makers. In 1919, he founded United Artists with CHAPLIN, FAIRBANKS and PICKFORD.

Gris, Juan [José Victoriano Gonzàlez] (1887–1927) Spanish painter. He settled in Paris in 1906, where he became an associate of PICASSO and BRAQUE, and one of the leading Cubist painters.

Gromyko, Andrei Andreyevich (1909–89) Soviet statesman and diplomat. He was Soviet foreign minister (1957–1985) and a Politburo member (1973–89) and adapted effortlessly to each stage of relations with the West, from Cold War through 1970s detente to the GORBACHEV era.

Grunewald, Matthias (*c*.1460–1528) German painter noted for his use of perspective, Gothic imagery, strong colour and an expressionistic style of distortion.

Guevara, Che [Ernesto Guevara] (1928–67) Argentinian-born Communist revolutionary. He joined Fidel CASTRO's forces in the Cuban revolution (1956–59). He subsequently led a guerrilla group in Bolivia, where he was killed by government troops.

Guinness, Sir Alec (1914–) English stage and film actor. Regarded as one of the most versatile stage actors of his generation, he became a household name through his films, e.g. *Kind Hearts and Coronets* and *Star Wars*.

Gulbenkian, Calouste Sarkis (1869–1955) Turkish Armenian-born British financier, industrialist, diplomat and philanthropist. He endowed the Gulbenkian Foundation for the arts and sciences. His son, **Nubar Sarkis Gulbenkian** (1896–1972), was an Iranian diplomat and a philanthropist.

Guthrie, Sir [William] Tyrone (1900–71) English actor and theatrical producer. His productions included a controversial Hamlet in modern dress and several important Shakespeare productions.

Guthrie, Woody [Woodrow Wilson Guthrie] (1912–67) American folksinger and writer. His songs, which attack racial bigotry and the economic exploitation of the poor and immigrants, were a strong influence on 1960s 'protest' singers.

Hadrian [Publius Aelius Hadrianus] (76–138) Roman soldier and emperor. He spent much of his reign travelling through the empire, the boundaries of which he was concerned to make firm. He built Hadrian's Wall in the north of England.

Hahn, Otto (1879–1968) German physical chemist. With MEITNER and others, he undertook significant research which led to the discovery of nuclear fission. He was awarded the 1944 Nobel prize for chemistry.

Haig, Douglas, 1st Earl (1861–1928) British field marshal. In World War I he was appointed commander in chief of the British forces on the western front (1915–18). The terrible losses of soldiers under his command led to fierce criticism of his tactics. He founded the British Legion.

Haile Selassie [title of Ras Tafari Makonnen] (1892–1975) emperor of Ethiopia (1930–36, 1941–74). He lived in Britain during the occupation of his country by Italy (1936–41). In the early 1960s he helped establish the Organization of African Unity. The famine of 1973 created unrest which led to his deposition in a military coup. He is worshipped as a god by the Rastafarian cult.

Haitink, Bernard [Johann Herman] (1929–) Dutch conductor, renowned as an interpreter of Bruckner and MAHLER.

Hall, Sir Peter [Reginald Frederick] (1930–) English stage director and theatre manager. He was director of the Royal Shakespeare Company (1960–68) and the National Theatre (1973–88).

Halley, Edmund (1656–1742) English astronomer and mathematician. In 1583, he calculated the orbit of the comet now named after him, and correctly predicted its return in following years.

Hals, Frans (*c.*1581–1666) Dutch painter. Noted for his lively and innovative group portraiture that moved away from formal trends. His most famous work is *The Laughing Cavalier*.

Hamilton, Alexander (1757–1804) American statesman. He founded the Federalist party in 1787 and, as first secretary of the Treasury (1789–95), founded the US federal bank.

Hammarskjöld, Dag [Hjalmar Agne Carl] (1905–61) Swedish secretary general of the the United Nations (1953–61). His period of office was a turbulent one, and he died in a plane crash during the Congo crisis. He was posthumously awarded the 1961 Nobel Peace Prize.

Hammerstein II, Oscar (1895–60) American songwriter and librettist, best known for his musicals written with Richard RODGERS, e.g. *South Pacific* and *The Sound of Music*.

Hammett, [Samuel] Dashiell (1894–1961) American novelist. He wrote realistic crime novels based on his own experiences as a Pinkerton detective. His best known are *The Maltese Falcon* and *The Thin Man*.

Hampden, John (1594–1643) English parliamentarian. Prosecuted in 1637 for refusing to pay CHARLES I's unpopular ship-money tax. He raised a regiment for Parliament during the Civil War and died of wounds received in battle.

Hancock, Tony [Anthony John Hancock] (1924–68) English comedian. His popular BBC radio and TV series, *Hancock's Half Hour*, established his well-known comic persona of the belligerent misfit. He committed suicide.

Handel, George Frederick [Georg Friedrich Händel] (1685–

1759) German-born English composer. He became court composer to the Hanover court in 1710 and wrote over 40 operas, e.g. *Semele*, and many concertos and oratorios, e.g. *The Messiah*, as well as chamber and orchestral music, e.g. *Water Music*.

Hannibal, (247–182 BC) Carthaginian general. During the Second Punic War with Rome, he invaded Italy and crossed the Alps in 218. For 15 years he campaigned in Italy but was finally defeated in 204.

Hardie, [James] Keir (1856–1915) Scottish Labour politician. He was the first leader of the parliamentary Labour Party (1906–7). A committed pacifist, he withdrew from politics following the failure of parties of the Left in Europe to oppose World War I.

Hardy, Godfrey Harold (1877–1947) English mathematician, noted for his work on analytic number theory.

Hardy, Oliver *see* LAUREL, STAN.

Hardy, Thomas (1840–1928) English novelist, short-story writer and poet. As well known for his influential novels, e.g. *Far from the Madding Crowd*, as for his poetry, he is now ranked, with ELIOT and YEATS, as one of the three great modern poets in English.

Harlow, Jean [Harlean Carpentier] (1911–37) American film actress who became one of the screen's main sex symbols of the 1930s, with her tough, wise-cracking 'platinum blonde' image.

Harriman, W[illiam] Averell (1891–1986) American diplomat. He was the main negotiator of the nuclear test-ban treaty of 1963, between the US, UK and USSR. He was also governor of New York (1955–58).

Harris, Sir Arthur Travers (1892–1984) English air force officer, nicknamed 'Bomber Harris' for his advocacy of heavy bombing raids on German cities during World War II. The policy lasted from 1942 to the firebombing of Dresden in 1944.

Harrison, George (1943–) English singer-songwriter. He played lead guitar for the Beatles (1962–70).

Hart, Lorenz [Milton] (1895–1943) American lyricist who is best known for his collaborations with the composer Richard RODGERS, e.g. *The Boys from Syracuse* and *Pal Joey*.

Hartley, L[eslie] P[oles] (1895–1972) English novelist, whose best-known works are subtle portrayals of social and sexual intrigue in Edwardian England, e.g. *The Go-Between*.

Harvey, William (1578–1657) English physician. Court physician to both JAMES VI and CHARLES I, he published his discovery of the circulation of the blood in 1628.

Hasek, Jaroslav (1883–1923) Czech novelist and short-story writer. His masterpiece is *The Good Soldier Svejk* (1925), based on his own experiences in the Austro-Hungarian army.

Hastings, Warren (1732–1818) British administrator in India. He was the first governor-general of Bengal (1773–85) and established the East India Company as one of the most powerful forces in India. He resigned office in 1784 and was impeached before the House of Commons in 1788 for corruption.

Haughey, Charles [James] (1925–) Irish Fianna Fáil politician. He was prime minister of the Republic of Ireland (1979–81, 1982, 1988–92) but was forced to resign after several scandals.

Havel, Vàclav (1936–) Czech dramatist and statesman. His plays satirized the brutality and corruption of Czech communism and he was imprisoned for several years after the Soviet invasion of 1968. He was elected his country's president in 1989 but resigned in 1992.

Hawke, Robert [James Lee] (1929–) Australian trades unionist and Labor statesman. He was prime minister (1983-92).

Hawking, Stephen William (1942–) English physicist. Widely regarded as perhaps the greatest physicist since EINSTEIN, his research into the theory of black holes has been highly acclaimed. He has suffered from a rare crippling nervous disease since the early 1960s and is confined to a wheelchair.

Hawks, Howard (1896–1977) American film director and producer. His films include several classics starring BOGART and Bacall, e.g. *The Big Sleep*, John WAYNE, and Marilyn MONROE.

Hawthorne, Nathaniel (1804–64) American novelist and short-story writer. New England Puritanism profoundly shaped his life and work, as in his masterpiece, *The Scarlet Letter*.

Haydn, [Franz] Joseph (1732–1809) Austrian composer. An innovative composer, he established the form of both the symphony and the string quartet. His huge oeuvre includes over 100 symphonies, 84 string quartets and the oratorio *The Creation*.

Hayek, Friedrich August von (1899–1992) Austrian-born British economist. A supporter of free-market policies and against government economic management, he shared the 1974 Nobel prize for economics with MYRDAL.

Hazlitt, William (1778–1830) English essayist and critic. Highly influential in his own day, he remains one of the most important literary critics, especially for his essays on his contemporaries.

Healey, Denis [Winston] (1917–) English Labour politician.

Chancellor of the exchequer (1974–79) and deputy leader of his party (1980–83), he is widely regarded as one of the most impressive modern British politicians.

Heaney, Seamus [Justin] (1939–) Irish poet and critic who is regarded by many critics as the finest Irish poet since YEATS.

Hearst, William Randolph (1863–1951) American newspaper publisher and politician. In the late 1920s he owned more than 25 daily newspapers and built a spectacular castle at San Simeon in California. He was congressman for New York (1903–7). WELLES' film, *Citizen Kane*, is a thinly disguised account of his life.

Heath, Edward [Richard George] (1916–) British Conservative statesman and prime minister (1970–74). A fervent pro-European, he negotiated Britain's entry into the Common Market in 1973. He has also been active and influential in world politics.

Hegel, Georg Wilhelm Friedrich (1770–1831) German philosopher. His highly influential works, which describe how the Absolute is being reached by man's evolving powers of consciousness, influenced Karl MARX.

Heidegger, Martin (1889–1976) German philosopher. He is usually described as an existentialist, despite his disclaimer of the label, and his concepts, such as 'angst', had a great deal of influence on existentialists such as SARTRE.

Heifetz, Jascha (1901–87) Lithuanian-born American violinist. His flamboyant and expressive interpretation of music from BACH to WALTON has been widely acclaimed.

Heine, Heinrich (1797–1856) German poet and critic. His masterpiece is his *Book of Songs* (1827), which includes some of the finest lyric poems ever written.

Heisenberg, Werner Karl (1901–76) German theoretical physicist. He was awarded the 1932 Nobel prize for physics for his work on quantum theory.

Heller, Joseph (1923–) American novelist. His most popular novel, *Catch–22* (1961), is a grim, surrealist satire on military life and logic.

Hemingway, Ernest [Millar] (1899–1961) American novelist and short-story writer, whose laconic narrative style made a big impression on his contemporaries. Major novels include *A Farewell to Arms* and *For Whom the Bell Tolls*. He was awarded the Nobel prize for literature in 1954. He committed suicide.

Hendrix, Jimi [James Marshall Hendrix] (1942–70) American rock guitarist, singer and songwriter. With his trio, the Jimi

Hendrix Experience, he became perhaps the most influential of all rock guitarists. He died of alcohol and drug abuse.

Henson, Jim [James Maury Henson] (1936–90) American puppeteer and film producer who created the engaging cast of 'muppets', including Kermit the Frog and Miss Piggy.

Henry VIII (1491–1547) king of England (1509–47). He acquired a European-wide reputation for his learning and patronage of artists and scholars such as HOLBEIN and ERASMUS. He declared his marriage to **Catherine of Aragon** (1485–1536) invalid (their only child became MARY I), thus precipitating the Act of Supremacy and schism from Rome. He subsequently married **Anne Boleyn** (c.1504–1536), the mother of ELIZABETH I, whom he had executed in 1536. Subsequent wives were **Jane Seymour** (c.1509–1537), who died after giving birth to Edward VI; **Anne of Cleves** (1515–57), whom he divorced; **Catherine Howard** (c.1521–42), whom he had beheaded for alleged adultery; and **Catherine Parr** (1512–48), who survived him. Originally violently opposed to LUTHER's Reformation (he was given the title Defender of the Faith by the pope for writing a tract against LUTHER), Henry established England as a Protestant state.

Henze, Hans Werner (1926–) German composer. His works, which often reflect his enthusiasm for left-wing causes, include the opera *Elegy for Young Lovers* with a libretto by AUDEN.

Hepburn, Katharine (1909–93) American film and stage actress, noted for her wit and versatility. She had a long personal and acting relationship with Spencer TRACY.

Hepworth, Dame [Jocelyn] Barbara (1903–75) English sculptor. She became one of Britain's leading abstract sculptors in the 1930s, noted for her strong, often monumental carving.

Herbert, George (1593–1633) English Anglican priest and poet. His poems are among the greatest devotional poems in the language, and are characteristic of metaphysical poetry in their subtle, paradoxical exploration of spiritual themes.

Herrick, Robert (1591–1674) English Anglican priest and poet. Many of the poems, which are often delicately sensual, are surprisingly direct in their sympathy for the traditional (virtually pagan) customs of English country life.

Hertz, Gustav Ludwig *see* FRANCK, JAMES.

Hertzog, James Barry Munnik (1866–1942) South African statesman. He founded the Nationalist Party (1913) and advocated noncooperation with Britain during World War I. He became prime minister (1924–39) and founded the Afrikaner Party in 1941.

Herzog, Werner (1942–) German film director. Bizarre enterprises, e.g. the building of an opera house up the Amazon in *Fitzcarraldo*, are a notable feature of his films.

Heseltine, Michael *see* THATCHER, MARGARET HILDA.

Hess, Dame Myra (1890–1965) English pianist. She was also a much acclaimed concert pianist and an influential teacher.

Hess, [Walter Richard] Rudolf (1894–1987) German Nazi politician. Deputy leader of Nazi party (1934–41). On the eve of Hitler's invasion of Russia, he flew to Scotland, apparently in the hope of negotiating peace terms with Britain. He spent the rest of his life imprisoned.

Hess, Victor Francis (1883–1964) Austrian-born American physicist. He shared the 1936 Nobel prize for physics with the American physicist **Carl David Anderson** (1905–) for his research into cosmic rays.

Hesse, Hermann (1877–1962) German-born Swiss novelist, short-story writer and poet. His fiction reflects his fascination with oriental mysticism, spiritual alienation and worldly detachment. He was awarded the Nobel prize for literature in 1946.

Heston, Charlton [John Charlton Carter] (1923–) American film and stage actor, renowned principally for his physique, noble profile and commanding presence in religious epics.

Heyerdahl, Thor (1914–) Norwegian anthropologist. His practical demonstration of his theory that South Americans emigrated to Polynesia on rafts of balsa wood caught the public imagination and he subsequently launched similar expeditions.

Hillary, Sir Edmund [Percival] (1919–) New Zealand explorer and mountaineer. He and the Tibetan sherpa, **Tenzing Norgay** (1914–86), made the first ascent of Mount Everest in 1953. His other exploits include an overland trek to the South Pole in 1958.

Himmler, Heinrich (1900–45) German Nazi leader. He was chosen by HITLER to head the SS in 1929, and by 1936 was in command of the German police structure. Through his secret police, the Gestapo, he organized repression first in Germany then in occupied Europe, and oversaw the construction of the Nazi concentration and death camp system and the genocide of the Jews.

Hindemith, Paul (1895–1963) German composer and violist. The Nazis banned his works for their 'impropriety', and he settled in the US in 1939. Highly prolific, he wrote operas, symphonies, song cycles, ballet and chamber music.

Hindenburg, Paul von Beneckendorff und von (1847–1934) German field marshal and statesman. He shared command of the German forces in World War I (1916–18), and became president of Germany (1925–34). He defeated HITLER in the presidential election of 1932 but was persuaded to appoint Hitler chancellor in 1933.

Hines, Earl [Kenneth] 'Fatha' (1903–83) American jazz pianist, bandleader and songwriter. He became one of the most influential jazz pianists of the 1930s and 1940s.

Hirohito (1901–89) Japanese emperor (1926–89). He ruled Japan as a divinity until her defeat in 1945, after which he became a constitutional monarch, known primarily for his marine biology research. He was succeeded by his son **Akihito** (1933–).

Hiss, Alger (1904–) American state department official. A highly respected public servant, he was jailed (1950–54) for spying for the USSR.

Hitchcock, Sir Alfred (1899–1980) English film director, based in Hollywood from 1940, whose suspenseful thrillers, e.g. *The Thirty-Nine Steps*, have long been regarded as masterpieces.

Hitler, Adolf (1889–1945) Austrian-born German dictator. He co-founded the National Socialist Workers' Party in 1919, and was jailed for nine months following his part in the failed Munich coup of 1923, during which time he wrote *Mein Kampf* ('my struggle'), an anti-semitic 'testament' of his belief in the superiority of the Aryan race. He was appointed chancellor by HINDENBURG in 1933 and consolidated his brutal regime through HIMMLER'S Gestapo. He allied himself temporarily with STALIN in 1939, in which year he invaded Poland, beginning World War II. He invaded Russia in 1941 and killed himself in Berlin in 1945. Hitler's war resulted in *c*.40 million dead.

Ho Chi Minh [Nguyen That Tan] (1890–1969) Vietnamese statesman. A Marxist nationalist, he led the Viet Minh forces, with US help, against the occupying Japanese during World War II and became president of Vietnam (1945–54), during which time he led his forces to victory against French colonial rule. He became president of North Vietnam (1954–69) after the country's partition at the 1954 Geneva conference.

Hockney, David (1937–) English painter and etcher. Associated with the Pop Art movement in his early work, he is now regarded as one of the world's leading representational painters.

Hodgkin, Sir Alan Lloyd (1914–) English physiologist. With

Sir Andrew Fielding Huxley (1917–) and Sir John Carew Ec-
cles, he shared the 1963 Nobel prize for physiology or medicine
for research into nerve impulses.

Hodgkin, Dorothy [Dorothy Mary Crowfoot] (1910–) English
chemist. She was awarded the 1964 Nobel prize for chemistry for
her work on the molecular structures of penicillin, insulin and vitamin B12.

Hofstadter, Robert *see* Mossbauer, Rudolf Ludwig.

Hogarth, William (1697–1764) English artist. Trained as an engraver in the rococo tradition, by 1720 he had established his own
illustration business. He then began his series of 'conversation
pieces' and was executing some fine portraits. He also produced
a remarkable series of paintings following a sequential narrative,
the best known of which is *Marriage à la Mode*. He wrote a treatise on aesthetic principles entitled *The Analysis of Beauty*.

Holbein, Hans (the Younger) (*c*.1479–1543) German painter.
He painted mainly portraits and religious paintings, the most
memorable of the latter being the *The Death of Christ* (1521). He
became court painter to Henry VIII.

Holiday, Billie 'Lady Day' [Eleanora] (1915–59) American
jazz singer. She became one of the most influential jazz singers
of her time, with her sad, elegiac and subtle interpretations of
popular songs.

Holly, Buddy [Charles Hardin Holley] (1936–59) American
rock singer, songwriter and guitarist. He was one of the first rock
singers to use the back-up of lead, rhythm and bass guitars, with
drums. He died in a plane crash.

Holst, Gustav [Theodore] (1874–1934) English composer of
Swedish descent. His best-known composition is *The Planets*
(1917). Much of his music was inspired by the English landscape
and by Thomas Hardy.

Homer (*c*.800 BC) Greek poet, author of the two great epic poems
The Iliad, the story of the Greek war against Troy, and *The Odyssey,* which describes the adventures of the Greek hero Odysseus
(known to the Romans as Ulysses) on his voyage home from the
war. The characters and events of the poems have had a profound
influence upon western literature.

Honecker, Erich (1912–) East German Communist politician.
Appointed head of state in 1976, he fell from power in 1989 following the wide social unrest that followed Gorbachev's statement that the USSR would no longer intervene in East German

affairs. He was charged in 1990 with treason and corruption following the re-unification of Germany.

Honegger, Arthur (1892–1955) French composer. One of the group of Parisian composers dubbed 'Les Six' his works include ballet music, symphonies, film scorces and *Pacific 231*, a musical portrait of a train.

Hoover, Herbert [Clark] (1874–1964) American Republican statesman and 31st president of the US (1929–33). He succeeded COOLIDGE as president in 1929, and was widely perceived as failing to cope with the crisis of the Great Depression.

Hoover, J[ohn] Edgar (1895–1972) American public servant and founder of the Federal Bureau of Investigation (1924–1972). He made the FBI into a highly effective federal crime-fighting force in the 1930s, but also used his organization's considerable powers against anyone perceived as 'radical' in politics.

Hope, Bob [Leslie Townes Hope] (1903–) English-born American comedian and film actor, known for his snappy wisecracks.

Hopkins, Sir Frederick Gowland (1861–1947) English biochemist. He shared the 1929 Nobel prize for physiology or medicine with EIJKMAN for his discovery of 'accessory food factors', which came to be called vitamins.

Hopkins, Gerard Manley (1844–89) English Jesuit priest and poet. A convert, he frequently expressed in his poems the keen conflict he felt between his desire to serve God as both priest and poet. None of his work was published in his lifetime.

Hopper, Edward (1882–1967) American artist. Regarded as the foremost realist American painter, his paintings have a still, introspective and often mysterious quality.

Horace [Quintus Horatius Flaccus] (65–8 BC) Roman poet and satirist. He looked to the literature of Greece for inspiration, but his sardonic, realistic and tightly controlled language is wholly Roman. His *Odes*, *Satires* and *Epistles* have been much imitated.

Housman, A[lfred] E[dward] (1859–1936) English poet and scholar. A distinguished classical scholar, his few works of poetry were published posthumously, e.g. *A Shropshire Lad*.

Howard, Catherine *see* HENRY VIII.

Howe, Sir Geoffrey *see* MAJOR, JOHN.

Hoyle, Sir Fred (1915–) English astronomer, mathematician, broadcaster and writer. He became the main proponent of the theory of the universe which holds that the universe is basically unchanging (as opposed to the big-bang theory).

Hubble, Edwin Powell (1889–1953) American astronomer. His discovery of galactic 'red shift' and other research established the theory of the expanding universe.

Hughes, Howard [Robard] (1905–76) American industrialist, aviator and film producer. He greatly extended his inherited oil wealth and made several epic flights, including a record round-the-world trip. He became increasingly eccentric and went into seclusion in 1966.

Hughes, Ted [Edward James Hughes] (1930–) English poet, noted for his violent poetic imagery drawn from the natural world. He was married (1956–63) to Sylvia PLATH. He was appointed poet laureate in 1984.

Hugo, Victor (1802–85) French novelist, dramatist and poet. His socially challenging dramas established Hugo as the leader of the French literary Romantics. His novels include *The Hunchback of Notre Dame* and *Les Misérables*.

Hume, David (1711–76) Scottish philosopher, economist and historian. An empiricist and sceptic, Hume disallowed human speculation much beyond what could be perceived by the senses. His works include *A Treatise of Human Nature*. He has been claimed by some modern economics to have been a pro-monetarist for his discussion of the 'hidden hand' guiding market forces.

Hunt, Leigh *see* KEATS, JOHN.

Hunt, William Holman (1827–1910) English painter. A founder of the Pre-Raphaelite movement, he sought inspiration in direct study from nature and natural composition.

Hussein, [Ibn Talal] (1935–) king of Jordan. He lost the West Bank of his country to Israel after the Six Day War of 1967, and has trod an uneasy diplomatic line between friendship with the West and his efforts on behalf of the Palestinians.

Hussein, Saddam (1937–) Iraqi dictator. He became president of Iraq in 1979, and established a reputation for ruthlessness in the suppression of his opponents. After his invasion of Kuwait in 1990, UN forces forced his withdrawal in the Gulf War of 1991.

Huston, John [Marcellus] (1906–87) American film director. His films include several classics, e.g. *The Maltese Falcon*, from a story by HAMMET. His last film, *The Dead*, from a short story by JOYCE, starred his daughter, the actress **Anjelica Huston** (1951–).

Hutton, Sir Leonard ('Len') (1916–90) English cricketer. A Yorkshire player throughout his long career, he became the first professional player to captain England regularly (1952–54).

Huxley, Sir Andrew Fielding *see* HODGKIN, SIR ALAN LLOYD

Huxley, Sir Julian [Sorell] (1887–1975) English biologist. He became one of Britain's best-known scientists and humanists and was the first director-general of UNESCO (1946–48). His brother, **Aldous [Leonard] Huxley** (1894–1963) was a novelist, short-story writer and essayist. His early work depicted the brittle word of 1920s English intellectual life, but his masterpiece is *Brave New World*, a chilling fable of a future totalitarian state.

Huxley, Thomas Henry (1825–95) English biologist. He became the most prominent scientific defender of DARWIN's theory of evolution. He gradually lost his belief in a deity and coined the term 'agnostic'.

Ibn Saud, Abdul Aziz (1880–1953) king of Saudi Arabia. He became the first king of Saudi Arabia (1932–53), and negotiated terms with American oil companies after the discovery of oil in his country (1938).

Ibsen, Henrik (1828–1906) Norwegian dramatist. His early verse dramas (e.g. *Peer Gynt*), plays of social realism (e.g. *Ghosts*), and later symbolic plays were all hugely influential on later dramatists, e.g. SHAW.

Ignatius Loyola, St (1491–1556) Spanish saint. A former solder who was severely wounded in action, he had a spiritual conversion and founded the Society of Jesus (the Jesuits) in 1534.

Ingres, Jean Auguste Dominique (1780–1867) French painter. One of the greatest exponents of neoclassical art, his excellent draughtsmanship influenced DEGAS, MATISSE and PICASSO.

Ionesco, Eugène (1912–) Romanian-born French dramatist. His plays, regarded as masterpieces of the Theatre of the Absurd, include *The Bald Prima Donna* and *The Lesson*.

Irving, Washington (1783–1859) American essayist and historian. His best-known stories are 'Rip Van Winkle' and 'The Legend of Sleepy Hollow'. He wrote a biography of WASHINGTON.

Isherwood, Christopher [William Bradshaw] (1904–86) English-born American novelist and dramatist. His best-known works are set in pre-World War II Berlin.

Ives, Charles Edward (1874–1954) American composer. His works are frequently experimental but based firmly within the American tradition.

Jackson, Glenda (1936–) English actress. Highly regarded on film and stage, she became a Labour MP in 1992.

Jackson, Jesse (1941–) American Democrat politician. A

Baptist minister and one of Martin Luther KING's aides, he campaigned twice for the Democratic presidential nomination.

Jackson, Michael [Joe] (1958–) American pop singer. The youngest of five brothers who as children formed the Jackson 5, he became a solo performer in the late 1970s.

Jagger, Mick [Michael Philip Jagger] (1943–) English singer and songwriter, and lead singer with the Rolling Stones rock group, the original members of which, with Jagger, were the guitarist and co-writer with Jagger of many of their songs, **Keith Richard** (1943–), bass guitarist **Bill Wyman** (1936–), drummer **Charlie Watts** (1941–) and guitarist **Brian Jones** (1944–69).

James, Henry (1843–1916) American-born British novelist, short-story writer and critic. Much of his work is concerned with the contrast between American innocence and the older, wiser European culture, e.g. *Daisy Miller.*

James, M[ontague] R[hodes] (1862–1936) English scholar and ghost-story writer. His stories are a mix of dry, scholarly wit with a horrifically reticent undertone of supernatural terror.

James, Dame P. D. [Phyllis Dorothy White] (1920–) English novelist. Her crime novels have been much admired for their wit.

James, William (1842–1910) American philosopher and psychologist. His works include *The Varieties of Religious Experience*, in which he coined the term 'stream of consciousness'.

Janácek, Leos (1854–1928) Czech composer. His works, heavily influenced by Czech folk music and culture, include the operas *The Cunning Little Vixen* and *The House of the Dead*, and two highly regarded string quartets.

Jefferson, Thomas (1743–1826) American statesman. He was the main creator of the Declaration of Independence in 1776 and became secretary of state (1790–93) under WASHINGTON. He was elected the 3rd president of the United States (1801–9).

Jenkins, Roy [Baron Jenkins of Hillhead] (1920–) Welsh Labour and Social Democrat politician. He resigned from the Labour Party in 1981 to co-found the Social Democratic Party. He was SDP MP for Glasgow Hillhead (1982–87).

Jenner, Edward (1749–1823) English physician. He investigated the traditional belief that catching cowpox gave protection against smallpox and discovered that vaccination was efficacious in preventing smallpox.

Jesus Christ (c.6 BC–c.30 AD) founder of Christianity. *The New Testament* records that he was born in Bethlehem, the son of

Joseph and Mary, and Christians have traditionally believed that he is the Son of God. The Book of Acts describes how the Christian gospel was spread through the Mediterranean world by his disciples, notably **Paul** and **Peter**, the latter being recognized as the founder of the Roman Catholic church.

Jiang Jie Shi *see* CHIANG KAI-SHEK.

Jiang Qing *see* CHIANG CH'ING.

Jinnah, Mohammed Ali (1876–1948) Pakistani statesman. An early member of the Indian Muslim League, he became convinced of the need for Indian partition into Hindu and Muslim states and was the first governor-general of Pakistan (1947–48).

Joan of Arc (*c*.1412–31) French patriot. From a peasant family, she had a vision when she was 13, urging her to free France from the invading English. She helped raise the siege of Orléans in 1429, and brought Charles VII to Rheims to be crowned king of France. Captured by the English in 1430, she was condemned for witchcraft and burned at the stake. She was canonized in 1920.

John, Augustus [Edwin] (1878–1961) Welsh painter who was a superb draughtsman and portraitist. His sister, **Gwen John** (1876–1939), was also a painter.

John Paul II [Karel Jozef Wojtyla] (1920–) Polish pope (1978–) The first Polish pope and first non–Italian pope for 450 years. His primacy has been notable for his conservatism in matters such as abortion and the celibacy of the priesthood.

Johns, Jasper (1930–) American painter, sculptor and printmaker. His work, especially his use of everyday images such as the stars and stripes, was very influential on later Pop Artists.

Johnson, Amy (1903–41) English aviator. She was the first woman to fly solo from England to Australia (1930). Her other records include a solo flight from London to Cape Town (1936). She was presumed drowned, after baling out over the Thames Estuary while serving as a transport pilot in World War II.

Johnson, Lyndon B[aines] (1908–73) American Democrat statesman. Following John F. KENNEDY's assassination in 1963, he became the 36th president of the US (1963–69). With Civil Rights agitation and the increasing unpopularity of the Vietnam War his time in office was a troubled one.

Johnson, Dr Samuel (1709–84) English critic, lexicographer and poet. One of the greatest literary figures of the 18th century who wrote on many subjects and was considered the moralist of the age. His works include the *Dictionary of the English Lan-*

guage (1755), an important edition of SHAKESPEARE, several essays and one novel. In 1763 he met **James Boswell** (1740–95) with whom he toured the Western Isles. Boswell's biography of Johnson is considered to be the finest in the language.

Jones, Brian *see* JAGGER, MICK.

Jonson, Benjamin (1572–1637) English dramatist. After a turbulent early life, during which he served as a soldier and killed a fellow soldier in a duel, he began writing comedies which are particularly noted for their satirical dialogue and use of the 'Theory of Humours' and which established him as a great dramatist. His plays include *Bartholomew Fair* (1614), *Volpone* (1616) and *The Alchemist* (1616). He became the first poet laureate in 1616.

Joplin, Scott (1868–1917) American pianist and composer. His ragtime compositions, e.g. *Maple Leaf Rag*, were enormously popular in the USA, selling over a million copies of sheet music.

Joyce, James [Augustine Aloysius] (1882–1941) Irish novelist and short-story writer. He left Ireland in 1902, returning briefly twice. His works include athe short-story collection *Dubliners* (1914), and two great novels, *Portrait of the Artist as a Young Man* (1914–15) and *Ulysses* (1922), the latter one of the key novels of the 20th century.

Joyce, William (1906–46) American-born British traitor (of Anglo-Irish descent). Dubbed 'Lord Haw-Haw' by the British public, he broadcast rabid Nazi propaganda to Britain during World War II and was executed for treason in 1946.

Juan Carlos (1938–) king of Spain from 1975. Nominated by FRANCO in 1969 as his successor, Juan Carlos carefully steered his country towards democracy after Franco's death in 1975.

Jung, Carl Gustav (1875–1961) Swiss psychiatrist. He began his career as a follower of Freud, but split with him after challenging his concentration on sex. His theory of the 'collective unconscious', and his use of the term 'archetype' to denote an image or symbol drawn from this store, has been highly influential.

Kafka, Franz (1883–1924) Czech-born German novelist and short-story writer. His novels, *The Trial* and *The Castle*, and several of his short stories, notably 'Metamorphosis', are established classics of 20th-century literature.

Kandinsky, Wassily (1866–1944) Russian-born French painter. He co-founded (with KLEE and MARC) the *Blaue Reiter* group in 1912, and is regarded as the first major abstract artist.

Kant, Immanuel (1724–1804) German philosopher. His works include *The Critique of Pure Reason* (1781), in which he adopts (in response to HUME's empiricism) an idealist position, arguing that our knowledge is limited by our capacity for perception, and *The Critique of Practical Reason* (1788), in which he expounds his theory of ethics based upon 'categorical imperatives'.

Karajan, Herbert von (1908–89) Austrian conductor. His recordings, notably of BEETHOVEN's symphonies, are held by some critics to be definitive.

Kauffmann, Angelica (1741–1807) Swiss painter. Influenced by neoclassicism, she settled in London in 1776 where she was noted for her portraits (of REYNOLDS and GOETHE among others) and history paintings. She was a founder of the Royal Academy.

Kaunda, Kenneth [David] (1924–) Zambian politician. He became president of Zambia when his country became independent in 1964.

Keaton, Buster [Joseph Francis Keaton] (1895–1966) American film comedian and director. Widely regarded as one of the all-time great comedians of the cinema, with his 'deadpan' expression and remarkable acrobatic skill, his silent comedy films include *The Navigator* (1924) and *The General* (1926).

Keats, John (1795–1821) English poet. His first sonnets were published by **Leigh Hunt** (1784–1859) in *The Examiner*, the weekly paper Hunt founded in 1808 with his brother **James Hunt** (1774–1848). Although savagely criticised early in his career, Keats went on to write some of the greatest works of English romantic literature.

Keller, Helen [Adams] (1880–1968) American writer. She became deaf and blind when 19 months old, and was taught to read and write by the partially sighted Anne Sullivan.

Kelly, Gene [Eugene Curran Kelly] (1912–) American dancer, choreographer and film director. Noted for his athleticism and witty dancing style.

Kelly, Grace [Patricia] (1929–82) American film actress. . She married **Prince Rainier III** (1923–) of Monaco in 1956, and gave up her career.

Kennedy, John Fitzgerald (1917–63) American Democratic politician, who became 35th president of the US (1961–63). He was the first Roman Catholic and the youngest man elected to the presidency. His period of office, cut short by his assassination in Dallas, was subsequently seen by many as a period of hope and social reform, with most of his 'New Frontier' legislation being implemented by Lyndon JOHNSON. His brother **Robert ('Bobby') [Francis] Kennedy** (1925–68), who became attorney general (1961–64) and senator for New York (1965–68) and furthered civil rights legislation, was assassinated. Another brother, **Edward [Moore] Kennedy** (1932–), became a senator in 1962, and was widely regarded as a future president until the 'Chappaquidick' incident of 1969, in which a girl passenger in his car was drowned.

Kenyatta, Jomo (c.1893–1978) Kenyan politician. He was jailed for six years (1952–58) for his leadership of the Mau-Mau rebellion. He became prime minister of Kenya on independence in 1963 and president (1964–78).

Kerenski, Alexsandr Feodorovich (1881–1970) Russian revolutionary leader. A member of the Social Democratic Party's liberal wing, he became prime minister of the Russian provisional government of 1917, but was deposed by LENIN's Bolsheviks.

Kern, Jerome [David] (1885–1945) American composer and songwriter. A highly prolific writer of music and songs, he had a huge influence on the American musical tradition.

Kerouac, Jack [Jean-Louis Lebris de Kérouac] (1922–69) American novelist and poet who was a much imitated central figure of the Beat Generation.

Keynes, John Maynard, 1st Baron (1883–1946) English economist. He argued that unemployment was curable through macroeconomic management of monetary and fiscal policies and advocated the creation of employment through government schemes.

Khomeini, Ayatollah [Ruholla] (1900–89) Iranian religious leader who established a theocratic dictatorship that crushed all dissent and declared his intention of 'exporting' the Shiite revolution to other Islamic countries. He aroused Western anger by proclaiming a death sentence against Salman RUSHDIE in 1989.

Khrushchev, Nikita Sergeyevich (1894–1971) Soviet politician. He was first secretary of the Communist Party (1953–64) and prime minister (1958–64). He promoted peaceful co-existence with the West and was deposed in 1964 in the Kremlin coup that brought BREZHNEV to power.

Kierkegaard, Søren Aabye (1813–55) Danish theologian and philosopher. Regarded as the founder of existentialism, he rejected the spiritual authority of organized religion and emphasized the centrality of individual choice.

Kim Il Sung (1912– 94) North Korean marshal and Communist politician. He became prime minister (1948–72) and president

(1972–94) of North Korea, establishing a Stalinist dictatorship based on a personality cult of himself as the 'great leader'. His son and proclaimed successor is **Kim Jong II** (1942–).

King, Billie Jean (1943–) American tennis player. Regarded as one of the finest women players ever, she won twenty Wimbledon titles between between 1965 and 1980.

King, Martin Luther, Jr (1929–68) American civil rights leader and Baptist minister. Influenced by GANDHI's policy of nonviolent resistance, he organized opposition to segregationist policies in the Southern US. He was awarded the 1964 Nobel Peace Prize and was assassinated in 1968.

Kinnock, Neil [Gordon] (1942–) Welsh Labour politician. Elected leader of the Labour Party in 1983 in succession to FOOT, he gradually moderated the Party's policies and had great success in marginalizing the hard left of the party.

Kipling, [Joseph] Rudyard (1865–1936) Indian-born English short-story writer, poet and novelist. Although best known for his stories for children (e.g. *The Jungle Book*), he was also a caustic observer of Anglo-Indian society and critical of many aspects of colonialism in his writing.

Kissinger, Henry [Alfred] (1923–) German-born American statesman. Shared the 1973 Nobel Peace Prize with the North Vietnamese negotiator **Le Duc Tho** (1911–) for the treaty ending US involvement in Vietnam. As secretary of state (1973–76) he fostered détente with the Soviet Union and China, and helped negotiate peace between Israel and Egypt in 1973.

Kitchener of Khartoum, [Horatio] Herbert, 1st Earl (1850–1916) Anglo-Irish field marshal. Commander in chief of the British forces during the Boer War of 1901–2, and of the British forces in India (1902–9), he was appointed secretary for war in 1914 and had mobilized Britain's largest-yet army by the time of his death by drowning when his ship hit a mine.

Klee, Paul (1879–1940) Swiss painter and etcher who developed a style of mainly abstract work characterized by doodle-like drawings. He was a member of the *Blaue Reiter* group.

Klemperer, Otto (1885–1973) German-born conductor. A great interpreter of both classical and contemporary works, he became director of the Los Angeles Symphony Orchestra in 1936 and director of the Budapest Opera (1947–50).

Klimt, Gustav (1862–1918) Austrian painter. An excellent draughtsman, his early works were influenced by Impressionism,

Symbolism and Art Nouveau. He was a founder of the Vienna Sezession and had a great influence on younger artists.

Knox, John (*c*.1513-1572) Scottish Protestant reformer. He was noted for his antagonistic relationship with MARY QUEEN OF SCOTS and for his single-minded determination in the pursuit of religious reformation.

Kodály, Zoltán (1882–1967) Hungarian composer. Like his friend BARTÓK, he was much influenced by the traditional music of his country. His works include the comic opera *Hary Janos*.

Kohl, Helmut (1930–) German Christian Democrat statesman. He became chancellor of West Germany (1982–90) and the first chancellor of reunited Germany in 1990.

Kokoschka, Oskar (1886–1980) Austrian-born painter and dramatist. A leading Expressionist painter, noted particularly for his landscapes and portraits, he fled to Britain in 1938.

Korda, Sir Alexander [Sandor Kellner] (1893–1956) Hungarian-born British film director and producer. His films include *The Private Life of Henry VIII* and *The Third Man*.

Kreisler, Fritz (1875–1962) Austrian-born American violinist and composer. ELGAR's violin concerto was dedicated to him, and he became one of the most popular violinists of his day.

Kubrick, Stanley (1928–) American film director and producer. His films include the anti-war classic *Paths of Glory* (1957), the black nuclear war comedy *Dr Strangelove* (1963), the innovative science fiction classic *2001: A Space Odyssey* (1968), and the still highly controversial *A Clockwork Orange* (1971).

Kundera, Milan (1929–) Czech novelist. His masterpiece is *The Unbearable Lightness of Being*, a love story set against the background of repression following the Russian invasion of Czechoslovakia in 1968.

Kurosawa, Akira (1910–) Japanese film director. His films include the samurai classics *The Seven Samurai* and *Yojimbo* (remade in the west as *The Magnificent Seven* and *A Fistful of Dollars*), and samurai versions of *Macbeth*, titled *Throne of Blood*, and *King Lear*, titled *Ran*. Kurosawa was happiest with the epic form, and also had a 'family' of actors he used regularly.

Kyd, Thomas (1558–94) English dramatist. His most important work is his revenge tragedy, *The Spanish Tragedy*, which served as a model for SHAKESPEARE's *Titus Andronicus*. A close associate of Christopher MARLOWE, he died in poverty after being accused of denying the divinity of Christ.

Laing, R[onald] D[avid] (1927–89) Scottish psychiatrist. He became a counterculture guru in the 1960s for his revolutionary ideas about mental disorders.

Lamarck, Jean [Baptiste Pierre Antoine de Monet, Chevalier de] (1744–1829) French naturalist. His theory of the evolution of species through the acquisition of inherited characteristics prepared the ground for DARWIN's theory of evolution.

Lamb, Charles (1775–1834) English essayist and critic. A friend of HAZLITT, WORDSWORTH and COLERIDGE, his writings display the great charm his friends describe. With his sister, **Mary Anne Lamb** (1764–1847), he adapted several of SHAKESPEARE's plays to prose form. In 1796, in a fit of insanity, Mary killed their mother, and Charles looked after her until his death.

Landseer, Sir Edwin Henry (1802–73) English painter. Highly regarded for his animal studies, his notable works include *The Monarch of the Glen* (1850) and the lions modelled for Trafalgar Square, London, in 1867.

Lansbury, George (1859–1940) English Labour politician. Noted for his support for women's suffrage and pacifism, he became leader of his party (1931–35) when MACDONALD joined the National Government. His daughter, **Angela Lansbury** (1925–) became a popular film actress in the 1940s.

Lardner, Ring [Ringgold Wilmer Lardner] (1885–1933) American journalist and short-story writer, whose stories of American low life are noted for their cynical wit.

Larkin, Philip [Arthur] (1922–85) English poet. Known for his dark, sardonic lyricism, he is regarded as one of the greatest of all modern English poets. He also wrote two novels and a collection of essays on jazz.

Larwood, Harold (1904–) English cricketer. His use of 'bodyline' tactics in the 1932–33 tour of Australia created great controversy, causing diplomatic tension in relations between Australia and the UK.

Lasdun, Sir Denys Louis (1914–) English architect. Influenced by LE CORBUSIER, his buildings include the University of East Anglia and the National Theatre in London.

Lasker, Emanuel (1868–1941) German chess player. His reign as world champion (1894–1921), is still a record.

Laski, Harold [Joseph] (1893–1950) English political scientist and socialist propagandist. He was a highly influential spokesman for Marxism through his position as teacher, writer and Labour Party power-broker (he was party chairman 1945–46), and through his friendships with politicians such as ROOSEVELT.

Lauda, Niki [Nikolas Andreas Lauda] (1949–) Austrian racing driver. World champion in 1975, 1977 and 1984, he suffered dreadful injuries in the 1976 German Grand Prix. He retired in 1985.

Lauder, Sir Harry [Hugh MacLennan] (1870–1950) Scottish music-hall comedian and singer, who made an international career out of his Scottish comedy routines and songs.

Laughton, Charles (1899–1962) English-born American stage and film actor, renowned for his larger-than-life performances in many memorable films, e.g. *The Private Life of Henry VIII*.

Laurel, Stan [Arthur Stanley Jefferson] (1890–1965), English-born American comedian, and **Oliver Hardy** (1892–1957) American comedian. Laurel began his career on the English music-hall stage (understudying CHAPLIN at one point), and Hardy performed with a minstrel troupe before going into films. They formed their Laurel (thin, vacant and bemused one) and Hardy (fat, blustering one) partnership in 1929, and made some very funny films, e.g. *Another Fine Mess* (1930).

Laval, Pierre (1883–1945) French statesman. Prime minister (1931–32, 1935–36, 1942–44), he sided openly during the occupation with the Germans and was executed for treason in 1945 by the victorious Free French.

Lavoisier, Antoine Laurent (1743–94) French chemist. Regarded as the founder of modern chemistry, he discovered oxygen and established its role in combustion and respiration.

Lawrence, D[avid] H[erbert] (1885–1930) English novelist, poet and short-story writer. His novels caused much controversy for their frank treatment of sex. *Lady Chatterley's Lover* (1928), was not published in its full form until 1960.

Lawrence, Gertrude [Gertrud Alexandra Dagmar Lawrence-Klasen] (1898–1952) English actress, noted for her professional relationship with Noel COWARD, many of whose plays had parts written especially for her.

Lawrence, Sir Thomas (1769–1830) English painter. The leading portraitist of his time, he was made court painter in 1792.

Lawrence, T[homas] E[dward] (1888–1935) Welsh-born Anglo-Irish soldier and author, known as 'Lawrence of Arabia'. In World War I, he helped the Arab revolt against the Turks and was instrumental in the conquest of Palestine (1918).

Lawson, Nigel *see* MAJOR, JOHN.

Leach, Bernard Howell (1887–1979) English potter, who revolutionized the production of pottery by creating reasonably priced, attractively designed studio pottery.

Leadbelly [Huddie Ledbetter] (1888–1949) American blues singer. Discovered in a Louisiana prison in 1933, he later recorded several songs that soon became recognized as blues/folk classics, e.g. 'Rock Island Line' and 'Goodnight, Irene'.

Leakey, Louis Seymour Bazett (1903–72) Kenyan-born British archaeologist and anthropologist, and **Mary Douglas Leakey** (1913–) English archaeologist. Married in 1936, the Leakeys made several important discoveries about humanity's origins in East Africa. Their son, **Richard Erskine Frere Leakey** (1944–), is also a prominent (Kenyan) archaeologist.

Lean, Sir David (1908–91) English film director. Highly regarded for his compositional skill and craftsmanship, his films include many classics, e.g. *Brief Encounter* and *Great Expectations*.

Leavis, F[rank] R[aymond] (1895–1978) English literary critic. With his wife, **Queenie Dorothy Leavis** (1906–81), he made a major impact on literary criticism from the 1930s attacking the modern age of mass culture and advertising.

Le Carré, John [David John Moore Cornwell] (1931–) English novelist. His popular novels are sombre anti-romantic narratives of Cold War espionage, e.g. *The Spy Who Came in from the Cold*.

Le Corbusier [Charles Edouard Jeanneret] (1887–1965) Swiss-born French architect and town planner. One of the most influential (and most praised and reviled) architects and planners of the century, his work is characterized by use of reinforced concrete and modular, standardized units of construction (based upon the proportions of the human figure), with the house famously defined as a 'machine for living in'.

Lederberg, Joshua (1925–) American geneticist. He shared the 1958 Nobel prize for physiology or medicine (with George Beadle and Edward TATUM) for his bacterial research.

Le Duc Tho *see* KISSINGER, HENRY.

Lee Kuan Yew (1923–) Singaporean politician. He became Singapore's first prime minister (1959–), establishing a strict regime noted for its economic achievements and authoritarianism.

Léger, Fernand (1881–1955) French painter. A leading Cubist, he was much influenced by industrial imagery and machinery.

Lehár, Franz (1870–1948) Hungarian composer and conductor, noted for his operettas, e.g. *The Merry Widow*.

Leibnitz *or* **Leibniz, Gottfried Wilhelm** (1646–1716) German philosopher and mathematician. Renowned for the range and depth of his intellect, he made important contributions to many different scientific fields.

Leigh, Vivien [Vivien Mary Hartley] (1913–67) Indian-born English stage and film actress. She became an international star with *Gone With the Wind* (1939), in which she co-starred with Clark GABLE.

Lenin, Vladimir Ilyich [Vladimir Ilyich Ulyanov] (1870–1924) Russian revolutionary leader and Marxist philosopher. He was instigator of the Bolshevik October Revolution which overthrew KERENSKI's government and leader of the Bolsheviks in the Civil War (1918–21). The failure of his economic policy after the war led to the institution of the New Economic Policy of 1921, which fostered limited private enterprise. He was a brilliant demagogue and an influential philosopher.

Lennon, John [Winston] (1940–80) English rock guitarist, singer and songwriter. With Paul MCCARTNEY, George HARRISON and Ringo STARR, he formed the Beatles, the most popular rock group ever. The success of the band was based on the songwriting partnership of Lennon/McCartney, whose songs achieved phenomenal popularity. He married **Yoko Ono** (1933–) and pursued a solo career after the Beatles split in 1969. He was assassinated in New York.

Leonardo da Vinci (1452–1519) Florentine painter, draughtsman, engineer, musician and thinker. The outstanding genius of his time, his greatest paintings include *The Last Supper* (1489) and his portrait of *Mona Lisa* (1504). His later years were devoted to scientific studies, and his work in mechanics, aeronautics, physiology and anatomy displays an understanding far beyond his times.

Le Pen, Jean-Marie (1928–) French politician. He founded the right-wing National Front in 1972, a crypto–fascist party with anti-immigrant policies.

Lermontov, Mikhail Yurievich (1814–41) Russian novelist and poet. His masterpiece is the novel *A Hero of our Time* (1840), a brilliant study of a disaffected, Byronic young aristocrat.

Lessing, Doris [May] (1919–) Iranian-born English novelist and short-story writer. Her novels include the 'Children of Violence' quintet series which explores the social and political undercurrents of modern society.

Lewes, George Henry *see* ELIOT, GEORGE.

Lewis, C[live] S[taples] (1898–1963) English novelist and critic. His works include studies of medieval literature (e.g. *The Allegory of Love*, works of Christian apologetics (e.g. *The Problem of Pain*), and science fiction novels (e.g. *Out of the Silent Planet*). He is best remembered for his enchanting Narnia stories for children (e.g. *The Lion, the Witch and the Wardrobe*).

Lewis, Jerry Lee (1935-) American rock singer and pianist noted for his flamboyant playing style and primitive rock 'n' roll lyrics.

Lewis, [Harry] Sinclair (1885–1951) American novelist. His work is particularly noted for its satirical view of small-town American life. He was the first American to win the Nobel prize for literature, in 1930.

Lewis, [Percy] Wyndham (1884–1957) English painter, novelist and critic. An influential writer with unfashionable right-wing views, he was also a leading member of the Vorticist group of artists. His best-known fictional work is the novel *The Apes of God*.

Lichtenstein, Roy (1923-) American painter and sculptor. He became the leading Pop Art painter of the 1960s with his highly coloured reproductions of sections of advertisements and cartoon strips.

Liddell, Eric Henry (1902–45) Scottish athlete, nicknamed the 'Flying Scot', who refused to compromise his sabbatarian principles by running on a Sunday during the 1924 Olympics (the subject of the award-winning film *Chariots of Fire*). He became a missionary and died in a Japanese prisoner-of-war camp.

Liddell Hart, Sir Basil Henry (1895–1970) English soldier and military historian, noted for his persistent advocacy of mechanized warfare and the development of air power after World War I.

Liebknecht, Karl *see* LUXEMBOURG, ROSA.

Ligeti, György Sándor (1923-) Hungarian composer. He fled to Vienna in 1956, where he soon became established as one of Europe's leading avant-garde composers.

Limbourg *or* **Limburg, Jean, Paul** and **Herman de** (all *fl.* 1400–16) Dutch illuminators. Their masterpiece, the unfinished *Les Tres Riches Heures*, is one of the greatest illuminated manuscripts of all time.

Lincoln, Abraham (1809–65) American statesman. From a poor background, he trained as a lawyer and became an Illinois congressman in 1846. He became the 16th president of the United

States in 1861 and led the Union to victory in 1865. Firmly opposed to slavery, he finally declared emancipation 1863. He was assassinated while attending the theatre.

Lindbergh, Charles Augustus (1902–74) American aviator. He became the first man to fly the Atlantic solo and nonstop with his 1927 flight in the monoplane *Spirit of St Louis*. The kidnap and murder of his infant son in 1932 made world headlines.

Lippi, Fra Filippo (*c*.1406–69) Florentine painter. He took up painting while a monk and later forsook his vows to marry the mother of his son, **Filippino Lippi** (1457–1504), who also became a painter. His lyrical and fluid style invest his paintings with a wistful melancholy. An innovative painter, he was one of the first artists to explore and develop the *Madonna and Child* theme.

Liszt, Franz *or* **Ferencz** (1811–86) Hungarian pianist and composer. Recognized as one of the greatest pianists of his day, he made several important contributions to musical form and was influential in his experimentation.

Littlewood, Joan (1914–) English theatre director. Her theatre company, Theatre Workshop, formed in 1945, became one of the major left-wing companies.

Livingstone, David (1813–73) Scottish missionary and explorer. His discoveries during his African expeditions include Lake Ngami (1849) and the Victoria Falls (1855). He was also a vigorous campaigner against the slave trade. His last expedition was a search for the source of the Nile, in the course of which he himself was 'discovered' by the Welsh-American adventurer **Henry Morton Stanley** (1841–1904).

Lloyd, Clive Hubert (1944–) Guyanian-born West Indian cricketer. A very fine batsman and fielder, he captained the West Indies team (1974–78, 1979–85).

Lloyd, Harold [Clayton] (1893–1971) American film comedian. He made hundreds of short silent films and is noted for his dangerous stunts.

Lloyd George, David, 1st Earl Lloyd George of Dwyfor (1863–1945) Welsh Liberal statesman. As chancellor of the exchequer (1908–15), he introduced far-reaching reforms in British society, notably the introduction of old-age pensions (1908) and the National Insurance Act (1911). Formerly a pacifist, he became minister of munitions (1915–16) and prime minister (1916–22) of coalition governments.

Lloyd Webber, Andrew (1948–) English composer. With the librettist **Tim Rice** (1944–), he composed several highly successful musicals, notably *Joseph and the Amazing Technicolour Dreamcoat*, *Jesus Christ Superstar* and *Evita*. Other successes were *Cats*, adapted from T. S. ELIOT's *Old Possum's Book of Practical Cats*, *Starlight Express* and *Phantom of the Opera*.

Locke, John (1632–1704) English philosopher. His influential theory of the political nature of man saw the social contract as resting on a 'natural law', which, if ignored by rulers, allowed them to be overthrown.

Lodge, David (1935–) English novelist and critic. His best-known novels are entertaining satires on academic life, e.g. *Small World*, and his novel *Nice Work* is a hybrid of the campus novel with the 19th-century 'condition of England' tradition.

Longfellow, Henry Wadsworth (1807–82) American poet. His narrative poems based on American legends and folk tales were among the most popular of the 19th century, e.g. *The Song of Hiawatha*, the hypnotic unrhymed rhythms of which were much parodied by later writers, e.g. CARROLL.

Lonsdale, Dame Kathleen (1903–71) Irish physicist, noted for innovative work in X-ray crystallography. She was the first woman to be elected a fellow of the Royal Society (1945).

Lorca, Federigo García (1899–1936) Spanish poet and dramatist. His dramatic masterpiece is his trilogy of tragedies on the plight of oppressed Spanish women, *Blood Wedding*, *Yarma* and *The House of Bernarda Alba*. He was killed by Fascist forces near the beginning of the Spanish Civil War.

Lorenz, Konrad [Zacharias] (1903–89) Austrian ethologist and zoologist. He shared the 1973 Nobel prize for physiology or medicine (with Niko TINBERGEN and Karl VON FRISCH) for his work on animal behaviour.

Lorre, Peter [Laszlo Lowenstein] (1904–64) Hungarian stage and film actor. His first major film part, as the pathetic child murderer, in LANG's *M* (1931) established him as a star. Other films include *Casablanca* and *The Maltese Falcon*.

Losey, Joseph (1909–84) American film director. Blacklisted during the MCCARTHY era, he came to work in England and had a great influence on the British film industry with films such as *The Servant*, *Accident* and *The Go-Between*.

Louis, Joe [Joseph Louis Barrow] (1914–81) American boxer, nicknamed the 'Brown Bomber'. He was world heavyweight champion for a record 12 years.

Lowei, Otto *see* DALE, SIR HENRY HALLETT.

Lowell, James Russell (1819–91) American poet, essayist and diplomat. His best-known verse was written in 'Yankee' dialect and inspired by his fervent abolitionism.

Lowell, Robert [Traill Spence] (1917–77) American poet. His verse is intensely personal and marked by private symbolism.

Lowry, L[aurence] S[tephen] (1887–1976) English painter. His paintings, which depict thin, dark 'matchstick' figures against a background of Northern Industrial life, became very popular in the mid–1960s.

Lowry, [Clarence] Malcolm (1909–57) English novelist and poet. His novels, e.g. *Under the Volcano*, often feature thinly veiled accounts of incidents from his own adventurous life.

Loyola, St Ignatius *see* IGNATIUS LOYOLA, ST.

Lully, Jean-Baptiste [Giambattista Lulli] (1632–87) French composer of Italian origin. He worked in the French court, where he composed many operas and comedy ballets. He died from an abscess after striking his foot with his conductor's baton.

Lumière, Auguste Marie Louis Nicolas (1862–1954) and **Louis Jean Lumière** (1864–1948) French chemists and cinematographers. They invented the first operational cine camera and projector and a colour photography process.

Luther, Martin (1483–1546) German religious reformer. An Augustinian monk, who suffered a crisis of faith that led to his proclaiming a break with Rome following the nailing of his '95 theses' on the church door of Wittenberg. The Lutheran Reformation spread rapidly throughout Germany. CALVIN, ZWINGLI and others subsequently preached their variants of the new religion.

Luthuli *or* **Lutuli, Chief Albert John** (1898–1967) South African nationalist. He became president of the African National Congress (1952–60), and was awarded the 1961 Nobel Peace Prize for his advocacy of nonviolent resistance to apartheid.

Lutoslawski, Witold (1913–) Polish composer and teacher. He has written extensively, including chamber, piano and vocal music, but is best known for his orchestral works, e.g. *Concerto for Orchestra*.

Luxemburg, Rosa (1871–1919) Polish-born German revolutionary and socialist theorist. With **Karl Liebknecht** (1871–1919) she founded the revolutionary Spartacus League in Berlin on the outbreak of World War I and later the German Communist Party. She and Liebknecht were killed after the failed revolt of 1919.

MacArthur, Douglas (1880–1964) American general. He was commander of the US Far East forces in 1941. When the Japanese forced him to withdraw from the Philippines in 1942, he pledged 'I shall return'. He was appointed supreme Allied commander in the southwest Pacific in 1942 and gradually rolled back the Japanese forces, accepting their surrender in 1945. He also commanded the UN forces at the beginning of the Korean War (1950–51), being dismissed his command by TRUMAN.

McCarthy, Joseph R[aymond] (1908–57) American politician He became a Republican senator in 1946 and embarked upon a crusade against supposed communist sympathizers in public life (1950–54). His wide and increasingly bizarre accusations against innocent people came to an end shortly after he was accused, during a televised hearing, of having no shame.

McCartney, Paul (1942–) English rock guitarist, singer and songwriter. He was a member of the Beatles (1961–70) with John LENNON, George HARRISON and Ringo STARR. With Lennon, he formed one of the most successful songwriting partnerships of the century. After the band's break-up, he formed the group Wings.

McCullers, Carson [Smith] (1917–67) American novelist and short-story writer. Her works, many of them filmed, usually centre on loners and misfits and include *The Heart is a Lonely Hunter* and *The Ballad of the Sad Café*.

MacDiarmid, Hugh [Christopher Murray Grieve] (1892–1978) Scottish poet and critic. Noted for his Communist and Nationalist sympathies, he influenced many Scottish writers, particularly with his masterpiece, *A Drunk Man Looks at the Thistle*.

MacDonald, [James] Ramsay (1866–1937) Scottish statesman. He became the first British Labour prime minister (1924, 1929–31) and was prime minister of the (mostly Conservative) coalition government of 1931–35.

MacGonagall, William (*c.*1830–*c.*1902) Scottish poet, renowned for his memorably awful doggerel verse.

Machiavelli, Niccolo (1469–1527) Italian statesman and political theorist. His treatise on the art of ruling, *The Prince* (1513), takes a dim view of human nature, seeing humanity as essentially corrupt and therefore best ruled by whatever method ensures the stability of the state, even if the method entails merciless cruelty.

McIndoe, Sir Archibald [Hector] (1900–1960) New Zealand plastic surgeon. One of the world's leading plastic surgeons, he pioneered facial surgery on burns victims.

Mackenzie, Sir [Edward Montague] Compton (1883–1972) English novelist, best known for his series of very popular comic novels set in the Scottish Western Isles, e.g. *Whisky Galore*.

Maclean, Donald *see* BURGESS, GUY.

McLuhan, [Herbert] Marshall (1911–80) Canadian critic and educator. His studies of mass culture and communication include the influential *The Medium is the Message*.

Macmillan, Sir [Maurice] Harold, 1st Earl of Stockton (1894–1986) English Conservative statesman and prime minister (1957–63) in succession to EDEN. Christened 'Supermac' by the cartoonist VICKY, he won the General Election of 1959 on the slogan 'You've never had it so good' and gained much international respect for his 'wind of change' speech in South Africa in 1958. His later years as premier were darkened by the PROFUMO scandal, and his manoeuvres against Rab BUTLER cost the latter the Tory leadership, which went to DOUGLAS-HOME. At the end of his life, he made a notably cutting speech in the House of Lords against THATCHER's privatization policies, 'selling the family silver'.

MacMillan, Sir Kenneth (1929–92) Scottish choreographer. He became the Royal Ballet's principal choreographer in 1977. He was also director of the Royal Ballet (1970–77).

MacNeice, [Frederick] Louis (1907–63) Irish poet and scholar. He was one of the leading AUDEN generation of poets, and his collections include *Letters from Iceland* (1937, written with Auden).

Maeterlinck, [Count] Maurice (1862–1949) Belgian poet, writer and playwright. Trained as a lawyer, he turned to writing poetry under the influence of the Symbolist poets. His masterpiece is *Pelléas et Mélisande* (1892), the basis for the opera by DEBUSSY. He was awarded the Nobel prize for literature in 1911.

Magritte, René (1898–1967) Belgian painter. He became a major Surrealist painter in Paris in the 1930s, devising a style dubbed 'magic realism' for its incongruous, dreamlike juxtaposition of carefully detailed everyday objects in dreamlike situations, e.g. men in bowler hats raining from the sky.

Mahler, Gustav (1860–1911) Austrian composer and conductor. Of Jewish birth, he became a Roman Catholic but remained subject to anti-semitic gibes while conductor of the Vienna State Opera (1897–1907). Regarded as both the last of the great Romantic composers of the 19th century and the first great composer of the modern era, his works include nine symphonies, song cycles, and the great symphonic song cycle, *The Song of the Earth* (1908).

Major, John (1943–) English Conservative politician. He became an MP in 1979 and was appointed a junior minister by THATCHER in 1981. His rise in the late 1980s was spectacular: he replaced **Sir Geoffrey Howe** (1926–) as foreign secretary in 1989, and later that year replaced **Nigel Lawson** (1932–) as chancellor. After Thatcher's resignation in late 1990, he was selected as Tory leader and prime minister.

Makarios III [Mikhail Khristodoulou Mouskos] (1913–77) Cypriot archbishop and statesman. Archbishop of the Orthodox Church in Cyprus, he became first president of Cyprus (1959–77) after independence.

Malan, Daniel F[rançois] (1874–1959) South African politician. A fervent believer in a racially divided society, he was prime minister (1948–54) and was responsible for the apartheid legislation.

Malcolm X [Malcolm Little] (1925–65) American black nationalist leader. A convert to Islam, he became an advocate of violence in response to racism only if used in self-defence.

Mallarmé, Stéphane (1842–98) French Symbolist poet. His impressionistic free-verse works and literary theorizing had a strong influence on the development of the Symbolist movement.

Malory, Sir Thomas (*fl.*15th century) translator, largely from French sources, of a collection of Arthurian legends. The work includes several episodes, e.g. the quest for the Holy Grail, that have been recycled by generations of writers.

Mandela, Nelson [Rolihlahla] (1918–) South African lawyer and nationalist leader. Leader of the banned African National Congress, he was imprisoned in 1964 for life by the South African government. Upon his release in 1990, he helped to dismantle apartheid and was elected president in the first free elections in 1994. He seperated from his second wife, **Winnie Mandela** (1934–) in 1992.

Mandelstam, Osip (1891–1938) Russian poet. Denounced for reading a satirical poem about STALIN, he and his wife, **Nadezhda Mandelstam** (1899–1980), were sent into exile in Siberia, where he died. Nadezhda later wrote accounts of their life together.

Manet, Edouard (1832–83) French painter. His direct approach and fresh, painterly style was influenced by the Impressionists, although he never exhibited with them.

Manley, Michael [Norman] (1923–) Jamaican statesman. He became leader of the socialist People's National Party in 1969, and prime minister (1972–80). He lost two subsequent elections, but won the 1989 election with a much less radical policy programme. He is regarded as a spokesman for the Third World.

Mann, Thomas (1875–1955) German novelist and critic, primarily concerned with the role of the artist and the purpose of artistic creation in modern society. His works include *Death in Venice* (1912), *The Magic Mountain* (1930), and *The Confessions of the Confidence Trickster Felix Krull* (1954), a comedy. He was awarded the Nobel prize for literature in 1929 and fled Nazi Germany in 1933.

Mao Tse-tung *or* **Mao Ze Dong** (1893–1976) Chinese Communist statesman and Marxist philosopher. He was a founder of the Chinese Communist Party (1922). Following the Japanese occupation (1937–45), during which Nationalists and Communists collaborated against the Japanese, the Communists won the resumed civil war and Mao established his People's Republic (1949). His dictatorship became murderous as he sought to break traditional patterns of Chinese family life and launched his 'Cultural Revolution' (1966–69).

Marat, Jean Paul (1743–93) French revolutionary and journalist. A prominent supporter of DANTON and ROBESPIERRE, he made repeated calls for increased executions during the establishment of the Revolution and was stabbed to death in his bath by the Girondist aristocrat **Charlotte Corday** (1768–93).

Marc, Franz (1880–1916) German painter. With KANDINSKY, he founded the *Blaue Reiter* group of expressionist artists.

Marceau, Marcel (1923–) French mime artist. Regarded as the world's leading mime artist.

Marciano, Rocky [Rocco Francis Marchegiano] (1923–69) American boxer. He became world heavyweight champion (1952–56), and never lost a professional fight.

Marconi, Guglielmo, Marchese (1874–1937) Italian physicist and electrical engineer. He shared the 1909 Nobel prize for physics for his development of wireless telegraphy and later developed short-wave radio transmissions.

Marcos, Ferdinand [Edralin] (1917–89) Filipino politician. He was president of the Philippines (1965–86). An autocratic ruler, he declared martial law in 1972, after which he ruled by oppressive and idiosyncratic decree. He was deposed in 1986 after the popular unrest that brought AQUINO to power, and lived in exile in Hawaii with his wife, **Imelda**.

Markiewicz, [Constance Georgine] Countess (1868–1927)

Irish nationalist. A member of Sinn Fein involved in the Easter Rising of 1916, she became the first woman to be elected to the British Parliament in 1918, but refused to take her seat.

Markova, Dame Alicia [Lilian Alicia Marks] (1910–) English ballerina. She was a member of DIAGHILEV's Ballet Russe (1924–29) and then of the Vic-Wells Ballet, where she became prima ballerina (1933–35).

Marks, Simon, [1st Baron Marks of Broughton] (1888–1964) English businessman. He inherited the Marks and Spencer chain of shops helped build it into a respected retail empire.

Marley, Bob [Robert Nesta Marley] (1945–81) Jamaican singer and songwriter. With his group, the Wailers, he became the world's leading reggae singer.

Marlowe, Christopher (1564–93) English dramatist and poet. He was one of the first English dramatists to use blank verse to great dramatic and poetic effect in his plays, the most famous of which are *Tamburlaine the Great* and his masterpiece, *Doctor Faustus*. He was probably a secret agent in the employ of the Elizabethan government and was killed in a tavern brawl.

Marshall, Alfred (1842–1924) English economist. His works have been of great influence on modern economics. He devised concepts such as 'elasticity', 'consumer surplus' and 'time analysis'.

Marshall, George C[atlett] (1880–1959) American general and statesman. He was chief of staff of the US army during World War II, and, as US secretary of state, oversaw the Marshall Aid Plan, for which he was awarded the 1953 Nobel Peace Prize.

Marvell, Andrew (1621–78) English poet. A (passive) supporter of Parliament during the English Civil War, he became member of parliament for Hull in 1659, a position he held until his death. His verse satires were much enjoyed by the wits of the day, even by those whose vices were attacked. His strange, metaphysical poems, e.g. 'The Garden' and 'Upon Appleton House', display a talent for symbolism and metaphor. His poem celebrating Oliver CROMWELL's suppression of the Irish rebellion, 'An Horatian Ode upon Cromwell's Return from Nature', is a great political poem, with its cool, restrained appreciation of Cromwell's stature.

Marx, Karl (1818–83) German philosopher. His theories on class struggle dominated 20th-century political thought from the Bolshevik Revolution to the collapse of the communist regimes of eastern Europe in 1989–91. *Das Kapital*, his study of the economics of capitalism, appeared in 1867; subsequent volumes, edited by **Friedrich Engels** (1820–95), appeared in 1885 and 1895. He also wrote *The Communist Manifesto* with Engels in 1848, and was one of the founders of the 'First International' in 1864.

Marx Brothers An American comedy group of brothers consisting of **Arthur Marx (Harpo)** (1893–1964), **Milton (Gummo)** (1894–1977), **Herbert Marx (Zeppo)** (1901–79), **Julius Marx (Groucho)** (1895–1977) and **Leonard Marx (Chico)** (1891–1961). The anarchic humour of the Marx Brothers' films was enormously popular with both critics and public, with Groucho in particular enjoying a cult status among intellectuals.

Mary I (1516–58) Queen of England. The daughter of Catherine of Aragon and HENRY VIII, she inherited the throne in 1553. A devout Roman Catholic, she was initially very popular. She gradually reintroduced her religion into England and married King Philip II of Spain in 1554. The last years of her reign were marked by increasing persecution of Protestants.

Masaccio [Tommaso di Ser Giovanni di Mone] (1401–*c*.1428) Florentine painter. A key figure of the early Renaissance and in the development of perspective.

Mascagni, Pietro (1863–1945) Italian composer. His works include the perennial favourite, the one-act *Cavalleria Rusticana*.

Masefield, John [Edward] (1878–1967) English poet, whose best-known poem, from *Salt-Water Ballads* (1902) is 'I must go down to the sea again'. Many later poems, e.g. *The Everlasting Mercy* (1911), caused scandal with their frank treatment of rural themes. He was appointed poet laureate in 1930.

Mata Hari [Margarethe Geertruida Zelle] (1876–1917) Dutch spy. A dancer in Paris with many lovers, she became a German spy and was shot for treason.

Matisse, Henri (1869–1954) French painter and sculptor. In the period before World War I he became a leading Fauvist. A superb draughtsman, he also designed ballet sets for DIAGHILEV. He continued to paint more abstract and decorative works, and made use of cut-outs and collages in simple compositions.

Matthews, Sir Stanley (1915–) English footballer. Regarded as one of the greatest wingers of all time (the 'Wizard of Dribble'), he won 54 international caps in a career that spanned 22 years.

Maugham, W[illiam] Somerset (1874–1965) English novelist and dramatist. Trained as a doctor, he used his experiences working in the London slums for his first novel, *Liza of Lambeth* (1897). His best-known novels are *Of Human Bondage* (1915) and *The Moon and Sixpence* (1919), the latter based on the life of the painter Paul GAUGUIN. He was a British secret agent during World War I, and his experiences then form the basis of his spy novel, *Ashenden* (1928).

Maxwell, [Ian] Robert [Robert Hoch] (1923–91) Czech-born British newspaper proprietor, publisher and politician. His mysterious death by drowning off the Canary Islands was followed by revelations of his mishandling of his companies' assets.

Mayer, Louis B[urt] [Eliezer Mayer] (1885–1957) Russian-born American film producer. He joined with GOLDWYN to form Metro-Goldwyn-Mayer in 1924, and became one of the most powerful of the Hollywood moguls.

Mead, Margaret (1901–78) American anthropologist. Her works, which include *Coming of Age in Samoa*, argue that cultural conditioning shapes personality, rather than heredity.

Medawar, Sir Peter Brian (1915–87) Brazilian-born British zoologist. He shared the 1960 Nobel prize for physiology or medicine with the Australian virologist **Sir Frank Macfarlane Burnet** (1899–1985) for his work on immunological tolerance.

Medici, Lorenzo de' (1449–92) Florentine aristocrat and statesman. Styled 'The Magnificent', he was a poet and a noted patron of the arts. His tomb in Florence was designed by MICHELANGELO.

Meinhoff, Ulrike (1934–76) German terrorist. With **Andreas Baader** (1943–77) and others, she founded the 'Red Army Faction' in 1970, an ultra-leftist terrorist organization dedicated to using violence to bring about the collapse of West German 'capitalist tyranny'.

Meir, Golda (1898–1978) Russian-born Israeli stateswoman. Active in the fight for a Jewish state, she was minister of labour (1949–56) and of foreign affairs (1956–66) before becoming Israel's first female prime minister (1969–74).

Meitner, Lise (1878–1968) Austrian-born Swedish physicist. She and Otto HAHN discovered the radioactive element protactinium (1918). With her nephew, Otto FRISCH, and others, she discovered the process of nuclear fission in the late 1930s.

Melba, Dame Nellie [Helen Porter Mitchell] (1861–1931) Australian soprano. Renowned for her light, pure voice, she became one of the world's leading prima donnas in the late 1880s.

Melville, Herman (1819–91) American novelist, short-story writer and poet. His masterpiece is the novel *Moby Dick* (1851), a complex and symbolic narrative featuring the revengeful Captain

Ahab. His short novel *Billy Budd, Foretopman* was made into an opera by BRITTEN.

Memling *or* **Memlinc, Hans** (*c.*1430–1494) German-born Dutch painter. He was a prolific and popular artist, and was a successful portraitist.

Mendel, Gregor Johann (1822–84) Austrian monk who was also a biologist and botanist. He discovered that traits such as colour or height had two factors (hereditary units) and that these factors do not blend but can be either dominant or recessive.

Mendelssohn, Felix [Jakob Ludwig Felix Mendelssohn-Bartholdy] (1809–47) German composer. The grandson of the philosopher **Moses Mendelssohn** (1729–86), he became one of the leading Romantic composers. His works include five symphonies, the opera *Elijah* (1846), songs and the overtures *A Midsummer Night's Dream* (1826) and *Fingal's Cave* (1832). His performance of BACH's *St Matthew Passion* resulted in a resurgence of interest in the composer.

Mengistu, Mariam Haile (1937–) Ethiopian dictator. He participated in the 1974 coup that toppled HAILE SELASSIE, and established a brutal dictatorship after a further coup in 1977.

Menotti, Gian Carlo (1911–) Italian-born American composer. His operas, for which he also wrote the librettos, employ a number of musical styles.

Menuhin, Sir Yehudi (1916–) American-born British violinist. An infant prodigy, he became one of the world's leading virtuosos and founded a school (in 1962) for musically gifted children.

Messerschmitt, Willy [Wilhelm Messerschmitt] (1898–1978) German aircraft designer and manufacturer. His planes include the first jet combat aircraft.

Messiaen, Olivier (1908–92) French composer and organist. His rhythmically complex works were often heavily influenced by religious mysticism.

Messmer, Otto (1894–1985) American cartoonist. His 'Felix the Cat' became the first cartoon superstar.

Meyerbeer, Giacomo (1791–1864) a German-born composer who visited Italy and wrote operas in the style of ROSSINI. His best-known work is *L'Africaine*.

Michelangelo Buonarotti (1475–1564) Florentine painter, sculptor, draughtsman, architect and poet, an outstanding figure of the Renaissance. His masterpiece was the ceiling paintings for the Sistine Chapel (1508–12). He also worked on the tombs of

Lorenzo and Giuliano de Medici, and on the rebuilding of St Peter's. He was an accomplished poet, and wrote fine sonnets.

Middleton, Thomas (*c*.1570–1627) English dramatist. His two powerful tragedies, *The Changeling* and *Women Beware Women*, are now highly regarded. His other works include the satirical comedy *A Trick to Catch the Old One* and a political satire, *A Game at Chesse*, which almost resulted in his imprisonment. He collaborated with many other dramatists.

Milhaud, Darius (1892–1974) French composer. A member of 'Les Six', he was a highly prolific composer. His works, were mostly polytonal and often influenced by jazz.

Mill, John Stuart (1806–73) English philosopher and economist. A follower of BENTHAM, he elaborated the philosophy of the 'greater good' in his philosophy of utilitarianism. His most popular work is the defence of personal freedom *On Liberty* (1859).

Millais, Sir John Everett (1829–96) English painter. Along with Holman HUNT and ROSSETTI, he founded the Pre-Raphaelite Brotherhood and was known for his posed, studied tableaux in clashing colours.

Miller, Arthur (1915–) American dramatist. His tragedies include three classics of the American stage: *Death of a Salesman*, *The Crucible*, a comment on McCarthyism in the USA, and *A View from the Bridge*, inspired by Greek drama. He was married to Marilyn MONROE (1955–61) for whom he wrote the screenplay for her last film, *The Misfits* (1961).

Miller, [Alton] Glenn (1904–44) American composer, bandleader and trombonist. His dance band became one of the most popular in the world.

Millet, Jean-François (1814–75) French painter. He earned his living as a portraitist, and exhibited his first major genre painting, *The Winnower*, in 1848. He was labelled a social-realist although his work had no direct political import.

Millett, Kate (1934–) American feminist. Her works are cornerstones of feminist fundamentalism.

Milligan, Spike [Terence Allan Milligan] (1918–) Anglo-Irish comedian and writer. With Peter SELLERS, the Welsh comedian and singer **Harry Secombe** (1921–) and the Anglo-Peruvian comedian **Michael Bentine** (1921–), he co-wrote and performed in the radio comedy series *The Goon Show* (1951–59), which became a highly influential comedy series, with its manic wit and surreal invention.

Millikan, Robert Andrews (1868–1953) American physicist. He was awarded the 1923 Nobel prize for physics for his determination of the charge on the electron.

Milne, A[lan] A[lexander] (1882–1956) English writer and dramatist. His children's books featuring Winnie the Pooh are much loved classics of children's literature.

Milton, John (1608–74) English poet. One of the most formidably learned of all English poets, he had a European-wide reputation by his late twenties. His early poems, e.g. the elegy *Lycidas* (1637), are steeped in the humanist tradition, which looked to classical literature for ethical principles and modes of expression, and to Scripture and the Christian tradition for faith. He supported Parliament during the Civil War and wrote tracts attacking royalty and episcopacy. His most famous prose work is the tract *Aeropagitica* (1644), a rousing defence of the liberty of free speech. His masterpiece is the great epic poem on the Fall of Man, *Paradise Lost* (1667–74). Other notable works include the verse drama *Samson Agonistes* (1671), in which the blind hero represents Milton himself in Restoration England.

Miró, Joan (1893–1983) Spanish painter. Influenced by PICASSO, his work became increasingly abstract over the years and was influential on the abstract expressionist painters.

Mitchell, R[eginald] J[oseph] (1895–1937) English aircraft designer. He designed the Supermarine Spitfire (1934–36).

Mitterrand, François [Maurice Marie] (1916–) French statesman. He became leader of the Socialist Party in 1971 and the first socialist president of France (1981–).

Mobuto, Sese Seko Kuku Ngbendu Wa Za Banga [Joseph Désiré Mobuto] (1930–) Zairean dictator. He assumed complete power over the Congo in 1965, changing the country's name to Zaire in 1971.

Modigliani, Amedeo (1884–1920) Italian painter and sculptor. His best-known works are his African-influenced sculptures of elongated figures.

Mohammed *or* **Muhammad** (*c.*570–*c.*632) Arab prophet and founder of Islam. Born in Mecca, the son of a merchant, he began having revelations, sometime after 600, that he was the last prophet of Allah and His channel of communication with the world. He gathered together a band of followers and established himself at Medina in 622, from where, after several battles, his forces conquered Mecca in 629, and shortly after all Arabia.

Molière [pseud. of Jean-Baptiste Poquelin] (1622–73) French dramatist. His great comedies are as popular now as when they were first performed; only SHAKESPEARE's plays have been more widely performed. The plays include *Tartuffe*, a satire on religious hypocrisy, *The Misanthrope*, a study of a cynic in love, and *The Imaginary Invalid*, a hilarious depiction of hypochondria and quack medicine.

Molotov, Vyacheslav Mikhailovich [Vyacheslav Mikhailovich Scriabin] (1890–1986) Russian statesman. He negotiated the non-aggression pact with Nazi Germany and became minister for foreign affairs (1953–56).

Mondrian, Piet [Pieter Cornelis Mondriaan] (1872–1944) Dutch painter. He developed a style of painting based on grids of lines against strong colours and co-founded the De Stijl group.

Monet, Claude Oscar (1840–1926) French Impressionist painter. His *Impression: Sunrise* gave its name to the movement. With RENOIR and SISLEY, he began the direct studies of nature and changing light that were to characterize their works. His works include the *Haystacks* (1891) and *Rouen Cathedral* (1894) series.

Monk, Thelonius [Sphere] (1920–82) American jazz pianist and composer. His compositions include the classic 'Round Midnight'.

Monroe, Marilyn [Norma Jean Baker *or* Mortenson] (1926–62) American film actress. She became the leading "dumb blonde" sex symbol in the movies with such films as *Gentleman Prefer Blondes* (1953). Her other films include *Bus Stop* (1956) and the classic comedy *Some Like It Hot* (1959). Her last film, *The Misfits* (1961), was written by her third husband, Arthur MILLER. Her death was apparently due to an overdose of sleeping pills.

Montaigne, Michel Eyquem de (1533–92) French essayist. The dominant theme in his work was antidogmatic scepticism and he did much to establish the essay as a literary form .

Montessori, Maria (1870–1952) Italian educationalist. Her method of encouraging the child to learn at her or his own pace without restraint, was very influential on modern pedagogy.

Monteverdi, Claudio Giovanni Antonio (1567–1643) Italian composer. He introduced many new elements to the opera form and is regarded as the first major opera composer. His works include *Orfeo* and *The Coronation of Poppea*.

Montgomery of Alamein, Bernard Law, 1st Viscount (1887–1976) English soldier. In World War II he was given command of the 8th Army in Egypt in 1942, and won the Battle of Alamein, a victory recognized by CHURCHILL as a turning point in the war. He later commanded the Allied land forces on D-Day.

Moore, Henry [Spencer] (1898–1986) English sculptor. His monumental sculptures, often semi-abstract in style but always based on organic form, resulted in him becoming the best known of modern sculptors.

More, Sir Thomas (1478–1535) English statesman and Roman Catholic saint. He was HENRY VIII's Lord Chancellor, and his refusal to recognize the annulment of Henry's marriage to Catherine of Aragon and declaration of supremacy over the Church in England led to his execution for treason. He was widely recognized as an honourable man, and his execution revulsed moderate opinion throughout Europe. His greatest work is his fantasy of a supposedly ideally organized state, *Utopia*. More was canonized in 1835, and has always been admired for his firm principles. His involvement in heresy trials, however, and his dispute with **William Tyndale** (*c*.1495–1536), English translator of the Bible, show a less attractive side of his character.

Morgan, Thomas Hunt (1866–1945) American geneticist and biologist. He was awarded the 1933 Nobel prize for physiology or medicine for his research into chromosomes and heredity.

Morisot, Berthe (1841–95) French painter, who exhibited in all but one of the Impressionist shows.

Moro, Aldo (1916–78) Italian Christian democrat statesman. He was prime minister (1963–68, 1974–76) and brought the Communist Party into close cooperation with his centre-left coalition shortly before his abduction and murder by the Red Brigade.

Morris, Desmond [John] (1928–) English zoologist. His studies of animal and human behaviour have been bestsellers.

Morris, William (1834–96) English poet, romance writer and artist. His influence on the arts and crafts movement was immense, as was his influence on the development and character of British socialism.

Morrison, Jim (1943–71) American rock singer and songwriter. His band, The Doors, became a huge cult after his death (from alcohol and drug abuse).

Morton, Jelly Roll [Ferdinand Joseph Lemott] (1885–1941) American jazz pianist, composer and bandleader who is regarded as one of the founders of New Orleans jazz.

Mosley, Sir Oswald [Ernald] (1896–1980) English Fascist

leader. First elected to Parliament as a Conservative (1918–22), he became an Independent (1922–24), then a Labour MP (1924, 1929–31), and finally founder and leader of the British Union of Fascists (1932–36). The thuggery and demagoguery of his movement failed to attract much support, and he was interned during World War II.

Mossbauer, Rudolf Ludwig (1929–) German physicist. He shared the 1961 Nobel prize for physics with the American physicist **Robert Hofstadter** (1915–) for his discovery of the 'Mossbauer effect', involving gamma radiation in crystals.

Mountbatten, Louis [Francis Victor Albert Nicholas], [1st Earl Mountbatten of Burma] (1900–79) British naval commander and statesman. Supreme Allied Commander in South-East Asia (1943–45) and viceroy of India (1947), he oversaw the transfer of power to the independent governments of India and Pakistan. He was assasinated by the IRA.

Moussorgsky, Modest *see* **Mussorgsky, Modest**.

Mozart, Wolfgang Amadeus (1756–91) Austrian musician and composer. A child prodigy, he began composing at the age of 5. One of the most lyrical of all composers, his works include the operas *The Marriage of Figaro*, *Don Giovanni*, *Cosi fan tutte* and *The Magic Flute*, over 40 symphonies, concertos, string quartets, sonatas, 18 masses, and the unfinished *Requiem*.

Mugabe, Robert [Gabriel] (1924–) Zimbabwean statesman. He became leader of the Zimbabwe African National Union and prime minister (1980–) following the end of white minority rule. He merged his ruling party with the Zimbabwe African People's Union in 1988 to form a one-party state.

Mulliken, Robert Sanderson (1896–1986) American chemist and physicist. He was awarded the 1986 Nobel prize for chemistry for his work on molecular structure and on chemical bonding.

Munch, Edvard (1863–1944) Norwegian painter. An Expressionist, his works, e.g. *The Scream*, are noted for their strong use of primary colours and emotions.

Munthe, Axel [Martin Frederik] (1857–1949) Swedish physicist and psychiatrist. His autobiographal book, *The Story of San Michele*, describing his experiences while practising medicine, became a world bestseller.

Murdoch, [Keith] Rupert (1931–) Australian-born American newspaper tycoon. He inherited an Australian newspaper group from his father and expanded his media empire in Britain and

America. His expansion into the US market necessitated his acquisition of US citizenship in 1985.

Musgrave, Thea (1928–) Scottish composer. Her early works were often on Scottish themes. Later compositions, often in serial form, include choral works and concertos.

Mussolini, Benito [Amilcare Andrea] (1883–1945) Italian dictator. Originally a socialist, he founded his fascist 'Blackshirt' party in 1919, and was elected to parliament in 1921, establishing himself as dictator ('Il Duce') in 1922. He formed the Axis with HITLER in 1937 and declared war on the Allies in 1940. He was deposed in 1943 and later executed by partisans.

Mussorgsky *or* **Moussorgsky, Modest Petrovich** (1839–81) Russian composer. His best-known works include the opera *Boris Godunov* and the piano piece 'Pictures at an Exhibition'.

Muzorewa, Bishop Abel *see* SMITH, IAN.

Myrdal, [Karl] Gunnar (1898–1987) Swedish economist. He shared the 1974 Nobel prize for economics with HAYEK, largely for his work on the application of economic theory to the economies of the Third World.

Nabokov, Vladimir (1899–1977) Russian-born American novelist, who wrote in both Russian and English. His most famous novel is *Lolita* (1955).

Nader, Ralph (1934–) American lawyer and consumer protectionist. Nader and his followers ('Nader's Raiders') publicized many such cases of consumer abuse in the late 1960s and 70s.

Nagy, Imre (1896–1958) Hungarian statesman. He was appointed prime minister (1953–55) and forced to resign after attempting to liberalize communist policies. He became premier again in 1956, but was replaced after the Soviet invasion of that year.

Nansen, Fridtjof (1861–1930) Norwegian explorer, scientist and statesman. He traversed Greenland (1888–89) and almost reached the North Pole in 1895, achieving a record latitude. He was appointed commissioner for refugees (1920–22) by the League of Nations and awarded the 1922 Nobel Peace Prize.

Napoleon I [Napoleon Bonaparte] (1769–1821) emperor of France (1804–15). A brilliant and ruthless military leader, he established an empire throughout Europe, defeating coalitions of the other major powers. His invasion of Russia in 1812, and the murderous campaign in the Pyrenees against WELLINGTON'S forces, led to the defeat of his armies at Leipzig in 1813 and Allied victory in 1814. Napoleon retired to Elba, from whence, in

1815, he came back to France, beginning the 'Hundred Days' campaign which resulted in his defeat at Waterloo, and subsequent banishment to St Helena, where he died.

Nashe, Thomas (1567–1601) English writer of pamphlets and tracts on various subjects, which were usually satirical and often contain barbs directed against his many literary and religious enemies. He was particularly virulent against the Puritans.

Nasser, Gamal Abdel (1918–70) Egyptian soldier and statesman. He took a leading part in the coup that deposed **King Farouk** (1920–65) in 1952, and became prime minister in 1954. He became president (1956–70) and precipitated the Suez Crisis by nationalizing the Suez Canal (1956).

Navratilova, Martina (1956–) Czech-born American tennis player. Regarded as the one of the world's greatest tennis players, she defected to the US in 1975.

Nehru, Jawaharlal (1889–1964) Indian nationalist leader and statesman. The son of the nationalist lawyer, **Motilal Nehru ('Pandit' Nehru)** (1861–1931), he joined the Indian National Congress in 1919 and was imprisoned many times in the 1930s and 40s for his nationalist views. He became the first prime minister of India (1947–64) following independence and the partition of the subcontinent into India and Pakistan. His daughter Indira GANDHI became prime minister in 1966.

Nelson, Horatio, [Viscount Nelson] (1758–1805) English naval commander. Renowned for his tactics, he became rear-admiral in 1797 after defeating the Spanish fleet at the battle of Cape St Vincent. The following year, he won a striking victory over the French at the battle of the Nile, and was killed by a sniper during his defeat of the French at Trafalgar in 1805.

Nero (37–68) Roman emperor. He succeeded CLAUDIUS in 54, and soon became infamous for his debauchery, vanity and paranoia. He had many people put to death or forced to kill themselves.

Nervi, Pier Luigi (1891–1979) Italian architect and engineer. An exponent of the virtues of reinforced concrete, his designs include the Pirellie skyscraper in Milan.

Newman, Cardinal John Henry (1801–90) English theologian. His spirited defence of his faith, *Apologia pro Vita Sua* (1864), was much admired by believers and non-believers alike.

Newman, Paul (1925–) American film actor. His films include *Hud* (1963), *Cool Hand Luke* (1967), *Butch Cassidy and the Sundance Kid* (1969) and *The Color of Money* (1986), the last earning him an Oscar. A political activist of the moderate left, he has also raised considerable sums of money for charity through sales of his own-name salad dressing.

Newton, Sir Isaac (1642–1727) English scientist, philosopher and mathematician. According to legend, observing the fall of an apple inspired him to discover the law of gravity. He also discovered (independently of LEIBNITZ) the differential calculus, the reflecting telescope, and devised the three laws of motion.

Nicholas II (1868–1918) Russian tsar (1895–1917). A weak ruler, alternating between bursts of liberalization and repression, his authority was seriously weakened by Russia's defeat in the war with Japan (1904–5). He was deposed by the Bolsheviks in 1917, who later murdered him and his family.

Nicklaus, Jack [William] (1940–) American golfer. One of the greatest golfers of all time, he won more major tournaments than any other player in history.

Nielsen, Carl [August] (1865–1931) Danish composer. The first prominent polytonal Danish composer, his works include six symphonies, two operas and concertos.

Niemöller, Martin (1892–1984) German Lutheran pastor. An outspoken opponent of HITLER and Nazi ideology, he was imprisoned in concentration camps (1937–45). He was president of the World Council of Churches (1961–68) and a prominent pacifist.

Nietzsche, Friedrich Wilhelm (1844–1900) German philosopher and poet, whose works were highly critical of traditional morality and Christianity and proclaimed the advent of the superman. He has been very influential on many 20th-century writers and was claimed by HITLER to be a spiritual forebear of Nazism, but Nietzsche, who despised anti-Semitism, would have rejected this.

Nijinsky, Vaslav (1890–1950) Russian ballet dancer and choreographer. He became a protégé of DIAGHILEV, and is regarded as one of the greatest ballet dancers of all time.

Niven, David [James David Graham Nevins] (1909–83) Scottish film actor who established himself as the model urbane Englishman in many Hollywood productions.

Nixon, Richard Milhous (1913–94) American Republican politician. The 37th president of the US (1969-74, he became the first president to resign from office, in 1974, following the 'Watergate' scandal. He was pardoned in 1974. While in office, he ended the Vietnam war and established rapprochement with China.

Nkrumah, Kwame (1909–72) Ghanaian statesman. He was the first president of Ghana (1957–66) after independence.

Nolan, Sir Sidney [Robert] (1917–92) Australian painter. His paintings draw heavily upon Australian history and folklore.

North, Frederick, 8th Lord North [2nd Earl of Guilford] (1732–92) English statesman. As prime minister (1770–82) during the reign of George III, he implemented the king's policy that led to the loss of the American colony.

Nostradamus [Michel de Notredame] (1503–66) French astrologer and physician. He published two books of cryptic prophecies in rhymed quatrains which enjoyed a huge vogue.

Novello, Ivor [Ivor Novello Davies] (1893–1951) Welsh songwriter, composer and actor. His songs include 'Keep the Home Fires Burning', which was hugely popular with British soldiers during World War I.. and 'We'll Gather Lilacs'.

Nuffield, William Richard Morris, 1st Viscount (1877–1963) English car manufacturer and philanthropist. He developed a Henry FORD-like system of mass production of cars, notably the Morris Oxford and the Morris Minor.

Nureyev, Rudolf (1939–93) Russian ballet dancer and choreographer. Regarded as the successor to NIJINSKY, he formed a famous partnership with FONTEYN in 1962.

Nyerere, Julius [Kambarage] (c.1922–) Tanzanian statesman. He became president (1962–85) and negotiated the union of Tanganyika and Zanzibar (1964), which formed Tanzania. Widely regarded as Africa's leading statesman. His invasion of Uganda in 1978 brought AMIN's dictatorship to an end.

Obote, [Apollo] Milton (1924–) Ugandan politician. He became Uganda's first prime minister (1962–66) after independence, and became president (1966–71) after deposing King Mutesa II. He was in turn deposed by AMIN and became president again (1980–85) after Amin's overthrow. He was deposed again in 1985.

O'Casey, Sean (1880–1964) Irish dramatist. His early plays, e.g. *Juno and Paycock*, reflect the patriotism that followed the Easter Rising of 1916.

Oistrakh, David Feodorovitch (1908–74) Russian violinist. A widely admired virtuoso whose son, **Igor Davidovitch Oistrakh** (1931–), also has an international reputation as a violinist.

Olivier, Laurence [Kerr], [Baron Olivier of Brighton] (1907–89) English stage and film actor and director. Regarded as the leading British actor of the modern era, he played all the major

SHAKESPEARE roles and became an international film star. He was director of the National Theatre (1962–73). His second wife (of three) was Vivien LEIGH.

O'Neill, Eugene [Gladstone] (1888–1953) American dramatist. His greatest play is *Long Day's Journey into Night* (1940–41), a study of family breakdown. He was awarded the Nobel prize for literature in 1936.

Ono, Yoko *see* LENNON, JOHN.

Oppenheimer, J[ulius] Robert (1904–67) American nuclear physicist. He resigned from the Los Alamos atom bomb project after the dropping of the bombs on Hiroshima and Nagasaki, and argued for cooperation with the USSR on the control of nuclear weapons.

Orff, Carl (1895–1982) German composer. His best-known work is the popular *Carmina Burana* (1937), a 'secular oratorio' based on medieval poems.

Ortega, Daniel (1945–) Nicaraguan politician. A leader of the Sandinista resistance movement that overthrew the dictatorship in 1979, he became president of Nicaragua (1985–90). The REAGAN administration gave backing to the right-wing 'Contra' forces in their guerrilla war against the Sandinistas and Ortega was defeated in the 1989 election.

Ortega y Gasset, José (1883–1955) Spanish philosopher who argued that democracy in the modern era could easily lead to tyrannies of either the left or right.

Orwell, George [Eric Arthur Blair] (1903–50) Indian-born English novelist and essayist. His two greatest novels have become classics: *Animal Farm* (1945), a grim allegory of the history of the Soviet Union, and *Nineteen Eighty-Four* (1949), an even grimmer picture of a totalitarian world.

Osborne, John [James] (1929–) English dramatist. His first play, *Look Back in Anger* (1956), gave its name to the 'Angry Young Men', a group of young playwrights who replaced the drawing-room comedies of 1950s British theatre with realistic dramas of working-class life.

Oswald, Lee Harvey (1939–63) American alleged assassin of President KENNEDY. He was arrested shortly after Kennedy's murder in Dallas in 1963, and was himself shot dead before he could come to trial by **Jack Ruby** (1911–64).

Ovid [Publius Ovidius Naso] (43 BC–*c*.17 AD) Roman poet. His sensual, witty love poems have always been admired, but his long narrative poem *Metamorphoses*, which describes myths in which characters change their forms, is of greater significance. It was used as a source book by many, e.g. SHAKESPEARE.

Owen, David [Anthony Llewellyn] (1938–) English politician. Founder of the Social Democratic Party with JENKINS and others. He refused to accept the merger of the SDP with the Liberal Party in 1987, but dissolved the SDP in 1990. He was made a life peer and worked as a UN peace negotiator in the Bosnian conflict of the early 1990s.

Owens, Jesse [James Cleveland Owens] (1913–80) American athlete. One of the finest athletes of his generation, he won four gold medals in the 1936 Berlin Olympics. Adolf HITLER left the stadium to avoid congratulating the black, non-Aryan athlete.

Padarewski, Ignace Jan (1860–1941) Polish pianist, composer and statesman. Widely regarded as the greatest pianist of his day, he served as prime minister for ten months in 1919.

Pahlavi, Mohammed Reza (1919–80) shah of Iran. He succeeded his father in 1941 and gradually established a dictatorship which was undermined by religious fundamentalists led by KHOMEINI and forced to flee his country in 1979.

Paine, Thomas (1737–1809) English-born American political theorist and pamphleteer. His highly influential pamphlet *Common Sense* (1776), which argued for American independence, was recognized by WASHINGTON as being a significant contribution to the Revolution. Paine returned to England in 1787 and published a defence of democratic principles, *The Rights of Man* (1791–92), in reply to Edmund BURKE's *Reflections on the Revolution in France*. In danger of arrest he moved to France where he was elected to the National Convention. He sided with the moderates, was imprisoned by ROBESPIERRE's faction, and released after 11 months, having narrowly escaped execution.

Paisley, Ian [Richard Kyle] (1926–) Northern Ireland Protestant clergyman and Unionist politician. A highly vocal opponent of Irish nationalism and Roman Catholicism.

Palestrina, Giovanni Pierluigi da (*c.*1525–1594) Italian composer. One of the greatest Renaissance composers, his compositions are practically all choral church works, including more than 90 masses, hymns, motets and madrigals.

Palmer, Samuel (1805–81) English painter and engraver, noted for his pastoral landscapes. He was a follower of Blake, who deeply influenced the visionary mysticism of his work.

Pankhurst, Emmeline (1858–1928) English suffragette and feminist. She and her daughter **Dame Christabel Harriette Pankhurst** (1880–1958) founded the Women's Social and Political Union in 1903, a campaigning organization for women's suffrage. Her daughter **Sylvia Pankhurst** (1882–1960) was also a suffragette as well as a pacifist.

Papandreou, Andreas George (1919–) Greek socialist politician and Greece's first socialist prime minister (1981–89).

Parker, Charlie *or* **Bird** [Charles Christopher Parker] (1920–55) American jazz alto saxophonist. He became the leading exponent of 'bop' jazz in the 1940s and worked with Dizzy GILLESPIE.

Parker, Dorothy [Rothschild] (1893–1967) American journalist, poet and short-story writer, noted for her dry wit and sharply ironic epigrams and satires.

Parnell, Charles Stewart (1846–91) Irish politician. An ardent Home Ruler, he became MP for Cork in 1880 and organized in parliament a masterly campaign of obstruction with the aim of disrupting Parliament and ultimately gaining Home Rule for Ireland. GLADSTONE became a convert to the cause, but in 1890, his career began to crumble after he was cited in a divorce case.

Parr, Catherine *see* HENRY VIII.

Pascal, Blaise (1623–62) French theologian, mathematician and physicist. He made important discoveries in hydraulics and invented a calculating machine.

Pasternak, Boris [Leonidovich] (1890–1960) Russian poet and novelist. A highly original and passionate lyric poet in a regime that demanded safe verse praising its achievements forced him to turn to translation for a living; his translations of SHAKESPEARE'S plays are still highly valued. His great novel *Dr Zhivago* was first published in Italy in 1958. He was awarded the Nobel prize for literature but was forced to decline it by the Soviet authorities.

Pasteur, Louis (1822–95) French chemist who discovered that fermentation is due to the presence of microorganisms and developed the process of pasteurization to destroy them. He also developed immunization processes against rabies and anthrax.

Patrick, Saint (*fl.* 5th century) British missionary. He was sold into slavery in Ireland as a youth, escaped to France and became a monk. He returned to Ireland as a missionary and converted many to his faith, and became the patron saint of Ireland.

Patton, George S[mith] (1885–1945) American general. In World War II he commanded the Allied invasion of North Africa

(1942–43), and led the 3rd US army across France and Germany to the Czech border (1944–45).

Paul, Saint (d. *c.*67 AD) Christian apostle and missionary to the Gentiles. A pharisee, he was a notable persecutor of Christians before his 'Damascus Road' conversion. Many of the Epistles in the New Testament are his. According to tradition, he was executed during the reign of Nero.

Pauling, Linus Carl (1901–94) American chemist. He was awarded the 1954 Nobel prize for physics for his research into chemical bonding and molecular structure, and the 1962 Nobel Peace Prize for his criticisms of nuclear testing and deterrence.

Pavarotti, Luciano (1935–) Italian tenor. He is regarded as one of the most powerful tenor singers of the modern era.

Pavlov, Ivan Petrovich (1849–1936) Russian physiologist. He was awarded the 1904 Nobel prize for physiology or medicine for his work on the physiology of digestion, and conducted experiments on the conditioning of reflexes.

Pavlova, Anna (1885–1931) Russian ballerina. FOKINE choreographed *The Dying Swan* for her. She also worked with DIAGHILEV, and became one of the most famous ballerinas in the world.

Pears, Sir Peter (1910–86) English tenor. A close associate of Benjamin BRITTEN, several of whose tenor opera roles were written for him.

Peary, Robert Edwin (1856–1920) American naval commander and Arctic explorer. He is credited with being the first man to reach the North Pole (1909).

Peel, Sir Robert (1788–1850) British statesman. He became Home Secretary in 1828 and founded the Metropolitan police. He was prime minister twice (1834–35, 1841–6). By his last year of office he had accepted and promoted the free-trade principles that disrupted the Tory party.

Peierls, Sir Rudolf Ernst (1907–) German-born British physicist. With Otto FRISCH, he demonstrated the feasibility of an atom bomb during World War II.

Pelé [Edson Arantes do Nascimento] (1940–) Brazilian footballer, universally recognized as one of the most skilful and entertaining players of all time.

Pepys, Samuel (1633–1703) English diarist and Admiralty official. His diary (written in code) was first published in 1825. The full uncensored version was published in 11 volumes (1970–83), and includes fascinating detail of life in 17th-century London.

Perón, Juan Domingo (1895–1974) Argentinian dictator. He was president (1946–55), was deposed by the army and lived in exile until re-elected president (1973–74). His success was based to a large extent on his first wife, **Eva [Duarte] Perón** (1919–52), an ex-actress nicknamed 'Evita'.

Perry, Fred[erick John] (1909–) English-born American tennis and table-tennis player. One of the most successful lawn tennis players of the 1930s, winning every major tournament.

Pétain, Henri Philippe Omer (1856–1951) French soldier and statesman. Appointed marshal of France in 1918 in recognition of his generalship during World War I, he headed the collaborationist Vichy government (1940–44) and was sentenced to death at the end of World War II (later commuted to life imprisonment).

Peter, Saint (died c.67 AD) Disciple of JESUS CHRIST and Christian apostle. A fisherman, he became one of Jesus's leading disciples and played an equally prominent role in establishing Christianity after the crucifixion and is regarded by Roman Catholics as the first pope. He is believed to have been martyred in Rome.

Peterson, Oscar [Emmanuel] (1925–) Canadian jazz pianist and composer. His Oscar Peterson Trio became one of the best-known small jazz groups of the 1950s.

Petrarch [Francesco Petrarca] (1304–74) Italian lyric poet and humanist. His work popularized the sonnet form, and he is recognized as the first major poet of the Renaissance.

Petronius [Gaius Petronius Arbiter] (d. AD c.66) Roman courtier and satirist. His great satirical novel, the *Satyricon*, is an important landmark in Western literature.

Philby, Kim [Harold Adrian Russell Philby] (1911–88) English diplomat, journalist and secret-service double agent. He became a Soviet agent in 1933 and was recruited to the British Secret Service in 1940. He became head of anti-communist espionage (1944–46) and worked in the British embassy in Washington DC (1949–51). He worked as a foreign correspondent (1956–63) before fleeing to the USSR.

Philip, Prince, [Duke of Edinburgh] (1921–) Greek-born British naval officer and prince consort. The nephew of MOUNTBATTEN, he married the then Princess ELIZABETH in 1947.

Piaf, Edith [Edith Giovanna Gassion] (1915–63) French singer and songwriter. Nicknamed 'Little Sparrow' for her small size and frail appearance, her songs include '*Non, je ne regrette rien*'.

Piaget, Jean (1896–1980) Swiss psychologist. His studies of children's intelligence and perception have been highly influential on modern educationalists.

Picasso, Pablo (1881–1973) Spanish painter and sculptor. Regarded as the most influential artist of the modern era, with BRAQUE, he was the founder of Cubism. His 'blue period' (1901–4) works include *The Blue Room* (1901); Cubist works include *Les Demoiselles d'Avignon* (1906–7). He designed costumes and scenery for DIAGHILEV from 1917, exhibited with the Surrealists in the mid–1920s, and created his strongest and perhaps best-known image *Guernica* (1937) in response to the fascist bombing of that Basque town during the Spanish Civil War.

Pickford, Mary [Gladys Mary Smith] (1893–1979) Canadian-born American film star. Known for her silent roles and as co-founder of the United Artists film studio (1919) with Charlie CHAPLIN and D. W. GRIFFITH.

Piero della Francesca (c.1416–92) Italian early Renaissance painter. While working in Florence he was deeply influenced by MASACCIO, who inspired the monumental grandeur of his subsequent works. From c.1460 he was working at the Urbino court, where he painted some of his finest works.

Pindar (c.518–c.438 BC) Greek lyric poet, noted for his odes and carefully constructed, elaborate poems which became influential in late-17th century England.

Pinochet [Ugarte], Augusto (1915–) Chilean general and dictator. He led the 1973 coup that deposed ALLENDE and became president (1974–90). He ruthlessly suppressed dissent and instituted monetarist economic polities.

Pinter, Harold (1930–) English dramatist, known for his halting, menacing dialogue and sinister pauses, e.g. *The Caretaker*.

Pirandello, Luigi (1867–1936) Italian dramatist and novelist. His two best-known plays are *Six Characters in Search of an Author* and *Henry IV*, both of which question theatrical conventions. He was awarded the Nobel prize for literature in 1934.

Pisano, Giovanni (c.1245–c.1314) Pisan sculptor. A leading sculptor of his time, his works are expressive and elegant in the Gothic tradition. His father **Nicola Pisano** (c.1220–c.1284) was also a notable sculptor and instrumental in the development of Christian art towards Roman rather than Gothic influences.

Pissarro, Camille (1830–1903) West Indian-born French Impressionist painter. Influenced by both CONSTABLE and TURNER, he exhibited in all eight Impressionist exhibitions.

Pitt, William [Pitt the Elder, 1st Earl of Chatham] (1707–88) English statesman. He led Britain to victory in the Seven Years War (1756–63) with France. He resigned in 1761, and served again 1766–68. His son **William Pitt** (the Younger) (1759–1806) became prime minister in 1783.

Planck, Max [Karl Ernst Ludwig] (1858–1947) German physicist. He formulated the quantum theory and was awarded the 1918 Nobel prize for physics.

Plath, Sylvia (1932–63) American poet and novelist. Her intense and highly expressive style has been very influential. She was married to Ted Hughes.

Plato (*c*.427–*c*.347 BC) Greek philosopher, regarded as the main founder of Western philosophy. Taught by SOCRATES, he was in turn ARISTOTLE's tutor. His many works, which take the form of dialogues, notably the *Symposium, Phaedo* and *The Republic*, have influenced almost every subsequent age and tradition.

Poe, Edgar Allan (1809–49) American short-story writer, poet and critic. His macabre, highly Gothic horror stories are studies in pathological obsession, and his detective stories, e.g. 'The Murders in the Rue Morgue', have been highly influential.

Pollock, [Paul] Jackson (1912–56) American painter. He became the leading exponent of action painting, a development of Abstract Expressionism, in the late 1940s.

Pol Pot *or* **Saloth Sar** [Kompong Thom] (1929–) Cambodian Communist politician. The establishment of his Maoist dictatorship cost the lives of up to three million people. The Khmer Rouge regime was overthrown by the Russian-backed Vietnamese invasion of 1979 but he remains a powerful figure.

Pompey *see* CAESAR, JULIUS.

Pompidou, Georges [Jean Raymond] (1911–74) French statesman. He was prime minister (1962–68), but was dismissed in 1968 by de Gaulle following the May student riots in Paris but elected president (1969–74).

Pope, Alexander (1688–1744) English poet. His mastery of the rhymed couplet, his deadly satire and gift for sustaining metaphor place him as one of the greatest English poets.

Popper, Sir Karl [Raimund] (1902–94) Austrian-born British philosopher. He established the concept of 'falsifiability' as the criterion by which to judge whether or not a particular proposition can be said to be scientific.

Porter, Cole [Albert] (1893–1964) American songwriter and composer. His highly popular songs, admired for their wit and lyricism, include 'Begin the Beguine' and 'Night and Day'.

Poulenc, Francis (1899–1963) French composer. A member of 'Les Six', he is particularly noted for his his settings of verses from poetry.

Pound, Ezra [Weston Loomis] (1885–1972) American poet and critic. A generous supporter of younger writers, e.g. T. S. ELIOT, HEMINGWAY, he lived in Italy from 1925 and broadcast propaganda against the Allies during World War II. He was committed to a US asylum after the war until 1958, when he returned to Italy.

Poussin, Nicolas (1594–1665) French painter who is noted for his carefully composed pictures in a classical style.

Powell, [John] Enoch (1912–) English Conservative politician. An outspoken opponent of immigration into Britain and of the Common Market. He was an Ulster Unionist MP (1974–87).

Powell, Michael (1905–90) English film producer and director. With the screenwriter **Emeric Pressburger** (1902–88), he made several films that have subsequently been hailed as important works, e.g. *The Life and Death of Colonel Blimp*.

Presley, Elvis [Aaron] (1935–77) American rock singer. He became one of the most popular singers in the world in the mid-1950s and was an outstanding interpreter of ballads.

Priestley, J[ohn] B[oynton] (1894–1984) English novelist and dramatist. His astute social commentaries made him one of the best-known literary figures of the day. His huge output includes the play *An Inspector Calls*.

Profumo, John Dennis (1915–) English Conservative politician. Secretary of state for war (1960–63), he resigned after admitting misleading the House of Commons about a sexual affair.

Prokofiev, Sergei Sergeyevich (1891–1953) Russian composer and pianist. His works include seven symphonies, ballets, piano and violin concertos, and the well-known orchestral 'fairy tale', *Peter and the Wolf* (1936).

Proust, Marcel (1871-1922) French novelist, essayist and critic, known for his long semi-autogiographic novel, *A la recherche du temps perdu*. By subjecting a mass of detail to an analytical eye and by using a circular form, Proust broke new ground in conveying the complexity of life and time and the importance of memory

Puccini, Giacomo (1858–1924) Italian composer. His operas, e.g. *La Bohème*, *Tosca*, *Madama Butterfly*, are regarded as the last great lyrical and dramatic works in the Italian tradition.

Purcell, Henry (*c*.1659–95) English composer. His works include incidental music for the theatre, songs, church music and six operas, notably *Dido and Aeneas* and *The Fairy Queen*.

Pushkin, Aleksandr Sergeyevich (1799–1837) Russian poet, novelist and dramatist. Widely regarded as Russia's greatest poet, the best known of his works are the verse novel *Eugene Onegin* and the historical tragedy *Boris Gudonov*. He died in a duel.

Qaddafi, Moammar al- *see* GADDAFI, MOAMMAR AL-.

Quant, Mary (1934–) English fashion designer. Her most famous design was the miniskirt, which became the symbol of 'swinging sixties' London.

Quayle, Sir [John] Anthony (1913–89) English actor and director. He appeared in several films, but was principally a stage actor, founding his own classical touring company, Compass.

Quisling, Vidkun (1887–1945) Norwegian Fascist leader. He was installed as prime minister (1942–45) by the Nazis, and was executed for treason after the war.

Rabelais, François (*c*.1494–*c*.1553) French monk, physician and satirist, noted for his huge, rambling and often licentious prose fantasy *Gargantua and Pantagruel*. The adjective 'Rabelaisian' is used to denote language that is robustly bawdy.

Rachmaninov, Sergei (1873–1943) Russian composer and pianist. Influenced by Tchaikovsky, his music was very much in the 19th-century romantic tradition. His works include three symphonies, four piano concertos, the *Rhapsody on a Theme by Paganini* (1934) and many songs.

Raleigh, Sir Walter (1552–1618) English courtier, poet and explorer. He became a favourite of ELIZABETH I after returning from a punitive expedition to punish Irish rebels in 1580, and organized unsuccessful attempts to colonize Virginia with English settlers in the 1580s. In 1595, he travelled to the Orinoco and participated in the English raid on Cadiz in 1596. He was imprisoned in after Elizabeth's death, was released to search for treasure on the Orinoco in 1616, and was executed on his return.

Rambert, Dame Marie [Cyvia Rambam] (1888–1982) Polish-born British ballet dancer, teacher and producer. After working with DIAGHILEV and NIJINSKY, she settled in Britain in 1917. She formed the Ballet Club in 1931, which, renamed Ballet Rambert in 1935, became the most influential ballet company in Britain.

Rameau, Jean Philippe (1683–1764) French composer, organist and harpsichordist. He published an influential textbook on harmony and composed motets and canatas. When he was 50, he started to write operas, with VOLTAIRE contributing several libretti.

Raphael [Raffaello Sanzio] (1483–1520) Italian painter. A leading figure of the High Renaissance, his portrayals of the Madonna and Holy Family combined Christian ideals with the grace and grandeur of classical antiquity.

Rasputin, Grigori Efimovich (*c.*1871–1916) Russian monk. Claiming to having healing powers, he became a cult figure among the Russian aristocracy, and an influential member of the royal household. He was assassinated in 1916.

Ravel, Maurice (1875–1937) French composer. He was one of the leading impressionist composers of his time. His works include the small orchestral piece *Boléro*.

Ravi Shankar (1920–) Indian sitar player and composer. Regarded as one of India's greatest modern musicians, he became world-famous after teaching George HARRISON to play the sitar.

Ray, Man (1890–1976) American photographer and painter, he was a leading exponent of Surrealist photography.

Ray, Satyajit (1921–92) Indian film director. His films, popular in art houses the world over, include the *Apu* trilogy of life in rural India, i.e. *Pather Panchali* (1955), *Aparajito* (1956) and *Apu Sansar* (1959), and *The Chess Players* (1977).

Reagan, Ronald [Wilson] (1911–) American film actor, Republican statesman and 40th president of the US (1981–89). He appeared in around fifty films and was president of the Screen Actors Guild (1947–52, 1959–60). As US president he pursued strong monetarist economic policies and a strong anti-communist foreign policy.

Redgrave, Sir Michael [Scudamore] (1908–85) English stage and film actor. One of the finest actors of his generation, with a distinctively intellectual approach to his craft. His daughter, **Vanessa Redgrave** (1937–), became a highly successful stage and film actress.

Reed, Sir Carol (1906–76) English film director. His films include *The Third Man* (1949), written by Graham GREENE and starring Orson WELLES, a bleak thriller set in postwar Vienna that is one of the most highly praised films ever made.

Reinhardt, Django [Jean Baptiste Reinhardt] (1910–53) Belgian guitarist, he formed the influential Quintette de Hot Club de Paris with GRAPPELLI.

Rembrandt Harmensz, van Rijn (1606–69) Dutch painter,

draughtsman and etcher. His remarkable series of self-portraits, painted over 40 years, reveal the depth and spiritual development of his work.

Renoir, Pierre Auguste (1841–1919) French Impressionist painter. His form of Impressionism developed the use of perspective, solidity of form and preliminary sketches. His son, **Jean Renoir** (1894–1979) was a film director. His memorable films, e.g. *La Grande Illusion* and *La Règle du Jeu*, are often described as 'humanist' for their compassion and sense of human unity.

Resnais, Alain (1922–) French film director. One of the best known of the French 'New Wave' directors, his films include the romance *Hiroshima mon amour* (1959) and the experimental, "Surrealist" *Last Year in Marienbad* (1961).

Reynolds, Albert (1933–) Irish politician. Elected in 1977 as a Fianna Fáil member, he held several posts under HAUGHEY but was sacked by him (1991). He eventually succeeded as *taoiseach* (prime minister) (1992).

Reynolds, Sir Joshua (1723–92) English painter and art theorist. A portraitist, influenced by his studies of Renaissance and Baroque painting and classical sculpture, he became first president of the Royal Academy.

Rice, Tim *see* LLOYD WEBBER, ANDREW.

Richard, Cliff [Harry Roger Webb] (1940–) Indian-born English singer and film actor, and an institution in British popular music.

Richard, Keith *see* JAGGER, MICK.

Richards, Viv (1952–) Antiguan-born West Indian cricketer. One of the best batsmen and fielders in modern cricket, he was captain of the West Indies (1985–91).

Richardson, Sir Ralph [David] (1902–83) English stage and film actor. Ranked with GIELGUD and OLIVIER as among the finest British actors of the 20th century, he was equally at home with the classics and modern roles. Notable film roles include Buckingham in Olivier's film of *Richard III*, the head of the secret service in *Our Man in Havana* and God in *Time Bandits* (1981).

Richardson, Samuel (1689–1761) English novelist. All his novels were written in epistolary form, and all were hugely popular. The first was *Pamela; or Virtue Rewarded*, in which a servant girl achieves an upwardly mobile marriage by resisting seduction (the work was attacked by FIELDING in his parody *Shamela* for its dubious morality). Richardson subsequently published *Clarissa Harlowe* and *Sir Charles Grandison*.

Richthofen, Manfred, Baron von (1882–1918) German fighter pilot, nicknamed the 'Red Baron'. He was credited with shooting down 80 allied aircraft.

Rimbaud, Arthur (1854–91) French poet. An early Symbolist, he stopped writing poetry at the age of nineteen. Some of the pieces in his collection of hallucinatory, vivid prose poems, *Les Illuminations*, were set to music by BRITTEN.

Rimsky-Korsakov, Nikolay Andreyevich (1844–1908) Russian composer. His music is typically Russian and he freely used local history, folk tunes, legends and myths as sources of inspiration. His works include 16 operas (e.g. *The Golden Cockerel*), three symphonies and numerous orchestral pieces.

Robeson, Paul [Le Roy] (1898–1976) American bass singer and actor. He qualified as a lawyer before becoming a highly popular stage actor in the 1920s. Notable performances include *Showboat* (1927) and *Othello* (1940). His warm, sensitive recordings of spirituals and folk songs were also very popular. A noted advocate of civil rights for Blacks, he came under strident attack in the US for supposed Communist sympathies and spent much of his life from the early 1960s in seclusion.

Robespierre, Maximilien Marie Isidore de (1758–94) French lawyer and revolutionary. He was elected to the National Assembly (1789) at the beginning of the French Revolution and became leader of the Jacobin group. He launched the infamous Reign of Terror, but was eventually guillotined himself.

Robinson, Mary (1944–) Irish barrister, politician and president (1990–) of the Republic of Ireland. Notably liberal in her policies, she won wide support from parties opposed to her opponent.

Rochester, John Wilmot, 2nd Earl of (1647–80) English poet and courtier. Renowned for his savage wit and depravity, his verse is among the most sexually explicit in English.

Rodgers, Richard [Charles] (1902–79) American composer. With the librettist Lorenz HART, he created musicals such as *The Pal Joey*). After Hart died, Rodgers collaborated with HAMMERSTEIN on several more successful musicals, e.g. *Oklahoma*.

Rodin, Auguste (1840–1917) French sculptor. He was responsible for reviving sculpture as an independent form rather than as an embellishment or decoration with works such as *The Thinker*.

Rogers, Ginger *see* ASTAIRE, FRED.

Rogers, Richard (1933–) Italian-born English architect. His designs include the Lloyds building (1979) in London, a steel and glass confection that typifies the controversial nature of his work.

Rolls, Charles Stewart (1877–1910) English motor car manufacturer and aviator. He joined Henry ROYCE in car manufacture in 1906.

Rommel, Erwin (1891–1944) German soldier. During World War II, he commanded the Afrika Korps in North Africa, earning the nickname the 'Desert Fox' for his brilliant tactics. He committed suicide after the discovery of his complicity in an assassination attempt on HITLER.

Roosevelt, Franklin D[elano] (1882–1945) American Democratic statesman. He became 32nd president of the US (1933–45) and, in order to deal with the crisis of economic collapse, instituted far-reaching 'New Deal' reforms. He was a popular and highly effective leader during World War II, dying shortly after the Yalta summit meeting with Churchill and Stalin. His wife, **[Anna] Eleanor Roosevelt** (1884–1962), was an active and popular First Lady, supporting her husband during his illness with polio. After his death she worked with the UN as US representative to the General Assembly (1946–52).

Roosevelt, Theodore (1858–1919) American Republican statesman. 26th president of the US (1901–9). He legislated against big business monopolies, intervened forcefully during the Panama civil war to protect the construction of the Panama Canal and won the 1906 Nobel Peace Prize for mediating the end of the Russo-Japanese war.

Rossetti, Christina Georgina (1830–94) English poet, noted for her reflective, occasionally melancholic religious poems. She also wrote for children. Her brother, **Dante Gabriel Rossetti** (1828–82), was both a poet and an artist, and a founder of the Pre-Raphaelite school of painting.

Rossini, Gioacchino Antonio (1792–1868) Italian composer, noted especially for his light operas, e.g. *The Barber of Seville*, *The Thieving Magpie*. His other works include a *Stabat Mater*.

Rostand, Edmond (1868–1918) French dramatist and poet. His best-known work is the verse drama *Cyrano de Bergerac* (1897).

Rostropovich, Mstislav (1927–) Russian cellist. One of the outstanding cellists of modern times, he has also given many recitals as a pianist, often accompanying his wife, the soprano **Galina Vishnevskaya** (1926–), in song recitals.

Rothko, Mark [Marcus Rothkovitch] (1903–70) Russian-born American painter. Having passed through Expressionism and Surrealism, he adopted the abstract expressionist style of painting, creating large canvases with almost luminous rectangles of colour.

Rousseau, Henri Julien ['Le Douanier'] (1844–1910) French painter. His naive style remained unaffected by all trends, and he defied conventions of colour and perspective in his exotic imaginary landscapes and painted dreams.

Rousseau, Jean-Jacques (1712–78) Swiss-born French philosopher. His most notable fictional works are the novels *Julie, or the New Héloïse* (1761) and *Emile* (1762), the former describing a highly improbable menage à trois, the latter a didactic work on how to educate children (whom he saw as naturally good). These works and others, notably the political tract *The Social Contract* (1762), which begins with the famous statement 'Man is born free, and is everywhere in chains', were profoundly influential on the intellectual ferment that led to the French Revolution. His very frank autobiography, *Confessions*, was published posthumously and set a fashion for this style of reminiscence.

Royce, Sir [Frederick] Henry (1863–1933) English engineer. In partnership with Charles ROLLS, he founded the car firm Rolls-Royce in 1906.

Rubens, Sir Peter Paul (1577–1640) Flemish painter and diplomat. He entered the service of the Duke of Mantua in Italy and became court painter to the Spanish viceroys in Antwerp. His masterpiece is the triptych *Descent from the Cross*. In 1629 he was sent to England to negotiate peace with Charles I, who knighted him.

Rubinstein, Artur (1888–1982) Polish-born American pianist. An outstanding concert pianist, he was particularly noted for his CHOPIN recitals.

Ruby, Jack *see* OSWALD, LEE HARVEY.

Rushdie, [Ahmed] Salman (1947–) Indian-born British novelist. After the publication of *Satanic Verses* (1988), Ayatollah KHOMEINI pronounced a death sentence for blasphemy on him.

Ruskin, John (1819–1900) English writer, artist and influential art critic. His works, which include *Modern Painters*, dictated Victorian taste for over half a century. He was an enthusiast for Gothic art, the Pre-Raphaelite movement and TURNER, and was a strong critic of the values and ugliness of Industrial England.

Russell, Bertrand [Arthur William] 3rd Earl Russell (1872–1970) British philosopher. He made notable contributions to mathematical and philosophical theory and, with the help of his student, WITTGENSTEIN, logical positivism. He was awarded the 1950 Nobel prize for literature.

Russell, Ken (1927–) English film director. He is especially noted for his film biographies of musicians, e.g. *Lisztomania*.

Rutherford, Ernest [1st Baron Rutherford of Nelson] (1871–1937) New Zealand physicist. He was awarded the 1908 Nobel prize for chemistry. In 1911 he deduced the existence of the atom's structure and was the first scientist to split the atom.

Sabin, Albert Bruce (1906–) Polish-born American microbiologist. He developed the Sabin polio vaccine in the mid–1950s.

Sadat, [Mohammed] Anwar El (1918–81) Egyptian statesman. He succeeded NASSER as president in 1970. After the 1973 war with Israel, he signed a peace treaty with BEGIN, for which they were awarded the 1978 Nobel Peace Prize. He was assassinated by Islamic fundamentalist soldiers during a military parade.

Sade, Donatien Alphonse François, Marquis de (1740–1814) French soldier and novelist. His highly licentious works include several novels, e.g. *Justine*. The term 'sadism' derives from the dominant theme in his life and work.

Sakharov, Andrei Dimitrievich (1921–89) Russian physicist and dissident. He developed the Russian hydrogen bomb in the 1950s and subsequently campaigned for international control of nuclear weapons. He was awarded the 1975 Nobel Peace Prize.

Saladin [Salah al-Din al-Ayyubi] (1137–93) Sultan of Egypt and Syria. The leader of the Arab world during the Crusades.

Salam, Abdus *see* WEINBERG, STEVEN.

Salk, Jonas Edward (1914–) American physician and microbiologist. He developed the Salk vaccine against polio.

Saloth Sar *see* POL POT.

Sappho (b. *c.*650 BC) Greek poet. The Greeks regarded her as one of the greatest of all lyric poets, but only short fragments of her work survivies.

Sartre, Jean-Paul (1905–80) French philosopher, novelist and dramatist. His attempts at reconciling Existentialist philosophy with Marxism are now of historical interest. His novels, however, e.g. *Nausea* (1938), are highly readable. Several of his plays, e.g. *Huis clos* (1944), are frequently performed.

Satie, Erik [Alfred Leslie] (1866–1925) French composer (his mother was a Scottish composer). His simple, classically inspired compositions were influential on DEBUSSY and RAVEL.

Saussure, Ferdinand de (1857–1913) Swiss linguist. Regarded as one of the founders of modern linguistics, he established the 'structuralist' approach to language as a social phenomenon, focusing on the arbitrary relationship between the word as 'linguistic sign' and the thing it signifies.

Schoenberg *or* **Schönberg, Arnold [Franz Walter]** (1874–1951) Austrian composer (US citizen from 1941). His early works, e.g. *Gurrelieder* (1900), are lush chromatic compositions in the late Romantic tradition. He then began composing atonal works and eventually developed his serial or 'twelve-tone method'.

Schopenhauer, Arthur (1788–1860) German philosopher. Renowned for his pessimistic outlook on life, he emphasized the active role of the will as the creative force in human thought.

Schubert, Franz [Peter] (1797–1828) Austrian composer. His works include nine symphonies, the eighth (in B minor) being the 'Unfinished', string quartets, and other chamber music. His songs, as in the song cycles *Die schöne Müllerin* and *Die Winterreise*, are regarded as some of the finest ever written, include settings of lyrics by HEINE and GOETHE, and others.

Schumacher, Ernst Friedrich (1911–77) German-born British economist. His book, *Small is Beautiful* (1973), became a founding text of the conservationist movement.

Schumann, Robert Alexander (1810–56) German composer. Noted for his espousal of Romantic values in music, his works include four symphonies, songs, and much fine piano music. His wife **Clara Schumann** (1819–96) was also a pianist and composer.

Schuschnigg, Kurt von (1897–1977) Austrian statesman. A staunch opponent of HITLER, he became chancellor in 1934 and was imprisoned by the Nazis (1938–45).

Scorsese, Martin (1942–) American film director. His films include *Taxi Driver* (1976), *Raging Bull* (1980) and *Goodfellas* (1990), these three films starring the actor most associated with Scorsese's work, Robert DE NIRO.

Scott, Robert Falcon (1868–1912) English explorer. He led two Antarctic expeditions (1901–4, 1910–12). He died with four companions on his last expedition, returning from the South Pole after having reached it a month after AMUNDSEN. His son, **Sir Peter [Markham] Scott** (1909–89), was a naturalist and artist whose television documentaries and many books were notably influential in promoting conservation.

Scott, Sir Walter (1771–1832) Scottish novelist and poet. His early, highly Romantic narrative poems, set in the Scottish past, e.g. *The Lady of the Lake*, established his popularity with both the reading public and the literary world, BYRON being particularly generous in his praise. His historical novels (a genre he refined and made into an art form), particularly *Waverley* (1814), *The Heart of Midlothian* (1818) and *Ivanhoe* (1819), were enormously influential and spawned a host of imitators.

Scriabin *or* **Skryabin, Alexander Nikolayevich** (1872–1915) Russian composer and pianist. His compositions often involved extra-musical effects, e.g. *Prometheus*, a piece for piano accompanied by coloured light projected on a screen. He envisaged all the arts coming together in one great performance.

Searle, Ronald [William Fordham] (1920–) English cartoonist and writer. Known primarily as the creator of the monstrous St Trinian's schoolgirls, who feature in several of his works, he is regarded, particularly in the US and France, as one of the finest graphic artists of the 20th century. His haunting book *To the Kwai—and Back: War Drawings 1939–45* is a record of his experiences as a Japanese prisoner of war.

Secombe, Harry *see* MILLIGAN, SPIKE.

Segovia, Andrés [Marquis of Salobreña] (1894–1987) Spanish guitarist. An internationally recognized virtuoso, he initiated a revival of interest in the classical guitar.

Sellers, Peter (1925–80) English actor and comedian. One of the founders of the Goon Show (*see* Spike MILLIGAN). He achieved further popularity as Inspector Clouseau in such films as *The Pink Panther* (1963).

Seneca [Lucius Annaeus Seneca] (*c*.4 BC–65 AD) Roman dramatist and Stoic philosopher. His verse tragedies were very influential on Elizabethan dramatists such as SHAKESPEARE.

Sennett, Mack [Michael Sinnott] (1880–1960) Canadian-born American film director and producer. He produced the manic 'Keystone Cop' comedies, which achieved international success. He also produced Charlie CHAPLIN's first films.

Seurat, Georges (1859–91) French painter, a leading neo-Impressionist. He developed the system of pointillism in which the painting is built up from tiny areas of pure colour.

Shackleton, Sir Ernest Henry (1874–1922) Anglo-Irish explorer. He served in Robert SCOTT's Antarctic expedition, and commanded two further expeditions (1908–09, 1914–16).

Shakespeare, William (1564–1616) English dramatist and poet.

His status as the greatest of all poets and dramatists has rarely been challenged. His plays are generally divided into three groups. The first group (late 1580s–*c*.1594) consists of histories, e.g. the *Henry VI* trilogy, early comedies such as *The Two Gentlemen of Verona*, and the tragedy of *Romeo and Juliet*. The second group (*c*.1595–*c*.1599) includes histories such as *King John, Henry IV Parts I and II*, the comedies *A Midsummer's Night's Dream* and *As You Like It*, and the tragedy *Julius Caesar*. The third group (*c*.1600–*c*.1612) includes the great tragedies *Hamlet, Othello, King Lear, Macbeth, Antony and Cleopatra, Coriolanus* and *Timon of Athens*, the so-called "dark comedies," *Troilus and Cressida, All's Well That Ends Well*, and *Measure for Measure*, and tragicomedies such as *The Winter's Tale* and *The Tempest*. Shakespeare's other major works are the narrative poems *Venus and Adonis* (1593) and *The Rape of Lucrece* (1594), and the magnificent *Sonnets*, which feature a romantic triangle between the poet (Shakespeare) a dark lady (identity unknown) and a beautiful young nobleman (possibly the Earl of Southampton).

Shankar, Ravi *see* RAVI SHANKAR.

Shankly, Bill [William Shankly] (1913–81) Scottish footballer and manager. Regarded as one of the outstanding football managers of the century, he transformed Liverpool into one of the most successful clubs of modern times. A renowned football fanatic, he once notoriously observed that football was more important than life or death.

Shaw, George Bernard (1856–1950) Anglo-Irish dramatist and critic. He began his literary career as a drama, literary and music critic in the 1880s, and after a false start in novel-writing, began writing plays in the 1890s. The plays, e.g. *Man and Superman* (1903), *Major Barbara* (1905) and *Pygmalion* (1913), have been very successful thanks to Shaw's mastery of witty dialogue. He was awarded the Nobel prize for literature in 1925.

Shelley, Mary Wollstonecraft (1797–1851) English novelist. Her masterpiece is *Frankenstein, or the Modern Prometheus* (1818), a Gothic fantasy that has also been hailed as the first science fiction novel.

Shelley, Percy Bysshe (1792–1822) English poet. His talent for public scandal emerged at Oxford University, where he was expelled for co-writing a tract entitled *The Necessity of Atheism* (1811), in which year he eloped with Harriet Westbrook. Two years later, he published his poem *Queen Mab*, which celebrates a future republican millenium of free love and vegetarianism. In 1814, he eloped with Mary Godwin (*see* Mary Wollstonecraft SHELLEY) and her step-sister, Jane 'Claire' Clairmont. Harriet committed suicide by drowning in 1816, in which year he married Mary. Shelley and his entourage moved to Italy in 1818, where he drowned in a sailing accident. His poems are among the greatest of English Romantic poetry. The highlights are: *Prometheus Unbound* (1820); *Adonais* (1821), his elegy on the death of KEATS; and several of the finest poems in the English language, notably *Ode to the West Wind* and *To a Skylark* (both 1820).

Sheridan, Richard Brinsley (1751–1816) Irish dramatist and politician, noted for his superb comedies of manners, *The Rivals* (1775) and *School for Scandal* (1777), both of which are firm repertory favourites. His other major play is *The Critic* (1779), a burlesque satirizing the conventions of tragedy. He was also highly regarded for his oratory in parliament.

Shockley, William Bradford (1910–89) American physicist. He shared, with BARDEEN and the Chinese-born American physicist **Walter Brattain** (1902–87), the 1956 Nobel prize for physics for his development of the junction transistor.

Shostakovich, Dimitri Dimitriyevich (1906–75) Russian composer. Many of his works, e.g. the opera *Lady Macbeth of Mtensk*, were attacked for their disregard of socialist realism. His works include 15 symphonies, 15 string quartets and song cycles.

Sibelius, Jean (1865–1957) Finnish composer. His works reflect his strong Finnish nationalism and often draw on the Finnish traditional epic, *Kalevala*.

Sidney, Sir Philip (1554–86) English poet, soldier and courtier. His works include *Arcadia* (1590), the first major English pastoral poem; the sonnet sequence *Astrophel and Stella* (1591), which inspired a host of imitations; and *A Defence of Poetry* (1595), a spirited defence of English as a medium for writing great poetry. His died in action against the Spaniards in the Netherlands.

Sihanouk, Prince Norodom (1922–) Cambodian statesman, formerly (elected) king of Cambodia (1941–55). He abdicated (in favour of his father) to become prime minister (1955–60) after independence from France in 1955, becoming head of state in 1960. He was deposed by a military coup in 1970 and fled to China, forming an alliance with POL POT's Khmer Rouge, who seized Cambodia in 1975. He again became head of state in 1975 and was deposed by Pol Pot the following year. After the Vietnamese invasion of 1979, Sihanouk formed a government in exile, in an uneasy alliance with the Khmer Rouge.

Sikorski, Wladyslaw (1881–1943) Polish general and statesman. Premier of the Polish government in exile during World War II and commander in chief of the Free Polish armed forces.

Sikorsky, Igor Ivan (1889–1972) Russian-born American aeronautical engineer. He built the first four-engined aircraft in 1913 and the first successful helicopter in 1939.

Simpson, Wallis *see* WINDSOR, DUKE OF.

Sinatra, Frank [Francis Albert Sinatra] (1915–) American singer and film actor. Regarded as one of the finest modern popular singers, with a finely tuned jazz-like sense of phrasing.

Singer, Isaac Bashevis (1904–91) Polish-born American Yiddish writer. Much of his fiction deals with the now vanished world of Polish Judaism, e.g. *The Magician of Lublin*. He was awarded the Nobel prize for literature in 1978.

Sisley, Alfred (1839–99) French painter of English extraction. Influenced by the Impressionists Renoir and Monet, he painted mainly carefully composed and sensitively coloured landscapes.

Skryabin *see* SCRIABIN.

Smith, Adam (1723–90) Scottish economist and philosopher. His book *Inquiry into the Nature and Causes of the Wealth of Nations* (1776), with its advocacy of free trade was of huge influence in the development of modern capitalist societies.

Smith, Bessie [Elizabeth Smith] (1895–1937) American blues singer, nicknamed the 'Empress of the Blues'. She became very popular with jazz audiences in the 1920s.

Smith, Ian [Douglas] (1919–) Zimbabwean politician. He was prime minister of Rhodesia (1964–79), and declared UDI (unilateral declaration of independence) from Britain in 1965 in order to maintain white minority rule. Majority rule came in 1979, with **Bishop Abel Muzorewa** (1925–) serving as caretaker premier (1979–80). MUGABE's Zanu party won the 1980 election. Smith resigned his leadership of his party in 1987.

Smith, Stevie [Florence Margaret Smith] (1902–71) English poet and novelist. Her graceful, melancholic, and occasionally fiercely funny verse has been much admired.

Smollett, Tobias [George] (1721–71) Scottish surgeon and novelist. He served in the Royal Navy as a ship's surgeon and took part in an attack upon a Spanish port in the West Indies. In the early 1740s, he set up a surgical practice in London. His picaresque novels, of which the most important are *The Adventures of Roderick Random*, *The Adventures of Peregrine Pickle*, and his masterpiece, *The Expedition of Humphrey Clinker*, are cleverly plotted satirical works rich in characterization, which achieved lasting popularity. His works influenced DICKENS.

Smuts, Jan Christian (1870–1950) South African statesman and philosopher. He commanded Boer forces during the Boer War, and became prime minister (1919–24, 1939–48).

Sobers, Gary [Sir Garfield St Auburn] (1936–) West Indian cricketer. Regarded as one of the finest all-rounders of all time.

Socrates (470–399 BC) Greek philosopher, the tutor of PLATO. The sources of his teachings are many and widely varied, but it is Plato's Socrates, with a gift for answering questions with another question, who has come down to posterity in Plato's 'Socratic' dialogues. The central theme in Socrates' thinking is a quest for truth through rigorous self-examination. He was forced to commit suicide by the Athenians for supposedly corrupting youths through teaching them 'impiety'.

Solti, Sir Georg (1912–) Hungarian-born British conductor. His recording of WAGNER's Ring cycle was particularly renowned.

Solzhenitsyn, Aleksandr Isayevich (1918–) Russian novelist and historian. He exposed the corruption and cruelty of Russian society in works such as *One Day in the Life of Ivan Denisovich* (based on his experiences in a Soviet labour camp and published in the USSR during a brief thaw in cultural restrictions), and *The First Circle* and *The Gulag Archipelago*, which had to be published abroad. He was awarded the Nobel prize for literature in 1970, and was deported from the USSR in 1974. He settled in Vermont in the USA, and returned to Russia in 1994.

Sondheim, Stephen [Joshua] (1930–) American songwriter and composer. He studied with HAMMERSTEIN and wrote the lyrics for BERNSTEIN's *West Side Story*, before writing the music and lyrics for several musicals, e.g. *A Funny Thing Happened on the Way to the Forum* and *Into the Woods*.

Sophocles (*c*.496–406 BC) Greek dramatist. Seven of his *c*.120 plays are extant. He was the most popular of the three great Athenian dramatists (the others being AESCHYLUS and EURIPIDES). The plays include *Oedipus Rex*, *Oedipus at Colonus*, and *Antigone*.

Sopwith, Sir Thomas [Octave Murdoch] (1888–1989) English aeronautical engineer. He designed and built the Sopwith Camel, one of the most successful fighter planes of World War I.

Southey, Robert (1774–1843) English poet. Closely associated with WORDSWORTH and COLERIDGE, he was poet laureate from 1813.

Spassky, Boris Vasilyevich (1937–) Russian chess player. He was world champion (1969–72).

Spence, Sir Basil (1907–76) Indian-born Scottish architect. He is famous for a few highly prestigious buildings, such as Coventry Cathedral, and notorious for some disastrous council housing.

Spencer, Lady Diana *see* CHARLES, PRINCE.

Spencer, Sir Stanley (1891–1959) English painter. An isolated figure in modern art, he is best known for his series of religious paintings, and, in his capacity as a war artist, his *Shipbuilding on the Clyde* series of panels.

Spenser, Edmund (*c*.1552–99) English poet, noted particularly for his long allegorical poem *The Faerie Queene*, which describes the adventures of 12 knights (who represent 12 virtues). Many of the adventures begin at the court of Gloriana, the Faerie Queen (an idealized version of ELIZABETH I).

Spielberg, Steven (1947–) American film director and producer. His many films include some of the most successful ever made, e.g. *Jaws*, *E.T.* and *Raiders of the Lost Ark*.

Spock, Dr [Benjamin McLane] (1903–) American pediatrician. He advocated a 'permissive', non-authoritarian approach to the raising of infants, which was popular in the 1960's.

Stalin, Joseph [Josef Vissarionovich Dzhugashvili] (1879–1953) Soviet dictator. Born in Georgia, he was expelled in 1899 from an orthodox seminary in Tiflis for expounding Marxism. After the Bolshevik Revolution, he manoeuvred his way into absolute power, shrewdly playing off his 'rightist' allies against TROTSKY and other 'leftists'. He forcibly collectivized Soviet agriculture in the 1930s and developed the Soviet Union's industrial base, using (and killing) many millions of prisoners as slave labour. His purges of the 1930s destroyed most of the surviving old Bolsheviks, as well as the army leadership. He signed a peace treaty with HITLER in 1939, and seized Poland's eastern territories after Hitler's September invasion. Forceful resistance from the Red Army, notably in the defence of Leningrad, the battle of Stalingrad, and in massive infantry and tank battles, led directly to the defeat of Hitler's regime and the occupation of eastern Europe by Stalin's forces.

Stanislavsky, Konstantin (1863–1938) Russian director and actor, who was co-founder of the Moscow Art Theatre in 1897.

The influence of his theory of acting (later dubbed 'method') has been immense. His theory is contained in such works as *An Actor Prepares* (1929) and *Building a Character* (1950).

Starr, Ringo [Richard Starkey] (1940–) English rock drummer and singer. He was the Beatles' drummer (1962–70).

Steel, Sir David [Martin Scott] (1938–) Scottish Liberal politician. He became leader of the Liberal Party in 1976 and, with David OWEN, the SDP (1981–88).

Steele, Sir Richard (1672–1729) Anglo-Irish essayist and dramatist. With ADDISON, he contributed many notable essays to the *The Tatler* and *The Spectator*. His plays were moral, Christian responses to the excess of Restoration drama and had a strong influence on 18th-century drama.

Steiner, Rudolf (1861–1925) Austrian philosopher. Influenced by theosophy, he formed his own movement of 'anthroposophy' in 1912, dedicated to developing the innate human capacity for spiritual perception, through activities such as art and dance.

Sterne, Laurence (1713–68) Irish-born English novelist. His novel *The Life and Opinions of Tristram Shandy* (1759–67) is noted for its eccentric style and humour.

Stevenson, Robert Louis [Balfour] (1850–94) Scottish novelist, poet and essayist. He trained as an advocate in Edinburgh, but decided in his twenties to be a writer. By the time his first important fictional work, *Treasure Island* (1883), had been published he had established himself as an author of note with essays, poems and two travel books, *Travels with a Donkey in the Cevennes* (1879) and *The Silverado Squatters* (1883). His masterpiece is *The Strange Case of Dr Jekyll and Mr Hyde* (1886), a disturbing story of dual personality. Other works include *Kidnapped* (1886), *The Master of Ballantrae* (1889), and the unfinished *Weir of Hermiston* (1896). He settled in Samoa, where he died.

Stewart, Prince Charles Edward [Louis Philip] (1720–88) also known as 'Bonnie Prince Charlie' or the 'Young Pretender', he led the Jacobite revolt against the Hanoverian King George III in 1745, fleeing Scotland when his Highland soldiers were defeated at Culloden in 1746. He died in Rome.

Stewart, Jackie [John Young Stewart] (1939–) Scottish racing driver. World champion 1969, 1971, 1973, he retired in 1973.

Stockhausen, Karlheinz (1928–) German composer. Regarded as the leading exponent of twelve-tone music, he also used electronic sounds in his work.

Stokowski, Leopold (1882–1977) British-born American conductor. A popularizer of classical music, he is best known for his collaboration with Walt DISNEY on the film *Fantasia*.

Stopes, Marie [Charlotte Carmichael] (1880–1958) Scottish scientist and birth-control pioneer. She began her career as a palaeobotanist, but the breakdown of her marriage led her to the study of sex education, in which field she soon became a world authority. She established a birth control clinic in Holloway in London (1920), which gave free contraceptive advice to the poor.

Stoppard, Tom (1937–) Czech-born British dramatist. His plays, e.g. *Rosencrantz and Guildenstern are Dead*, are noted for their sharp, witty wordplay and fast, cleverly plotted action.

Stowe, Mrs Harriet [Elizabeth] Beecher (1811–96) American novelist. Her great anti-slavery novel *Uncle Tom's Cabin, or, Life Among the Lowly* (1852) has been described as a factor leading to the American Civil War.

Strauss, Richard (1864–1949) German composer and conductor. His works include a series of richly orchestrated tone poems, e.g. *Also Sprach Zarathustra*, several operas, e.g. *Elektra* and *Der Rosenkavalier*, and *Four Last Songs*.

Strauss, Johann (the Younger) (1825–99) Austrian violinist, conductor and composer. One of a musical family, he wrote light music, especially Viennese waltzes, e.g. the 'Blue Danube' waltz, and 16 operettas, e.g. *Die Fledermaus*.

Stravinsky, Igor Fyodorovich (1882–1971) Russian composer. He composed ballet scores for DIAGHILEV, e.g. *Petrushka* (1911) and *The Rite of Spring* (1913), the first performance of the latter provoking a riot but now regarded as a milestone in modernist music. He later composed several austerely neoclassical works, such as the opera-oratorio *Oedipus Rex* (1927), which also displayed the influence of SCHOENBERG's serial techniques.

Strindberg, Johan August (1849–1912) Swedish dramatist and novelist. His highly innovative works, e.g. the play *Miss Julie*, have influenced many 20th-century dramatists.

Stubbs, George (1724–1806) English painter and engraver, best known for his paintings of horses.

Sun Yat-sen *or* **Sun Zhong Shan** (1866–1925) Chinese nationalist leader and statesman. He played a leading role in the overthrow of the Manchu dynasty and became the first president of the Republic of China in 1911–12.

Sutherland, Dame Joan (1926–) Australian soprano. She became one of the world's leading bel canto operatic sopranos.

Sutherland, Graham [Vivian] (1903–80) English painter. He was an official war artist (1941–45) and subsequently became a portrait painter of note.

Swift, Jonathan (1667–1745) Anglo-Irish divine, poet and satirist. His first important satirical works, published in 1704, were *The Battle of the Books*, a defence of the merits of classical literature against the claims of the moderns, and *A Tale of a Tub*, an attack on religious extremism. In politics, Swift began as a Whig but soon became a staunch Tory. He became Dean of St Patrick's Cathedral in Dublin in 1713 and published several tracts defending the Irish poor against their overlords, including the savage *A Modest Proposal* (1729). His masterpiece is *Gulliver's Travels* (1726), which culminates in Gulliver's voyage to the Houyhnhnms ('whinims'), intelligent horses whose nobility is contrasted with the brutality of humanity.

Swinburne, Algernon [Charles] (1837–1909) English poet and critic, noted for his sensuous verse which frequently created scandal, not just for their sexuality but for the author's clear dislike of Christianity.

Synge, [Edmund] John Millington (1871–1909) Irish dramatist, noted for his poetic rendering of Irish peasant speech. His masterpiece is *The Playboy of the Western World* (1907), a highly controversial comedy.

Tagore, Rabindranath (1861–1941) Indian poet and philosopher. Regarded by many Bengalis as their greatest writer, he was awarded the 1913 Nobel prize for literature.

Tati, Jacques [Jacques Tatischeff] (1908–82) French actor and film director. An ex-rugby player, he became an international comedy star with his Monsieur Hulot creation, an engagingly incompetent character at odds with the modern world. Five Hulot films were made, including *Mr Hulot's Holiday* and *Mon Oncle*.

Tatum, Art[hur] (1910–56) American jazz pianist. He was an acclaimed virtuoso of jazz piano music in the 'swing' mode.

Tatum, Edward Lawrie (1909–75) American biochemist. With the American geneticist **George Wells Beadle** (1903–89), he demonstrated that biochemical reactions in cells are controlled by particular genes. With LEDERBERG, he discovered the phenomenon of genetic recombination in bacteria. All three shared the 1958 Nobel prize for physiology or medicine.

Tavener, John Kenneth (1944–) English composer. He studied under Lennox BERKELEY, and became noted particularly for his religious compositions, e.g. the cantata *Cain and Abel*.

Taverner, John (*c.*1490–1545) English composer. He taught at Oxford University and is best known for his religious works.

Taylor, A[lan] J[ohn] P[ercivale] (1906–90) English historian. Often a controversial figure (he argued that World War II was produced by accident as much as by HITLER's design), he was admired by his peers for his research and insight into modern European history, and became the historian best known to the British public through his live lectures to television audiences.

Taylor, Elizabeth (1932–) English-born (of American parents) American film actress. Her films as a child include *National Velvet* and *Little Women*. Regarded as one of the most beautiful film stars of her generation, her films include *Cat on a Hot Tin Roof* and *Who's Afraid of Virginia Woolf?* The latter film co-starred her 5th husband, Richard BURTON, whom she married twice.

Tchaikovsky, Peter Ilyich (1840–93) Russian composer. Notable for his strong melodic sense and rejection of an overtly nationalistic and 'folk' approach to composition, his works include tone poems, a violin concerto, operas, e.g. *Eugene Onegin*, the ballets *Swan Lake* and *The Sleeping Beauty*, and the so-called 'Pathétique Sixth Symphony.

Teilhard de Chardin, Pierre (1881–1955) French Jesuit theologian, philosopher and palaeontologist. He developed a theory of evolution which he claimed was compatible with Roman Catholic teaching.

Te Kanawa, Dame Kiri (1944–) New Zealand soprano. She is regarded as one of the world's leading operatic sopranos.

Telemann, George Philipp (1681–1767) German composer. A highly prolific composer of the Baroque era, his works include over 40 operas and over 40 Passions.

Teller, Edward (1908–) Hungarian-born American physicist. Known as the 'father of the hydrogen bomb' for his ground-breaking work in that field.

Temple, Shirley (1928–) American film actress and Republican politician. She became the world's leading child film star and later developed a career in politics.

Teng Hsiao-p'ing *see* DENG XIAO PING.

Tennyson, Alfred Lord [1st Baron Tennyson] (1809–92) English poet. He first came to public notice with *Poems, Chiefly Lyrical* (1830). Subsequent volumes established him as a highly popular poet, and he was appointed poet laureate in in 1850, the year in which he published his great elegy for his dead friend A. H. Hallam, *In Memoriam*. He became a much respected public figure, with several of his poems, e.g. 'Locksley Hall' (1842), being regarded as oracular statements on the spirit of the age.

Tenzing Norgay *see* HILLARY, EDMUND.

Thackeray, William Makepeace (1811–63) Indian-born English novelist and essayist, noted particularly for the witty social satire of both his novels and his non-fiction works, e.g. *The Book of Snobs* (1846–47), a funny description of the varieties of snobbery. His masterpiece is *Vanity Fair* (1847–48), a decidedly non-moralistic tale of the opportunistic 'anti-heroine' Becky Sharp, set during the Napoleonic wars. His other works include the novels *Pendennis* (1850) and *Henry Esmond* (1852).

Thatcher, Margaret Hilda (1925–) English Conservative stateswoman. She became MP for Finchley in 1959 and, as secretary of state for education and science (1970–74) ended provision of free school milk. She defeated HEATH in the Tory leadership campaign of 1975, becoming the first woman to lead a major British political party. As prime minister (1979–1990), she launched an ideological crusade (dubbed 'Thatcherism') against what she perceived as the entrenchment of socialism in Britain, the principal elements of her attack being free-market policies and the privatization of nationalized industries. Her period of office was marked by rising unemployment and by the Falklands War of 1982, the success of which many believed to be the decisive factor in the Conservative's huge election victory of 1983 over FOOT's Labour party. Her policies were widely disliked by her political opponents and by moderate Tories, the latter forming small resistance groups around figures such as Heath and **Michael Heseltine** (1933–). Increasing dissension within her cabinet, over such issues as the highly controversial Community Charge (or Poll Tax) and the disarray of the Health Service, led to her resignation in 1990 and the election of MAJOR as prime minister.

Theresa of Calcutta, Mother [Agnes Gonxha Bojaxhiu] (1910–) Yugoslavian-born Roman Catholic nun and missionary. She founded the Order of the Missionaries of Charity in 1950. Venerated by many people as a living saint, her work in Calcutta with orphans and the dying led to her being awarded the 1979 Nobel Peace Prize.

Thomas, Dylan [Marlais] (1914–53) Welsh poet. His best-known single work is *Under Milk Wood* (1954), a radio drama in poetic prose.

Thomas à Becket *see* BECKET, THOMAS À.

Thomas Aquinas, Saint (*c*.1225–74) Italian theologian and philosopher. His writings established the need for both reason and faith in Christianity, and have become a cornerstone in the teachings of the Roman Catholic Church.

Thomson, Sir George Paget (1892–1975) English physicist. He shared the 1937 Nobel prize for physics with the American physicist **Clinton Joseph Davisson** (1881–1958) for their (independent) discovery of the diffraction of electrons by crystals.

Thomson, Sir Joseph John (1856–1940) English physicist. He was awarded the 1906 Nobel prize for physics for his discovery (1906) of the electron, one of the most significant discoveries in physics. Seven of his assistants went on to win Nobel Prizes.

Thoreau, Henry David (1817–62) American philosopher whose advocacy of self-sufficiency and passive resistance to tyranny has been very influential, GANDHI being his most notable admirer.

Thurber, James [Grover] (1894–1961) American humorist, cartoonist and essayist, much of whose work first appeared in *New Yorker* magazine, including his most famous story, 'The Secret Life of Walter Mitty'.

Tiepolo, Giambattista (1696–1770) Italian artist, the greatest decorative fresco painter of the Rococo period.

Tillich, Paul [Johannes] (1886–1965) German-born American theologian and philosopher. His highly influential writings address the problems of matching traditional Christianity with an increasingly secular society.

Tinbergen, Jan (1903–) Dutch economist (brother of Niko TINBERGEN). He shared the 1969 Nobel prize for economics with the Norwegian economist **Ragnar Frisch** (1895–1973) for their work in the field of econometrics.

Tinbergen, Niko[laas] (1907–88) Dutch ethologist (brother of Jan TINBERGEN). He shared the 1973 Nobel prize for physiology or medicine (with LORENZ and Karl von FRISCH) for his groundbreaking studies of animal behaviour.

Tintoretto, Jacopo (1518–94) Venetian painter noted for his dynamic, highly imaginative use of lighting and highlighting.

Tippett, Sir Michael (1905–) English composer. His works include several operas, e.g. *The Midsummer Marriage*, the oratorio *A Child of our Time*, symphonies, song cycles and chamber music.

Titian [Tiziano Vecelli] (c.1490–1576) Venetian painter, one of the great figures of world art. He studied with Giovanni BELLINI and worked with GIORGIONE, whom he succeeded as the master of Venetian painters for some 60 years.

Tito, Marshal [Josip Broz] (1892–1980) Yugoslav statesman. He fought with the Bolsheviks during the Russian civil war and became secretary-general of the Yugoslav Communist Party in 1937. In 1941, after the German invasion of Yugoslavia, he organized a partisan force to fight the occupiers and succeeded in diverting British aid from other guerrilla forces to his own. After the war, he established a Communist government and broke with STALIN. He succeeded in preserving a fragile Yugoslav unity, but 11 years after his death the break-up of the Yugoslav state began with Slovenia, then Croatia, declaring independence from the Serbian-dominated state in 1991.

Tojo, Hideki (1885–1948) Japanese soldier. He became minister of war (1940–44) and prime minister (1941–44). He resigned in 1944, and was executed as a war criminal.

Tolkien, J[ohn] R[onald] R[euel] (1892–1973) South African-born British fantasy writer and scholar. Probably the most influential (and best-selling) fantasy writer, the works on which his fame rests are *The Hobbit* and *Lord of the Rings*.

Tolstoy, Count Leo [Nikolayevich] (1828–1910) Russian novelist, dramatist, short-story writer and philosopher. His spiritual self-questioning resulted in some of the world's greatest works of fiction, notably *War and Peace*, a panoramic epic of the Napoleonic invasions of Russia, and *Anna Karenina*, a tragic tale of adulterous love which raises profound questions about personal social morality.

Torvill, Jayne (1957–) and **Dean, Christopher** (1958–) English ice-dance skaters. They became world champions (1981–83) and Olympic champions (1984).

Toscanini, Arturo (1867–1957) Italian conductor. Regarded as one of the most authoritarian conductors of all time, he was renowned for his devotion to authenticity and for his remarkable musical memory.

Toulouse-Lautrec, Henri [Marie Raymond] de (1864–1901) French painter and lithographer. Influenced by VAN GOGH and DEGAS, his subjects were café clientele, prostitutes and cabaret performers in and around Montmartre.

Tracy, Spencer (1900–1967) American film actor. Noted for his straightforward, yet commanding, performances, he had a long personal and professional relationship with Katharine HEPBURN.

Trevelyan, George Macaulay (1876–1962) English historian. His highly readable works include *History of England* (1926) and *English Social History* (1944) and several biographies.

Trollope, Anthony (1815–82) English novelist, whose more than 50 books are dominated by two main novel sequences: the 'Barsetshire' novels, which focus on the provincial lives of the gentry, clergy and middle classes and the 'Palliser' novels of political life. His mother, **Mrs Frances Trollope** (1780–1863), was also a prolific author.

Trotsky, Leon [Lev Davidovich Bronstein] (1879–1940) Russian revolutionary. An advocate of 'permanent revolution', he believed that socialism could not be built in one country alone, and supported the Mensheviks against Lenin's Bolsheviks. Forced into exile by STALIN in 1929, he was later assassinated by a Russian agent.

Trueman, Freddy [Frederick Sewards Trueman] (1931–) English cricketer. He was a notable fast bowler.

Truffaut, François (1932–84) French film director, critic and actor. One of the *Cahiers du Cinema* group of film critics, his first film, the semi-autobiographical *The Four Hundred Blows*, was widely praised. His other films include *Jules et Jim* and *The Last Metro*. He has acted in several films, e.g. SPIELBERG'S *Close Encounters of the Third Kind*.

Truman, Harry S (1884–1972) American Democratic statesman. He became 33rd president of the US (1945–52) after Franklin D. ROOSEVELT'S death, and authorized the dropping of the atom bombs on Hiroshima and Nagasaki. He initiated the change in US foreign policy towards the Soviet Union expressed as the 'Truman doctrine', a policy of containment of communism and aid towards groups or nations resisting communism, and approved the MARSHALL Plan of aid for Britain and Western Europe.

Turgenev, Ivan Sergeyevich (1818–83) Russian novelist, short-story writer and dramatist. His novels, e.g. his masterpiece *Fathers and Sons* (1862), explore such major issues of Russian life as serfdom and revolutionary change. The best known of his plays is *A Month in the Country* (1850).

Turing, Alan Mathison (1912–54) English mathematician. Regarded as one of the most important computer theoreticians, he developed the concept of an idealized computer called the 'Universal Automaton' (later called the 'Turing Machine'). The computer, he posited, would be able to modify its own program through a sequence on paper tape of 1s and 0s. Turing also took part in the vitally important code-breaking project at Bletchley Park in World War II, which deciphered the German 'Enigma' codes. He committed suicide.

Turner, Joseph Mallord William (1775–1851) English painter. Precociously talented, he exhibited his first work aged 15. After a trip to Italy in 1819 he became interested in gradations of shifting light and atmosphere. The works of the next two decades represent his finest period, CONSTABLE describing paintings such as *The Fighting Téméraire* (1839) as 'airy visions painted with tinted steam'. He found an influential champion in RUSKIN.

Twain, Mark [pseud. of Samuel Langhorne Clemens] (1835–1910) American novelist, short-story writer and humorist. His two most famous novels, *The Adventures of Tom Sawyer* (1876) and *The Adventures of Huckleberry Finn* (1884), have become classics of children's literature.

Tyndale, William *see* MORE, SIR THOMAS.

Ustinov, Sir Peter [Alexander] (1921–) British actor, director, dramatist and raconteur (of Russian-French parentage). His plays include *The Love of Four Oranges* (1951) and *Romanoff and Juliet* (1956). Other works include an autobiography, *Dear Me* (1977). He is best known as an engaging raconteur.

Valentino, Rudolph [Rodolfo Guglielmi di Valentina d'Antonguolla] (1895–1926) Italian-born American film actor. He became the leading screen personification of the romantic hero in many films, e.g. *The Son of the Sheik*. He died of peritonitis.

Van Allen, James Alfred (1914–) American physicist. He discovered, through detectors on the US satellite *Explorer I*, the Van Allen radiation belts outside the Earth's atmosphere.

Vanbrugh, Sir John (1664–1726) English dramatist and architect, noted for his witty comedies, e.g. *The Relapse* and *The Provok'd Wife*. He was also one of the finest architects of his day, the most famous of his buildings being Blenheim Palace.

Van der Post, Sir Laurens [Jan] (1906–) South African novelist, travel writer and mystic. His works are strongly influenced by JUNG and display a strong sympathy for the 'primitive' peoples of the world. His novels include *The Seed and the Sower* (1963), based on his experiences a a prisoner of war of the Japanese in World War II and filmed as *Merry Christmas, Mr Lawrence*. His travel books include two African classics, *Venture to the Interior* and *The Lost World of the Kalahari*.

van Eyck, Jan (*c*.1385–1441) Dutch painter. A master in the medium of oil painting, his paintings are both realistic and charged with a serene, spiritual atmosphere.

Van Gogh, Vincent *see* GOGH, VINCENT VAN.

Varèse, Edgard (1883–1965) French-born American composer and conductor. His compositions are noted for their combination of the extreme registers of instruments with taped and electronic sounds.

Vasari, Giorgio (1511–74) Italian painter, writer and architect, noted particularly for his *Lives of the Most Eminent Painters, Sculptors and Architects*, an invaluable source book for the lives of Renaissance artists.

Vaughan Williams, Ralph (1872–1958) English composer. Like HOLST, he was heavily influenced by traditional English music, particularly English folk song. His works include the choral *Sea Symphony*, *Fantasia on a Theme by Thomas Tallis*, operas, ballet music and song cycles.

Velàzquez *or* **Velàsquez, Diego Roderiguez de Silva y** (1599–1660) Spanish painter. His earliest paintings were *bodegones*, a type of genre painting peculiar to Spain, consisting largely of domestic scenes, e.g. *An Old Woman Cooking Eggs* (1618). On RUBENS' advice he travelled to Italy in 1628, where he was influenced by TITIAN and TINTORETTO, developing a lighter palette and finer brushwork. His works include the portrait of *Pope Innocent X* (1650) and *Surrender of Breda* (1634–35).

Verdi, Giuseppe (1813–1901) Italian composer. His post-1850 operas, which include *Il Trovatore* (1853), *La Traviata* (1853), *La Forza del Destino* (1862), *Aida* (1871), *Otello* (1887) and *Falstaff* (1893), were hugely popular and remain constant favourites within the repertory of most opera companies. He became a deputy in the first Italian parliament of 1860.

Verlaine, Paul (1844–96) French poet, regarded with his friend and lover RIMBAUD as an early Symbolist. Collections of his verse include *Romances Without Words*.

Vermeer, Jan *or* **Johannes** (1632–75) Dutch painter. He is best remembered for his small-scale intimate interior scenes, carefully composed and lit, usually by daylight through a window.

Verne, Jules (1828–1905) French novelist, whose innovative fantasy novels, e.g. *Voyage to the Centre of the Earth* (1864) and

20,000 Leagues Under the Sea (1969), are regarded as the earliest great science fiction novels.

Verwoerd, Hendrik Frensch (1901–66) South African politician and prime minister (1958–66). He fostered apartheid, banned the African National Congress (1960) and took South Africa out of the Commonwealth in 1961.

Vicky [Victor Weisz] (1913–66) German-born British cartoonist. He was one of the leading left-wing political cartoonists and caricaturists of his day.

Vidal, [Eugene Luther] Gore (1925–) American novelist, dramatist and critic. His American historical fiction provides an unofficial and waspishly entertaining alternative history of the US and its leaders, e.g. *Burr* (1973) and *1876* (1976). His work includes several important essay collections, e.g. *The Second American Revolution* (1982) and *Armageddon* (1987).

Villa-Lobos, Heitor (1887–1959) Brazilian composer and conductor. His popular works combined elements of traditional Brazilian music with the European classical tradition.

Virgil [Publius Vergilius Maro] (70–19 BC) Roman poet. One of the most influential poets of all time, his masterpiece is the epic poem the *Aeneid,* which charts the progrss of the Trojan hero Aeneas from the fall of Troy to the founding of the Roman state.

Visconti [di Modrone], Count Luchino (1906–76) Italian film director. He began his career as a stage designer, then worked as an assistant to RENOIR. His films include *The Damned* (1969) and *Death in Venice* (1971), both starring BOGARDE.

Vishnevskaya, Galina *see* ROSTROPOVICH, MSTISLAV.

Voltaire [pseud. of François Marie Arouet] (1694–1778) French philosopher, poet, historian, essayist, dramatist and essayist. Regarded as one of the most important of the French philosophers of the Enlightenment, his most influential single work is the *Philosophical Letters* (1734), a collection of witty, acerbic attacks on the tyranny of the *ancien régime*. His writings, with those of ROUSSEAU (with whom he disputed bitterly), are often described as the main intellectual roots of the French Revolution. His other works include the remarkable novel *Candide* (1759), which takes a markedly pessimistic view of human endeavour.

von Braun, Wernher (1912–77) German-born American rocket engineer, he designed the V–1 and V–2 rocket bombs for Germany and later the Saturn moon rockets in the US.

Wagner, [Wilhelm] Richard (1813–83) German composer. He

achieved great success with his third opera, *Rienzi* (1842). The operas which followed, *The Flying Dutchman* (1843) and *Tannhäuser* (1845) were not so popular, and, in trouble with the authorities for his radical sympathies, he fled to Paris. He established his own theatre in Bayreuth in 1876, where he staged his *Ring of the Niebelung* cycle. His strongly Romantic works revolutionized opera, with their use of leitmotif and dramatic power.

Walcott, Derek [Anton] (1930–) St Lucian-born West Indian poet and dramatist who has lived most of his life in Trinidad. His poetry includes *Omeros*, a reworking in a Caribbean setting of themes from HOMER's *Odyssey* and *Iliad* and DANTE's *Divine Comedy*. His plays draw on Creole traditions and imagery. He was awarded the Nobel prize for literature in 1992.

Waldheim, Kurt (1918–) Austrian diplomat. After service as a Nazi intelligence officer in World War II, he entered the Austrian diplomatic service and became secretary-general of the United Nations (1972–82) and president of Austria (1986–). Revelations about his role in the Nazi genocide machine in Yugoslavia during the war surfaced in the late 1980s.

Walesa, Lech (1943–) Polish trade union leader and statesman. He became the leader of the free trade union, Solidarity, in 1980, which forced substantial concessions from the Polish government. After the imposition of martial law in 1981, Solidarity was banned and he was imprisoned (1981–82). After his release, he was awarded the 1983 Nobel Peace Prize. A skilled negotiator, Walesa succeeded in getting Solidarity re-legalized, and, in 1989, in the first free elections in eastern Europe since the 1940s, a Solidarity government was formed with Walesa as president.

Wallace, Alfred Russel (1823–1913) Welsh naturalist. Independently of DARWIN, he devised a theory of evolution by natural selection, which Darwin acknowledged.

Waller, Fats [Thomas Wright Waller] (1904–43) American jazz pianist and composer, he was an exponent of the 'stride' school of jazz piano and noted for his humorous lyrics.

Wallis, Sir Barnes [Neville] (1887–1979) English aeronautical engineer. He designed the 'bouncing bombs' used in the famous 'Dambuster' bombing raids of 1943.

Walpole, Sir Robert, [1st Earl of Orford] (1676–1745) English statesman. As Chancellor and First Lord of the Treasury he was, effectively, Britain's first prime minister from 1721–42, George I having little interest in the government of Britain. His son

Horace Walpole [4th Earl of Orford] (1717–97) was an author, noted for his vast correspondence and for his fascination with the 'Gothic', which expressed itself in his conversion of his house, Strawberry Hill, into a pseudo-medieval castle, and the Gopthic novel *The Castle of Otranto*, which spawned a host of imitations.

Walter, Bruno [Bruno Walter Schlesinger] (1876–1962) German-born American conductor. Noted for his concerts and recordings of the great German Romantic composers, he is particularly associated with the works of his friend MAHLER.

Walton, Sir Earnest *see* COCKCROFT, SIR JOHN DOUGLAS.

Walton, Izaak (1593–1683) English author, best known for *The Compleat Angler*, a treatise on the art of angling.

Walton, Sir William [Turner] (1902–83) English composer. His works include a setting of Edith Sitwell's poem *Façade* for voice and instruments. His other works include the oratorio *Belshazaar's Feast* (1930–31), and several film scores, e.g. for OLIVIER's *Henry V* (1944).

Warhol, Andy [Andrew Warhola] (1930–87) American pop artist and film-maker. He became the prime exponent of Pop Art in the early 1960s with his deliberately mundane works such as his reproductions of Campbell's soup cans and his repetitive portraits of contemporary icons, such as PRESLEY, MAO and Marilyn MONROE. His films include the three-hour *Sleep*.

Washington, George (1732–99) American general and 1st president of the United States (1789–97). He became commander of the American armed forces during the War of Independence in 1785 and led them to victory. After the Philadelphia Convention of 1787, he was president of the new country (1789–97).

Watson, James Dewey (1928–) American biologist. He and Francis CRICK discovered the 'double helix' structure of DNA, for which they shared (with Maurice WILKINS) the 1962 Nobel prize for physiology or medicine.

Watson-Watt, Sir Robert Alexander (1892–1973) Scottish physicist. He played a major role in the development of radar.

Watt, James (1736–1819) Scottish engineer. His improvements to the steam engine led directly to the rapid expansion of the Industrial revolution.

Watteau, Jean-Antoine (1684–1721) French painter, an outstanding exponent of Rococo art. His work is noted for a delicacy of colour and sensitivity of composition not achieved by his imitators.

Watts, Charlie *see* JAGGER, MICK.

Waugh, Evelyn [Arthur St John] (1903–66) English novelist known for his brilliant satires, e.g. *Vile Bodies* (1930) on the brittle postwar world of upper-class England, *Scoop* (1938) on war reporting, and *The Loved One* (1948) on Californian burial practices. His work also had a deeper tone, resulting from his conversion to Catholicism in 1930. His best-known novel, *Brideshead Revisited* (1945), although still a satire displays a growing spiritual concern. His masterpiece is his *Sword of Honour* trilogy, based on his own experiences with the Communist partisans in Yugoslavia in World War II.

Wayne, John [Marion Michael Morrison] (1907–79) American film actor. A screen actor of outstanding presence, he is best known as the star of many classic westerns.

Webb, Beatrice [Potter] (1858–1943) and **Webb, Sidney James,** [Baron Passfield] (1859–1947) English social reformers and economists. Married in 1892, the Webbs were, with George Bernard SHAW and H. G. WELLS, the leading propagandists of Fabian socialism. They co-founded the London School of Economics (1895), founded the *New Statesman* (1913) and produced many of pamphlets and articles.

Weber, Carl Maria Ernst von (1786–1826) German composer, conductor and pianist. He is considered to be the creator of German romantic opera, using French opera as a framework and introducing German themes. He had a colossal influence on subsequent composers up to, and including, WAGNER. His works include the operas *Der Freischütz, Euryanthe* and *Oberon*, two symphonies, concertos, piano sonatas and many songs.

Weber, Max (1864–1920) German sociologist. Regarded as one of the founders of sociology, he devised the concept of 'ideal types' of real situations for comparative purposes.

Webern, Anton von (1883–1945) Austrian composer, and one of the leading exponents of the serial form of composition.

Webster, John (*c.*1578–*c.*1632) English dramatist, noted for two very powerful tragedies, *The White Devil* and *The Duchess of Malfi*. His bleak and chilling dialogue has rarely been matched.

Weil, Simone (1909–43) French philosopher. From an intellectual Jewish family, she chose to live as a farm and industrial labourer during the 1930s, and worked for the Republican forces during the Spanish Civil War. She later developed a strong interest in Roman Catholic mysticism. She worked for the French Resistance in London, where she starved herself to death in sympathy with the inmates of the Nazi camps.

Weill, Kurt (1900–1950) German composer, noted especially for his collaborations with BRECHT, e.g. *The Threepenny Opera* (1928). He fled from Germany in 1935, settling in the US.

Weinberg, Steven (1933–) American physicist. He devised a theory of the unity of the forces operating on elementary particles that was independently arrived at by the Pakistani physicist **Abdus Salam** (1926–), and later developed by the American physicist **Sheldon Glashow** (1932–). All three shared the 1979 Nobel prize for physics.

Weizmann, Chaim [Azriel] (1874–1952) Russian-born chemist and Israeli statesman. A distinguished scientist, he participated in the negotiations for a Jewish homeland and became first president of Israel (1949-52).

Welles, [George] Orson (1915–85)American stage and film director and actor. He achieved notoriety with his radio production of WELLS's *War of the Worlds* in 1938, which sparked off mass panic in the US. He co-wrote, produced and directed one of the greatest films of all time, *Citizen Kane*, based on the life of HEARST. His other films include *The Magnificent Ambersons*, *Macbeth* and *Othello*. His other acting roles include, most notably, Harry Lime in REED's masterpiece, *The Third Man*.

Wellington, 1st Duke of [Arthur Wellesley] (1769–1852) Anglo-Irish soldier and statesman, nicknamed the 'Iron Duke'. He distinguished himself as a commander in India, and was appointed commander of the British forces during the Peninsular War of 1808–14 and led the Allied forces to victory against NAPOLEON at Trafalgar in 1815. Respected for defeating Napoleon, he became Tory prime minister (1828–30) and opposed reform.

Wells, H[erbert] G[eorge] (1866–1946) English novelist and short-story writer. His science fiction works include several classics, e.g. *The Time Machine* (1895), *The War of the Worlds* (1898) and *The Shape of Things to Come* (1933). He was a propagandist with the WEBBS and others for Fabian socialism, and his novels on contemporary themes generally address their subject matter from a 'progressive' viewpoint, e.g. *Ann Veronica*, and sometimes with a comic or satirical element, e.g. *Love and Mr Lewisham*and *The History of Mr Polly*.

Wesley, John (1703–91) English evangelist. The 15th son of the poet and clergyman, **Samuel Wesley** (1662–1735), he joined a small group of devout Anglicans, formed by his brother **Charles Wesley** (1707–88), who subsequently became known as 'Methodists', which name was used to describe the expanding movement, and which remained within the Church of England in Wesley's lifetime.

West, Mae (1892–1980) American vaudeville artist, dramatist and film actress. Several of her plays were banned for obscenity, notably *Sex*, for which she was also briefly imprisoned. She became a major star, renowned for her sardonic wit and powerful sexuality, with such films as *She Done Him Wrong*.

Whistler, James Abbott McNeill (1834–1903) American painter. He settled in London in 1859, where he was influenced by the Pre-Raphaelites and by Japanese art. He became famous as a portraitist, with works such as *Arrangement in Grey and Black*, a portrait of the his mother. He became involved in a court case with RUSKIN, who had sneered at Whistler's work in a review of an 1877 exhibition (Whistler was awarded a penny damages).

Whitman, Walt[er] (1819–92) American poet. His collection, *Leaves of Grass*, was first published in 1855 and the book is regarded as the most important single volume of poems in American literature.

Whittle, Sir Frank (1907–) English aeronautical engineer. He designed the first operational jet engine for aircraft and the first successful flight was made in a Gloster in 1941.

Wilberforce, William (1759–1833) English philanthropist and politician. His long campaign to end the British slave trade led to its abolition in 1807.

Wilde, Oscar [Fingal O'Flahertie Wills] (1854–1900) Irish dramatist, poet, essayist and wit. He first came to notice in the late 1870s, and lived up to the 'Bunthorne' image of an aesthete presented in GILBERT and Sullivan's comic opera *Patience*. After the publication of *Poems* (1881), he made a highly successful tour of America, published his children's stories *The Happy Prince and Other Tales* in 1888, with his only novel *The Picture of Dorian Gray* following in 1890. The first of his great plays, *Lady Windermere's Fan* appeared in 1892. The succeeding plays, *A Woman of No Importance* (1893), *An Ideal Husband* (1895) and *The Importance of Being Earnest* (1895) established him as the most important dramatist of the age, with their superbly witty dialogue and biting satire. He was jailed for homosexuality (1895–57), and during his imprisonment wrote *De Profundis*. After his release, Wilde fled to France, where he wrote *The Ballad of Reading Gaol* (1898) and died in poverty.

Wilder, Billy [Samuel Wilder] (1906–) Austrian-born American film director and screenwriter. He emigrated to the US in the 1930s, winning Oscars for *The Lost Weekend*, *Sunset Boulevard* and *The Apartment*. Other films include *Double Indemnity*, *The Seven Year Itch* and *Some Like it Hot*.

Wilkins, Maurice Hugh Frederick (1916–) New Zealand physicist and biologist. His research into DNA structure resulted in CRICK and WATSON's discovery of the 'double helix' structure of DNA, for which Wilkins, Crick and Watson shared the 1962 Nobel prize for physics.

Williamson, Malcolm (1931–) Australian-born British composer. Master of the Queen's Music since 1975, his works include several operas and music for film and television.

Wilmot, John *see* ROCHESTER, 2ND EARL OF.

Wilson, Sir [James] Harold [Baron of Rievaulx] (1916–) English Labour statesman. He served in World War II as a civil servant and became an MP in 1945. He held various ministerial posts before succeeding GAITSKELL as Labour leader in 1963. He was prime minister (1964–70, 1974–76). Originally on the soft left of his party, he became a strong defender of US policy on Vietnam and imposed a statutory incomes policy to deal with the a balance of payments crisis in the mid–1960s. He unexpectedly resigned in 1976, with CALLAGHAN succeeding him as prime minister.

Wilson, [Thomas] Woodrow (1856–1924) American Democratic statesman. He was 28th president of the USA (1913–21). Re-elected in 1916 on a policy of neutrality, he declared war on Germany following the sinking of US vessels. His 'fourteen points' speech of January 1918 set out US conditions for ending the war, including the disbandment of the German, Austro-Hungarian and Ottoman empires, and imposed the armistice with Germany on Britain and France.

Windsor, Duke of [formerly Edward VIII] (1894–1972) English monarch, (1936). Highly popular with the British public for his apparent concern at the lot of the unemployed, he abdicated to marry the American divorcée, **Wallis Simpson** (1896–1986), after BALDWIN had made plain his opposition to the notion of Mrs Simpson becoming queen. He married her in 1937, after which they lived in exile, the Duke becoming governor of the Bahamas during World War II.

Wittgenstein, Ludwig [Josef Johann] (1889–1951) Austrian-born British philosopher. He studied under Bertrand RUSSELL (1912–13), who observed that he was soon learning as much from his pupil as he had taught him. On the outbreak of World War I, he returned to Austria to serve as an artillery officer and was captured. While a POW, he wrote and sent to Russell his *Tractatus Logico-Philosophicus*, a series of aphoristic propositions on the boundaries of language and philosophy in relation to the world. During the 1920s, influenced by TOLSTOY's asceticism, he gave his considerable inherited wealth away and worked as a schoolteacher. His posthumous *Philosophical Investigations* retracts the confident assertions of the *Tractatus*, focusing instead on the concept of language as a series of games in which 'The meaning of the word is its use in language.'

Wodehouse, P[elham] G[renville] (1881–1975) English novelist and short-story writer. His most famous literary creations are Bertie Wooster and his butler Jeeves.

Wollstonecraft, Mary *see* SHELLEY, MARY WOLLSTONECRAFT.

Wolsey, Cardinal Thomas (c.1475–1530) English cleric and statesman. He was made a privy councillor (1511) by HENRY VIII, who then appointed him archbishop of York (1514–30) and lord chancellor (1515–29). Instructed by the king in 1527 to negotiate with the pope the annulment of the king's marriage, his failure after two years of pressurizing Rome led to his dismissal as lord chancellor (being succeeded by Sir Thomas MORE). He died on the journey from York to London to face charges of treason.

Wood, Sir Henry [Joseph] (1869–1940) English conductor. He founded the London Promenade Concerts (the 'Proms') in 1895, which he conducted until his death.

Woolf, [Adeline] Virginia (1882–1941) English novelist and critic. Her novels, including *To the Lighthouse* and *Orlando*, are written in a fluid, poetic style using stream of consciousness narration and are recognized as being among the most innovative of the 20th century.

Wordsworth, William (1770–1850) English poet. The main figure of the English Romantic movement, his work successfully blended the personal with the natural and social worlds into a coherent whole. He became poet laureate in 1843.

Wright, Orville (1871–1948) and **Wright, Wilbur** (1867–1912) American aviators and brothers. Cycle manufacturers, they designed and built the first heavier-than-air flying machine.

Wycherley, William (1641–1715) English dramatist noted for the witty dialogue of his popular Restoration comedies.

Wyman, Bill *see* Jagger, Mick.

Yeats, W[illiam] B[utler] (1865–1939) Anglo-Irish poet and dramatist. His early works reflect his concern with Irish myth and legend. His play, *Cathleen ni Houlihan* (1902) demonstrated his support of Irish patriotism, and he later feared it had sent men to their deaths against the British. Following Irish independence, he became a member of the Irish senate. He was awarded the Nobel prize for literature in 1923. His brother, **Jack Yeats** [John Butler Yeats] (1870–1957) was an illustrator, particularly of comic strips and children's books, before turning to painting and writing.

Yeltsin, Boris Nikolayevich (1931–) Russian politician. A member of the Communist party since 1960, he was brought into the Soviet Politburo by Gorbachev in 1985, in which year he was appointed head of the Moscow party organization. His subsequent assault on the ingrained inefficiency and corruption of that body resulted in his demotion from the post and from the Politburo. In the free elections of 1989, he was elected to the Congress of People's Deputies, and won an overwhelming majority of votes in the Russian presidential election of 1990.

Zeffirelli, Franco (1923–) Italian stage and film director and designer. His films include *Romeo and Juliet* and the TV film *Jesus of Nazareth*.

Zhivkov, Todor (1911–) Bulgarian Communist statesman. Prime minister (1962–71) and president (1971–89). Under his rule, Bulgaria became the most servile of the satellites of the Soviet Union.

Zhou En Lai *see* Chou En-Lai.

Zola, Emile (1840–1902) French novelist. Regarded as the most prominent exponent of Naturalism in the novel, and a highly able propagandist for socialism and for social justice.

Zwingli, Huldreich or **Ulrich** (1484–1531) Swiss religious reformer. After Luther and Calvin, he became the most influential of the Protestant reformers.

KINGS AND QUEENS

Saxons and Danes	*Reign*
Egbert (d. 839)	802–39
Aethelwulf (d. 858)	839–58
Aethelbald (d. 860), son of Aethelwulf	858–60
Aethelbert (d. 865), second son of Aethelwulf	860–65
Aethelred (d. 871), third son of Aethelwulf	865–71
Alfred (849–99), fourth son of Aethelwulf	871–99
Edward (the Elder) (d. 924), son of Alfred	899–924
Athelstan (895–939), son of Edward	924–39
Edmund (921–46), third son of Edward	939–46
Edred (d. 955), fourth son of Edward	946–55
Edwy (d. 959), son of Edmund	955–57
Edgar (*c*.944–975), younger son of Edmund	957–75
Edward (the Martyr) (*c*.963–78), son of Edgar	975–78
Aethelred (the Unready) (*c*.968–1016), younger son of Edgar	978–1016
Edmund (Ironside) (*c*.993–1016) son of Aethelred	1016
Canute (*c*.994–1035), king of Denmark (1014–28) and England	1016–35
Harold I (Harefoot) (d. 1040), illegitimate son of Canute	1035–40
Harthacanute (*c*.1019–42), son of Canute	1040–42
Edward (the Confessor) (*c*.1003–66), younger son of Aethelred	1042–66
Harold II (1020–66), brother-in-law of Edward	1066

House of Normandy	
William I (the Conqueror) (1028–87), by conquest	1066–87
Wiliam II (Rufus) (1060–1100) third son of William I	1087–1100
Henry I (1068–1135), youngest son of William I	1100–35

House of Blois	
Stephen (*c*.1097–1154), grandson of William I	1135–54

House of Plantagenet	
Henry II (1133–89), grandson of Henry I	1154–89
Richard I (Coeur de Lion) (1157–99), third son of Henry II	1189–99
John (1166–1216), youngest son of Henry II	1199–1216
Henry III (1207–72), son of John,	1216–72
Edward I (1239–1307), son of Henry III	1272–1307
Edward II (1284–1327), son of Edward I	1307–27
Edward III (1312–77), son of Edward II	1327–77
Richard II (1367–1400), grandson of Edward III	1377–99

House of Lancaster	
Henry IV (1367–1413), grandson of Edward III	1399–1413
Henry V (1387–1422), son of Henry IV	1413–22
Henry VI (1421–71), son of Henry V	1422–61, 1470–71

House of York
Edward IV (1442–83), great-grandson of Edward III	1461–70, 1471–83
Edward V (1470–1483), son of Edward IV	1483
Richard III (1452–85), brother of Edward IV	1483–85

House of Tudor
Henry VII (1457–1509), descendant of Edward III	1485–1509
Henry VIII (1491–1547), son of Henry VII	1509–47
Edward VI (1482–1553), son of Henry VIII	1547–53
Mary I (1516–58), daughter of Henry VIII	1553–58
Elizabeth I (1533–1603), younger daughter of Henry VIII	1558–1603

House of Stuart
James I (1566–1625) (James VI of Scotland), son of Mary Queen of Scots	1603–25
Charles I (1600–49), son of James I	1625–49

Commonwealth and Protectorate
Council of State	1649–53
Oliver Cromwell (1599–1658), lord protector	1653–58
Richard Cromwell (1626–1712), lord protector	1658–59

House of Stuart (restored)
Charles II (1630–85), son of Charles I	1660–85
James II (1633–1701), younger son of Charles I	1685–88
William III (1650–1702), grandson of Charles I (ruled jointly with Mary II ,1689–94)	1689–1702
Mary II (1662–94), daughter of James II, (ruled jointly with William III)	1689–94
Anne (1665–1714), younger daughter of James II	1702–14

House of Hanover
George I (1660–1727), great-grandson of James I	1714–27
George II (1683–1760), son of George I	1727–60
George III (1738–1820), grandson of George II	1760–1820
George IV (1762–1830), son of George III	1820–30
William IV (1765–1837), third son of George III	1830–37
Victoria (1819–1901), granddaughter of George III	1837–1901

House of Saxe-Coburg/Windsor (the family name changed from Saxe-Coburg to Windsor during World War I)
Edward VII (1897–1972), son of Victoria,	1901–10
George V (1865–1936), son of Edward VII	1910–36
Edward VIII (1894–1972), son of George V	1936
George VI (1894–1952), second son of George V	1936–52
Elizabeth II (1926–), daughter of George VI	1952–

ART, MUSIC AND LITERATURE

This section of the *Concise Encyclopedia* provides essential information on terms used in the worlds of art, music and literature to enable a better understanding of these important subjects. The entries are in A to Z order, and there are cross-references, indicated in SMALL CAPITALS, to enable you to relate one term to another to improve understanding. When the name of a person is preceded by the mark ◊, you will find information on that person in the FAMOUS PEOPLE section.

*

A the sixth NOTE of the SCALE of C; it is the note to which instruments of an orchestra are usually tuned (*see* TUNING).

abbandono (*Italian*) 'passionately'.

abbreviations are employed in music for terms of expression, as *dim.* for DIMINUENDO, *f.* for FORTE; as arbitrary signs, such as two DOTS on either side of an oblique line for repetition of a group of NOTES; or as numerals, which serve as shorthand symbols for various CHORDS in FIGURED BASS.

absolute music *or* **abstract music** instrumental music that exists purely as music and does not attempt to relate to a story or image. It is the opposite of PROGRAMME MUSIC.

absolute pitch *or* **perfect pitch** the sense by which some people can exactly identify, or sing without an accompanying instrument, any NOTE they hear.

abstract art art that intentionally avoids representation of the observed world. Abstraction has long been a feature of the decorative arts and to a large degree continues to dominate 20th-century art. There are two distinct trends: one towards an ordered, hard-edged CONSTRUCTIVISM, the other leaning to a freer, more expressionistic reduction of forms.

abstract expressionism art that is based on freedom of expression, spontaneity and random composition and is characterized by loose, unrestrained brushwork and often indistinct forms, usually on large canvases. The works may or may not be figurative. The term mainly applies to an art movement of the 1940s in New York, although it was first used in 1919 with reference to the early abstract work of ◊Kandinsky. Inspired by SURREALISM, the movement represented a breakaway from the REALISM hitherto dominant in American art and went on to influence European art in the 1950s.

abstract music *see* ABSOLUTE MUSIC.

Absurd, Theatre of the a form of theatre, developed in the 1960s, that characterizes the human condition as one of helplessness in the face of an irrational, 'absurd' universe. ◊Beckett, ◊Pinter and ◊Ionesco, whose characters communicate with one another in disjointed, inconsequential language, are among the best-known practitioners of the form, whose roots go back to DADAISM. Absurdist drama reacts strongly against the conventions of naturalism. However, the only absurdist dramatist to become president of a country, Vaclav ◊Havel, has argued that the form is in fact a very efficient vehicle for describing life realistically in a totalitarian society.

a cappella *or* **alla capella** (*Italian*) literally 'in the chapel style'; it is a term that has come to mean unaccompanied choral singing.

accel. the abbreviation for ACCELERANDO.

accelerando (*Italian*) 'quickening'; a term used to indicate a gradual speeding up of pace (abbreviation ACCEL.).

accent the emphasis given to specific notes to indicate the RHYTHM of a piece of music.

acciaccatura (*Italian*) an ornamental or auxiliary NOTE, normally the SEMITONE below, played just before, or at the same time as, a regular note. An *acciaccatura* is written in small type before the regular note and has a stroke through its tail. From the Italian *acciacciare*, to crush.

accidental a NOTE in a piece of music that departs by one or two SEMITONES from the KEY SIGNATURE. It is indicated by a SHARP, FLAT or NATURAL sign before it. An accidental holds good throughout a BAR unless contradicted.

accompaniment music supporting a soloist or CHOIR. An accompaniment may be provided by an orchestra, organ or, most usually, a piano.

accordion a portable REED ORGAN, which was invented in Germany in the early 19th century. Air is forced through the reeds by means of bellows that are operated by the player's arms, and notes and chords are played by pressing buttons. The *piano accordion* has a keyboard (operated by the right hand) for playing MELODY NOTES, and buttons (operated by the left hand) for simple chords. The accordion is associated with informal or FOLK music, but it has been used by serious composers.

Acmeist group a school of Russian poetry which first emerged as a coherent group in Leningrad in 1911. In part a reaction to the more obscure aspects of SYMBOLISM, the group proclaimed the virtue of clarity of expression. It was founded by the poet Anna Akhmatova (1889–1966) whose ex-husband was executed by the Bolsheviks in 1921 and whose son was arrested and imprisoned several times during Stalin's terror.

acoustic guitar *see* GUITAR.

acoustics (1) a branch of physics that is concerned with SOUND. The main characteristics of a sound are its PITCH, intensity, RESO-

NANCE and quality. (2) the characteristics of a hall or auditorium that enable speech and music to be heard without the sounds being distorted. In a concert hall with good acoustics, sounds from the stage can be heard clearly in all quarters.

acrostic a type of poem, in which the initial letters of each line form a word reading downwards. The form was used by Roman poets, and the Elizabethan poet and statesman Sir John Davies (1569–1626) devised in *Hymns of Astraea* (1599) 26 verses, each spelling out the name of Elizabeth I ('Elisabetha Regina').

acrylic paint a versatile synthetic paint that is quick-drying and can be used in thick, heavy layers or thin washes on almost any surface. A range of matt or gloss finishes can be achieved by the use of additives.

action (1) the mechanism of a keyboard instrument that links the keyboard to the strings or, in the case of an ORGAN, to the PIPES and STOPS. (2) the gap between the strings and FINGERBOARD of a stringed instrument as dictated by the height of the BRIDGE.

action painting a form of ABSTRACT EXPRESSIONISM in which the paint is applied to the canvas in the course of a series of actions or movements by the artist. This may involve dancing, cycling or rolling about on the canvas to spread and mix the wet paint. In a less random technique the artist might paint the silhouette of a model in various poses against the canvas.

act tune *or* **curtain music** an instrumental piece of music that is played between the acts of a play while the curtain is down. It is usually associated with 17th- and 18th-century music. *See also* ENTR'ACTE; INTERLUDE; INTERMEZZO.

ad lib. abbreviation for AD LIBITUM.

ad libitum (*Latin*) literally 'at pleasure' and usually abbreviated to AD LIB. In music, the term is used to indicate that, when playing a piece, a performer can: (a) alter the TEMPO or RHYTHM; (b) choose an alternative PASSAGE by the composer; (c) improvise a CADENZA; and (d) include or omit a passage if he or she so chooses.

adagietto (*Italian*) (1) 'slow' but not as slow as ADAGIO. (2) a short composition in an adagio TEMPO.

adagio (*Italian*) (1) literally 'at ease', i.e. at a slow TEMPO. (2) a slow movement.

adagissimo (*Italian*) 'very slow'.

added sixth a frequently used CHORD created by adding the sixth note from the ROOT to a MAJOR or MINOR TRIAD; for example, in the KEY of C major, A is added above the triad of C-E-G.

additional accompaniments new or revised PARTS for extra in-struments written by later composers and added to 17th- and 18th-century works in order to increase fullness. In many cases, the additions did not match the quality of the original music, but ◊Mozart once wrote additional music for ◊Handel's MESSIAH when an organ was not available.

a due corde (*Italian*), **à deux cordes** (*French*) 'on two strings'; when applied to music for stringed instruments, the term means that a piece should be played on two strings, not just on one.

Aeolian harp a type of ZITHER which has strings of similar length but of different thickness. The instrument is not actually played but left outside to catch the wind; different CHORDS are sounded according to the speed of the wind, which makes the strings vi-brate faster or slower (*see* VIBRATION). The name is derived from Aeolus, who was the Greek god of the wind.

Aeolian mode a MODE that, on the PIANO, uses the white NOTES from A to A.

Aesthetic movement a cultural movement which developed in England in the late 19th century, characterized by a very affected and mannered approach to life and the arts, a fondness for orientalism and decadence, archaic language and pseudo-medievalism. The character Bunthorne in ◊Gilbert and Sillivan's comic opera *Patience* (1881) is a conflation of all the features found ridiculous in the movement by contemporaries: 'Though the Philistines may jostle, you will rank as an apostle in the high aesthetic band, / If you walk down Piccadilly with a poppy or a lily in your medieval hand.' Oscar ◊Wilde is the most prominent literary figure of merit associated with the movement.

aesthetics an area of philosophy concerning the ideals of taste and beauty and providing criteria for critical study of the arts. The term was coined in the mid-18th century by the German phi-losopher Alexander Baumgarten, and in the 20th century came to include a wider theory of natural beauty.

affettuoso (*Italian*) 'tender' or 'affectionate', i.e. an indication that a piece of music should be played with tender feeling.

African art a term generally used to describe African tribal art in the countries south of the Sahara Desert. Much of this art is of a group nature, in that it has cultural and religious significance at its heart rather than individual ambition. Examples of typical art forms include richly carved wooden masks and figures. Body art is also important in tribal ritual and may involve scarring, tattooing or disfigurement of parts of the body, although it can also make use of paint, beads and feathers. Brightly coloured batiks and printed fabrics are a more recent feature of this rich heritage. African tribal art had a marked influence on 20th-century art styles, as in the works of ◊Picasso and ◊Cézanne.

agitato, agitatamente (*Italian*) literally 'agitated', 'agitatedly', i.e. an indication that a piece should be played restlessly or wildly.

Agnus Dei (*Latin*) 'O Lamb of God'; the concluding part of the Latin MASS. Numerous musical settings have been made for it.

air (1) a simple TUNE or SONG. (2) a melodious BAROQUE composition.

air brush an atomizer, powered by compressed air, that is used to spray paint. It is shaped like a large fountain pen and produces a fine mist of colour, giving delicate tonal gradations and a smooth finish. Its principal use is in the fields of advertising and graphic design.

alabaster a fine-grained type of gypsum that can be translucent, white or streaked with colour. It is soft and easy to carve and is therefore a popular medium for decorative artefacts and statues. It is not as strong or weather-resistant as marble, and is not often used for outdoor works.

Alberti bass a simple accompaniment to a MELODY consisting of 'broken' or spread CHORDS arranged in a rhythmic pattern. It is so called because the Italian singer, composer and harpsichordist Domenico Alberti (1710–40) used it in his keyboard SONATAS.

alborada (*Spanish*) literally 'morning song'; a form of popular Spanish music for BAGPIPES and SIDE DRUM.

Albumblatt (*German*) literally 'album leaf'; a popular title given by 19th-century composers to short, instrumental compositions (often for the PIANO) and of a personal nature.

Aldeburgh Festival an annual music FESTIVAL held in June, which was founded by ◊Britten and the tenor Peter ◊Pears at Aldeburgh, Suffolk, in 1948. It maintains its strong association with Britten, many of whose works were first performed there.

aleatory music music which contains unpredictable or chance elements so that no two performances of a piece are ever similar. It is a form explored since 1945 by composers such as ◊Cage in his *Music of Changes*, and ◊Stockhausen.

alienation effect an effect which is supposed to occur upon an audience when the audience is reminded by action, dialogue or song that it is in fact an audience watching a play, and not, for example, waiting for a bus. The intention is to confront the audience with the artificiality of dramatic representation, through devices such as interrupting the action to address the audience, or by bursting into song, or by stylizing the stage set or action. The theory is especially associated with ◊Brecht, who claimed that his plays created an 'alienating', distancing effect, enabling the audience to resist identifying emotionally with the characters on stage and therefore more capable of absorbing the message of plays, e.g. that traditional notions of morality simply represent 'bourgeois' morality. 'Alienation effects' of the kind described by Brecht have existed in drama since before ◊Aristophanes, and form an important element in the Theatre of the ABSURD.

alla (*Italian*) 'in the style of'.

alla breve (*Italian*) (1) an instruction that a piece of music should be performed twice as fast as the NOTATION would suggest. (2) 2/2 TIME.

allargando (*Italian*) literally 'getting broader', i.e. an indication that a piece should be played grandly whilst at the same time getting slower.

alla tedesca (*Italian*) an abbreviation of *alla danza tedesca,* meaning 'in the style of a German dance'. *See* ALLEMANDE.

allegory a form of narrative in which the characters and events symbolize an underlying moral or spiritual quality, or represent a hidden meaning beneath the literal one expressed. ◊Bunyan's *Pilgrim's Progress* is the greatest English-language example of a sustained allegory.

allegretto (*Italian*) a term indicating light and moderately quick movement, but not as fast as ALLEGRO.

allegro (*Italian*) literally 'lively', i.e. in a quick TEMPO. The term is often used as the title of a bright composition or MOVEMENT.

allemande (*French*) an abbreviation of *danse allemande* or 'German dance', of which there are two forms. (1) a moderately slow dance used by 17th- and 18th-century composers as the first MOVEMENT of a SUITE of four contrasting dances. (2) a brisk dance of the 18th and 19th centuries, similar to the WALTZ.

allentando (*Italian*) 'slowing down', i.e. a term used to indicate that the TEMPO of a piece of music should be slowed down.

all' ongarese (*Italian*) 'in the style of Hungarian [gypsy] music'.

alphabet the letters used in music as they occur in the natural SCALE are C, D, E, F, G, A, B. The oldest HARPS and shepherd PIPES are believed to have had seven TONES, to which the Greeks gave the names of letters, A being the lowest. Greek NOTATION became highly complicated with the development of the MODES, and Pope Gregory the Great (540–604) changed church notation, again employing the first seven letters, indicating the lower OCTAVE by capitals, and the upper by small letters. NOTES were gradually added to the lower A, and when the modern scale was adopted in the 16th century, the lowest tone had become C instead of A. In addition, Germans use H for B natural, B for B flat.

Alphorn (*German*) a primitive type of HORN with no valves, traditionally played by Swiss herdsmen to call in their cattle in the evening. Made from wood and bark, alphorns usually have an upturned bell which rests on the ground, and they can be up to 3 metres (10 feet) long.

al segno (*Italian*) 'to the sign' (i.e. to a standard symbol used in musical NOTATION). The term is used in two ways: it can instruct the player either to go *back* to the sign and start again, or to *continue* until the sign is reached.

alt an abbreviation of the Latin phrase *in alto,* which means 'high'. It is used for the NOTES in the OCTAVE rising from G above the TREBLE CLEF; the notes in the octave above that are said to be *in altissimo*.

Altamira the site in northern Spain of prehistoric rock paintings dating from about 13000 BC, in 1879 the first ever to be discovered. Originally dismissed as forgeries, their age and authenticity were accepted as genuine only in the early 20th century. A variety of animals painted in a lively, naturalistic manner are depicted, including bison, aurochs and wild horses.

altarpiece a decorated wall, screen or sectional painting set behind the altar of a Christian church, a feature of church decor from the 11th century. There are two forms: a *retable* can be fairly large and complex, rising from floor level; a *reredos* is often smaller and may stand on the altar itself or on a pedestal behind it.

alto (*Italian*) 'high' (1) the highest adult male VOICE, which is now used only in male-voice CHOIRS. (2) an addition to the name of an instrument to indicate that it is one size larger than the SOPRANO member of the family; for example alto CLARINET. (3) a low female voice that has a greater compass than the male alto voice (usually, and more properly, called CONTRALTO).

Amati the name of a famous family of violin-makers who worked in Cremona, Italy, in the 16th and 17th centuries.

Ambrosian chants a collection of CHANTS or PLAINSONG, used in Milan Cathedral, which are named after St Ambrose (*c.* 340–97), Bishop of Milan, who greatly influenced church singing and may have introduced the antiphonal singing of the Syrian church. Despite bearing his name, the earliest surviving chants were composed long after his death.

amen (*Hebrew*) 'so be it'.

American organ *or* **cabinet organ** a REED ORGAN, similar to a HARMONIUM except that air is sucked through the reeds instead of being blown through them.

amoroso (*Italian*) 'lovingly', indicating that a piece should be played with warm affection.

amplifier any device, particularly an electric one, which renders a sound louder.

anabasis (*Greek*) a succession of ascending tones.

anacrusis (*Greek anakrousis*, literally 'a prelude') an unstressed NOTE or grouping of notes at the beginning of a musical PHRASE; it can also mean an unstressed syllable at the beginning of a SONG.

Ancients, The a group of Romantic artists working in England between 1824 and the early 1830s. Samuel ◊Palmer was a leading member of the group. Their work was mainly pastoral in theme, much inspired by ◊Blake's illustrations of ◊Virgil.

ancora (*Italian*) 'again', 'yet' or 'still', as in *ancora forte* meaning 'still loud', and *ancora più forte* meaning 'yet louder'.

andante (*Italian*) 'going' or 'moving'; it is usually used to indicate a moderate TEMPO or a walking pace. *Più andante* means 'moving more' or slightly faster. Andante is sometimes used as a title for a moderately slow piece of music.

andantino (*Italian*) 'less slow' (i.e. slightly faster) than ANDANTE.

Anfang (*German*) 'beginning'; *Anfangs* means 'from the beginning'.

anglaise (*French*) short for *danse anglaise* or 'English dance', i.e. a lively dance in quick time, such as a HORNPIPE.

Anglican chant a characteristically English way of setting to music prose, psalms and canticles, in which the number of syllables per line can vary. To accommodate this irregularity, the first NOTE of each musical PHRASE is a RECITING NOTE which is timeless and is used to sing as many syllables as necessary before moving on to notes which are sung in time and which normally carry one syllable each. It is basically a simple form of GREGORIAN CHANT.

Anglo-Saxon art a term for works of art produced in England between AD 5 and 1066. The major source of surviving artefacts is the 7th-century excavation site at Sutton Hoo, and much of the Anglo-Saxon jewellery collection at the British Museum comes from there. The abstract plant and animal designs show the influences of Celtic art typical of Anglo-Saxon craft. The late 7th and early 8th centuries saw the production of the Lindisfarne Gospels in the kingdom of Northumbria. These are famous for their delicate interwoven designs, reminiscent of Irish illuminations, as in the Book of Kells. The other centre for manuscript production was the Winchester school of the 10th century.

Angry Young Men a rather imprecise term used in mid-1950s Britain to denote a group of English writers who had little in common apart from vaguely leftish sympathies and a hatred of English provincialism and intellectual pretentiousness ('madrigalphobia'). Other characteristics of Angry Young Men included a liking for jazz, polo-neck sweaters, coffee bars, and compliant women – like their American counterparts, the ◊Beat Generation writers, Angry Young Men regarded women as appendages.

anima (*Italian*) 'soul' or 'spirit', as in *con anima,* which means that a piece should be played 'with soul' or 'with emotion'.

animato (*Italian*) 'animated'.

animo (*Italian*) 'spirit', so *con animo* indicates that a piece should be performed 'with spirit'.

animoso (*Italian*) 'spirited'.

answer the second entry of the main SUBJECT (theme) of a FUGUE which is played a FIFTH higher or lower than the first entry. In a *real answer,* the subject and answer are identical; in a *tonal answer,* the intervals in the answer are changed.

anthem the Anglican equivalent to the Roman Catholic MOTET. An anthem is usually an elaborate musical setting of non-liturgical words sung by a church CHOIR without the congregation; SOLO parts are common and accompaniment by an ORGAN is usual.

anticipation the sounding of a NOTE (or notes) of a CHORD before the rest of the chord is played.

antinovel *see* novel.

antiphon the sacred words, sung in PLAINSONG by two CHOIRS, before and after a PSALM or CANTICLE in a Roman Catholic service. *Antiphonal* is an adjective applied to the musical effect achieved by two choirs (or groups of instruments) which are positioned in different parts of a hall and sing (or play) alternately, one 'answering' the other.

Antique, The remains of ancient art, in particular Greek and Roman statues, which were taken as a standard of classical order and beauty in the representation of the human form by RENAISSANCE and NEOCLASSICAL artists.

anvil a PERCUSSION INSTRUMENT consisting of steel bars that are struck with a wooden or metal mallet. It is meant to sound like a blacksmith's anvil being struck with a hammer and was used by both ◊Verdi (in *Il Trovatore*) and ◊Wagner (in *Das Rheingold*).

a piacere (*Italian*) 'at pleasure', meaning that the performer of a piece of music is permitted to take a certain amount of liberty, particularly with TEMPO, while playing it. *See also* AD LIBITUM.

appassionato, appassionata (*Italian*) 'impassioned' or 'with passion or feeling', hence the title *Sonata appassionata* which was given to ◊Beethoven's Piano Sonata in F Minor (Op. 57).

applied art art that serves a useful purpose or that ornaments functional objects; often a synonym for *design*. Subjects included under this term are architecture, interior design, ceramics, furniture, graphics, etc. These are usually contrasted with the *fine arts* of painting, drawing, sculpture, printmaking, etc, and the division became more distinct at the time of the Industrial Revolution and the emergence of AESTHETICS. This division is still a matter of important debate.

appoggiando (*Italian*) 'leaning'; when applied to NOTES, this implies that they should pass very smoothly from one to the next.

appoggiatura (*Italian*) a term for a 'leaning' NOTE (*see also* APPOGGIANDO), indicated in the SCORE. (1) a *long appoggiatura* is a note of varying length that is different from the HARMONY note. (2) a *short appoggiatura* is a very short note of indefinite length, sometimes accented, sometimes not. (3) a *passing appoggiatura,* as used in the 18th century, normally occurs when the principal notes of a MELODY form a sequence of thirds and it is played before the beat.

aquarelle the French term for watercolour painting, where a water-based paint is applied to dampened paper in thin glazes that are gradually built up into areas of varying tone.

aquatint an etching technique where a resin-coated metal plate is placed in a bath of acid that bites into the resin, producing a pitted surface. The depth of tone intensifies the longer the plate remains in the acid, and areas required to be lighter in tone are 'stopped out', using washes of varnish. The finished print resembles a watercolour wash, and the technique of overlaying separate plates of different colours can be used to build up a range of depth and colour. The process is often combined with linear etching.

arabesque (1) a florid treatment of thematic music. (2) a lyrical piece of music that employs an exaggerated and elaborate style, as used by ◊Schumann and ◊Debussy.

Arabian Nights Entertainments *or* **The Thousand and One Nights** a compilation of stories, the earliest of which probably originated in Persia, that were translated into Arabic in the mid-9th century AD, and have become classics of Arab and world literature. The stories are told by Scheherazade to her husband, a king who has killed each previous bride following the consummation of the marriage. Scheherazade saves her life by keeping the king in suspense, postponing the conclusion of each story until the following night.

Arcadia a region of ancient Greece which became the archetypal setting for rural bliss and innocence in the arts. ◊Virgil's *Eclogues* in the 1st century BC established the use of Arcadia as a literary device for this purpose, but the ironic undertone in Virgil's work (Arcadia is largely barren) is usually missing from later writers' use of the myth. Virgil's dark undertone returns to Western culture in the work of several 16th and 17th-century painters, e.g. ◊Poussin, with reference to the phrase *Et in Arcadia Ego* ('And I [i.e. death] also in Arcadia').

archet (*French*) a BOW, such as is used to play a stringed instrument.

archi (*Italian*) 'bows', a term that refers to all stringed instruments played with a BOW.

arco (*Italian*) the singular of ARCHI. It is the usual instruction to play with the BOW after playing PIZZICATO.

ardito (*Italian*) 'bold', 'energetic'.

aria (*Italian*) a SONG or AIR. Originally the term was used for any song for one or more voices but it has come to be used exclusively for a long, SOLO song as found in ORATORIO and OPERA.

arioso (*Italian*) 'like an ARIA'. (1) a melodious and song-like RECITATIVE. (2) a short AIR in an OPERA or ORATORIO. (3) an instrumental piece that follows the style of a vocal arioso.

Armory Show the international exhibition of modern art held at the 69th Regimental Armory in New York in 1913, one of the most influential exhibitions ever shown in the US. Effectively two exhibitions in one, it represented not only a fine cross-section of contemporary American art but also a massive selection of modern European art, a total of around 1,600 works. It toured the US, arousing great controversy and excitement among the 250,000 people who paid to see it, but it served the function of restoring the life and vitality of contemporary art and critical debate in the US.

arpeggiare (*Italian*) 'to play the HARP', i.e. to play CHORDS 'spread out' as they are on the harp. *See also* ARPEGGIO.

arpeggio (*Italian*) 'HARP-wise', i.e. an indication that the NOTES of a CHORD should be played in rapid succession, as they are on a harp, and not simultaneously.

arrangement an adaptation of a piece of music for a medium different from that for which it was originally composed.

ars antiqua (*Latin*) the 'old art', i.e. music of the 12th and 13th centuries as opposed to **ars nova**, the new style of music that evolved in the 14th century.

Art Autre *or* **Art Informel** a name coined by art critic Michel Tapie in *Un Art Autre* (1952); he used it to describe nongeometric ABSTRACT EXPRESSIONISM.

Art Brut the work of anyone not linked to the art world either as professional or amateur, for example psychiatric patients or prisoners, etc. The term can also include graffiti and the work of young children. It refers to any work uninfluenced by the art world and its fashions.

Art Deco the decorative art of the 1920s and 1930s in Europe and North America, originally called *Jazz Modern*. It was classical in style, with slender, symmetrical, geometric or rectilinear forms. Major influences were ART NOUVEAU architecture and ideas from the ARTS AND CRAFTS MOVEMENT and the BAUHAUS. The simplicity of style was easily adaptable to modern industrial production methods and contemporary materials, especially plastics. This resulted in a proliferation of utility items, jewellery and furniture in an elegant streamlined form, as well as simplification and streamlining of interior decor and architecture.

Art Nouveau a style of decorative art influential and popular between 1890 and World War I in Europe and North America. Art Nouveau was primarily a design style with its main effects being seen in applied art, graphics, furniture and fabric design, and in architecture. In the fine arts it represented a move away from historical realism, but was not as vigorous or dominant as IMPRESSIONISM or CUBISM. Art Nouveau design is characterized by flowing organic forms and asymmetrical linear structures, although architectural and calligraphic forms were more austere and reserved. Its principal exponents were the Scottish architect and designer Charles Rennie Mackintosh (1868–1928) and the American designer Louis Comfort Tiffany (1848–1933).

Arts and Crafts Movement an English movement in the decorative arts towards the end of the 19th century. It was based on the ideas of the art critic John ◊Ruskin and the architect Augustus Pugin (1812–52), with reference to the medieval guilds system, and took its name from the Arts and Crafts Exhibition Society formed in 1888. The motive was to re-establish the value of handcrafted objects at a time of increasing mass-production and industrialization. Designers in the movement, with a variety of styles, attempted to produce functional objects of an aesthetically pleasing nature. The most active and important leader of the movement was William ◊Morris.

ascription *see* ATTRIBUTION.

Ashcan School a group of American painters of urban realism between 1908 and 1918. Their aim was to declare themselves primarily American painters, and they painted what they saw as American life, rejecting subject matter of academic approval. Among their influences were the works of ◊Daumier and ◊Goya.

assai (*Italian*) 'very', as in *allegro assai,* 'very fast'.

assemblage any sculptural type of construction using found objects, from pieces of painted wood to old shoes. *See also* COLLAGE.

assez (*French*) 'moderately', as in *assez vite,* 'moderately quick'.

atelier the French term for an artist's studio. In 19th-century France, an *atelier libre* was a studio where artists could go to paint a model. No formal tuition was provided, and a small fee was charged.

a tempo (*Italian*) 'in time', a term that indicates that a piece should revert to its normal TEMPO after a change of speed.

athematic music music that does not have any THEMES or TUNES as such; it is concerned with exploring the unconventional possibilities of sounds.

atonal music music that is not in any KEY. Atonal music is particularly associated with the works of ◊Schoenberg, although he preferred to use the word *pantonality,* meaning a synthesis of all the keys.

attacca (*Italian*) 'attack', i.e. start the next MOVEMENT without a pause.

attribution *or* **ascription** the assigning of an unsigned picture to a painter, using similarity of style or subject as the basis.

aubade (*French*) 'morning music', as opposed to a SERENADE.

augmentation the lengthening of the time values of NOTES in melodic parts with the result that they sound more impressive and grand. The opposite of augmentation is DIMINUTION.

augmented interval the INTERVAL formed by increasing any perfect or MAJOR interval by a SEMITONE.

augmented sixth a CHORD based on the flattened SUBMEDIANT that contains the augmented sixth INTERVAL.

augmented triad a TRIAD of which the FIFTH is augmented.

a una corda (*Italian*) 'on one string' (*compare* A DUE CORDE), meaning left-hand PEDAL (of a piano), i.e. reducing the volume.

Authorized Version *or* **King James Bible** a translation of the Bible published in 1611 in the reign of James I of England. The powerful and poetic language of the Authorized Version has made it perhaps the most influential book on writers in English from the early 17th century on. Although it is often said to be the greatest book ever written by a committee, the work is based for the most part on the great translation of 1525 by William Tyndale (*c*.1495–1536).

autograph in art, a term used to denote a painting by one artist only, and not assisted by pupils or assistants.

autoharp a type of ZITHER in which CHORDS are produced by pressing down KEYS (1) that dampen some of the strings but let others vibrate freely. The instrument was invented in the late 19th century and was popular with American folk musicians.

Automatistes a Canadian group of painters formed in the 1950s whose ideas were based on the spontaneity of creativity. One of its main proponents was Paul Emile Borduas (1905–60).

avant-garde (*French*) 'vanguard', a term applied to music (or any other art) that is considered to break new ground in style, structure, or technique.

Ave Maria (*Latin*) 'Hail Mary', a prayer to the Virgin Mary used in the Roman Catholic Church. It has been set to music by numerous composers.

B (1) the seventh note of the scale of C major. (2) abbreviation for bass or for Bachelor (as in B. Mus., Bachelor of Music).

baby grand the smallest size of grand PIANO.

Bach trumpet a 19th-century valved TRUMPET which was designed to make it easier to play the high-pitched parts that were originally composed by BACH and his contemporaries for a natural (unvalved) trumpet.

back the lower part of the sounding box of string instruments, connected in VIOLS to the sounding board or belly by a sound post set beneath the bridge. Its construction and material vitally affect the quality of the TONE (3) produced.

bagatelle (*French*) 'trifle', a short, light piece of music, usually for piano, for example, ◊Beethoven's FÜR ELISE.

bagpipes a reed instrument in which air is supplied to the PIPE or pipes from an inflated bag. Bagpipes are known to have existed for 3000 years or more and hundreds of different types are found today. The best known form of bagpipe is played in Scotland and consists of a *bag* which is inflated through a pipe and is held under the arm; a CHANTER (a REED pipe with finger holes) on which the MELODY is played; and several DRONE pipes, each of which is tuned to a different note. Air is rhythmically squeezed from the bag by the arm (and is then replenished with more breath) and is forced out through the chanter and drone pipes.

balalaika (*Russian*) a FOLK instrument of the GUITAR family, with a triangular body. It is of Tartar origin and usually has just three strings and a fretted FINGERBOARD. Balalaikas are made in several sizes and are often played in concert with one another.

ballabile (*Italian*) 'in a dancing style'.

ballad a narrative poem or song in brief stanzas, often with a repeated refrain and frequently featuring a dramatic incident. The songs sold by the vagabond Autolycus in Shakespeare's *As You Like It*, describing battles, public executions and the like, are typical examples of the sort of *broadside ballad* popular with the common people up to (and a bit beyond) Victorian times. In 1765, the antiquary Thomas Percy (1729–1811) published his *Reliques of Ancient English Poetry*, a collection of ancient and not-so-ancient traditional English poems, songs and folk ballads that was to prove immensely influential.

Examples of what has been termed the *literary ballad* soon began to appear. Notable examples include ◊Coleridge's 'Rime of the Ancient Mariner' and ◊Keats' 'La Belle Dame sans Merci'.

Among the greatest examples of the form are the *Border ballads*, which stem from the violent world of the English/Scottish borders from the late Middle Ages to the 17th century. Their merit had been recognized by Sir Philip ◊Sidney in his *Defence of Poesie* (1595), but his opinion was to remain a minority one until the late 18th century, when the rediscovery of the great ballad heritage coincided with the birth pangs of the Romantic movement, and with enthusiasm for the 'noble' and 'simple' truths of the world of traditional songs throughout Europe. Representative examples of the Border ballads are the laments 'Sir Patrick Spens' and 'The Bonny Earl of Murray', the haunting song of fairyland 'Thomas the Rhymer', and the macabre 'Twa Corbies'. The most important collection of Border ballads is that issued by Sir Walter Scott in 1802–3, *Minstrelsy of the Scottish Borders*. Many of the ballads here were written down at the dictation of the singers of the old songs themselves.

In music, a ballad is also a sentimental 'drawing-room' song of the late 19th century (sometimes referred to as a *shop ballad* to differentiate it from a broadside ballad) or a narrative song or operatic ARIA.

ballade a type of medieval French poetry, often set to music by TROUBADOURS. In music, it is a 19th-century term, coined by CHOPIN, for a long, romantic instrumental piece. Chopin wrote four outstanding ballades.

ballad opera popular OPERA composed of dialogue and SONGS with tunes borrowed from FOLK music, popular songs, and sometimes opera. They first appeared in the 18th century in England, probably the best-known being *The Beggar's Opera*.

ballet a dramatic entertainment in which dancers in costume perform to a musical ACCOMPANIMENT. Mime is often used in ballet to express emotions or to tell a story. Ballet has a long history that dates back to before the Middle Ages. In the 16th and 17th centuries, ballets often included singing and consequently were closely linked to OPERA. By the end of the 18th century, however, ballet had evolved more gymnastic qualities and, although it was still included as an integral part in many operas, it also kept a separate existence. In the 19th century, ballet achieved new heights of popularity in France and spread to Italy and Russia where several schools of ballet were established that incorporated traditional dancing into their teaching. ◊Tchaikovsky's ballet scores (e.g. *Swan Lake* and *The Sleeping Beauty*) had a massive influence on Russian ballet and greatly added to its international appeal. The Russian choreographer and entrepreneur Sergei Diaghilev (1872–1929) encouraged young composers such as ◊Stravinsky and ◊Ravel to write ballet scores. At the start of the 20th century, ballet became immensely popular in England. ◊Vaughan Williams, ◊Bliss and ◊Britten all composed notable pieces for ballet, and the outstanding British choreographers Sir Frederick Ashton

(1904–88) and Sir Kenneth Macmillan (1929–92) helped to maintain the interest. In the USA, the choreographer George Balanchine (1904–83) had an equally powerful influence, and many American composers, such as ◊Copland and ◊Bernstein, have since written ballet music. Meanwhile, ◊Prokofiev's masterpieces (e.g. *Romeo and Juliet*) maintained Russia's tradition in dancing. Today, ballet is witnessing a new revival, with SCORES being produced by young composers and with energetic companies establishing new dancing techniques.

band a term used to describe virtually any group of instrumentalists except a concert ORCHESTRA, for example dance band, JAZZ band, POP band, MILITARY BAND.

banjo a GUITAR-like, stringed instrument of Black American origin. It comprises a shallow metal (sometimes wood) drum with parchment stretched over the top while the bottom is (usually) left open. Banjos can have between four and nine strings, which are played by plucking either with the fingers or a PLECTRUM.

bar (1) a vertical line (bar line) drawn down one or more STAVES of music. (2) the space between two bar lines.

barber-shop quartet a quartet of amateur male singers who perform CLOSE-HARMONY arrangements. The tradition originated in barber shops in New York in the late 19th century.

Barbizon School a group of French landscape painters in the 1840s who based their art on direct study from nature. Their initial influences included ◊Constable as well as some of the Dutch landscape painters. Their advanced ideas represented a move away from academic conventions, and their interest in daylight effects and their bold use of colour helped prepare the way for IMPRESSIONISM.

barcarolle (*French*) a boating song with a rhythm imitating that of songs sung by gondoliers.

bard a Celtic minstrel, part of whose job it was to compose SONGS for his master. Bards traditionally held annual meetings (*Eisteddfods*) in Wales and these have been revived in recent times as competition festivals.

baritone (1) a male voice, midway between BASS and TENOR with a range of approximately two OCTAVES. (2) a BRASS INSTRUMENT of the SAXHORN family.

Baroque a cultural movement in art, music and science in the 17th century. In terms of art history, the area of reference is slightly broader and takes in the late 16th and early 18th centuries. It specifically indicates the stage between the MANNERISM of the late High RENAISSANCE and ROCOCO, into which Baroque developed. As a style it is characterized by movement, rhetoric and emotion, stemming from the achievements of the High Renaissance, and it represented a reaction away from Mannerist attitudes and techniques. ◊Caravaggio was among its leading figures when it first began in Rome, and ◊Rembrandt's work reflected Baroque trends for part of his career. Adjectivally, *baroque* can also be used to describe art from any age that displays the richness and dynamism associated with the movement.

barrel organ a mechanical ORGAN of the 18th and 19th centuries in which air was admitted into PIPES by means of pins on a hand-rotated barrel. It was restricted to playing a limited number of tunes but was nonetheless frequently used in church services. *See also* MECHANICAL INSTRUMENTS.

bass (1) the lowest adult male VOICE. (2) an abbreviation for DOUBLE BASS. (3) an addition to the instrument name to indicate the largest member of a family of instruments (except where CONTRABASS instruments are built).

bassa (*Italian*) 'low'.

bass-bar a strip of wood glued as reinforcement under the BRIDGE (1) inside the BELLY of instruments of the VIOLIN family.

bass clarinet a single-REED instrument built an OCTAVE lower than the CLARINET, with a crook and upturned bell.

bass clef *see* CLEF.

bass drum a large PERCUSSION INSTRUMENT consisting of a cylindrical wooden hoop which is usually covered on both sides with vellum. It is common in MILITARY BANDS in which it is suspended vertically from the shoulders and beaten with two sticks.

basset horn an ALTO CLARINET.

bass flute an ALTO FLUTE with a PITCH a FOURTH lower than a 'concert' or normal flute.

basso continuo *see* FIGURED BASS.

bassoon a double-reed instrument of the 16th century, consisting of a wooden tube doubled back on itself. It has a compass from B flat below BASS CLEF to E on the fourth line of the TREBLE CLEF.

basso ostinato (*Italian*) 'obstinate bass', a GROUND BASS, i.e. a bass FIGURE that is repeated many times throughout a composition (or part of a composition) while the upper parts vary.

baton the stick used by a CONDUCTOR to give commands to performers.

batterie (*French*) (*also* **battery**) (1) a 17th- and 18th-century term for ARPEGGIO. (2) the PERCUSSION section of an ORCHESTRA.

battuta (*Italian*) *see* BEAT.

Bauhaus a German school of architecture and applied arts founded by the architect Walter Gropius (1883–1969) at Weimar in 1919. One of its aims, as with the ARTS AND CRAFTS MOVEMENT, was to narrow the gap between fine and APPLIED ARTS; another was to focus on architecture as the environment of art. Each student took a six-month foundation course in practical craft skills such as weaving, glass painting and metalwork. Among the first masters were the EXPRESSIONIST painters ◊Klee and ◊Kandinsky. A more CONSTRUCTIVIST influence came when the Bauhaus moved to Dessau in 1925. Later came a shift in emphasis from craftsmanship towards industrialized mass-production. Gropius resigned from the Bauhaus in l928; it was moved to Berlin in 1932 and was closed by the Nazis in 1933. A number of Bauhaus masters emigrated to the US, where their ideas were influential.

Bayreuth a town in Germany where WAGNER arranged for the building of a festival theatre which has subsequently become internationally famous for staging his operas. Built to resemble a Greek amphitheatre, the theatre holds 1,800 people, and the special feature of a hood surrounding the orchestra pit gives the auditorium an acoustical excellence ideal for Wagner's music.

beat (1) a unit of rhythmic measure in music, indicated to a CHOIR (2) or ORCHESTRA by the movement of a conductor's BATON. The number of beats in a BAR depends on the TIME-SIGNATURE. (2) a form of 20th-century POPULAR MUSIC with a steady and powerful RHYTHM.

Beat Generation a term invented by ◊Kerouac to describe a group of American writers, artists and musicians in the 1950s. Notable Beat writers included Kerouac himself, whose novel *On the Road* (1952) became the 'Beat bible', the poets Allen Ginsberg (1926–) and Lawrence Ferlinghetti (1919–), and the novelists Neal Cassady (1926–68) and William ◊Burroughs. The Beat writers were anti-Western in their values; they dabbled in communalism, loved modern jazz and took drugs. The term 'Beat' was said to denote (a) the weariness of struggling against materialist society, (b) jazz rhythm, which they tried to capture in their prose, (c) beautitude. The last quality is somewhat dubious.

bebop a JAZZ development of the 1940s in which complex RHYTHMS and harmonic sequences were carried out against rapidly played melodic IMPROVISATION. It is particularly associated with the jazz saxophonist, Charlie ◊Parker.

Bebung (*German*) 'trembling', i.e. a VIBRATO effect caused by shaking a finger holding down a KEY (1) of a CLAVICHORD.

Bechstein a company of German piano manufacturers established in Berlin in 1856 by Friedrick Wilhelm Karl Bechstein (1826–1900). Branches of his firm were subsequently formed in France, England and Russia.

bel a unit used to measure the intensity of SOUND, named after Alexander Graham ◊Bell. *See also* DECIBEL.

bel canto (*Italian*) 'beautiful singing', a style of singing characterized by elaborate technique, associated with 18th-century Italian OPERA.

bells (*orchestral*) cylindrical metal tubes (*tubular bells*) of different lengths which are suspended from a frame and struck with a wooden mallet.

belly the upper part of the body or soundbox of a stringed instrument.

ben, bene (*Italian*) 'well', as in *ben marcato* meaning 'well marked', 'well accented'.

Benedicite (*Latin*) a CANTICLE known as the *Song of the Three Holy Children;* it is used during Lent as an alternative to the TE DEUM in the Anglican service of Morning Prayer.

Benedictus (*Latin*) (1) the second part of the SANCTUS of a Roman Catholic MASS. (2) the CANTICLE 'Benedictus Dominus Israel' or 'Blessed be the Lord God of Israel'.

berceuse (*French*) a cradle SONG.

bergamasca (*Italian*), **bergomask** (*English*) *or* **bergamasque** (*French*) (1) a popular 16th- and 17th-century dance from Bergamo in Italy. (2) a 19th-century dance in quick 6/8 TIME.

Bible, The *see* Authorized Version.

Biedermeier a style in art and architecture in Austria and Germany between 1815 and 1848. It took its name from a fictional character of the time, Gottlieb Biedermeier, who personified the philistine artistic taste of the middle classes. Architecture associated with the style is solid and utilitarian, paintings are meticulous and devoid of imagination.

big band a large BAND, most commonly associated with the SWING era. Such bands were famed for the strong dance RHYTHMS they produced.

Bildungsroman (*German*) 'education novel', a novel that describes the growth of a character (usually based on the author) from youthful naivety to a well-rounded maturity. The term derives from ◊Goethe's *Wilhelm Meister's Apprenticeship*. Two notable examples in English are ◊Dickens' *David Copperfield* and ◊Joyce's *Portrait of the Artist as a Young Man*.

binary form a structure, common in BAROQUE music, consisting of two related sections which were repeated. SONATA FORM evolved from it.

bis (*French*) 'twice', 'again'.

bitonality the use of two keys simultaneously.

blanche (*French*) 'white'; the French word for a MINIM.

blank verse a term sometimes used to denote any form of unrhymed verse but normally applied to unrhymed verse in iambic pentameters, i.e. a line of verse with five short-long 'feet', e.g. the actress Mrs Siddons's reputed remark: 'You brought me water, boy; I asked for beer' (she was known to speak unconsciously in blank verse). The form was developed in English by the Earl of Surrey (*c*.1517–47), and reached its highest peak in ◊Shakespeare's plays. Other notable works written in blank verse include ◊Milton's *Paradise Lost* and ◊Wordsworth's *Prelude*.

Blaue Reiter, Der (*German*) 'The Blue Rider', the name, taken from a painting by ◊Kandinsky, of a group of German EXPRESSIONISTS formed in Munich in 1911. Leading members were ◊Kandinsky and ◊Klee, who, although their working styles were diverse, were united by a philosophy of the creative spirit in European art. They organized two touring exhibitions in Germany in 1911 and 1912, and produced an *Almanac* (1912), which included major European avant-garde artists as well as tribal, folk and children's art. The idea of the *Almanac* was to unite music, art and literature in a single creative venture. It was intended to be the first in a series, but the group disbanded in 1914.

block chords a harmonic procedure in which the NOTES of CHORDS are moved simultaneously in 'blocks'.

Bloomsbury Group a group of artists, writers and intellectuals who lived or worked in the Bloomsbury area of London in the early decades of the 20th century and whose members included Virginia ◊Woolf and John Maynard ◊Keynes.

bluegrass a type of FOLK music originally from Kentucky, USA, (where Kentucky bluegrass grows); *see* COUNTRY AND WESTERN.

blues a 20th-century Black American SONG or lamentation following an essentially simple form of twelve BARS to each verse.

Blues music formed the basis for JAZZ; musicians favoured such instruments as the GUITAR and HARMONICA.

Bluestocking an originally disparaging term denoting members of small, mostly female groups in English 18th-century social life, who held informal discussion groups on literary and scholarly matters. The term derives from the blue stockings worn by a male member of the groups, the botanist Benjamin Stillingfleet.

bocca chiusa (*Italian*) literally 'closed mouth', i.e. humming.

body paint *see* gouache.

Boehm system an improved system of KEYS (2) and levers for the FLUTE (1) which is named after its German inventor, Theobald Boehm (1794–1881). The system is also applied to other instruments, for example, the clarinet.

bolero (*Spanish*) a moderately fast Spanish dance in triple TIME. ◊Ravel's *Bolero* (1928), a spiralling crescendo based on a repeated theme, was the music for a ballet choreographed by ◊Nijinsky.

bones a pair of small sticks (originally bones) that are held in the hands and clicked together rhythmically.

bongos pairs of small, upright Cuban DRUMS that are often found in dance BANDS. They are played with the hands.

boogie-woogie a JAZZ and BLUES style of piano playing in which the left hand plays a persistent bass RHYTHM while the right hand plays a MELODY.

Book of Common Prayer the once-official book of services for the Church of England, first published in 1549. The most loved version is that of 1662, the language of which, like that of the AUTHORIZED VERSION, has been very influential on English prose and poetry.

bop short for BEBOP.

Border ballad *see* BALLAD.

bouche fermée (*French*) *see* BOCCA CHIUSA.

bourrée (*French*) a lively French dance of the 17th century.

bouzouki a Greek stringed instrument with a long, fretted neck. Its six strings are plucked, often as an ACCOMPANIMENT to songs. The sound of the bouzouki reached a worldwide audience with the film music of the Greek composer Mikis Theodorakis (1925–).

bow a wooden stick which is strung with horse-hair and used to play instruments of the VIOLIN and VIOL families.

bowed harp a primitive VIOLIN, dating back to at least the twelfth century. It was held on the knee and played vertically.

bowing the technique of using a BOW to play an instrument.

brace the vertical line, usually with a bracket, which joins two STAVES of music to indicate that they are played together.

branle (*French*) a French FOLK DANCE from the 15th century, which had a swaying movement.

brass band a type of BAND, particularly associated with the north of England, which consists of BRASS INSTRUMENTS and DRUMS only. Brass bands have been popular in England since the beginning of the 19th century.

brass instruments a family of WIND INSTRUMENTS which are made of metal but not always brass. Instruments with REEDS and those which used to be made from wood (such as the FLUTE) are excluded. A characteristic of the family is that sound is produced by the vibration of the lips which are pressed into a funnel-shaped MOUTHPIECE. A selection of NOTES can be produced by effectively lengthening the tubing, either with a slide (as in the TROMBONE) or with valves (as in the TRUMPET). Brass instruments include the trombone, CORNET, BUGLE, trumpet, French HORN, TUBA, and EU-PHONIUM.

bravura (*Italian*) literally 'bravery', as in a 'bravura passage', a passage that demands a VIRTUOSO display by the performer.

break (1) in JAZZ, a short, improvised, SOLO passage. (2) the point in a vocal or instrumental range where the REGISTER changes.

breit (*German*) 'broadly' or 'grandly', a term used to describe the manner in which a piece should be played.

breve originally the short NOTE of music (*c*.13th century), but as other notes have been introduced, it is now the longest note and is only occasionally used.

bridge (1) a piece of wood that stands on the BELLY of stringed instruments and supports the strings. (2) a passage in a COMPOSI-TION (1) that links two important THEMES together.

brindisi (*Italian*) 'a toast', a drinking song in an opera during which toasts are often given.

brio (*Italian*) 'vigour', so CON BRIO means 'with vigour'.

brisé (*French*) 'broken'; a term which indicates that a CHORD should be played in ARPEGGIO fashion, or that music for stringed instruments should be played with short movements of the BOW.

broadside ballad *see* ballad.

broken octaves a term used to describe a passage of NOTES that are played alternately an OCTAVE apart; they frequently occur in piano music.

bronze a metal alloy of bronze mixed with tin and occasionally lead and zinc, which has been used as a medium for sculpture since ancient times, when it was cast solid using wooden models. Modern techniques use hollow casting methods of sand casting or *cire perdue* ('lost wax').

Brücke, Die (*German*) 'The Bridge', an association of German artists founded in 1905 in Dresden. The name derives from ◊Nietszche's idea that a man can be seen as a bridge towards a better future, and in this the artists saw themselves as a link with the art of the future, in a move away from REALISM and IMPRESSIONISM. They also wanted to integrate art and life, and so lived together in community in the tradition of the medieval guilds system. Their influences included AFRICAN tribal art and the works of Van ◊Gogh and FAUVISM. Their painting was mainly EXPRESSIONIST, although comprehending a variety of styles and techniques. They concentrated initially on figures in landscape and portrait, and made use of texture, clashing colour and aggressive distortion to powerful effect. They helped found the Neue SEZESSION in 1910, then split away and exhibited as a group with Der BLAUE REITER. In 1913 the group disbanded because of conflicts over aims and policies in relation to the development of CUBISM.

brushwork the 'handwriting' of a painter, i.e. the distinctive way in which he or she applies paint, either smoothly or roughly, thinly or thickly, in long strokes or short. Like handwriting, brushwork is individual to a painter.

bugle a simple BRASS INSTRUMENT with a conical tube and a cup-shaped MOUTHPIECE which was widely used for giving military signals. *See also* LAST POST.

bull roarer *see* THUNDER STICK.

burla, burlesca (*Italian*) a short and jolly piece of music.

Byzantine music music of the Christian Church of the Eastern Roman Empire which was established in AD 330 and lasted until 1435. It influenced Western church music.

C (1) the key-note or TONIC of the SCALE of C major. (2) an abbreviation for CONTRALTO; c*on* (with); *col, colla* (with the).

c.a. abbreviation for *coll' arco,* meaning 'with the BOW', as opposed to PIZZICATO (with reference to a stringed instrument).

cabaletta (*Italian*) a term for a simple ARIA with an insistent RHYTHM, or an emphatically rhythmical ending to an ARIA or DUET.

cabinet organ *see* AMERICAN ORGAN.

caccia (*Italian*) a 'hunt', as in c*orno da caccia,* hunting horn. Also a 14th-century hunting poem about country life set to music.

cachucha a Spanish solo dance in 3/4 time, resembling the BOLERO.

cacophony a discordant muddle of SOUND or DISSONANCE.

cadence literally a 'falling', a term used to describe the concluding PHRASE at the end of a section of music.

cadenza (*Italian*) literally 'cadence', but it has come to have two specific meanings: (1) an elaborate ending to an operatic ARIA. (2) a flourish at the end of a PASSAGE of SOLO music in a CONCERTO.

calando (*Italian*) 'diminishing', i.e. in both volume and speed.

calcando (*Italian*) 'pressing forward', i.e. a term used to indicate an increase in speed.

calypso a kind of song with SYNCOPATED RHYTHMS from the West Indies, notably Trinidad; calypso LYRICS are usually witty and topical, and are often vehicles for political satire.

cambiata (*Italian*) an abbreviation for *nota cambiata*, CHANGING NOTE.

camera (*Italian*) literally a 'room', but in musical terms it refers to a type of music that can be performed in a place other than a church, music hall, or opera house, etc; *see* CHAMBER MUSIC.

campanelli (*Italian*) *see* GLOCKENSPIEL.

campanology the art of bell-ringing or the study of bells.

campus novel a NOVEL with a university setting. They are invariably satirical and are equally invariably written by former or practising academics. An early example is Kingsley ◊Amis's *Lucky Jim* (1954). Some novelists, such as David ◊Lodge, whose *Small World* is perhaps the definitive example, have made a speciality of the genre. Another notable example is *The History Man* (1975) by Malcolm Bradbury (1932–). American examples tend towards anguish and 'relationships'; the British are more concerned with casting a cold eye on the harsh world of academic politics.

cancan a Parisian music-hall dance of the late 19th century in quick 2/4 time.

cancel (*US*) *see* NATURAL.

cancrizans a type of music that makes sense if it is played backwards; RETROGRADE MOTION.

canon a COUNTERPOINT composition in which one part is imitated and overlapped by one or more other PARTS, for example, a SOPRANO lead with a TENOR follow-up. In a 'strict' canon, the imitation is exact in every way.

cantabile (*Italian*) 'song-like', a term applied to instrumental pieces indicating that they should be played in a singing style.

cantata originally a piece of music of the BAROQUE period that is sung (as opposed to a SONATA, a piece which is played). It has come to be a term used to describe a vocal or CHORAL piece with an instrumental accompaniment. German cantatas were generally religious works. In many ways, the form is similar to OPERA and ORATORIO, but it tends not to be so elaborate.

canticle a HYMN that has words from the Bible, other than a PSALM.

cantor (*Latin*) a 'singer'; nowadays the term refers to the chief singer in a CHOIR or the lead singer of liturgical music in a synagogue.

cantus firmus (*Latin*) 'fixed song', i.e. a MELODY in POLYPHONIC music, often taken from PLAINSONG, with long NOTES (1) against which COUNTERPOINT tunes are sung.

canzone, canzona, canzon literally 'song'; a vocal work, or an instrumental piece that is modelled on music for the VOICE.

canzonet (1) a short kind of CANZONE. (2) a type of MADRIGAL or a simple SOLO SONG.

capotasto (*Italian*) the 'head of the fingerboard', i.e. the raised part or 'nut' at the top of the FINGERBOARD of a stringed instrument that defines the lengths of the strings. A moveable capotasto, comprising a wood or metal bar that can be clamped to the fingerboard, is occasionally used on fretted instruments to shorten all the strings at the same time, thus raising the PITCH.

cappella, a *see* A CAPPELLA.

capriccio (*Italian*) 'caprice'; a short, lively piece.

caricature a drawing of a person in which his or her most prominent features are exaggerated or distorted in order to produce a recognizable but ridiculous portrait, possibly suggesting a likeness to another object. The technique was pioneered in the late 16th century and flourished in the 18th and 19th centuries.

carillon (1) a set of bells, usually in a bell tower, which can be played by electrical or mechanical means to produce a tune. (2) an ORGAN STOP which produces a bell-like sound.

carol originally, any medieval English song with a refrain, but now generally a song associated with Christmas.

cartoon (1) a drawing, or series of drawings, intended to convey humour, satire or wit. Cartoons were commonly used from the 18th century onwards in newspapers and periodicals as a vehicle for social and political comment, and in comic magazines for children and adults in the 20th century. (2) a full-size preparatory drawing for a painting, mural or fresco. The drawing was fully worked out on paper and then mapped out on to the surface to be painted.

castanets a Spanish PERCUSSION INSTRUMENT comprising two shell-like pieces of wood which are clicked together by the fingers. In orchestras, they are occasionally shaken on the end of sticks.

castrato (*Italian*) an adult male singer with a SOPRANO or CONTRALTO voice produced by castration before puberty. Castrati were popular singers in the 17th and 18th centuries. The practice was abandoned during the 19th century.

catch a ROUND for three or more VOICES. The words are often humorous and frequently contain puns, for example, *Ah, how Sophia* which, when sung, sounds like 'Our house afire'.

Cavalier Poets a loose grouping of lyric poets associated with the court or cause of Charles I during his clashes with the English Parliament and the ensuing Civil War. (Poets such as Marvell and Milton who supported Parliament, however, are not known as Roundhead poets.) The most notable Cavalier poets are ◊Herrick, Sir John Suckling (1609–41), Thomas Carew (*c*.1595–1640) and Richard Lovelace (1618–*c*.1658). The latter's witty and graceful 'To Althea' is perhaps the most loved of the Cavalier poems.

cavatina (*Italian*) a short and often slow SONG or instrumental piece.

Cave Paintings see Altamira; Lascaux.

CB an abbreviation for *contrabasso* (DOUBLE BASS).

cebell a 17th-century English dance similar to the GAVOTTE.

Cecilia, St the patron saint of music who was martyred in the second or third century. Since the 16th century music festivals to commemorate her have been annual events. Her feast day is 22 November.

ceilidh (*Gaelic*) a gathering at which SONGS, FOLK music and dances are performed; ceilidhs are particularly associated with Scotland and Ireland.

celesta a small keyboard instrument in which HAMMERS are made to strike metal bars suspended over wooden resonators; the sound produced has an ethereal, bell-like quality. ◊Tchaikovsky included a celesta in the' Dance of the Sugar-Plum Fairy' in his ballet *The Nutcracker*.

cello *see* VIOLONCELLO.

cembalo (*Italian*) (1) a DULCIMER. (2) an abbreviation of *clavicembalo*, which is the Italian for HARPSICHORD.

CF abbreviation for CANTUS FIRMUS.

chaconne (*French*) a slow dance in triple time that is thought to have originated in Mexico.

chalk a soft stone, similar to a very soft limestone, used for drawing. *Crayon* is powdered chalk mixed with oil or wax.

chalumeau (*French*)) (1) a generic term for a type of REED-PIPE. (2) a term now used for the lower REGISTER of the CLARINET.

chamber music originally, chamber music was a term used to describe any type of music that was suitable for playing in a room of a house as opposed to a church or concert hall. However, it has come to mean music for a small number of instruments (for example, flute and piano) or group of performers (for example, STRING QUARTET, SEXTET, etc.), with one instrument to each part.

chamber orchestra a small orchestra, sometimes solely of stringed instruments, for performing CHAMBER MUSIC.

change-ringing an English method of ringing a peal of church bells; the bells are rung in an established order, which then passes through a series of changes.

changing note *or* **cambiatta** a dissonant PASSING NOTE which is a third away from the preceding note, before being resolved.

chanson (*French*) a song for either a SOLO VOICE or a CHOIR. In some contexts it can also mean an instrumental piece of song-like quality.

chant a general term for a type of music which is sung as part of a ritual or ceremony. It is a term which is used particularly for unaccompanied singing in religious services.

chanter the pipe of a BAGPIPE, on which the MELODY is played.

chanterelle (*French*) literally the 'singing one', i.e the highest string on a bowed, stringed instrument (for example, the E string on a VIOLIN).

character piece a term used by composers for a short instrumental piece, such as may attempt to describe a specific mood. Examples are ◊Schumann's *Fantasiestücke*, *Nachtstücke*, and *Albumblätter*.

charcoal the carbon residue from wood that has been partially burned. Charcoal will make easily erasable black marks and is used mainly to make preliminary drawings, e.g. on walls. When used on paper it has to be coated with a fixative to make the drawing permanent.

charleston a ballroom dance, similar to the FOXTROT, which was evolved by black Americans of the Southern USA.

chest voice the lower REGISTER (2) of VOICE (1), so called because NOTES seem to emanate from the chest. *Compare* HEAD VOICE.

chevalet (*French*) the BRIDGE of a stringed instrument.

chiaro, chiara (*Italian*) 'clear', 'distinct'.

chiaroscuro (*Italian*) literally 'light-dark', used to describe the treatment of light and shade in a painting, drawing or engraving to convey depth and shape. It is particularly used of works by painters like ◊Caravaggio or ◊Rembrandt.

chinoiserie In the 16th and 17th centuries, trade with the Far East created a European market for Chinese art and influenced the development of a vogue for things Chinese. Pagodas and stylized scenes, plants and animals conceived to be in the Chinese style began to decorate pottery, furniture, fabrics and ornaments. These were finally mass-produced, both in Europe and the Far East, specifically for this market. A familiar product in this style is the famous Willow Pattern pottery range.

chitarrone (*Italian*) a large LUTE.

choir (1) the place, defined by special seats or 'choir stalls', in a large church or cathedral where singers are positioned. (2) a body of singers, such as a male-voice choir, church choir. (3) (US) a section of the orchestra, for example 'brass choir'.

choirbook a large medieval volume that (usually) included both words and music and was designed to be read by various members of a CHOIR (2) while it was stationed on a centrally placed lectern.

choir organ the section of an ORGAN that is played from the lowest MANUAL and is soft enough to accompany a church CHOIR (2).

choral an adjective used to describe music that involves a CHORUS, for example CHORAL SYMPHONY.

chorale a HYMN-tune of the Lutheran Church, but dating back to the 15th century.

chorale cantata a CANTATA that was written to be performed in a (Lutheran) church.

choral symphony (1) a SYMPHONY in which a CHORUS is used at some point (or, indeed, a symphony written entirely for voices). (2) the popular name of ◊Beethoven's symphony no. 9 in D Minor, which ends with 'An die Freude' ('Ode to Joy') for chorus and soloists.

chord a combination of NOTES played simultaneously, usually not less than three.

chorus (1) a body of singers. *See* CHOIR. (2) music written for a body of singers (usually to follow an introductory piece). (3) a REFRAIN that follows a SOLO verse.

chromatic (from Greek *chromatikos,* 'coloured') a term used to describe NOTES which do not belong to a prevailing SCALE, for example, in C major all SHARPS and FLATS (1) are chromatic notes. The 'chromatic scale' is a scale of twelve ascending or descending SEMITONES; and a 'chromatic CHORD' is a chord that contains chromatic notes. *See also* TWELVE-NOTE MUSIC.

ciaccona (*Italian*) *see* CHACONNE.

cimbal, cimbalom *see* DULCIMER.

cinquecento the Italian term for the 16th century.

circular breathing the technique of sustaining a NOTE when playing a WIND INSTRUMENT by breathing in through the nose while sounding the note.

cittern a pear-shaped stringed instrument of the GUITAR family popular from the 16th century to the 18th century It was similar to the LUTE except that it had a flat back and wire strings, and was easier to play.

clappers virtually any kind of PERCUSSION INSTRUMENT comprising two similar pieces that can be struck together, for example BONES, spoons, sticks.

clarinet a single-REED WOODWIND instrument dating back to the 17th century. It has a cylindrical tube and nowadays comes in two common sizes: B flat and A. It is an instrument common to both CLASSICAL music and JAZZ.

clàrsach (*Gaelic*) a small harp of the Scottish Highlands and Ireland.

classical (1) a term used to describe a certain form of music which adheres to basic conventions and forms that are more concerned with carefully controlled expression rather than unrestrained emotion. (2) a term used to describe 'serious' music as opposed to popular music.

Classicism a style of art based on order, serenity and emotional control, with reference to the classical art of the ancient Greeks and Romans. It eschews the impulsive creativity and sponteneity of Romanticism in favour of peace, harmony and strict ideals of beauty. Figures drawn in the classsical style were usually symmetrical and devoid of the normal irregularities of nature. *See also* NEOCLASSICISM.

clavecin (*French*) *see* HARPSICHORD.

claves short sticks that are held in the hand and clicked together to emphasize a BEAT (1) or RHYTHM. They originated in Cuba.

clavicembalo (*Italian*) *see* HARPSICHORD.

clavichord a keyboard instrument dating from the 15th century in which the strings are struck by a brass 'tangent' and can be made to sound a note of variable PITCH until the KEY (1) is released. However, the sound is soft and the keyboard is limited; the instrument fell out of favour with the introduction of the PIANO.

clavier (1) a practice keyboard which makes no sound save clicks. (2) any keyboard instrument that has strings, for example, the CLAVICHORD, the HARPSICHORD, the PIANO.

clef a symbol positioned on a line of a STAVE which indicates the PITCH of the line and consequently all the NOTES on the stave. Three clefs are commonly used: ALTO (TENOR), TREBLE and BASS.

Clerihew a verse form invented by Edmund Clerihew ◊Bentley with two rhymed couplets of variable length and often encapsulating an unreliable biographical anecdote: 'Mr Michael Foot/ Had lots of loot;/ He loved to gloat/ While petting his stoat.'

close harmony HARMONY in which the NOTES of the CHORDS are close together. In singing, this means that each VOICE remains fairly close to the MELODY.

coda (*Italian*) literally a 'tail', meaning a PASSAGE at the end of a piece of music which rounds it off.

col, coll', colla, colle (*Italian*) literally 'with the', so *col basso* means 'with bass'; *colle voce*, 'with voice'.

collage a piece of art created by adhering pieces of paper, fabric, wood, etc, on to a flat surface. The technique was popular with the Cubists, Braque and Picasso, and is a precursor of the more sculptural methods of assemblage.

coloratura (*Italian*) the florid ornamentation of a melodic line, especially in opera.

colour (1) in art, an effect induced in the eye by light of various wavelengths, the colour perceived depending on the specific wavelength of light reflected by an object. Most objects contain pigments that absorb certain light frequencies and reflect others, e.g. the plant pigment chlorophyll usually absorbs orange or red light and reflects green or blue, therefore the majority of plants appear to be green in colour. A white surface is one where all light frequencies are reflected and a black surface absorbs all frequencies. Artists' colours are made by combining pigments of vegetable or mineral extraction with an appropriate medium, e.g.

linseed oil. The rarity of some mineral pigments has a direct effect on the prices of particular colours. (2) in music, the TONE quality of instruments and voices.

colour field painting a movement begun by abstract expressionists towards a more intellectual abstraction. Their paintings were large areas of pure, flat colour, the mood and atmosphere being created by the shape of the canvas and by sheer scale.

colourist a term in art criticism referring to an artist who places emphasis on colour over line or form. For example, ◊Titian and ◊Giorgione have been called the 'Venetian Colourists'. The term is, however, too vague to be applied consistently.

combination tone a faint (third) NOTE that is heard when two notes are sounded simultaneously; also called a 'resultant tone'.

combo an abbreviation of 'combination', especially a collection of musicians that make up a JAZZ BAND.

comedy a form of drama, usually of a light and humorous kind and frequently involving misunderstandings that are resolved in a happy ending. The first major examples known, those by ◊Aristophanes, are still among the greatest, and became known as *old comedy*. The roots of Aristophanes' work are ancient, based on fertility rituals, and often involve ferocious attacks on named individuals, e.g. ◊Euripedes and ◊Socrates. The outrage caused by Aristophanes' plays led to the Athenians banning the ridicule of named individuals on stage. The so-called *new comedy* that then developed in Greece is known to us largely through adaptations of lost Greek originals by Roman dramatists. It is this new comedy, based upon Aristotle's opinion that the business of comedy is with people of no significance (who can be safely ridiculed), that was to prevail on the stage until the advent of ◊Chekhov, ◊Ibsen and ◊Strindberg, with their downbeat comedies of middle-class life. These latter comedies may loosely be described as *tragicomedies*, although the term is normally reserved to denote those plays of the Jacobean period, such as Beaumont and ◊Fletcher's *Philaster* (1609) and *A King and No King* (1611), and ◊Shakespeare's 'dark comedies', e.g. *Measure for Measure* (1604), in all of which the action seems to be leading inexorably towards a tragic ending, but resolves itself (more or less) happily at the end, after trials, tests and tribulations. Other notable forms of comedy include the comedy of HUMOURS, the COMEDY OF MANNERS, SENTIMENTAL COMEDY and COMMEDIA DELL'ARTE. *See also* MELODRAMA, *compare* TRAGEDY.

comedy of humours see HUMOURS, THEORY OF.

comedy of manners a form of comedy that features intrigues, invariably involving sex and/or money, among an upper region of society. The central characters are usually witty sophisticates, and there is often much mockery of characters from inferior stations who try to imitate the behaviour of their betters, e.g. a merchant trying to live the lifestyle of a gallant. The form is associated particularly with RESTORATION dramatists such as William Congreve (1670–1729), Sir George Etherege (*c.*1634–91) and ◊Wycherley. The finest of these Restoration comedies is Congreve's *The Way of the World* (1700).

comic opera an OPERA that has an amusing plot, or (sometimes) an opera that includes some spoken dialogue.

commedia dell'arte a form of Italian comedy, popular from the RENAISSANCE until the 18th century, that used stock farcical characters (such as Harlequin and Columbine) and plots as a basis for improvization. Actors wore masks representing their particular characters, and were often skilled acrobats. The COMMEDIA DELL'ARTE form was given new life by ◊Goldoni.

common chord a MAJOR or MINOR CHORD, usually consisting of a keynote and its third and FIFTH.

comodo (*Italian*) 'convenient', as in *tempo comodo,* meaning at a 'convenient speed'.

compass the musical RANGE of a VOICE or instrument.

composition in art, the arrangement of elements in a drawing, painting or sculpture in proper proportion and relation to each other and to the whole. In music, (1) a work of music. (2) the putting together of sounds in a creative manner. (3) the art of writing music.

compound interval an INTERVAL which is greater than an OCTAVE.

compound time musical TIME in which each BEAT (1) in a BAR is divisible by three, for example 6/8, 9/8 and 12/8 time.

computer-generated music music that is created by feeding a formula or program into a computer, which then translates the program into sounds.

con (*Italian*) 'with', so *con amore* means 'with love', i.e. lovingly, tenderly.

concert a public performance of secular music other than an OPERA or BALLET.

concert grand a large GRAND PIANO that is used in concert halls.

concertina a type of ACCORDION, hexagonal in shape, with small studs at each end which are used as keys.

concertmaster (*US*) the first violinist, or leader of an orchestra.

concerto (*Italian*) (1) originally, a work for one or several voices with instrumental ACCOMPANIMENT. (2) a work for several contrasted instruments. (3) an orchestral work in several movements, containing passages for groups of SOLO instruments (*concerto grosso*). (4) a piece for a solo instrument and an accompanying orchestra.

concert overture an orchestral piece of one MOVEMENT, similar to an opera OVERTURE, but written solely for performance in a concert hall. It originated in the 19th century. Examples are ◊Mendelssohn's *Hebrides* and ◊Tchaikovsky's *Romeo and Juliet*.

concert pitch the internationally agreed PITCH, according to which A above middle C (in the middle of the TREBLE CLEF) is fixed at 440 hertz (cycles per second).

Concertstück, Konzertstück (*German*) a short CONCERTO.

concitato (*Italian*) 'agitated'.

concord a combination of sounds (such as a CHORD) that are satisfactory and sound agreeable. The opposite of DISSONANCE.

concrete art a term used to describe severely geometrical abstract art.

concrete music *see* MUSIQUE CONCRÈTE.

conducting the art of directing and controlling an ORCHESTRA or CHOIR (or operatic performance) by means of gestures. As well as indicating the speed of a piece, a conductor, who often uses a BATON to exaggerate his or her arm movements, is also responsible for interpreting the music.

conga (1) a tall, narrow DRUM which is played with the hands. (2) an entertaining dance in which the participants form a long, moving line one behind the other.

conjunct a succession of NOTES of different PITCH.

conservatory a school that specializes in musical training. The term originates from the kind of charitable institutions for orphans, called *conservatorii* in 16th- and 17th-century Italy, where music was taught to a high standard.

consort an old spelling of the word 'concert', meaning an ENSEMBLE of instruments, for example, a consort of VIOLS.

Constructivism a movement in abstract expressionism concerned with forms and movement in sculpture and the aesthetics of the industrial age. It began in post-World War I Russia with the sculptors Antoine Pevsner (1886–1962), his brother Naum Gabo (1890–1979) and Vladimir Tatlin (1885–1953). Their work, which made use of modern plastics, glass and wood, was intentionally nonrepresentational. Their ideas were published in Gabo's *Realistic Manifesto* (1920). Gabo and Pevsner left Russia in 1922 and 1923 respectively and went on to exert great influence on western art. Tatlin remained to pursue his own ideals of the social and aesthetic usefulness of his art.

Constructivist theatre a form of theatre devised by Vsevolod Meyerhold (1874–1940), Russian theatrical producer and director. By the time the Bolsheviks came to power in 1917, Meyerhold was recognized as the most prominent exponent of avantgarde ideas and productions on the Russian stage. Among the plays he produced at his Meyerhold Theatre were those of Mayakovsky (*see* FUTURISM). His productions (which were strongly influential on ◊Brecht) cheerfully abandoned traditional conventions, such as the proscenium arch, and broke plays up into episodic segments. Stage sets were determinedly Constructivist, i.e. they used technological artefacts derived from industrial processes to emphasize the kinetic, active nature of the stage (in large part, a development from Russian Futurism). Actors were encouraged to think of themselves as 'biomechanisms', and to study circus acrobatics and the conventions of COMMEDIA DELL' ARTE. Meyerhold's ideas inevitably proved intolerable to the Soviet cultural commissars of Socialist realism and he was executed.

continuo (*Italian*) an abbreviation of *basso continuo*. *See* FIGURED BASS.

contrabass (1) (adjective) an instrument that is an OCTAVE lower than the normal BASS of the family, for example, contrabass TUBA. (2) (noun) a DOUBLE BASS.

contralto the lowest female VOICE, which usually has a range of about two OCTAVES.

contrapuntal relating to COUNTERPOINT.

contratenor the 14th- and 15th-century word for a VOICE with approximately the same range as a TENOR.

contredanse (*French*) a French corruption of 'country dance', i.e. a lively dance.

cor (*French*) *see* French horn *under* HORN.

cor anglais (*French*) literally 'English horn', but it is neither English nor a HORN. It is in fact an ALTO OBOE pitched a FIFTH below the standard oboe.

coranto (*Italian*) *see* COURANTE.

corda (*Italian*) a 'string', as in 'piano string'; the term *una corda* literally means 'one string', an indication to use the 'soft' PEDAL on the PIANO.

cornet (1) a BRASS INSTRUMENT with three valves that has a quality of TONE (3) lying between a HORN and a TRUMPET; it has great flexibility and is often used in MILITARY and JAZZ BANDS. (2) an ORGAN STOP used for playing flourishes.

cotillion a popular ballroom dance of the early 19th century.

cottage piano a small upright PIANO.

counterpoint the combination of two or more independent melodic lines that fit together to create a coherent SOUND texture. The CLASSICAL (1) conventions of HARMONY are based on counterpoint.

counter-subject a MELODY, found in a FUGUE, that is CONTRAPUNTAL to the main THEME (SUBJECT), i.e. after singing the subject, a VOICE (2) carries on to sing the counter-subject while the answer is sung.

counter-tenor the highest natural male VOICE (not to be confused with FALSETTO).

country and western a generic term for a form of 20th-century American folk music, originating from the southeast of the USA, with Nashville, Tennessee, as its traditional home. It is usually played by small BANDS using FIDDLES, GUITARS, BANJOS and DRUMS etc. The songs are typically of a sentimental, sometimes tragic, nature. Lively BLUEGRASS music is a form of country and western.

couplet (1) the same as DUPLET. (2) a two-note SLUR. (3) a SONG in which the same music is repeated for every STANZA.

courante (*French*) short for *danse courante* or 'running dance', a lively Baroque dance in triple time.

cow bell as used as a PERCUSSION INSTRUMENT in an orchestra, it is an ordinary square cow bell with the clapper taken out. It is played with a drumstick.

crayon *see* CHALK.

credo (*Latin*) 'I believe', the first word in the Roman Catholic Creed.

crescendo (*Italian*) 'increasing', i.e. getting gradually louder.

croche (*French*) a QUAVER.

crook (1) a detachable section of tubing that was inserted into a BRASS or WOODWIND INSTRUMENT between the MOUTHPIECE and the body of the instrument to give it a different KEY (by increasing the length of the air-column). Performers often had as many as twelve crooks but the introduction of valved instruments in the 1850s virtually dispensed with their necessity. (2) a curved metal tube between the mouthpiece and the body of large wind instruments such as the BASSOON and BASS CLARINET.

crooning a soft, sentimental style of singing, often to DANCE MUSIC. Bing ◊Crosby was a noted 'crooner'.

cross rhythms rhythms that appear to have conflicting patterns and are performed at the same time as one another.

crotchet (*US* 'quarter note') a NOTE with a quarter of the time value of a whole note (SEMIBREVE).

Cruelty, Theatre of a form of theatre devised by the French actor and theatre director Antonin Artaud (1896–1948) which uses non-verbal means of communication such as pantomine, light effects and irrational language, to project the pain and loss fostered by the modern world. His aim was to use drama to subvert the idea of art as a set of concepts separate from real life and he has had a lasting effect on Western drama.

crumhorn *see* KRUMHORN.

Cubism an art movement started by ◊Picasso and ◊Braque, and influenced by AFRICAN tribal masks and carvings, and by the work of ◊Cézanne. They moved away from REALIST and IMPRESSIONIST trends towards a more intellectual representation of objects. Hitherto, painters had observed subjects from a fixed viewpoint, but the Cubists also wanted to represent a more cerebral understanding of their subject. The result was an explosion of multi-viewpoint images, often broken up into geometric shapes and realigned to suggest faces full on and in profile together, to explain the three-dimensional variety of an object or to imply movement. Such fragmented images could be highly complicated. Cubism had an enormous and continuing influence on 20th-century art.

cuckoo a short PIPE with a single finger hole; it gives two notes that imitate the sound of the bird.

cue a catchword or note on a score, used to indicate the entrance of a voice or instrument.

curtain music *see* ACT TUNE.

curtall a small BASSOON of the 16th and 17th centuries.

cycle a series or sequence of pieces of music, by a single composer, which have a common THEME or idea.

cymbalo *see* DULCIMER.

cymbals PERCUSSION INSTRUMENTS comprising two metal plates which are held in the hands and clashed together. They are mounted on stands for JAZZ and POPULAR MUSIC DRUM KITS, where they are operated by pedals or struck with sticks.

czárdás a Hungarian dance with two parts (a slow section and a fast section) that alternate.

D (1) the second NOTE of the SCALE of C major. (2) abbreviation for DOMINANT, and for doctor (as in D.Mus., Doctor of Music).

da capo (*Italian*) 'from the head'; it is an instruction to repeat the beginning of the piece (abbreviation: DC).

Dada an art movement that began in Zurich in 1915, its name randomly chosen from a lexicon. Dada represented a reaction to postwar disillusion with established art. Leading figures included Jean ◊Arp and the poet Tristan Tzara (1896–1963), and, when the movement spread to New York, Francis Picabia (1879–1953) and ◊Duchamp. Its aim was to reject accepted aesthetic and cultural values and to promote an irrational form of non-art, or anti-art. The random juxtapositions of collage and the use of ready-made objects suited their purpose best. A notable example is Duchamp's *Fountain* (1917), which was an unadorned urinal. Dada gave way to NEUE SACHLICHKEIT around 1924 as the artists associated with the movement diversified. It led, however, to the beginnings of SURREALISM and is the source of other movements in ABSTRACT ART, such as ACTION PAINTING.

dal segno (*Italian*) 'from the sign', i.e. go back to the point in the music marked by the relevant symbol and repeat the music which follows it (abbreviation: DS).

damp to stop the vibrations of an instrument by touching it, or part of it, for example the strings of a HARP, the skin of a DRUM.

Dämpfer (*German*) a MUTE.

Danube School a school of German painters who developed the art of landscape painting as a genre in its own right. Its most prominent member was Albrecht Altdorfer (1480–1538) whose work is characterized by a fantastic inventiveness, distortion of figures and brilliant effects of colour and light.

DC *see* DA CAPO.

début (*French*) 'beginning', i.e. a first appearance.

decibel one tenth of a BEL, a unit for measuring SOUND. A decibel represents the smallest change in loudness that can be detected by the average human ear.

deciso (*Italian*) literally 'decided', i.e. with decision or 'play firmly'.

Deconstruction *see* STRUCTURALISM.

decrescendo (*Italian*) 'decreasing', i.e. getting gradually softer.

degree a step of a SCALE; the position of each NOTE on a scale is identified by its degree.

delicatamente (*Italian*) 'delicately'.

delicato (*Italian*) 'delicate'.

descant (1) a soprano part, sometimes improvised, sung above a HYMN TUNE while the tune itself is sung by the rest of the congregation or CHOIR. (2) (spelt **discant** by music scholars) a general term for all forms of POLYPHONY used from the 12th century.

De Stijl *see* STIJL, DE.

deus ex machina a Latin term meaning 'god from the machine', i.e. a god introduced into the action of a play to resolve some intractable situation in the plot. The device was used commonly in both Greek and Roman drama. In Greek drama, the intervention took the form of the god being lowered onto the stage via some kind of stage machinery. ◊Euripides seems to have been particularly fond of the device, but it was rarely used by ◊Aeschylus and ◊Sophocles. The term has come to denote any twist in a plot which resolves or develops the action in an unexpected way. The device became an extremely common feature of Victorian literature and drama, in the form of legacies from long-lost relatives enabling otherwise impossible marriages to take place and foiling innumerable wicked schemes. The device has been rarely used in modern serious literature, except for ironic effect, as at the end of David ◊Lodge's novel *Nice Work*.

deux temps (*French*) in 2/2 TIME. *Valse à deux temps* is a WALTZ which has only two dance steps to every three BEATS of the BAR.

development the expansion or changing in some way of parts of a THEME of music that have already been heard, e.g. by varying the RHYTHM or elaborating the PHRASE to give it new impetus.

diapason (1) the term given to a family of ORGAN STOPS which are largely responsible for the TONE of the instrument. (2) (*French*) a TUNING FORK; *diapason normal* means the same as CONCERT PITCH.

diatonic belonging to a SCALE. The diatonic NOTES of a major scale consist of five TONES (T) and two SEMITONES (S), arranged TTSTTTS. *Compare* CHROMATIC.

dièse (*French*) sharp.

Dies Irae (*Latin*) 'Day of Wrath', a part of the REQUIEM MASS, with a PLAINSONG MELODY which has often been used by ROMANTIC composers such as ◊Berlioz, ◊Liszt, and ◊Rachmaninov.

digital (1) one of the KEYS on the keyboard of a PIANO or ORGAN. (2) in sound recording, a method of converting audio or analogue signals into a series of pulses according to their voltage, for the purposes of storage or manipulation.

diminished interval a PERFECT or MAJOR INTERVAL reduced by one SEMITONE by flattening the upper NOTE or sharpening the lower one.

diminished seventh chord a CHORD which covers a MINOR SEVENTH diminished by one SEMITONE, i.e. C-B flat diminished to C-A. (This is in fact equivalent to a major sixth, but the term 'diminished seventh' is often used.) It is frequently employed as a means of TRANSITION into another KEY.

diminished triad a MINOR TRIAD in which the FIFTH is flattened (diminished), for example in the KEY of C major, C-E-G flat.

diminuendo (*Italian*) 'diminishing', i.e. getting gradually quieter.

diminution the shortening of NOTE TIME-values, so that a MELODY is played more quickly, usually at double speed.

diptych a pair of paintings or carvings on two panels hinged together so that they can be opened or closed.

direct a sign placed at the end of a line or page of old music that indicates the PITCH of the following NOTE or notes.

discant *see* DESCANT.

discord a CHORD or combination of NOTES which creates an unpleasant or jarring sound that needs to be resolved.

dissonance the creation of an unpleasant sound or DISCORD.

distemper an impermanent paint made by mixing colours with eggs or glue instead of oil.

divertimento (*Italian*) an 18th-century term for a piece of music that was intended to be a light entertainment, i.e. a diversion. ◊Mozart wrote many divertimenti.

divertissement (*French*) (1) a short ballet incorporated into an opera or play. (2) a short piece that includes well-known tunes taken from another source. (3) a DIVERTIMENTO.

divisé (*French*) *see* DIVISI.

divisi (*Italian*) 'divided'; a term used to indicate that, where a PART is written in double NOTES, performers should not attempt to play all the notes but should divide themselves into groups to play them. It is particularly used in music for STRINGS.

division (1) a 17th-century type of VARIATION in which the long NOTES of a MELODY were split up into shorter ones. (2) an obsolete term for long vocal RUNS used by composers such as ◊Bach and ◊Handel.

Divisionism *see* POSTIMPRESSIONISM.

'Dixieland' a simple form of traditional JAZZ which originated in New Orleans at the start of the 20th century.

do (*Italian*) *see* DOH.

dodecaphonic relating to dodecaphony, the TWELVE-NOTE SYSTEM of composition.

doh the spoken name for the first NOTE of a MAJOR SCALE in TONIC SOL-FA.

dolce (*Italian*) 'sweet' or 'gentle'.

dolcissimo (*Italian*) 'very sweet'.

dolente (*Italian*) 'sorrowful'.

doloroso (*Italian*) 'sorrowfully'.

domestic tragedy a form of tragedy that appeared in the Elizabethan period, which focuses on the crises of middle-class domestic life in an unpatronizing and sympathetic manner. An early example is the anonymous *Arden of Faversham* (1592). *The London Merchant* (1731) by George Lillo (1693–1739), which was much admired and very influential throughout Europe, established the genre as a highly popular (and profitable) one. The form is closely related to sentimental comedy, and was also influential on the development of melodrama.

dominant (1) the fifth NOTE above the TONIC of a MAJOR or MINOR SCALE. (2) the name given to the RECITING NOTE of GREGORIAN CHANTS.

doppio (*Italian*) 'double', as in *doppio movimento*, meaning 'twice as fast'.

Dorian mode a term applied to the ascending SCALE which is played on the white keys of a PIANO beginning at D.

dot a MARK used in musical NOTATION. When it is placed after a NOTE, it makes the note half as long again; when it is placed above a note it indicates STACCATO.

dotted note *see* DOT.

double (1) a word used to describe certain instruments that are built an OCTAVE lower than normal, for example a double BASSOON (also called a *contrabassoon*) is built an octave lower than a standard bassoon. (2) a term used to describe a type of VARIATION found in 17th-century French instrumental music in which MELODY NOTES are embellished with ornamentation.

double bass the largest and lowest-pitched of the bowed string instruments. It used to have three strings but now it has four (sometimes five).

double counterpoint COUNTERPOINT in which the two PARTS can change places, i.e. the higher can become the lower and vice versa.

double fugue (1) a FUGUE with two SUBJECTS. In one type of double fugue both subjects are introduced at the start; in another type the second subject appears after the first and the two are eventually combined.

down-beat the downward movement of a conductor's BATON or hand which usually indicates the first BEAT of a BAR.

Doxologia Magna (*Latin*) the 'Gloria in Excelsis Deo'. *See* GLORIA.

D'Oyly Carte Company a company founded by the English impresario Richard D'Oyly-Carte (1844-1901) to perform the operas of ◊Gilbert and Sullivan (whom he had brought together) and for which he built the Savoy Theatre in London.

drama (1) a PLAY for the stage, radio or television. (2) dramatic literature as a genre.

dramatic irony a situation in which a character in a PLAY, NOVEL, etc, says or does something that has a meaning for the audience or reader, other than the obvious meaning, that he or she does not understand. Its use is common in both COMEDY and TRAGEDY.

drone a PIPE that sounds a continuous NOTE of fixed PITCH as a permanent BASS. The BAGPIPES, for example, have several drone pipes. Also, a similar effect produced by stringed instruments fitted with 'drone strings'.

drum a PERCUSSION INSTRUMENT of which there are numerous types, including BASS DRUM, SIDE DRUM, TABOR, TENOR DRUM and TIMPANI. Most drums consist of a hollow metal or wood cylinder over which is stretched a skin. Sound is produced by beating the skin with drumsticks or with the hands.

drum kit a set of DRUMS and CYMBALS arranged in such a way that they can all be played by one person sitting on a stool. Some of the instruments (such as the BASS DRUM) are played with a foot PEDAL, but most are struck with sticks or wire brushes. They are used by JAZZ and POP drummers and can vary enormously in size.

DS abbreviation for DAL SEGNO.

due corde (*Italian*) literally 'two strings'; a term used in VIOLIN music indicating that a PASSAGE that could theoretically be played on one string should nevertheless be played on two to produce the desired effect.

duet a combination of two performers or a composition for such a pair, for example, piano duet.

dulcimer *or* **cymbalo** an ancient instrument which was introduced to Europe from the East in the Middle Ages. It consists of a shallow box over which strings are stretched. The instrument is placed on the knees and the strings are struck with small HAMMERS. In the USA, an instrument similar to the ZITHER is sometimes called a dulcimer.

dulcitone a keyboard instrument containing TUNING FORKS which are struck with HAMMERS, as in a PIANO.

duplet a group of two NOTES of equal value which are played in the time normally taken by three.

duple time a form of musical TIME in which the number of BEATS in a BAR is a multiple of two, for example 2/4 (2 CROTCHETS) and 6/8 (6 QUAVERS in two groups of three).

dur (*German*) 'major', as in MAJOR KEY.

dynamic accents ACCENTS which correspond to the regular RHYTHM of a piece of music, as indicated by the TIME SIGNATURE.

E the third note (MEDIANT) of the SCALE of C major.

écossaise abbreviation of *danse écossaise*, i.e. 'Scottish dance', although in fact the term has little to do with Scottish dancing and merely refers to a quick dance in 2/4 TIME.

Eight, The a group of American painters, for the most part REALIST painters who campaigned vigorously on the development of progressive art away from the strictures of academic tradition. *See also* ASHCAN SCHOOL.

eighth-note (US) a QUAVER.

electronic instruments a generic term for instruments that convert electrical energy into sound, such as the SYNTHESIZER.

embouchure (1) the mouthpiece of a BRASS or WIND INSTRUMENT. (2) the correct tensioning of the lips and facial muscles when playing woodwind and brass instruments to create good TONE.

encore (*French*) 'again', the call from an English audience (the French equivalent is BIS) for more music. If the performance does continue, the additional music is also known as an 'encore'.

end pin *see* TAIL PIN.

engraving a technique of cutting an image into a metal or wood plate using special tools. When ink is applied to the plate, the raised parts will print black and the engraved parts white. The term is also used for a print produced in this way.

enharmonic intervals INTERVALS that are so small that they do not exist on keyboard instruments; an example is the interval from A sharp to B flat.

ensemble (*French*) literally 'together'; a term meaning a group of players or singers, a MOVEMENT in OPERA for several singers, or the precision with which such a group performs together.

entr'acte (*French*) the music played between the acts of a play or OPERA. *See also* ACT TUNE, INTERLUDE, INTERMEZZO.

epic (1) a very long narrative poem dealing with heroic deeds and adventures on a grand scale, as ◊Homer's *Iliad*. (2) a novel or film with some of these qualities.

episode (1) in A FUGUE, a PASSAGE that connects entries of the SUBJECT. (2) in A RONDO, a contrasting section that separates entries of the PRINCIPAL THEME.

epistolary novel a novel in the form of a series of letters written to and from the main characters, sometimes presented by the author in the anonymous role of 'editor'. The form flourished in the 18th century, an example being Samuel ◊Richardson's *Pamela* (1741). The best parody is Jane ◊Austen's *Love and Freindship* (written when she was 14), closely followed by Fielding's (much larger) *Shamela Andrews* (1741). Jane Austen toyed for a while with the form: *Lady Susan* (written 1793–4), a minor work by her own high standards, ends with a lovely send-up of the form's conventions in the 'Conclusion', and the first draft of *Sense and Sensibility* (1797–8), entitled *Elinor and Marianne*, was originally in epistolary form, but the form was too weak for what she planned to write.

equal temperament a convenient, but technically incorrect, way of tuning a keyboard in which all SEMITONES are considered equal, for example F sharp and G flat are taken to be identical NOTES when theoretically they are not. Such a system makes complex MODULATIONS practicable.

escapement the mechanism in a PIANO which releases the HAMMER, allowing a string to vibrate freely after it has been struck.

espressivo (*Italian*) 'expressively'.

esquisse (*French*) a 'sketch', a title sometimes given to short instrumental pieces.

estinto (*Latin*) literally 'extinct', i.e. as soft as possible.

etching a technique of making an engraving in a metal plate, using acid to bite out the image rather than tools. Tones of black or grey can be produced, depending on the extent the acid is allowed to bite. The term is also used for a print produced in this way.

étude (*French*) a 'study' or piece of music evolved from a single PHRASE or idea. Studies are also written purely as exercises to improve technique or FINGERING.

euphonium a large BRASS INSTRUMENT, a tenor TUBA, which is mainly used in BRASS and MILITARY BANDS.

eurhythmics a system of teaching musical RHYTHM by graceful physical movements. It was invented in 1905 by the Swiss composer and teacher Émile Jaques-Dalcroze (1865–1950).

evensong *see* NUNC DIMITTIS.

Existentialism a philosophical position based on a perception of life in which man is an actor forced to make choices in an essentially meaningless universe that functions as a colossal and cruel Theatre of the ABSURD. The main writers associated with Existentialism are French, notably ◊Sartre and ◊Camus, and the bilingual ◊Beckett. The roots of Existentialism are complex; one important source is NIHILISM, the influence of which is apparent in Camus' novel *The Outsider* (1942), described by its author as 'the study of an absurd man in an absurd world'. Another important source is the Danish theologian Søren Kierkegaard (1813–55), who observed that life must be lived forwards but can only be understood backwards. Life is therefore a continual act of faith in which choices are made for a series of actions, the consequences of which must remain unclear. Camus' quest for meaning in life and art led him to an accommodation with Christianity, detailed in his essay *The Rebel* (1951), whereas Sartre came to an uneasy alliance with Marxism; Beckett, however, kept on ploughing his unique and lonely furrow, free of political or religious comfort, until his death.

exposition (1) in the SONATA FORM, the first section of a piece in which the main THEMES are introduced before they are developed. (2) in FUGUE, the initial statement of the SUBJECT by each of the PARTS.

Expressionism a term, derived from the character of some 20th-century Northern European art, which was coined in a description of an exhibition of FAUVIST and CUBIST paintings at the Berlin SEZESSION in 1911 but quickly came to be applied to the works of Die BRÜCKE and Der BLAUE REITER. Expressionist works represented a move away from the observational detachment of REALISM and, to an extent, IMPRESSIONIST trends, and were concerned with conveying the artist's feelings and emotions as aroused by his subject. Any painting technique that helped to express these feelings was considered a valid medium and included bold, free brushwork, distorted or stylized forms, and vibrant, often violently clashing, colours. The term expressionist also refers to an expressive quality of distortion or heightened colour in art from any period or place. *See also* ABSTRACT EXPRESSIONISM. In music it is used to imply the expression of inner emotions.

extemporization *see* IMPROVISATION.

F (1) the fourth note (or SUBDOMINANT) of the scale of C major. (2) in abbreviations, *f* means *forte* (loud); *ff*, *fortissimo* (very loud) and *fp, forte piano* (loud and then soft).

fa In the TONIC SOL-FA, the fourth degree in any major scale.

fado (*Portuguese*) a type of melancholy song with a guitar accompaniment.

false relation in harmony, the occurrence of a note bearing an ACCIDENTAL, which is immediately followed, in another part, by the same note which does not bear an accidental, or vice versa.

falsetto (*Italian*) an adult male voice, used in the register above its normal range. It has often been used to comic effect in operas.

fancy *see* FANTASIA.

fandango a lively Spanish dance, thought to be South American in origin, in triple time. It is usually accompanied by guitar and castanets. Composers who have included or adapted the fandango form include ◊Gluck in his *Don Juan* ballet, ◊Mozart in *The Marriage of Figaro*, and ◊Rimsky-Korsakov in his *Capriccio Espagnol*.

fanfare a flourish of trumpets, or other instruments (for example, the organ) that imitate the sound of trumpets.

fantasia (*Italian*) a piece in which the composer follows his imagination in free association rather than composing within a particular conventional form; when such a piece is played, it can sound as if it is being improvised. It is also a composer's adaptation or use of another's theme or of a known song, for example. ◊Vaughan Williams's *Fantasia on a theme by Thomas Tallis*.

Fantasie (*German*), **fantaisie** (*French*) a FANTASIA.

Fauvists a group of French painters, including ◊Matisse and ◊Derain, who painted in a particularly vivid and colourful style. The term *fauve* ('wild animal') was coined as a form of derogatory criticism of an exhibition held at the SALON d'Automne of 1905. Their use of strong, bright colours to express their response to the fierce light of the Mediterranean coast owes something to the influence of ◊Gauguin and Van ◊Gogh, but they were less interested in representing what they saw and more concerned to express their own feelings in the boldness and freedom of their compositions. Although Matisse continued to explore Fauvist techniques, the other artists soon diverged, and the movement as such was fairly short-lived. It was, however, influential in CUBIST and EXPRESSIONIST art.

fauxbourdon (*French*) a 15th-century continental technique of improvising a bass part for a PLAINSONG melody.

feminine cadence an ending in which the final chord occurs on a weak beat of the bar and not the more usual strong beat.

fermata (*Italian*) *see* PAUSE.

ff *see* F (2).

fiddle (1) a generic term for a range of primitive stringed instruments played with a bow, as used in parts of Asia, Africa and Eastern Europe. (2) a colloquial term for a violin, especially in folk music.

fife a small flute still used in 'drum and fife' bands.

fifth an INTERVAL of five notes (the first and last notes are counted) or seven semitones, for example, from C to G.

figurative art *or* **representational art** art that recognizably represents figures, objects or animals from real life, as opposed to ABSTRACT ART.

figure a short musical phrase that is repeated in the course of a composition.

figured bass the bass part of a composition which has numerical figures written below the notes to indicate how the harmony above should be played. It is, in effect, a type of musical shorthand in which the bass line and melody are written down while the numbers indicate which chords should be played. The system was used during the 17th and early 18th centuries.

finale (*Italian*) (1) the last movement of a work. (2) the concluding section of an opera act.

fine arts *see* APPLIED ARTS.

fingering a type of notation that indicates which fingers should be used to play a piece of music.

fino (*Italian*) 'as far as', so *fino al segno* means 'as far as the sign'.

fioritura (*Italian*) 'flowering', i.e. an embellishment.

fipple flute *see* FLAGEOLET; RECORDER.

Five, The the name given to a group of nationalistic 19th-century Russian composers who were known in Russia as *moguchaya kuchka* (The Mighty Handful). The five were ◊Rimsky-Korsakov,

Mily Alexeyevich Balakirev (1837–1910), Aleksandr Borodin (1833–87), César Antonovich Cui (1835–1918) and ◊Mussorgsky.

flageolet a small, end-blown FLUTE with six holes, four in front and two at the back, popular in the 17th century.

flamenco a generic term for a type of Spanish song from Andalusia, usually sad and often accompanied by guitar and dancing. Flamenco guitar playing relies heavily on the strumming of powerful, dynamic rhythms.

flat (1) a note which is lowered by one semitone as indicated by the flat sign (*see* Appendix). (2) a note (or notes) produced at too low a pitch and hence 'out of tune'.

flirts and straights a distinction between authors who specialize in showing off to their readers (flirts) and those whose main concern is getting on with telling the story (straights). A flirt will play with conventions and expectations, and disrupt the narrative with disquistions on the meaning of life or on what the author had for breakfast. A straight will, for the most part, maintain the agreed conventions between author and reader. A writer of detective stories, in which genre the conventions are fairly rigorous, is almost always a straight, though inferior crime writers will make their heroes secret readers of ◊Proust or ◊Nietzsche. Many writers combine both elements: George ◊Eliot is a straight in character development, but a flirt in digression.

flue pipes all ORGAN pipes that have narrow openings, or flues, into which air passes; the other pipes are REED PIPES.

Flügelhorn (*German*) a soprano brass instrument similar to a bugle in shape, but with three pistons.

flute (1) the tranverse or German flute is a member of the WOODWIND family of instruments, although these days it is normally made of silver or other metal. One end of the instrument is stopped and sound is produced by blowing across the mouthpiece formed around an aperture cut into the side of the instrument at the stopped end. The pitch is controlled by means of a lever system. (2) the English flute is a beaked, end-blown, wind instrument with finger holes, now more usually called the RECORDER.

folia (*Portuguese*) 'the folly', a wild and noisy Portuguese dance.

folk dance any dance, performed by ordinary people, in a pre-industrial society, that has evolved over the years and gained a traditional form. Folk dances differ widely in character and some have symbolic significance, such as war dances, etc.

folk song properly, any song that has been preserved by oral tradition. Many composers and pop musicians have written new compositions that imitate old folk songs.

form the structure of a composition. The basic elements of musical composition which define a given piece's form are repetition, variation and contrast. Examples of recognized forms include FUGUE, RONDO, SONATA FORM, etc.

forte (*Italian*) 'loud' (abbreviation *f*).

fortepiano (*Italian*) an early word for PIANOFORTE. Not to be confused with *forte piano* (loud then soft).

fortissimo (*Italian*) 'very loud' (abbreviation *ff*).

forza (*Italian*) 'force', so *con forza* means 'with force'.

forzato (*Italian*) 'forced'.

found object *or* **objet trouvé** a form of art that began with Dada and continued with Surrealism, where an object, either natural or manufactured, is displayed as a piece of art in its own right.

fourth an INTERVAL of four notes (including the first and last) or five semitones, for example C to F.

foxtrot a dance, originating in the USA, in duple time. It first became popular in the ballroom from about 1912 and was at the height of its popularity in the 1930s and 1940s, by which time it had acquired two variations, the quick and the slow foxtrot.

fp abbreviation for FORTE PIANO (*Italian*) 'loud then soft'.

free reed a type of REED found in such instruments as the ACCORDION and HARMONICA. It consists of a small metal tongue that vibrates freely in a metal slot when air is blown over it. The pitch of the reed is determined by its thickness and length.

found object *or* **objet trouvé** a form of art that began with DADA and continued with SURREALISM, where an object, either natural or manufactured, is displayed as a piece of art in its own right.

French horn *see* HORN.

French sixth *see* AUGMENTED SIXTH.

fresco a painting directly painted on to a wall that has previously been covered with a damp, freshly laid layer of lime plaster, the paint and plaster reacting chemically to become stable and permanent. Fresco painting worked particularly well in the warm, dry climate of Italy, where it reached its peak in the 16th century.

fret (*French*) one of a series of thin pieces of metal fitted into the wooden fingerboard of a stringed instrument to make the stopping of strings easier and more accurate. Each fret represents the position of a specific note.

front man the person who stands at the front of the stage during a performance of JAZZ and who is therefore the focus of the audience's attention. He or she is often, but not always, the leader or singer of the band.

fugue a contrapuntal composition for two or more parts (commonly called 'voices') which enter successively in imitation of each other. The first entry is called the 'SUBJECT' and the second entry (a fifth higher or lower than the subject) is called the 'ANSWER'. When all the voices have entered, the EXPOSITION is complete and is usually followed by an EPISODE which connects to the next series of subject entries. A COUNTER-SUBJECT is a melodic accompaniment to the subject and answer, and is often in DOUBLE COUNTERPOINT. A fugue may be written for voices, instruments or both. The form dates back to the 17th century. Possibly the greatest exponent of the fugue was Johann Sebastian ◊Bach, and his *Art of Fugue* is the fullest statement of the form.

full close *see* CADENCE.

full organ a term used in ORGAN music to indicate that all the loud stops are to be used together.

funk a form of heavily syncopated, rhythmic black dance music, originating in the United States. The adjective, often used in JAZZ terminology, is *funky*.

fuoco (*Italian*) 'fire', so *con fuoco* means 'with fire'.

furioso (*Italian*) 'furious'.

Futurism a movement of writers and artists, originating in early 20th-century Italy, that extolled the virtues of the new, dynamic machine age, which was reckoned to have rendered the aesthetic standards of the past redundant. The founding document of the movement is the poet Filipo Marinetti's (1876–1944) *Futurist Manifesto* of 1909, which, in literature, called for the destruction of traditional sentence construction and the establishment of a 'free verse in free words' (*parole in libertà*) owing nothing to the literary standards of the past; the new relationship between words was to be in terms of analogy alone. The English variant of Futurism is VORTICISM, which included writers such as Wyndham ◊Lewis and Ezra ◊Pound. The Russian variant, *Russian Futurism*, was led by the poet Vladimir Mayakovsky (1893–1930), whose curious love affair with the Soviet dictatorship ended with his suicide (Lenin described him as 'incomprehensible'; once he was safely dead, Stalin lauded him as a great Bolshevik poet).

Futurism became a spent force by the 1930s, largely because of its close association with Fascism and the establishment of the

Futurist hero Mussolini's dictatorship in Italy (Marinetti's vision of war as 'the hygiene of the world' is also Mussolini's).

In art, Boccioni was among the painters in the group, whose aim was to convey a sense of movement and dynamism, as in Boccioni's *The City Rises* (1910). As a group, the Futurists published manifestos on various aspects of the arts, and exhibitions toured Europe during 1911–12. The original group of painters had broken up by the end of World War I, but their work and ideas had a resounding influence on subsequent art movements.

fz abbreviation for FORZATO.

G the fifth note (or DOMINANT) of the scale of C major.

galant (*French*) 'polite'; a term applied to certain graceful styles of court music, especially of the 18th century.

galanterie an 18th-century German term for a keyboard piece in the GALANT style.

galliard (*French*) a lively court dance, usually in triple time, which dates back to the 16th century.

galop a lively dance in duple time that originated in Germany and was popular in the 19th century.

gamelan a type of traditional orchestra found principally in Indonesia and South-East Asia. Although such an orchestra includes strings and woodwind instruments, it is the array of gongs, drums, chimes, xylophones and marimbas that produces the unique and highly complex rhythms of gamelan music. ◊Debussy was especially influenced by gamelan.

gamut (1) the note G on the bottom line of the bass clef. (2) an alternative (now obsolete) word for the key of G. (3) the whole range of musical sounds, from the lowest to the highest.

gavotte an old French dance, originally of the upper Alps, in 4/4 time, which usually starts on the third beat of the bar. It was favoured by ◊Lully in his ballets and operas and was revived in the 20th century by such composers as ◊Prokofiev and ◊Schoenberg.

gedämpft (*German*) 'muted'.

Generalpause (*German*) a rest of one or more bars for all the members of an orchestra.

genre a distinctive type or category of artistic or literary composition.

genre painting a painting that has as its subject a scene from everyday life, as opposed to a historical event, mythological scene, etc. Genre paintings appear in the backgrounds of medieval paintings, but it was the Dutch painters, e.g. ◊Bruegel, ◊Bosch and ◊Vermeer, who were the first to specialize in them and to continue the tradition. In France, Jean-Baptiste Chardin (1699–1779) used genre scenes to great effect, but they did not become really popular with painters until the REALISTS, e.g. ◊Courbet and ◊Millet. British painters, e.g. ◊Hogarth, ◊Gainsborough and ◊Wilkie, painted genre scenes, but gradually the distinction between such scenes and other genres of painting has blurred.

German sixth *see* AUGMENTED SIXTH.

gigue (*French*) a lively dance or jig.

giocoso (*Italian*) 'merry'.

gioioso (*Italian*) 'joyful'.

giusto (*Italian*) 'exact', as in *tempo giusto*, which can mean either 'strict time' or 'appropriate speed'.

Glasgow Boys *or* **Glasgow School** a group of painters centred in Glasgow in the 1880s and 90s. They represented a move away from academic strictures and were inspired by the plein air BARBIZON SCHOOL. They established an outpost of the European vogue for NATURALISM and ROMANTIC lyricism in landscape painting, and their influence extended into the 20th century.

glass harmonica at its simplest, a set of goblets that are played by rubbing a moistened finger around the rims. This idea was taken further by the American scientist and statesman Benjamin ◊Franklin, who invented a glass harmonica in which a gradated series of glass bowls is fixed to a rotating spindle and played with the fingers. Both ◊Beethoven and ◊Mozart wrote music for the instrument, which produces a high-pitched humming sound.

glee a simple, unaccompanied composition for male voices in several sections.

glissando (*Italian*) 'sliding'; a rapid sliding movement up or down a scale.

Glockenspiel (*German*), **Campanelli** (*Italian*) literally 'a play of bells', an instrument, produced in a variety of sizes, comprising steel bars of different lengths that are arranged like a keyboard; each bar sounds a different note. Played with hammers, it produces sounds that have a bell-like quality. It is used in orchestras and military bands (in which it is held vertically).

Gloria (*Latin*) the first word of *Gloria in excelsis Deo* ('Glory to God in the highest'), the hymn used in both Roman Catholic Masses and in Anglican services. Many composers have set it to music. It is also the first word of the doxology *Gloria Patri* ('Glory be to the Father'), sung after a psalm.

gong a PERCUSSION INSTRUMENT that originated in the Far East. Gongs are made in many sizes and shapes, but an orchestral gong consists of nothing more than a large sheet of metal with a pronounced rim. Sound is produced by striking it with a hammer.

gospel song a type of popular religious song originated by black American slaves who sang hymns to pulsating BLUES rhythms. Such songs, which are still sung fervently today in religious services, were one of the originating forces of JAZZ.

Gothic a style of architecture that lasted from the 12th to the 16th centuries in Northern Europe and Spain. Its effect on art was to produce the INTERNATIONAL GOTHIC style.

Gothic novel a type of NOVEL that was enormously popular in the late 18th century, combining elements of the supernatural, macabre or fantastic, often in wildly ROMANTIC settings, e.g. ruined abbeys or ancient castles. The heroes and/or heroines, whether medieval or modern, for the most part speak in a formal, stilted language curiously at odds (for the modern reader) with the appalling situations they find themselves in. Horace ◊Walpole's *The Castle of Otranto* (1764) and *The Mysteries of Udolpho* (1794) by Ann Radcliffe (1764–1823), are among the best-known examples of the genre. Jane ◊Austen's *Northanger Abbey* (1818) remains the definitive parody.

gouache *also called* **poster paint** *or* **body paint** an opaque mixture of watercolour paint and white pigment.

GP an abbreviation of GENERALPAUSE.

grace note an ornamental, extra note, usually written in small type, used to embellish a melody.

grandioso (*Italian*) 'in an imposing manner'.

grand opera a term originally used to distinguish serious opera, sung throughout, from opera that contained some spoken dialogue. The term is now also used to describe a lavish production.

grand orchestre (*French*) a full orchestra.

grand orgue (*French*) a great ORGAN (as opposed to a swell organ, etc).

grand piano *see* PIANOFORTE.

grave (*Italian*) 'slow' or 'solemn'.

grazia (*Italian*) 'grace'.

grazioso (*Italian*) 'gracefully'.

great stave a STAVE created by pushing the stave with the treble clef and the stave with the bass clef closer together so that both clefs can be located on one exaggerated stave.

Gregorian chant a term that refers to the large collection of ancient solo and chorus PLAINSONG melodies preserved by the Roman Catholic Church. They are named after Pope Gregory I (*c.* 540-604) but date from about 800. Until recently they were sung at specific ceremonies, such as baptism, Mass, etc.

grisaille a monochrome painting made using only shades of grey, often used as a sketch for oil paintings.

grotesque a term for a style of ornamentation that began in Roman times and reached its height with ROCOCO. It consisted of a series of figurative or floral ornaments in decorative frames that are linked by festoons.

ground bass a BASS line that is constantly repeated throughout a composition, as a foundation for variation in the upper parts.

grupetto (*Italian*) a 'little group'; a general term used to describe various ORNAMENTS of one or more decorative notes.

Guarneri *or* **Guarnerius** a violin made by one of several members of a famous Italian family of violin-makers who were based in Cremona in the 17th and 18th centuries.

guitar a plucked STRING instrument, which may have been introduced to Spain from North Africa. Unlike the LUTE, it has a flat back and usually carries six strings suspended over a fretted finger-board (twelve-string guitars were favoured by certain BLUES musicians). The acoustic ('soundbox ') guitar has been played by classical, flamenco and folk musicians for generations, but the electric guitar is a comparatively new development. The body may be hollow (or 'semi-acoustic') or solid, with 'pick-ups' (electrically motivated resonators that respond to the vibration of the strings) mounted under the BRIDGE. The vibrations received by the pick-ups have to be electrically amplified or else they are virtually featureless. Electric guitars have a huge COMPASS.

gusto (*Italian*) 'taste', so *con gusto* means 'with taste'.

H (*German*) B natural.

habanera (*Spanish*) a dance of Cuban origin with a powerful, SYNCOPATED RHYTHM, most usually associated, however, with Spain.

Hague School a school of Dutch landscape painters, one of whose prominent leaders was Anton Mauve (1838–88).

haiku a 17-syllable sequential verse form devised by the Japanese poet Basho (1644–94). A Basho haiku gave Ian ◊Fleming the title for one of his novels, *You Only Live Twice*.

half note (US) a MINIM.

half step (US) a SEMITONE.

Hallé Orchestra an internationally famous orchestra founded in Manchester in 1848 by the German-born conductor and pianist Sir Charles Hallé (1819–95).

halling a lively Norwegian dance, in 2/4 TIME, during which men leap high into the air.

hammer that part of the PIANO mechanism which strikes the strings; a mallet for playing the DULCIMER; the clapper of a BELL.

Hammond organ the brand name of an electric ORGAN first produced by the Hammond Organ Company, Chicago, in 1935. The sound it produces is electronically manufactured and attempts to reproduce the sound of the PIPE ORGAN. It cannot be said to succeed in this, but its unique temperament has been exploited by JAZZ, POP and music-hall musicians the world over.

handbells bells, of various pitch, that are held in the hands of a group of performers and rung in sequence to create a tune.

hardanger fiddle a Norwegian VIOLIN used in FOLK music. It is somewhat smaller than an ordinary violin and has four SYMPATHETIC STRINGS.

harmonica a small, FREE-REED instrument commonly called the *mouth organ*. Although it is a small and apparently inconsequential instrument, many BLUES and FOLK musicians have illustrated its potential by exploiting its emotive power.

harmonic minor MINOR SCALE containing the minor sixth with the MAJOR SEVENTH, in which ascent and descent are without alteration.

harmonics the sounds that can be produced on stringed instruments by lightly touching a string at one of its harmonic nodes, i.e. at a half-length of a string, quarter-length and so on.

harmonium a small, portable REED-ORGAN developed in the 19th century. Air is pumped to the REEDS (which are controlled by STOPS and KEYS) by PEDALS worked continuously by the feet.

harmony (1) the simultaneous sounding of two or more NOTES, i.e CHORDS. A harmonious SOUND is an agreeable or pleasant sound (CONCORD); but harmonization may also produce sounds which, to some ears at least, are unpleasant (*see* DISCORD). (2) the structure and relationship of chords.

harp an instrument, of ancient origin, consisting of strings stretched across an open frame. It is played by plucking the strings, each of which is tuned (*see* TUNING) to a separate NOTE.

harpsichord a keyboard instrument, developed in the 14th and 15th centuries, in which the strings are plucked (not struck) by quills or tongues (PLECTRA). The tongues are connected to the KEYS by a simple lever mechanism. The harpsichord went out of favour during the late 18th century due to the introduction of the PIANO. However, it has seen a revival in the 20th century, and new compositions exploiting its 'twangy' sound have been written for it.

hautbois (*French*) 'high' or 'loud wood'. *See* OBOE. From the Elizabethan period to the 18th century, the English equivalent was *hautboy*.

Hawaiian guitar a style of GUITAR playing in which a steel bar is moved up and down the strings (as opposed to the more usual STOPPING of strings with the fingers) to produce a distinctive slurred sound. The guitar is usually played horizontally.

head voice the upper register of a VOICE, so called because the sound seems to vibrate in the head of the singer. *Compare* CHEST VOICE.

Heckelphone a double-REED instrument which is effectively a baritone OBOE. It was used by Richard ◊Strauss in his opera *Salomé*.

Heldentenor (*German*) a 'heroic tenor ', i.e. a tenor with a strong voice suitable for ◊Wagner's heroic roles.

hemiola a RHYTHM in which two BARS in triple TIME are played as though they were three bars in DUPLE TIME.

hemisemidemiquaver the sixty-fourth NOTE, i.e. a note with a value of a quarter of a SEMIQUAVER or $1/64$th of a SEMIBREVE.

heroic tragedy a form of tragedy that became very popular during the RESTORATION. Such tragedies were usually written in bombastic rhymed couplets and featured the adventures in love and war of noble characters in exotic locations, past and present. The characteristic conflict at the heart of such plays was the clash between the equally imperious commands of love and duty.

heterophony (*Greek*) literally 'difference of sounds', i.e. two or more performers playing different versions of the same MELODY simultaneously.

hexachord a SCALE of six NOTES which was used in medieval times.

High Mass MASS that is sung throughout, as distinguished from Low Mass, which is said.

history painting a genre of painting that takes as its subject a scene from history, religious or mythological legend, or from great works of literature, e.g. by ◊Dante or ◊Shakespeare.

hocket (*French*) the breaking-up of a MELODY into very short PHRASES or single NOTES, with RESTS in between them.

homophony a term applied to music in which the PARTS move 'in step' and do not have independent RHYTHMS. *Compare* POLYPHONY.

hook the black line attached to the stem of all NOTES of less value than a CROTCHET.

hootenanny a US term for a small festival of FOLK music.

horn a BRASS INSTRUMENT consisting of a conical tube coiled into a spiral and ending in a bell. The lips are pushed into a funnel-shaped MOUTHPIECE. The modern orchestral horn is called the *French horn* (because that is where it was developed) and is fitted with three (sometimes four, sometimes seven) valves which open and close various lengths of tubing so that the PITCH of the NOTES can be changed. There are two common 'horns', which are in fact WOODWIND instruments, the BASSET HORN (ALTO CLARINET) and the English horn or COR ANGLAIS (alto OBOE).

hornpipe (1) a single-REED WIND INSTRUMENT played in Celtic countries. (2) a 16th-century dance in triple TIME, originally accompanied by the hornpipe and later erroneously associated with sailors.

Hosanna (*Hebrew*)'Save now', part of the SANCTUS in the MASS.

Hudson River School a group of American landscape painters active in the mid-19th century whose work was concerned with the beauty and mysticism of nature, expressed in romantic terms on a grand and noble scale. They were influenced by the writers Fenimore ◊Cooper and Washington ◊Irving as well as by ◊Turner.

humoresque (*French*), **Humoreske** (*German*) a word used by, e.g. ◊Schumann, as the title for a short, lively piece of music.

humours, theory of (in medieval medical theory) any of the four body fluids: blood, phlegm, yellow (choleric) bile, and black (melancholic) bile. This theory is the basis for the *comedy of humours*, notably Ben ◊Jonson's *Every Man in his Humour* (1598), in which the characters have names and behaviour appropriate to their eccentrically dominant 'humour' or personality trait. For humour in the modern sense *see* wit.

hurdy-gurdy a medieval stringed instrument, shaped like a VIOL. A wooden wheel, coated in RESIN, is cranked at one end to make all the strings resonate. The strings are stopped by rods operated by KEYS. The hurdy-gurdy was often used to provide dance music.

hymn in the Christian Church, a poem sung to music in praise of God.

icon *or* **ikon** a religious image, usually painted on a wooden panel, regarded as sacred in the Byzantine Church and subsequently by the Orthodox Churches of Russia and Greece, where they survive. The word comes from the Greek *eikon*, meaning 'likeness', and strict rules were devised as to the subject, generally a saint, and to the form of the painting and its use, so although icon painting flourished in the 6th century it is extremely difficult to date icons painted then or later. A reaction to what was considered idolatry took place in the 8th century, resulting in *iconoclasm*, the destruction of such images.

iconography, iconology the study and interpretation of representations in figurative art and their symbolic meanings. It is particularly important in the understanding of Christian art, especially of the medieval and RENAISSANCE periods, e.g. the dove signifying the Holy Spirit, or the fish symbolizing Christ.

idée fixe (*French*) 'fixed idea', i.e. a recurring theme.

idiophone any instrument in which SOUND is produced by the VIBRATION of the instrument itself, for example, CYMBALS, BELLS, CASTANETS etc.

ikon *see* ICON.

Imagism a poetry movement of the early 20th century which advocated using everyday language and precise representation of the image of the subject discussed. Imagist poems were short and to the point, anti-ROMANTIC and anti-Victorian in tone, and could be on any subject under the sun. Prominent Imagists included ◊Pound and Amy Lowell (1874–1925), whose *Tendencies in Modern American Poetry* (1917) has the best introduction to the movement.

imitation a device in COUNTERPOINT whereby a PHRASE is sung successively by different VOICES.

impasto an Italian word used to describe the thickness and textures that can be achieved with acrylic or oil paint.

imperioso(*Italian*) 'imperiously'.

impetuoso (*Italian*) 'impetuously'.

Impressionism an art movement originating in France in the 1860s, centred on a fairly diverse group of artists who held eight exhibitions together between 1874 and 1886. The main artists were ◊Cézanne, ◊Degas, ◊Manet, ◊Monet, Morisot, ◊Pissarro, ◊Renoir and ◊Sisley, although they did not all show paintings at all eight exhibitions. The name of the movement was coined by critics from a painting by Monet in the 1874 exhibition entitled *Impression: Soleil Levant.* Members of the group were variously influenced by the BARBIZON SCHOOL, the works of ◊Turner and

◊Constable, and the REALISM of ◊Courbet. The advent of photography and scientific theories about colour also had their impact on the painters' approach to their work. The Impressionists were concerned with representing day-to-day existence in an objective and realistic manner, and they rejected the ROMANTIC idea that a painting should convey strong emotions. They wanted to record the fleeting effects of light and movement, and so their usual subjects were landscapes or social scenes like streets and cafés. They chose unusual viewpoints and painted 'close-ups', probably influenced by photography. They were on the whole much freer in their use of unusual colours and a lighter palette; their subject matter was also less weighty, and they came in for some criticism over the lack of intellectual content of their painting. Impressionism has had an enormous influence on almost every subsequent major art movement: on CUBISM via ◊Cézanne; on the synthetic art of ◊Gauguin through ◊Seurat and the NEOIMPRESSIONISTS, and on EXPRESSIONISM through the works of Van ◊Gogh. This influence has continued in a large proportion of 20th-century art.

By analogy, Impressionism is also used to identify certain types of atmospheric music, such as the music of ◊Debussy and ◊Ravel.

impromptu a type of PIANO music that sounds as if it has been improvised, i.e. written in a free and easy style.

improvisation the art of playing or 'inventing' music that has not already been composed, i.e. spontaneous composition. Some forms of music (especially JAZZ) often rely heavily on the ability of performers to improvise certain sections. It has the same meaning as *extemporization*.

in alt *see* ALT.

incalzando (*Italian*) 'pressing forward', i.e. working up speed and force.

incidental music music written to accompany the action in a play, but the term is also commonly applied to OVERTURES and INTERLUDES.

inciso (*Italian*) 'incisive', hence an instruction that a strong RHYTHM is required.

indeciso (*Italian*) 'undecided', i.e. the pace of a piece of music can be varied according to the performer's feelings.

indeterminacy a term used by John ◊Cage to describe music that does not follow a rigid NOTATION but leaves certain events to chance or allows performers to make their own decisions when performing it.

inflected note a NOTE with an ACCIDENTAL placed before it, i.e. it is sharpened or flattened.

inner parts the PARTS of a piece of music excluding the highest and lowest; for example, in a work for SOPRANO, ALTO, TENOR and BASS, the alto and tenor roles are inner parts.

In nomine (*Latin*) ('In the name of the Lord') a type of CANTUS FIRMUS used by English composers of the 16th century. It was first used by ◊Taverner in his setting of *In nomine Domini* for one of his Masses.

instrument in music, a device on which or with which music can be played. There are five traditional categories of instrument: WOODWIND, BRASS, PERCUSSION, KEYBOARD, and STRING. However, ELECTRONIC and MECHANICAL INSTRUMENTS also exist.

instrumentation *see* ORCHESTRATION.

intaglio the cutting into a stone or other material or the etching or engraving on a metal plate of an image; the opposite of RELIEF. Intaglio printing techniques include ENGRAVING and ETCHING.

interior monologue a form of STREAM OF CONSCIOUSNESS narrative technique employed by the English novelist Dorothy Richardson (1873–1957) which anticipated ◊Joyce's use of the technique in *Ulysses* (the device was not really new; similar effects can be found in, e.g. ◊Dickens).

interlude a title sometimes used for a short PART of a complete composition, e.g. a piece of music performed between the acts of an opera. *See also* ACT TUNE, ENTR'ACTE, INTERMEZZO.

intermezzo (*Italian*) (1) a short piece of piano music. (2) a short comic opera performed between the acts of a serious opera, especially in the 16th and 17th centuries. *See also* ACT TUNE, ENTR'ACTE, INTERMEZZO.

International Gothic a predominant style in European art covering the period between the end of the Byzantine era and the beginning of the RENAISSANCE, i.e. *c*.1375–*c*.1425. Some variations in styles occurred regionally, but the most influential centres were Italy, France and the Netherlands. Ideas spread widely due to an increase in the art trade, to travelling artists, and to a certain amount of rivalry over royal commissions. The Dukes of Berry and Burgundy were among the major patrons of the time. International Gothic style was characterized by decorative detail and refined, flowing lines; figures were often elongated or distorted to increase an appearance of elegant charm and the use of gilts and rich colours figured strongly. Scale and perspective were more symbolic than naturalistic, although naturalism began to take hold in the later works of the period.

interpretation the way in which a performer plays a piece of composed music. No composer can possibly indicate exactly how a piece should be played and, to some degree, it is up to the performer to play it as he or she thinks fit.

interval the gap or 'sound distance', expressed numerically, between any two NOTES, i.e. the difference in PITCH between two notes. For example, the interval between C and G is called a FIFTH because G is the fifth note from C. *Perfect intervals* are intervals that remain the same in MAJOR and MINOR KEYS (i.e. FOURTHS, fifths, OCTAVES.)

intonation a term used to describe the judgement of PITCH by a performer.

intone to sing on one NOTE. A priest may intone during a Roman Catholic or Anglican service.

introduction a section, often slow, found at the start of certain pieces of music, notably SYMPHONIES and SUITES.

Introit an ANTIPHON, usually sung in conjunction with a PSALM verse, in the Roman Catholic and Anglican LITURGIES.

invention a title used by ◊Bach for his two-part keyboard pieces in CONTRAPUNTAL form.

inversion a term which literally means turning upside-down. It can refer to a CHORD, INTERVAL, THEME, MELODY or COUNTERPOINT. For example, an *inverted interval* is an interval in which one NOTE changes by an OCTAVE to the other side, as it were, of the other note.

Ionian mode a MODE which, on the PIANO, uses the white NOTES from C to C.

irlandais (*French*) 'in Irish style'.

isorhythm a term used to describe a short RHYTHM pattern that is repeatedly applied to an existing MELODY which already has an distinct rhythm.

Italian sixth *see* AUGMENTED SIXTH.

italiano (*Italian*), **italienne** (*French*) 'in Italian style'.

Jacobean tragedy a development of revenge tragedy in the Jacobean period. The distinction between Jacobean and REVENGE TRAGEDY is a disputed one, hinging on the supposed wave of cynicism and pessimism that is alleged by some historians to have accompanied the accession of James VI of Scotland to the English throne, and the end of the Elizabethan era. The debate is a complex one, but it is undoubtedly the case that tragedies such as ◊Shakespeare's *Hamlet*, ◊Middleton's *The Changeling*, and ◊Webster's *The White Devil* and *The Duchess of Malfi*, are obsessed with political and sexual corruption. The language of these plays is highly sophisticated, ironic, and coldly brilliant.

jam session a 20th-century slang expression for an occasion when a group of musicians join forces to improvise (*see* IMPROVISATION) music. It is usually only appropriate to JAZZ, BLUES and ROCK music.

Janissary music the music of Turkish MILITARY BANDS which influenced European composers during the 18th century. It is particularly associated with CYMBALS, DRUMS and TAMBOURINES.

jazz a term used to describe a style of music that evolved in the Southern States of the USA at the turn of the century. It owes a great deal to the RHYTHMS and idioms of BLUES and SPIRITUALS, but many of the favoured instruments (for example, SAXOPHONE, TRUMPET and TROMBONE) were European in origin. Jazz traditionally relies upon a strong rhythm 'section', comprising BASS and DRUMS, which provides a springboard for other instruments. Jazz developed from being a form of music played in the back streets of New Orleans to a sophisticated art form performed by small dedicated groups as well as 'BIG BANDS' or 'jazz orchestras'.

Self-expression, and therefore IMPROVISATION, has always been a crucial aspect of jazz and this has allowed many individuals (such as Louis ◊Armstrong and Benny ◊Goodman) to blossom and further its cause. *See also* BEBOP.

Jazz Modern *see* ART DECO.

Jeune France ('Young France') the name adopted by a group of French composers, including ◊Messiaen, who identified their common aims in 1936.

Jew's harp a simple instrument consisting of a small, heart-shaped metal frame to which a thin strip of hardened steel is attached. The open-ended neck of the frame is held against the teeth and the strip is twanged to produce sound, which is modified by using the cavity of the mouth as a soundbox.

jig a generic term for a lively dance. *See also* GIGUE.

jingle a short, catchy piece of music with equally catchy LYRICS, often used to enliven the commentary of radio stations broadcasting popular music.

jingles an instrument consisting of a number of small bells or rattling objects on a strap, which are shaken to produce sound.

Jugendstil the German form of ART NOUVEAU.

juke box an automatic, coin-operated, machine that plays records.

K when followed by a number, a reference to either a catalogue of ◊Mozart's works compiled by an Austrian scientist Ludwig von Köchel (1800–77), or a catalogue of ◊Scarlatti's works compiled by Ralph Kirkpatrick.

Kapellmeister (*German*) literally 'master of the chapel', i.e. director of music to a noble court or bishop.

kazoo a simple instrument consisting of a short tube with a small hole in the side which is covered with a thin membrane. When a player hums down the tube, the membrane makes a buzzing sound. It is usually considered a children's instrument although it is frequently used by FOLK and JAZZ musicians.

kettledrum *see* TIMPANI.

key (1) on a piano, harpsichord, organ etc., one of the finger-operated levers by which the instrument is played. (2) On woodwind instruments, one of the metal, finger-operated levers that opens or closes one or more of the soundholes. (3) a note that is considered to be the most important in a piece of music and to which all the other notes relate. Most pieces of Western music are 'written in a key', i.e. all the chords in the piece are built around a particular note, say F minor. The concept of a key is alien to certain types of music, such as Indian and Chinese.

key note *see* TONIC.

key signature the sign (or signs) placed at the beginning of a composition to define its KEY. A key signature indicates all the notes that are to be sharpened or flattened in the piece; should a piece move temporarily into another key, the relevant notes can be identified with ACCIDENTALS.

kinetic art an art form in which light or balance are used to create a work that moves or appears to move. More complicated kinetic art objects are made to move by electric motors.

King James Bible *see* AUTHORIZED VERSION.

kit a miniature violin which was particularly popular with dancing masters of the 17th and 18th centuries, who could carry one in the pocket and thereby provide music for lessons.

Klangfarbenmelodie (*German*) literally, 'melody of tone colours'; a term used by ◊Schoenberg to describe a form of composition in which the pitch does not change; colour is achieved by adding or taking away instruments.

klavier *see* CLAVIER.

koto a Japanese zither which has 13 silk strings stretched over a long box. The strings pass over moveable bridges and are played with plectra worn on the fingers. The instrument is placed on the ground and produces a distinctive, somewhat harsh, sound.

Krumhorn *or* **Krummhorn** (*German*) *or* **crumhorn** a double-reed instrument, common in the 16th and early 17th centuries. The tube was curved at the lower end and the reed was enclosed in a cap into which the player blew. It was made in several sizes: treble, tenor and bass.

Kyrie Eleison (*Greek*) 'Lord have Mercy', the formal invocation at the start of the Mass and communion service.

la *or* **lah** (1) the note A. (2) In the TONIC SOL-FA, the sixth note (or SUBMEDIANT) of the major scale.

lacrimoso (*Italian*) 'tearful'.

lai (*French*) a 13th- and 14th-century French song usually consisting of 12 irregular stanzas sung to different musical phrases.

lambeg drum a large, double-headed bass drum from Northern Ireland.

lament a Scottish or Irish folk tune played at a death or some disaster, usually on the bagpipes.

lamentoso (*Italian*) 'mournfully'.

lampon (*French*) a drinking song.

Lancers, The a type of QUADRILLE in which 8 or 16 couples take part.

Ländler a country dance in slow 3/4 time from Austria and Bavaria, from which the WALTZ was probably derived.

langsam (*German*) 'slow'.

languido (*Italian*) 'languid'.

largamente (*Italian*) 'broadly', meaning slowly and in a dignified manner.

larghetto (*Italian*) 'slow' or 'broad', but not as slow as LARGO.

largo (*Italian*) literally 'broad', meaning slow and in a dignified manner.

Lascaux the site, in Dordogne, France, of some outstanding Paleolithic cave paintings and rock engravings. Dating from *c.*15000 BC, they have survived in remarkably good condition and depict local fauna, etc, on a large scale and in a bold, direct style.

Last Post, The a bugle call of the British Army to signal the end of the day at 10 p.m. It is also played at military funerals.

lay a song or ballad.

lay clerk an adult male member of an Anglican cathedral choir.

lead (1) the announcement of a subject or theme that later appears in other parts. (2) a sign giving the cue or entry of the various parts.

leader (1) in Britain, the title of the principal first violin of an orchestra or the first violin of a string quartet or similar ensemble. (2) the leader of a section of an orchestra. (3) In the USA, an alternative term for conductor.

leading motif *see* LEITMOTIF.

leading note the seventh note of the scale; it is so called because it 'leads to' the TONIC, a semitone above.

ledger lines *see* LEGER LINES.

legato (*Italian*) 'smooth'.

leger lines *or* **ledger lines** short lines added above or below a STAVE to indicate the pitch of notes that are too high or low to be written on the stave itself.

leggiero (*Italian*) 'light'.

legno (*Italian*) 'wood'; *col legno* is a direction to a violinist to turn the bow over and to tap the strings with the wood.

leise (*German*) 'soft' or 'gentle'.

leitmotif *or* **Leitmotiv** (*German*) literally a 'leading theme', i.e. a recurring theme of music, commonly used in opera, that is associated with a character or idea, thus enabling the composer to tell a story in terms of music. It has been used by many composers, including ◊Mozart and ◊Berlioz, but it is particularly associated with ◊Wagner. In the last act of *Götterdämmerung*, for example, every leitmotif associated with Siegfried is woven into the death march.

lentamente (*Italian*) 'slowly'.

lento (*Italian*) 'slow'.

LH an abbreviation for 'left hand', found in piano music.

liberamente (*Italian*) 'freely', i.e. as the performer wishes.

libretto (*Italian*) literally 'little book'. It is a term used for the text of an opera or oratorio.

licenza (*Italian*) 'licence' or 'freedom'; *con alcuna licenza* means 'with some freedom'.

Lied, Lieder (*German*) 'song, songs'. The term is now used for songs by the German romantic composers, for example ◊Brahms, ◊Schubert, ◊Strauss, etc.

ligature (1) a 12th-century form of notation for a group of notes. (2) a slur indicating that a group of notes must be sung to one syllable. (3) the tie used to link two notes over a bar line. (4) the metal band used to fix the reed to the mouthpiece of a clarinet, etc.

limerick a humorous five-lined piece of light verse, with the first two lines rhyming with each other, the third and fourth lines ryming with each other, and the fifth line rhyming with the first line. Usually there are three stressed beats in the first, second and fifth lines and two stressed beats on the third and forth lines. Traditionally the name of a place is mentioned in the first line and may be repeated in the last line. The English humorist and painter Edward Lear (1812–88) made the form popular in the 19th century. Limerick is a town in Ireland, but the name of the verse is probably derived from a Victorian custom of singing nonsense songs at parties.

lira da braccio, lira da gamba Italian stringed instruments of the 15th and 16th centuries. The *lira da braccio* had seven strings and was played like a violin; the *lira da gamba* was a bass instrument played between the knees, and had up to sixteen strings.

lira organizzata a type of HURDY-GURDY that included a miniature organ.

literary ballad *see* ballad.

literary criticism the formal study, discussion and evaluation of a literary work.

liturgy a term for any official, and written down, form of religious service.

loco (*Italian*) 'place'. It is used in music to indicate that a passage is to be played at normal pitch, after a previous, contrary instruction, i.e. the music reverts to its original place on the stave.

lontano (*Italian*) 'distant'.

loure a type of bagpipe played in northern France, especially Normandy.

lunga pausa (*Italian*) a 'long pause'.

lusingando (*Italian*) 'flattering', i.e. in a cajoling manner.

lustig (*German*) 'merry'.

lute a plucked stringed instrument with a body resembling that of a half-pear. It is thought to have a history dating back some three thousand years and was particularly popular during the 16th and 17th centuries; it has since been revived by 20th-century instrument makers. It has a fretted fingerboard with a characteristic 'pegbox' (a string harness) bent back at an angle to the fingerboard. A lute can have up to 18 strings. It was traditionally used as an instrument for accompanying dances, but many solo works have also been written for it.

Lydian mode (1) a scale used in ancient Greek music, the equivalent of the white notes on a piano from C to C. (2) From the Middle Ages onwards, the equivalent of a scale on the white notes on a piano from F to F.

lyre an instrument familiar to the ancient Greeks, Assyrians and Hebrews. It comprised a small, hollow box from which extended two horns that supported a cross bar and anything up to 12 strings, which could be plucked or strummed. It is traditionally taken to represent a token of love (Orpheus played the lyre).

lyric a short poem, or sequence of words, for a song. The term has a particular application to 20th-century musicals and pop songs. A 'lyricist' is the person who writes the words to a popular tune.

m *abbreviation for* MAIN, MANO, MANUAL.

m (me) in TONIC SOL-FA. the third note (or MEDIANT) of the major scale.

ma (*Italian*) 'but', as *andante ma non troppo*, 'slow, but not too slow'.

machete a small Portuguese guitar.

madrigal a musical setting of a secular poem for two or more voices in COUNTERPOINT, usually unaccompanied. The first madrigals date back to the 14th century, and the first publications were made in Italy about 1501. The art of madrigal spread to every part of Europe, with the result that a wealth of polyphonic vocal music was created and reached a high art before the development of instrumental music. In the 17th century madrigals were superseded by CANTATAS.

maestà the Italian word for 'majesty', used in art to denote a depiction of the Virgin and Child enthroned in majesty and surrounded by angels or saints.

maestoso (*Italian*) 'majestic' or 'dignified'.

maestro (*Italian*) literally 'master', a term used for a master musician, particularly a conductor.

maestro sostitutto (*Italian*) 'substitute conductor', an assistant conductor responsible in opera for an offstage chorus or band. Also, a RÉPÉTITEUR.

maggiore (*Italian*) 'major mode'.

magic realism a term devised in the 1920s to describe the work of a group of German painters, part of the NEUE SACHLICHKEIT, whose work exhibited a disquieting blend of surreal fantasy with matter-of-fact representationalism. In literature, the term is often applied with particular reference to the work of certain South

American novelists, notably the Peruvian novelist Mario Vargas Llosa (1936–) and the Colombian Gabriel Garcia Marquez (1928–), whose work combines deadpan description of the everyday world with (often equally deadpan) excursions into fantasy. Some European novelists have been characterized as 'magic realists', e.g. ◊Calvino and ◊Rushdie. The techniques of magic realism have a long ancestry; ◊Chesterton's novel *The Man Who Was Thursday* is a notable early 20th-century example, and there are clear links with the GOTHIC NOVEL.

Magnificat (*Latin*) short for *Magnificat anima mea Dominum* ('My soul magnifies the Lord') the canticle of the Virgin Mary sung at Roman Catholic Vespers and Anglican Evensong. It is usually chanted, but many composers, such as ◊Bach, have set it to their own music.

main (*French*) 'hand', so *main droite* means 'right hand' (particularly in piano music).

major (*Latin*) 'greater', as opposed to MINOR or 'lesser'. Major scales are those in which a major third (INTERVAL of four semitones) occurs in ascending from the tonic; while the minor scales involve a minor third (three semitones). A major tone has the ratio 8 : 9 while a minor tone has the ratio 9 : 10.

malapropism the incorrect use of a word, often through confusion with a similar-sounding word. It is called after Mrs Malaprop, a character in ◊Sheridan's comedy *The Rivals* (1775) whose name is derived from the French mal a propos, 'not apposite'. Some of her malapropisms include 'She's as headstrong as an allegory on the banks of the Nile' and 'Illiterate him quite from your mind'.

malinconia (*Italian*) 'melancholy'.

mancando (*Italian*) 'decreasing' or 'fading away'.

Manchester School the name applied to a group of British composers who studied music at the Royal Manchester College during the 1950s. They include Harrison ◊Birtwhistle and Peter Maxwell ◊Davies, among others.

mandolin, mandoline a stringed instrument, similar to the lute, but smaller, usually played with a plectrum. It has four pairs of strings and is occasionally used as an orchestral instrument.

mano (*Italian*) 'hand'.

Mannerism an exaggerated and often artificial sense of style found in Italian art between *c*.1520 and 1600, i.e. between the High RENAISSANCE and BAROQUE periods. It represents a reaction against the balanced forms and perspectives of Renaissance art and is characterized by uncomfortably posed, elongated figures and contorted facial expressions. Harsh colours and unusual modes of perspective were also used to striking effect. The major artists of the period were able to create emotional responses of greater power and sophistication, and they paved the way for the development of Baroque art.

manual a keyboard on an organ or harpsichord; organs may have four manuals, named *solo*, *swell*, *great* and *choir*.

maracas a pair of Latin-American percussion instruments made from gourds filled with seeds, pebbles or shells. Sound is produced by shaking the gourds.

march a piece of music with a strict rhythm, usually 4/4 time but sometimes in 2/4, 3/4 or 6/8 time, to which soldiers can march. The pace varies with the purpose of the piece, from the extremely slow *funeral* or *dead march* to the *quickstep* (with about 108 steps a minute) and the *Sturm Marsch* or *pas de charge* with 120 steps a minute.

marcia (*Italian*) 'march', so *alla marcia*, 'in a marching style'.

mariachi (*Spanish*) a Mexican folk group of variable size; it normally includes violins and guitars.

marimba a Latin American instrument which may have originated in Africa. It is similar to a large XYLOPHONE and can be played by up to four people at the same time.

mark a sign or word used in NOTATION to indicate the time, tone, accent or quality of a composition, or the pace at which it should be performed.

martelé (*French*) *see* MARTELLATO.

martellato (*Italian*) literally 'hammered'; a term used mainly in music for strings to indicate that notes should be played with short, sharp strokes of the bow. The term is also occasionally used in guitar and piano music.

marziale (*Italian*) 'warlike'.

masque a spectacular court entertainment that was especially popular during the 17th century. It combined poetry and dancing with vocal and instrumental music to tell a simple story that invariably flattered its aristocratic audience.

Mass (*Latin* **Missa**, *Italian* **Messa**, *French* and *German* **Messe**) in musical terms, the setting to music of the Latin Ordinary of Mass (those parts of the Mass that do not vary). The five parts are the KYRIE ELEISON, GLORIA, CREDO, SANCTUS with BENEDICTUS, and AGNUS DEI.

Master of the Queen's Musick an honorary position (in Britain) awarded to a prominent musician of the time; it is his (or her) duty to compose anthems, etc, for royal occasions.

mastersinger *see* MEISTERSINGER.

Matins the name given to the first of the canonical hours of the Roman Catholic Church. The term also refers to morning prayer in the Anglican Church.

mazurka a Polish folk dance of the 17th century for up to 12 people. The music can vary in speed and is often played on bagpipes. ◊Chopin, amongst other composers, was influenced by the music and wrote some 55 'mazurkas' for piano.

me in the TONIC SOL-FA, the third note (or MEDIANT) of the major scale.

measure (1) a unit of rhythm or notes and rests included between two bars. (2) a stately dance of the minuet or pavanne type. (3) (US) a BAR (of music).

mechanical instruments instruments that can play complex music through the programming of their mechanism (e.g. by punched paper or pins on a spindle) when supplied with power (through foot pedals, clockwork, steam power, electricity, etc).

mediant the third note in a major or minor scale above the TONIC (lowest note), e.g. E in the scale of C major.

medium a material used in art, e.g. OIL in painting, PENCIL in drawing, or BRONZE in sculpture. The term is also used to denote a method, e.g. painting as opposed to sculpture.

Meistersinger (*German*) 'mastersinger', the title of highest rank in the song schools or guilds that flourished in German cities from the 14th century until the 19th century. Where the MINNESINGERS drew their members from the aristocracy, mastersingers were usually craftsmen or tradesmen who composed poems and music and who formed themselves into powerful guilds. They were doubtless of great value as a means of extending musical culture, but in their latter days their original purpose tended to be defeated by pedantic restrictions, as satirized in ◊Wagner's great opera, *Die Meistersinger von Nürnberg*.

melodica (*Italian*) a free-reed instrument which was developed from the harmonica. It is box-shaped and has a small keyboard; the player blows down a tube and plays by pressing the keys.

melodic minor scale *see* SCALE.

melodic sequence *see* SEQUENCE.

melodrama a form of drama (from the Greek for 'song' plus 'drama') that seems to have arisen in 18th-century France and that contained elements of music, spectacle, sensational incidents and sentimentalism (*see* SENTIMENTAL COMEDY). The form reached its peak in the popular theatre of 19th-century England, when quite spectacular stage effects often accompanied the action, and villains became blacker than black in their persecution of pure heroes and heroines, e.g. in *The Miller and his Men* (1813) by Isaac Pocock (1782–1835), a Gothic melodrama with splendid bandits, virtuous and faithful young lovers, battles, a wild ravine, and an exploding bridge at the climax. *See also* DOMESTIC TRAGEDY.

melody a succession of notes, of varying pitch, that create a distinct and identifiable musical form. Melody, HARMONY and RHYTHM are the three essential ingredients of music. The criteria of what constitutes a melody change over time.

membranophone the generic term for all instruments in which sound is produced by the vibration of a skin or membrane, for example, DRUM, KAZOO.

meno (*Italian*) 'less', so *meno mosso* means 'slower' (less speed).

menuet (*French*) MINUET.

Messa, Messe *see* MASS.

mesto, mestoso (*Italian*) 'sad'.

metallophone an instrument that is similar to a XYLOPHONE but has metal bars (usually bronze).

metaphysical painting an art movement begun in Italy in 1917 by Carlo Carré (1881–1966) and de ◊Chirico. They sought to portray the world of the subconscious by presenting real objects in incongruous juxtaposition, as in their *Metaphysical Interiors* and *Muses* series (1917). Carré soon abandoned the movement, and by the early 1920s both artists had developed other interests. Although short-lived, the movement did have some influence.

meter (1) in verse, the measured arrangement of syllables according to stress in a rhythmic pattern. (2) in music a rhythmic pattern. *See* RHYTHM.

metaphysical poetry a poetry movement of the 17th century, noted for intense feeling, extended metaphor and striking, elaborate imagery, often with a mystical element. ◊Donne is regarded as the first important metaphysical poet.

method acting a style of acting, devised by Konstantin ◊Stanislavsky, which involves an actor immersing himself in the 'inner life' of the character he is playing, and, using the insights gained in this study, conveying to the audience the hidden reality behind the words. Stanislavsky's theories were adopted and adapted by the American director Lee Strasberg (1901–82), whose method style of acting achieved world fame (or notoriety) through pupils such as James ◊Dean and Marlon ◊Brando.

metronome an instrument that produces regular beats and can therefore be used to indicate the pace at which a piece of music should be played. The first clockwork metronome was invented patented in 1816 and had a metal rod that swung backwards and forwards on a stand. The speed of ticking could be altered by sliding a weight up or down the rod. Electronic metronomes are also manufactured today.

mezzo (*Italian*) literally 'half', so *mezzo-soprano* means a voice between soprano and contralto.

mf abbreviation for *mezzo forte*, (*Italian*) 'moderately loud'.

microtones INTERVALS that are smaller than a SEMITONE in length, for example, the quarter-tone.

middle C the note C which occupies the first ledger line below the treble staff, the first ledger line above the bass staff, and is indicated by the C clef.

military band a band in the armed forces that plays military music, usually for marching. There are many different types of military band, and the number of players varies. Most bands comprise a mixture of brass, woodwind and percussion instruments.

minim a note, formerly the shortest in time-value, with half the value of a SEMIBREVE; the equivalent of a half-note in US terminology.

Minnesingers the poet-musicians of Germany in the 12th and 13th centuries, who were of noble birth, like the TROUBADOURS of France, and who produced *minnelieder*, or love songs. ◊Wagner's Tannhäuser is a minnesinger. They were succeeded by the MEISTERSINGERS.

minor (*Latin*) 'less' or 'smaller'. Minor intervals contain one semitone less than MAJOR. The minor third is characteristic of scales in the minor mode.

minstrel a professional entertainer or musician of medieval times. Such people were often employed by a royal court or aristocratic family.

minuet a French rural dance in 3/4 time that was popular during the 17th and 18th centuries. It was incorporated into classical sonatas and symphonies as a regular movement.

miracle play *see* MYSTERY PLAY.

mirliton (*French*) any wind instrument in which a thin membrane is made to vibrate and make a noise when the player blows, hums or sings into it. It is now known as the KAZOO.

mirror music any piece of music that sounds the same when played backwards.

Miserere (*Latin*) short for *Miserere mei Deus* ('Have mercy upon me, O God'), the first line of the 51st Psalm. It has been set to music by several composers, including ◊Verdi.

Missa (*Latin*) 'Mass', so *Missa brevis* means 'short Mass'; *Missa cantata* means 'sung Mass'; *Missa pro defunctis* is Mass for the dead, or Requiem; and *Missa solemnis* is solemn or high Mass.

misterioso (*Italian*) 'mysteriously'.

misura (*Italian*) 'measure'; equivalent to a BAR.

Mixolydian mode (1) the set of notes, in ancient Greek music, which are the equivalent of the white notes on a piano from B to B. (2) in church music of the Middle Ages onwards, the equivalent of the white notes on a piano from G to G.

mixture an organ stop that brings into play a number of pipes that produce HARMONICS above the pitch corresponding to the actual key which is played.

mobile a type of moving sculpture devised by the American sculptor Alexander Calder (1898–1976) who originally trained as an engineer.

moderato (*Italian*) 'moderate' (in terms of speed).

modes the various sets of notes or SCALES, which were used by musicians until the concept of the KEY was accepted (*c*.1650). Modes were originally used by the ancient Greeks and were adapted by medieval composers, especially for church music. Modes were based on what are now the white notes of the piano.

modulation the gradual changing of key during the course of a part of a composition by means of a series of harmonic progressions. Modulation is *diatonic* when it is accomplished by the use of chords from relative keys; *chromatic* when by means of non-relative keys; *enharmonic* when effected by the alteration of notation; *final*, or *complete*, when a new tonality is established; and *partial*, or *passing*, when the change of key is only transient.

moll (*German*) 'minor' (as opposed to 'major', *dur*).

molto (*Italian*) 'very', so *allegro molto* means 'very fast'.

monochrome a drawing or painting executed in one colour only. *See also* grisaille.

monodrama a dramatic work for a single performer.

monody a type of accompanied solo song which was developed during the late 16th and early 17th centuries. It contained dramatic and expressive embellishments and devices, and consequently had an influence on OPERA.

monothematic a piece of music that is developed from a single musical idea.

monotone declamation of words on a single tone.

montage an art technique similar to COLLAGE, where the images used are photographic.

morbido (*Italian*) 'soft' or 'gentle'.

morceau (*French*) a 'piece' (of music).

mordent a musical ornament whereby one note rapidly alternates with another one degree below it; this is indicated by a sign over the note.

morendo (*Italian*) 'dying', i.e. decreasing in volume.

moresca (*Italian*) a sword dance dating from the 15th and 16th centuries, which represents battles between the Moors and the Christians. It was the origin of the English MORRIS DANCE. It has been included in OPERAS, often to a marching rhythm.

morisco (*Italian*) 'in Moorish style'.

morris dance a style of English dance, the music for which is provided by pipe and tabor. It was orginally a costume dance, the characters often being those from the Robin Hood ballads. Of Moorish or Spanish origin, the dance later became associated with many tunes, some in 4/4, others in 3/4 time.

mosso (*Italian*) 'moved', so *piu mosso* means 'more moved', i.e. quicker, and *meno mosso* 'less speed'.

motet a musical setting of sacred words for solo voices or choir, with or without accompaniment. The first motets were composed in the 13th century.

motif *or* **motive** a small group of notes which create a melody or rhythm, e.g. the first four notes of ◊Beethoven's 5th symphony.

motion the upward or downward progress of a melody. It is said to be *conjunct* when the degrees of the scale succeed each other; *disjunct* where the melody proceeds in skips; *contrary* where two parts move in opposite directions; *oblique* when one part moves while the other remains stationary; and *similar*, or *direct*, when the parts move in the same direction.

moto (*Italian*) 'motion', so *con moto* means 'with motion' or 'quickly'.

motto theme a short theme that recurs during the course of a composition. In this way, it dominates the piece.

mouth organ *see* HARMONICA.

movement a self-contained section of a larger instrumental composition, such as a symphony or sonata.

mp abbreviation for *mezzo piano* (*Italian*), meaning 'half-soft'.

muffled drum a drum with a piece of cloth or towelling draped over the vibrating surfaces. It produces a sombre tone when struck and is usually associated with funeral music.

musette (*French*) (1) a type of small BAGPIPE popular at the French court in the 17th and 18th centuries. (2) an air in 2/4, 3/4 or 6/8 time that imitates the drone of the bagpipe. (3) a dance tune suitable for a bagpipe. (4) an organ reed stop.

musica (*Italian*) 'music'.

musica ficta *or* **cantus fictus** (*Latin*) 'feigned music' or 'feigned song'; it is a term for ACCIDENTALS used in MODE music.

musical a type of play or film in which music plays an important part and the actors occasionally sing, for example, *My Fair Lady*, *West Side Story*.

musical box a clockwork MECHANICAL INSTRUMENT in which a drum studded with small pins plays a tune by plucking the teeth of a metal comb.

musical comedy a term used between 1890 and 1930 to describe a humorous play with light music and singing in it.

music drama a term first used to describe the operas of ◊Wagner, where the action and music are completely interlocked, with, e.g. no pauses for applause after an aria, or repetition within a piece.

musicology the scientific study of music.

musique concrète a term coined by the French composer Pierre Schaffer in 1948 to describe a type of music in which taped sounds are distorted or manipulated by the composer. The term ELECTRONIC MUSIC is now more generally used.

muta (*Italian*) 'change', a musical direction: (1) that the key be changed in horn or drum music; (2) that the MUTE be used.

mutation stops organ stops that produce sound, usually a HARMONIC – which is different from the normal or octave pitch corresponding to the key that is depressed.

mute any device used to soften or reduce the normal volume, or alter the tone, of an instrument. With bowed instruments, a small clamp is slotted onto the bridge; in brass instruments a hand or bung is pushed into the bell; in the piano the soft (left) pedal is pressed; and with drums, cloths are placed over the skins, or sponge-headed drumsticks are used.

mv abbreviation for *mezzo voce*.

mystery play *or* **miracle play** a form of dramatic entertainment based on sacred subjects and given under church auspices which was used before the development of either OPERA or ORATORIO.

Nabis a group of painters working in France in the 1890s. Influenced by the works and ideas of ◊Gauguin and by oriental art, they worked in flat areas of strong colour, avoiding direct representation in favour of a symbolic approach of mystical revelation.

nachdruck (*German*) 'ACCENT' or 'emphasis'.

Nachschlag (*German*) 'after beat', a grace or ORNAMENT, like a short APPOGGIATURA, but occurring at the end instead of at the beginning of a NOTE.

nachspiel (*German*) a POSTLUDE.

Nachtmusik (*German*) 'night music', that is, music suitable for performing in the evening or suggestive of night.

naive art works by untrained artists whose style is noted for its innocence and simplicity. Scenes are often depicted literally, with little attention to formal perspective and with an intuitive rather than studied use of pictorial space, composition and colour. Naive painters work independently of contemporary trends or movements in art, and their works are often fresh and invigorating by comparison.

naker the medieval English name for a small KETTLEDRUM (often with snares, *see* SIDE DRUM) of Arabic origin, from which TIMPANI developed. Nakers were always used in pairs.

national anthem a SONG or HYMN that is formally adopted by a country and sung or played at official occasions.

nationalism a late 19th-century and early 20th-century music movement in which a number of composers set out to write work which would express their national identity, often by reference to FOLK music and by evocation of landscape. It was in part a reaction to the dominance of German music.

natural a NOTE that is neither sharpened nor flattened.

Naturalism a term deriving from the late-19th French literary movement of the same name, denoting fiction characterized by close observation and documentation of everyday life, with a strong emphasis on the influence of the material world on individual behaviour. Naturalistic NOVELS therefore tended to adopt a very deterministic approach to life and fiction, and most practitioners of the form would have described themselves as socialists or social Darwinists. The influence of the school on writers in English was patchy; there are strong elements of naturalism in Arnold ◊Bennett.

natural key KEY of C major.

Nazarenes an art movement based on the Brotherhood of St Luke formed in Vienna in 1809. It involved painters of German and Austrian origin, who worked mainly in Italy. Inspired by the medieval guild system, they worked cooperatively with a common goal of reviving Christian art. Influences included German medieval art and Italian RENAISSANCE painting.

neck the narrow projecting part of a stringed instrument that supports the FINGERBOARD; at the end of the neck lies the PEG-BOX which secures the strings and enables them to be tuned.

nel battere (*Italian*) on the BEAT or down stroke (DOWN-BEAT).

Neoclassicism a term denoting any movement in the Arts emphasizing the virtues of imitating the style and precepts of the great classical writers and artists (Neoclassicist principles in literature derive mostly from the writings of ◊Aristotle – principally the *Poetics* – and some observations by the Roman poets, ◊Virgil and ◊Horace). The hallmarks of Neoclassicism are traditionally defined as balance, moderation, attention to formal rules – such as the dramatic *Unities*, in which time and space is strictly ordered around a sequential plot with a beginning, middle and end – avoidance of emotional display and distrust of enthusiasm, and the assumption that human nature has changed little since CLASSICAL times. Neoclassicism is frequently contrasted with ROMANTICISM, and, interestingly, the strongest period of Neoclassicism in art and architecture is contemporary with the peak period of Romanticism, the late 18th and early 19th centuries.

In literature, Neoclassicism is generally held to have begun with ◊Petrarch in the mid-14th century. The greatest Neoclassical English poets are ◊Dryden and ◊Pope; the greatest Neoclassical English critic is sometimes said to be Dr ◊Johnson, but his espousal of Neoclassical virtues was heavily qualified, particularly in response to French criticism of ◊Shakespeare as virtually a 'literary savage'. Neoclassicism had been a powerful influence on French literature of the 17th century, but has never won wide acceptance among writers in English, not even in the 18th century.

In art and architecture, Neoclassicism was the dominant style in Europe in the late 18th and early 19th centuries. It followed on from, and was essentially a reaction against, BAROQUE and RO-COCO styles. Classical forms were employed to express the reasoned enlightenment of the age, and Neoclassical painters adhered to the Classical principles of order, symmetry and calm. At the same time, they felt free to embrace Romantic themes.

In music, Neoclassicism was a 20th-century movement that reacted against the overtly Romantic forms of the late 19th century. Composers who adhered to the philosophy (in particular ◊Stravinsky, ◊Hindemith, ◊Poulenc and ◊Prokofiev) attempted to create new works with the balance and restraint found in the work of 18th-century composers, especially J. S. ◊Bach.

Neoimpressionism *see* POINTILLISM.

Neoplatonism a synthesis of Platonic and mystical concepts that originated in the Greek-speaking Mediterranean world of the 3rd century. Plotinus (*c*.205–*c*.270) was the main figure behind the synthesis. His ideas, such as the notion of a world soul and the perception of the poet as an inspired prophet who sees the real world behind the shadowy illusions of the material world, have been influential on many English writers, notably ◊Shelley.

neume a sign used in musical NOTATION from the 7th to 14th centuries before the invention of the STAVE. It indicated PITCH.

Neue Sachlichkeit (*German*) 'new objectivity', the title of an exhibition of postwar figurative art which then came to represent any art concerned with objective representation of real life, such works being the opposition to EXPRESSIONIST subjectivity.

new comedy *see* comedy.

Nibelungenlied an anonymous medieval German epic recounting the hero Siegfried's capture of a hoard of gold belonging to a race of dwarfs (the Nibelungs). The epic forms the basis for Wagner's great opera cycle, *The Ring of the Nibelungs*, and was influential on ◊Tolkien's *Lord of the Rings*.

niente (*Italian*) 'nothing'; used in *quasi niente* 'almost nothing', indicating a very soft tone.

Nihilism a philosophical movement originating in mid-19th century Russia that rejected all established authority and values. The revolutionary Bazarov in ◊Turgenev's *Fathers and Sons* is the first significant fictional portrait of a nihilist. Much of ◊Dostoevsky's work, e.g. *The Possessed*, is concerned with exposing the essential shallowness and banality of nihilism. Nihilist characters crop up frequently in English fiction of the late 19th and early 20th century, e.g. in Joseph ◊Conrad's *The Secret Agent*.

ninth an INTERVAL of nine NOTES, in which both the first and last notes are counted.

No *see* Noh.

Nobel prize any of the annual awards endowed by the Swedish chemist Alfred Nobel (1833–96) for significant contributions in the fields of chemistry, physics, literature, medicine or physiology and peace, with economics added later. Winners of the Nobel prize for literature include ◊Kipling (1907), ◊Yeats (1923), ◊Shaw (1925), T. S. ◊Eliot (1948), ◊Pasternak (1958), ◊Hemingway (1954), ◊Beckett (1969), ◊Golding (1983) and ◊Walcott (1992).

nobile, nobilmente (*Italian*) 'noble, nobly'.

nocturne literally a 'night piece', i.e. a piece of music, often meditative in character and suggesting the quietness of night. The form was invented by John ◊Field and later perfected by ◊Chopin.

Noh *or* **No** a form of highly stylized drama originating in 14th-century Japan. The typical Noh play is short, slow-paced, draws heavily on classical Japanese symbolism, and usually involves song, dance, mime and intricately detailed costume.

noire (*French*) literally 'black', a CROTCHET or quarter note.

nomenclature *see* NOTATION.

nonet a group of nine instruments, or a piece of music for such a group.

normal pitch standard PITCH.

nota (*Latin, Italian*) 'NOTE', so *nota bianca* means 'white note' or half-note; *nota buona* is an accented note; *nota cambita* or *cambiata* is a CHANGING NOTE; *nota caratteristica* is a LEADING NOTE; *nota cattiva* is an unaccented note.

notation *or* **nomenclature** the symbols used in written music to indicate the PITCH and RHYTHM of NOTES, the combination and duration of TONES, as well as the graces and shades of expression without which music can become mechanical.

note (1) a SOUND that has a defined PITCH and duration. (2) a symbol for such a sound. (3) the KEY of a PIANO or other keyboard instrument.

novel a sustained fictional prose narrative. Although most of the essential characteristics of the form can be found in ancient texts, such as the Greek Romances of the 3rd century, and in the works of writers of the Roman world, the novel as the term is generally understood, with complex characterization and multilayered strands of plot and character development, is essentially a creation of 18th-century writers in English, particularly ◊Defoe, ◊Richardson and ◊Fielding.

In the early years of the 19th century, the dual tradition of the novel – adventure in the great world outside, and exploration of personality – reached striking new levels in the novels of Sr Walter ◊Scott and Jane ◊Austen respectively, with the latter setting standards of characterization that have rarely been matched. In the course of the 19th century, writers throughout Europe and America, e.g. ◊Dickens, ◊Stendhal, George ◊Eliot, ◊Tolstoy, ◊Dostoyevsky, ◊Balzac, ◊Melville and Henry ◊James, developed the novel into a highly sophisticated vehicle for exploring human consciousness. The 20th century has seen many adaptations of the traditional form of the novel, from the use of the STREAM OF CONSCIOUSNESS technique by Joyce and Woolf, to the MAGIC REALISM of South American writers, with such oddities as the so-called *antinovels* of writers such as the French novelist Alain Robbe-Grillet (1922–) occurring along the way.

novella a short version of the NOVEL; a tale usually leading up to some point, and often, in early versions of the form, of a satirical or scabrous nature.

nuance a subtle change of speed, TONE, etc.

number (1) an integral portion of a musical composition, particularly in opera where it can mean an ARIA, DUET, etc. (2) one of the works on a programme.

Nunc Dimittis (*Latin*) the Song of Simeon, 'Lord, now lettest Thou Thy servant depart in peace', which is sung at both Roman Catholic and Anglican evening services. It has been set to music by numerous composers.

nursery rhyme a (usually traditional) short verse or song for children. Many nursery rhymes, e.g. 'Ring a Ring a Roses' (which refers to the Great Plague) have their roots in ancient and occasionally unsavoury events.

nut (1) the part of the BOW of a stringed instrument that holds the horsehair and that incorporates a screw that tightens the tension of the hairs. (2) the hardwood ridge at the PEG-BOX end of a stringed instrument's FINGERBOARD that raises the strings above the level of the FINGERBOARD.

o when placed over a NOTE in a musical SCORE for strings, indicates that the note must be played on an open string or as a harmonic.

ob abbreviation for OBOE and OBBLIGATO.

obbligato (*Italian*) 'obligatory', a term that refers to a PART that cannot be dispensed with in a performance (some parts can be optional). However, some 19th-century composers used the word to mean the exact opposite, i.e. a part that was optional.

ober (*German*) 'over', 'upper', as OBERWERK.

objet trouvé *see* FOUND OBJECT.

oblique motion two parallel MELODY lines, or PARTS: one moves up or down the SCALE while the other stays on a consistent NOTE.

oboe a WOODWIND instrument with a conical bore and a double REED. The instrument has a history dating back to ancient Egyptian times. SHAWMS evolved from these Egyptian predecessors and became known as HAUTBOIS instruments in the 17th and 18th centuries. The modern oboe (the word is a corruption of 'hautbois') dates from the 18th century. The established variations of the instrument are: the oboe (TREBLE), the COR ANGLAIS (ALTO), or the BASSOON (tenor), and the double bassoon (BASS).

ocarina a small, egg-shaped WIND INSTRUMENT, often made of clay, which is played in a way similar to a RECORDER. It was invented in the mid-19th century and is still made, mainly as a toy.

octave an INTERVAL of eight NOTES, inclusive of the top and bottom notes, e.g. C to C.

octet a group of eight instruments or VOICES, or a piece for such a group.

octobass a huge kind of three-stringed DOUBLE BASS, some four metres in height, which incorporated hand- and pedal-operated levers to STOP the immensely thick strings. It was invented by J.B. Vuillaume in Paris in 1849, but proved impractical.

oeuvre (*French*) a 'work' (OPUS).

offertory an ANTIPHON sung (or music played on the ORGAN) while the priest prepares the bread and wine at a communion service.

ohne (*German*) 'without', hence *ohne worte*, 'without words'.

oil paint a paint made by mixing colour pigments with oil (generally linseed oil) to produce a slow-drying, malleable sticky substance. Oil paint has been the dominant medium in European art since the 15th century because of the range of effects that can be produced.

old comedy *see* comedy.

Ondes Martenot *or* **Ondes Musicales** an ELECTRONIC musical instrument patented in 1922. It was used by ◊Messiaen.

Op, op abbreviation for OPUS.

Op Art *or* **Optical Art** an abstract art that uses precise, hard-edged patterns in strong colours that dazzle the viewer and make the image appear to move.

open harmony *see* HARMONY.

open note (1) in stringed instruments, an OPEN STRING. (2) in BRASS or WOODWIND instruments, a NOTE produced without using VALVES, CROOKS, or KEYS.

open string any string on an instrument that is allowed to vibrate along its entire length without being stopped (*see* STOPPING).

Oper (*German*) 'opera'.

opera a dramatic work in which all, or most of, the text is sung to orchestral ACCOMPANIMENT. It is a formidable musical form, and has a history dating back to Italy in the 16th century. This Italian form of opera reached its culmination in the operas of ◊MONTE-VERDI, in particular his *Orfeo*, but thereafter developed into a rigidly prescribed form of art. The growth of the science of HARMONY and the development of the modern ORCHESTRA led to a revolt against Italian opera, headed by ◊Gluck, ◊Mozart and, later, by ◊Weber in Germany. ◊Wagner gave a new impetus to operatic composition. His approach assumed that music that detracted from interest in the progress of the drama was bad music, and that the purpose of music, as of architecture, of lighting, of costume, and of acting, was to enforce the damatic interest of the text.

Opera demands a LIBRETTO, an orchestra, singers, an ample stage and, only too often, considerable funds to produce. It also requires a suspension of disbelief, for opera is the convention of unreality, but in that unreality lies its ability to work magic.

opéra-bouffe (*French*), **opera buffa** (*Italian*) similar to OPÉRA COMIQUE but with the dialogue sung throughout and spoken only occasionally in *opera buffa* modelled on the French style.

opéra comique (*French*) literally 'a comic OPERA', but in fact an opera consisting of dramatic pieces with music and dancing and instrumental ACCOMPANIMENT, often along tragic rather than comic lines. Like the German SPINGSPIEL, all or nearly all the dialogue is spoken.

opera seria (*Italian*) 'serious OPERA', as usually applied to work of the 17th and 18th centuries.

operetta a short OPERA or, more usually, a term taken to mean an opera with some spoken dialogue and a romantic plot with a happy ending.

Optical Art *see* OP ART.

opus (*Latin*) 'work'; a term used by composers (or their cataloguers) to indicate the chronological order of their works. It is usually abbreviated to Op. and is followed by the catalogued number of the work.

oratorio the musical setting of a religious or epic LIBRETTO for soloists, CHORUS and ORCHESTRA, performed without the theatrical effects of stage and costumes, etc. Oratorio had its beginnings in the MYSTERY PLAYS of the Middle Ages. At first they were performed in MADRIGAL style, and became popular throughout Italy. From Italy, where it was soon overshadowed by OPERA, the oratorio spread to the rest of Europe. The church CANTATAS of J. S. ◊Bach and his PASSIONS can be regarded as its highest expression in northern Germany. In England it was ◊Handel's recourse when opera was no longer profitable or was forbidden. His *Messiah* and ◊Haydn's *Creation* and *The Seasons* were the culmination of the form, but later composers also wrote oratorios, for example ◊Mendelssohn's *Elijah*, and ◊Elgar's *Dream of Gerontius*.

orchestra a group of instruments and their players. The word comes from Greek and means 'dancing place'. This was a space in front of the stage, in which a raised platform was built for the accommodation of the CHORUS. The early composers of OPERA applied the name to the place allotted to their musicians, and it is now used to designate the place, the musicians or the instruments. Orchestras have grown over the centuries in response to larger auditoriums. A standard, modern orchestra contains four families of instruments: STRINGS, WOODWIND, BRASS and PERCUSSION. The exact number of players within each section can vary, and extra instruments can be called for by a particular SCORE.

orchestration the art of writing and arranging music for an OR-CHESTRA.

organ a keyboard wind instrument, played with the hands and feet, in which pressurized air is forced through PIPES to sound NOTES. PITCH is determined by the length of the pipe. There are essentially two types of pipe; FLUE PIPES, which are blown like a WHISTLE, and REED PIPES in which air is blown over vibrating strips of metal. Flue pipes can be 'stopped' (blocked off at one end) to produce a sound an OCTAVE lower than when open. There are a number of keyboards on an organ, one of which is operated by the feet (PEDAL board). Those operated by the hands are called MANUALS, and there are four common categories: the solo (used for playing SOLO MELODIES), the swell (on which notes can be made to sound louder or softer, *see also* SWELL ORGAN), the great (the manual that opens up all the most powerful pipes), and the choir (which operates the softer sounding pipes, *see also* CHOIR ORGAN). In addition there are a number of 'STOPS' (buttons or levers) that can alter the pitch or TONE of specific pipes. The organ dates back to before the time of Christ and has gone through many stages of evolution. ELECTRONIC organs (*see* HAMMOND ORGAN) have been invented and these tend to produce sounds rather different from those in which pumped air is actually used.

organum (1) (*Latin*) 'ORGAN'. (2) measured music, as opposed to unmeasured PLAINSONG, an early form of POLYPHONY.

ornaments and graces embellishments to the NOTES of a MELODY, indicated by symbols or small notes. They were used frequently in the 17th and 18th centuries.

Orpheus the legendary poet and musician of Greek mythology whose name has been adopted by numerous musical societies, etc, and has also been used as the title of several collections of vocal music. The story of Orpheus and his search in the underworld for his wife Eurydice has been the subject of many musical forms.

Orphism *or* **Orphic Cubism** a brief but influential art movement developed out of Cubist principles. Their aim was to move away from the objectivity of CUBISM towards a more lyrical and colourful art. The artists were influenced in part by Italian FUTURISM, and typical works use juxtaposed forms and strong colours. The movement had a deep influence on some of the German EXPRESSIONISTS and on SYNCHROMISM.

oscillator an ELECTRONIC INSTRUMENT that converts electrical energy into audible sound.

ossia (*Italian*) 'or', 'otherwise', 'else'; used to indicate an alternative PASSAGE of music.

ostinato (*Italian*) 'obstinate'; a short PHRASE or other pattern that is repeated over and over again during the course of a composition.

ottava (*Italian*) OCTAVE.

overblow to increase the wind pressure in a WOODWIND instrument to force an upper PARTIAL note instead of its fundamental note, thus producing a harmonic.

overtones *see* HARMONICS.

overture a piece of music that introduces an an OPERA, ORATORIO, BALLET or other major work. Overtures may be built out of the principal THEMES of the work that is to follow, or may be quite independent of them. ◊Beethoven composed no fewer than four overtures to his only opera, *Fidelio*, and ◊Verdi's *Otello* and other operas have no overture whatever. Overtures are nearly always in the SONATA FORM, being, in fact, similar to the first MOVEMENT of a SYMPHONY, on a somewhat larger scale. The CONCERT OVERTURE is often an independent piece, written for performance in a concert hall.

p (1) abbreviation for PIANO (*Italian*), meaning 'soft'. (2) abbreviation for 'PEDAL' (ORGAN).

pandora a plucked stringed instrument of the CITTERN family. It was particularly popular in England during the 16th century.

panpipes a set of graduated PIPES, stopped at the lower end, which are bound together by thongs. Each pipe makes a single NOTE, and sound is produced by blowing across the open end. They are popular in South America and parts of Eastern Europe.

pantomime a combination of dancing and gesticulation by which a drama may be represented without words, although accompanied by music. In Britain, the term is now applied to a musical show with dialogue, traditionally based on a fairy tale and performed at Christmas time.

pantonality *see* ATONAL.

parameter a 20th-century term used to describe aspects of SOUND that can be varied but which nevertheless impose a limit. It is particularly applied to ELECTRONIC MUSIC with regard to volume, etc.

part a VOICE or instrument in a group of performers, or a piece of music for it.

parte (*Italian*) 'PART', so *colla parte* means 'with the part'.

part-song a composition for unaccompanied VOICES in which the highest part usually sings the MELODY while the lower parts sing accompanying HARMONIES.

passacaglia (*Italian*) a type of slow and stately dance originating in Spain, for which keyboard music was written in the 17th century. It has come to mean a work in which such a THEME recurs again and again.

passage a FIGURE or PHRASE of music; a RUN.

passage work a piece of music that provides an opportunity for VIRTUOSO playing.

passamezzo (*Italian*) 'half-step'; a quick Italian dance in DUPLE TIME that became popular throughout Europe in the late 16th century.

passepied (*French*) a French dance in triple TIME, like a quick

MINUET, that is thought to have originated in Brittany. It was incorporated into French ballets of the mid-17th century.

passing note a NOTE that is dissonant with the prevailing HARMONY but that is nevertheless useful in making the TRANSITION from one CHORD or KEY to another.

Passion music the setting to music of the story of Christ's Passion (the story of the Crucifixion taken from the Gospels). The first dramatic representation of the Passion is said to have been made in the 4th century by St Gregory Nazianzen (329–89), bishop of Antioch. It was sung throughout. From the 13th century, the Passion was changed to PLAINSONG melodies by priests in churches during Holy Week. The most celebrated of later Passions are those of Johann Sebastian ◊Bach, the *St John Passion* and the *St Matthew Passion*.

pastel a paint medium of powdered colour mixed with gum arabic to form a hard stick. When applied to paper, the colour adheres to the surface. Pastel was used to great effect by ◊Degas.

pasticchio (*Italian*) literally 'pie', a dramatic entertainment that contains a selection of pieces from various composers' works.

pastoral any piece of literature celebrating the country way of life. The first pastoral poems of any significance are those of Theocritus (*c*.310–*c*.250 BC), a Greek poet whose work established the standard frame of the form: shepherds and shepherdesses singing to one another of their loves in a world of peace and plenty in which the sun always shines. Death, however, is occasionally present in the form of a shepherd lamenting the death of a friend (◊Shakespeare's 'Dead shepherd' couplet from *As You Like It* is a moving, later example of this convention being used as a tribute to Christopher ◊Marlow. Theocritus' form was used by ◊Virgil in his *Eclogues*, so establishing a tradition that lasted for centuries. Later practitioners of the form include ◊Petrarch, ◊Milton and ◊Shelley.

pastorale (1) a vocal or instrumental MOVEMENT or composition in COMPOUND triple TIME, which suggests a rural subject; it usually has long BASS notes that imitate the sounds of the BAGPIPE drone. (2) a stage entertainment based on a PASTORAL.

patter song a kind of comic SONG that has a string of tongue-twisting syllables and is usually sung quickly to minimal ACCOMPANIMENT. It is often found in opera.

Pauken (*German*) KETTLEDRUMS.

pausa (*Italian*) 'REST'.

pause a symbol over a NOTE or REST to indicate that this should be held for longer than its written value.

pavan, pavane a stately court dance, normally in slow DUPLE TIME, which was occasionally incorporated into instrumental music in the 16th century.

pavillon (*French*) literally a 'tent', so, with reference to the shape, the bell of a BRASS INSTRUMENT.

peal a set of church bells or, as a verb, to ring a set of church bells.

ped abbreviation for PEDAL.

pedal the part of an instrument's mechanism that is operated by the feet, such as on a PIANO, ORGAN or HARP. The *forte*, or loud, pedal on a piano by raising the dampers enriches the TONE. The *piano*, or soft, pedal enables the player to strike only one or two strings or to reduce the volume of tone. Harp pedals sharpen, flatten or neutralize one NOTE throughout the COMPASS. Organ pedals produce notes of the lower register independently of the MANUAL or alter the arrangement of the registers.

peg-box the part of a stringed instrument that houses the pegs that anchor and tune the strings.

pencil a mixture of graphite and clay in stick form and covered by a hard casing. The greater the clay element, the harder is the pencil. Graphite replaced lead as the principal component in the 16th century. Until the end of the 18th century, the word 'pencil' also denoted a fine brush.

penny whistle *see* TIN WHISTLE.

pentatonic scale a SCALE composed of five notes in an octave. It is found in various types of folk music from Scottish to Chinese.

per (*Italian*) 'by' or 'for'.

percussion (1) the actual striking of a DISCORD after it has been prepared and before its RESOLUTION. (2) the mechanism by which the tongue of a REED is struck with a HAMMER as air is admitted from the wind chest, thus ensuring immediate 'speaking'.

percussion instrument an instrument that produces TONE when struck, such as the PIANO or XYLOPHONE, but more especially one of the family of instruments that produce SOUND when struck or shaken, for example, MARACAS, DRUMS, TRIANGLE.

perdendosi (*Italian*) 'losing itself', i.e. dying away both in volume of TONE and in speed.

perfect interval *see* INTERVAL.

period a complete musical sentence (*see* PHRASE).

perpetuum mobile (*Latin*) 'perpetually in motion', i.e. a short piece of music with a repetitive NOTE pattern that is played quickly without any PAUSES.

perspective in art, the representation of a three-dimensional view in a two-dimensional space by establishing a vanishing point in the distance at which parallel lines converge, the objects or figures in the distance being smaller and closer together than objects or figures nearer the viewer. Perspective is demonstrated in the works of ◊Giotto, and its rules were formulated by the Italian writer, architect, sculptor and painter Leon Battista Alberti (1404–72) in *De Pictura* (1435), but by the 20th century these were being abandoned by artists.

pesante (*Italian*) 'heavy', 'ponderous' or 'solid'.

PF abbreviation for PIANOFORTE, PIANO FORTE, and PIÙ *forte*.

Phantasie (*German*) *see* FANTASIA.

philharmonic (*Greek*) literally 'music loving'; an adjective used in the titles of many orchestras, societies, etc.

phrase a short melodic section of a composition, of no fixed length, although it is often four BARS long.

piacere (*Italian*) 'pleasure', so *a piacere* means 'at [the performer's] pleasure'.

piacevole (*Italian*) 'pleasantly'.

piangevole (*Italian*) 'sadly'.

pianissimo (*Italian*) 'very quiet'.

piano (1) (*Italian*) 'soft'. (2) the common abbreviated form of PIANOFORTE.

piano accordion *see* ACCORDION.

piano à queue. (*French*) a grand PIANO.

piano carré. (*French*) a square PIANO.

pianoforte, piano a keyboard instrument that was invented by Bartolomeo Cristofori in Florence in 1709 and for which important works were being written by the end of the 18th century. Most modern instruments usually have 88 KEYS and a COMPASS of $7^1/_3$ OCTAVES, although it is possible to find larger versions. The keys operate HAMMERS that strike STRINGS at the back of the instrument. These strings can run vertically (*upright piano*) or horizontally (*grand piano*). Most pianos have one string for the very lowest NOTES, two parallel strings for the middle REGISTER notes and three strings for the highest notes. Normally, when a NOTE is played, a damper (*see* DAMP) deadens the strings when the key returns to its normal position, but a sustaining (right) PEDAL suspends the action of the dampers and allows the note to coninue sounding. The soft (left) pedal mutes the sound produced, either by moving the hammers closer to the strings so that their action is diminished, or by moving the hammers sideways so that only one or two strings are struck. On some pianos, a third, SOSTENUTO pedal, allows selected notes to continue sounding while others are dampened.

pianola *see* PLAYER PIANO.

pibroch (*Gaelic*) a type of Scottish BAGPIPE music with the form of THEME and VARIATIONS.

picaresque novel a type of NOVEL in which the hero (very rarely, the heroine – ◊Defoe's Molly Flanders is the best-known example in English) undergoes an episodic series of adventures. The term derives from the Spanish *picaro*, a rogue or trickster. Many examples appear in 16th-century Spanish literature, when the genre first established itself, but picaresque novels have been appearing since the very earliest days of the novel. The first major English example is Thomas ◊Nashe's lurid *The Unfortunate Traveller*, which appeared in the 1590s along with other, lesser examples. Several great novels of the 18th and 19th centuries, e.g. ◊Smollett's *Roderick Random*, ◊Fielding's *Tom Jones* and ◊Dickens' *Pickwick Papers*, have picaresque elements but inhabit an entirely different emotional and moral world from that of the earlier examples of the genre. Thus, Tom Jones will have a characteristically picaresque sexual escapade with Molly Seagrim, but will not abandon her to the mob, as his scabrous fictional predecessors would cheerfully have done.

piccolo a small FLUTE with a PITCH an OCTAVE higher than a concert flute. It is used in orchestras and MILITARY BANDS.

pick a common expression for plucking the strings on a GUITAR.

pietà the Italian word for 'pity', used in art to denote a painting or sculpture of the body of the dead Christ being supported by the Virgin, often with other mourning figures.

pipe a hollow cylinder in which vibrating air produces SOUND. On many instruments, the effective length of the pipe can be altered to produce a range of NOTES by means of holes that are opened or closed by the fingers.

pipe organ an American term for a real ORGAN, as opposed to an AMERICAN ORGAN.

pistons the VALVES on BRASS instruments that allow players to sound different NOTES.

pitch the height or depth of a SOUND, which determines its position on a SCALE.

più (*Italian*) 'more', so *più* ALLEGRO means 'faster', and *più* FORTE 'more loudly'.

pizz. an abbreviation of PIZZICATO.

pizzicato (*Italian*) 'plucked' (with specific reference to using the fingers to pluck the STRINGS on a bowed instrument).

plainsong the collection of ancient MELODIES to which parts of Roman Catholic services have been sung for centuries. The best-known is GREGORIAN CHANT. Plainsong is usually unaccompanied and sung in UNISON. It is also in free RHYTHM, i.e. it does not have BARS but follows the prose rhythm of the PSALM or prayer.

Platonism the theory of forms devised by ◊Plato in which objects as we perceive them are distinguished from the idea of the objects, a theory that has had a strong influence on many writers, e.g. ◊Donne, ◊Wordsworth, and, most of all, ◊Shelley (*see also* NEOPLATONISM). Plato's speculations are contained in dialogue form in several works, e.g. the *Symposium* and *Phaedo*, and in *The Republic* (an examination of the principles of good government).

player piano *or* **pianola** a mechanical PIANO operated pneumatically by a perforated roll of paper.

plectrum a small piece of horn, plastic or wood that is used to pluck the STRINGS of a GUITAR, MANDOLIN, ZITHER, etc.

plein air (*French*) 'open air', used of paintings that have been produced out of doors and not in a studio. Plein air painting was particularly popular with the BARBIZON SCHOOL and became a central tenet of IMPRESSIONISM.

poco (*Italian*) 'little' or 'slightly', so *poco* DIMINUENDO means 'getting slightly softer' and *poco a poco* means 'little by little'.

poem an arrangement of words, especially in METER, often rhymed, in a style more imaginative than ordinary speech.

poet laureate a poet appointed to a court or other formal institution. In Britain, the post is held for life and the poet laureate is expected, although not forced, to write a poem to commemorate important events. Ben ◊Jonson held the post unofficially, being succeeded by Sir William Davenant (1606–68). The first official poet laureate was ◊Dryden, who was also the first to lose the post before his death, in the upheaval surrounding the 'Glorious Revolution'. Dryden's successor in 1689 was Thomas Shadwell (*c*.1642–92). Nahum Tate (1652–1715) held the office from 1692, and Nicholas Rowe (1674–1718) from 1715. Laurence

Eusden (1688–1730) succeeded in 1718, more for political reasons than for poetic ones. He is better known for being mentioned in ◊Pope's *Dunciad* for his drinking habits than for any skill as a poet. His successor in 1730, the actor and dramatist Colley Cibber (1671–1757), also became a target of the *The Dunciad*, Pope personifying him as 'Dullness' in the final edition. The appointment in 1757 of the dramatist William Whitehead (1715–85) also attracted satirical comment. Thomas Warton (1728–90) held the post from 1785, and Henry James Pye (1745–1813) from 1790. The reputation of the post revived a little with the appointment of ◊Southey in 1813 and considerably with ◊Wordsworth (1843–50) and ◊Tennyson (1850–92) but suffered a setback with the appointment of Alfred Austin (1835–1913) in 1896. The 20th-century holders of the post were Robert Bridges (1844–1930) from 1913, ◊Masefield (1930–67), ◊Day-Lewis (1968–72), ◊Betjeman (1972–84), and Ted ◊Hughes (1984–).

poi (*Italian*) 'then', so SCHERZO DA CAPO, *poi la* CODA means 'repeat the scherzo, then play the coda'.

point the tip of a BOW; the opposite end to the part that is held (the heel).

point d'orgue (*French*) 'ORGAN point'. It can indicate a harmonic PEDAL (a NOTE sustained under changing HARMONIES); the sign for a PAUSE; or a CADENZA in a CONCERTO.

pointillism a scientific and logical development of IMPRESSIONISM pioneered by the pointillist painters, notably ◊Seurat and ◊Pissarro. The brokenly applied brushwork of ◊Monet and ◊Renoir was extended and refined to a system of dots of pure colour, applied according to scientific principles, with the intention of creating an image of greater purity and luminosity.

In music, the term was borrowed to describe a style in which NOTES seem to be isolated as 'dots' rather than as sequential parts of a MELODY. It is applied to the works of certain 20th-century composers, such as ◊Webern.

polacca (*Italian*) *see* POLONAISE.

polka a ROUND DANCE in quick 2/4 TIME from Czechoslovakia. It became popular throughout Europe in the mid-19th century.

polonaise (*French*), **polacca** (*Italian*) a stately ballroom dance of Polish origin in moderately fast 3/4 TIME. It was used by ◊Chopin in sixteen strongly patriotic piano pieces.

polyphony (*Greek*) literally 'many sounds', i.e. a type of music in which two or more PARTS have independent melodic lines, arranged in COUNTERPOINT. The blending of several distinct MELODIES is what is aimed for, rather than the construction of a single melody with harmonized ACCOMPANIMENT.

polyptych a painting, usually an ALTARPIECE, consisting of two or more paintings within a decorative frame. *See also* DIPTYCH, TRIPTYCH.

polytonality the use of two or more KEYS at the same time.

ponticello (*Italian*) 'BRIDGE' (of a stringed instrument).

Pop Art a realistic art style that uses techniques and subjects from commercial art, comic strips, posters, etc. The most notable exponents include ◊Lichtenstein, ◊Oldenburg, and Robert Rauschenberg (1925–).

pop music short for 'popular' music, i.e. 20th-century music specifically composed to have instant appeal to young people. There are many types of pop music, with influences ranging from JAZZ and FOLK to ROCK and REGGAE.

portamento (*Italian*) literally 'carrying'; an effect used in singing or on bowed instruments in which sound is smoothly 'carried' or slid from one NOTE to the next without a break.

portraiture the art of painting, drawing or sculpting the likeness of someone, either the face, the figure to the waist, or the whole person. Portraits vary from the idealized or romanticized to the realistic.

position a term used in the playing of stringed instruments for where the left hand should be placed so that the fingers can play different sets of NOTES; e.g. first position has the hand near the end of the strings, second position is slightly further along the FINGERBOARD.

poster paint *see* GOUACHE.

posthorn a simple (valveless) BRASS instrument similar to a BUGLE, but usually coiled in a circular form.

Postimpressionism a blanket term used to describe the works of artists in the late 19th century who rejected IMPRESSIONISM. It was not a movement in itself, and most of the artists it refers to worked in widely divergent and independent styles. They include ◊Braque, ◊Picasso, ◊Cézanne, ◊Gauguin, Van ◊Gogh and ◊Matisse. The name was coined by the English art critic Roger Fry (1866–1934), an enthusiastic supporter of modern art, who organized the first London exhibition of Postimpressionist painters in 1912.

postlude the closing section of a composition.

Poststructuralism *see* STRUCTURALISM.

pot-pourri (*French*) a medley of well-known tunes played at a concert.

pp, PP an abbreviation for PIANISSIMO, 'very soft'; *ppp* means 'even softer'.

precentor the official in charge of music, or the leader of the singing, at a cathedral, monastery, etc. *See also* CANTOR.

precipitato, precipitoso (*Italian*) 'precipitately', hence also 'impetuously'.

prelude an introductory piece of music or a self-contained PIANO piece in one MOVEMENT.

Pre-Raphaelite Brotherhood a movement founded in 1848 by Holman ◊Hunt, ◊Millais and ◊Rossetti, who wanted to raise standards in British art. They drew their imagery from medieval legends and literature in an attempt to provide an escape from industrial materialism. They sought to recreate the innocence of Italian painting before ◊Raphael, and were influenced by the works of the NAZARENES. They had a large following, partly due to the support of the critic John ◊Ruskin, which included William ◊Morris. The movement broke up in 1853.

presto (*Italian*) 'lively'; *prestissimo* indicates the fastest speed of which a performer is capable.

prima donna (*Italian*) the 'first lady', i.e. the most important female singer in an opera.

primary colours the colours red, blue and yellow, which in painting cannot be produced by mixing other colours. Primary colours are mixed to make orange (red and yellow), purple (red and blue) and green (blue and yellow), which are the *secondary colours*.

primo (*Italian*) 'first', as the first or top PART of a PIANO DUET (the lower part being termed *secondo*, 'second').

principal (1) the LEADER of a section of an orchestra (e.g. principal HORN). (2) a singer who regularly takes leading parts in an OPERA company, but not the main ones (e.g. a principal TENOR).

principal subject the first SUBJECT in a SONATA FORM or a RONDO.

Prix de Rome (*French*) an annual prize awarded by the French government to artists of various disciplines who had been sent to study in Rome for four years. ◊Berlioz, ◊Bizet and ◊Debussy were all winners, but ◊Ravel failed after many attempts. It was first awarded in 1803, and was discontinued in 1968.

programme music music that attempts to tell a story or evoke an image. The term was first used by ◊Liszt to describe his SYM-

PHONIC POEMS. ◊Beethoven made occasional incursions into the realm of programme music, notably in his symphony no. 6 in F (1808), the *Pastoral Symphony*, each of the five movements of which has an evocative title: '1. *Allegro ma non molto*, The pleasant feelings aroused in the heart on arriving in the country; 2. *Andante con moto*, Scene at the brook; 3. *Allegro*, Jovial assembly of country folk, interrupted by 4. *Allegro*, thunderstorm; 5. *Allegretto*, pleasurable feelings after the storm, mixed with gratitude to God'.

progression MOTION from NOTE to note, or from CHORD to chord.

Promenade Concerts an annual season of concerts given in London's Royal Albert Hall. The 'Proms' were instituted in 1895 by Robert Newman and were conducted until 1944 by Sir Henry ◊Wood. Cheap tickets are available for standing-room; people do not, however, walk about. Several cities around the world (such as Boston, Massachusetts) have similar concert seasons.

psalm a poem (song) from the Old Testament's Book of Psalms. Attributed to King David, psalms were inherited by the Christian churches from the earlier service of the Jews. The word is from Greek, and means 'to pluck a string', hence HARP song.

psalmody the singing of PSALMS to music or the musical setting of a psalm.

psalter a book of PSALMS and psalm tunes.

psaltery a medieval stringed instrument, similar to the DULCIMER except that the STRINGS are plucked and not struck. It is usually trapezium-shaped and is generally played horizontally.

pulse *see* BEAT.

Pult (*German*) 'desk', i.e. the music stand that two orchestral players share.

punta (*Italian*) 'POINT'; so *a punta d'arco* means 'at the point of the BOW', indicating that only the tip of the bow should be used to play the strings.

quadrille a French dance that was particularly fashionable in the early 19th century. It comprised five sections in alternating 6/8 and 2/4 time.

quadruple counterpoint four-PART COUNTERPOINT so constructed that all the parts may be transposed.

quadruplet a group of four NOTES of equal value played in the time of three.

quadruple time *or* **common time** the TIME of four CROTCHETS (quarter notes) in a BAR, indicated by the time signature 4/4 or C.

quarter note (US) *see* CROTCHET

quarter tone half a SEMITONE, which is the smallest INTERVAL traditionally used in Western music.

quartet a group of four performers; a composition for four SOLO instruments or for four VOICES.

quasi (*Italian*) literally 'as if' or 'nearly'; so *quasi niente* means 'almost nothing', or as softly as possible.

quattrocento an Italian term that refers to 15th-century Italian art, often used descriptively of the early RENAISSANCE period.

quaver a NOTE that is half the length of a CROTCHET and the eighth of a SEMIBREVE (whole note).

quickstep a MARCH in quick TIME, which also developed into the modern ballroom dance.

quintet a group of five performers; a composition for five SOLO instruments or for five VOICES.

quintuple time five BEATS, usually CROTCHETS, in a BAR, i.e. 5/4 TIME.

quodlibet (*Latin*) 'what you will'; a term used to describe a collection of tunes that are cleverly woven together to create an amusing entertainment.

R an abbreviation for RIPIENO or for 'right'.

racket *or* **rackett** *or* **ranket** a WOODWIND instrument with a double REED used between the late 16th and early 18th centuries. It came in four sizes (SOPRANO, TENOR, BASS, double bass) and created a distinctive buzzing sound.

rag a piece of RAGTIME music, notably as developed by ◊Joplin.

raga a type of Indian SCALE or a type of MELODY based on such a scale. Each raga is associated with a mood and with particular times of the day and year.

ragtime a style of syncopated (*see* SYNCOPATION) popular dance music, dating from the late 19th century, which was adopted by many composers, e.g. ◊Debussy with *Cakewalk*, and ◊Stravinsky with *Ragtime*. The combination of ragtime and BLUES led to the development of JAZZ. Scott ◊Joplin was a famous ragtime composer.

rallentando (*Italian*) 'slowing down'.

ranket *see* RACKET.

rap a term for an influential type of POP MUSIC of the late 20th century, which has a pulsating RHYTHM and in which LYRICS for SONGS are usually spoken to the BEAT and not sung.

rattle a type of PERCUSSION INSTRUMENT that traditionally consists of a hollowed-out gourd filled with seeds that rattle when shaken.

An alternative type is a contraption in which a strip of wood held in a frame strikes against a cog-wheel as the frame is twirled round. It is occasionally required as a percussion instrument in orchestras.

re *or* **ray** in the TONIC SOL-FA, the second NOTE of the MAJOR SCALE.

Realism in literature, a true and faithful representation of reality in fiction. Once defined, discussion of the term usually breaks down into personal prejudices of various kinds. The process of distinguishing the term from NATURALISM is particularly fraught; any artist must select from the chaos of life in order to create, and in the process of choosing must impose some personal, even if banal, vision on the world, and in the process either convince the reader that the world portrayed is a real one, or fail. In the last analysis, there is only good writing and bad writing. ◊Balzac is regarded as the founding father of literary realism.

In art, Realism is taken to be, in general, the objective representation of scenes. The term is used particularly of the 19th-century French painters, e.g. ◊Daumier and ◊Courbet, who broke away from CLASSICISM and ROMANTICISM.

rebec *or* **rebeck** a small instrument with a pear-shaped body and, usually, three strings that were played with a BOW. It developed from the Arabian *rebab* and was used in Europe from the 16th century.

recapitulation *see* SONATA FORM.

recit. an abbreviation of RECITANDO or RECITATIVE.

recital a public concert given by just one or two people, e.g. a singer with PIANO ACCOMPANIMENT.

recitando (*Italian*) 'reciting', i.e. speaking rather than singing.

recitative a way of singing (usually on a fixed NOTE) in which the RHYTHM and lilt are taken from the words, and there is no tune as such. It is commonly used in OPERA and ORATORIO.

reciting note in PLAINSONG, the NOTE on which the first few words of each verse of a PSALM are sung.

recorder a straight, end-blown FLUTE, as opposed to a side-blown (concert) flute. Notes can be played by opening or closing eight holes in the instrument with the fingers. Recorders come in CONSORTS (families): DESCANT, TREBLE, TENOR and BASS.

Redskins and Palefaces a distinction between authors who write about outdoor, manly topics such as men at war (Redskins), and those who write about the problems and relationships of indoors, 'cultivated' people. It was formulated by an American academic, Leslie Fielder, and works easily in terms of much American literature, e.g. ◊Hemingway is as obviously a Redskin as Henry ◊James is a Paleface. It is less helpful elsewhere.

reed the small part found in many blown instruments that vibrates when air is blown across it and actually creates the sound. It is usually made of cane or metal. In single-reed instruments (e.g. CLARINET, SAXOPHONE), the reed vibrates against the instrument itself; in double-reed instruments (e.g. COR ANGLAIS, BASSOON), two reeds vibrate against each other; in free-reed instruments (e.g. HARMONIUM, CONCERTINA), a metal reed vibrates freely within a slot.

reed organ the generic term for a number of instruments that have no PIPES and use FREE REEDS to produce their NOTES. Examples are the ACCORDION and the HARMONIUM.

reed pipe an ORGAN pipe with a metal reed in the mouthpiece, which vibrates when air is passed over it.

reel a Celtic dance, usually in quick 4/4 TIME and in regular four-BAR PHRASES.

refrain the CHORUS of a BALLAD.

regal a portable REED ORGAN of the 16th and 17th centuries.

reggae a type of Jamaican POP MUSIC with a heavy and pronounced RHYTHM and strongly accented UPBEAT. Its best-known exponent was Bob ◊Marley.

register (1) a set of ORGAN PIPES that are controlled by a single STOP. (2) a part of a singer's vocal COMPASS, e.g. CHEST register, HEAD register, etc. The term is also applied to certain instruments.

related keys *see* MODULATION.

relative major, relative minor terms used to describe the connection between a MAJOR KEY and a MINOR KEY that share the same KEY SIGNATURE, e.g. A minor is the relative key of C major.

relief a sculptural form that is not freestanding. The three-dimensional shape is either carved, e.g. in stone, wood, ivory, etc, or built up, as in metal, etc. Relief sculpture can be *low relief* (*basso relievo* or *bas-relief*), where the depth of the pattern is less than half; *medium relief* (*mezzo relievo*), where the depth is roughly half; or *high relief* (*alto relievo*), where practically all the medium has been removed. The extremely low-relief technique of *stiacciato*, 'drawing in marble', was devised by ◊Donatello.

Renaissance in literature, the revival of the arts that occurred in Europe in the 14th-16th centuries, as a result of the rediscovery of the writing of the great classical writers, notably the works of

◊Plato and ◊Aristotle. In the case of the latter, the 'rediscovery' occurred in terms of reinterpretation; instead of taking the texts of Aristotle as literal, unchallengable authority, as medieval scholars had tended to do, the new thinkers, such as Francis ◊Bacon (the father of modern scientific method) approached written authority with a new, sceptical eye. The Renaissance period in England is usually given as 1500–1660, i.e. from the visit of ◊Erasmus in 1599 to the RESTORATION.

In art, the early Renaissance was established in Italy with the works of ◊Giotto, in a spectacular move away from Gothic conventions and ideals. The sculptors ◊Pisano and ◊Donatello emulated Greek and Roman sculpture in an expression of the new humanist and aesthetic values of the 'age of reason'. The movement reached a peak between 1500 and 1520 with the works of ◊Leonardo da Vinci, ◊Michelangelo and ◊Raphael. The Northern Renaissance took place as ideas spread to Germany, the Netherlands and the rest of Europe during the early 16th century.

repeat two or four DOTS in the spaces of the STAVE that indicate that the PASSAGE so marked is to be played through twice.

répétiteur (*French*) a person hired to teach musicians or singers their PARTS, particularly in OPERA.

replica (*Italian*) 'repeat', so *senza replica* means 'without repetition'.

representational art *see* FIGURATIVE ART.

reprise a musical repetition; it is often found in musical comedies when songs heard in one act are repeated in another.

reredos *see* ALTARPIECE.

Requiem a MASS for the dead in the Roman Catholic Church, so called because of the opening words at the beginning of the INTROIT, *Requiem aeternam dona eis, Domine* ('Grant them eternal rest, O Lord'). It is sung annually in commemoration of the dead on All Souls' Day and may also be sung at the funeral and on the anniversary of the death of an individual. Besides the Introit, the other chief divisions are the KYRIE; the Gradual, *Requiem aeternam* and tract, *Absolve Domine*; the *Sequence*, DIES IRAE; the *Offertorium, Domine Jesu Christi* ('Lord Jesus'); the SANCTUS; the BENEDICTUS; the AGNUS DEI, the *Communion, Lux aeterna* ('Light eternal'); and sometimes the *Responsorium, Libera me* ('Deliver me'); and the *Lectio, Taedet animam meam*.

Notable settings of the Requiem have been composed by ◊Palestrina, ◊Mozart, ◊Brahms, ◊Beethoven and ◊Verdi.

resolution a term for a process in HARMONY by which a piece moves from DISCORD to CONCORD.

resonance the intensification and prolongation of a SOUND or a musical NOTE produced by sympathetic VIBRATION.

responses the PLAINSONG replies of a CHOIR or congregation to SOLO CHANTS sung by a priest.

rest a sign employed in NOTATION indicating silence.

Restoration (1) the re-establishment of the British monarchy in 1660, following the return to England of Charles II in that year. (2) the period of Charles II's reign (1660–85). The characteristics of Restoration literature are wit, salaciousness, and religious and philosophical questioning.

Restoration comedy *see* COMEDY OF MANNERS.

resultant tone *see* COMBINATION TONE.

retable *see* ALTARPIECE.

retardation a SUSPENSION in which a DISCORD is resolved upwards by one step rather than downwards.

retrograde motion a term for music that is played backwards.

revenge tragedy a form of tragedy that appeared in the late Elizabethan period, heavily influenced by the bloodthirsty language and plots of ◊Seneca's plays, in which revenge, often for the death of a son or father, is the prime motive. Thomas ◊Kyd's *The Spanish Tragedy* (1588–9) is the earliest example, ◊Shakespeare's *Hamlet* (1602) the greatest. ◊Marlowe's *The Jew of Malta* (1592) is another notable example. *See also* JACOBEAN TRAGEDY.

reveille (pronounced 'revally') a BUGLE call used by the British Army to awaken soldiers.

rf, rfz abbreviations for RINFORZANDO.

RH abbreviation for 'right hand'.

rhapsody the title commonly given by 19th- and 20th-century composers to an instrumental composition in one continuous movement. Rhapsodies are often based on FOLK tunes, and are nationalistic or heroic in tone.

rhythm the regular recurrence of beat, accent or silence in the flow of sound, especially of words and music. In MUSIC NOTATION, rhythm is determined by the way in which NOTES are grouped together into BARS, the number and type of BEATS in a bar (as governed by the TIME SIGNATURE), and the type of emphasis (ACCENT) that is given to the beats. Along with MELODY and HARMONY, it is one of the essential characteristics of music.

rhythm and blues a type of POP MUSIC that combines elements of BLUES and JAZZ. It developed in the USA and was widely accepted by white audiences and pop musicians. ROCK'N' ROLL evolved from rhythm and blues.

rhythm-names *see* TIME-NAMES.

rhythm section the name given to the PERCUSSION and DOUBLE BASS section of a JAZZ band; it provides the all-important BEAT.

ribs the sides uniting the back and belly of an instrument of the VIOLIN family.

rigaudon *or* **rigadoon** a jaunty dance from southern France that has two or four BEATS to the BAR. It was used in French ballets and operas, and it became popular in England in the late 17th century.

rigoroso (*Italian*) 'rigorously', i.e. in exact TIME.

rinforzando (*Italian*) literally 'reinforcing', i.e. a sudden strong ACCENT on a NOTE or CHORD.

ripieno (*Italian*) literally 'full'; a term used to describe PASSAGES that are to be played by the whole BAROQUE orchestra, rather than only a soloist.

risoluto (*Italian*) 'resolute' or 'in a resolute manner'.

rit. an abbreviation of RITARDANDO.

ritardando (*Italian*) 'becoming gradually slower'.

ritenuto (*Italian*) 'held back' (in TEMPO), i.e. slower.

ritmo, ritmico (*Italian*) 'RHYTHM', 'rhythmic'.

ritornello (*Italian*) literally a 'small repetition'. (1) a short PASSAGE for the whole orchestra in a BAROQUE ARIA or CONCERTO, during which the soloist is silent. (2) a short instrumental piece, played between scenes in early OPERA.

rock a type of POP MUSIC that evolved from ROCK 'N' ROLL in the USA during the 1960s. It mixes COUNTRY AND WESTERN with RHYTHM AND BLUES and is usually played loudly on electric instruments.

rock 'n' roll a type of POP MUSIC, with a strong, catchy RHYTHM, that evolved in the USA during the 1950s and is often associated with 'jiving' (fast dancing that requires nimble footwork). Elvis ◊Presley was one of its greatest early exponents.

Rocky Mountain School an American school of painters who painted landscapes of this formidable countryside in the middle of the 19th century. Its principal member was Albert Bierstadt (1830–1902), a German-born American landscape painter.

Rococo a style in art following on from BAROQUE and even more exaggerated in terms of embellishments and mannered flourishes. It became established around the beginning of the 18th century and spread throughout Europe, lasting up until the advent of NEOCLASSICISM in the 1760s. The main exponents of the style were ◊Fragonard and ◊Watteau in France and, to a lesser extent, ◊Tiepolo in Italy and ÿHogarth in England. It continued in some areas to the end of the century, particularly in church decoration.

Music from the same period is sometimes similarly termed.

roll a TRILL on PERCUSSION INSTRUMENTS produced by sounding NOTES so rapidly that they overlap and appear to produce a continuous sound.

romance a love SONG or composition of a romantic character.

Romanticism a term denoting any movement in the arts which emphasizes feeling and content as opposed to form and order. The Romantic movement can be roughly dated from the late 18th century to the early 19th century, although the contrast between the need to express emotion and the desirability of following artistic rules dates back as far as the great Athenian dramatists. Other distinctive features of the Romantic movement are: the supremacy of individual over collective judgment; a 'progressive' faith in the reformability and essential goodness of humanity; the supremacy of 'natural' and 'organic' virtues over society's artifical construction. The extent and meaning of Romanticism in 18th-century English literature is still a matter of hot debate. It is certainly true that elements of what we call Romanticism can be found in poets such as ◊Cowper and ◊Smart, and even in Dr ◊Johnson's writings, but the first great works of Romantic literature are ◊Blake's works of the 1790s and ◊Wordsworth and ◊Coleridge's *Lyrical Ballads* (1798). Other prominent Romantic poets are ◊Byron, ◊Shelley, ◊Keats, ◊Heine and ◊Scott. *Compare* NEOCLASSICISM.

In art, the movement dates from the late 18th until the mid-19th century. It was a reaction to the balanced harmony and order of Classicism, and identified with the Romantic writers of the age. In response to increasing industrialization, Romantic painters viewed nature from a nostalgic point of view, imbuing landscapes with powerful emotions, often in a melancholic or melodramatic way. Notable Romantic artists include ◊Fuseli, ◊Goya, ◊Delacroix, ◊Géricault, ◊Friedrich, ◊Constable, ◊Turner and the visionary Blake.

In music, Romanticism lasted from *c*.1820 to *c*.1920. During this phase music tended to be more poetic, subjective and individualistic than previously. Lyricism, drama and often nationalistic feeling were characteristic of Romantic music.

Rome, Prix de *see* PRIX DE ROME.

ronde (*French*) literally 'round', as a noun a SEMIBREVE.

rondo a form of instrumental music that incorporates a recurring THEME, either in an independent piece or (more usually) as part of a MOVEMENT. It usually starts with a lively tune (the 'SUBJECT'), which is repeated at intervals throughout the movement. Intervening sections are called EPISODES, and these may or may not be in different keys from the subject. Rondo forms often occur in the final movements of SYMPHONIES, SONATAS and CONCERTOS.

root the lowest ('fundamental' or 'generating') NOTE of a CHORD. Hence, for example, the chord C-E-G has a root of C

rosin a hard resin that is applied to the hair of BOWS used to play VIOLINS, etc. It causes increased friction between the hairs of the bow and the strings.

round a short CANON in which each PART enters at equal INTERVALS and in UNISON.

round dance a dance in which partners start opposite each other and subsequently form a ring.

roundelay a poem with certain lines repeated at intervals, or the tune to which such a poem was sung.

rubato (*Italian*) literally 'robbed', i.e. the taking of TIME from one NOTE or PASSAGE and passing it on to another note or passage.

rumba a sexually suggestive and fast Afro-Cuban dance in syncopated (*see* SYNCOPATION) 2/4 TIME.

run a SCALE or succession of NOTES rapidly played, or, if vocal, sung to one syllable.

Russian Futurism *see* FUTURISM.

S abbreviation for SEGNO, SENZA, SINISTRA, SOLO, SORDINO, SUBITO.

sackbut an instrument of the 15th century, probably originating in Spain. It is similar to the TROMBONE, but smaller.

sacra conversazione (*Italian*) 'holy conversation', in art denoting a painting in one panel of the Virgin and Child with saints.

St Cecilia *see* CECILIA, ST.

Saite (*German*) a 'string'.

salon (*French*) 'room', now also denoting an art exhibition. In the 19th century, the Salon was the annual exhibition of the ACADÉMIE FRANÇAISE, whose powerful and conventional jury increasingly refused to show the work of innovative artists. In 1863 Napoleon III ordered that there be an exhibition of artists' work rejected by the Salon, the Salon des Refusés.

saltando (*Italian*) literally 'leaping', i.e. an instruction to the string player to bounce the BOW lightly off the string.

saltarello a festive Italian FOLK dance in 3/4 or 6/8 TIME.

samba a Brazilian carnival dance in 2/4 TIME but with syncopated (*see* SYNCOPATION) rhythms.

samisen *see* SHAMISEN.

sämtlich (*German*) 'complete', as in *sämtliche Werke,* the 'complete works'.

Sanctus (*Latin*) 'Holy, holy, holy'; a part of the Ordinary of MASS in the Roman Catholic Church. It has been set to music by many composers.

sarabande (*French*) a slow dance in 3/2 or 3/4 TIME, which came to Italy from Spain.

Satz (*German*) a 'MOVEMENT' or 'piece of music'.

sautille (*French*) a SALTANDO.

Savoy Operas a name for the light operas written by ◊Gilbert and Sullivan, which were first performed at the Savoy Theatre in London by the D'OYLY CARTE company.

saxhorn a family of BUGLE-like BRASS instruments patented by the Belgian instrument-maker Adolphe Sax (1814–94) in 1845. They were innovative in that they had VALVES, as opposed to the KEYS normally associated with the bugle family.

saxophone a family of instruments patented by Adolphe Sax (*see* SAXHORN) in 1846 which, although made of brass, actually belong to the WOODWIND group because they are REED instruments. Saxophones come in many different sizes (e.g. SOPRANO, TENOR) and are commonly used in JAZZ bands as well as orchestras.

scala (*Italian*) 'staircase', from which the Teatro alla SCALA gets its name, but in music a RUN or SCALE.

Scala, La *or* **Teatro alla Scala** Milan's, and Italy's, premier opera house, which was opened in 1778.

scale an ordered sequence of NOTES that ascend or descend in PITCH. The most frequently used scales in European music are the MAJOR and MINOR scales, which use TONES (whole notes) and SEMITONES (half-notes) as steps of progression.

scat singing a type of singing used in JAZZ in which nonsense SOUNDS rather than words are sung.

scena (*Italian*) 'scene', a division of an act marked by a change of scenery. In OPERA, a solo movement of dramatic purpose, generally an extended aria.

scherzando, scherzoso (*Italian*) 'playful', or 'lively', as of a phrase or movement.

scherzetto (*Italian*) a short SCHERZO.

scherzo (*Italian*) 'joke', i.e. a cheerful, quick piece of music, either vocal or instrumental. The third MOVEMENT (of four) in many SYMPHONIES, SONATAS, etc, often takes the form of a scherzo.

schnell (*German*) 'quick'.

school in art, a group of artists who hold similar principles and work in a similar style. In art history, it also denotes that a painting has been executed by a pupil or assistant. In music, the characteristics of certain composers, whose style made a school.

Schottische (*German*) 'Scottish'; a ROUND DANCE, similar to the POLKA, that was popular in the 19th century. It is not in fact Scottish, but is so called because it is what those on the Continent thought a Scottish dance should be like.

Schrammel quartet a Viennese ENSEMBLE usually comprising two VIOLINS, a GUITAR and an ACCORDION, or the music composed for such an ensemble. It takes its name from Joseph Schrammel (1858–93), who wrote WALTZES for such a group.

scordatura (*Italian*) 'mistuning', i.e. the TUNING of stringed instruments to abnormal NOTES, so as to produce special effects.

score music written down in such a way that it indicates all the PARTS for all the performers, i.e. the whole COMPOSITION. A *full* or *orchestral score* is one with separate STAVES for each part. A *piano score* is one in which all the instrumental parts are represented on two staves. A *vocal score* is a piano score with two additional staves for the vocal parts. A *short close* or *compressed score* has more than one part to the stave.

scoring the writing of a SCORE.

Scotch snap the name for a RHYTHM that leaps from a short NOTE to a longer note. It is found in many Scottish FOLK tunes.

scraper a PERCUSSION INSTRUMENT in which SOUND is produced by scraping a stick over a series of notches cut into a piece of wood or bone.

scroll the decorative end of the PEG-BOX of a VIOLIN (or other stringed instrument), which may be carved into a curl resembling a scroll, or an animal head.

sec (*French*), **secco** (*Italian*) 'unornamented', 'plain'.

secondary colours *see* PRIMARY COLOURS.

Section d'Or a group of painters in France who associated between 1912 and 1914 and whose aim was to hold group exhibitions and to encourage debate of their aesthetic ideals. They admired the work of ◊Cézanne and drew inspiration from FUTURISM.

segno (*Italian*) 'sign', used in NOTATION to mark a repeat, usually as *al segno*.

segue (*Italian*) 'follows', i.e. a direction to start playing the following MOVEMENT without a break.

seguidilla a Spanish dance in 3/8 or 3/4 TIME in the style of the BOLERO, but much faster.

semibreve a 'half of a BREVE'; the NOTE with the longest time-value normally used in modern Western NOTATION. In US notation, this is called a 'whole note'.

semidemisemiquaver a name for a HEMIDEMISEMIQUAVER or sixty-fourth note.

Semiotics *see* STRUCTURALISM.

semiquaver a NOTE with half the time-value of a QUAVER, and a sixteenth the time-value of a SEMIBREVE. In US NOTATION, it is called a 'sixteenth-note'.

semitone 'half a TONE'; the smallest INTERVAL regularly used in modern Western music.

semplice (*Italian*) 'unornamented', 'in a simple manner'.

sempre (*Italian*) 'throughout', 'continually'; as *sempre* FORTE, 'loud throughout'.

sentimental comedy a form of English COMEDY that arose in the early 18th century, focusing on the problems of middle-class characters. The plays always end happily and feature strongly contrasting good and bad characters and high emotional peaks. The form was developed by Richard ◊Steele in a conscious reaction to the excesses of Restoration comedy (see COMEDY OF MANNERS). Examples include Steele's *The Tender Husband* (1705) and, notably, *The Conscious Lovers* (1722). The form led on to MELODRAMA (*see also* DOMESTIC TRAGEDY).

senza (*Italian*) 'without', so *senza* SORDINO means 'without MUTE' (in music for strings).

septet a group of seven performers or a piece of music written for such a group.

septuplet a group of seven NOTES of equal time-value to be played in the time of four or six.

sequence (1) the repetition of a short PASSAGE of music in a different PITCH. (2) a form of HYMN in Latin used in the Roman Catholic Mass, such as DIES IRAE and STABAT MATER.

serenade (1) a love SONG, traditionally sung in the evening and usually accompanied by a GUITAR or MANDOLIN. (2) a DIVERTIMENTO performed during an evening entertainment.

serenata (*Italian*) an 18th-century form of secular CANTATA or a short OPERA composed for a patron.

serialism a method of composition developed by ◊Schoenberg in which all SEMITONES are treated as equal, i.e. tonal values are eliminated. *See also* TWELVE-NOTE MUSIC.

serpent an obsolete BASS WOODWIND instrument with several curves in it (hence its name). It was used during the 16th century in church orchestras and MILITARY BANDS.

seventh an INTERVAL in which two NOTES are seven steps apart (including the first and last), for example F to E.

sevillana a Spanish FOLK DANCE originally from the city of Seville. It is similar to the SEGUIDILLA.

sextet a group of six performers or a piece of music written for such a group.

sextolet *or* **sextuplet** a group of six notes to be performed in the time of four notes.

Sezession (*German*) 'secession', adopted as a name in the 1890s by groups of painters in Austria and Germany when they broke away from official academies to work and exhibit in contemporary styles, e.g. IMPRESSIONISM. In Germany, the first German Sezession was in Munich in 1892, followed by the Berlin Sezession of 1899, which in turn in 1910 repudiated Die BRÜCKE, which resulted in the latter forming the *Neue Sezession*. In Austria, the Vienna Sezession was organized by ◊Klimt in 1897.

sf *or* **sfz** abbreviation for SFORZANDO.

sforzando (*Italian*) 'forcing', i.e. a strong ACCENT placed on a NOTE or CHORD.

sfumato a subtle modelling of light and shade between figures and background, deployed by ◊Leonardo da Vinci when it represented a remarkable departure from the RENAISSANCE art stress on strong lighting and outline.

shake an alternative term for TRILL.

shamisen *or* **samisen** a Japanese long-necked LUTE with three strings. It has no FRETS and is plucked with a PLECTRUM.

shanai a double REED instrument from India, similar to a SHAWM.

shanty a SONG, with a pronounced RHYTHM, that was sung by sailors to help them coordinate their actions in the days of sailing ships. Shanties usually follow a format in which SOLO verses are followed by a CHORUS.

sharp the sign that raises the PITCH of the line or space on which it stands on a STAVE by a SEMITONE.

shawm *or* **shawn** a double-REED WOODWIND instrument that dates from the 13th century. It was developed from Middle Eastern instruments and produced a coarse, shrill sound. It was a forerunner of the OBOE.

sheng a sophisticated Chinese mouth organ (*see* HARMONICA), dating back some 3000 years.

shift a change of position of the hands when playing on a string instrument.

shofar *or* **shophar** an ancient Jewish WIND INSTRUMENT made from a ram's horn, which is still used in synagogues.

shop ballad *see* BALLAD.

siciliano a slow dance from Sicily in 6/8 or 12/8 TIME, with a characteristic lilting RHYTHM.

side drum *or* **snare drum** a cylindrically shaped DRUM that is the smallest usually used in an orchestra. Snares, made of gut or sprung metal, are stretched across the bottom parchment and vibrate against it when the upper membrane of parchment is struck; this gives the drum its characteristic rattling sound. The snares can be released so that a more hollow sound is produced.

signature *see* KEY SIGNATURE; TIME SIGNATURE.

signature tune a few BARS of catchy music that are associated with a performer or broadcast show.

similar motion the simultaneous PROGRESSION of two or more PARTS in the same direction.

simple interval any INTERVAL that is an octave or less. *Compare* COMPOUND INTERVAL.

simple time *see* COMPOUND TIME.

sine tone an electronically produced NOTE that is entirely 'pure'.

sinfonia (*Italian*) 'SYMPHONY', i.e. an instrumental piece. It is also a term used for a small orchestra.

sinfonietta a short SYMPHONY or a symphony for a small orchestra.

singing the act of producing musical TONE by means of the VOICE.

single chant *see* ANGLICAN CHANT.

Singspiel (*German*) literally 'sing-play', i.e. a comic opera in German with spoken dialogue replacing the sung RECITATIVE.

sinistra, sinistro (*Italian*) 'left', as in MANO *sinistra*, 'left hand'.

sistrum an ancient type of RATTLE in which loose wooden or metal discs are suspended on metal bars strung across a frame.

sitar a type of Indian LUTE, which is believed to have originated in Persia. It has movable metal FRETS and three to seven 'MELODY' strings; below these strings lie twelve or so SYMPATHETIC STRINGS, which create a droning sound. The sitar is plucked with a long wire PLECTRUM. It has a distinctive 'twangy' sound and is usually played in consort with the TABLA. Ravi ◊Shankar is perhaps the world's best player of the sitar.

Six, Les (*French*) 'The Six', the name given in 1920 to six young French composers by the poet and music critic Henri Collet who, with another of their champions, Jean ◊Cocteau, was passionately anti-◊Wagner. The six were Georges Auric (1899–1983), Louis Durey (1888–1979), ◊Honegger, ◊Milhaud, ◊Poulenc and Germaine Tailleferre (1892–1983). Subsequently a number of other composers became members of the group, but it ceased to have an effective function after 1925.

sixteenth-note (US) *see* SEMIQUAVER.

sketch in art, a preliminary drawing made by an artist to establish points of composition, scale, etc. In music, a short PIANO or instrumental piece.

skiffle a type of POP MUSIC played in England during the 1950s. Skiffle BANDS relied on American idioms (for example BLUES) and attempted to become 'authentic' by incorporating home-made instruments (such as tea-chest 'basses') into their outfits.

slancio, con (*Italian*) 'with impetus'.

sleigh bells small metal bells with steel balls inside which are mounted together in groups to produce a richly textured jingling sound. They are traditionally hung on sleighs, but are occasionally used in orchestras to create special effects.

slide (1) a passing from one to note to another without an INTERVAL. (2) a mechanism on the TRUMPET and TROMBONE that lengthens the tube to allow a new series of harmonics.

slide trombone *see* TROMBONE.

slide trumpet an early form of TRUMPET that had a slide similar to that used in the TROMBONE. It became obsolete when the VALVE trumpet was invented.

slur a curved line that is placed over or under a group of NOTES to indicate that they are to be played, or sung, smoothly, that is, with one stroke of the BOW (VIOLIN music) or in one breath (singing).

smorzando (*Italian*) 'fading' or 'dying away', i.e. the music is to become softer and slower.

snare drum *see* SIDE DRUM.

soave (*Italian*) 'soft' or 'gentle'.

soca music a type of powerful, rhythmic dance music from the English-speaking islands of the Caribbean. It evolved from soul (hence *so*) and calypso (*ca*).

socialist realism the name given to official art in the former Soviet Union, which was intended to glorify the achievements of the Communist Party.

social realism a form of realism, in which an artist's political viewpoint (usually on the left) affects the content of his work.

soft pedal *see* PIANO.

soh in the TONIC SOL-FA, the fifth NOTE (or DOMINANT) of the MAJOR SCALE.

solemnis (*Latin*) 'solemn', as in MISSA *Solemnis,* 'Solemn Mass'.

solenne (*Italian*) 'solemn'.

solennelle (*French*) 'solemn'.

sol-fa *see* TONIC SOL-FA.

solfeggio (*Italian*) a type of singing exercise in which the names of the NOTES are sung. *See* TONIC SOL-FA.

solo (*Italian*) 'alone', i.e. a piece to be performed by one person, with or without ACCOMPANIMENT.

solo organ a manual on an ORGAN with strong, distinctive STOPS, used for individual effect.

sonata originally a term for any instrumental piece to distinguish it from a sung piece or CANTATA. However, during the 17th century two distinct forms of sonata arose: the *sonata da* CAMERA (chamber sonata), in which dance movements were played by two or three stringed instruments with a keyboard ACCOMPANIMENT, and the *sonata da chiesa* (church sonata), which was similar but more serious. In the 18th century the sonata came to be a piece in several contrasting movements for keyboard only or for keyboard and one SOLO instrument.

sonata form a method of arranging and constructing music that is commonly used (since *c*.1750) for SYMPHONIES, SONATAS, CONCERTOS, etc. There are three sections to sonata form: the EXPOSITION (in which the SUBJECT or subjects are introduced), the DEVELOPMENT (in which the subject(s) are expanded and developed), and the 'recapitulation' (in which the exposition, usually modified in some way, is repeated).

sonata-rondo form a type of RONDO, popular with such composers as BEETHOVEN, which is a combination of rondo and SONATA FORM.

sonatina a short SONATA.

song (1) a musical setting of poetry or prose. (2) a poem that can be sung. (3) a name used to designate the second SUBJECT of a SONATA.

song cycle a set of SONGS that have a common THEME or have words by a single poet. ◊Schubert, ◊Schumann and ◊Mahler wrote notable song cycles.

sopra (*Italian*) 'above', so *come sopra* means 'as above'.

soprano the highest PITCH of human VOICE, with a range of about two OCTAVES above approximately middle C. The term is also applied to some instruments, such as soprano SAXOPHONE (the highest pitched saxophone). *See also* MEZZO.

sordino (*Italian*) 'MUTE'.

sospirando (*Italian*) 'sighing'.

sospiro (*Italian*) literally 'sigh', in music meaning a CROTCHET rest

sostenuto (*Italian*) 'sustained'.

sotto (*Italian*) 'below', as in *sotto voce,* which literally means 'under the VOICE' or whispered.

soul music a type of emotionally charged music developed by black musicians in America. 'Soul', as it is usually called, derives from BLUES and GOSPEL music with the addition of ROCK RHYTHMS.

sound a term in ACOUSTICS for TONES resulting from regular VIBRATIONS, as opposed to noise.

sound hole the opening in the BELLY of a stringed instrument, e.g. the f-shaped holes in a violin or the round hole in a guitar.

soundpost a piece of wood connecting the BELLY of a stringed instrument (such as a VIOLIN) to the back. It helps to distribute VIBRATIONS through the body of the instrument.

sousaphone a giant TUBA that encircles the player's body which was designed for his band by the American bandmaster and composer John Philip Sousa (1854-1932) who formed a successful MILITARY-style BAND that toured the world giving concerts.

Spanish guitar the classic GUITAR with a narrow waist, six strings and a central SOUND HOLE.

special effects a non-specific term used of any extraordinary noises or SOUNDS that may be required of an orchestra, or part of an orchestra, to satisfy the demands of a composer, such as COW BELLS, etc.

species a discipline used in teaching strict COUNTERPOINT, developed by Johann Fux (1660–1741), who listed five rhythmic patterns ('species') in which one VOICE PART could be combined with another.

spinet a type of small HARPSICHORD.

spirito (*Italian*) 'spirit', so *con spirito* means 'with spirit'.

spiritual a type of religious FOLK SONG or HYMN that was developed by black (and white) Americans in the 18th and 19th centuries. Spirituals are characterized by strong SYNCOPATION and simple MELODIES. They were superseded by GOSPEL music.

Sprechgesang (*German*) literally 'speech-song', i.e. a type of singing that is half speech. It was used by ◊Schoenberg in his song cycle *Pierrot Lunaire*.

Stabat Mater (*Latin*) 'The Mother stood', the initial words of a hymn describing the sorrows of the Virgin at the Crucifixion. It was set to music, other than its original PLAINSONG, by, for example, ◊Palestrina; later settings include those by ◊Haydn, ◊Schubert and ◊Rossini.

stabile a non-moving MOBILE, as devised by Alexander Calder.

staccato (*Italian*) 'detached', i.e. NOTES should be shortened and played with brief INTERVALS between them.

staff *see* STAVE.

stave *or* **staff** a set of horizontal lines (usually five) on which music is written. Each line, and the gaps between them, represent a different PITCH.

steel drum a PERCUSSION INSTRUMENT ('pan') made by West Indian musicians (particularly from Trinidad) out of discarded oil drums. Each DRUM can be tuned to play a range of notes by beating and heat-treating different sections of the 'head', i.e. the top of the drum.

Steinway a firm of piano manufacturers founded by Henry Steinway [originally Heinrich Steinweg] (1797–1871) in New York in 1853. A London branch opened in 1875.

stem the line, or 'tail', attached to the head of all notes smaller than a SEMIBREVE.

stesso (*Italian*) 'same', so *lo stesso* TEMPO means 'the same speed'.

stiacciato *see* relief.

Stijl, De a group of Dutch artists, founded to spread theories on ABSTRACT ART, principally through the *De Stijl* magazine, which was published 1917–28. The group rejected the representational in art, believing that art's object was to convey harmony and order, achieved by the use of straight lines and geometrical shapes in primary colours or black and white. Their ideas had great influence, particularly on BAUHAUS, on architecture and on commercial art.

still life a genre of painting depicting inanimate objects such as fruit, flowers, etc, begun by Dutch artists seeking secular commissions after the Reformation and the loss of Church patronage. Within the genre, the *vanitas* still life contains objects symbolic of the transcience of life, e.g. skulls, hour-glasses, etc, while others contain religious symbols, such as bread and wine. In the 18th century, new life was given to the form by the French painter Jean-Baptiste Chardin (1699–1779) and in the 19th century ◊Cézanne's use of it in his experiments with structure was very influential on the CUBISTS.

stomp a BLUES composition in which the BEAT is literally stamped on the floor.

stop a handle or knob on an ORGAN that admits or prevents air from reaching certain PIPES and that can therefore be used to modify the potential output of the MANUALS and PEDALS.

stopping on stringed instruments, the placing of fingers on a string to shorten its effective length and raise its PITCH.

Stradivari *or* **Stradivarius** a violin made by Antonio Stradivari (1644-1737) an Italian violin-maker whose instruments are unsurpassed for the quality of their sound.

strathspey *see* REEL.

stream of consciousness a term coined by William ◊James in his *The Varieties of Religious Experience* (1902) which has been adapted by literary critics to denote a fluxive method of narration in which characters voice their feelings with no 'obtrusive' authorial comment and with no orthodox dialogue or decription. The term has particular reference to the work of ◊Joyce and ◊Woolf.

Streichquartett (*German*) a 'STRING QUARTET'.

strepitoso (*Italian*) 'boisterously'.

stretto 'close together', i.e. a quickening of TEMPO.

stride (piano) a JAZZ piano technique characterized by the use of single bass notes on the first and third beats and chords on the second and fourth.

string a vibrating cord for the production of tone, in the piano of drawn cast steel wire, in instruments of the violin family of catgut or spun silk, and in the guitar of catgut or wire.

stringendo (*Italian*) 'tightening', i.e. increasing tension, often with accelerated TEMPO.

string quartet a group of four performers who use stringed instruments (two VIOLINS, VIOLA and CELLO); or a piece of music written for such a group.

strings a general term for the stringed instruments of the VIOLIN family.

Stroh violin a VIOLIN made of metal (invented by Charles Stroh in 1901) that incorporates a TRUMPET bell and does not have a normal violin body.

Structuralism in literary criticism, a critical approach to literature in which the text being studied is viewed as a 'cultural product' that cannot be 'read' in isolation and in which the text is held to absorb its meaning from the interconnected web of linguistic codes and symbols of which it is but a part. The process of studying the codes, etc., and their relation to each other, is called *Semiotics*. A Structuralist approach to the novels of Fennimore ◊Cooper, for example, would include recognition of the linguistic and cultural conventions underlying the author's use of language, with particular reference to the significance of both the 'Noble Savage' myth in Western culture and the emerging frontier myth in American culture. The heroic persona of the Deerslayer, and his portrayal as a transient figure between the mythic world of primitive America and the swelling wave of modern civilization, results in a creative tension ripe for hours of happy exploration and parallel.

Figures associated with the development of Structuralist theory are the Canadian critic Marshall ◊McLuhan, whose studies of mass culture and communication include *The Gutenberg Galaxy* (1962) and *The Medium is the Message* (1967); the linguist Ferdinand de ◊Saussure; the anthropologist Claude Levi-Strauss (1908–); the critic Roland ◊Barthes; and the psychoanalyst Jacques Lacan (1901–81). Structuralism is thus an approach drawing on a wide range of disciplines, with some critics, e.g. followers of Lacan, focusing on the play between unconscious and conscious concepts, while others, e.g. followers of Saussure, will focus on the linguistic relativism that emerges between the *signifier* (the spoken word) and the *signified* (the mind's concept of the word). *Deconstruction*, a concept developed by the French philosopher Jacques Derrida (1930–), is a term for the process or 'strategy' of examining the elements (signs) of language in isolation from other elements, thus exposing the contradictions inherent within language. It is also called *Poststructuralism*.

The psychologist Jean ◊Piaget usefully defines structure as composed of wholeness, transformation and self-regulation. Thus, ◊Homer's *Iliad*, for example, (a) is a work with a unity of structure conforming to the conventions of EPIC poetic form; (b) includes recognizable 'types' of characters who appear in other such works, e.g. warriors, who may also behave in ways outside the expected form, as when the young Achilles hides himself amongst women dressed as a girl; (c) can alter its meaning according to external factors, e.g. the reader's understanding of the characters' behaviour can vary at different times, as fresh experiences alter the reader's perception.

Stück (*German*) 'piece'.

study in art, a drawing or painting of a detail for use in a larger finished work. In music, a piece written to demonstrate technique in playing a musical instrument or using the voice.

subdominant the fourth NOTE of the MAJOR or MINOR SCALE.

subito (*Italian*) 'suddenly', as in PIANO *subito,* meaning 'suddenly soft'.

subject a musical THEME on which a composition (or part of a composition) is constructed, e.g. the first and second SUBJECTS in the EXPOSITION in SONATA FORM; the subject in a FUGUE; also the leading VOICE (first PART) of a fugue.

submediant the sixth NOTE of the MAJOR or MINOR SCALE.

subsidiary theme any THEME that is less important than the main theme(s) of a composition.

suite a collection of short pieces that combine to form an effective overall composition; the BAROQUE suite was a set of (stylized) dances.

sul, sull' (*Italian*) 'on' or 'over', so *sul ponticello* means 'over the BRIDGE' (in VIOLIN bowing).

Suprematism a Russian art movement based on principles of nonobjectivity. It was begun by the painter Kasimir Malevich (1878–1935) in 1913 and evolved on a parallel with Constructivism. *White on White* by Malevich is typical of the work of the movement. The influence of Suprematism spread through the BAUHAUS to Europe and the US.

Surrealism an avant-garde art movement of the 1920s and 1930s in France, which grew out of DADA and was inspired by the dream theories of Sigmund ◊Freud and by the literature and poetry of ◊Rimbaud and ◊Baudelaire. Surrealism took from Dadaism a love for the juxtaposition of incongruous images, the purpose of which in the Surrealist view was to express the workings of the unconscious mind. The term 'Surrealism' had been coined by the poet Guillauime ◊Apollinaire, but the movement really got going with the publication by the poet André Breton (1896–1966) of his first *Surrealist Manifesto* in 1924. According to Breton (who was much influenced by Freud), the 'higher reality' could only be achieved in art by freeing the mind from the lower world of superficial rationality.

In art, its influences include the works of de ◊Chirico. There were two main trends: *automatism*, or *free association*, was explored in the works of ◊Miró, ◊Ernst and others, who sought deliberately to avoid conscious control by using techniques of spontaneity to express the subconscious. The world of dreams was the source of inspiration for the incongruously juxtaposed, often bizarre, but precisely painted imagery of ◊Dali, and ◊Magritte.

suspension a device used in HARMONY, in which a NOTE sounded in one CHORD is sustained while a subsequent chord is played (or sung), producing a DISSONANCE that is then resolved.

sustaining pedal *see* PIANO.

swell organ a MANUAL on an ORGAN. The notes played on this manual can become louder and softer by the opening and closing of the shutters on the swell box, which encloses the PIPES.

swing a type of American POPULAR MUSIC of the 1935-45 era; it was played by BIG BANDS and had an insistent RHYTHM. Glenn ◊Miller and his ENSEMBLE were influential in its development.

Symbolism in literature, a French poetry movement of the late 19th century that rejected the dictates of both Realism and naturalism by seeking to express a state of mind by a process of suggestion rather than by attempting to portray 'objective reality'. As ◊Mallarmé put it, 'not the thing, but the effect produced'. Other prominent poets associated with Symbolism include ◊Verlaine and ◊Rimbaud. The movement has strong links with the world of Impressionist composers, such as ◊Debussy. Poets outside the French-speaking world who were influenced by Symbolism include T. S. ◊Eliot, ◊Pound, ◊Rilke, and, notably, ◊Yeats, whose superb epigram 'Three Movements' serves as an epitaph both for the movement and for his own involvement with it. Several important plays of the late 19th century, e.g. ◊Chekhov's *The Seagull* (1895) and ◊Ibsen's *The Master Builder* (1896), also display the influence of Symbolism.

In art, also in late 19th-century France, Symbolism represented a response to the intrinsically visual work of the Impressionists and fell into two distinct trends: some painters were inspired by the images of Symbolist Literature, while others, including ◊Gauguin, Van ◊Gogh and the NABIS explored the symbolic use of colour and line to express emotion.

sympathetic strings strings on certain instruments, such as the SITAR, which are not actually plucked or bowed, but which are set in sympathetic VIBRATION and produce a NOTE without being touched, when the same note is played on a 'melody' string.

symphonic poem *or* **tone poem** an orchestral composition, a form of PROGRAMME MUSIC, usually in one MOVEMENT, which attempts to interpret or describe an emotion, idea, or story. The term was coined by ◊Liszt.

symphony in essence, a prolonged or extended SONATA for an orchestra. Most symphonies have four MOVEMENTS (sections) that, although interrelated, tend to have recognized forms, for example, a quick first movement, a slow second movement, a MINUET third movement, and a vibrant fourth movement (FINALE).

Synchromism an art movement originating in the US in 1913 the members of which were concerned with the balanced arrangement of pure colour, or 'colours together'. The movement influenced a number of American painters.

syncopation an alteration to the normal arrangement of accented BEATS in a BAR. This is usually done by placing ACCENTS on beats or parts of a beat that do not normally carry an accent.

synthesizer an ELECTRONIC instrument, operated by a keyboard and switches, that can generate and modify an extensive range of SOUND.

tabla a pair of Indian DRUMS, beaten with the hands, which are often used to accompany the SITAR in classical Indian music.

table an alternative name for the upper surface, or BELLY, of instruments of the VIOLIN family.

tabor an early type of SIDE DRUM.

tace (*Italian*) 'silent'.

Tafelmusik (*German*) 'table music', i.e. music sung during a banquet as an entertainment.

tail the STEM attached to the head of a MINIM (half-note) or a smaller NOTE.

tail piece the piece of wood at the base of a VIOLIN to which the strings are attached.

tail pin the metal rod at the bottom of a CELLO or DOUBLE BASS, which can be pulled out to adjust the height of the instrument above the floor.

Takt (*German*) 'TIME', so *im Takt* means 'in time'.

talon (*French*) the 'nut' or heel of a BOW.

tambourin (1) a lively 18th-century piece in the style of a FOLK DANCE from Provence, usually in 2/4 TIME. (2) a narrow DRUM, played along with a PIPE, as the ACCOMPANIMENT to dancing.

tambourine a small, shallow DRUM with a single skin fastened over a circular frame. Small metal CYMBALS (jingles) are slotted into the frame and rattle when the instrument is shaken or beaten with the hand.

tampon a drumstick that has a head at each end, held in the middle to produce a DRUM ROLL.

tango a Latin-American dance in moderately slow 2/4 TIME, originating from Argentina. It makes use of syncopated RHYTHMS (*see* SYNCOPATION) and became popular in Europe in the 1920s.

tanto (*Italian*) 'so much', as in ALLEGRO *non tanto*, meaning 'quick, but not too quick'.

Tanz (*German*) 'dance'.

tap dance a dance in which the feet are used to tap out a RHYTHM. Tap dancing was made popular by performances in films by Fred ◊Astaire during the 1930s. Special shoes with steel plates at the toe and heel are usually worn.

tarantella a very fast, wild FOLK DANCE from southern Italy in 6/8 TIME, and gradually increasing in speed. ◊Chopin used the form in a concert piece.

tasto (*Italian*) the keyboard of a PIANO or the FINGERBOARD of a stringed instrument.

tattoo originally a night DRUM beat calling soldiers to their quarters, now a military display.

Te Deum laudamus (*Latin*) 'We Praise Thee, O God'; a Christian HYMN sung at MATINS. Numerous composers (e.g ◊Purcell, ◊Handel, ◊Verdi) have set it to music.

tempera a paint medium made by mixing colour pigments with egg. It was much used until the 15th century and the development of oil paint.

temperament the way in which INTERVALS between NOTES have been 'tempered', or slightly altered, in Western music so that the slight discrepancy in seven OCTAVES is distributed evenly over the range. In EQUAL TEMPERAMENT an octave is divided into twelve SEMITONES, which means that, for example, D SHARP is also E FLAT:

this is a compromise, for strictly there is a marginal difference between D sharp and E flat.

tempo (*Italian*) 'TIME'. The time taken by a composition, therefore the speed at which it is performed, hence the pace of the BEAT. *A tempo* means 'in time'. Tempo can also mean a movement of a SONATA or SYMPHONY, as in *il secondo tempo*, 'the second MOVEMENT'.

ten. (*Italian*) an abbreviation for TENUTO.

tenor (1) the highest adult male VOICE with a range an OCTAVE to either side of middle C. (2) as a prefix to the name of an instrument, it indicates the size between an ALTO member of the family and a BASS, for example tenor SAXOPHONE. (3) the RECITING NOTE in PSALM singing. (4) an obsolete term for a VIOLA (tenor VIOLIN).

tenor drum a DRUM, frequently used in MILITARY BANDS, between a SIDE DRUM and BASS DRUM in size and PITCH, and without snares.

tenor violin see VIOLONCELLO.

tenuto (*Italian*) 'held'; a term that indicates that a NOTE should be held for its full value, or in some cases, even longer.

ternary form a term applied to a piece of music that is divided into three self-contained parts, with the first and third sections bearing strong similarities.

ternary time *see* TRIPLE TIME.

terzett, terzetto (*Italian*) *see* TRIO.

tessitura (*Italian*) 'texture'; a term that indicates whether the majority of NOTES in a piece are high up or low down in the range of a VOICE (or instrument).

tetrachord a group of four NOTES.

theme the MELODY, or other musical material, that forms the basis of a work or a MOVEMENT and which may be varied or developed. It may return in one form or another throughout a composition.

thirty-second note (US) a DEMISEMIQUAVER.

thorough bass *see* FIGURED BASS.

thunder stick *or* **bull roarer** *or* **whizzer** an instrument consisting of a flat piece of wood fastened to a piece of string. When the piece of wood is whirled around the head, it creates a roaring sound.

tie a curved line that joins two NOTES of the same PITCH together, indicating that they should be played as one long note.

timbre (*French*) the quality of TONE, or the characteristic SOUND of an instrument.

time the rhythmic pattern (number of BEATS in a BAR) of a piece of music, as indicated by the TIME SIGNATURE. DUPLE TIME has two beats in a bar, triple time has three beats in a bar, and so on.

time-names *or* **rhythm-names** a French method of teaching TIME and RHYTHM, in which beats are given names, such as 'ta', 'ta-te', etc.

time signature a sign placed at the beginning of a piece of music that indicates the number and value of BEATS in a BAR. A time signature usually consists of two numbers, one placed above the other. The lower number defines the unit of measurement in relation to the SEMIBREVE (whole note); the top figure indicates the number of those units in a bar, for example, 3/4 indicates that there are three CROTCHETS (quarter notes) in a bar.

timpani *or* **kettledrums** the main orchestral PERCUSSION INSTRUMENTS, consisting of bowl-shaped shells over which the membrane is stretched. The shell is supported on a frame at the base of which, in 'pedal timpani', is the foot PEDAL that can alter the PITCH of the drum as it is played. The drum can also be tuned (*see* TUNING) by screws, which alter the tension of the membrane.

Tin Pan Alley the nickname given to West 28th Street in New York, where the popular-song publishing business used to be situated. It consequently became a slang expression for the POPULAR MUSIC industry.

tin whistle *or* **penny whistle** a metal whistle-FLUTE, similar to a RECORDER but with six finger holes. It produces high-pitched sounds and is commonly used to play FOLK music.

toccata (*Italian*) 'touched'; a type of music for a keyboard instrument that is intended to show off a player's 'touch' or ability.

tonality the use of a KEY in a composition.

tondo the Italian word for 'round', used in art to denote a circular picture or sculpture.

tone (1) an INTERVAL comprising two SEMITONES, for example the interval between C and D. (2) (US) a musical NOTE. (3) the quality of SOUND, for example good TONE, SHARP tone, etc. (4) in PLAINSONG, a MELODY.

tone poem *see* SYMPHONIC POEM.

tonguing in the playing of a WIND INSTRUMENT, this means interrupting the flow of breath with the tongue so that detached NOTES are played, or the first note of a PHRASE is distinguished.

tonic the first NOTE of a MAJOR or MINOR SCALE.

tonic sol-fa a system of NOTATION and sight-singing used in training, in which NOTES are sung to syllables. The notes of the major scale are: DOH, RE, ME, FAH, SOH, LA, TE, DOH (doh is always the TONIC, whatever the KEY). The system was pioneered in England by John Curwen (1816–80) in the mid-19th century.

tosto (*Italian*) 'rapid', as in PIÙ *tosto*, 'quicker'.

trad jazz literally 'traditional JAZZ'; a term referring to the type of comparatively simple jazz, with a strong MELODY, as played in New Orleans, which preceded the development of BEBOP.

tragedy a form of drama in which a hero or heroine comes to a bad end. The cause of the protagonist's failure can be either a personal flaw or a circumstance beyond his or her control, or both. The earliest tragedies known, those by ◊Aeschylus, ◊Sophocles and ◊Euripides, are still among the greatest. The first critical study of the form is in ◊Aristotle's *Poetics*, where Aristotle defines tragedy as an imitation (*mimesis*) of a serious, complete action on a grand scale, 'grand' meaning a momentous action involving highly placed characters in society. The protagonist will make an 'error of judgment' (*hamartia*, often been rendered, a bit misleadingly, as 'tragic flaw') but the protagonist's main fault is as often the result of having to undertake a certain action at a certain time, as in any character defect; thus, in Sophocles' *Antigone*, the heroine is in the position of having to choose between divine and human law. The protagonist is usually a good person, but not perfect, and progresses from happiness to misery. Another important concept in the *Poetics* is that of catharsis, the 'purging' (or purification, cleansing) of the emotions of pity and fear aroused in the spectators by the play.

The great tradition of the Greek tragedians was filtered through the plays of ◊Seneca to the dramatists of the Renaissance, although Renaissance tragedies, such as those of ◊Shakespeare, differ significantly from those of the past. The interplay in Shakespeare's tragedies between the heroic and the ironic or comic commonplace worlds, e.g. the banter between the rustic clown and Cleopatra at the end of *Antony and Cleopatra*, is profoundly foreign to the world of the *Poetics*, just as the pagan and fate-haunted world of the Greeks was ultimately alien to Renaissance dramatists brought up in the Christian tradition.

Several 20th-century dramatists, e.g. Arthur ◊Miller and ◊O'Neill, have tried, with debatable results, to adapt the form of Athenian tragedy to the modern stage. The most that can be said for these is that they may result in effects similar to those of the originals. The fact that such dramas invariably have as subtext the notion that this state of affairs is reformable, and the equally invariable ironic presentation of the protagonists as 'losers of history', rather than as victims of forces as permanent as they are merciless, puts such plays as Miller's *Death of a Salesman* at a further remove from the Athenian drama than, say, Shakespeare's *King Lear*, with its bleak vision of a fallen world in which bloody tyranny is an everpresent threat. *See also* DOMESTIC TRAGEDY, HEROIC TRAGEDY, JACOBEAN TRAGEDY, REVENGE TRAGEDY.

tragicomedy *see* COMEDY.

tranquillo (*Italian*) 'calm'.

transcription *see* ARRANGEMENT.

transition (1) the changing from one KEY to another during the course of a composition. (2) a PASSAGE linking two sections of a piece, which often involves a change of key.

transposing instruments instruments that sound NOTES different from those actually written down, e.g. a piece of music in E flat for the B flat CLARINET would actually be written in F.

transposition the changing of the PITCH of a composition. Singers sometimes ask accompanists to transpose a SONG higher or lower so that it is better suited to their voice range.

treble the highest boy's VOICE.

treble clef G CLEF on the second line of the STAVE, used for TREBLE VOICES and instruments of medium or high PITCH, such as VIOLINS, FLUTES, OBOES, CLARINETS, HORNS and TRUMPETS.

trecento the Italian term for the 14th century.

tremolando (*Italian*) 'trembling'.

tremolo (*Italian*) the rapid repetition of a single NOTE, or the rapid alternation between two or more notes.

triad a CHORD of three NOTES that includes a third and a FIFTH.

triangle a PERCUSSION INSTRUMENT comprising a thin steel bar bent into a triangle but with one corner left unjoined. It is normally struck with a thin metal bar.

trill *or* **shake** an ORNAMENT in which a NOTE is rapidly alternated with the note above. It is used in both vocal and instrumental pieces.

trio (1) a group of three performers, or a piece of music written for such a group. (2) the middle section of a MINUET, as found in SONATAS, SYMPHONIES, etc. It was originally a section scored for three PARTS.

triplet a group of three NOTES played in the time of two notes.

triptych a painting, usually an altarpiece, consisting of three hinged parts, the outer two folding over the middle section. *See also* diptych, polyptych.

tritone an INTERVAL consisting of three WHOLE TONES.

tromba marina a long, stringed instrument of the 15th century. It consisted of a long, tapered box with one string, mounted on top, which was played with a BOW; inside the box were some twenty SYMPATHETIC STRINGS.

trombone a BRASS instrument that has changed little for 500 years. The body of the instrument has a cylindrical bore with a bell at one end and a MOUTHPIECE at the other. A U-shaped SLIDE is used for lengthening or shortening the tubing and therefore for sounding different NOTES. TENOR and BASS trombones are often used in orchestras.

trope (*Latin*) an addition of music or words to traditional PLAIN-SONG LITURGY.

troppo (*Italian*) 'too much', as in ALLEGRO *non troppo*, meaning 'fast but not too fast'.

troubadour a poet-musician of the early Middle Ages who originally came from the South of France and sang in the Provençal language.

trumpet a BRASS instrument that has a cylindrical bore with a funnel-shaped MOUTHPIECE at one end and a bell (flared opening) at the other. The modern trumpet has three valves (operated by PISTONS) which bring into play extra lengths of tubing and are therefore used to change the pitch of the instrument. Trumpets are used in orchestras, JAZZ BANDS and MILITARY BANDS. 'Trumpet' is also a generic term used to describe any number of very different wind instruments that are found all over the world.

tuba a large BRASS instrument with a wide conical bore, a large cup-shaped MOUTHPIECE, and a large bell that faces upwards. It can have between three and five valves and comes in three common sizes: TENOR (EUPHONIUM), BASS and double bass. Tubas are found in orchestras and military bands.

tubular bells *see* BELLS.

tune a MELODY or AIR.

tuning the adjusting of the PITCH of an instrument so that it corresponds to an agreed note, for example, an orchestra will usually have all its instruments tuned to the note of A.

tuning fork a two-pronged steel device that, when tapped, will sound a single, 'pure' note. It was invented by John Shore in 1711 and is used to tune instruments, etc.

tutti (*Italian*) 'all'; in orchestral music, a *tutti* passage is one to be played by the whole orchestra.

twelve-note music *or* **twelve-tone system** a method of composition formulated and advanced by ◊Schoenberg. In the system, the twelve CHROMATIC NOTES of an OCTAVE can only be used in specific orders, called 'note rows'; no note can be repeated twice within a note row, and the rows must be used complete. In all, there are forty-eight ways in which a note row can be arranged (using INVERSION, RETROGRADE MOTION and inverted retrograde motion), and it is with note rows that compositions are constructed.

ukelele a small, four-stringed GUITAR that was developed in Hawaii during the 19th century. It was a popular music-hall instrument during the 1920s.

unison the sounding of the same NOTE or its OCTAVE by two or more VOICES or instruments.

Unities *see* NEOCLASSICISM.

up beat the upward movement of a conductor's BATON or hand, indicating the unstressed (usually the last) BEAT in a BAR.

upright *see* PIANO.

Urtext (*German*) 'original text'.

Utopian novel a form of NOVEL developed from *Utopia* (1516) a fantasy of a supposedly ideally organized state written by Sir Thomas ◊More. The work spawned a host of imitations throughout the centuries but the impact of 20th-century totalitarianism has lessened enthusiams for the form. Aldous ◊Huxley's *Island* (1962) is a modern example of a Utopian novel; the same author's *Brave New World* (1932) is an example of its opposite, a 'dystopia' or 'bad place'.

Utrecht School a movement in Dutch art begun by Gerrit van Honthorst (1590–1656), Hendrick Terbrugghen (1588–1629) and Dirck van Baburen (*c.*1595–1624), who were in Rome between 1610 and 1620 and were strongly influenced by ◊Caravaggio, whose style they took back to the Netherlands, thus influencing in turn such northern masters as ◊Vermeer and ◊Rembrandt.

V an abbreviation for VIOLINO, VOCE, VOLTA.

VA an abbreviation of VIOLA.

valse (*French*) *see* WALTZ.

valve a device attached to horns, trumpets and other brass instruments to lengthen or reduce the extend of tubing, hence lowering or raising the pitch respectively, to complete the scale.

vamp to improvise an ACCOMPANIMENT.

variation the modification or DEVELOPMENT of a THEME.

vaudeville (*French*) originally a type of popular, satirical SONG sung by Parisian street musicians. In the 18th century these songs (with new words) were incorporated into plays, and the word came to mean the last song in an opera in which each character sang a verse. In the 19th century stage performances with songs and dances were called 'vaudevilles', and the Americans used the term to describe music-hall shows.

veloce (*Italian*) 'fast'.

Venite (*Latin*) the first word of PSALM 95, '*Venite, exultemus Domino*' ('O come let us sing unto the Lord'), which is sung as a prelude to psalms at Anglican MATINS.

verismo (*Italian*) 'realism'; the term is used to describe a type of opera that was concerned with representing contemporary life of ordinary people in an honest and realistic way, e.g. *Cavalleria Rusticana* by ◊Mascagni.

verse (1) a line of poetry or a stanza of a poem. (2) a composition in METER, especially of a light nature. (3) a short section of a chapter in the Bible.

versification (1) the art of making verses. (2) the METER or verses of a poem.

Vespers the seventh of the Canonical Hours (services of the day) in the Roman Catholic Church. Many composers (such as ◊Mozart) have written musical settings for the service.

vibraphone *or* **vibes** an American instrument, similar to the GLOCKENSPIEL, which consists of a series of metal bars that are struck with mallets. Underneath the bars hang tubular resonators, which contain small discs that can be made to spin by means of an electric motor. When the NOTES are sustained the spinning discs give the sound a pulsating quality.

vibration a term in ACOUSTICS for the wave-like MOTION by which a musical TONE is produced. Sound vibrations are mechanical; radio vibrations are electro-magnetic and inaudible.

vibrato (*Italian*) literally 'shaking', i.e. a small but rapid variation in the PITCH of a NOTE.

vierhändig (*German*) 'four-handed', i.e. a piano duet.

villanella (*Italian*) literally a 'rustic SONG', a popular PART-SONG of the 17th century.

Vingt, Les a group of 20 Belgian painters who exhibited together in Brussels for ten years from 1884. Their exhibitions also included works by innovative French painters, e.g. ◊Seurat, ◊Gauguin, ◊Cézanne and Van ◊Gogh.

viol a family of stringed instruments played with a BOW, which were widely used in the 16th and 17th centuries. The instruments came in several sizes and designs, but they all usually had six strings and FRETS. Although they were similar in appearance to members of the VIOLIN family, they were constructed differently and gave a much softer sound.

viola originally a general term for any bowed stringed instrument. However, it is now the name of the ALTO member of the VIOLIN family. It has four strings.

viola da braccio (*Italian*) literally an 'arm VIOL'; a generic term for any stringed instrument played on the arm. It came to mean a VIOLIN or VIOLA.

viola da gamba (*Italian*) literally a 'leg VIOL', a term originally used of those members of the viol family played vertically between the legs or on the lap, but it came to be used exclusively for the BASS viol.

viola d'amore (*Italian*) literally a 'love VIOL', i.e. a tenor VIOL with seven strings (instead of six) and seven or fourteen SYMPATHETIC STRINGS, so called because it had a particularly sweet TONE.

violin a stringed instrument, played with a BOW, which was introduced in the 16th century. It was developed independently of the VIOL from the medieval FIDDLE. It has no FRETS and just four strings. The violin family includes the violin itself (TREBLE), VIOLA (ALTO) and VIOLONCELLO or 'cello' (TENOR). The DOUBLE BASS developed from the double BASS VIOL, but it is now included in the violin family.

violoncello, cello the tenor of the VIOLIN family, dating from the 16th century. It is held vertically between the legs of the seated player, and the TAIL PIN rests on the ground. It has four strings, which are played with a BOW.

virginal a keyboard instrument dating from the 16th century in which the strings are plucked by quills. It was similar to the HARPSICHORD, except that it had an oblong body with strings running parallel to the keyboard. The word has also been used to describe any member of the harpsichord family.

virtuoso (*Italian*) a skilled performer on the VIOLIN or some other instrument. The word was formerly synonymous with 'amateur'.

vivace (*Italian*) 'lively'.

vivamente (*Italian*) 'in a lively way'.

vivo (*Italian*) 'lively'.

vocalization control of the VOICE and vocal sounds, and the method of producing and phrasing NOTES with the voice.

vocal score *see* SCORE.

voce (*Italian*) 'VOICE', as in *voce di petto*, 'CHEST VOICE'.

voice (1) the SOUND produced by human beings by the rush of air over the vocal chords, which are made to vibrate. There are three categories of adult male voice (BASS, BARITONE and TENOR); three female categories (CONTRALTO, MEZZO-SOPRANO and SOPRANO); and two boy categories (TREBLE and ALTO). (2) Parts in contrapuntal (*see* COUNTERPOINT) compositions are traditionally termed 'voices'.

volti subito (*Italian*) 'turn over quickly' (of a page).

voluntary (1) an improvised piece of instrumental music (16th century). (2) an ORGAN SOLO (sometimes improvised) played before and after an Anglican service.

Vorticism a short-lived English Cubist art movement devised by Wyndham ◊Lewis, who also edited the two issues of its magazine *Blast* (1914, 1915). *See* FUTURISM.

waltz a dance in triple TIME. Waltzes evolved in Germany and Austria during the late 18th century and became particularly popular in Vienna.

watercolour a paint medium of colour pigments mixed with water-soluble gum arabic. When moistened, a watercolour paint produces a transparent colour that is applied to paper, usually white, the paper showing through the paint.

wedding march a tune played at the start or end of a wedding service. The two most famous wedding marches are ◊Mendelssohn's 'Wedding March' from his incidental music to *A Midsummer Night's Dream*, and ◊Wagner's 'Bridal Chorus' (better known as 'Here Comes the Bride') from the opera *Lohengrin*.

whistle (1) a toy FLUTE. (2) the making of a musical sound with the lips and breath without using the vocal cords, the hollow of the mouth forming a RESONANCE BOX. Whistling PITCH is an OCTAVE higher than is generally supposed.

whizzer *see* THUNDER STICK.

whole note (US) a SEMIBREVE.

whole-tone scale a SCALE in which all the INTERVALS are whole-tones, i.e. two SEMITONES.

wind instrument a musical INSTRUMENT the SOUND of which is produced by the breath of the player or by means of bellows.

wit 'What oft was thought but ne'er so well expressed' (◊Pope,

An Essay on Criticism). The term has had many meanings and shades of meanings down through the years, and can denote either the thing itself or a notable practitioner of it. The main shifts of meaning to bear in mind are: (a) Elizabethan usage, meaning intelligence or wisdom; (b) early 17th-century usage, meaning ingenious thought, 'fancy', and original figures of speech, as in ◊Donne's verse and METAPHYSICAL POETRY; (c) the period relevant to Pope's definition, roughly from the mid-17th century to the last half of the 18th, which is discussed below; (d) 19th-century to modern times usage, meaning an amusing, perhaps surprising observation, usually involving paradox.

Wit as defined by Pope must be distinguished from what we now regard as humour: wit can be malicious, humour is benevolent amusement. ◊Swift is witty, ◊Addison and ◊Steele, who set the pattern for the future, are both witty and humorous. Wits tended to congregate in groups of like-minded intellectuals sharing similar political, social and religious views.

By the late half of the 18th century, the term largely ceased to be used to describe intellectual groups, implying as it did either heartless frivolity or political faction. Intellectual groupings became looser, although certainly no less formidable: a literary gathering in 1780 London, for example, could include figures as diverse as ◊Sheridan, Dr ◊Johnson, ◊Burke and Edward ◊Gibbon, all of whom could be described as sharp-witted heavyweight thinkers and controversialists, although not 'wits' in the previous sense of the term.

woodwind a term for a group of blown instruments that were traditionally made of wood (some of which are now made of metal, e.g. FLUTES, OBOES, CLARINETS and BASSOONS, etc.

xylophone a PERCUSSION INSTRUMENT made up of hardwood bars arranged like a keyboard on a frame. It is played by striking the bars with mallets. Xylophones used in orchestras have steel resonators suspended beneath each bar.

zarzuela a type of Spanish comic opera that has a satirical theme and includes dialogue. It usually comprises just one act.

zither the generic term for a range of stringed instruments. The European zither consists of a flat box that is strung with a variety of different kinds of string (up to 40). The player uses a PLECTRUM to play MELODIES on one set of strings while the fingers on the other hand pluck a series of open strings to form a DRONE ACCOMPANIMENT.

*

EARLY CIVILIZATIONS OF ASIA

Before History

Origins – Scientists estimate that the earth was formed some 4600 million years ago. Fossils of the simplest animals and plants have been found in rocks dating from 1000 million years later. The early development of life within those ancient seas was inconceivably slow. The first land plants and animals evolved in the Silurian age, over 400 million years ago. The great dinosaurs ruled the earth for the 160 million years of the Mesozoic Era, which ended some 65 million years BC. The extinction of these giants provided the opportunity for the family of mammals to begin their colonization of the planet.

Some two million years ago several groups of primates, living around the forest edge in Africa, began to show characteristics which might be called 'human'. These creatures began to plan their hunting expeditions and their use of weapons. Other animals use tools – no other animals make tools for something they plan to do tomorrow!

Still, the development of man into the species *homo sapiens* remained immensely slow. Some evolutionary pathways proved to be dead ends. But the spread of the family of man was relentless. For hundreds of thousands of years, small bands of these evolving people moved into new environments, hunting and gathering their food as they went. The animal, man, proved remarkably adaptable, surviving the cold of the ice ages and the heat of the tropics.

The First Agricultural Revolution – The last ice age rolled back some 12,000 years ago, leaving the world with much the same climate that it has retained until today. Comparatively shortly afterwards some people began to introduce major changes into the timeless pattern of life.

Wild wheat and barley live naturally in the area between eastern Turkey and the Caspian Sea. At some time people – probably the women – learnt that it was possible to plant the seeds and so reduce the work of gathering. Soon these new farmers began to select which seeds produced the best crop, and so improved the quality of the crops.

The introduction of cereal farming had radical effects on hu-

WORLD HISTORY

In contrast to the previous sections of the *Concise Encyclopedia*, this section is laid out chronologically and thematically in order to include a précis of the enormous panorama that the history of the world represents, from the earliest beginnings of human civilization to the upheavals of the 1990s.

man life. Tribal groups lost their mobility as they had to settle in one place to tend the crops. When, in time, one group began to produce a surplus, it had to defend its goods against attack. Settlements then needed to be fortified and a military class grew up within the community. Once a community was producing a surplus of food, some people could undertake specialised roles within the community.

The domestication of animals was, no doubt, a long process. There was no sharp dividing line between the time when the people followed herds of wild animals as hunters, and the time when they drove the animals as herders. During the same years after the last ice age, people of southern Asia and Europe domesticated sheep, cattle and pigs. In the millennia that followed, tribesmen from the mountains of northern Iran and the steppes of Central Asia tamed the horse and camel.

Scholars differ about the pattern of development of settled agriculture. The traditional view was that all innovation happened in the Fertile Crescent of the Middle East, and skills spread outward, like ripples on a pond. Others hold that settled agriculture was discovered in many different places as conditions favoured it. Certainly the new methods appeared across Europe, as well as in India and Africa in the millennia which followed. Developments in the Far East and the Americas, at least, were independent of those in the Fertile Crescent. Millet and rice were cultivated in China and South East Asia from about 6000 BC. Here chicken, water buffalo and, again, pigs were domesticated. Change came later in the Americas, where maize, the potato and other important crops were added to the world's store.

The Growth of Cities

As the agricultural age continued, so people began to gather into yet larger communities. The earliest discovered is Jericho, which grew up before 8000 BC. Two thousand years later, Catal Hüyük, in Anatolia, covered 32 acres. These cities provided protection and allowed for greater specialization of role for the inhabitants.

New skills were, indeed, needed. Copper was smelted in Anatolia in about 7000 BC, introducing the age of metals. The earliest known pottery and evidence of the first woollen textiles have both been found in Catal Hüyük.

City life also provided a centre for religious worship. A temple lay at the heart of the community, and religion and government were always closely allied to each other. The change in lifestyle brought with it a change in religious practice. Cave paintings, such as those of southern France, give a glimpse of the cults of the hunter gatherers, which focused on animals and sacred places. These have much in common with the practices of people, like some North American Indians, who lived similar lives within historical times.

Settled agriculture brought with it a new emphasis on birth and fertility, symbolised by the mother goddess figures found from widely dispersed areas of this early civilized world.

Sumerian Civilization

Irrigation – As would be expected, the earliest developments in city life happened in regions which had adequate natural rainfall. Some time after 5000 BC, however, groups from the north began to settle in the dry land of Mesopotamia. Here they drained the marshes and used the water from the twin rivers Tigris and Euphrates to irrigate the fertile land.

The Rise of the Sumerian Cities – It appears as though two of the most vital inventions in the history of man – the wheel and the plough – were made in Mesopotamia in around 3500 BC. These enabled farmers to cultivate the irrigated land in a more concentrated manner, so increasing the surplus production, leading to a spectacular flourishing of cities.

The most famous city, Ur of the Chaldes, was only one; also prominent were Eridu, Uruk, Bad-tibira, Nippur and Kish. Each city had its own special deity, and it served as the centre for a surrounding region of villages and farm land.

The Invention of Writing – In about 3100 BC the people of these Sumerian cities learnt how to represent their spoken language by the use of writing. The earliest characters were pictographic, and remain largely undeciphered. The Sumerians later developed the more flexible cuneiform script. The invention of writing marks the beginning of history, but the earliest documents were unremarkable. Written on tablets of clay are lists showing the ownership of jars of oil and bundles of reeds. They do show, however, that some of the inhabitants were gathering serious wealth, which could be measured in hundreds and thousands of units.

Life in Sumeria – The cities were walled, but it appears that, in the early centuries, this was not a world of warring cities. Disputes were controlled by the exchange of embassies and by dynastic marriages, rather than by conflict. The laws which governed behaviour were not particularly strict.

The area was short of both wood and stone, and the Sumerian people depended heavily on clay for building and many other functions. The skills of the artisans became ever more refined. Gold, silver, bronze and polished stones were made into fine objects for the decoration of people, homes and temples. Weavers, leather workers and potters followed their specialised crafts. The scribes of later centuries wrote down a fine oral tradition of myths, epics and hymns. The world in which small family groups of hunters lived in co-operation had now been left far behind. Everyday life was controlled by a highly developed bureaucracy, which, for good or ill, was to become a hallmark of civilization. Kings were now divine beings, who were buried with treasure, and also with their whole retinue to see them into the next life.

Egypt

In about 3200 BC King Menes united the whole of the land of the lower Nile. The deserts which stretched on both sides of the river largely protected the Egyptians against the invasions which plagued Mesopotamia. Egyptian rulers had to face the armies of Assyria and 'The People of the Sea' from the Mediterranean, but the remarkable endurance of Egyptian civilization owes much to its isolation. Despite this, the Egyptians owed much to the Sumerians. In particular, they borrowed the early Sumerian system of writing, and adapted this into their own pictorial script. *Hieroglyphics* means 'the writing of the priests' and the art remained a closely guarded secret within the priestly caste.

For more than 2000 years dynasties followed one another; the country experienced bad times as well as good, but a continuity was maintained, unparalleled in the history of the world. Even when the land later fell under foreign rulers, Egyptian culture retained its remarkable integrity.

The Nile Waters – Egypt depended on the Nile. This was a kindlier river than the Tigris and Euphrates because each year it flooded the land on either side, providing natural irrigation for the fertile soil. The whole of Egyptian life was attuned to the rise and fall of the great river. The ruler – or pharaoh, as he would later be called – was the owner of the land and the giver of its life, and the ceremonials of kingship centred on the fertility of the land. The Book of Exodus describes how the rulers of Egypt were able to organize the storage of surpluses from good years to guard against crop failures in bad years.

The Calendar – The Egyptians studied the movements of the sun and stars, and they were the first to work out the year, consisting of $364\frac{1}{4}$ days. For the farmer, this year was divided into three parts, each of four months – one of flooding, one of planting and one of harvesting.

The Capital Cities – Menes set up his capital in Memphis. Later pharaohs moved it to Thebes, but neither were true cities, like those of Sumeria. Their role was more as a centre of religion than a focus for daily life. The wide deserts provided more protection from enemies than any city walls. Because of this physical isolation, Egyptian life could remain focused on the villages, rather than on larger centres of population.

Monuments and Art – The massive monuments of ancient Egypt remain objects of wonder. Imhotep, builder of the Step Pyramid at Saqqara, has left his name as the first architect known to history. Many thousands were marshalled to build these tombs, working without winches, pulleys, blocks or tackles.

A modern visitor will look with awe at the pyramids and other great stone monuments, but it is the more modest paintings which give insight into the daily lives of the people. They show scenes of busy rural life, where peasants gather crops and hunt wild fowl by the Nile. They are happily free from the scenes of carnage and inhumanity, which is all too common in much of the art of the period. It was a world in which women had a high status and beauty was admired. No doubt the peasants had to work hard to keep not only themselves but the whole apparatus of royal and priestly rule, but the river was kind and the land was fertile, and there was usually enough for all.

Migration and Trade

Semites and Indo Europeans – The Semites were herders of sheep who originated in the Arabian peninsula. They were a warrior people, reared in the stern disciplines of life at the desert edge. The most powerful group in those early years them were a people called the Amorites. They founded cities to the north of Sumeria – Babylon, Nineveh and Damascus. The Indo-Europeans were mainly cattle herders, who made their way into Mesopotamia from the north. Their gods emerge in the Pantheon of Greece and in the Vedic deities of India.

The Indo-Europeans had learned how to tame horses from their Asian neighbours. Most importantly, they brought iron. Iron weapons and chariots gave them a technological advantage over the earlier inhabitants of Mesopotamia. Control of iron therefore became an essential precondition of political power. The slow spread of iron technology had other important effects. An iron plough could break in land which had hitherto been too hard for agriculture. This created a rise in production, and hence an increase in population.

The Growth of Trade – Newcomers from both north and south were drawn into Mesopotamia by the rich lifestyle of the cities, but it happened that the area had no significant iron deposits and was poor in other metals. The need for raw materials was to be the driving force for the development of trade in the ancient world.

Money – It is remarkable how much trade was carried on before the development of currency as a method of exchange. Merchants from the civilized Fertile Crescent were able to take a range of manufactured goods to exchange for metals and other raw materials. Goods were also moved around the world as tribute, taxes and offerings to temples. The first coins date from about 700 BC, but their use spread slowly. Egypt, for instance, did not introduce a currency until about 400 BC.

Land Transport – The wheel was of no value in a world without roads. Columns of pack animals began to spread out into the highlands of Iran and through the Balkans into metal-rich Europe, opening up trade routes which would be trampled for centuries.

Sea Transport – Improvements in the design of ships followed. Oars and sails were developed and rigging improved; decks were made watertight. The Red Sea and Persian Gulf became navigable all the year round, and the Mediterranean at least in summer. The growth in sea transport would ultimately change the centre of gravity of early civilizations away from inland rivers towards coastal regions. Ideas and empires could now spread along sea as well as land routes.

Against this background, the empires of the ancient Near East rose and fell.

Babylon, Assyria and the Hittites

Babylon – In 1792 BC a ruler called Hammurabi came to power in the Semite city of Babylon. He can be looked upon as the first great emperor in the history of the world. Hammurabi's armies carried Babylonian power across most of the Fertile Crescent, from the Persian Gulf and the old Sumerian cities in the east, to the edge of mountains of Asia Minor and the borders of Syria in the west. Conquest was undertaken to secure essential supplies by the control of trade routes, and the exaction of tribute. Carvings show endless lines of conquered people bearing products to swell the stores of the great king, and the riches of Babylon became famous throughout the region.

Hammurabi was an absolute ruler, but he was anxious that his subject should know the laws under which they had to order their lives. He set up pillars in the temples on which were engraved all the laws which governed his kingdom, so that his subjects would be able to come and refer to them. This Code of Hammurabi was the first statement of the principle of 'An eye for an eye'.

Astrology played a vital role in all decision taking, and this led the Babylonians to study the stars closely. By 1000 BC their astrologers had plotted the paths of the sun and the planets with great accuracy, and they were able to predict eclipses. They instituted the system under which the circle is divided into 360 degrees and the hour into 60 minutes.

The first great period of Babylonian power ended when the city was destroyed by the Hittites in 1600 BC After that, Babylon remained an important centre of trade and culture, but a thousand years would pass before the city would achieve a late flowering of political power, under the great king Nebuchadnezzar.

The Hittites, who destroyed the first Babylon, were an Indo-European people who had come into the area from the north, probably through the Balkans. After defeating Babylon, they dominated an even larger empire than that of Hammurabi, across the sweep of the fertile crescent, from their homeland in Anatolia, Asia Minor to the Persian Gulf and the borders of Egypt. The power of the Hittites was based on skill with iron. It was they who carried iron technology across the region.

Hittite power collapsed in its turn under pressure from the 'People of the Sea', who were also harassing Egypt. These People of the Sea, however, did not follow up their successes by founding an empire. Rather, they left a vacuum which was to be filled by the most terrible of the empires of the Ancient Near East.

Assyria – The centre of power now moved to the city of Nineveh on the middle reaches of the Tigris. Monuments of the great kings of Assyria, like Tiglath-Pileser I and Ashurbanipal show an empire based on brute military force and the use of terror to control conquered people. Whole populations, like the lost ten tribes of Israel, were moved from their homeland and resettled in other parts of the empire. In this way they lost the identity on which national resistance could be built.

Assyrian armies dominated the region from the 12th to the 7th centuries BC They marched north into the highlands of modern Turkey and Iran, looking for metals and other necessary supplies. They conquered Syria and Palestine, and, under Ashurbanipal in the mid 7th century, they even drove the Pharaohs of Egypt out of the Nile delta.

The Hebrews

Among the Semite invaders into the Near East was a group known as the Hebrews. The Bible record tells how Abraham, the father of the people, left the city of Ur to return to a purer nomadic way of life. His descendants experienced a period of bondage in Egypt, from which they emerged in about 1300 BC.

The Hebrews made their home in Palestine, and they had set up a monarchy by about 1000 BC. Hebrew power reached its peak under King Solomon, who died in 935 BC The kingdom then split; Israel, the northern kingdom, was destroyed by Assyria in 722 BC and Judah, the southern, by Babylon in 587 BC.

The Hebrews do not feature in world history by virtue of their political success, but because of their religious faith. They proclaimed a single deity whom they called Yahweh. Their sacred writings have been one of the major influences on the subsequent history of the world, so some themes need to be identified.

Monotheism – Initially Yahweh was seen as the God of the Hebrews, who was set over the gods of other peoples of the area. In time, however, Yahweh began to develop a uniqueness which challenged the existence of other gods. A writer from the period of the Babylonian exile pronounced Yahweh to be the god of the non-Hebrew, as well as the Hebrew people.

Divine Law – The rulers of Babylon and Assyria were absolute monarchs, whose word was law, and whose actions therefore could not be judged by any superior authority. The Hebrew prophetic tradition, in contrast, made it clear that a king, no less than any other person, operated under a divine law. Here, a ruler, who has unjustly taken a common man's vineyard, can be challenged by a prophet with the words 'Thou art the man!'

Man and Nature – The Hebrew creation myth, which was handed down verbally for many centuries before being written into the Book of Genesis, clearly sets man apart from the rest of creation. He is made in the image of God and given dominion over the beasts. The Bible has been the vehicle which has transmitted this perspective into Western culture.

Male-centred Religion – The Old Testament narrative describes the fierce rejection of female fertility gods of the Fertile Crescent, which were described as The Abomination of Desolation. For the Hebrews divinity was uncompromisingly male, and woman is depicted as a secondary creation, born out of man's side. This rejection of the female strand of religion would later be modified in the Catholic Christian cult of the Virgin, but it has been influential in defining western attitudes on the relationship of the sexes.

Persia

In about the year 1000 Aryan people moved south into the land which is now Iran (the land of the Aryans). There were two dominant tribes: the Medes occupied the north of the country, while the Persians occupied the south.

In the early centuries the Medish tribes were subject to the Assyrians, but they rebelled against their masters, and in 612 BC Nineveh was sacked and the Assyrian Empire was destroyed by the army of the Medes. The success of the Medes, as of the Persians after them, was based on their successful harnessing of the horse as an instrument of war.

The power centre shifted south when the Persian King Cyrus united Medes and Persians to form what was to become the greatest empire of the Near East. At its height, it extended from Greece and North Africa in the west to the Indus valley and the edge of the Central Asian steppe in the east. Darius the Great had problems at either edge of the empire – with Greeks in the west and Scythians in the east, but the bulk of the empire held together well until 330 BC.

The official Persian religion was Zoroastrianism. This emphasised the struggle of good and evil, and was to give the Semites the concept of angels and hell fire. It did not, however, seek converts, and the people of the empire were left in peace with their own gods. Cyrus was greeted by the Jews as the instrument of Jahweh, and he even rebuilt King Solomon's temple.

Darius was not as successful a conqueror as Cyrus, but he was an administrator of genius. Once a region had been brought within the empire, the royal satrap worked to win the trust and loyalty of the conquered people. Regional traditions were respected and local people were given responsibility in managing their own affairs. The country was bound together by roads which could be used for trade and even postal services as well as for armies.

India

At its peak, the Persian Empire reached as far as the Indus valley. This was the home of another, distinct Asian civilization.

The Harappa Culture – Remains have been found in the Indus Valley of cities, dating from about 2550 BC. The pictogram writing of these early Harappa people has not been deciphered, but archaeologists have discovered houses, with bathrooms, built of burnt brick. There are remains of canals and docks, and Indian products from this period have been excavated in Mesopotamia. Rice was grown, which may indicate that the cities had contact with the Far East. Here is the first evidence of cultivated cotton.

The Harappan cities had houses, granaries and temples, but no palaces. This suggests that the civilization was centred on the priests, rather than on warrior kings, and therefore ill equipped to challenge invaders.

The Aryans – In about 1750 BC Indo-European Aryans began to penetrate into the land from the north. They herded cattle, which were to become sacred creatures. Their religion is enshrined in the oldest holy books of the world, the Vedas. From these it is possible to get an image of nomadic people, standing round a camp fire, chanting hymns to the sun and other forces of nature.

The Aryans overran the northern part of the continent, but they did not completely destroy the people who had been there before them. They slowly spread from the Indus, clearing the dense forest of the Ganges Valley and founding cities, such as Benares.

Hindu Castes – The racial structure of Aryan and non-Aryan people became enshrined in the caste system of India. There were three 'twice-born' castes, which are assumed to originate from the Aryan invaders: *Brahmins* were priests, *Ksahiyas* were warriors and the *Varsyas* were farmers and merchants. Only members of these castes were permitted to take part in the Vedic rituals.

The *Sudras*, who came below the lowest member of the twice-born castes, accommodated the conquered people. Below them were the unclean *outcasts*, who did not enjoy any caste status.

The Cults – As time passed, people looked for religious expressions which could engage the emotions more fully than the Vedic hymns. The cults surrounding the gods *Vishnu* and *Shiva*, with their consorts, fulfilled their needs. It appears that Shiva, at least, was drawn from older pre-Aryan India. The cult of Shiva, who represented the great cycle of birth and death, life and destruction, was to express the Hindu world view most completely.

Buddhism – In the early 6th century BC a prince of the warrior caste, called Siddartha Buddha, left his home to seek enlightenment. He followed strict Hindu practices of fasting but did not achieve his objective. He found that true enlightenment could only be discovered by 'letting go' of his own self and accepting that, in life, all things are change. The Buddha rejected the caste system and his teachings took his followers out of Hinduism.

Although Hinduism and Buddhism separated, any contest for supremacy lay in the mind, for there were no wars of religion, like those which were to mark the West. The two religions share the same root. Both see man as an integral part of the natural world, not as a creature set apart from, and above it, as in the Hebrew tradition.

Buddhism received a great impetus with the conversion of the north Indian king Ashoka in 260 BC. He abandoned his career of conquest and administered his kingdom in the light of the teaching, providing the people with social works and good laws. In the end, Hinduism was to retain its hold on the sub-continent, apart from Ceylon in the south and the mountains of Tibet in the north, while Buddhism made its impact farther east.

Central Asia

Across the Himalayas from India lay the great land mass of central Asia. This can be divided into three bands. Farthest north was the great wall of the forests of Siberia. The centre consists of the Asian grasslands. In the south are the deserts and mountains. The last two are influential in world history from the earliest times until about 1500 AD.

In the grasslands of the steppe lived a selection of nomadic tribes. They survived in marginal land, much as, in later times, the Plains Indians would survive on the American prairie. The nomadic life could take peoples right across the grasslands, and they often fought each other for the control of land. Because the plain could only support a small population, drought, war or other impulses could set whole peoples on the move. This would produce a knock-on effect. Ripples could grow to waves. These would then break onto the boundaries of the lands which bordered onto the steppes.

These were illiterate people, so their names and history is confused, but they appear in history as the Hsiung-nu or Huns, the Avars, the Scythians, the Turks and the Mongols. They were terrible foes, who won their battles by great mobility and superb mastery of the horse.

Farther south, in the desert region, lay the trade routes. From very early times Bactrian camels and horses carried goods along these routes, creating a link between Europe and the Near East to the west and China to the east. Most of the goods moved from east to west. At an early date, the Chinese learnt to make fine fabric from the web of the silk worm. Pepper and other spices also made light and high-value loads. It was an immense and dangerous journey, but the profits were incentive enough to keep the caravans moving.

China

Isolation and Contact – the people of China have long known of their nation as *Chung-hua,* the 'central nation'. Educated people knew well of the existence of other cultures, but they were looked on as subordinate, and, indeed, tributaries of the great nation. Although the Chinese did maintain contact with the outside world, they were little influenced by it. Chinese culture was therefore able to establish a structure in the early centuries which remained little altered throughout history.

The immediate concern of Chinese rulers, again from very early times, was to defend the northern borders against the steppe nomads. This border, which would be marked by the world's greatest building work, The Great Wall, lay along the line where the decline in rainfall made settled agriculture impracticable.

Culture and Language – The huge country centred on three rivers, the Hwang-Ho, the Yangtse and the Hsi. They were divided by great mountain ridges. A wide range of climates could be found within the nation. China has been politically divided for long periods, but she has maintained a unity of culture, beyond that achieved by any other people. An important reason for this is that, while the people of the west came to use to a phonic script, China retained the use of pictograms. The difference is fundamental. A phonic script is easily learned, but it needs to reflect the sounds of a language. People of different languages are therefore unable to communicate with each other without learning each other's language. A pictogram script, in contrast, is hard to learn, but it is not linked to the sound of language. It can therefore be used to bind people who speak differently. China therefore developed a power to absorb and civilize the conquerors who, from time to time, spilled over her frontiers. Literacy was the property of a cultured elite, whose whole education had, of necessity, been centred on diligence rather than creativity. This gave Chinese culture the twin characteristics of breadth and stability.

The State – Around 1700 BC the first historical dynasty, the Shang, gained control of the northern Hwang-Ho river valley. Even a this early stage, the court had archivists and scribes. Like their successors of later dynasties, the kings saw themselves as the bringers of civilization to barbarian peoples.

About 1100 BC the Shang were overthrown by the Chou who carried royal power to the central Yangtse river valley. Then, around 700 BC, the Chou in their turn were overthrown by pastoralists from the north. This brought in the time graphically known as the Period of the Warring States.

Confucianism – During this period there lived K'ung-fu-tsu, who became known to the world as Confucius. He looked back from that period of unrest to an earlier time when the world was at peace and believed that the problems of his times arose from the fact that people had forgotten their proper duty. In an ordered world, everyone had a place in society. Some – rulers, parents, husbands – were 'higher'; others – subjects, children, wives – were 'lower'. Everyone, high and low, was bound together in ties of mutual duty and respect. The high had no more right to oppress the low than the low had to be disrespectful of the high. When these bonds were broken, the times became out of joint.

Confucianism therefore placed emphasis on 'conservative' institutions – the state, the civil service, scholarship, and, above all, the family. It was not a religion in the sense of teaching about God, but it brought a religious dimension to the worship of ancestors.

Social Structure – K'ung-fu-tsu accepted the most fundamental division in Chinese society. The common peasants were not allowed to belong to a clan, and they therefore had no ancestors to worship. Their lives consisted of an endless round of toil.

For those who were, more fortunately, born into a clan, China would become a land of opportunity. Even boys from poor homes could study to pass the examinations that would open up the coveted civil service jobs. For those with more modest aspirations, growing cities offered opportunities in trade and the crafts.

The fortunate lived in an assurance that Chinese customs and the Chinese way offered the model of excellence, and all other people had to be judged according to the way in which they measured up to this standard.

MEDITERRANEAN CIVILIZATION

Early Sea-going People

Conquering the Oceans – The earliest civilizations centred around major river valleys. The rivers provided water and arteries of communication. Then the technology of sails and ship building improved to a level which enabled men to venture onto the oceans. From early times, the Red Sea and the Persian Gulf provided important communication routes, which were orientated towards the east. The Mediterranean, particularly in winter, is subject to violent storms. Further advances in marine engineering, such as the construction of watertight holds and improvements in sails and rigging, were needed before sailors could master this environment.

By about 500 BC ships were able to move freely in the Mediterranean, at least in summer, so providing easier communication than was possible on land. There was then no distinction between a fertile north and an arid north shore. The whole region was fertile. Traders and rulers therefore saw the Mediterranean basin as a single unit, bound together by its ocean highway.

Minoa and Mycenae – In about 1900 BC a civilization grew up on Crete, which has been named after its king, Minos. Its earliest writing has not been deciphered, but excavations reveal fine palaces and developed communities. Their cities stood beside the sea, and the builders were already confident enough in the control of their ships over the eastern Mediterranean to dispense with fortifications.

Objects found in Crete and Egypt show that there was a lively trade between the two cultures. The Minoan sailors probably traded in timber, wood, olive oil and grapes over the whole of the Mediterranean area.

Inhabitants of the Minoan cities were the first people to enjoy the benefits of piped drains and sewers, and wall paintings show them dancing and playing sports.

The Minoans set up colonies on the mainland, of which the most important seems to have been at Mycenae. This is the name which is given to Minoan civilization as it is found on the mainland. The culture spread across the Aegean to the coast of Asia Minor and to the city of Troy at the mouth of the Bosphorus.

The first Minoan civilization was destroyed by Indo-European people who poured into the region from the north. Some of these invaders settled in the Ionian peninsula to become Greeks. A later resurgence of Minoan civilization is thought to have been under Greek influence.

The stories which were written down centuries later by the poet Homer tell of the struggles between the Mycenaens of Troy and the less advanced Indo-European invaders.

The Phoenicians – Semite people, in general, liked to keep their feet on dry land. The exception were the people who lived in the area known as Phoenicia, which is now Lebanon and southern Syria. They developed remarkable skills as sailors and for centuries their ships dominated the trade routes. Phoenician sailors reached the Atlantic Ocean and traded with tin miners in distant Cornwall. The Greek historian Herodits even reports that one expedition rounded the southern cape of Africa.

The Phoenicians planted colonies to protect their trade routes. Most important, about 800 BC they founded the city of Carthage. The colony was strategically placed to protect the ships which brought metal from Western Europe.

Phoenicia was never a power on land, and when, in 868 BC the Assyrian king 'washed his weapons in the Mediterranean' Phoenicia lost its independence. But the rulers of the great empires needed these fine sailors, and the Phoenicians therefore exercised influence beyond their military power.

Phoenicia is best known for its sailors. It did, however, make another major contribution to western culture, by creating a phonic alphabet. The words Alpha, Beta and Gama are derived from the Phoenician words for an ox, a house and a camel.

The Greeks

In Mycenaean times, an iron-working Aryan people were moving south into the Greek peninsula. Myths of early battles with

Mycenaean Troy are preserved in the works of the story teller – or tellers – given the name of Homer.

The early culture was oral, but, in around 750 BC the Greeks adopted and modified the Phoenician alphabet and committed the ancient legends to writing. These were to provide the starting point for the world's first great literary culture.

The beginning of Greek civilization was dated from the first Olympian Games, held in 776 BC. This event, held once every four years, drew together people who shared the Greek language and culture. The participants did not, however, come under one unified government.

Government – The Greek political structure was dictated by the geography of the region in which they settled. This was a land of mountain ranges, with small coastal plains, which faced outwards to the sea. Each of these plains was settled by a self-governing community, which initially contained only as many people as the land would support. This was the basis of the *polis*, or city state.

The *Iliad* provides a picture of an early feudal society of kings, nobles and common fighting men. Each city then followed its own course in working out the structure of government. The first struggle lay between the kings (monarchy) and the nobles (aristocracy). Then pressure came from other influential citizens (oligarchy) and from the mass of free male citizens (democracy). When a state plunged into chaos, a strong man (tyranny), often benevolent and public-spirited, would emerge to bring order.

The Greek concept of democracy was specific to the confined structure of the city state. It did not operate through representative institutions but through the direct participation of citizens in the decision-taking process. The meeting place, or *agora*, not the temple or the royal palace, was now the centre of city life. The citizens who met here provided the city with its law courts and its political assembly. Debate and persuasion became vital skills. People could on occasion be swept away by the power of a demagogue, but within this forum they learned to listen and to analyse argument.

The fractured nature of Greek society did not provide peace and stability. The city states might join together in games, but they were as often at war with each other. The people remained fiercely independent, more ready than any other people before, and perhaps even since, to question the structure of the society within which they lived.

Colonization – Since geography prevented expansion inland, the

Greeks had an impetus to expand outwards, along the sea routes. Greek communities were established along the west and south coasts of Asia Minor, on the islands of the Aegean and as far east as Cyprus and westwards to Sicily and southern Italy, and even farther into North Africa, France and Spain. These colonies were self-governing, but they often had links with powerful city states, such as Corinth or Athens. They served as an overspill for excess population and as trading bases across the Mediterranean Sea.

The Persian Wars – the conflict between Greece and Persia has been depicted as a struggle between an oppressive empire and a freedom-loving people. Reality is more complex. Close links had long existed between the Greeks and the Persians, and many Greeks served in the Persian army. The trouble started when Greek city states in Asia Minor rebelled against Persian rule and Darius moved to put down the insurrection. The Asians were supported by the European Greeks, and this brought the Persian Empire into conflict with an alliance of Greek cities, led by Athens and Sparta. The army of Darius was defeated at Marathon in 490 BC and the navy led by his successor Xerses failed ten years later at Salamis. This war drew the boundary of the Persian Empire to the east of the area of Greek settlement.

Athens and Sparta – The alliance which had defeated Persia did not survive the victory. Athens was much the largest of the city states, with a larger population than its farm land could support. Prosperity was based on the control of silver mines worked by thousands of slaves. The city's survival depended on a structure of trade and colonies. Whatever freedom may have been enjoyed by Athenian citizens within their city, their rule of others was often oppressive. The Athenians demanded heavy tribute from client states and put down rebellion as violently as any Persian army.

Other trading states, like Corinth, felt themselves continually threatened by Athenian power. They found allies in the conservative, agricultural state of Sparta. The Peloponnesian War lasted for 27 years, and ended with the defeat of Athens in 404 BC. This led to a reaction against an over-mighty Sparta, and the destructive sequence of wars continued into the 4th century. The Greeks may have provided the world with a vocabulary of politics and an ideal of democracy, but its outstanding achievement lies, not in politics, but in broader fields of culture.

Religion – Greek myth is drawn from the common Indo-European root, which created the Vedas in India. It has provided a fertile source of inspiration for western art and literature for more than 2000 years, but it is harder to look back through the twin filters of Semitic religion and rationalism, which have shaped modern attitudes, to understand what the world of gods meant to the Greeks themselves. On the one side, there was a piety of the common man, which condemned Socrates for blaspheming against the gods; on the other side was a free-thinking strain expressed by the philosopher of 7th-century Miletus, who declared 'If an ox could paint a picture, its god would look like an ox'. The Greek religious tradition was real, but it was not an all-demanding way of life like that of the Hebrews.

Philosophy and Science – The Greeks invented organized abstract thought and took it to a level which would dominate the philosophy of the Near East and Europe until very recent times. In the Greek perspective, there was no distinction between the arts, the sciences, and, indeed, religion. All were a part of the search for truth. In the 6th century, Pythagoras did not distinguish mathematics from philosophy and religion. The two greatest Greek thinkers defined the twin, often opposing, channels through which all philosophy, and later, all theology, would flow.

Plato, a pupil of Socrates, was 23 years old when his home city of Athens was defeated by Sparta. His attempt to achieve a mental order was therefore born of the political disorder of the post war years. Plato is the apostle of the *ideal* – the abstract of perfection, whether it be for the state, the individual, or in a mathematical equation. In his philosophy, all life is a striving towards an ideal of the good, containing truth, justice and beauty, which was the only reality in an imperfect world. Plato's Academy can lay claim to being the world's first university.

Aristotle came to Plato's Academy at the age of 17 and remained his master's devoted disciple. His interests, however, took him in the opposite direction, as he came to emphasize enquiry and experiment as the source of knowledge. While Plato stressed the *ideal*, Aristotle stressed the *real*; while Plato was drawn into the abstractions of mathematics, Aristotle found himself fascinated by the complexities of biology and literary criticism. For him, truth lay not in a distant abstract, but in a 'happy medium'. Aristotle is therefore seen as the father of the scientific method.

The Arts – 5th-century Athens provided the most fertile environment for classical Greek culture. The architecture of the Parthenon, the sculptures of Praxiteles and Pheidias provide an illustration in stone of the Platonic ideal. They provided generations of architects and artists, particularly from Europe, with a standard of perfection. Literature also flourished. Aeschylus, Sophocles and Euripides used the ancient myths to explore depths of the human experience and create tragic drama, while the irreverent Aristophanes, pioneered the tradition of comedy. The disasters of the Peloponnesian Wars also inspired Thucydides to become the world's first scientific and literary historian.

The contribution of Greece to the world's cultural store is a fundamental theme of history. By the middle of the 4th century, however, the advances were largely confined to the Greek speaking world. The diffusion of Greek culture into a wider world would be the work of a young and brilliant student of Aristotle.

The Hellenistic World

Alexander the Great – The state of Macedon lay to the north of Greece, crossing the boundary which divided the civilized world from the barbarians. Philip II of Macedon developed his army into an efficient fighting machine and conquered the Greek city states. Philip died in 336 BC and was succeeded by Aristotle's pupil, his son, Alexander.

Alexander inherited his father's army and the Greek power base. The problem he faced was how he could pay the soldiers who had served Macedon so well. This search for money took Alexander on spectacular campaigns. There was ample booty to be won across the Aegean in the Persian Empire. In 334 BC the Macedonian army defeated the Persians at Issus then marched south into Egypt, where Alexander founded the city which was to carry his name. He returned north, defeated the Persians once more and sacked the capital, Persepolis. Not content, he took his army eastward into Afghanistan and the Punjab. He would have gone further, but his soldiers insisted that the time had come to turn back.

The young man was one of the great soldiers of all time. The importance of his conquests, however, was that they were the catalyst which brought together the old civilizations of the Near East and the newer Greek culture. Alexander was Greek, but he was drawn to Eastern ways. He himself married the Persian emperor's daughter, and, in a great symbolic gesture, he married 9000 of his soldiers to eastern women.

The Division of the Empire – Alexander died in Babylon in 323 BC at the age of 32, leaving no heir to succeed to his enormous empire. The land was divided between his generals. The Ptolemies based their power in Egypt, the Seleucids in the region of Syria and the Attalids around Pergamum. Parthia later became independent of the Seleuchids. These were centralized states, under absolute monarchs. The age of debate and democracy was certainly past. Over most of the Hellenistic world, this was a time of economic growth, but the Greek cities themselves declined.

Hellenistic Culture – Greek was now the official and commercial language of the whole area. The learning of the scholars became widely known and great libraries were set up at Alexandria and Pergamum. Among the books preserved were many of the writings of Plato and Aristotle. Scholars in the Greek tradition worked in different parts of the Hellenistic world. Science flourished, as it would not do again for over 1500 years. In Alexandria Euclid laid the foundation of geometry. Aristarchus correctly deduced the structure of the solar system 1800 years before Copernicus and Eratosthenes measured the circumference of the earth. Archimedes of Syracuse had the widest ranging genius of all.

Philosophers, such as the stoics, could no longer question the ways of government, so they turned their thoughts towards the inner life of man. They led a quest for virtue and true contentment. Classical Greek styles provided powerful models for painters and sculptors, but Hellenistic artists retreated from the Platonic search for an ideal and worked instead to project the humanity of their subjects.

Religion – Greek religion was too restricted a vehicle for this new, expansive world. Mystery cults began to spread which demanded a more active devotion from their followers. Two of these became increasingly dominant. From Egypt came the myth of Isis and Osiris. This told of a dying and a rising god. From Zoroastrianism came the mystery of Mithras, with its powerful image of redemption through blood.

The End of the Hellenistic World – The Hellenistic empires in their turn fell to a new power from further west in the Mediterranean. The Roman victory at Actium in 31 BC marked the end of the era. No battle, however, could put an end to Greek culture. The Roman poet Horace summed it up by saying that, although Greece was defeated, it took its conquerors prisoner.

Republican Rome

The Etruscans – In the years before 509 BC central Italy was dominated by a people called the Etruscans. They can be seen in lifelike tomb sculptures, but little is still known about their culture. They appear to have been an Indo-European people, who achieved dominance over other people by bringing iron working to a high level of perfection. Etruscan kings, the Tarquins, ruled in Rome until they were expelled, according to tradition in 509 BC. The expulsion of the kings remained a powerful myth within the Roman state. Men looked back to the days of the Tarquins as the time when the rights of the citizen were subjected to the will of a single individual.

The Structure of the State – The new Roman state was based on agriculture. Indeed, *pecunia*, the name for a flock or herd of animals, became the Latin word for money.

There were different groups within society. The old families, who took pride in their status as *patricians*, assumed power in place of the deposed kings. The remaining free people were known as the *plebs*. At first they were poor farmers with little say in affairs of state. As Rome grew, many plebeians became more wealthy and they began to look for a share in the running of affairs.

Romans, be they patricians or plebs, took immense pride in their status as citizens. Roman citizenship became a unique badge of belonging to a pure and strong society, free from the softness and corruption of the Hellenistic world around them. Every man was liable to military service which could be for as long as 16 years in the infantry or 10 years in the cavalry. Warlike virtues were admired by society and inculcated in boys through the home and education. At best, this could breed a self-sacrifice to the common good; at worst it could bring a lust for battle and bloodshed.

The organization of the Roman Republic was not unlike that of a Greek polis. The Roman forum took the place of the Greek agora. The senate, which was an assembly of patricians, wielded the real power. Two consuls, elected from its ranks, commanded the army in war and were responsible for government in time of peace. The demand of the plebs to be represented was met by the appointment of two tribunes. It therefore became possible for an unusually talented man, from a low family, to rise in the state. This structure lasted for 450 years. It carried Rome from being a small city state to dominance in the Mediterranean basin.

Early Expansion – In the early centuries, Roman armies were occupied with winning control over the Italian peninsula. If there was a ruthless character to Roman expansion, there could also be generosity in the terms given on surrender. Conquered people were given Roman citizenship and allowed a large measure of self-government. Once within Roman rule, they too were expected to provide troops for the army.

The Punic Wars – As Rome expanded, she had only one serious rival. Carthage had expanded beyond North Africa. Her ships controlled the sea and Carthaginian colonies were established in Sicily, Southern Italy and Spain. The two powers were bound to clash for supremacy in the western Mediterranean. The Romans built up a navy, and in the First Punic War (264 – 241 BC) they defeated the Carthaginians at sea and won Sicily.

The Second Punic War (218 – 201 BC) marked the decisive struggle between the two powers. When Hannibal crossed the Alps and defeated Roman armies at Lake Trasimene and Cannae, it seemed as though Roman power would be broken. In 202, however, Hannibal was in turn defeated at Zama and Carthaginian power was destroyed. In 149 BC Rome took an excuse to fight a third Punic War. This time Carthage was flattened and the ground on which the city had stood was ploughed over.

The Rise of the Generals – Victory over Carthage had been bought at a high cost, and that cost was paid by the poor. Many peasant farmers, who were citizens sold their land to the rich and so lost their means of support. This led to internal unrest.

Wars were now being fought far from home, in the Hellenistic east and to the north in the land they called Gaul. Roads were built across the empire, which enabled the army legions to move swiftly from one trouble spot to another. These distant armies could no longer be commanded by consuls, with a term of office of two years.

There therefore arose a new breed of professional generals. These men often became fabulously rich on the booty of war, and, with a loyal army at their back, they could pose a threat to the traditional institutions of the Republic. Marius made his name in Africa and Gaul, and then Sulla in the eastern Mediterranean. Julius Caesar was the most successful in this line of successful generals. In 49 BC he took an irrevocable step when he crossed the river Rubicon, which marked the boundary of Italy, and marched on Rome at the head of his army. By this action he started the chain of events, which led to his murder, and the founding of imperial Rome.

Christianity

Origins – The early years of the Roman Empire were to see the beginnings of another of the great religions of the world. The Jewish people had maintained a stubborn refusal to dilute their religion to meet the demands of Hellenistic rulers. At the time of Jesus of Nazareth, sects like the Essenes and the Zealots maintained a resistance to Roman rule.

Jesus was a Jew, but he appears to have rejected the path of political resistance and taught instead a message of the relationship of the individual to God and other men, closer to the teaching of some later rabbis. The content of Jesus' teaching was indeed to be influential, but his significance lay not in what he said but in what his disciples declared him to be.

The share of responsibility for his execution can not be determined from the documents preserved, so it is unclear whether he was executed as a danger to the Roman state or as a critic of Jewish practice. Whichever it was, his disciples declared that they had witnessed his resurrection, and proclaimed that he was the Son of God. They picked up the words of the writer from the Babylonian exile and announced him as the saviour of the world, and not just of a chosen people. The holy books of the new religion were written down in the Greek language of the Hellenistic world, rather than in the more restricted Aramaic language which Jesus himself spoke.

Christianity and the Mysteries – Paul of Tarsus carried the message in a series of missionary journeys through the Greek speaking world. There he spoke the language of the popular mysteries – of redemption through blood and of a dying and rising god. With Christianity, however, it was different, he declared. While the mysteries were based in mere images, Christianity was rooted in historical fact.

Paul and other missionaries always sought to found a Christian cell, which they called an *ecclesia*, the word used for the meeting of the Greek polis. Hellenistic culture provided a language for the new religion; Rome provided a structure which enabled it to spread. Missionaries could make use of the Roman roads, and they were not likely to be molested by bandits on the way.

There was no doubting the enthusiasm of the converts, but, for a long time, an outsider would not have readily recognized a fundamental difference between this religion and the mysteries. Heresies, like Gnosticism and Manichaeism were pulling Christianity away from its Semitic roots into the maelstrom of Hellenistic religion. The Roman army generally favoured Mithras. A long path of persecution lay ahead before Christianity would emerge as the dominant religion of the region.

Imperial Rome

The Emperor – At the battle of Actium in 31 BC, Julius Caesar's great-nephew, Octavian, brought Egypt into the empire and ended the years of civil war. Four years later he was given the title of Augustus and made consul for life. He was careful to preserve the honoured republican institutions, but the senate lapsed into impotence and all power now lay with him.

No rule of inheritance was ever established for the position of emperor. In the centuries which were to follow, incompetents would be matched by administrators and generals of ability, imbeciles by philosophers. Most emperors died violently. Succession first passed through the house of Caesar. During one century of good government, it became the practice for an emperor to adopt his successor. For long periods, however, power fell to the general who could command the largest army. But the mass of people would never see the emperor in person. For them, success or failure had to be judged on whether he was strong enough to prevent the huge empire from breaking into civil strife.

The practice of emperor worship was imported from the old Persian tradition. The act of reverence due to the god-ruler was the symbol which bound together the hugely diverse people who now lay under Roman rule. Pious Jews refused to perform this ritual, but this was recognized to be a part of their ancient tradition and it was generally overlooked. The refusal of Christians, who came from all parts and races, was looked upon as a serious threat to the unity of the empire.

Buildings – The great monuments of Rome date from the Imperial age. Augustus himself restored 82 temples, and boasted, 'I found Rome of brick and left it of marble'. Aqueducts, arches and the huge Colosseum still stand as monuments to imperial glory. The Romans were content to copy Greek styles, to which they added impressive engineering skills.

The more prosperous built homes, such as have been preserved at Pompeii and excavated across the empire. Here they built for comfort, and artists, working in paint and mosaic, expressed a less pretentious view of life with humour and grace.

Natural frontiers – The Roman armies had now carried the empire across Europe, Asia and Africa, until it had ten thousand miles of land frontier. Beyond lay barbarians, ever willing to invade and plunder. The task of defence was made easier by natural boundaries – the African and Arabian deserts and the great rivers Rhine and Danube. This line of defence had two weak points, lying on either side of the Black Sea. In Asia the entrance to the steppes lay open across the land of the Parthians. In Europe generals were tempted to go beyond the Danube, across what is now Rumania to the Carpathian Mountains. Roman armies suffered heavy defeats in both of these sectors. Claudius also carried the empire across the natural frontier of the North Sea to Britain. The expedition was designed to bring the glory of conquest and to win control of fabled metal mines of the wild island.

The City of Rome – By imperial times, Rome had grown to be a huge city. Since most of the work was done by slaves, much of the population was unemployed, and the citizens had become accustomed to a life style supported by tribute from conquered peoples. No emperor could contemplate unrest in Rome, so the citizens had to be fed and kept amused on the famous diet of bread and circuses. Entertainments were on a massive scale. The Circus Maximus alone seated 190,000 people. Claudius built the huge harbour at Ostia, where grain, wild beasts and slaves were constantly being unloaded to feed the stomachs and the jaded palates of the people. The city gave nothing back to its empire.

East and West – Gradually a distinction began to emerge between the eastern and the western parts of the empire. The West, centred on Rome itself, covered western Europe and the old Carthaginian lands of North Africa. The east included the old Hellenistic world of Greece, Asia Minor, the Near East and Egypt.

The eastern side of the empire had a better balance to life. It contained ancient cities, but none dominated the region. It was self-sufficient in grain, wood, oil, wine and other essentials, with a surplus to buy in metal from the west and luxuries from the east.

The western part of the empire was not an area of ancient civilization. Since Carthage had been flattened, it had no cities to balance metropolis of Rome, which constantly sucked in products, so upsetting the economic balance of the region.

In 285 the Emperor Diocletian appointed a co-Emperor to rule the western sector. There was now an Empire of the East and an Empire of the West. In 324 Constantine accepted the dominance of the east by taking his capital to his new city of Constantinople.

The Triumph of Christianity – By this time, Christianity had established itself as a growing force. Diocletian tried to stem the tide, but Constantine accepted the new faith. Emperor worship may now have ceased, but even a Christian emperor could not shed the concept that he was the fountain of religion. He declared himself to be the thirteenth apostle and sat as chairman of the Council of Nicea, which established Christian doctrine. This set a precedent for the control of the church by the state.

At about the same time a group of hermits came together in Egypt to form the first monastery in the Christian tradition. This was destined to grow into an influential movement, capable of confronting the ambitions of Christian rulers.

The Barbarian Invasions – The century after Constantine saw increasing pressure on the European frontier of the Western Empire. Far away in the east, the Huns were on the move, and this created pressure on western tribes. The Huns themselves erupted into Europe under Attila in 440, to be defeated at Troyes in 451, but ahead of them, as if a prow wave, came Goths, Ostrogoths, Visigoths, Franks and Vandals.

The Romans found it difficult to defend the long land frontier and they recruited barbarians to strengthen the army. In 376 about 40,000 armed Visigoths were allowed across the frontier. Then in 410 the Goths sacked Rome. Vandals, who left their name for mindless destruction, crossed through Spain into North Africa and then returned for an even more destructive assault on the great city.

In northern Europe, Angles, Saxons and Jutes crossed the North Sea, first to ravage and then to settle in the British Isles. The Celtic inhabitants, no longer protected by Roman legions, were driven back to the highland area of the West, and into Ireland, where the Christian faith survived and flourished.

Byzantium

Her Frontiers – With the ancient capital in barbarian hands, the Roman Empire can be said to have fallen. Those who lived in the Empire of the East, however, recognized no such catastrophe. In

483 Justinian succeeded in Constantinople, and he set about the task of winning back the lost western lands. His armies recovered North Africa, Italy and Southern Spain. It appeared for a time as though the Roman Empire was still a reality. His conquests, however, were ephemeral. From his time onwards, the Empire of the East was under continual pressure.

In the East, Persia was a power of consequence once again, and behind her the steppe nomads were ever menacing. In the south the empire faced growing Arab power. In the north, Slav people were pressing into the Balkans. The Emperor Heraclius led the Imperial armies in more successful campaigns, but the pressure was ever inwards towards what was to be the Byzantine heartland of Asia Minor, Greece, the Balkans and southern Italy.

Cultural Life – The people saw themselves as being direct inheritors of the old empire. Citizens of Constantinople still visited the bath houses; they still followed the chariot races with the passion of a modern football supporter. Justinian completed the work of centuries of Roman jurists by compiling the authoritative digest of Roman law.

Byzantium, however, soon developed a distinctive character which set it apart from the old empire. This drew both from the Greco-Roman and from Eastern traditions. Constantinople remained a home of classical scholarship. Plato was particularly popular, but his thinking became overlaid by layers of mysticism. Classical features were used in buildings, but the great dome which rose over Justinian's Church of the Holy Wisdom demonstrated new skills and a new aesthetic. Secular artists still worked within Hellenistic traditions, but religious artists, in paintings and mosaics, were beginning to express a particularly eastern Christian piety.

Religion – The eastern church early developed a distinction between secular (living in the world) and religious (living out of the world) clergy. Secular clergy worked at the parish level and were allowed to marry. The ideal was set by the many hermits and monks who expressed their piety in extreme self sacrifice. Religious icons became the focus of devotion for ordinary people.

The emperor maintained Constantine's position at the head of the church. Patriarchs, bishops and priests lay under his power. Emperors decided doctrine and mercilessly persecuted many of their subjects who held 'heretical' beliefs. .

In the centuries after Justinian, the eastern and the western churches drew gradually further apart. In the west, the Bishop of Rome claimed primacy and began to build a centralized structure. The church finally divided into western and eastern parts in the Great Schism of 1054. This was partly about authority, partly about abstruse issues of theology, but it mainly stemmed lack of understanding of each other's piety.

The Arabs

Mecca – The desert land of the Arabian peninsula was inhabited by fierce and independent-minded Semitic tribes people known as Arabs. They led a nomadic life of great hardship. A trade route between the Mediterranean and the Indian Ocean crossed this land, passing through Mecca. The city was also a centre for pilgrimage to the sacred stone or *kaba*. The citizens of Mecca jealously guarded the revenues of both the trade and the pilgrimage.

Early in the 7th century a merchant, called Mohammed, had a vision and started preaching the message 'There is no god but Allah'. He came into conflict with the citizens of Mecca, and in 622 he left the city to live in Medina. This is the date from which the Arab world numbers its calendar.

Islam – The prophet Mohammed had met Christians and Jews and read many of their books and the religion which he founded lies within the Semitic tradition. He preached one god, which for him, ruled out the Christian concept of the Trinity. The word 'Islam' means 'submission', for the duty of the Moslem is to submit to the will of the one god. He gave his followers the five duties – daily prayers, alms, fasting, the keeping of Friday as holy day, and the pilgrimage – but the message was one of great simplicity. Very quickly, the feuding tribes of the peninsula were given that sense of community, which has ever since been the distinguishing feature of Islam.

Mohammed taught his followers that Christians and Jews were 'people of the book'. They and their religion had, therefore to be treated with respect. Once they accepted Moslem rule, they might be taxed, but they should not be persecuted or converted by force.

The Arab Conquests – Once the Arabs were united, they started raiding towards the north in search of booty, into the lands controlled by Byzantium and Persia. Their invasions had startling and unexpected success. This was partly because the two empires had weakened one another by endless warfare. More important, however, was that taxation and religious persecution had made their governments deeply unpopular with ordinary people. To 'heretical' Christians, the tolerant Moslem invaders seemed greatly preferable to either emperor.

The Persian Empire collapsed and Byzantium was pressed ever further backwards. Jerusalem fell in 638. It seemed as though Constantinople itself would fall, but in 717 the Arab armies were driven back from the city walls. By this time the Arabs not only controlled the Near East, but also North Africa and the whole of Spain. Their armies were even crossing the Pyrenees into the plains of Europe. Here, however, they found themselves in an alien environment of cold weather and barbarous people, so they turned back towards the south. The Arab armies carried Islam over this wide empire. Many conquered people converted; indeed Christianity disappeared from its old stronghold in North Africa.

The ultimate authority within the Islamic world lay with the caliphs. In 750 the ruling Umayyad house was overthrown and the new Abbasid rulers moved the capital to Baghdad.

Arab Culture – The Arabs possessed a powerful poetic tradition before the time of Mohammed and Islamic culture was founded in literature. The Koran, with its religious message, and its classical language provided a powerful unifying bond for one of history's more stable empires. Since the depiction of the human form was forbidden, art developed as elaborate geometric pattern. As the centre of empire moved out of the Arabian peninsula to Baghdad, so eastern influences became increasingly powerful. The Arabic language remained, however, the cement of the Islamic world. Although local dialects might vary, scholars from all parts continued to use the pure language of the Koran.

The Moslems did not come as the destroyers of civilization. The men from the desert quickly absorbed the cultures which they conquered. Their scholars read the Greek philosophers and united them with the astronomy, mathematics and medicine of the east, so serving as the main channel for the ancient learning in a troubled world. Moslem civilization reached one of its peaks in Spain, where the university of Cordova was a major centre of learning.

The eastern Mediterranean remained the centre of thriving trade. War might bring temporary disruption, but trading links with the East were never long severed. From India came spices, pepper and sugar; from China came porcelain and silks. The wealthy of Byzantium had an insatiable taste for luxury goods and the Arabs soon came to share these sophisticated tastes. Byzantium controlled the overland routes to China, which ended at the Black Sea ports. The Arabs controlled the sea routes by the Persian Gulf and the Red Sea to India, with links beyond to China and the Spice Isles.

Threats to Arab Civilization – In time, Byzantium ceased to be a threat to the Islamic Empire; indeed it seemed only a matter of time before Constantinople must fall. From the 11th century, for some 300 years, Arab civilization would be subjected to assaults by Christian crusaders from Europe and successive waves of nomadic invaders from the steppes of Asia. The latter were by far the more threatening of the two, and it was they who finally brought the great days of Near Eastern civilization to an end.

THE FORMATION OF EUROPE.

Church and State

The Papacy – In the year 590 a new Bishop of Rome was elected who would later be known as Gregory the Great. He was a Roman from a senatorial family, but, in the chaos of his day, he had made the choice to become a monk. For a devout Christian the monastic life seemed the only safe course to heaven in a violent and turbulent world. But Gregory saw that it was pointless to live with regrets for past glories of Rome or hopes for help from Byzantium. The church now had a mission to the restless and threatening barbarian world. Gregory selected monks as missionaries and sent them to bring Christianity to the barbarian tribes. Best known of these was Augustine of Canterbury. At the same time, missionaries from Ireland were moving south from Scotland into England and northern Europe. The missionaries from Rome, however, succeeded in linking the growing church back to Rome.

For Gregory's successors the first priority was to establish the primacy of the bishopric of Rome, or papacy. Popes claimed that, since they stood in a direct line from St Peter, they had inherited his 'power to bind and loose'. A pope could therefore control men's eternal destiny by the weapon of excommunication. In an extreme situation, he could even place an interdict, which forbade the performance of any sacraments, on a whole country. In an age of faith this was a formidable sanction.

The Popes had first to bring the Christian clergy under their control. Ordinary parish priests were generally illiterate peasants; bishops were temporal lords who used the church as a means of expanding family lands. Most were married men, who expected to pass their lands and livings on to their children. Their prime allegiance was therefore to the king or chief, rather than to a distant pope.

Monasticism – Only the monks were free from these temporal ties. The Rule of St Benedict, which imposed poverty, chastity and obedience, was now widely accepted. The monks were also almost alone in being literate in an uncultured world. This meant that they could reach positions of influence in church and state.

The popes used monks as their representatives, and, wherever possible, promoted them to high positions within the church. In time the popes worked to extend their control over the secular clergy by forbidding clerical marriage altogether.

A Time of Turbulence – In the early centuries after the fall of Rome, the pope and his monks were able to establish respect and authority because they provided the only apparent stability in a troubled society. Groups of barbarians roamed through Europe, bound to their leaders in simple tribal ties. When they settled down and adopted Christianity, much of the old way of life continued. Society still had no recognizable political structure, in the modern sense. Disputes were still settled by traditional 'rough justice', such as the ordeal and trial by battle.

Change continued slow in the dark forests of Germany. In time, however, the Franks and other groups in the western part of the European mainland adopted a form of Latin as their language, and paid some respect to the Roman legal system. The tribes who were more cut off in the British Isles, continued to speak their own German language, and developed law, based on past rulings, as preserved in the minds of the elders. So developed the divisions between the romance and Anglo-Saxon languages, and between Roman and common law which were to become important in later western civilization.

Political and social order was beginning to emerge by the end of the 8th century, but then Viking ships brought new danger to European coasts. It is never easy to say why a people go on the move, but it appears as though population growth and weather problems disturbed the balance of marginal Scandinavian farming. Certainly the feared Norsemen set off on 'land takings' and voyages of plunder. Their ships spread out across the North Atlantic to Iceland, Greenland and North America; they emerged into the Mediterranean; they sailed down the great rivers of central Asia, setting up the Russian state, and reaching Constantinople; they won control of northern Britain and Normandy. In 1066 a family of Norse descent won the crown of England.

The Norsemen were not the only raiders. Men from the steppes, this time the Magyars, were pillaging from the east and Moslem Saracen raiders came from the south. Hardly any part of Europe escaped. The unfortunate monks of Luxeil had their monastery burned by Norsemen, Hungarians and Saracens.

The Empire – For a brief period a new power arose in Europe. In 771 the ruthless and talented Charlemagne succeeded to the whole of the Frankish kingdom. For the next 40 years he led his armies to victories on all his borders, even mounting the first counter attack against Islam in Spain. Charlemagne was more than a conqueror. He was a devout Christian, and did much to spread the faith – by the sword if necessary – across Europe. He also respected learning, and he could read himself, although writing defeated him. He encouraged the clergy to respect books and learning, founded schools and brought the best minds of the day to his court.

On Christmas Day, 800, he was crowned by Pope Leo III in the church of St Peter in Rome. The people cried, 'to Charles Augustus, crowned by God, great and peaceful Emperor of the Romans, Life and Victory.' A new Roman Empire had been proclaimed.

The empire was based on one man's will, and, like Alexander's, it fell apart on Charlemagne's death. It was divided into three parts. The central kingdom did not survive, but the two other halves would ultimately become France and Germany. Charlemagne's eastern successor retained the title of Holy Roman Emperor, but his lands remained a loose confederacy. In 940 the Comte de Paris, Hughes Capet, won the French crown and established a monarchy which survived until the French Revolution. His family was the first European dynasty to establish the concept of a hereditary monarchy.

Powers Temporal and Spiritual – After Pope Leo III had placed the crown on Charlemagne's head, he stretched himself on the ground as a sign of honour to the Emperor. Laster popes would regret this gesture. The first objective of the Popes was to win control within the church. This involved taking the right to appoint bishops away from the temporal rulers.

In the 11th century, Pope Gregory VII and Emperor Henry IV came into conflict in the Investiture Controversy. Gregory was victorious, forcing Henry to stand barefoot in the winter snow as a sign of submission. Gregory then formulated the extreme claim that all power came from the pope, and he therefore had the right to appoint and depose kings and emperors. The Investiture Controversy was the first of a series of disputes between church and state. They involved not only the Holy Roman Emperor but also kings of France and England.

King, Lord and Parliament

The Feudal System – In those troubled times, people were prepared to sacrifice liberty in the interest of security. Kings and emperors were remote figures, so free men bound themselves to their local lord, who could give assistance when danger was near. When a man took an oath of loyalty he gave his lands to the lord, and then received them back as the lord's vassal. He had the obligation to follow the lord to war, but as a mounted knight, to set him apart from the common serfs. The lord, in his turn, bound himself to a higher lord, and the king stood at the apex of the pyramid. Only the serfs were nobody's vassal, because they had nothing to give in exchange for protection. These common people were not allowed to leave their villages, to go to school or to get married without their lord's permission.

By the end of the 9th century, this feudal system had spread to all but the most remote areas of Europe. Kings, like other lords, were concerned to extend their lands wherever they could by war and dynastic marriage. The two-way nature of the feudal compact served as a check on royal power. In France, the Capetian kings stood at the apex of the pyramid, but for long periods their actual power did not extend beyond their own lands around Paris. So, when the King of England married a French heiress, he did homage to the French king for his lands in Aquitaine, but he did not permit any interference within his territory.

The Hundred Years War between France and England was fought sporadically from 1337 to 1453. The English king may have laid claim to the crown of France, but it remained in essence a struggle between a dynastic monarch, determined to establish direct control over feudal lands on the one side, and an over-mighty subject on the other. It was one of the catalysts which defined the meaning of the modern nation state. Some 200 years later, Shakespeare put words of nationalistic fervour into the mouths of John of Gaunt and Henry V. Such wordss would have been incomprehensible in the time of Charlemagne or William the Conqueror, but they were beginning to have some meaning to their supposed speakers.

King and Parliament – William the Conqueror gave English kings more direct authority within their own realms. The feudal system was constructed to ensure that no lord could become 'over mighty'. Vassals, for their part were concerned that the king should not achieve unlimited power. In 1215 the lords forced King John to sign Magna Carta, which laid down two basic rights – that no free man could be imprisoned without a trial and the king could not raise taxes without the consent of a Great Council. In 1295, King Edward I called what became known as the Model Parliament, because it set the pattern for future parliaments. Representation was by estates – the Lords temporal, the Lords Spiritual and the Third Estate, with the first two sitting together in an upper house. It was also established that parliament had the responsibility to act as the highest court in the land, to give advice to the king, to make laws and to vote taxes.

The Rise of the Towns – The inclusion of the third estate in Edward's Model Parliament was testament to the growing importance of trade in the European economy. Wealth was no longer the preserve of landowners and the church, so, to achieve maximum income, it was now necessary to consult with the representatives of the growing towns.

As towns grew in importance, kings gave them charters, which assured them freedom from interference by local landowners. Their walls were the symbol of their independence, and magnificent churches the evidence of their wealth. Trade provided a means by which low born men could rise to positions of power within their own community, and even within the state. Different occupations were organized into guilds, which controlled terms of entry, quality standards and gave members a social structure.

The cities were often natural allies to kings who wanted to centralize power. Overmighty nobles might flourish in conditions of civil war, but merchants needed the peace, which only a strong government could provide. Kings, for their part, recognized that the growing wealth, which was the basis for national strength as well as royal revenue, was generated, not on noble estates, but inside the town walls.

The Cloth Trade – The Lord Chancellor of England, still sits in the House of Lords of a Woolsack. This was a reminder to parliament that the nation's wealth rested on the woollen trade. England, however, stood in the lowly position of a primary producer; the business in finished cloth centred round Flanders. Flemish weavers jealously guarded the trade secrets which made their cloth the most sought after in Europe. From the 13th century, the economy of northern Europe became increasingly sensitive to fluctuations in the fortunes of the cloth trade.

The Crusades

The First Crusade – In 1095 the Byzantine emperor appealed to the pope for assistance against the Turks. The pope answered the call by preaching a Holy War. The motives of those, both noble and common folk, who took the cross, were very mixed. Many of the Norman lords who took the lead saw the opportunity of a new land taking, like those of their Viking ancestors. But there was also a real devotion. The two were not incompatible. When the army arrived first in Byzantium and then in the Arab lands, they appeared like barbarians, with nothing to recommend them but their brute courage. Jerusalem fell to the crusaders, who waded through blood to give thanks for the victory.

Outremer – The crusaders established states in the conquered land. The Moslems resented these Christian enclaves in their territory and they were under constant pressure. In 1187 Saladin reconquered Jerusalem and the crusaders were unable to win it back. In 1291 the last Christian outpost fell to the army of Islam. The crusades gave the West two centuries of contact with a higher culture. Knights returned home with a taste for oriental luxury goods; some picked up an interest in learning and mathematics; methods of castle construction and siege warfare were modernized on Arab models.

The Later Crusades – Eight campaigns between the 11th and the 13th centuries are known as crusades, and include the tragic 'children's crusade' of 1212. The movement turned inwards against European heretics. The simple crusaders were not always able to distinguish which enemy they should fight. The Venetians encouraged the fourth crusade to turn on Byzantium. In 1204 Constantinople was captured by the crusaders and the city remained in Christian hands until 1261. Although the rump of empire would survive into the 15th century, Byzantium never recovered from the disaster.

Spain – At the same time, Christian forces were counter-attacking against the Moslem Moors in Spain. In 1212 the Moors were defeated and driven back to Grenada. The reconquest of the peninsula was completed in 1492. A great culture was replaced by a fanatical Christian state, in which the Inquisition was used as a tool of persecution against Moors, Jews and many Christians whose views did not please the authorities.

Learning, Art and Society

Scholarship and Authority – As long as there was no nation state, there were no sharply defined national boundaries. Latin provided a lingua franca and the church a broadly based structure within which the educated of their day could communicate.

Through the troubled times any learning remained behind monastic walls. The books of early Christian fathers were copied and became the intellectual authorities of the new world. Men had lost confidence in their own ability to reach conclusions, either through logic or through experiment, and all argument therefore referred back to authority. Even quite trivial issues of dispute would be decided by the weight of authority which could be mustered on the one side or the other.

The authors of antiquity were largely unknown until around the 12th century. Then translations began to be made into Latin from copies preserved in Islamic Spain and Sicily. The ancient dichotomy between Plato and Aristotle began to be reflected in arguments between nominalist and realist theologians. Thomas Aquinas, in particular, baptised Aristotle. This did not, however, lead to an increase in experiment; classical authors joined the Christian fathers as valid sources of authority. In southern Europe, men still lived amidst the ruins of classical civilization. The classical and the Christian came together until, as in Dante's Inferno and Michelangelo's Sistine Chapel, they became indistinguishable from each other.

By the 12th century, learning was coming out from monastic walls into the more open atmosphere of universities. The first to be opened was at Salerno, where Islamic and Byzantine influence was strong. Then came Bologna, Paris, Oxford and many others. Crowds would follow teachers, like Peter Abelard, who spoke a new and more restless language. Students at university were in religious orders of some sort, but the educational impetus continued outwards into the wider population. By later medieval times, an increasing number of lay people, particularly in the towns, were acquiring literacy.

Architecture and Painting – In early medieval times most stone buildings were either castles or monasteries. Many were fine buildings, but they added little to the techniques of antiquity. By the 12th century architects were developing their own signature. The Romanesque style of Southern Italy was based closely on a study of classical models. In northern France and England there rose magnificent cathedrals in the Gothic style. Here the pointed arch and the flying buttress enabled them to give their structures both height and light.

Most painting, likewise, remained dedicated to the church. Altar pieces showed the Virgin and child, with patrons and saints; frescoes and stained glass windows reminded illiterate worshippers of Bible stories; monks, copying psalters and books of hours, under no pressure of deadlines, painted exquisite decoration. In Italy, the school of Sienna worked under direct influence from Byzantium. But painters, like architects and stone masons, were craftsmen who were happy to work for any patron, and, as the centuries passed, an increasing number of commissions were available for secular work.

Literature – Medieval literature, like that of any other period, was made up of different strands – folk tales and myths, national histories, historical chronicles, love poems and works of devotion. Early vernacular literature, like Norse sagas and the Anglo-Saxon Beowolf, helped to create national language areas. In the early centuries, however, Latin was the language of both secular and religious writing.

By the 14th century a new vernacular literature was emerging. The supreme example of in English is *The Canterbury Tales*, written by soldier and customs officer, Geoffrey Chaucer, for an audience of other lay people.

Times of Change

The Black Death – A sickness new to the human race was first reported in the Yangtze Valley in 1334 and, according to one estimate, some 13 million Chinese died in the following years. Relentlessly it spread from east to west, leaving devastation in India and across Asia. In 1347 the plague spread across Northern Italy, and in the following years it is estimated that between a quarter and a third of the population of Europe perished. This first outbreak was the worst, but the disease returned periodically until the second half of the 17th century. Although it was a world wide phenomenon, its effects have been most closely studied in Europe.

Initially it brought economic collapse; prices of all goods fell sharply and much farm land returned to nature. As life recovered, employers were faced with an acute labour shortage. This created strains within the social structure of both town and country. Guild regulations were flouted and the feudal structure began to crumble. There were major peasant uprisings, in France in 1358, in Florence in 1378 and in England in 1381.

The Late Medieval Church – Pious Christians could not understand why God had created such destruction. The plague accentuated a Christian piety which identified God as judge and destroyer and the saints, particularly the Virgin Mary, as protector.

The church, like all institutions, moves through cycles of corruption and reformation. In early medieval times, reformation came from within. The last of these reforming movements was the founding of the friars by Francis of Assisi in 1209. Now the impetus for reform had grown weak. In the 14th century popes taxed the faithful heavily to maintain a lavish lifestyle. After the Black Death these taxes fell all the more heavily on a smaller population. One fund raising technique was the offer of indulgences, by which punishment in the next world was remitted in exchange for payment in this world. During the 14th century the church lost its independence when it moved under the protection of the King of France in Avignon. The Great Schism, when rival popes competed from Rome and Avignon, further undermined spiritual authority. Some Franciscans denounced papal luxury and were burned as heretics but their message was heard by the people.

Before the end of the 14th century John Wyclif in England and Jan Hus in Bohemia were preaching that man did not need the apparatus of the church to make contact with God. Hus founded what was to be the first protestant church, and Wyclif translated the Bible into English.

The Reformation – In the early 16th century the pope set out to raise money for the building of St Peter's by selling indulgences. In 1517, the university lecturer Martin Luther challenged the papal representative to a debate by nailing 95 theses to the door of Wittenberg cathedral. The church authorities sought to have him condemned, like heretics of old, but he found protection from German princes. The protestant movement soon won followers, particularly in the trading towns and in Northern Europe.

Luther did not initially see himself as the leader of a movement which would split the western church, but, as he preached the supremacy of the Bible and faith over the sacraments and traditional authority, the division quickly became irreconcilable. He found himself leading a mass movement, based on individual piety. Luther was the catalyst for another round in the ancient struggle between lay and secular powers. He survived to preach only because he was adopted by German princes, who saw his movement as a useful weapon against the power of the church.

Eastern Europe

Russia – It appears as though the Norsemen who settled the rivers of Russia brought no women with them, so the process of assimilation was rapid. In 980 Vladimir established the kingdom of Kiev and he married a sister of the Byzantine emperor. It is said that Russian envoys visited Constantinople and the West to decide which form of Christianity should be adopted. They were overwhelmed by the splendour of Constantinople, and the eastern link was forged. Kiev was destroyed in 1169 and the centre of power was driven northwards to Moscow. Trading and cultural ties with Byzantium were largely lost, and Russia was increasingly isolated until it was overrun by the Mongols in the 13th century. Russian independence can then be dated to the victory over the Tartars in 1380. The Grand Princes of Moscow emerged as rulers and Ivan III (1462-1505) adopted the title of Tsar (Caesar) and the double headed eagle, to substantiate the claim that, with Constantinople in Ottoman hands, the Russian monarchy had now inherited the imperial tradition.

Poland – When Vladimir made his choice of the eastern church, the Poles on his western frontier had just turned in the other direction. The missionaries who brought western Christianity to Poland also acted as forerunners for waves of land-hungry German invaders, led by the fearsome Teutonic Knights. In late medieval times, a Polish state lay across the central European plain, with its prosperity based on grain exports to the west through the port of Danzig. It was, however, already showing signs of the damage that would be caused by its geographical location as a buffer between Western Europe, the Scandinavian north, Russia and the East and the disturbed cauldron of Slavs and Magyars in the Balkan south.

In both Russia and Poland the serfs lived in great poverty, under the control of a wealthy landed class. Rulers were faced with a perpetual challenge from overmighty subjects without being able to look for the support of any considerable middle class.

THE WIDER WORLD

Asia Before the Mongols

India – For centuries after Ashoka, the Indian sub-continent was divided into warring states. The south, behind its mountain barrier, remained the home of non-Aryan people. They maintained contact with the Mediterranean civilizations through the Red Sea and Persian Gulf trading routes. In the north-west, the frontier and Indus valley remained open to Asian invaders. Invading Hunas, probably Huns, devastated this region, as they did lands both to east and west.

In about 320 AD the Guptas united the whole of northern India. This marked the great age of Hindu culture. In the 5th century, the decimal system was invented, so opening new areas of mathematics. Sculpture and literature flourished, both achieving a broad unity of style, characterized by a warm sensuality. Buddhist culture declined as Hinduism spread across Asia and into the islands of the Pacific. The island of Bali remains today a marker of this great expansion.

The Hindu Empire was in time challenged by the rise of Islam. Moslem traders – always effective missionaries for the Prophet – would have visited the western ports in the 7th century. By the 8th century invaders were crossing the open north western frontier. By the 12th century, they controlled the Punjab and a century later they dominated the Ganges valley. The fateful religious divide was now established.

China – China was united more effectively by language and culture than it was by its political structure. The two most powerful dynasties were Han (c. 205 BC – 220 AD) and T'ang (618 – 907). Their empires were comparable to that of Rome at its most powerful. During the T'ang Dynasty trade flourished, and China became a major sea power, with trade reaching from the Persian Gulf in the west to Indonesia in the east. The great Chinese dynasties had an expectation of life of about 300 years. They were founded by a great individual who combined military and administrative skills. In later years, as the succession passed to lesser men, the state would come under pressure from nomads to the north and rebellion at home. Imperial authority was upheld by officials, who preserved the traditions of K'ung-fu-tsu. Their main tasks were to take the census and keep the land register up to date. Beyond that, they maintained only a broad supervision over local lords, who raised taxes and performed the day to day tasks of administration themselves.

Great civil works were undertaken. The country was now bound together by canals, most important of which was the Great Canal, which linked Peking with Hang-chou. Huge irrigation projects were undertaken to provide food for the ever growing population. The casting of iron, printing, the magnetic compass, the use of paper money and explosives were all pioneered in China, but the conservative structure of society militated against the fullest exploitation of her inventions.

In the periods between the great dynasties, the country relapsed into warring states. There were times of disaster, when armies ravaged large areas, but in general, conditions changed little for the mass of peasants, whose life was always more closely governed by local lords than by distant emperors. But, while Europe remained divided into her warring states, China could always be drawn together once again by a dynamic new dynasty.

The Sung Dynasty (960 – 1279) was never as powerful as its great predecessors and in 1127 it lost the northern part of the country to Chin invaders. In the following century and a half the Southern Sung Dynasty lacked military power, but the period is viewed by many as the high point of Chinese culture. The Imperial capital of Hang-chou was a centre of wealth, culture and leisured living, far beyond any other city in the world.

Sung art was influenced by the Zen school of Buddhism. Painters, such as Ma Yuan, worked with an economy of line and colour to make a visual statement about man's position within the world order. Potters made dishes which looked 'like ivory, but were as delicate as thin layers of ice'.

The Seljuk Turks – The name 'Turk' is given to widely dispersed people, originating on the Asian steppes, who spoke a common language. In the 10th century a chief called Seljuk settled with his people near Samarkand and was converted to Islam. The tribe organized an army based on slaves, mainly recruited from southern Russia and the Caucusus, who were known as mameluks. Backed by these fearless warriors, Seljuk's grandsons built an empire, from Azerbaijan and Armenia, into the ancient lands of Middle East. They overran Persia, captured Baghdad, Jerusalem and Egypt and invaded Byzantine lands in Asia Minor.

Later Seljuks rulers found it difficult to hold this vast empire together. While their efforts were largely directed against European crusades, they faced trouble in other parts of the empire. In Egypt, for instance, mameluke soldiers established a virtually independant government. The Seljuk Empire therefore became vulnerable to another and greater threat from the Asian steppes.

The Mongols

Genghis Khan and his Successors – In 1206 a chief called Temujin, better known to the world as Genghis Khan, united the Mongol tribes who lived in the area today called Mongolia. These were wild, nomadic peoples in the tradition of the horsemen who had come from the steppes throughout recorded history. He then established dominance over the more numerous Turkish peoples from the land to the north of the Himalayas. Genghis Khan came to believe that he was destined to rule the world, and he embarked on the greatest programme of conquest in history. His followers were magnificent horsemen. As a nomad people, they could survive on dried milk and the blood of their horses. Released from the constraints of supply, they were therefore uniquely mobile. They were also utterly ruthless. Cities which accepted them were often treated with leniency; those that resisted were liable to be levelled to the ground, and the population massacred. As the reputation of the Mongol horde was carried ahead, rulers capitulated to avoid the dreadful destruction.

By the time that Genghis died in 1227, the Chin Empire of northern China had fallen, and Mongol armies had swept across the open grasslands of Asia as far as Russia and the Caucasus. Still the advance continued. In 1237-8 the Russian state was overwhelmed by horsemen who rode down the frozen rivers, achieving the winter conquest that later eluded both Napoleon and Hitler. When a Great Khan died, the armies returned to their homeland to debate the issue of succession. Europe might have been overrun had Genghis Khan's successor not died in 1241. The armies did not again threaten Europe; to the Mongols, it seemed a poor land, hardly worth conquering. They did, however, return to the Middle East, capturing Baghdad and destroying the caliphate in 1258. The tide of conquest finally turned here too when, in 1260, the mamelukes of Egypt organized the armies of Islam to defeat a Mongol army at Ain Jalut, near the town of Nazareth.

Mongol China – The Mongol Empire was now divided into four, with the eastern section the portion of Genghis' grandson, Kublai. He led a Mongol assault on the Southern Sung Empire, which fell in 1279. Further expeditions were launched into South East Asia and even, unsuccessfully, against Japan. While his grandfather Genghis had devastated the north, Kublai respected the civilization which he conquered. Although he spoke little Chinese, he was a patron of literature and, like conquerors before him, he adopted Chinese ways. Mongol rule had now united the whole territory between Europe and China under a single authority and the ancient overland routes were opened once again. In 1275 members of the Polo family from far away Venice reached the court of Kublai Khan. When the young Marco Polo finally returned to Venice in 1299 he gave the west its first information about the civilization of the east. Readers in the more primitive Europe found it hard to believe that such a land of riches could exist far to the east, but some two centuries later a Genoan sailor called Christopher Columbus would own and make notes on a copy of the Venetian's narrative.

For the Chinese, however, the Mongols remained a dynasty of foreigners. Prosperity declined sharply and there was a wave of unrest, and the Mongols were overthrown in 1367 by a new Ming Dynasty. This survived its allotted three centuries until in 1644 it was in turn overthrown by new invaders from Manchuria, who established the Manchu Dynasty.

Later Mongol Conquests – In about 1370 Timur the Lame, a chief from the region of Samarkand, proclaimed that he was the man to revive the Mongol Empire. In the next 30 years, he ravaged the Middle East, Asia Minor, Southern Russia and Northern India with a brutality only matched by his distant kinsman Genghis Khan. The ancient lands of the Fertile Crescent, so long the focus of world civilization, never recovered from his invasion. The Mongol Khanate of the Golden Hoarde in Russia was fatally weakened. He died in 1405, when on his way to carry his conquests into China.

In time the Mongol people of Central Asia and the Middle East came to accept the religion of Islam. The weakness in Mongol power lay in the fact that there was no established law of succession. Timur's successors, like other Mongols, were concerned with domestic issues as they contested succession. Fifth in line from Timur was the more attractive Babur. The kingdoms of northern India were at that time in a state of permanent warfare. In 1526 Babur won a series of victories, and by his death in 1530 he had established Mongol – or Mogul – rule in northern India.

Mogul India

Akbar – In 1556 Babur's 14-year-old grandson, called Akbar, inherited a weak and divided empire as a boy of 14. He also inherited the ancestral belief that no empire can survive unless it is continually expanding, and throughout his reign he kept his armies constantly on the offensive. He continued old Mongol tactics. When a city, like Chittor, resisted it could be utterly destroyed and its people massacred; when people accepted his authority, they found him a generous ruler. By 1600 his Mogul Empire controlled the whole of the subcontinent, except for Ceylon and Vijayanagar in the south. Akbar built a huge capital at Fathpur-Siki, which was to be the model for Mogul public buildings of incomparable grandeur, culminating in Shah Jahan's Taj Mahal.

The country was divided into provinces, but all authority sprang directly from the Emperor himself. Although a ruthless conqueror, Akbar was anxious to bind his people together effectively, and he was concerned at the religious division which existed between his Hindu and Moslem subjects. He was suspicious of all dogmatism, and devout Moslems accused him of backsliding when he abolished the poll tax payable by Hindus, and worked to find a compromise between the two religions.

The Decline of the Mogul Empire – Akbar was an outstanding ruler, but his empire suffered from weaknesses inherited from his Mongol tradition. In Europe, structures of government were coming into existence which transcended the personality of the ruler. In Mogul India, however, authority continued to be over-dependant on the ability of one man. In his last years, even Akbar was plagued by rebellious sons. The instability of the empire is illustrated by events at the end of the reign of Shah Jehan. In 1657 he fell ill, triggering a ferocious civil war between his sons. The victorious Aurangzeb was a devout and intolerant Moslem and under his rule the united empire created by Akbar began to fall apart.

The Ottomans

The Foundation of Empire – Mongol successes in central Asia created more movement of nomad tribes out of the grasslands. In the late 13th century. one Ertughrul led a band of followers, who were equally devoted to Islam and to plunder, into the Seljuk lands of the Middle East. Ertughrul's son, Othman overthrew the Seljuk sultans, and founded the great empire which was to bear his name.

Othman's successors defeated the Byzantine army. They captured Asia Minor, and, in 1361, crossed into Europe to establish Ottoman power in the Balkans. Constantinople was now an isolated fortress in Ottoman lands, and in 1453 it fell to the Sultan Mehmet II.

The Spread of Empire – Ottoman power reached its peak in the century after the fall of Constantinople. In the early 16th century Selim I marched southwards, defeating the Mamelukes of Egypt and capturing Mecca, where he was proclaimed Caliph of the Islamic world. His successor Suleiman I, the Magnificent, turned north. In 1526 he defeated the Hungarian army at the great battle of Mohacs. Three years later his armies laid siege to Vienna.

Africa

Trans-Saharan Trade – Historians of early sub-Saharan Africa are restricted by the lack of written records and the destructive capacity of termites, working on wood and mud brick. The continent, however, was far from isolated. A thriving trade existed across the Sahara trade routes between North Africa and the grassland region which lies across the continent from near the Atlantic to the Nile.

The staple product being carried southward was salt – an essential commodity for people living in a hot climate. The Moslem traders who crossed the desert carried various luxury goods, and also brought their religion and literacy in Arabic script. On the return journey they carried gold, slaves and leather goods. Before the time of Columbus, Europe was heavily dependant on African gold and 'Morocco leather' has always originated south of the Sahara. A key focal point of this trade was Timbuktu, on the Niger, which became famous as the meeting point of the camel and the canoe. The town was already well enough known to be marked on a Spanish map in the late 14th century.

The gold, and probably most of the slaves, came from the forest region still farther south, so trade reached out in both directions. Among the most active traders were the Hausa people, who were based on city states, such as Kano and Zaria. They would be late recruits to Islam and never organized into larger political units.

African Empires – Broadly based political structures did, however, come into existence in the Southern Sudan to control the two-way trade. The Empire of Ghana (8th – 11th centuries), was succeeded by Mali (12th – 14th centuries) and Songhai (14th –

16th centuries). Kings like Musa Mensa, who ruled Mali in the early 14th century, were well known for their wealth and learning across the Islamic world, and even beyond. The trade in gold appears also to have stimulated the growth of forest kingdoms, such as Benin and Oyo. These would grow in importance with the arrival of European ships on the coast in the 15th century. Far to the east, the kingdom of Ethiopia maintained its isolated Christian tradition, again with power based on trade with the north by way of the Nile.

There was also traffic in gold and slaves down the coast of East Africa. The unique stone ruins of Zimbabwe provide evidence to support the reports of inland states in this region.

America

America was the last continent to be settled by man and it remained the most isolated. Traditional hunter/gatherer lifestyles were successfully followed by people of widely differing culture across wide areas of North America and within the many forest regions of North America until they suffered under the impact of European invaders. The cultivation of maize and then of other crops, however, made possible the development of more complex civilizations.

Central America – The earliest civilization was that of the Olmecs, which flourished on the coast of the Gulf of Mexico in the 7th century BC Many of the characteristics of later civilizations of the region can already be recognized in these people. In their capital of Teotihuacan they built huge pyramids, apparently dedicated to the same gods which would be worshipped by people of the region in later generations.

The most accomplished civilization of the region was the Maya, centred on the Yukatan peninsula, which reached its peak in the 9th century BC The Mayans used a pictogram form of writing. Like the Babylonians, they laid emphasis on the calendar and the heavenly bodies and they developed great skill in mathematics and astronomy, working out the duration of the year and learning how to predict eclipses. They were the first people in the world's history to achieve a sense of the vast span of time. Mayan sites, like those of ancient Egypt, are not cities, but vast complexes of temples and other ceremonial buildings.

The Maya were succeeded by the Toltecs, and they were overthrown in their turn by the Aztecs, who dominated the region from the 13th century. They appear to have been the first to introduce mass human sacrifice. This practice came to dominate the whole of Aztec strategy for the region. As victims were best found in warfare, they had no motivation to create conditions of peace, but rather encouraged a general unrest among subject people.

The Aztecs had a tradition that the white skinned and bearded god Quetzalcoatl would one day return from the east. When the invading Spaniards appeared to fulfil this prophesy, there were many subject people who were prepared to take their side against their feared Aztec masters.

The Andes – The long spine of the Andes is perhaps the most improbable setting for any of the world's civilizations. Between 600 and 1000 AD a people called the Huari brought some political unity to this area. In the 12th century, the Inca, based on Cuzco in modern Peru, were only one of many smaller groupings. They then conquered an empire which by the 15th century stretched 2000 miles from Quito in modern Equador to the deserts of Chile.

The Incas were a non-literate people. Instructions were carried to distant parts of the empire by messengers. Again, lacking the wheel, these messengers travelled on foot over a road network, built with great engineering skill. Inca power was centred on heavily fortified cities, where invading Spaniards were to find a wealth of beautiful objects made of gold and stone.

The Incas were not as oppressive to their subject people as the Aztecs, but there were still many who were prepared to support the small force of Spaniards who arrived in 1531 to conquer and loot the empire.

THE TRIUMPH OF EUROPE

The Background to Conquest
New Perspectives – The Mappa Mundi, in Hereford Cathedral, illustrates the medieval perspective of the world. Jerusalem lies in the centre of the world, with the three known continents – Asia, Africa and Europe – arranged around the Mediterranean Sea. Phoenician and Viking ships may have sailed the wider oceans, but these lay at the edge of the known universe.

By the 15th century, changes were taking place. The reports of Marco Polo's travels in the East were becoming widely known. No profit orientated merchant could ignore his descriptions of markets loaded with silks, velvets and damasks. He had travelled beyond China to the islands of the Pacific and described how cheaply spices could be obtained. It was still impossible to keep meat animals alive through the European winter, so all except the breeding stock was slaughtered and salted down at Michaelmas. By spring it was barely edible without pepper, cinnamon and nutmeg to disguise the taste.

In 1400 also a copy of the Hellenistic Ptolemy's *Geography* was brought from Constantinople and published in the west. It contained many errors, but did show that the world was round and not a flat dish. During the century, this became the accepted view of scholars.

The Ottoman conquests helped stimulate interest in alternative routes to East Asia. Thorough medieval times the majority of luxury goods had been brought by the Asian overland routes. These were now threatened by a hostile power. The Genoese, traditional allies of Byzantium, were particularly threatened by the new developments. Ottomans and Venetians alike combined to shut them out from the profitable business.

Logic demanded that traders should turn their attention to the oceans that lay beyond the enclosed Mediterranean world. Luxury goods were high value and low bulk cargo. Projected returns on investment on one cargo reaching Europe were astronomical.

Technical advance – During the 15th century major technical advances were also made in Europe, which brought such a project within the bounds of the possible. Before that time European ships had been square rigged on a single main mast. Such a ship could be manned by a small crew, but could not sail efficiently into the wind. Arab ships used a lateen sail. This could sail into the wind, but such a large crew was needed that it could never go far from land where food could be obtained. Ship builders now constructed multi-masted vessels, with both square and lateen sails, which could both be handled by a small crew and sail into the wind.

If ships were to sail far out from land, then navigational techniques needed to improve. By 1500 European sailors were skilled in the use of the magnetic compass, either re-invented or brought from China, and in measuring latitude. Almost 200 years more years would pass before similar advances were made in calculating longitude. Great advances were also made in cartographical techniques, with the Dutch leading the way.

European craftsmen also developed gunnery to new levels. King John II of Portugal took particular interest in the problems of mounting modern guns on board ship. Success in these experiments meant that European ships could command the seas. In previous centuries ships came together with grappling hooks to allow soldiers to fight a conventional battle. Now the European ship could sink an enemy ship without allowing it to come close enough to bring the soldiers into action.

Population and Prices – The intellectual climate was favourable, commercial incentives were strong, and the required technology was available. As with Norsemen and Mongols, however, a further 'push factor' was needed to trigger off a major movement of European people. Demographers have shown that Western Europe had recovered from the Black Death and a cyclical population increase was in progress. Pauperism was on the increase, and also, in populations organised on the basis of primogeniture, landless younger sons of gentry families were looking for any way of making a fortune.

Historians now link the population rise with an inflationary trend which persisted through the 16th century. On average, prices quadrupled between 1500 and 1600. Since wages and savings did not always keep up with the rising prices, this created conditions of hardship which could make emigration attractive.

Religion – Christians of the period generally held that unbelievers possessed no rights. The Pope declared that Christian kings had a right to conquer heathen lands. Some Catholic friars and, later, Jesuits did identify with the cause of the native people, but even their mission stations were instruments of colonial control. The Protestant record was, if anything, worse. 300 years would pass before protestant Christians made any serious attempt to protect the rights of and to share their faith with non European people.

Asia

The Portuguese – By 1400 Portugal was free from Moslem rule and had established itself as a separate country from Spain. Its geographical position made it a natural Atlantic pioneer. In the first half of the 15th century, the king's brother, Henry 'The Navigator' established a school for sailors at Sagres, by Cape St Vincent, and sent out expeditions to explore ever further south into the Atlantic. Slowly they pushed the boundaries of exploration beyond the Azores and to Senegal.

In 1487, 27 years after Henry's death, Bartholomew Diaz rounded the Cape of Good Hope and established that the way to India lay clear. In 1498 Vasco da Gama took his ship to Calicut in south India. Indian merchants were happy to sell to the newcomers as they offered higher prices than the Arabs. He returned with a cargo of pepper, cinnamon, ginger, cloves and tin. It was reported that the King of Portugal and Vasco da Gama's other backers made a 6000% return on their investment. A century of human and financial investment had finally paid it dividend. In 1503 the Portuguese established a permanent base in India, at Cochin, followed in 1510 by Goa, and later by Seurat.

In 1509 the Arabs sent a fleet, manned by 15,000 men, to drive the Portuguese from their seas, but the European superiority in ships and gunnery proved decisive in a battle off Diu. From that time European fleets exercised control over the world's oceans. Arab and oriental sailors could no longer confront them in battle, but only operate as pirates.

In 1517 the first Portuguese ship arrived off the coast of China and according to European custom fired their guns in salute. The Chinese found these barbaric Europeans 'crafty and cruel', but had to respect their guns which 'shook the earth'. In 1521 Portuguese ships had reached the Spice Islands. In 1557 they established their trading base at Macao, off the Chinese mainland.

The Dutch – The Portuguese successfully protected their Africa route against encroachment by other European nations until the last years of the 16th century. Then in 1594 a group of Dutch businessmen fitted out four ships to sail to the Far East. They carried the products of Europe – woollen and linen fabrics, glassware, ornaments and different kinds of ironware, including armour. The ships reached East Asia and found that the people welcomed their quality goods. In 1602, the Dutch parliament, the Estates, set up the Dutch East India Company to follow up this initiative. The Malacca Strait, in modern Indonesia, became the focus of the empire, with headquarters on the island of Java. The Dutch then set about driving the Portuguese out of their Asian empire. Only a few Portuguese outposts, such a Goa and Macao survived the assault.

Once in control, the Dutch traders ruthlessly set about eliminating all competition. In 1623 ten English merchants were tortured and killed at Amboyna. But they were not content to exclude other European competition from their market. Chinese junks were shut out of their traditional markets as even local trade was channelled into Dutch ships. By now Europe was becoming glutted with spices, so the Dutch governor, Jan Coen set about controlling production to keep prices high. On one occasion he destroyed all the nutmeg trees on the Banda Islands and either killed or sold into slavery the entire population of 15,000 people. He burnt villages along the coast of China in an attempt to control the whole region, but complained that China, like India, was 'too extensive for discipline'.

The English – The English East India Company was founded two years earlier than the Dutch, but it lost the race to control the Spice Islands. After Amboyna, the Dutch and the English were bitter commercial rivals. The English had to accept that the prize of the Pacific trade was closed to them and had to make do as a second best with establishing themselves in India. The trade in coffee, tea and cotton goods was of lower value than that from further east, but the English trading stations at Madras, Bombay and Calcutta grew in importance tea gained status as a fashionable drink. When Dutch power waned in the later years of the 17th century, English ships were able to use their Indian bases for trading with China and the Pacific Islands.

The French – The French East India Company had now replaced the Dutch as the main competition. French merchants, however, operated under difficulties. They came from a nation whose power was centred on its land army. While naval and commercial interests were influential in London, they carried little weight in Paris. In time of war, French ships were exposed to the powerful English navy, and French overseas outposts were at all times starved of resources.

It long seemed impossible that any European nation would establish political control in the sub-continent. Then the death of Aurangzeb in 1707 marked the end of the Mogul Empire as an effective force, and the sub-continent split into warring states. From that time, the trading companies became increasingly involved in politics.

America

The Spanish – On January 2nd 1492 the troops of the 'Catholic Monarchs' Isabella of Castile and her husband, Ferdinand of Aragon finally drove the Moors out of Grenada. In the cheering crowd was a Genoese sailor, Christopher Columbus. Like another Genoese, John Cabot, he had decided that the Indes could best be reached by sailing westwards. Both turned to western European monarchs, with a natural interest in Atlantic trade. Columbus won the support of Isabella and in August his three ships sailed from Palos, to reach San Salvador on 12 October.

Columbus was bitterly disappointed that he did not find the eastern markets described by Marco Polo. In later voyages he explored the Caribbean Islands and reached the mainland. He died in 1506, still convinced that he had reached the Indes. Before then, however, another Italian, Amerigo Vespucci, this time in Portuguese pay, had established that this was indeed the continent which subsequently carried his name. In the year that Columbus sailed, the Spanish Pope, Alexander VI issued a Bull, awarding to Spain and Portugal all lands already discovered or to be discovered 'in the West, towards the Indes or the ocean seas, with the dividing line between the two on the line of longitude 45⁰ West. This ruling gave Brazil to Portugal and the rest of the continent to Spain. The Spanish, however, never established effective control to the north of a line from modern Georgia in the east to California in the west.

In 1519 Magellan led an expedition to explore this new world. When the remains of his expedition returned in 1522, having circumnavigated the globe, the basic facts of world geography were finally established.

Meanwhile the Spaniards were establishing their power in the New World. In 1513 Balboa crossed the Isthmus of Panama and reached the Pacific Ocean. In the east, Portuguese guns could win naval battles, but they could never bring down great empires. In the west, however, the Spaniards found that civilizations crumbled before them. There was too large a gap between the technology of the 'New World' on one side and the firearms, horses and armour of the 'Old World' on the other. Perhaps most important, the American 'Indian' people were psychologically ill equipped to confront the brutal European soldiers. Many were killed by the newcomers; many lost the will to live when forced to work in unfamiliar ways; even more died of the plague and other diseased for which they lacked immunity. According to one estimate, 25 million people lived in what was to become New Spain when Columbus landed, but only 1¹/2 million survived a century later.

The Spaniards may not have found silks and spices, but they found gold. What to the native Americans was a decorative metal was, to the Spaniards, the basic unit of exchange and measurement of wealth. For gold Cortes and Pizarro destroyed the Aztec and Inca civilizations. Unsuccessful searches for gold established Spanish rule in what is now the south of the United States, from Florida to the Great Plains, and the Californian coast. All kinds of gold objects were melted down and shipped back to Spain, where the new riches funded the emergence of Spain as a major power.

The gold was soon plundered and no significant mines were discovered. A sustainable flow of wealth was, however, established by the opening of silver mines in Peru. Spain now controlled both sides of the Isthmus of Panama and a merchant fleet was built on the westward, Pacific side. A trading base was established at Manila in the Philippines, and galleons carried trading goods across the wide Pacific. These luxury goods from the Orient, along with silver from Peru, were then carried across the Isthmus of Panama and loaded onto the Atlantic treasure fleet for Spain.

In the early years of colonization few women left Spain for the New World, and settlers took Indian wives. The culture, and even the religion of New Spain therefore developed a syncretism between Spanish and Indian traditions. In time the importation of black slaves from Africa further complicated the ethnic mix. It has, however, remained generally true into modern times that the social position and wealth of any individual could be gauged by skin colour.

The English – John Cabot was convinced that Columbus had got his sums wrong. He believed correctly that China was far out of range of any ship following a southerly route. By his calculation, the journey could be made at a more northerly latitude. Sailors from Bristol, England were already fishing the Newfoundland banks and knew the North Atlantic well. Cabot therefore won support from King Henry VII of England and in 1496 reached the coast of North America. It was not obvious that the north of the continent was embedded in the Arctic ice and Cabot's son, Sebastian led a long line of English sailors in search of the North West Passage. The English sea dogs, Drake and Hawkins preferred the warm waters of New Spain to the cold northern seas. They first operated as traders, and then, after being attacked by Spaniards, as privateers.

The gold of New Spain and the luxury trade of the Orient offered instant riches. Returns on investment in North America were likely to be less spectacular. By the 1580s, however, Sir Walter

Raleigh and others were advocating colonization of the land of Virginia, which was now claimed by England. Attempts were made to establish colonies in 1585 and 1589, but both failed. The first successful colony was made at Jamestown in 1607. In 1620 a group of 'Pilgrim' refugees set up a colony at New Plymouth, Massachusetts, and later moved to the better site of Boston.

The English settlements were based on a farming economy. Disease, spreading from New Spain had recently ravaged the native American tribes, leaving much of the land vacant. The surviving people practised a mixed hunting and farming economy, based on shifting cultivation, so to newcomers much of the land appeared to be empty. As land hungry settlers kept on arriving and pushing inland towards the Appalachian Mountains conflict with the Indian people was inevitable.

The Dutch – In 1614 the United New Netherlands Company established a colony at the mouth of the Hudson River. The Dutch recognized the potential of the trade in beaver fur and used the Hudson to make contact with Indian people of the interior. This settlement divided the English colonies of Virginia and New England and hostility between the two Protestant countries, aroused in the far Spice Islands, spilled over in the New World. In 1664 the English drove the Dutch from North America.

At the height of their powers, the Dutch carried their assault on the Portuguese Empire into the New World by annexing Brazil in 1637. The Portuguese settlers rebelled against them and they were driven out in 1654, leaving Brazil as the western outpost of a once great Portuguese Empire.

The French – In 1603 the French explorer de Champlain sailed into the St Lawrence River. He too was still searching for the elusive route to the east. He established settlements which were to become Montreal and Quebec and pressed on to explore the inland waterways of the interior. The French settlers were comparatively few in number and they received little support from their home government. Champlain and those who came after him exploited Indian rivalries to establish a flourishing trading empire, based on the fashion trade in beaver fur. As the animals were hunted to near extinction in the east, the 'beaver frontier' moved west, taking the hardy French after them.

French explorers followed the Great Lakes waterway into the interior and then the Mississippi to the Gulf of Mexico. Here they established the French outpost of New Orleans. The North American empire, named Louisiana, after Louis XIV, now followed the waterways in a huge, but lightly populated arc. At first the French and English colonists only came into contact with each other in the Hudson Valley. The risk of conflict grew, however, when the French tightened the noose around the English colonies by taking control of the Ohio River. At the time, however, colonial wars, which decided the fate of India and North America, were seen as little more than a sideshow beside the main European conflicts.

The Old Colonial System – The Dutch can be credited with the development of mercantilism, which became known as the old colonial system. This was not developed specifically for North America, but, when applied by the English in their American possessions, it became a root cause of later conflict between the colonists and the mother country. It was assumed that overseas colonies existed to promote the interests of the mother country, by extending its economic base. Colonists were expected to produce cash crops. Some, like rice from the Carolinas or tobacco from Virginia, could not be produced in northern Europe. Softwood timber from New England was also of vital strategic importance for ship building at a time when European forests were finally disappearing. Buying these goods from a national source saved the mother country the foreign exchange, which would be required to purchase them from abroad. By selling these crops, the colonists earned money, which would be spent on the manufactured goods. This in turn assisted the manufacturing industries and strengthened the merchant marine of the mother country. Any business between the colony and a third country had to transacted through the mother country. This had the further benefit of boosting customs revenue.

The trade-off was that the mother country was responsible for providing the colonists with protection, be it from local populations or from hostile Europeans. This involved the Westminster government in the expense of funding wars against the French and their Indian allies. The system came under pressure when the colonies began to develop out of their original role as providers of raw materials to develop their own manufactures.

Africa
The Atlantic Slave Trade – The Portuguese were the first to discover that West Africa had human resources, which were to be exploited in a slave trade, which continued for some 350 years. A

base was established on the coast as early as 1448, from which relatively small numbers of slaves were shipped back to Portugal.

An acute labour problem then began to develop in the new American plantations. The obvious solution was to recruit American Indians. Heavy field work, however, proved alien to them. Many died, often by suicide, when forced to work on European plantations. European labour was also brought in, both by the forcible transportation of convicts, and by indentured labour schemes, under which immigrants were bound to their masters for a given number of years. Again, however, expectation of life was short, and the labour problem remained unresolved.

Portuguese ships then began to take slaves direct to their colony of Brazil. In 1562 John Hawkins began the English slave trade between West Africa and the Caribbean. Dutch, French, Danes and later sailors from both North and South America joined in the business. European nations established forts on the West African coast to protect the interests of their slave traders.

It is estimated that some eight to ten million slaves were carried across the Middle Passage to America. The economies of European cities, such as Nantes, Bristol and later Liverpool were based on slaving, and the business was accepted as a part of the national commercial interest.

The individual suffering of slaves would ultimately receive wide publicity; the impact the trade had on African society is harder to quantify. European sailors rarely penetrated inland to find their own captives. Domestic slavery already existed on the continent, and Africans initially sold their own slaves to purchase European goods. In time, however, demand outstripped this source of supply. Military confederacies, such as Dahomey and Ashanti, grew up to fulfil the double function of protecting their own members, and feeding slaves to the European forts. When Europeans later penetrated the continent, they discovered that these states often acted with a savagery untypical of African society further inland. The demand for slaves created an endemic state of war which penetrated inland, far beyond any direct European contact. The resulting depopulation appears, however, to have been largely balanced by improvements in the African diet as a result of the importation of American crops, such as the yam and cassava.

Colonization – The first African colonies had the prime function of protecting and providing staging posts for national ships on the eastern trade routes. The Portuguese early established the outposts in Mozambique and Angola which would achieve the distinction of being the longest-lasting European overseas colonies. In 1652 Jan van Riesbeck set up the Dutch colony at the Cape of Good Hope, to serve the eastern convoys as a 'tavern of the seas'. In the 18th century, the French established an interest in the Indian Ocean island of Madagascar, along with Mauritius, and Reunion. The slave coast of West Africa remained unattractive for colonization. European slavers and soldiers suffered a high mortality rate from tropical diseases, particularly yellow fever and malaria.

East Africa – At this time, East Africa lay off the main trading routes, and the region offered little to attract European merchants. Arab dhows still sailed undisturbed to Zanzibar and their caravans penetrated deep inland. Here again, slaves featured prominently as a trading commodity alongside gold and ivory. The area remained an Arab area of influence until European missionaries and traders penetrated the area in the 19th century.

THE NATIONS OF EUROPE

Italy and the European Powers
The City States and the Papacy – In the 15th century, the northern half of Italy was the most advanced part of Europe. The great trading cities of Genoa and Venice brought in wealth and broad contact was maintained, both through trade and cultural exchange with Arab and Byzantine civilizations. The country probably benefited from the fact that it was never brought under unitary political control.

The broken terrain of Tuscany and Umbria suited the development of independent city states, not unlike those of ancient Greece. Florence and Sienna, like Athens and Sparta of old, built up confederacies to counterbalance the power of the other. In the late 14th century, the banking family of Medici took power in Florence. Times were not always easy, but they led the city to its unique flowering of culture.

In the north another ring of states, with Milan as the most powerful, controlled the trading routes across the Alps. In the centre, the pope ruled the Papal States as any other temporal monarch, and involved himself in the politics of the peninsula, attempting always to extend the patrimony of St Peter. During this period the lifestyle of the popes was little different from that of any other monarch. They led troops into battle, promoted family interests, including those of their children, and built themselves enormous monuments. Julius II's decision to build himself a tomb set off the chain of events which triggered the Reformation in distant Germany; the tomb would be too large for St Peter's, so the church had to be rebuilt; this involved raising money by the granting of indulgences.

The Theory of Kingship – Within this turbulent world of Italian politics, only the fittest survived. Nicolo Machiavelli worked for the Florentine state, travelling widely as a diplomat. He wrote a book, called *The Prince*, which was based on these experiences, which contained advice for the Medici family on the theory and practice of government. Political decisions, he argued, could only be taken on a cool, indeed callous, assessment of the security needs of the state and of its ruler. Medieval concepts of the mutual duties of ruler and subjects were cut away in this first exposition of what would later come to be called 'real politik'.

Medieval monarchy was based on a feudal alliance between king and his tenants in chief. In the 16th century power was being drawn to the centre, at the expense of both the magnates and of representative institutions. For Machiavelli's prince, power was its own justification. The theory of centralization was later taken further with the formulation of the concept of the divine right of kings. Rulers, it was said, held power directly from God. Rebellion was a sin and criticism of the royal will was tantamount to treason.

Foreign Invasion – In 1494 Charles VIII of France crossed the Alps at the head of an army of 30,000 men. He laid claim to the Kingdom of Naples and on his way south, through Rome itself, his army left a trail of destruction. Other foreign armies followed. Artists still worked on, producing some of the greatest works known to man, but the days of the city state were over and Italy would henceforth be a pawn in the real politik of the great powers. In 1527 the ragged, unpaid and hungry army of the great emperor, Charles V, ran wild in the streets of Rome, and the city was sacked for the first time since the barbarian invasions.

The Empire of Charles V – Throughout medieval times, kingship was fundamentally a matter of family inheritance. Charles was the ultimate beneficiary of this dynastic system. From his mother, the mad Joanna, he inherited his grandparents' crowns of Castile and Aragon. On the paternal side, he inherited from his grandfather the title of Holy Roman Emperor, and from his grandmother the lands of the Duchy of Burgundy. As king of Castile he controlled Spanish land in the New World; as Emperor he ruled Austria, Hungary, Bohemia and much of Germany; as Duke of Burgundy he possessed the Netherlands, which was the richest part of all Europe. His empire was larger than that of Charlemagne.

France was now shut in on all sides, and its king was determined not to let Italy fall to Charles' empire. The crusading spirit was finally laid to rest as Pope and King of France allied with the Ottoman Turks against Charles.

This great empire, like that of Charlemagne, carried the seeds of its own destruction. Charles was unable to function adequately as ruler of such dispersed lands, and resentment grew, particularly in the Netherlands, at the taxes raised to support Italian wars. Charles was also depressed at his inability to control the spread of protestantism within his own lands. He abdicated in 1556 and the empire was divided. The title of Emperor passed to his brother Ferdinand I, while the more valuable western share, consisting of Spain and the old Burgundian lands, went to his son, Philip II. There were now two Hapsburg dynasties in Europe.

Protestantism and the Counter Reformation

The Spread of Protestantism – Luther's new beliefs found most followers in northern Europe, particularly in Germany and Scandinavia. The impetus behind the further spread of protestantism came not from Germany but from Geneva. John Calvin was French, but he achieved prominence in the Swiss canton. He preached a harsh form of protestantism; since God was all powerful, he had predestined a minority of people – the elect – to salvation and the rest to damnation. The elect had to show their status by a strict adherence to a way of life. In Geneva moral sins, like adultery and even disobedience by a child, were severely punished. Calvinism proved to be a more militant faith than Lutheranism. It appealed in the Netherlands, England and the west coast of France, in Scotland and later in the Lutheran heartland of Germany.

All Protestantism stressed the direct communion of the individual with God, and it is not surprising that it early showed a capacity to fragment. In 1532 an extreme group, the Anabaptists, took control of the German city of Münster, preaching not only rejection of infant baptism but polygamy and a radical social gospel. In the extreme Protestant sects, authority lay not in any higher political or ecclesiastical power, but in the local 'gathered church'. These separatist churches were persecuted in Protestant and Catholic countries alike, but it was this tradition that would ultimately implant itself in the New England colonies of North America, and profoundly influence the development of American society.

Toleration was not a cherished ideal in 16th century Europe, but by 1530 it had become clear that protestantism was too powerful a movement to be readily suppressed. In that year the Peace of Augsburg laid down the principle of 'cuius regio, eius religio' – the country would follow the religion of the ruler. This left rulers free to persecute within their own dominions.

Sweden and England Break with Rome – Two European monarchs took their nations out of communion with the Roman church. Both were motivated by national and financial, rather than by religious reasons. In 1523 the young Swedish nobleman, Gustavus Vasa, succeeded in his struggle to make Sweden independent from Denmark, and was proclaimed king. Lutheranism had already made progress among his people. In 1527 he broke with Rome as a symbol of the new national independence, and he enriched his hard-pressed government with church lands.

Henry VIII of England had showed no personal inclination towards the reformed religion; indeed, he had written a pamphlet attacking Luther and had persecuted Protestants. In 1530, however, he became involved in a dispute with the pope over his divorce from Catherine of Aragon. Using selective intimidation, he won the support of parliament for a breach with Rome and then for the plundering of monastic lands. The Church of England, reformed in doctrine, but conservative in practice, was the creation of Henry's Archbishop of Canterbury, Thomas Cranmer. After a return to catholicism under Mary I, Elizabeth, declared that the English church should be a home for all men of goodwill. Separatist Protestants and politically active Catholics were still persecuted, but England did escape the worst violence of these years.

The Counter Reformation – The Roman church had been on the defensive against an aggressive protestantism for 25 years when Pope Paul III called his bishops together for the Council of Trent. Paul represented a new generation of Pope, anxious to clear away the scandals of the past, and re-establish the western church on a firm footing. The discussions were dominated by bishops from Spain and Italy, where protestantism had found no foothold. The Council brought in reforms, but it made no concessions to Protestant faith. By the time that the Council had finished its debates in 1563, the lines of division were clearly drawn.

Catholicism was now on the counter-offensive. As in the past, monasticism provided the papacy with its front line troops. In 1540, Ignatius Loyola, who had been a fellow student in Paris with John Calvin, established the Society of Jesus, or Jesuits. Members were bound to total loyalty to the Pope, and this provided the reforming papacy with a means of circumventing special interests within the church. Jesuits became particularly prominent in education and in missionary work.

Spain and the Netherlands

The Expulsions – Even without Charles' eastern lands, Philip II's Spain remained the dominant power in Europe. He controlled southern Italy and Sicily and succeeded in conquering Portugal. Spain's European power was now underpinned by the revenues of a two huge overseas empires.

The nation's weakness was not clearly evident at the time. When the Moors were finally defeated, Moslems and Jews had been promised security within the Christian state. The presence of infidels, however, proved too much for Catholic rulers still driven by the intolerance of the Inquisition. Moors, Jews and converted Moors, the Moriscos, were all driven out of the country. These, however, were the very tradespeople and skilled craftsmen on whom the economy rested. As a result, Spain became heavily dependent on imported goods, particularly from the prosperous Netherlands. On occasions the Panama fleet had to be diverted and sailed direct to unload its treasure in the Netherlands.

The Spanish Netherlands – The old Burgundian lands covered both the modern states of Belgium and Holland. The greatest centres of prosperity, Antwerp outstanding, lay in the south. The northern part, mostly consisting of land drained from the Rhine delta, contained the finest farmland in Europe, but, even with intensive agriculture, it could not feed the growing towns. Calvinist protestantism had won adherents in the north and in the south.

Charles V was born in the Netherlands and during his reign the two religions co-existed with reasonable tolerance. The accession of Spanish-born Philip II, however, brought change. As king, he was determined to bring the old Burgundian noble families under his control, and, as a faithful son of the church, he meant to stamp out heresy in his land. The Spanish Duke of Alva was sent with an army to bring the area under control.

Dutch Independence – In 1572 William Prince of Orange led the People of the Netherlands in revolt. As Spanish armies established control of the south, many Protestants moved north behind the protection of the dykes, and the religious division between the Catholic south and the Protestant north was established. In 1581 the followers of William of Orange declared their independence from Spain. No matter how bitter the fighting, the trade between Spain and her rebellious provinces never ceased. Philip was in no position to cut off this channel of supplies and the Dutch were happy to drain the enemy of wealth. William was murdered on Philip's orders in 1584, but the struggle continued until Spain made a truce in 1609. Almost forty years would pass before Spain finally recognized the independence of the Dutch people, but in practice Holland had established its independence from its traditional ruling house.

The Dutch Republic – The new nation was unique in that power was based on trade rather than on inherited land. A successful Dutchman did not plan for the day when he would put aside the cares of trade and live as a gentleman; his objective was to hand a thriving business to his heirs. People lived by a strict work ethic and made the most of the limited resources of their small land.

National wealth was founded on north-south trade, carrying products such as grain, timber and iron from the Baltic to the overpopulated Mediterranean lands. Dutch flyboats, little more than floating holds, plied the oceans. 'Norway was their forest, the banks of the Rhine and the Dordogne their vineyard; Spain and Ireland grazed their sheep; India and Arabia were their gardens and the sea their highway.' Scholars also provided information for sailors and laid the foundation of modern geography.

The Decline of Spain – The loss of the Netherlands was the clearest marker of Spain's fall from its position as Europe's dominant power. In 1588 a Spanish naval armada was also defeated by the English fleet. In 1640 Portugal re-established her independence under the house of Breganza. The nation could have overcome military reverse; the basic problem was that Philip II and his successors concentrated on military and colonial affairs at the expense of the economy, shattered by the mass expulsions.

The French Wars of Religion
The French Monarchy – In the middle of the 16th century, French royal power stood at a low ebb. Financial stringency led to offices being sold to the highest bidder, and, partly as a result,

the size and independence of the aristocracy was ever increasing. Calvinism was strong in Brittany and Normandy, and growing in power further south on the Atlantic coast, and in Languedoc. Its strength was based on craftsmen and some poorer nobles, followed by a growing number of peasants. By 1562 there were over 1500 'Huguenot' congregations, many led by Geneva-trained pastors. The Catholics themselves were divided: the moderates, led by the Regent, Catherine de Medici, who planned to keep the peace by giving a measure of toleration to the Protestants, and an extreme Catholic party, who wanted to see heresy stamped out.

The Wars – Fighting broke out after extremist Catholics massacred a Huguenot congregation at Vassy in 1562. The ensuing wars were fought with great ferocity on both sides. In 1572, 3,000 Huguenots were massacred in Paris on St Bartholomew's Day, and in 1588 the king was ejected from his own capital by extreme Catholics. In 1584 the Huguenot Henry of Navarre became heir to the throne. He succeeded in bringing the war to an end by turning Catholic and reaching agreement with his former Protestant followers in the Edict of Nantes. This left the Huguenots with freedom of worship in large areas of the country as well as certain fortified cities, now effectively outside royal control.

Germany

The Empire after Charles V – Charles V's brother Ferdinand saw himself as a faithful Catholic and soldier of the Counter Reformation. His own lands and the south of Germany remained Catholic. The Protestant forces set against him were divided. In the north were the Lutheran powers of Denmark, Saxony and Brandenburg. The Calvinist stronghold lay to the west around the Rhine. Ferdinand dreamed of winning back the whole of Germany to catholicism, while at the same time bringing it once again under imperial rule, but he was unable to achieve his ambition because his empire was exposed on its eastern flank. In the south, the Ottoman Empire reached the peak of its power under Suleiman I, and even threatened Vienna itself. In the north, Sweden was establishing control of the Baltic Sea while Poland and Russia both pressed on German land.

The Thirty Years War – In the early 17th century the religious divisions became more sharply fixed. In 1608-9 the Catholic League and the Calvinist Union were set up as rival military blocks. The first of a series of wars broke out in 1618, when the Calvinist

Elector Palatine was elected King of Bohemia. The Catholic armies, led by virtually independent war lords, won early successes, but this rallied the Lutheran armies to the Protestant cause. The Protestant champion turned out to be Gustavus Adolphus, King of Sweden, who won a series of battles before he was killed at Lützen in 1632.

By now the religious battle lines were becoming blurred. Catholic France, under Cardinal Richelieu, was prepared to fund Protestant armies and even to intervene directly to prolong the war and so prevent and re-emergence of imperial power in Germany. This brought in Catholic and Hapsburg Spain on the imperial side.

The war was a disaster for the people of Germany. Roaming armies stripped the countryside of food; the devastation caused by the imperial sack of Magdeburg in 1629 rivalled that of a Mongol army. When the war limped to a close in 1648, the countryside was impoverished and depopulated. Ferdinand's ideal of a Catholic Germany, united under the empire was destroyed. Protestantism was unassailable in the north and the effective power of the emperor in the German-speaking lands was henceforth limited to his Austrian heartland. In the Treaties of Westphalia the Emperor had to accept the independence of Switzerland – a reality since the end of the 15th century – and the King of Spain that of the Netherlands. France and Spain both made achieved territorial gains in German lands. Most significant for the future, the new power of Brandenburg had emerged in the north.

Brandenburg – Prussia – In 1640 'The Great Elector' Frederick William, of the House of Hohenzollern, inherited Brandenburg and the eastern territory of Prussia. A man of great energy, he set about creating a well-run, modern state. His twin tools were an efficient civil service and a highly disciplined army, which served as a model for later German armies. The Great Elector's work was consolidated a century later by Frederick II 'the Great'. He had no vision of a united Germany, but he ruthlessly expanded his family lands at the expense of the Empire.

The Hegemony of France

Richelieu – Henry IV was assassinated in 1610, leaving a country at peace, but with many problems. The Huguenots were a state within a state; the nobles were over-powerful and contributed little to the nation; the peasants were desperately poor and over-taxed.

In 1624 his successor, Louis XIII, appointed Cardinal Richelieu as head of the royal council. For 18 years, he worked single-mindedly to establish royal power within the nation. He had no wish to persecute the Protestants, but he destroyed the independent Huguenot fortresses. He made examples at high level to bring the nobles under his control. Regional government was delegated to directly appointed intendants, who exercised the complete range of royal power.

Richlelieu's foreign policy was directed at limiting the power of Spain and improving national security by achieving 'natural frontiers' at the Rhine and Alps. For this, he was prepared to ally with Protestants and to prolong the misery of the Thirty Years War.

Richelieu represented the apotheosis of the Machiavellian ideal; his policy was driven by a cold analysis of *raison d'état*. He did not recognize that an improvement in the lot of the poor was essential if the state was to be securely based. Shortly after Richelieu and his royal master died in 1642-3, there was a series of popular uprisings, known as the Frondes, across the country.

Louis XIV – The young king who succeeded ruled the country until 1715. His domestic and foreign policy was a continuation of that laid down by Richelieu. All real power lay in the hands of non-noble ministers and intendants, while the nobles were emasculated by being drawn into the glittering court of Versailles.

Unlike Richelieu, however, Louis determined that he would not rule over heretics. He revoked the Edict of Nantes, facing protestants with the choice of conversion or expulsion. Like Isabella of Castille, he was hereby driving a productive group out of the nation. Economic conditions did improve, but the poor continued to suffer harshly enforced penal taxation.

Much tax revenue was spent on foreign wars. As France had organized leagues to limit the power of Spain, so now others united to contain France. The driving force in the anti-French Grand Alliance was William of Orange, Stadholder of the Netherlands. His power strengthened when, in 1688, he also became king of England as William III. The War of the Grand Alliance (1689-97) was followed by the War of the Spanish Succession (1701-14), which sought to prevent Louis from unifying the crowns of Fence and Spain by dynastic succession.

18th-century France – In 1715 France was clearly the leading power in Europe. Major losses of overseas territory to England in India and North America during the Seven Years War (1756-73) did not appear as significant at the time as they were later to become. Financial weakness, however, underlay the pageantry of the monarchy. The huge noble class – estimated at up to 250,000 strong – had lost political power but not financial and legal privilege. The state sank ever more deeply in debt but had no means of tapping the huge reserves of noble wealth. Here lay the seeds of revolution.

England

Sea Power – When Roman soldiers were posted to Britain, they considered that they were being consigned to the edge of the civilized world. Through medieval times, the British Isles remained on the periphery of the known world. The discovery of America moved the centre of gravity from the Mediterranean towards the Atlantic Ocean. Geography therefore now favoured England.

As an island nation, the English were perforce a seafaring people. By 1500, however, this seafaring tradition had not been converted into naval power. The defeat of the Spanish Armada in 1588 proved to be a turning point. The battle was won by strategy rather than by fighting force, but the Elizabethan sea-dogs created a national myth which would survive into modern times. Governments, reluctant to involve troops in European land battles, laid the greatest stress on building up naval power and securing naval supplies. The navy provided protection for the island, maintained links with overseas colonies, and secured trade routes against competition.

Monarchy and Parliament – The Tudor monarchs, Henry VIII and his daughter Elizabeth, dominated 16th-century English politics. The nobility were few in number, and were generally content to concentrate their efforts on field sports and the efficient management of their estates. While parliamentary government was withering on the continent, in England the old institutions remained robust. Henry found it convenient to use the House of Commons as his ally against the Church, and Elizabeth was able to manage parliament, even if sometimes with difficulty, both as a source of revenue, and as a channel of government.

When Elizabeth died in 1603, the succession passed to the Scots House of Stuart, which, through family and cultural ties, was more influenced by the French model. Very early, James I became involved in disputes with both the legal and parliamentary establishment. James proclaimed the divine right of kings, which, he claimed, gave the king the power to appoint and dismiss judges and to raise taxes. Jurists recovered documents such as Magna Carta from obscurity to defend ancient privileges against the new royal pretentions. Implicit in their arguments lay the notion that royal power was derived from the consent of the people – however the people might be defined. The conflict was made more acute by the fact that personality did not match pretention. The Tudors had maintained authority through the force of their personalities rather than through modern concepts of kingship. James was intelligent but personally unimpressive; his son Charles I was an inadequate recluse.

The Civil War – Charles I soon found himself in direct confrontation with parliament. In 1628 parliament presented a Petition of Right against the use of arbitrary royal power; in 1629 Charles dissolved parliament and began 11 years of direct rule. Many aspects of royal government were unpopular to influential subjects. An attempt was made to impose 'high church' worship, not only on England but also on Calvinist Scotland. An increasing number of cases were heard in royal prerogative courts rather than in the courts of common law. Direct taxes were levied without parliamentary approval. It seemed to many as though Charles would soon follow Richelieu's example and centralize all government.

The outbreak of war in Scotland brought financial disaster and Charles was forced to recall parliament in 1640. A struggle for power led to the outbreak of war in 1642. Historians have long argued the economic, religious and social issues which lay behind the conflict; certainly it was very different in nature from the violent upheavals which would later shake France and Russia. Parliamentary power was based in the rich southeast, while the king's was centred in the poorer north and west. The parliamentary victory was due both to this difference in resources and to the leadership of Oliver Cromwell, who emerged as the outstanding general in the conflict. He kept his New Model Army under such firm control that it could march across countryside and leave fields and property as they had been before the army passed.

The Commonwealth – The parliamentary broke into factions after the defeat of the king. In 1648 one faction seized power, with army support and staged the trial of Charles I. The execution of the king in 1649 provoked a shocked response across Europe. No action could have expressed the rejection of divine kingship more vividly. In 1653, Cromwell staged a military coup and assumed power as Lord Protector. Cromwell died in 1658, and a brief attempt was made to continue the protectorate under his son. This failed, however, and in 1660 the army again was responsible for bringing Charles II back to London.

The Glorious Revolution – The saga of the conflict between the Stuarts and their parliaments was not, however, over. Charles was mistrusted, both for his French sympathies and for his leaning towards catholicism, but he still depended on parliament for revenue. In 1685 he was succeeded by his Catholic brother, James II. Three years later James was forced to leave the country, to be replaced by his Protestant daughter, Mary and her husband, the Dutch William of Orange, who exercised the practical power. William was more interested in securing the English alliance against France than he was in pursuing power struggles with the English parliamentso he accepted laws which established that the king would henceforth require parliamentary consent to raise money and keep a standing army in peace time. It was also agreed that he could not alter or suspend any act of parliament.

In 1714 the English throne passed to the German house of Hanover. Since the new king could not speak English, day-to-day government passed to a prime minister and a cabinet, drawn from the majority party in the House of Commons. Political power had now finally passed from the monarchy to the property owning classes, who were represented in parliament. In the century which followed parliament largely used its power to improve the position of the landowning class, often at the expense of the poor. English politics had, however, run against the European tide, which favoured greater centralization in the hands of the monarch.

The Act of Union – Throughout history there had been strife between England and her smaller, poorer northern neighbour, Scotland. The union of the crowns in 1603 did not end this. In 1707, however, the two countries became formally united in the Act of Union. Two clan uprisings followed in 1715 and 1745 in favour of the exiled Stuarts but were suppressed. Scots engineers, doctors and scholars were shortly after to make a major contribution to the great surge in national prosperity of the united Great Britain.

Russia

Boyars and Serfs – Across the continent, the Russian state was following a very different pattern of development. The noble boyars held their land from the Tsar in return for defined services. Since Russia had no law of primogeniture, this class was getting ever larger, and most of its members poorer, as estates were split one generation after another. The mass of the people remained in the medieval condition of serfdom. Families were owned by their masters, had no right to move of their own free will and had no redress except in their masters' court.

The relationship of Tsar and boyars was often marked by bloody conflict. Ivan IV 'The Terrible' allied himself with the merchant class and the common people in an attempt to break noble power. He achieved many real reforms before mental disorder led him, in the latter years of his reign, to behaviour which anticipated that of Joseph Stalin in the 20th century.

National Objectives – Russian development was hindered by the lack of a warm-weather outlet to the ocean. The port of Archangel was ice-bound in winter, and all year the journey round northern Scandinavia was long and dangerous. The port of Rostov in the south was of little use as long as the Ottomans controlled the mouth of the Sea of Azov and the Dardanelles. National policy therefore became directed at winning a port on the Baltic Sea. This brought Russia into conflict with the advanced military state of Sweden, which guarded the Baltic as a Swedish lake.

The Russian Tsar could mobilize huge armies, by raising levies, but there was no adequate support structure. Forces were sent to war with the vague hope that they would be able to live off the land. Often countless thousands starved, and those who survived were in no condition to fight the world's most efficient army.

Peter the Great – Peter succeeded to the throne in 1682 at the age of 10, and suffered huge indignities from guards and boyars while still a child. Once a man, he announced his intention to bring his nation up to date and orientate it towards the West. A man of little education but enormous energy, he immersed himself in every detail of western science and technology. In a famous visit to the west he was equally at home working in disguise as a dock worker in Holland and meeting with scientists in England. His methods of enforcement were effective, if sometimes eccentric.

The vindication of Peter's work came in 1709 when his army won a decisive victory over the Swedish army under Charles XII at Poltava. Russia had won its outlet to the Baltic Sea, and here Peter decided to build his capital of St Petersburg.

Peter's great failure was that, like Louis XIV in France, he did nothing to improve the lot of the Russian poor. Someone had to pay for wars against Turkey and Sweden, for the modern weapons, for new ships and for the fine capital city. The poor were taxed and taxed again until they were left with the barest minimum necessary to stay alive. It is a measure of the depth of the misery and the capacity of the Russian people to absorb suffering that revolution did not erupt in violence for another 200 years.

THE WESTERN MIND

The Renaissance

Italy – The word *renaissance* was coined in the 19th century to describe the rebirth in Italy of the classical ideal in art, architecture and letters. The Middle Ages was looked upon as a dark period before the great transformation of the 15th and early 16th centuries. Recent study has shown that the picture was more complicated; classicism remained strong throughout the Middle Ages, and there was more cross-fertilization between Europe north and south of the Alps than had been assumed.

Any gallery visitor can, however, see the astonishing change which happened in visual perception within a comparatively few years. Across northern Italy artists experimented with new forms. In the words of Vasari, Giotto 'restored the art of design'. In Umbria, Piero della Francesca used mathematics to work out laws of perspective, well beyond any classical achievement. In Florence, Michelangelo combined an analytical eye with his huge talent to create a new vision of the human form. Even when painters and sculptors continued to work on church commissions, they now used live models to give a new sense of naturalism.

There was a keen awareness among the artistic community that they were living in an exciting new age. The Medici and other patrons commissioned works with secular themes, often drawn from Greek mythology. Artists were no longer faceless craftsmen who had produced so many medieval treasures. Art had found a new self-consciousness.

The same secular, driven innovation was reflected in music and literature. There was a passionate interest in all aspects of antiquity. Some sculptors even buried their own work and dug it up again, claiming it as a classical discovery. Old manuscripts were found in monastic libraries or brought from the east and studied with a new intensity. Enthusiasm for antiquity did not preclude Christian belief; rather the classical tradition was seen as one element in divine revelation, so producing a syncretism which alarmed conservative churchmen.

By the mid 16th century the Italian renaissance was losing its impetus. The first unique burst of innovation could not be maintained. The Counter Reformation church now demanded a more orthodox treatment of subject matter, both in literature and in painting. Much great work continued to be done, particularly in the Veneto. Paladio used Roman models in creating the architectural style which would bear his name, while Titian and his contemporaries were laying the foundations of what would become the baroque style. Generations of artists and patrons continued to travel to Italy to absorb the culture both of its classical past and of the present.

The Northern Renaissance – Some of the great painters of the Flemish school crossed the Alps and were much admired by Renaissance artists. Perhaps because they were not surrounded by antiquities in their home environment, however, they never made the sharp break with the gothic. Italian styles took many years to become established north of the Alps.

Northern Europe's unique contribution came in the field of scholarship and literature. Here writers were free from the restrictions of the Counter Reformation and fear of the Inquisition. Protestants wanted to make the Bible available to all. The translations of the scriptures by Martin Luther and William Tyndale were immensely influential in formalizing the written forms of German and English respectively. Traditional interpretations of the Bible were challenged when Erasmus of Rotterdam produced a version of the New Testament in the original Greek. Latin was now ceasing to be the universal language of scholarship. While a return to the vernacular liberated learning from the cloisters of the church, it also fractured the international culture, which had reached its peak in the 12th century.

A strong secular tradition now flourished in England. Chaucer had already written for the newly educated merchant class. In 1510 John Colet, Dean of St Paul's Cathedral and close friend of Erasmus, made a gesture to the secularisation of learning when he closed his cathedral school and re-founded it under the control of a trading guild. The combination of Tyndale's language and renaissance scholarship had created a uniquely favourable environment when in 1585 an actor called William Shakespeare left his native Stratford to chance his fortune in London.

The great flowering of French literature came in the 17th century. Corneille and Racine were still in essence renaissance writers, handling classical themes with a paladian sense of form and style.

Printing – Most importantly, the re-invention of printing by movable type provided the means of dissemination of both religious and secular literature. Whether the innovation be credited to Guttenberg of Maintz or Coster of Haarlem, the technique provided the means of dissemination of the works of any author. Books became cheaper as print runs grew longer. In the following centuries print was used to promote colonies, to circulate scurrilous pamphlets to produce works on magic as well as to disseminate works of scholarship, religion and literature. In 1702 *The Courant*, the world's first daily newspaper, was published in London. Soon afterwards works of popular fiction began to come off the presses. Print had become an integral part of Western life.

The Advancement of Science

The Copernican Revolution – In Hellenistic times the idea had been posited that the earth rotated round the sun, but this had not won general acceptance and in 16th century it was still generally accepted that the heavenly bodies rotated around a stationary earth. In 1543, however, the Polish scholar Copernicus published a book arguing the theory of heliocentric astronomy.

Copernicus' theory received little attention. During this time, however, Dutch craftsmen were experimenting with glass lenses. They made spectacles and also telescopes for use at sea. One of these telescopes fell into the hands of the Italian teacher, Galileo Galilei, and he turned the instrument towards the skies. By studying sun spots, the phases of Venus and the rings of Jupiter, he provided clear proof that Copernicus had been correct.

Galileo delayed publishing his findings because he recognized that they must arouse a storm of controversy. Authority, both of the Bible and of ancient authors clearly supported a geocentric universe, and the church still held to authority as the arbiter of truth. He published his findings in 1632, but, faced with the terror of the Inquisition, he recanted in 1633.

Descartes – The Turning Point – Tradition states that, after formally accepting that the earth remained stationary, Galileo muttered 'it goes on moving'. Certainly the scientific impetus continued. In 1637 the French philosopher Descartes published *Discours de la Method*, which laid down what has become known as the Cartesian method. He argued that the experimental scientific process was the arbiter of truth. The pursuit of truth now involved breaking down knowledge into ever smaller areas of study. Medicine, for instance, became concerned with analysing the symptoms of disease in minute detail – arguably at the expense of a more integrated approach to the healing process.

In his dictum, *cogito ergo sum*, Descartes proclaimed the individualism which was to be the hallmark of modern European society. Western man had at last emerged from the shadow of past authorities, religious or classical. Personally a devout Catholic, Descartes rejected authority as an arbiter of faith and proclaimed that it had to be discovered through the human intellect. This was recognized as a fundamental challenge to the church, and Louis XIV personally ensured that Descartes was denied Christian burial.

Northern Europe – The condemnation of both Galileo and Descartes, and continued activities of the Inquisition, placed scientists who lived in Catholic countries in an invidious position. In Protestant countries scientists might meet hostility from those who defended religious authority, but not persecution. The impetus for scientific innovation therefore passed to Northern Europe.

The first protestant scientist was the German, Kepler, who provided information on the movements of planets. Dutch scientists, continuing their work with lenses, developed the microscope. This opened up whole new areas of study in such areas as the biological sciences. In England the cause of experimental science was argued by the Lord Chancellor, Francis Bacon, who had early visions of its potential. In 1619, William Harvey demonstrated the mechanism of the circulation of the blood.

The advances in navigation, first in Holland, and then in France and, above all, in England, drove forward skills in cartography and geographical study. Progress in astronomy and in the construction of clocks were spin-offs from this. Landsmen could now own clocks and watches which told the time with great accuracy. People began to organize their lives around them, and to treat the hours and minutes of the day with a new respect.

The revolution started by Copernicus was completed by Isaac Newton, who published his *Principia Mathematica* in 1687. While Galileo argued the structure of the universe, Newton demonstrated the gravitational mechanism by which it worked.

Until Newton's time, man was an uncomprehending plaything of fate or divine providence. Now he began to understand that the everyday events of life were driven by a structure of causation. Later generations of scientists have maintained the process.

Mendel worked out the structure of genetic inheritance, Darwin illustrated the mechanism evolution, Pasteur demonstrated the causes of disease; Crick and Watson unravelled the DNA code. These and many other insights make up the intellectual baggage of Western man.

Enlightenment to Romanticism

The Philosophes – The new enlightenment was to find its home in France, but the pattern of thinking owed much to 17th century British writers, notably John Locke, who published his *Essay Concerning Human Understanding* in 1690. Locke said that many religious issues were beyond human knowledge, and he argued for tolerance and reliance on reason and reasonableness. His work reflected a wide change of mood, singnalling the end of two centuries of religious strife; never again would the battle lines of Europe's terrible wars be drawn along religious lines.

The scientific advances of the 17th century encouraged philosophers of the following century to see the world as an ordered machine, much like one of the new clocks. There was an optimistic view that the universe was driven by a well-oiled logic, and, if people could only behave in a reasonable manner, the world's problems could be readily overcome. Past religious passions now appeared irrelevant. Many thinkers no longer saw God as an imminent cause of good or evil, but as a great watchmaker, an ultimate mover, who no longer had immediate relevance to life.

The dominant personality among the *philosophes* was the Frenchman, Voltaire. He was a satirist, rather than an original thinker, and he turned his barbed pen on anything which he saw as repressive or pretentious. Voltaire had problems with the French authorities, but he and his circle sewed seeds of scepticism about the old order which would have immense repercussions in the later years of the century.

Evangelicalism – The first reaction against the intellectual emphasis of the age came with a religious revival, which developed in parallel in England and her North American colonies, both within and outside the Church of England. John Wesley set the emotional tone of the movement, sharply in contrast with the language of the *philosophes*, when he described how he 'felt his heart strangely warmed'. This new protestantism appealed primarily not to authority, but to the conversion experience. Until then, the Protestant churches had left missionary work almost entirely to the Catholic orders, but, by the end of the century, the worldwide tide of Protestant missions was beginning to flow, with incalculable effects on non-European cultures.

Romanticism – If John Wesley represented the religious, Swiss-born philosopher, Jean Jacques Rousseau, led the secular reaction against Cartesian intellectualism. He proclaimed that man was pure when in the simple state, be that the uncorrupted form of a noble savage, or a new born child. The quest for goodness therefore involved a return to nature. Rousseau, more than any other person, taught people to look on their environment as a place of beauty; since the time of Hannibal travellers had crossed the Alps, without pausing to recognize them as anything other than a barrier on the road to Italy. Now, as if overnight, Rousseau's Swiss mountains were discovered as majestic things of beauty.

As romanticism emphasised the emotions above the intellect, so it elevated the creative artist, as the person most able to express those emotions. The great milestones of the movement, such as Wordsworth and Coleridge's *Lyrical Balads*, Beethoven's *Eroica Symphony*, the late paintings of Turner, explored new forms and emotions. This could lead to excess, but it also opened the way to the achievements, such as those of French impressionist painters and the great romantic composers.

Social Reform – At about the same time, first clearly surfacing in the 1770s, a transformation began to occur in attitudes to social issues. For centuries, Europeans had been shipping Africans to slavery with no apparent compunction. Now powerful anti-slavery movements made themselves heard in France, Denmark, England and other countries. Movements for the reform of vicious penal systems, the abolition of the 'hanging codes' and for the humane treatment of the insane can be dated to the same time. Educational reform also became a cause for the future.

Credit for this new mood of social reform has been given to the pen of Voltaire, the preaching of Wesley and the ideals of Rousseau. All played their part. In education, for instance, evangelical passion to bring truth to the poor led directly to the opening of ragged schools, while Rousseau was laying the foundations for the quite separate development of child centred learning, which was carried forward by the Swiss educator, Pestalozzi. The cause of reform was uniquely in the air and the traditional political structures were ill equipped to contain it. Europe was ready for the cataclysm of the French Revolution.

REVOLUTION.

The French Revolution

The Estates General – In 1776 the British government was faced with a major revolution in its American colonies. King Louis XVI of France, recognizing this as an opportunity of regaining some of the ground lost in the Seven Years War, involved France in the conflict. In military terms the intervention was successful; in financial terms it was a disaster. The French government, always in financial straits, was now unable to function. The shortfall could no longer be met by the time honoured device of increasing taxes on the poor, but those able to pay could only be taxed with their own consent. Members of the aristocracy recognized an opportunity of winning concessions from the monarchy in return for money, and they insisted that Louis should recall the French parliament, the *Estates General*, which had not met for 150 years.

The body met in three separate houses – aristocracy, clergy and the third estate. This last house represented the property owning middle classes and was largely made up of professional men. They had no vision of themselves as revolutionaries, but they were influenced by the ideas of the *philosophes* and of the American Declaration of Independence. Louis anticipated doing his business with the other two houses before disbanding the body, but the Third Estate had equal representation with the other two, and could count on considerable support in the House of Clergy. In the summer of 1789 the Third Estate declared that it constituted a National Assembly. Louis gave way before its demands and the body set about a huge programme of constitutional, administrative and social reform.

Popular Unrest – Since the time of the Frondes, French kings had been acutely aware of the dangers of uprisings among the poor, who remained unrepresented in the National Assembly. There was unrest in many parts of the countryside, where chateaux were attacked and hated rent books burned. The most immediate danger, however, came from the poor of Paris, who found themselves caught in a spiral of inflation, most crucially in the price of bread. By the 14th July, it was estimated that only three days supply remained in the storehouses of the capital.

The mob possessed armaments, but little ammunition. This lay under close guard in the royal castle of the Bastille. On the 14th

July the mob stormed the Bastille, leaving Louis quite helpless. He could not use his army because the loyalty of rank and file soldiers was in doubt. Many of the aristocracy were now fleeing France and in June 1791 Louis and his family made their bid to escape. They were captured and brought back as prisoners to the capital. The Assembly maintained the King as a figurehead until he and signed the new Constitution in September. The body disbanded itself to make way for the new Legislative Assembly.

War and the Terror – Since the National Assembly had barred any of their number from seeking re- election, the new body was made up of inexperienced men. The dominant figures were Danton, who surrounded himself with members from the Gironde, in southern France, and the little lawyer Robespierre, whose power was based on the Jacobin Club. Protagonists of the new order now felt under siege. The King could still serve as a focal point for a royalist counter-revolution, and both Austria and Prussia were issuing threats. Robespierre argued that peace should be preserved, but Danton believed that the nation could only be united by war. He urged his fellow countrymen to 'dare and dare and dare again' and Frenchmen responded to his cry that the *patrie* was in danger. In April 1792, France declared war on Austria, and Prussia came in on the side of Austria. Early news from the war was disastrous and the capital was gripped in a fever. On 30th July a contingent marched into the capital, singing the song which would become the national anthem. They demanded that Louis should be dethroned and a republic proclaimed. The men of Marseilles were soon joined by a huge citizen army which, chanting the Marseillaise, threw itself on and routed the mercenary enemy soldiers at Valmy on 20th September. Two days later, France was declared a republic. Louis was placed on trial in December and executed on 21st January 1793.

The citizen's army swept across the Netherlands and at last achieved the 'natural frontiers' which had been beyond the reach of the armies of Louis XIV. The victors proclaimed liberty and equality for the poor of all lands, but in practice all too often they laid new tax burdens on those same poor to pay the cost of war.

In February 1793 France faced a coalition of Britain, Austria, Prussia, Holland, Spain, Sardinia and Italian states. Action taken against the Catholic church also provoked civil war in the conservative regions of the Vendée and Brittany. Effective power now passed from the Assembly to a Committee of Public Safety.

In June, Danton's Gironde fell to Robespierre's Jacobins and the period, known as the Reign of Terror, began. Among the victims were successive waves of politicians, including both Danton and his Girondins and Robespierre and the Jacobins. As a result, power passed to a new generation of second rate men, who could not command the respect of the nation.

Meanwhile, the French citizen army, now reinforced by the first use of conscription in modern times, was more than holding its own in the war. Britain, formidable at sea, was poorly equipped for a land war and the old enemies, Prussia and Austria, failed to co-ordinate their effort. The French armies, now led by a new generation of generals, remained firmly entrenched on the Rhine.

The Empire

The rise of Napoleon – In May 1798 a French army, led by the Corsican Napoleon Bonaparte, was sent to invade Egypt in an attempt to cut British trade routes. Land victories were made worthless when the British fleet, commanded by Admiral Nelson, destroyed the French supply fleet and so cut the army off from Europe. In August 1899 Napoleon abandoned his army and returned to France to challenge the discredited leaders of the nation. His gambler's throw succeeded, and on November 9th he staged a coup d'etat and assumed the title of First Consul. He set about centralizing power in his own hands; in 1802 he became consul for life, and in 1804, he followed the example of Charlemagne by crowning himself Emperor as Napoleon I. Any dismay at this negation of the ideals of the revolution was overwhelmed by the relief of ordinary people at the return of ordered and firm government.

Imperial Government – Napoleon had a genius for administration. After an initial purge of remaining Jacobins, he set about healing old divisions and re-uniting the country. He recognized that the continuing civil war in the Vendée could not be brought to an end unless the state came to terms with the Catholic church, so the old religion was restored to its position as the national faith. He set about recruiting the ablest men into government, regardless of whether they held republican or royalist sympathies. Most enduringly, he personally supervised a detailed revision of the whole of the French legal system into the *Code Napoleon*. Had Napoleon been content to hold the Rhine frontier and bring sound administration to France, his rule could have been outstandingly successful. But he was by instinct a general and the symbolic identification with Charlemagne at his coronation illustrated his determination to build the greatest empire that the world had seen. 'I am destined to change the face of the world,' he declared. But Napoleon, like Louis XVI, discovered that wars could only be fought at a financial cost, which had to be passed on in taxes to the people of France and the conquered countries.

The Napoleonic Wars – The great struggles of previous centuries had achieved little more than change the line of a frontier here and there. In the three years from 1805 Napoleon completely redrew the map of Europe. He owed his success to the army which he had inherited from the revolution. Opposing generals recognized that the citizens' armies of France were carried forward on a tide of national energy, which had been released by the revolution. Napoleon added to this a military professionalism, identified with the magnificent Imperial Guard. The surge of victories carried the army across Europe as far as Bohemia, north into Scandinavia and south into Italy and Spain. Ancient rulers were replaced by members of the Bonaparte family or army generals. Even then, however, Britain, Spain and Russia remained as weak points remained in the French Continental System.

Giving priority to the invasion of Britain, Napoleon gathered barges at the channel ports. Any hope of carrying out this operation, however, ended in 1805 when the French fleet was destroyed at the Battle of Trafalgar. Britain therefore remained an implacable foe across the Channel.

The victorious French army in Spain found itself unable to overcome a fierce guerilla resistance which made full use of the broken terrain. The British despatched a force under the general who would later become the Duke of Wellington. In August 1812, after a relentless campaign, Wellington led his army into Madrid.

As Madrid fell, Napoleon was on the other side of Europe, leading 450,000 men on his disastrous campaign against Russia. He had already heavily defeated the Russian army and he believed that serfs would flock to join him once they heard that he had proclaimed their emancipation. He defeated the Russian army again at Borodino and marched on across the scorched countryside to occupy Moscow. But, when the Russians burned their own capital city around his army, and winter began to set in, he was forced to order the terrible retreat. In the end, only a tenth of his great army survived the ordeal. The Imperial Guard was reduced to some 400 men; 80,000 horses had died, leaving the emperor with no effective cavalry to put in the field.

Defeats in Spain and Russia shattered the myth of invincibility and by 1814 Napoleon had lost everything. Paris fell on the 30th March and he abdicated his imperial crown on 11th April. In France, however, loyalty to the deposed emperor remained strong, and when he escaped from exile in 1815, men flocked to join his army. The hundred days adventure ended when he was defeated by the combined British and Prussian armies at Waterloo on 18th June.

Napoleon passed the remainder of his life in well-guarded exile, but the Napoleonic legend lived on. As French power declined, people remembered that it was the Little Corporal who had led them to glory.

Reaction and Revolution

The Return of the Old Order – After the defeat of Napoleon, members of the old ruling houses moved back into their palaces. The statesmen met in Vienna to reorganize the continent. The treaty took little account of nationalist aspirations. Poland was awarded to Russia; Venice and Lombardy to Austria; the Rhineland was taken from France and given to Prussia; the southern Netherlands were incorporated into Holland; Norway was made a part of Sweden.

The Austrian Prince Metternich was the main architect of this restoration of the old order. He fully recognized the huge changes in political consciousness brought about by the French Revolution, but he believed that these had to be suppressed, and that structures should return to return to their dynastic roots. He opposed all representative institutions, and established the Holy League as a coalition of powers dedicated to suppress ideas of liberty and nationalism, wherever they might show themselves. Of the major powers, only Britain -itself, however imperfectly, a representative government – stood apart to uphold a more liberal tradition.

The policy of intervention was successfully invoked when the Spanish people rose in rebellion in 1820. Austria also put down rebellion in her Italian possessions. Metternich was wise enough to see himself as the defender of a dying way of life. In 1821 the people of Greece rose against their Turkish masters. True to his principles, Metternich gave Austrian support to the Ottoman

Turks, but the rebels won backing from Russia and Britain and achieved their independence in 1830.

Also in 1830 the people of Paris rose again and replaced the conservative king with his more liberal cousin, Louis Philippe, and revolutions broke out in Poland and across Germany. In the same year, the Catholic Belgians rebelled against their Dutch masters. The conservative powers threatened to intervene, but Britain, in a gesture which would be called in 84 years later, guaranteed Belgian independence.

The Year of Revolutions – The unrest of 1830 was a prelude to much greater upheavals of 1848. In January, rebellion broke out in Sicily. In February the people of Paris drove Louis Philippe, now a figure of fun, into exile. In March, Venice, Parma, Milan and Sardinia all rose against Austria. As the year progressed, there was revolution in Poland and Hungary. Smaller German princes fell, most never to return. Uprisings in Berlin and Vienna even brought the powerful Prussian and Austrian states to the point of collapse, and the elderly Metternich had to follow Louis Philippe into exile.

The Hughes Capet French monarchy was finished for ever, and, after a period of civil war, the French people turned again to the magic name of Napoleon in the person of his nephew, Louis Napoleon. He followed family tradition by staging a coup d'état and assuming the title of Emperor Napoleon III. Across the rest of Europe, ruling houses re-established control over their dominions.

New Nations

The Unification of Italy – A decade later, Camillo Cavour, a statesman in the Italian kingdom of Savoy, set about achieving by political means what had been beyond the powers of the revolutionaries. In 1858 he met Napoleon III to discuss how Austrian rule might be ended and Italy unified under his king, Victor Emmanuel of Savoy. In 1859 French armies inflicted heavy defeats on the Austrians at Magenta and Solferino. In 1860, the popular soldier Garibaldi led 'the thousand' against the rulers of Sicily and Naples. He handed these territories over to Victor Emmanuel. For a time Austria held on to Venice, but the city fell in 1866. Finally the Papal States were brought into a united Italy in 1870. The political task was complete, but the new country faced formidable problems of poverty, and large numbers, particularly from the south, emigrated to find a better life.

The Unification of Germany – In 1862 Otto von Bismark, a noble-man of Junker descent, became Prime Minister of Prussia. His first speech was ominous for the future of European peace. 'The great issues of our day cannot be solved by speeches and majority votes, but by blood and iron.' The German-speaking people were already showing a formidable potential, but to achieve all they had to be united into a nation. Only Austria or Prussia could be the focus of that state; Bismark determined that it should be Prussia.

In 1864 the two powers collaborated to annex the German-speaking lands of Schleswig and Holstein from Denmark. Then two years later Prussia went to war with Austria. On 3rd July 1866 the Hapsburg army was devastatingly defeated at Sadowa. The Hapsburg monarchy retained Austria, but Germany was now effectively united. In 1870 Germany went to war with France and the Napoleonic legend was laid for ever on the field of Sedan.

As Bismark's army occupied Paris, there could no longer be any doubt that Germany was the dominant power in continental Europe. The violent methods by which this had been achieved were no innovation in European politics. The new state was based on admirable organization. German cities were models of organization and sanitary efficiency; a state school place was provided for every child, and illiteracy rates became the lowest in the world; the poor, who until that time had emigrated in large numbers, now showed their confidence in the government of their country by staying at home, and by playing their part in con-structing the impressive industrial base of the new nation.

A CHANGING WORLD

The Infrastructure of Change

Population – The population of Europe had been growing re-lentlessly since the time of the Black Death. Demographers have argued why, for instance, the increase was particularly pro-nounced in the 16th century. It appears as though women started marrying younger, so having a longer child bearing life, but this leaves unanswered why such a social change should have oc-curred. The 18th century again saw a steady increase across west-ern Europe, which pre-dated major medical advances of the fol-lowing century. A modest alleviation of the harsh conditions of rural life, the improvement of the housing stock, and some ad-vances in public health may all have contributed to a reduction in the death rate.

Rulers generally welcomed a rising population; it provided an larger man-power pool for the military, and increased the tax base of the nation. In 1798, however, an English clergyman, called Thomas Malthus, published his *Essay on Population*. The world, he argued, possesses limited resources. As population grows, so the most vulnerable – the poor – must inevitably experience disaster and hunger. Malthus' work was influential, but his warnings were not, in the short term, authenticated by events. The reason for this was that, at the same time that the population was increasing, Europe was experiencing a green revolution, which greatly increased the amount of food available to meet the growing demand.

The Second Agricultural Revolution – The first great change in farming practice came with the introduction of settled agriculture at the beginning of historical times. Even in Babylonian cities, farming families had to produce a surplus to feed craftsmen, priests and warriors. By the beginning of the 18th century, little had changed. It is estimated that in England eight out of ten people still lived in the countryside and that, on average, one farming family had to keep one other family from the produce of its land. People still ate bread baked from their own wheat and drank beer brewed from their own barley. Animals, except for breeding stock were still slaughtered and salted down for the winter.

Once again, change originated in small, highly urbanized, 17th century Holland. Dutch farms had to be more efficient than those of their larger neighbours, and major improvements were pioneered, particularly in the development of root vegetables, largely for animal winter feed, and in high yield artificial grasses, such as alfalfa and lucerne.

In the 18th century, the English gentry, unlike their neighbours in France, lived on their estates and it became fashionable to take an interest in farming. George III set the tone by contributing articles to a farming journal. Some began to introduce the Dutch innovations on their estates. New crops and methods of rotation were introduced and selective breeding produced remarkable improvements in the quality of livestock.

These improvements could not be introduced without radical changes in the organization of the countryside. Improved agriculture could not be successfully introduced in the old communal fields, so enclosures, which had been taking place for two centuries, were given a new impetus. In the change from peasant holdings to larger farms, worked by landless labourers, many lost land and ancient rights. The production of food, however, became a much more efficient process. By the late 18th century British farmers were in a position to support a huge increase in the nation's urban population.

Financial and Human Resources – Any major economic expansion needs to be built on a sound financial base. Britain's growing international trade brought prosperity, and her island position meant that wealth did not have to be dissipated on the maintenance of a large standing army. By the standards of the time, she also had a sophisticated and well-capitalized banking industry.

It is harder to establish a link between the skills required for technological advance and the social and educational structure of the day. Few of the innovators of the new age came form the conventional academic background, which had produced Isaac Newton; they were more typically self taught, or the products of Scottish or dissenting education.

Economic Theory – In 1776 Adam Smith published *The Wealth of Nations*, which laid the basis of modern economics. He argued the benefits of competition in a free economy, against both state control and the abuses of monopoly powers. His arguments were influential both in government and business circles, initially in Britain and later in the United States and elsewhere.

The First Industrial Revolution

Iron and Coal – Since the time of the Hittites, iron working had been centred on the great forests. The charcoal used in the smelting process consumed large quantities of timber, which was also vital for building and naval supplies. Over the centuries, the forests receded to the more remote areas. By the end of the 17th century, Britain faced something of a crisis. In the 14th century, German craftsmen of the Rhineland had learnt how to make cast iron, so that the metal could now be used to make a wider range of products, but there was an acute shortage of wood to drive the blast furnaces.

Early in the 18th century the Darby family of Shropshire finally solved the problem of how iron could be smelted from coal. As this technique became widely known, industry moved from the forests to the great coal fields, which lie across Europe in a band from mid Russia to Wales. Surface coal was soon exhausted and deep mines were sunk to exploit the seams. Iron goods could now be produced in bulk.

Steam Power – As early as Hellenistic times, it had been recognized in theory that steam could be used to drive an engine, but the technological basis was lacking. The need for pumps to drain the new deep mines made progress all the more essential. The Scottish engineer, James Watt made the essential break-through when he separated the cylinder from the condenser. As a result, industry could now be liberated, not only from the forests, but also from the banks of fast flowing rivers.

Water Transport – Before the 18th century, land transport was rudimentary over most of Europe. Once again, the Dutch had pioneered the use of the canals which drained their country for transporting loads. The French government also constructed the magnificent Canal du Midi, designed to prevent goods having to be carried around the coast of Spain. France also had a high quality road network, built by forced labour, but these, like those of the Romans, were built for military use.

In 1861 the Duke of Bridgewater opened a canal which linked his coal mine at Worsley with the growing town of Manchester. The potential for improved communications to lubricate economic growth was illustrated when the price of coal in Manchester fell immediately by a half. The great revolution occurred, however, when steam power was applied to locomotion. Here the initiative was taken in the United States, where inland waterways provided the essential communication links for the new nation. In 1807, Robert Fulton sailed *The Steamboat* from New York to Albany in 32 hours – a journey which had previously taken four days. Two years later, steam power was applied to ocean navigation.

Railways – The world's first commercial railway was opened in Britain in 1825, between Stockton and Darlington. Huge sums of money were invested in railway building in many nations, but, despite massive construction programmes, especially in the United States and Germany, Britain retained her initial advantage. The age of cheap and rapid communication brought important social as well as economic change, as the structure of society began to reflect the new mobility.

Cotton and the Factory System – There had long been a market for fine fabrics in western Europe. By the early 18th century a substantial silk industry had grown up in France, which reduced dependence on imports. At this time, cotton was still a luxury fabric, and ready woven cloth was imported from India. Entrepreneurs then began to import raw cotton, which was put out for manufacture to domestic workers. Whole families worked immensely long hours at carding, spinning and weaving to earn a modest subsistence. The early machines were invented by enterprising craftsmen to help boost domestic output.

The first large spinning factory was built by Richard Arkwright at Cromford, near Derby in 1771. By the early 19th century all the stages of cotton cloth production had been brought within the factory system. Britain, backed by her huge merchant marine, had established a dominant position in the world supply of textiles. One machine, tended by a woman or a girl, could now do the work of many domestic workers, and traditional producers, from Britain itself to India, lost their livelihood.

Despite being a closely guarded secret, the new technology was bound to become known. The United States was already showing itself a fertile ground for industrial development and a substantial industry grew up in New England.

Urban Growth – The population of Europe continued to grow rapidly throughout the 19th century, but the increase was now concentrated in the urban centres. In the 19th century, the population of London increased from about 900,000 to some 4.7 million, that of Paris from 600,000 to 3.6 million; small country towns turned into conurbations. This growth in Europe was matched by comparable expansion of New York and the midwestern cities of the United States.

The urban centres grew faster than their service infrastructure, and so the industrial revolution became identified with slum housing, malnutrition and cholera, on a scale which remains common in the burgeoning cities of modern developing countries. For most of the workers, however, the change from rural to urban poverty was not the disaster that has often been painted. The poor had always lived on the edge of subsistence; there were indeed reverses, as during the 'hungry forties', but the overall tendency was towards an improvement in living standards. Pasteur's discovery of the germ causation of disease stimulated major sewage and other sanitation projects in the second half of the century.

The Second Industrial Revolution

The Decline of Britain – Visitors to the Great Exhibition, which was held in London in 1851, would not have readily recognized that the age of British industrial supremacy was already nearing its end. Britain possessed half the world's mileage of railway lines, and half its merchant marine. Five years later, the British inventor, Henry Bessemer, would present his Convertor, which made possible the mass production of steel. The nation's lead still appeared unassailable.

In hindsight it is possible to recognize the signs of decay. Too much investment lay in the industries of the first industrial revolution, which were vulnerable to competition from low cost countries; the educational system, both for the rich and poor was ill equipped to train in the more technical skills needed to meet the ever growing complexities of industry; British industry was already at times failing to capitalize on the skills of the inventors.

Germany and the United States – In the second half of the century two powers demonstrated great economic potential. German military expenditure funded the expansion of the mighty firm of Alfred Krupp, which was soon competing with British companies for the supply of railway and shipyard equipment. The electric dynamo was invented simultaneously in Britain and Germany, but the German firm of Siemens reaped the benefits. In 1885 Carl Benz produced the first working automobile using the internal combustion engine, so initiating the greatest transport revolution in the world's history.

The United States was also showing both creativity and economic power. Inventive geniuses, like Bell and Edison, found that the young nation, with its growing market base, provided an ideal environment for the exploitation of new technology. The telegraph, the telephone, the domestic sewing machine, mechanised agricultural machines, the safety lift, air conditioning, the electric light, the phonograph, the cine camera and the aeroplane were all American contributions to the more sophisticated second phase of industrialisation. Andrew Carnegie and Henry Ford also showed the American capacity to build great operations on the inventions of others.

Capital and Labour

Trades Unions – Throughout history, there had always been a sharp divide between the rich and the poor, but the working people within the new factory system became acutely aware of the polarization between those who owned the means of production and their employees. By gathering workers together in large units of production, the owners made it practicable for them to organize in defence of their living conditions.

Robert Owen, a working man turned successful cotton master, attempted to establish a model industrial society at New Lanark, Scotland; he introduced schools and all kinds of leisure activities for the working people, and still was able to show a profit for the mill. He became dissatisfied with this paternalistic approach and set up a co-operative venture in New Harmony in America. This proved less successful, and he returned to Britain, where he founded the ambitious Grand National Consolidated Trades Union. This was a bid to harness the power of the working people, so that they could control the industries in which they worked. Owen's union failed, as did most of the early attempts to organize labour. Unskilled workers, faced by organized management, lacked credible bargaining power. Over much of Europe, they were further weakened by being divided between opposing Christian and socialist unions.

The battle between capital and labour could be seen in its rawest state in the United States. The owners mobilized city and state authorities and hired private armies to break strikes. Also there were as yet no anti-trust laws to prevent employers from combining to achieve their objectives. The workers responded by organizing themselves into violent secret societies, like the Molly Macguires of the Pennsylvania coal mines. At Andrew Carnegie's Homestead works at Pittsburgh in 1892, the two sides confronted each other in pitched battle.

At Homestead, as elsewhere, management emerged victorious because there was always unskilled 'blackleg' labour on hand to fill the jobs of those who went on strike. At the end of the century, however, there emerged a new generation of union leaders who recognized that progress could best be made by organizing the skilled labour, which was now vital for the more sophisticated industries. In The United States, in 1886, Samuel Gompers organized these skilled trades into the more successful American Federation of Labour. In the years which followed, the rights of organized labour were increasingly recognized by the legal systems of the industrialized nations.

Socialism – During the time that Robert Owen was experimenting with new structures, continental thinkers were beginning to challenge the laissez-faire theories of Adam Smith. Most influential was the French nobleman, Claude de Saint-Simon, often looked on as the founder of socialism, who published his critique of the new industrial age in the 1820s. He argued for the replacement of the existing ruling elite by a 'meritocracy', which would manage the economy for the general good of the population, rather than for individual gain.

Saint-Simon's ideas gained ground in France. In 1848 Paris experienced two distinct revolutions. The first unseated the king; the second was a bloody confrontation between workers, proclaiming the new socialists ideas, and the bourgeoisie, who defended traditional property rights.

Communism – Karl Marx watched the destruction of the Paris workers in 1848 with distress but without surprise. He had been associated with the revolutionary movement in his native Germany before being forced into exile. He believed that history showed two struggles. The first, as in all earlier revolutions, had been between the feudal authorities and the bourgeoisie. The second, in his own day, lay between the bourgeoisie and the proletariat.

Marx held that the value of goods lay in the labour which had been expended in its production, and the interests of the proletariat lay in winning a fair return for that labour. That was in conflict with the interests of the owners, or bourgeoisie, who were dedicated to achieving a profit on the product. Within a capitalist society the proletariat was therefore alienated from the production process, and both sides were inevitably locked in class war. The objective for the proletariat was to win control of the machinery of government by revolution, and then to use the new communist state to control the 'commanding heights of the economy' – land, transport, factories and banks.

Marx and his friends tried to gather the revolutionary movement into the unity without which he believed it could never be effective. In 1864 the First International of the Communist party was held in London, with delegations from France, Germany, Italy, Switzerland and Poland, as well as Britain. The party, however, early showed its capacity for splitting into factions. When, by the beginning of the next century, none of the great industrial nations had fallen, many thought that the communist challenge had passed away. It was not anticipated that the revolution would come in Russia which, under Marx's definition, still lay within the feudal stage of development.

Change and Society

Education – The movement for educational reform can be traced to the late 18th century, but another century had to pass before change affected the lives of working people. In Germany and the United States, and later in Japan, politicians recognized that, if a nation were to remain competitive in the new world, it needed an educated labour force. All across the industrial world there was a huge increase, not only in basic education but in the provision of higher education. Literacy and numeracy were at last seen as functional skills, rather than as the prerogative of a privileged elite.

The Women's Movement – Before the middle of the 19th century individual voices had been raised to protest against the subjugation of women in western society, but the origin of a formal movement can be placed in 1848, the year of revolutions. In that year a group of women, with men supporters, met at Seneca Falls in New York State and laid out a programme which was to be the blueprint for the women's movement. The resolutions demanded voting rights, equality before the law, the right to hold property, justice in marriage, equal opportunity in education, free access to jobs and an end to the pervasive double standard in morality. The political struggle became identified with the names of Susan Anthony in the USA and later with the Pankhurst family in Britain. Many advances were made, particularly in educational provision, but the radical change came with World War One. Women who undertook a wide range of men's work could no longer be denied basic rights.

Leisure – Towards the end of the century working hours began to be reduced and, perhaps for the first time in history, the less privileged found themselves with time for leisure activities. Virtually all the major sports, which are popular across the world today, were codified during these decades, and this happened mainly in Britain, where the industrial achievements brought the earliest benefits. By the beginning of the 20th century, the bicycle and the railway excursion were giving urban dwellers a new sense of freedom. Many problems remained, but those who lived in the industrial societies experienced a genuine improvement in the quality of life. This improvement made the programmes of the revolutionaries less attractive than Karl Marx and his followers had anticipated.

AMERICA

The Birth of the United States

The Causes of Conflict – When the Seven Years War ended in 1763 it appeared that Britain had achieved her aims in the New World. The French colonies in Canada had fallen under British rule and the stranglehold on the Thirteen Colonies by French forts on the Ohio River had been broken. Very shortly, however, it became clear that strains were building up in the relationships between the American colonists and the mother country.

Under the mercantilist system, it was taken for granted that the colonies existed for the benefit of the other country. As American economies strengthened, however, they began to generate their own momentum. Slaving ships from New England, for instance, now competed directly with those from Bristol on the Guinea Coast.

The American colonists had already developed the westward momentum, which remains a feature of the nation today. Pioneers were penetrating into the rich lands to the west of the Appalachians. Britain, as the colonizing power, was responsible for security, and the London government therefore had to decide whether to expand budgets to provide protection to these pioneers. To the annoyance of many colonists, a decision was taken that a limit should be drawn along the ridge of the Appalachians. The government further decided that the American colonies should be taxed to help pay security costs. When the traditional colonial assemblies refused to vote the funds, the British government decided to establish the principle of its right to impose direct taxation. The Stamp Act, the Sugar Act and the duty on tea were all stages in the deteriorating relationships. None were in themselves onerous, but they created genuine anxiety. Sugar molasses, for instance, was turned into rum which was the staple of the slave trade. Any tax could be used to make American ships uncompetitive with their British rivals.

Independence – Tension centred on the largest city and trading port of Boston, where fighting started in 1775. In the following year representatives from the Thirteen colonies, now to become states, met in Philadelphia to declare themselves independent.

The famous and highly influential Declaration of Independence, drafted by Thomas Jefferson, justified the act of rebellion in terms which drew from Locke and the *philosophes*. It declared that government derives from the consent of the governed and the misgovernment, listed in detail, broke that tie of consent.

The colonists faced serious problems in organizing themselves to fight a major European power; there was little natural unity, and money to fund the conflict proved as hard to raise as it had been under British rule. American success was largely the result of the outstanding leadership qualities of George Washington and the ability of the colonists to adapt to a guerilla style of warfare, well suited to the heavily forested terrain. In 1781, the British army surrendered at Yorktown and two years later, Britain accepted defeat.

The Constitution – It was not immediately clear, however, whether one or thirteen new nations had emerged from the conflict. Many of Washington's army remained unpaid and no mechanism existed for a central government to raise money from the states. The Constitutional Convention of 1787 was faced with serious division between the interests of large and of small states, and between those who wanted to see a strong central government and those who preferred to see real power continue to lie with the individual states. The final document, which was ratified in 1788, steered a compromise course between the interests. The Executive, Legislature and Judiciary all had their own spheres of responsibility, and acted as a control on one another by a complex structure of checks and balances.

Canada

The successful rebellion by the American colonies left the British government reluctant to expend further effort and resources on colonization. Many loyalists from the south had moved north, and the division between the French and English population remained deep. The colonies covered much sparsely populated territory and communications remained poor. The people were united only in a common hostility to any threat of annexation by the more powerful neighbour to the south.

In the first half of the 19th century, progress was made towards the establishment of a confederacy. In 1867 The British North America Act brought together four provinces into a federal Dominion of Canada. To protect minority French interests, language and education remained provincial concerns and other provinces joined the federation in subsequent years. In 1885 the last rivet was driven into the Canadian Pacific Line, bringing together east and west and opening up the prairies for agricultural development.

Latin America

To the south, the countries of Latin America remained under the colonial control of Spain and Portugal. The successful rebellion of the British colonies was shortly followed by the collapse of the old monarchies in the face of Napoleon's army. Links with the old countries were cut during the European wars, and this generated an outburst of nationalist fervour.

Spain fought a series of devastating wars to recover control of her American empire. In 1810, the Mexican priest Manuel Hidalgo y Costilla led the poor in a rising, but independence was not finally won until 1821. Power then passed, not to the poor, but to the wealthy classes of Spanish descent. Rulers like Santa Anna treated the country as a personal *hacienda*, and the situation of the poor became, if anything, worse than it had been in colonial days.

In 1811 Venezuela declared its independence under the 'Great Liberator', Simon Bolivar. He had travelled in Europe and was particularly influenced by the writings of Voltaire, and he now saw himself as the George Washington who would bring unity to the Spanish speaking countries of South America. He won a series of victories against Spain and independence seemed assured, provided the conservative European powers did not follow Metternich's plan and intervene to uphold the old order. This was prevented by American President Monroe, who warned off any intervention by proclaiming his doctrine of 'hands off America'.

Bolivar seemed on the verge of creating a United Republic of Columbia, which could be a comparable power to the U. S. A. He was, however, unable to hold the new country together, and one part of the country after another broke off to form new nations. As in Mexico, the privileged classes preserved power to themselves. The European nations competed to invest, particularly in Argentina, and there was a steady stream of immigration from the Old World, but the old inequalities remained, and the economies of many of the new Latin American countries became dangerously dependent on single primary products.

The path to independence was smoother in Brazil. The Portuguese royal family decided not to defend its rights, and in 1822 the country was declared an independent empire by consent. Here too old social inequalities remained and, as late as 1888, Brazil was the last American country to abolish the Atlantic slave trade.

Slavery and the Civil War

King Cotton – Dr Samuel Johnson spoke for many when he poured scorn on American ideals of liberty, which were denied to the black slave population. The continuance of the institution was one of the issues discussed in the Constitutional Convention. There were three broad points of view. Opponents of slavery wished to see the institution outlawed in the new nation; representatives of the southern states would not contemplate joining a union which deprived them of their property; moderates, like Washington himself, opposed slavery, but they believed that they could let history take its course. Slavery, they argued, was outdated and it would wither away of its own accord. Events proved them wrong.

The new English cotton mills created an insatiable demand for raw cotton. The native short staple cotton was an uneconomic crop until in 1793 Eli Whitney invented a gin, which enabled it to be cleaned in large quantities. In the decades which followed huge areas of the south was given over to cotton cultivation. This created a demand for slaves. The Atlantic slave trade was declared illegal, but many were smuggled into the country; others were 'sold down the river' by plantation owners from the more northerly slave states.

This resurgence of slavery led to widespread unrest. Slave risings broke out and an increasing number of slaves used the freedom road to escape north. White and black activists combined in a highly organized anti-slavery movement. Anger rose when in 1850 Congress passed the Fugitive Slave Law, which gave southern owners the right to pursue their property into the free northern states.

Slave and Free States – The House of Representatives, elected by population, was dominated by the free states. The Senate was more finely balanced. As new states were added to the Union, the balance was maintained. California and Oregon tilted the balance towards the free states. 'Bleeding' Kansas, a fierce bone of contention, fell to the slave party. When, in 1860, a republican from

Illinois called Abraham Lincoln was elected president, the slave states felt that the political balance had swung irretrievably against them. In March 1861 eleven southern states declared their secession from the Union and the following month they attacked the federal Fort Sumter. *The Civil War.* Over 600,000 men died in the four years of war which followed. The southern armies were highly motivated and generally well commanded, but they were bound to lose a long war of attrition. The industrial north had a larger population, more industrial production and more miles of railway. This was the first major war in history fought with armaments which were the products of the industrial revolution, and great battles, like Antietam and Gettysburg presaged the terrible loss of life at Verdun and on the Somme half a century later. When the war ended in April 1865, the south lay devastated. Lincoln was assassinated five days later.

Civil Rights – The war had been fought over the right of the south to secede from the Union. Slavery was abolished in the process. Lincoln's emancipation decree was given the force of law by the Thirteenth Amendment of 1865 and further amendments wrote civil rights into the constitution. In the years of reconstruction black legislators took their seats and it appeared as though political and social equality might be close. Gradually, however, by a process of manipulation and terrorisation, the white supremacists regained control of the southern states. The liberal fervour of the anti-slavery years was now spent, and the Supreme Court proved unwilling to uphold even most clearly defined constitutional rights. Disillusioned, many blacks migrated to the booming industrial cities of the north, where they encountered new forms of discrimination.

The situation only began to improve with the great Civil Rights movement of the 1960s, when Dr Martin Luther King provided a rallying point for his people's aspirations and liberal white sympathizers were again mobilized, as they had been a century before in the anti-slavery campaign.

The Westward Movement

Thomas Jefferson – Of all the founding fathers, Jefferson had the clearest vision that the new nation could become a great power, and that this had to be based on an exploitation of the great potential of the continent. He was the architect of the system whereby new states could be added to the Union. By 1803

Napoleon had decided that the Mississippi lands of Louisiana, which remained French, were of no value and Jefferson, now president, negotiated to buy them for $15,000,000 – and so double the land area of the United States. In 1804 he sent out an expedition led by Lewis and Clark to cross the continent and report back on its potential.

Jefferson's vision of the west as the land of opportunity gradually captured the American imagination. It was argued that the American people – by which was meant the white American people – had a 'manifest destiny' to possess the continent from the Atlantic to the Pacific Oceans.

The Dispossession of the Indian People – During the early years of the 19th century, Americans of European origin were pushing into traditional Indian territory beyond the Appalachians. Every expedient was used, from purchase to forced expulsion, to drive the Indian people back into the western grasslands, which remained unattractive to white settlement.

The nomadic buffalo culture of the plains Indians was based on horses originally acquired form the southern Spanish settlements, and it was therefore a comparatively recent development. In the middle of the century, migrants were attracted, not to the featureless plains with their extremes of climate, but to the far west. For a brief period, wagon trains and nomadic Indians were able to coexist. By the 1870s, however, the white men began to move into these last hunting grounds. The buffalo were hunted, depriving the Indian people of their livlihood and providing food for railway construction workers; then the railway link with the eastern markets made the grasslands attractive for cattle farming. Finally new agricultural machinery and irrigation techniques made large scale wheat farming economic. With buffalo herds destroyed and their whole way of life undermined, the surviving Indian people were driven back into ever more arid and infertile reservations.

Oregon Country – Lewis and Clark reported on fertile land on the Pacific coast around the mouth of the Columbia River. Many Americans were prepared to go to war with Britain over British Columbia, but agreement was reached on the 49th parallel boundary. This left ample scope for colonization in the north west. The wagon trains which followed the Oregon trail brought farming families into this attractive region.

The South West – The new Mexican state claimed the whole of the south west of the country, from Texas to California and as far north as Utah and southern Wyoming. Spanish settlement had been based on missions, which were often widely dispersed, and the non-Indian population of the region remained low. Between 1836 and 1847 the United States and Mexico were in an intermittent state of war, which ended with the capture of Mexico City and defeat for Mexico. Under the treaty the United States won the whole of the southwest. Existing property rights of the Spanish speaking people were, in theory, protected, but, in practice, they had no means of protecting them against the newly arrived 'Anglos', who controlled the courts.

Shortly before the treaty was signed, gold was discovered at Sutter's Mill in Northern California. This set off the Gold Rush, which brought fortune hunters flocking to California from the east, and, indeed, from many parts of the world. The influx of population in turn created a farming boom and California was rapidly converted from a thinly populated region, largely consisting of mountains and desert, to the world's most rapidly expanding economy.

Immigration

From Europe – Any measurement of the population rise of Europe from the middle of the 18th to the end of the 19th centuries should properly include, not only statistics on those countries themselves, but also of the millions who emigrated to destinations in many parts of the world – as well as their descendants. Figures can not be collated, but people of European stock took over great areas of the world, often at the expense of the indigenous population.

In order to overcome human reluctance to disrupt living patterns, there needs to be a 'push factor' propelling people from their homes, and a 'pull factor' drawing them to a new environment. As in the early years of colonization, the growing wealth of the United States drew economic, political and religious refugees from Europe. The British still came. Many of the Mormons who pulled their handcarts across the plains to Utah originated from among the cotton mills of Lancashire. The depopulation of the Scottish glens provided a new stream, although most preferred to go to Canada. The Catholic Irish, angered by English protestant rule and by unjust land laws had long been ready recruits; the disastrous potato famine of 1845-6, which is estimated to have claimed the lives of a million people, turned the stream into a flood.

People now came from new countries of origin. Norwegian families, long accustomed to extremes of climate, left their marginal fiord farms to farm in the harsh environment of Wisconsin and the Dakotas. Germans fled from the political and social upheavals of their country. Peasants from southern Italy, condemned to live on the brink of subsistence under rapacious landlords, took the boat to America. Towards the end of the century, people were coming from further east. Russian Jews fled the pogroms; Poles fled Russian oppression. All funnelled through Ellis Island to emerge, often penniless, and speaking no English, onto the streets of New York. They worked as they could, in clothing sweatshops, on construction, in domestic service. Each new national group faced discrimination as those who were settled in jobs and homes tried to protect their position from the work-hungry newcomers.

The New Immigration – The capture of the south west brought a significant Spanish speaking population within the United States. Civil war in Mexico and an increasing divergency of the standards of living brought an increasing number of immigrants across the border. Most came as migrant workers, following the crops into California and far beyond. In good times, they were welcomed as cheap labour, but in times of depression they proved easy targets for discrimination. In the 20th century immigrants from Puerto Rico and other Caribbean islands have also increased the Hispanic population of the eastern side of the country.

Asian immigration began when Chinese labourers were recruited to work in the 1849 Gold Rush. Distinctive in those early days in their 'queues' and national clothing, they found themselves at the bottom of the immigrant 'heap', increasingly shut out from desirable employment and property ownership by Chinese Exclusion Acts. They, like subsequent Asian immigrants, preserved a respect for education, which enabled them to improve their status rapidly when the legal discrimination was brought to an end.

The United States Abroad

The Continent – The Monroe Doctrine was originally proclaimed to protect emerging Latin nation seeking to establish independence from European colonial powers. In the later years of the century it was used to promote the continent as a sphere of U.S. interest.

One major thrust lay through the Caribbean towards South America. In 1903 effective control over the Isthmus of Panama was wrested from Columbia and the Panama Canal linking the two oceans was opened in 1914. War with Spain in 1898 also ended with the acquisition of Puerto Rico and Cuba.

American interests also led expansion across the Pacific. Alaska was purchased from Russia in 1867, providing the west-ward bridge of the Aleutian Islands. Midway Island was won in the same year, followed by Samoa and the Hawaiian group. The war with Spain finally brought Guam and the Philippines within the American empire.

Although the United States was no longer a new country, the need to absorb waves of immigrants fostered an introversion and at times an aggressive nationalism. Many American statesmen, wishing to distance their country from what they saw as the de-structive quarrels of the old world, proclaimed a policy of isola-tionism. The history of the 20th century was to show that the world's greatest power could not successfully stand back from international events.

THE AGE OF IMPERIALISM

India

The East India Company – The battles in the 18th century be-tween rival trading companies were fought, not to win territory, but to establish trading advantage. In 1757, however, the British East India Company's army in Bengal first captured the French trading station and then defeated the Nawab's army at Plassey. The company then found itself, by default, the inheritor of Mogul power. Now irretrievably involved in politics, it gradually ex-tended its control over large areas of the sub-continent.

Company officials never lost sight of the fact that their objec-tive was to turn in a profit. As the company extended its control over all internal as well as external trade, the standard of living of many Indians declined. Company officials took the opportunity of amassing private fortunes, often by corrupt means. In the days before steam ships and the opening of the Suez Canal, India was far distant from home. Men travelled out as bachelors and many took local women and lived much as Indian princes.

After the American revolution, the British government was reluctant to become involved in further colonial expansion. To bring the Company under control, however, it assumed dual control of the Indian possessions in 1784. The writings of Adam Smith had discredited the old mer-cantilist ideas, which had been the justification for early colonization. In line with prevailing doctrines of free trade, the company therefore lost its monopoly trading rights and was reduced to an administrative organization.

Modernization – The evangelical fervour of the age brought protestant missionaries of many denominations to the sub-continent. Most had a simple desire to replace the traditional religions of Hinduism and Islam. They started schools which offered western education and encouraged converts to adopt western dress and habits. These missionaries looked to the Christian rulers for protection and active encouragement.

The new generation of administrators was less directly motivated by the profit motive and more by a desire to bring the benefits of modern life to the people of India. Many had a genuine, albeit paternalistic, respect for Indian culture, and they resisted the missionaries' attempt to overturn traditional ways. These administrators did, however, believe in reform. Laws, based on western practice, were introduced to stamp out traditional practices, such as the burning of widows and the killing of infant girls. The products of the industrial revolution, such as the electric telegraph and railways were also enthusiastically introduced.

The Mutiny – The modernization programme inevitably created tension. Railways, for instance, were looked upon as a threat to the caste system. There was also powerful resentment against British acquisition of new land, particularly in the northern province of Oudh. The introduction of a new form of greased cartridge was the immediate cause of the Indian Mutiny of 1857. This was as much a traditionalist reaction against modernization as it was a rebellion against the ever expanding foreign rule. Many educated Indians, like the operators of the Delhi telegraph, died at the hands of the mutineers. The mutiny was put down with as much ferocity as it had been waged. The British parliament at last accepted direct responsibility for government. In 1877 Queen Victoria was proclaimed Empress of India and rule over the sub-continent became the symbol of British power. The true age of imperialism had begun.

The Raj – The new rulers determined that mistakes which had led to the mutiny should not be repeated. They therefore took care to respect the rights of the traditional ruling class. When early representative institutions were introduced, this ruling class was called upon to represent the Indian people. The aspirations of the rising intelligentsia were therefore overlooked. Indeed, the contempt for the educated 'westernized native' which was to be characteristic of British imperialism, was first shown in India. The first meeting of the Indian National Congress was held in Bombay in 1885, but a further 20 years would pass before independence appeared on the Congress agenda.

Throughout history, India, like China, had shown a capacity to absorb its conquerors; the British alone resisted assimilation. The new rulers of the Indian Civil Service were drawn from the elite and many acquired a knowledge of Indian language and customs, but, in the wake of the Mutiny, a barrier existed between the two races which could not be crossed. Fast and comfortable steam ships now linked Europe and India, and the journey time was much reduced when the Suez Canal opened in 1869. Administrators and traders increasingly kept their roots in Britain, while serving tours of duty overseas. Also men were now joined in India by their womenfolk. Few of these *memsahibs* had work which brought them into contact with Indian people, so their cultural values were never seriously challenged.

In the second half of the century new concepts of racial superiority were fashionable, particularly in northern Europe. Europeans had long treated other races as inferior, but they had not theorised about it. Now concepts of racial superiority were becoming fashionable, partly based on popular Darwinianism. The European rulers of India, as of other colonized people, were therefore ill equipped to understand the nationalist aspirations when they did come to the surface.

China
The Manchu Empire – In the middle of the 17th century, invaders from Manchuria overthrew the Ming emperor and established the foreign Manchu (Ch'ing) Dynasty. Following the ancient pattern, the early rulers were able men who established a working relationship with the mandarin administrators, and for more than a century the land experienced one of its more prosperous periods.

By the end of the 18th century, however, problems were growing. It is estimated that the population trebled, from 100 to 300 million between 1650 and 1800, and it would reach 420 million by 1850. In China, Malthus' forecasts on the effects of population growth proved accurate. All available land was already under cultivation, so production could not match increased demand. The situation became disastrous in the terrible northern famine of 1887-9, when some ten million people starved to death. As social problems became worse, so the quality of imperial government deteriorated into corruption and mismanagement. Resentment boiled and people remembered that the Manchu were a foreign race.

In 1786 rebellion broke out in Shantung, and this was followed in 1795 by the White Lotus Uprising on the borders of Szechwan and Shensi. These were the preludes of a century of peasant unrest on a scale far beyond anything experiences in human history before that time. It is estimated, for instance, that more people died in the T'ai-p'ing Rebellion of 1850-64 than World War One, while huge Islamic risings of the north and south west left wide areas of the country devastated. The Manchu Dynasty, however, managed to cling to power through all these upheavals.

China and the West – Since the earliest times, China had always had a favourable balance of trade with Europe. There was a demand in the West of porcelain and silks, but, apart from a few clocks and toys, Europe had little to offer in return. Towards the end of the 18th century the balance took a turn for the worse. There was a fashion in Europe for Chinoiserie, reflected in some of the art of the period. More important, tea became the staple drink of many Europeans. This could only be bought by a steady drain of bullion.

Western merchants were convinced a huge Chinese market, was waiting to be opened up, but contact was strictly controlled through a few merchants in Canton. Attempts to open the market ended in frustration. In 1793 George III of Britain sent an emissary to the Manchu court with gifts. The Emperor thanked King George for his "submissive loyalty in sending this tribute mission" from "the lonely remoteness of your island, cut off from the world by intervening wastes of sea", but the mission achieved nothing of substance.

The Opium Wars – In the early years of the 19th century British traders found that the drug opium could right the adverse balance of trade. A great deal of Indian farmland was placed under the crop and the flow of bullion into China was quickly reversed. Apart from the direct damage done by the opium, the Chinese government found that the drain of wealth quickly created financial crisis. The opium trade was a breach of Chinese law, and in 1839 a large quantity was destroyed. In the following First Opium War the Chinese forces proved ill equipped to fight a modern war, and they were defeated. In 1842, China was forcedly opened up to foreign trade and missions, and Britain won control of the trading outpost of Hong Kong.

Thirteen years later, the British Prime Minister, Lord Palmerston, decided to assert British authority once again. His declared policy that half civilized governments such as those of China "all need a dressing every eight or ten years to keep them in order" made him popular at home. He was prepared to defend British citizens against the valid operation of foreign law and in 1856 he defied parliament to take Britain, with French help, to war with China again. The imperial army was weakened by the T'ai-p'ing Rebellion and in 1860 the allied army marched into Peking and burned the Imperial palace.

European Influence and Reaction – Although China herself remained nominally independent, her influence in Asia was much reduced. Russia used the British and French invasion as a cover for occupying the northern Amur river, so winning the Pacific outlet of Valdivostok; Britain won Burma, against fierce local opposition; France defeated Chinese armies to win Indo-China; Korea won its independence, later to fall to Japan; Japan conquered Taiwan; even the United States closed in by conquering the Philippines, again in the face of fierce nationalist resistance. Within China itself, the European powers jockeyed for privileges. Even more threateningly, the country was now open to western missionaries who, along with the Christian gospel, brought cultural assumptions profoundly at odds with traditional Confucian values.

The End of the Manchu Empire – By the last years of the century the ancient civilization was in collapse. In 1898 the young emperor and his advisers decided that China must follow the Japanese example and adopt western ways. The experiment was short lived as the dowager Empress led the faction of reaction. She imprisoned the emperor and gave support to the xenophobic Boxers, who were attacking mission stations and other western interests across the country, and the embassy area of Peking was besieged. The western powers replied by sending a combined army to relieve the city. Still the Manchu rulers clung to power, but they were threatened from two directions. The army war lords were now unreliable, and outside the country, young foreign educated men plotted to overthrow the dynasty. In 1911-2 the two combined to bring down the Manchu Dynasty. The foreign educated Sun Yat-sen became president, but one year later he gave way to one of the military commanders.

Japan

The Shogunate – In 1603, at a time when the imperial family had lost effective power, the military leader, or Shogun, Tokugawa Ieyasu established power over the whole of Japan. In the centuries which followed, the Tokugawa shogunate closed Japan off from the outside world. The Japanese were prohibited from travelling abroad; Jesuit missionaries were expelled and their converts persecuted; only a few Dutch traders were allowed to operate from the city of Nagasaki. For Japanese urban entrepreneurs, however, the cost was a small price to pay for the peace and prosperity brought by the powerful shoguns. Educational reforms created a high level of literacy and a vigorous free enterprise economy was permitted to flourish in the growing towns. The growing prosperity of the towns was not matched in the countryside, where both the traditional lords, and the peasants tended to become poorer.

The Opening of Japan – In 1854 the navy officer, Matthew Perry, was commissioned by the President of the U. S. A. to open up the Japanese market. His Treaty of Kanagawa brought the years of isolation to an end. The shogunate did not long survive it, and the Emperor resumed direct power in 1868. There was now a fierce debate within Japan as to whether the country should adopt western ways wholeheartedly, or follow the example of China and remain separate. The reformers were able to point to the disastrous results of conservative policies, as applied in China. The largest feudal families voluntarily surrendered their rights and the government systematically set about the modernization of their country. The changes were based on the solid structure, bequeathed by the Tokugawa shogunate, but there remains no example in history of a comparable change in social life within a single generation. By 1900 an advanced system of state education had been constructed, western experts were imported to train the people in engineering, and young Japanese students were sent to study overseas. At first the new industries, like textiles and shipbuilding, were faithful copies of western prototypes, but they gained an increasing share in world markets. By the 1920s Japan was a formidable industrial competitor to the European nations.

Japanese Expansionism – The era of peace had left the samurai caste deprived of employment. They bequeathed an aggressive nationalism to the new state. The Japanese also recognized that European world domination had been based the use of force. The now popular motto 'Asia for the Asians' was intended as a Munroe Doctrine for a Japanese sphere of influence.

Russian power was particularly menacing. The transcontinental railway had now reached Vladivostok, and the Russians were showing interest in the newly independent Korea. In 1902 Japan concluded a treaty with Britain, which provided security against intervention and two years later she attacked Russian shipping in the Manchurian Port Arthur. The city fell in January of the next year and the Russian Baltic fleet was destroyed in the Tsushima Straits in May.

This victory of an Asian over an essentially European power in the Russo-Japanese War marked the end of the European military domination of the world, which had survived since the 15th century. In the years which followed, Japan continued to build an empire, first by the annexation of Korea and then by the acquisition of wide Chinese lands. These conquests were accepted as a fait accompli by the European powers at the Treaty of Versailles in 1919.

The Pacific

The Aborigines of Australia – Some time before 50,000 years ago great ice caps in the polar regions made the world's seas lower than they are today. The Indonesian islands formed a great peninsula, and Australia was joined to Tasmania and New Guinea in a single land mass. At this time the ancestors of the Australian aborigines arrived in their isolated home. Despite the lower waters, they had still crossed a wide stretch of ocean, making them possibly the world's first seafaring people. These early settlers brought their dogs, but the other animals would have provided a strange sight to people accustomed to the fauna of Asia. In their new home, they adopted a hunter-gatherer lifestyle, delicately in balance with the unique environment.

The Polynesians – Much later, some 4-3,000 years ago, a different race of people began to spread out across the islands of the Pacific Ocean. The methods by which they navigated their great canoes are little understood; they probably followed the paths of migrating birds, and it is suggested that they could feel the current off distant land masses on the surface of the water with their hands. Certainly they made successful voyages of up to 2000 miles to colonize unknown islands. It appears that they went via Fiji and Samoa to the remote Marquesas Islands, from where they fanned out, north to Hawaii, south east to Easter Island and south west to New Zealand, which they called Ao-te-roa, or Long White Cloud. The earliest settlers were probably fleeing from war, but in time warfare followed them to their new homes.

The Arrival of the Europeans – Australian aborigines and Polynesian islanders alike were for long protected from European ships by unfavourable trade winds. In the 17th century several Dutch sailors, operating from the East Indes, made voyages in the area, but they were not attracted by what they saw as the region offered no prospect of profitable trade. In 1770 the English Captain James Cook sailed along the east coast of Australia and landed at Botany Bay. He later commanded two more voyages through the Pacific Islands. The sailors found the Pacific island societies to be living examples of the 'noble savage' existence, extolled by writers such as Rousseau – and bequeathed the devastations of syphilis to the islanders.

Australia

The Penal Colony – The war with the American colonies shut Britain off from the penal colonies of Georgia and the Carolinas, and so gave the British government the problem of how to dispose of its surplus criminal population. As long as the war was in progress, convicts were kept in hulks, moored in river estuaries.

One of those who had landed off Cook's ship in Botany Bay was a geographer and scientist, called Joseph Banks. In the years which followed he had become the driving force behind an exploration movement, intended to open new areas of the world to British trade. Banks argued the case for establishing a penal colony in Botany Bay. The land was good, he argued, the climate mild and the natives few in number.

The first convoy sailed in 1787, under the command of Captain Arthur Phillip, carrying 571 male and 159 female convicts, supervised by over 200 marines. Most of those transported were hard core criminals, but there were also a significant number of political prisoners, particularly from rebellious Ireland. Large numbers of enforced immigrants suffered dreadfully on the long journey and in the penal settlements, and many continued to nurse resentment against the 'old country' and the forces of law and order.

Exploration – By the end of the century it was established that New South Wales in the east was linked to New Holland in the West in a single continent. In 1813 pioneers crossed the Great Dividing Range, which hemmed in the eastern coastal plain to discover the broad grasslands of the interior. By 1859 the landmass of the continent had been divided into six colonies.

It is said that, when these first white men appeared on the central plain, an aborigine scrambled into a tree and let out a long, high-pitched shriek. The establishment of European civilization in Australia was an immense achievement, but, yet again, the heaviest price would be paid by indigenous people in the age-old clash of interests between nomadic hunter-gatherers and settled agriculturalists.

Economic growth – The earliest settlers did not readily find cash crops to make the colony self sufficient. Lieutenant John Macarthur is credited with recognizing the immense potential of the interior for sheep farming. He developed new breeds which would flourish in the New South Wales grasslands and was able to live in the style of an English country gentleman. His example was followed by emancipated convicts and a new generation of free settlers. The influx of cheap Australian wool to the home country stimulated the Yorkshire woollen industry at a time when woollen fabrics were gaining popularity in world markets. Towards the end of the 19th century the development of refrigerated ships boosted the meat trade. Then, in the early years of the 20th century, strains of wheat were developed to suit the dry climate.

It was also early established that the continent possessed great mineral wealth. Gold and copper mines were in operation by the middle of the 19th century, and the great Broken Hills complex was opened up in 1883. Despite such development in the interior, the cities proved to be the main beneficiaries. By 1901, 65 per cent of the population lived in the six capital cities.

Political Development – Progress with self-government in Canada encouraged the British government to devolve increasing political responsibility in its colonies of European settlement. In 1901 the six colonies became states to form the Commonwealth of Australia. Old links proved decisive when Australian soldiers fought with the British army in the wars of the 20th century.

During World War Two, however, the nation's leaders, recognizing that Britain could contribute little against an expansionist Japan, turned to the United States for support. Since the war, extensive non-British immigration into Australia, and the increasing orientation of Britain towards Europe has further weakened traditional ties.

New Zealand

European Settlement – In 1814 a group of missionaries arrived in the land which had been described by Captain Cook. It is estimated that, at that time there was a population of about a quarter of a million Maori people, who had lived in complete isolation for many centuries. In 1839 Edmund Gibbon Wakefield established the New Zealand Company, with a view to buying land off the tribes and organizing settlements. The British government, hoping to control the movement, formally annexed the country in the following year.

The British proclaimed equality between Maori and European people, but practice never matched theory, and the colonists' land hunger provoked the Land War of 1845-8. After further settlers arrived, many from Scotland, war broke out again in the 1860s. By 1870 the Maori people had effectively lost control of their land.

Constitution and Economy – The country was granted a constitution in 1852 and in 1907 it became a self governing dominion within the British Empire. Its dependence on agriculture, however, left it heavily dependant on the British economy. Early prosperity was based on wool and gold, but the introduction of refrigerated shipping in the last years of the 19th century favoured low cost New Zealand farmers, at the expense of their British competitors. This brought a period of prosperity, and ties with Britain were reinforced by disproportionate contribution made in two world wars. As with Australia, these have weakened in the second half of the 20th century, during which time the country has suffered from its heavy dependence on primary products.

Japan and The United States

By 1914 Britain was withdrawing from direct involvement in the Pacific region but neither the emerging Australia or New Zealand were showing potential as a regional power. The Dutch still controlled the East Indes, modern Indonesia, but only at the cost of a series of major struggles against an emerging nationalism on Bali, Sumatra, and Java. Two powers now faced each other; the United States, with forward bases in Samoa, Guam and the Philippines, and the emerging power of Japan. The foundations of a major regional conflict were already laid.

North Africa

Egypt – In classical times, North Africa had been an integral part of Mediterranean civilization. After the early flowering of Islamic civilization, however, it became increasingly cut off from the countries on the northern, Christian shore of the inland sea. Egypt was for centuries isolated under mameluke rule. When Napoleon led an army into Egypt in 1798, he took with him not only fighting men, but also scholars, who would be able to interpret the remains of the country's fabled ancient civilization.

French interest in the area survived the fall of Napoleon, and, when Mehemet Ali broke the power of the mamelukes and established effective independence from Ottoman rule, French influence remained powerful. Under Mehemet Ali and his grandson Ishmael, Egyptian power was taken south into the Sudan and along the Red Sea. Ishmael contracted with France for the construction of the Suez Canal, which was opened in 1869. He staved off financial collapse, however, by selling a controlling interest in the canal to Britain, who now controlled this lifeline to India. In 1881 the Egyptian government was threatened by a nationalist rising in Egypt and by the Mahdi in the Sudan, and Britain responded by sending a force to protect the canal. It was not intended as an army of occupation, but Britain became involved in a protracted war in the Sudan and in administering a protectorate over Egypt.

Algeria – The coast of Algeria to the west was had long been the home of Barbary pirates. In the 1830s, France began a major advance into the area. The pirates were driven from their harbours, and the French moved south to the Atlas mountains. Here they met fierce resistance, led by Abd el Kadir, but they won control of the mountain passes. Military success was followed by an influx of French settlers into the coastal region.

Sub-Saharan Africa

An Unknown Continent – For centuries the interior of Africa had been viewed by the outside world as little more than a source of human merchandise. European merchants had shipped slaves by the million out of the west coast; Bedu and Tuareg tribesmen had driven them across the Sahara to the markets of North Africa; they had been carried across the Red Sea in dhows by Arab traders; they had been beaten into submission by Dutch settlers in the south. The slave trade had had a profoundly brutalising effect on African life, far beyond the boundaries of foreign exploration.

Yet in the early 19th century, Africa had its own political movements. In the grasslands of West Africa, an aggressive Islam was expanding in Hausaland under the Fulani Uthman dan Fodio and in Futa Jallon, under Al-hajj Umar. Far away, in the south west, the Bantu people were experiencing a period of unrest. Shaka founded the Zulu kingdom in 1818, setting neighbouring people on the move.

European Explorers and Missionaries – In the early days of the industrial revolution, there was a general view, vigorously fostered by Joseph Banks, that Africa was a land of unbounded wealth, which offered untapped opportunities for trade. Since Britain had most to sell, British interests funded the earliest explorers. Early explorers, such as Mungo Park, acted as commercial travellers, carrying samples of Lancashire textiles and other manufactures. Results were disappointing but some solid business was established on the coast in products such as palm oil.

By the middle of the century European interest was increasingly focused on 'the dark continent', and explorers, such as David Livingstone and H. M. Stanley became major celebrities. Livingstone maintained an interest in 'legitimate trade', which he hoped would displace the continuing traffic in slaves in Central Africa, but he travelled as a missionary. European civilization had now achieved an unassailable self-confidence. Romantic concepts of the noble savage were forgotten and it was readily assumed that Africa was in need of Christianity, Western customs, and the post-industrial working practices which alone could provide the basis for economic advance.

Explorers, mainly following the routes of the great rivers, penetrated deep into the continent. They were followed by missionaries from a wide range of denominations from Europe and America, who were at times almost as much at competition with each other as they were with traditional practice. Expectation of life for explorers, traders and missionaries in malarial West Africa could be measured in months until quinine was introduced as a prophylactic in the 1840s and even afterwards the coast was still considered unfit for European settlement.

The Scramble for Africa – In 1880 active European political interest in Africa was limited to the French colony in Algeria in the north and the British Cape Colony in the south. The old Portuguese colonies, various ex-slaving trading outposts and settlements of freed slaves retained only tenuous links with Europe. By 1914 in the whole continent, only Ethiopia was a truly independent nation. In the intervening decades the continent was divided up between colonizing powers. Lines were drawn on maps in European capitals; boundaries sometimes followed rivers, often placing a village in one country and its farm land in another. The colonizing movement was in places the focus of national policy; elsewhere it was the product of adventurers or commercial companies working on their own initiative.

The British assumption of control in Egypt provoked the jealousy of other European countries. In particular, the French army was suffering from the humiliation of the defeat at Sedan in 1870. Africa offered a forum for the recovery of lost military prestige.

France and Britain were the main protagonists in the northern half of the continent. French colonization followed two thrusts. The first came south across the Sahara from Algeria into the grasslands of West Africa. The second went east from Senegal along the upper Niger to Lake Chad towards the Nile. The British also had a dual thrust, south from Egypt and north from South Africa. The imperialist Cecil Rhodes dreamed of establishing an unbroken chain of British possessions from the Cape to Cairo. French and British forces met where the thrusts intersected at Fashoda in the southern Sudan in 1898, when for a time it seemed likely that the two countries would be involved in a colonial war.

Meanwhile the British had also established West African colonies, based on their old slaving stations. The Germans were active in West, South West and in East Africa. King Leopold of the Belgians gained control of the Congo as a private venture. This was taken over by the Belgian state in 1908. Spain won control of much of the north western Sahara and shared influence in Morocco with France. Italy belatedly joined the scramble by invading Libya in 1911.

In the early years colonization was largely bloodless, but the process became increasingly violent. Britain faced African revolts as far apart as the Gold Coast and Rhodesia and France the Niger and Madagascar. The brutality of King Leopold's exploitation of the Congo was exposed in 1904. In the same year a major rebellion broke out against the Germans in South West Africa, which ended when they drove the Herero people to virtual extinction in the desert. The Italian invasion of Libya was also conducted with widespread brutality. By the beginning of 1914 the re-drawn map of Africa could be seen as a symbol of a dangerously aggressive and expansionist mood within Europe.

South Africa

The Great Trek – During the Napoleonic Wars Britain occupied the Cape of Good Hope, and the territory was retained, as the Cape Colony, in 1814 for its strategic value in controlling the sea routes to the east. At that time, however, there were no British settlers, the land being shared between nomadic Bushmen and Hottentots and Afrikaner speaking Boers of Dutch and French Huguenot origin. Soon the new government began to bring in thousands of British settlers. The Boers were angered when their black slaves were freed and laws were introduced which they considered to be unduly favourable to the previously subject black people. In 1835 some 10,000 Boers left their homes at the Cape and settled on land of the Vaal and Orange Rivers. More Boers followed when the British annexed their republic of Natal. The settlers set up the new republics of Transvaal and the Orange Free State where they could live free from British interference.

The movement of the Boers from the south coincided with migrations of Bantu people, displaced by the Zulu kingdom. The two people clashed, but the main losers were the native nomadic people, who were driven to a precarious existence in the desert.

The Boer War – Resentment between Boers and the British continued to grow. The British briefly annexed the Transvaal, and, although they withdrew, this left the Boers feeling that they would never be left in peace. Then, in 1886, gold was discovered in the Transvaal, and, within a few years, a new city of Johannesburg had grown to a population of 100,000. Most of the newcomers were British, but they were excluded from the running of the republic. Angry that the world's great empire, the modern Rome, could be frustrated by a small number of intransigent Boer farmers, Cecil Rhodes provoked a confrontation. President Kruger of the Transvaal, an implacable opponent of British rule, responded with an ultimatum, and war broke out in 1899.

Liberal opinion in Britain and Europe saw the Boers as an oppressed minority, and, when they were finally defeated in 1902, there was pressure for a generous settlement. A few voices were raised in the British parliament to defend the rights of the black peoples, but these found no support. In 1909 the four territories were brought together into the self governing Union of South Africa, which lost little time in passing laws which discriminated against the non-white peoples. In 1948 the Afrikaner speaking people won power within the country and put in place the formal structure of apartheid.

THE NATION STATE IN CRISIS

The Eastern Question

The Decline of Ottoman Power – In 1683 armies of the Ottoman empire laid siege to the city of Vienna for the second time and Europe was threatened once more from the East. The armies withdrew, but the Emperor at Istanbul still controlled almost three quarters of the Mediterranean coastline – North Africa, the Arab lands of the Middle East, the homeland of Turkey, Greece and the Balkans.

By the 18th Century statesmen recognized that the Ottoman Empire, like other empires before it, was in decline. Administration was clumsy, and the sultan had to rely on local rulers, whose loyalty was often in doubt. Also, the social military structure of the empire was becoming increasingly out of date.

Russian Objectives – Russian statesmen took the closest interest in the Ottoman decline. Peter the Great had won a warm water port, but, for both trade and strategic reasons, the country still badly needed an outlet into the Mediterranean Sea. In 1768-74 Catherine the Great fought a successful war against the Turks and won the Crimea and other territory on the north bank of the Black Sea along with rights of navigation into the Mediterranean. She also established that Russia had the right to act as protector of eastern Christians within the Turkish dominions.

Russia continued too make advances after the defeat of Napoleon. She won control of the ancestral Ottoman homeland in the grasslands east of the Caspian Sea, taking her empire as far as the mountain passes of the Himalayas. Still further east, she won the

Pacific port of Vladivostok from the Chinese. Russian territorial ambitions were backed by huge military forces, and other European powers perceived her as an aggressive imperial power.

Concern focused on the fate of the Turkish European territories. In a private conversation with the British ambassador, Tsar Nicholas 1 described Turkey as 'the sick man of Europe'. He implied that it would be better for the powers to consider how to share the sick man's possessions, rather than to wait and fight over them when he died. Other powers, however, preferred to support Turkey so that it could continue to act as a check on Russian ambitions in Eastern Europe.

In 1841 the European powers came together in the Convention of the Straits to guarantee Turkish independence. It was agreed then that the Bosphorus should be closed to all ships of war. This shut Russia out of the Mediterranean, and meant that she could not protect her merchant ships, now carrying increasing grain exports by the Black Sea.

The Crimean War – In 1851 Russia invaded Turkey's Danube lands, and in 1853 her navy sank the Turkish fleet, so winning back her outlet to the Mediterranean. Excitement ran high in Paris and London. Napoleon III was looking for a way of rebuilding the family's military prestige. Britain was concerned for her links with India, for, although the Suez Canal was not yet built, traffic was already following the Mediterranean route. In March 1954 the two powers declared war on Russia in support of Turkey. Combined forces were despatched to capture the Russian naval base at Sevastopol in the Crimea. The huge Russian army was unable to dislodge the invading force and in 1856 she was forced to accept peace on the terms that she would keep no fleet in the Black Sea and build no bases on its shores.

The battles of the Crimean War were made famous because the armies were followed by a journalist, who published detailed reports in the London *Times*. For the first time in history, the public was able to read first hand reports of the sufferings of the soldiers. The modern profession of nursing dates itself from the work done by Florence Nightingale and her staff in this campaign.

Disintegration – Victory over Russia in the Crimean War could not long delay the final disintegration of the Ottoman Empire. France and Britain, who had fought as allies of the Turks, were happy to help themselves to territory in North Africa. Britain also occupied Cyprus and extended her influence in the Middle East. Russia continued her forward movement in the less sensitive territory to the east of the Caspian Sea. In Eastern Europe, Greece was already independent and in the half century after the end of the Crimean War, Serbia, Rumania and Bulgaria would also break free. Russia, always ready to stand as protector of the oppressed Slav peoples, went to war with Turkey again in 1877. For a time Europe stood on the brink of another war as the powers prepared to shore up the tottering empire once again. In 1878, however, Russia, faced by the combination of Prussia, Austria and Britain, was forced to accept terms at the Congress of Berlin.

In 1907 rebellion broke out in Turkey itself. A group, who called themselves the Young Turks, demanded constitutional reforms, along European lines. In 1909 the long reigning Abdul-Hamid was deposed. The new rulers dressed their government as a constitutional monarchy, but it was effectively a dictatorship, dedicated to reviving Turkish power, at home and in the remaining Ottoman lands of the Middle East.

Nationalism

Western Europe – The Napoleonic conquests and the reactions against them had aroused fierce emotions of nationalism, which were to influence European politics. Germany and Italy began their discovery of a national identity, but the mood also affected smaller peoples, such as Belgians and Norwegians. Britain had her own problems in Ireland. The situation was complicated by the fact that Westminster politicians had to reconcile two vocal nationalist groups. The majority Catholics considered themselves to be under a foreign power, discriminated against in their religion and insecure in their land holding. The minority Protestants of the north, mostly of Scots descent, used their political connections with English conservatives to defend accustomed privileges. After 1848, however, concern on issues of nationality centred on eastern Europe.

Poland – Russia might stand as the liberator of oppressed Slav peoples in the Balkans, but, on her own western frontier, she was the oppressor. The decline of Poland began with long wars against Sweden, which ended in 1709. Depopulated and weakened, with no natural frontiers, she stood between aggressive powers to east and west. In the last decades of the 18th century, she was partitioned between Russia, Austria and Prussia. A supposedly free Poland, created in 1815, was effectively a Russian colony. A series of nationalist rebellions were a failure and Russian administrators tried to eliminate all traces of Polish nationalism, insisting that even primary school children should be taught in the Russian language.

The Austro-Hungarian Empire – Metternich recognized very clearly that the new nationalism could undermine the whole structure of the Austrian empire. The house of Hapsburg ruled over different nationalities, speaking a wide range of languages. Defeat by Prussia and then the loss of Italy pushed the western boundaries of the once great empire back to the Austrian heartland. Alone of all the major European powers, land-locked Austria was not in a position to participate in the scramble for colonial possessions. Any expansion had to be towards the east, and foreign policy now focused on the Danube and the Balkans.

The new nationalists of the region, however, saw Austria, as much as Turkey as a threat to their aspirations. The Hungarians exploited the weakness of the Empire after the Prussian victory at Sadowa to negotiate a new Covenant with Vienna. The Hapsburgs now ruled a dual Austro-Hungarian empire, in which military and foreign policy was co-ordinated, but in other ways the eastern part had virtual self government. The new Hungarian section of the Empire contained a number of national minorities, and trouble was never far from the surface.

In 1878, after the war between Russia and Turkey, Bosnia and Herzegovina were placed under Austrian administration, and in 1908 they were annexed by Austria. The independent Serbia, with Russian support, now stood as the focus of pan-Slavic aspirations, and so as protector of the nationalist movements in the two territories. The Austrian government, angry at this subversion, looked for an opportunity of crushing Serbia.

Russia

Despotism – In the decades before the Crimean War, Russia was ruled by the autocratic Tsar, Nicholas I. He tried to keep all western ideas of liberalism and socialism at bay by a suffocating censorship. At the same time the administration became ever more corrupt and inefficient. The repression of this period was primarily directed against the intelligentsia, who were traditionally close to developments in the west. Nicholas did recognize, however, that the position of the serfs had become such an anomaly that it endangered the Russian state. As in France before the Revolution, these poorest people had to carry by far the bulk of the load of taxation. Nicholas declared a desire to make changes and he did make progress in codifying peasants' rights and bringing them within the legal system. He was unable, however, to tackle the medieval structure of serfdom, which tied the mass of the people to their villages, and left them as the virtual possessions of their masters.

Emancipation and Reform – Nicholas was succeeded by his son, Alexander II during the Crimean War. The failure of the superior Russian armies and the humiliating nature of the peace, left no doubt that the state needed radical overhaul. Although conservative by nature, the new Tsar supervised a major overhaul of the army, the law and the administrative system.

Most difficult, he put in train the process of emancipation for the serfs. "Better," he said, "to abolish serfdom from above, than to wait till it begins to abolish itself from below. " Emancipation was pronounced in 1861, but problems still remained to be solved. Landlords needed to be compensated and a system had established whereby the peasants could buy their own land. This took the form of a tax, which left many, in practice, worse off than they had been before emancipation.

The Prelude to Revolution – The first shot was fired at Alexander only five years after his emancipation decree; he was assassinated in 1881. The reforms of his reign were matched with a continued autocracy, which aroused profound frustration, particularly amongst the intelligentsia. The education system, in particular, was subject to the tightest control by a reactionary bureaucracy. During these years also individuals within government gave support to pogroms against the Jews. After the murder of Alexander in 1881, government fell increasingly into the hands of the opponents of reform.

Opposition was divided between liberals, socialists and groups of nihilists, all of whose leaders were drawn from the intelligentsia. They appealed first to the suffering peasants, demanding a programme of land reform. Towards the end of the century, however, large numbers of peasants were leaving the land to make up the industrial proletariat of the long delayed industrial revolution. Revolutionary activists now found it productive to work in the growing slums of the cities, building up revolutionary cells of workers.

Success is the ultimate justification of autocratic government, and defeat by Japan in 1905 brought the imperial government to the brink of collapse. The battleship *Potemkin* mutinied and terrorised the Black Sea. Massive strikes, particularly by railway workers, crippled the economy. In October 1905 the Socialist groups organized themselves into the First Soviet, based on the principle of the cells which had been established in the factories. Nicholas II, like Louis XVI before him, was forced to attempt to rally national unity by calling a national parliament, or *duma*. Experiments in representative democracy were, however, half-hearted and failed. In the years which followed, the weak Tsar shut himself increasingly within his family circle, now increasingly dominated by the eccentric Rasputin. When the European war broke out in 1914, Russia was ill prepared for such a disaster.

The Armed Peace

The Alliances – In the years after 1871, there were two fixed points in European diplomacy. Austria and Russia faced each other over the control of the liberated Turkish lands in the Balkans. Fighting could break out at any time within the region, leading to the risk of 'superpower involvement'. France also, smarting from defeat at Sadowa and the occupation of Paris, was chronically hostile to Germany. She was, however, militarily weak and the autocratic powers of Austria and Russia looked on her as a threat, and so she remained isolated and impotent.

In previous centuries, alliances had been formed under the immediate threat of war, and they had disintegrated immediately after the threat was over. During these decades, however, the European powers began to form themselves into permanent alliances, committed to help each other in the event of war. By the beginning of the 20th century, a new alignment of powers had become established. Germany allied with Austria, and they were later to be joined by Italy to form the Triple Alliance. To meet this threat, France and Russia joined to form the Dual Alliance. Britain was not a significant continental power, and as late as 1898 the two countries narrowly avoided a colonial war. In 1904, however, policy changed dramatically as Britain concluded a non-binding *entente cordiale* with France, which was followed by a similar agreement with Russia. Hostility towards Germany increased as the German government set about a major naval construction programme, which was interpreted as a direct threat to Britain.

The British government responded with its own programme, and a major arms race was under way.

Military Strategy – With Europe organized into armed camps, the generals considered strategy in the event of conflict. Failing to take account of the bloody attrition of the American Civil War, they assumed that events would be settled, as in Bismark's wars, by one swift, decisive campaign. Germany was faced with the prospect of fighting on two fronts. Strategists decided that, while the Russian war machine was massive, the bureaucratic inefficiency would prevent rapid deployment of forces. They therefore developed a plan that, in the event of impending war, the German army would make a first strike to knock out France, so that it could then give full attention to the eastern front.

In the early years of the century, there was a mood of militarism throughout Europe, fed by accounts of colonial wars and victories against non European people. It was most evident in Germany, where theorists declared that war was the natural state of man, but it spread much wider. In Britain, for instance, metaphors of war and sport were subtly mingled in the public school education of the nation's elite.

The Outbreak of War

Austria and Serbia – By the summer of 1918 Serbian support for rebels in Bosnia and Herzegovina had brought relationships with Austria to a low state. On the 28th June the heir to the throne, the Archduke Franz Ferdinand and his wife were murdered in the Bosnian capital of Sarajevo. Encouraged by her ally Germany, Austria used this as a pretext for invading Serbia. On the 30th July Tsar Nicholas II ordered mobilization, not only in the Balkans, but along the whole border.

First strike – It appears that, at the last moment, Kaiser Wilhelm II of Germany may have had doubts about plunging Europe into war. The British foreign minister tried to gather support for a conference to localize the conflict, but the German war machine was now moving under its own impetus. On the 3rd August Germany attacked France through undefended neutral Belgium. Italy declared that the conflict was none of her concern, so the central powers of Germany and Austria faced France and Russia. Britain had no treaty obligation to enter the war on behalf of France, but did consider herself bound by guarantee the guarantee made to Belgium after the 1830 uprising. Her formal position for taking up arms was therefore as defender of the rights of small nations. Italy later entered the war on the side of the Allies, as they were now called, while Turkey and Bulgaria aligned themselves with the Central Powers. Military enthusiasts forecast a short war, to be decided by Christmas, but the British Foreign Secretary, Sir Edward Grey warned, "The lamps are going out all over Europe. We shall not see them lit again in our lifetime. "

War and Revolution

Stalemate – The German first strike strategy involved high risk. Russia mobilized more rapidly than anticipated the and German army was defeated at Grumbinnen on the 20th August. In early September the western offensive became bogged down on the Marne. Germany was fighting the war on two fronts, which her generals had feared. On the western front, the opposing armies dug in for their long years of attrition. The new German navy remained in port as the British fleet set about sapping German resistance by blockade. Allied attempts to break the stalemate by offensives in the Dardanelles and Salonika, were unsuccessful.

The Russian Revolution – The huge open spaces of the eastern front kept war more mobile. Early Russian success was undermined by the failure of the political structure. In March 1917 a wave of unrest swept the Tsar from power. The opposition was divided between liberal politicians, who now set up a provisional government and the socialist Soviet – itself divided between the moderates and a radical Bolshevik wing. The moderate provisional government pledged itself to continue the war, but in April the Bolshevik, Vladimir Ilyich Lenin, returned from exile and announced the arrival of world revolution. Russian workers, he claimed, should not be dying in a bosses' war. The provisional government staked every-thing on a last great offensive, but this failed, and on the 7th November, Lenin staged a Bolshevik coup d'état. In March 1918 he concluded peace between his newly born Soviet Union and the Central Powers at Brest Litovsk.

American Intervention – Germany now had to fight on only one front, but, during this period, another, even more formidable enemy had been drawn into the war. Desperate at the success of the British naval blockade, the German navy mounted its own submarine blockade of Britain. To be successful it had to attack American ships which were carrying supplies to Britain. This brought the United States into the conflict in April 1917. The

German High Command recognized that the intervention of American troops would tilt the battle against the Central Powers, but it staked everything on defeating Britain and France before the Americans arrived. 1917 and 1918 saw huge and costly offensives from both sides on the western front. In the Autumn of 1918 Germany's allies, Austria and Bulgaria began to crumble, the German fleet mutinied and there was increasing unrest in the German cities. Finally the Kaiser abdicated and the generals sued for peace.

The World of Versailles

The Cost of War – All the major continental nations emerged weakened from the war. Russia, involved in civil war, was no longer a factor in international politics. France, though victorious, had suffered grievously. Austria was now not a power of significance. Germany, although defeated, was no longer surrounded by serious rivals. Loss of life had been severe in all the combatant nations, but wealth had also drained away. The United States was the main beneficiary of the war at a cost of fewer casualties than had been suffered by the Dominion of Australia. In the past she had been a major debtor nation, but now she moved into a period of being the world's main creditor.

A New World – The war was also an emotional and intellectual landmark. It was as if the great optimism, which had buoyed up a successful and expansionist Europe was suddenly pierced. The belief an inevitable tide of progress, prevalent since the time of Descartes, no longer seemed tenable in the face of sustained barbarity on European soil. Liberal thinkers, in disciplines such as theology as well as in politics, found themselves on the defensive. New absolutisms, of both left and right, emerged in confrontation, both threatening to overwhelm traditions of representative government.

The conflict had also brought permanent changes in the structure of society. Women, who had been mobilized to fill men's jobs, could no longer be denied political and a growing economic emancipation. The war brought technological advances in areas such as aeronautics and the development of motor vehicles. Output had increased to meet the demands of a technological war, and, in the process, labour unions had established a stronger position for themselves. Many felt threatened by the rapid social change, evident in almost every field of life.

In the years before the war, artists had already been working in strange and disturbing new forms. Stravinsky's *Rite of Spring* and Picasso's *Demoiselles d'Avignon* created scandal in their fields. In 1922, Joyce's *Ulysses* dispensed with the convention of the English novel. It seemed as though all recognisable values were now fractured as creative artists abandoned both classical and romantic forms to explore abstraction and an inner life, now provided with a whole new vocabulary by the works of Sigmund Freud. The arrival of jazz from America, exploiting the interaction between African and European popular music, only served to heighten the alarm of traditionalists.

The Treaties – The Treaty of Versailles, ratified by Germany in July 1919, was the first of a series of treaties imposed on the defeated Central Powers. The leading architects of the new order were President Wilson of the U. S. A., Clemenceau of France and Lloyd George of Britain. Clemenceau, recognizing the continuing potential of Germany, pressed for financial reparations, intended to retard industrial recovery, the return of Alsace-Lorainne to France, and the demilitarisation of the Rhineland. The map of eastern Europe was re-drawn, with Poland, Hungary, Czechoslovakia and Yugoslavia created as new nations. In the north, Finland, which had won independence from Russia in 1917, was joined by the three newly independent Baltic States. The pattern of nationalities was, however, more complex than could be accommodated within national boundaries, and all of these nations had substantial minorities. Of greatest significance for the future, substantial numbers of German speaking people found themselves within Czechoslovakia and Poland. The treaties attempted to protect minority rights, but there was considerable movement of peoples across national boundaries. The largest movement came at the end a war between Greece and Turkey from 1920 to 1922. In particular Greek people left the coast of Asia Minor, where they had lived since ancient times. The two communities continued in uneasy co-existence in Cyprus.

The treaties also changed the wider world. Germany's East and West African possessions were divided between Britain and France, while South West Africa, the future Namibia, was placed under the trusteeship of South Africa. The concept of trusteeship was also used to extend western influence over the old Ottoman territories of the Middle East.

The League of Nations – President Wilson hoped that his country, with its democratic tradition could take the lead in creating a new atmosphere of goodwill. He therefore proposed a League of Nations, which would serve as guardian of world peace. Wilson was to be bitterly disappointed when his own Congress refused to let the United States join the new body. Unhappy about the way in which their country had ben plunged into European affairs, the majority of Americans were anxious to return to a traditional isolationism. It became evident that the new body lacked credibility as early as 1920, when Poland successfully seized Vilna from Lithuania. Later incidents reinforced the fact that successful international collaboration to repel aggression could not be organized through the League. The Italian government took full advantage when, in Europe's final African venture, it launched an attack on Ethiopia in 1935.

Ireland – Attempts by pre-war liberal administrations to give home rule to Ireland had been frustrated by the collaboration of Ulster protestants and conservative politicians. Prime Minister Lloyd George now faced destructive guerilla warfare from nationalists. In 1921 the moderate nationalists accepted partition of the island, which left a significant Catholic minority within the Protestant dominated northern provinces. This led to civil war within the new Irish Free State, and laid the foundations of continuing strife in the north.

The World Economy

The Post-War Boom – During the 1920s world trade appeared to be returning to its pre-war vigour, but, even during these boom years, there were signs of problems ahead. The war had created an increased potential for production, but demand was stagnant. The Soviet Union was in no position to import goods from abroad, and new nations raised tariff barriers to protect fledgling industries. The United States now produced over half of all the world's manufactures, but American consumers, like the Japanese 70 years later, showed little desire to buy goods from abroad and domestic industry was protected by import duties.

As industry boomed, so the price of raw materials, including agricultural products, declined, creating problems for primary producers. At the same time, the fact that workers did not share the profits of their industries, brought outbursts of industrial unrest, such as the British General Strike of 1926.

The Great Depression – By 1928 world trade had become

heavily dependent on American finance. In that year Wall Street experienced The Great Bull Market as the price of shares rose to unrealistic heights. Then, on October 28 1929, the stock market crashed. American capital for investment dried up, leading to a rapid world wide collapse of industrial confidence. Governments took what action they could to protect their own industries against imports, so further inhibiting world trade. It is estimated that at the depth of the recession in 1932 industrial production in the United States and Germany was only half of what it had been three years earlier. Unemployment reached record levels in all the industrial countries, bringing times of great hardship.

The New Deal – In America, the parties divided over the political response to the problems. The Republicans, favouring a traditional *laissez-faire* approach, were defeated in the 1932 elections by a Democratic party, led by Franklin Roosevelt. He instituted a New Deal, based on substantial public investment. The showpiece was the publicly owned Tennessee Valley Authority. Designed to provide an industrial infrastructure for one of the country's poorest regions. Roosevelt won great popularity, going on to win an unprecedented four presidential elections, but the improvement brought by the New Deal was as much psychological as practical, and real recovery had to await the stimulus of a second world war.

The Rise of the Dictators

Italy – In the elections of 1921 a new party won just 36 seats in the Italian parliament. Its leader, Benito Mussolini had a background as a socialist, but he now proclaimed that he would save Italy from the menace of communism. The party appealed to ancient Rome in its extended arm salute and the symbol of the *fasces*, which gave the movement its name. The black shirted fascists used intimidation, first to come to power and then to eliminate all political opposition. Mussolini's rule achieved some legitimacy when, in 1929, he negotiated a treaty with the highly conservative papacy.

Germany – The Austrian-born Adolf Hitler became leader of the German National Socialist, or Nazi, party in 1921. Having failed in an early attempt to take control of the Bavarian government, he set about reorganizing his party as a military movement, not hesitating to purge his own followers. He directed his appeal to a German people, who were frustrated by military defeat, humiliated by the loss of empire and European territory, and, in many cases, impoverished by hyper-inflation. Hitler's philosophy was laid out in his early book *Mein Kampf*. This described both his military ambitions for Germany, and his obsessive hatred of the Jewish people.

The struggle appeared to lie between Hitler's new right, and the parties of the left. But the left was divided. The communists, taking their orders from Moscow, attempted, and sometimes succeeded, in fomenting revolution. The social democrats were therefore forced into alliance with conservative military leaders. Capitalizing on these divisions and on the economic problems brought by the Depression, Hitler took his Nazi party to power in 1933. He then quickly set up a reign of terror. While the Jews were the prime target, political opponents, gypsies, the handicapped, and anybody not considered to be of true Aryan descent also suffered. Despite this, his popularity remained high among most Germans. His armaments and other public works programme appeared to be bringing a return of prosperity, while military success retrieved national pride.

The Soviet Union – The Bolshevik revolution of 1917 was followed by three years of civil war, during which White Russian armies, supported by foreign troops, tried to overthrow the new communist state. Lenin and his followers emerged successful, but at huge cost. It is estimated that some 13 million died in the war and the famine it caused; economic life was at a standstill. In 1921, as a emergency measure, Lenin largely freed the economy and recovery followed rapidly.

Lenin died in January 1924, leaving two men contending the succession. Trotsky proclaimed that the new society could only flourish within a communist world, and the prime task was therefore to export the revolution. His opponent, Stalin, argued that the priority was to rebuild the Soviet Union, by creating 'communism within one state'. When Stalin emerged victorious, it appeared as though the forces of moderation had prevailed.

Stalin assumed autocratic power and created a personality cult, not dissimilar to those constructed around the fascist dictators. He set himself the objective of changing the Soviet Union from a largely medieval economy, to a major modern state within a few decades. This involved the conversion of agriculture from its peasant structure by wholesale collectivization, and the rapid development of heavy industry. The programme was forced through at huge human cost. Industrially the results were dramatic. Production of coal, iron and steel and other basics increased many times over. The expansion of heavy industry was, however, bought at the expense of consumer goods, and the people, were constantly disappointed in the promised general improvement in living standards. Peasants on the collective farms, also resentful at being expected to produce low cost food for the growing cities for little return, remained obstinately unproductive.

Stalin's increasingly paranoiac behaviour was now demonstrated in a series of show trials and purges. Virtually all the old political leaders and a high proportion of military officers were executed to ensure that nobody would be able to challenge for power. Millions more suffered and died in labour camps. The new administrators of the country were tied to Stalin by a common guilt, and by an increasing web of petty corruption.

Spain – By the 1930s the days in which Spain had been a great European power were long past, and she had therefore avoided involvement in the First World War. In 1933 a right wing government came to power, which provoked rebellion by national minorities. In early 1936 a left wing government was elected with a large majority. General Franco, modelling himself on the fascist dictators, led a mutiny of the army in Morocco and invaded the mainland. The army, the political right and the Roman Catholic church aligned with Franco, while left wing groups and the national minorities aligned with the elected government. Franco received assistance from the fascist states, while the government was supported by the Soviet Union and a variety of international volunteers. The bitter war lasted until 1939, when Franco achieved the position of dictator, which he held until his death in 1975.

The Second World War in the West

German Expansion – From the beginning Hitler, followed a programme for the creation of a German empire in central Europe. His first objective was to win back land lost at Versailles; he then planned to conquer the whole of mainland Europe, including European Russia, and create an empire in which 'lower' races, such as the Slavs, would be reduced to a servile status. He exploited the weakness of the League of Nations, American isolationism, and lack of unity among other European powers in a series of successes – the recovery of the Saarland by plebiscite, the remilitarisation of the Rhineland, unification with Austria, and finally the dismemberment of Czechoslovakia. When Britain and France acquiesced to the last of these at Munich, it appeared as though no other power had the will to frustrate his ambitions.

In 1939 Hitler and Stalin concluded the Nazi-Soviet Pact to preserve Russian neutrality. The Soviet Union was awarded eastern Poland and took the opportunity to advance further into the Baltic States and Finland, where Russian armies were halted by fierce national resistance. Unlike Czechoslovakia, Poland was protected by treaty links with Britain and France, and the German invasion provoked a joint ultimatum and war. Mussolini took the opportunity of entering the war in support of Germany and invading Greece.

German Successes – After defeating Poland, in 1940, the German army repeated the 1914 tactic of invading France across Belgium. This time Paris fell and a puppet government was installed in southern France. Successful campaigns to the north and south reduced Denmark, Norway, Yugoslavia and Greece. In early 1941 the Afrika Corps landed in Libya and within two months was threatening Cairo and the Suez Canal. Britain, now rallied by the charismatic leader, Winston Churchill, held off an air offensive, intended to prepare the way for invasion, in the Battle of Britain.

On 22 June 1941 Hitler launched Operation Barbarossa against an unprepared Soviet Union. The invasion followed the logic of Hitler's master plan, but it dangerously overstretched German resources. The imbalance was made greater when the Japanese attack on Pearl Harbour brought the United States into the war in December of the same year. Stalin demonstrated his character as a national leader in rallying his people for a massively costly defence. The war turned in November 1942, when the Russians broke the German front at Stalingrad and a British army defeated the Afrika Corps at El Alamein. Once the Allies had re-established a western front with the Normandy landings of June 1944, the final defeat in 1945 was inevitable.

The years from 1939-45 gave a new and terrible meaning to warfare. The Germans mobilised conquered people for slave labour, and perpetrated mass genocide on European Jewry; the Russians deported whole national populations for alleged collaboration; residential areas of cities were targeted in indiscriminate bombing by both sides. Among some 50 million dead were an estimated 27 million Russians, 6 million Jews and 4¹/2 million Poles.

Europe Divided

The Yalta Settlement – The future political shape of Europe was negotiated in February 1945 at a conference at Yalta in the Crimea, attended by Stalin, Roosevelt and Churchill. Germany was to be partitioned and the countries of Eastern Europe were to form a zone of Russian influence. In the event, Austria and Greece – the latter after civil war – remained within the western sphere.

The Recovery of Western Europe – At the end of the war, western Europe was in a state of serious economic collapse. Once again, there were large movements of displaced people, and food shortages continued for years after the war. In June 1947, the U. S. Secretary of State, George Marshall, announced a major aid programme, directed, "not against any country or doctrine, but against hunger, poverty, desperation and chaos". The Soviet Union was offered the chance of participating but turned it down. The Marshall Plan provided much needed capital for reconstruction.

The United Nations – During the last years of the war, thought was given to the reasons why the League of Nations had failed to preserve world peace. In 1945 representatives of the nations met in San Francisco to set up the new United Nations. In its constitution, great influence was given to the Security Council, which had five 'great powers' as permanent members and representatives of other nations. The right of veto was given only to the great powers, but at least all the major powers were now involved in the organization and debates were subject to the scrutiny of the world media.

The European Community – Some European leaders now argued that the nation state was no longer capable of providing a secure structure for world peace. In particular, the long standing enmity between France and Germany was no longer tolerable. In 1952, the Federal Republic of Germany, France, Italy, Holland, Belgium and Luxembourg, formed the European Economic Community. This was designed to be both a trading group, capable of competing with the new super-powers, and also a stabilizing influence on the volatile European political scene.

The Cold War in Europe – It soon became clear that European nationalism had run its destructive course, and the danger to world peace now lay in the confrontation of the United States and the Soviet Union. In the words of Winston Churchill, an 'iron curtain' had descended across Europe.

The Soviet Union emerged from the Second World War in control of a vast empire. It had inherited imperial conquests, and had further added the Baltic Republics. It also now controlled puppet regimes in Eastern Europe, bound together in the Warsaw Pact, which maintained huge land forces on its western front. Stalin's policy was still primarily directed at preserving national security, which had been so devastatingly violated by Hitler's army. He and later Soviet leaders therefore felt threatened by American superiority in nuclear weapons. A crash nuclear programme was put in hand and advances in rocketry were clearly illustrated when, in April 1961, Yuri Gregarin became the first man to be launched into space.

America and her allies in the North Atlantic Treaty Organization (NATO) relied heavily on nuclear superiority. The Americans responded to the Russian space programme and, in July 1969, with a wondering world watching on television, men were placed on the moon.

Berlin, divided between the four occupying powers, lay exposed within the Russian area of influence and in 1948-9 conflict loomed as the Russians shut off western communications with the city. A later crisis ended with the building of the Berlin Wall in 1961. This stood for the next 28 years as a potent symbol of the Cold War and the division of Europe into two hostile camps.

AFTER EMPIRE

The Expansion of Japan

The Beginnings of Aggression – The 1914-18 war brought prosperity to the rising Japanese economy. European competition in Asian markets was reduced and Japanese factories were able to export to the combatants. During this period, heavy industries, such as shipbuilding, were able to build up a firm base. Competition returned in the post-war boom years, but Japan continued to export successfully. During the boom years, companies re-invested profits in preparation for more difficult times. Japanese industry, none the less, suffered badly in the Depression. With foreign markets closed and the home market as yet undeveloped, industry worked at only a fraction of capacity. The weakness was exacerbated by the country's lack of raw materials. Foreign policy therefore became directed at the winning control of the export markets and natural resources of East Asia. China was the first target for expansion.

China's Weakness – After the fall of the Manchu Empire in 1912, China plunged back into chaos. Sun Yat-Sen's Nationalist (Kuomintang) party struggled for power with independent war lords. During this time communist cells were coming into existence. Following Marxist orthodoxy, they initially concentrated on the cities, but later, under the influence of the rising Mao Tse-tung, they worked increasingly among the mass of the peasants, who had suffered greatly during the upheavals. Under his influence, the communists built up communes in scattered and remote areas. Sun Yat-Sen died in 1925, to be succeeded as Kuomintang leader by the more conservative Chiang Kai-shek. After a period of collaboration, Chiang attempted to exterminate the communist opposition. Driven from their southern bases, the communists only survived by coming together in the Long March of 1934-5 and establishing a new northern headquarters, based on Yenan.

The War in the East.

The Attack on China – Japan exploited the weakness and growing corruption of the Kuomintang government by strengthening its control over Manchuria and areas of the north in the early 1930s. In 1936 the Kuomintang and the communists made common cause against the foreigners, but in the following year, Japan launched a major assault on China. In December 1937 the Japanese army captured the capital at Nanking and the Chinese government had to retreat to remote Szechwan, leaving the Japanese in control of the north, and most of the Pacific coast, including the major industrial cities.

Victory brought Japan into conflict with the Pacific colonial powers, and their concessionary ports were blockaded. The Americans and British responded by supplying Chiang Kai-shek along the Burma Road, and the United States renounced its commercial agreement with Japan.

Control of the Pacific – Japanese foreign policy was now set on winning control over the whole of the Pacific rim. With the outbreak of war in Europe, she allied herself with Germany. Then in 1941, as German troops were sweeping into Russia, she launched her first attack on French Indo-China. On the 7th December 1941 her air force suddenly attacked the American navy in Pearl Harbour, Hawaii, and, at the same time, she launched assaults on the Dutch in Indonesia and the British in Mayalsia and Burma. The campaigns were brilliantly successful and by mid 1942 both India and Australia were under threat.

Defeat and the Atom Bomb – The attack on Pearl Harbour put and end to isolationism and united Americans behind President Roosevelt. As the world's greatest industrial power became geared for war, the tide turned against Japan. In June 1942 the Japanese fleet suffered a reverse at the battle of Midway Island, and thereafter a relentless American offensive drove them from their Pacific conquests, while the British also fought back through Burma. From November 1944 the Japanese cities came under direct air attack. The war ended with the use of the new atomic weapon on the cities of Hiroshima and Nagasaki in August 1945.

Decolonization – The Japanese victories, and, in particular, the fall of Singapore on the 15th February 1942, involved a profound loss of face for the colonizing powers. The invading armies were seen by many Asians as liberators from western regimes. Many of those who had assumed control, under Japanese direction, now became prominent in independence movements. The United States handed over political control of the Philippines in 1946 after negotiating a continued miliary presence. The Dutch, themselves newly liberated, at first fought to preserve their possessions but in 1948 they accepted the independence of the Republic of Indonesia. The British fought a communist rebellion in Malaya before handing over to a more acceptable national government in 1957. The French became involved in a long war for Indo-China before being defeated in 1954.

China and her Neighbours

Communist China – The fall of Japan left the two forces of the Kuomintang and the communists vying for the control of China. China's miseries continued when civil war broke out in 1947. In one battle, half a million men were engaged on each side. By 1949 the communists were gaining the upper hand and in May 1950 Chiang Kai-shek retreated to Taiwan with his government.

The new communist government was faced by a huge task of reconstruction. According to Mao's estimate, some 800,000 'enemies of the people' were executed, largely from the old village landlord class. The communists had long experience with the collectivization of agriculture within their own territories, and they did not follow Stalin's example of imposing it from above. Peasants were organized to control their own operations and, despite set-backs, the conditions of life for the mass of people improved.

Mao Tse-tung capitalized on the age-old Chinese respect for authority to provide a strong central government, which had for so long been lacking. He adapted western Marxist ideology to traditional thought patterns, and showed a strong hostility to western culture, which was given full rein in the Cultural Revolution, which he launched in 1966.

To western eyes, China appeared now to be a part of a united Communist bloc, intent on achieving world dominance. In practice, however, Mao had largely rejected the Russian brand of communism. By the 1960s, acute strains were appearing in the relationship between the two countries. When China developed its own nuclear capability in 1964, it was primarily as a deterrent against potential Russian aggression. The Chinese reconquest of the old province of Tibet also led to a successful war with India in 1962.

The Korean War – In 1945 the Japanese colony of Korea was occupied by Russian troops from the north and Americans from the south. This led to partition, with both governments claiming the whole country. In 1950 the northern armies invaded the south. The United States and other western nations, with the backing of a United Nations resolution, responded by sending forces to support the south.

For a time it appeared as though the north would be defeated, but China, concerned at her own security, sent an army across the border. The American President Truman refused to become involved in a war on Chinese soil, and the war was concluded in 1953 by an armistice, which perpetuated partition.

Conflict of Ideologies – American analysts saw the communist strategy in South East Asia and being a process of 'slicing the salami'. Territories were to fall to communism, not in one major conflict, but one by one. The communist uprisings, which faced almost every nation of South East Asia in the coming decades, were in fact little co-ordinated and variously owned allegiance to Moscow, Peking or neither. That in the new nation of Indonesia was put down with great violence.

American policy became dedicated to holding the line against communism in the region. This involved providing support to non-communist regimes, including Chinese nationalist government in Taiwan. The United States was therefore deeply involved in the politics of the region.

The French defeat in Indo-China left the new country of Vietnam divided, with a communist regime under the old nationalist Ho Chi Minh established in the north. The United States became increasingly involved in the struggle, supporting unstable non-communist administrations, based in the southern capital of Saigon. In 1965, faced with the possibility of the defeat of the client regime by the northern backed Viet Cong guerilllas, President Johnson authorized massive involvement in the conflict. The weight of American firepower proved ineffective against a highly motivated enemy. In 1973 the American government, confronted by a mounting anti-war campaign at home, withdrew from the conflict. In the next two years the three countries of Indo-China fell to the communists. The people of Cambodia, having experienced American bombing, now suffered from the worst aberrations of Marxism, as interpreted by the Pol Pot regime.

The Pacific Rim

Japanese Reconstruction – United States troops occupied Japan, in an enlightened manner, from 1945 until 1952. The first objective was to ensure that the expansionist phase was over. A new democratic constitution was established, the Emperor renounced his divinity, and expenditure on defence and armaments was radically curtailed. As with Germany, industrial reconstruction followed fast. After the humiliation of defeat, both nations needed to experience success. Also, the imposed limitation of defence expenditure proved a powerful boost to the civilian economy.

The Technological Revolution – Soon Japan was no longer a low cost economy and her heavy industries began to suffer some of the problems experienced in the West. By this time, however, the nation had developed skills, which enabled it to take the lead in the third, technological phase of world industrialization. Automobile production boomed, winning markets in Europe and North America, and Japanese labour and management skills proved highly suitable to the detailed work involved in the production of hi-tech goods. Supported by a huge balance of payments surplus, she has established a position of dominance in world markets in a wide range of product areas.

An Area of Growth – In the last decade of the 20th century it is clear that the region of the Pacific rim is established as a formidable competitor to the established industrialized regions of western Europe and North America. It remains, however, a region of wide diversity. South Korea, Taiwan, Singapore and – at least until re-unification with China in 1997 – Hong Kong have participated in the economic prosperity pioneered by Japan. At the other extreme, peoples of many of the nations of South East Asia continue to survive on low per capita incomes. China herself emerged from the isolation of the Cultural Revolution to re-build international links, but, unlike communist regimes to the west, it has successfully repressed those who wished to liberalize the political structure of the nation.

The Indian Sub-Continent

The Independence Movement – Indian troops made a significant contribution to the allied victory in the World War One, and in 1918 nationalist politicians looked to see their country start its progress towards the self government which had already been given to the white dominions. In 1919, however, a British general ordered troops to fire on a demonstration in Amristar, killing some 400 and injuring many more. Although the government disavowed the act, many British residents were loud in support, fuelling bitterness between the two communities. One of those radicalised by the Amristar massacre was Mohandas Gandhi, known as Mahatma (Great Soul). During the next decades, he led a civil disobedience movement, based, if not always successfully, on non-violent principles.

In the face of opposition at home, as well as from residents in India, the British government slowly moved towards accepting the principle of granting dominion status to India, and the Government of India Act of 1935 gave substantial power to elected representatives. The movement for complete independence, however, continued to grow. With the outbreak of the World War Two, some Indians sided with Japan in the hope of bringing down the colonial power.

Partition – The independence movement still faced the problem of reconciling the two major religious groupings of the sub-continent. Mohammed Ali Jinnah emerged as leader of the Muslim

League, which now demanded that an independent state of Pakistan should be established at independence for the Islamic community. In 1945 a Labour government was returned in Britain and in March 1946 it made an offer of full independence. As disputes continued, it announced that Britain would withdraw not later than June 1948. Faced with this ultimatum, the Hindu leaders accepted partition – for which decision Gandhi was assassinated by an extremist Hindu.

The new state of Pakistan was established in two blocks in the north west and north east. The rulers of princely states on the boarder of the two nations were permitted to decide their allegiance, leaving Kashmir as disputed territory. Independence was marked by communal rioting, which left some half a million dead, and the mass movement of peoples in both directions across the frontier.

Independence – Jinnah died in 1948 and a decade later the army took control of Pakistan. Leadership of India fell to Jawaharlal Nehru and later passed to his daughter, Indira and grandson Rajiv Gandhi. The new country faced formidable problems. Independence was quickly followed by famine in 1951, and, with rising population it appeared as though Malthusian disaster was imminent. A combination of a reduction in the rate of population growth and an agricultural 'green' revolution has, however, improved the supply of food. The fragile ecology of eastern Pakistan, however, continued to bring disasters and a cyclone in 1970 led to rebellion, which, with Indian help, brought into being the separate Islamic state of Bangladesh.

Partition did not bring the end of India's communal problems. Indira Gandhi was assassinated by discontented Sikh nationalists, and her son Rajiv by Tamils of the south. Mahatma Gandhi allied himself with outcasts and hoped to see the end of the caste system, but this has been frustrated by a resurgence of Hindu fundamentalism. For all its problems, however, India remains the world's largest democracy.

Sub-Saharan Africa

Decolonization – British governments of both parties continued the policy of giving independence to colonies, which had begun with India. The sheer size of the British Empire had meant that expatriate manpower was spread thinly. The second layer of administration was already staffed by African personnel and a machinery of local government was in place. Riots in the Gold Coast in 1948 gave notice of a growing nationalist movement. In 1957 the Gold Coast became the first independent country, within the British commonwealth, under its new name, Ghana. Three years later the much larger Nigeria became a sovereign state.

Across the continent, in Kenya and Rhodesia the problem was complicated by the presence of a white settler population, bitterly opposed to any move towards majority rule. The most serious challenge was posed by the Mau Mau disturbances in Kenya of 1952-6. Many of the white minority left the country when it received its independence in 1963. Two years later the white minority government of Southern Rhodesia declared unilateral independence and seceded from the British commonwealth. The British government failed to take effective action against this colonial rebellion and war continued between the white government and black nationalist groups, until the latter won to set up the state of Zimbabwe in 1976.

French governments, disillusioned by prolonged war in Indo-China and Algeria, gave independence at an even faster pace. In 1960 the Sub-Saharan colonies were offered either complete separation, in which case, they would receive no continued assistance, or association with France, within a French Community.

The two largest African empires were therefore dismantled within a few years with comparatively little strife. Independence for the remaining colonies proved a more painful process. In 1960, the Belgians withdrew from the Congo, which became the state of Zaire. Until that time, Africans held no positions of responsibility, and there was little preparation for the event. When the mineral-rich area of Katanga attempted to secede, the Cold War super-powers became involved in the ensuing civil war.

The last African empire was also the oldest. The Portuguese colonies of Guinea Bissau, Mozambique and Angola only achieved independence after prolonged struggle.

After Independence – The emergent nations faced formidable problems. Some new nations spent unwisely on military prestige projects, but even where this was avoided, as, for instance, in Tanzania, falling world commodity prices led to a serious reduction in government revenue. Industrialization has proved unattainable, both through lack of capital, but also because it has proved hard for products from new nations to break into the controlled markets of the developed world.

Independent African nations found themselves caught in the Malthusian nutcracker of increasing population and falling revenue. This led to a decline in already low living standards and a failure by governments to deliver the public health and education programmes expected within a newly liberated nation. This exacerbated traditional communal rivalries, which in turn frequently erupted into civil war, like the Nigerian Biafra War of 1967-70 and later struggles in the Sudan, Ethiopia and the Horn of Africa. Political instability led to the emergence of authoritarian, often military, regimes. An already difficult situation has been made worse for nations immediately south of the Sahara by climatic change and desertification, which have destroyed large areas of productive land.

South Africa – The violently imposed apartheid system led to South Africa being increasingly ostracized from the world community. She withdrew from the British Commonwealth in 1961, and was later expelled from the United Nations. Economic sanctions imposed by the U. S. A. and a world sporting boycott had an effect and in the early 1990s the legal apparatus of apartheid was dismantled, but, with the white community continuing to control the police and armed forces, the political structure of a future multiracial nation remained unresolved. In 1990, however president F.W. de Klerk, instigated the release from prison of Nelson Mandela, the leader of the banned African National Congress. In 1994. the first free elections were held and Nelson Mandela was elected president. The economic sanctions against South Africa have since been lifted and relations with the international community restored.

Latin America

Capital and Industrialization – In the years before World War One there was heavy European involvement in the economy of Latin America. The war then led to a drying up of European capital and the United States became the main investor in the region.

The world depression of the 1930s hit the region hard. The price of primary products, the mainstay of the economies, collapsed. After the war many of the larger nations instituted industrialization programmes, at times with a degree of success, but this was achieved only by borrowing the required capital, which left the nation with a heavy burden of debt and vulnerable to currency and interest rate fluctuations on the international market.

Economic problems created political instability. The rural poor had always lived in conditions of poverty, but they did not pose the same immediate problem to political stability as the growing and highly volatile urban populations.

Political Structures – The economic problems of the region meant that reforming governments did not have the revenue to deliver the social programmes needed to combat deprivation. When reforms were attempted they created inflation which weakened the economic base of society. Reforming democracies have therefore been under constant pressure from more authoritarian sys-tems of government. These took three broad forms – popularist leaders, military regimes and revolutionary governments.

The archetype polularist leader was Getulio Vargas, who came to power in Brazil in 1930, and the best known Juan Peron, who ruled the Argentine from 1943-55 and then returned briefly in 1973. Both drew comparison with European dictators, but they had wide support among the urban poor, who believed that they alone could take on powerful vested interests on behalf of the people. They depended, however, on army support, and both were vulnerable when this was withdrawn.

Cuba and Revolution – The revolutionary movement had early roots in Mexico, but it became focused on Cuba with the success of Fidel Castro's revolution in 1959. An attempt by the United States to undermine the revolution came to disaster at the Bay of Pigs in 1961. In the following years Cuba, now aligned with Russia, exported revolution into Latin America. Che Guevara, a symbol to the new left across the world, was killed fighting with Bolivian guerillas in 1967. The United States became involved, supporting anti-communist regimes within the region, even when these had a poor human rights record. The democratic left wing government of Salvadore Allende in Chile, for instance, was overthrown by the military in 1973 with American support. Contra rebels against the Cuban inspired government of Nicaragua were funded from Washington, and the government of the island of Grenada was overthrown by American invasion in 1983.

The Missile Crisis – In 1962 Cuba was the focus of the most dangerous crisis of the Cold War. In October intelligence reports showed that sites were being built on Cuba from which missiles would be able to reach any city in the United States. President Kennedy demanded that all missiles in Cuba should be withdrawn and announced that ships bringing more would be intercepted. The super-powers stood poised for nuclear confrontation, but the Russian President Khrushchev broke the crisis by agreeing to withdraw the missiles. President Kennedy had successfully reasserted the Munroe Doctrine that the American continent would remain an area of United States influence, and the powers would not again come so close to open war.

The Middle East and North Africa

The New Turkey – In 1918, a proposal was put forward that Turkey itself should be divided into French, British and Italian spheres of influence. The successful general, Mustafa Kemal, led resistance against Greek and French forces, and established independence for the new, smaller nation. He set about a process of modernization of the nation, which went as far as westernizing its script and converting the country into a secular state. His people gave him the name of Ataturk – father of the Turks.

The Mandates – The old Ottoman lands of the Islamic Middle East, now finally separated from the Ottoman Empire, had acquired new strategic importance with the early development of oil reserves – although the scale and future importance of these were not as yet recognized. National boundaries were drawn up and the region was divided between France and Britain under the mandate of the League of Nations. This implied that the newly defined countries were destined to move towards self governing status. France was awarded Lebanon and Syria, although she had to take possession of the latter by force, and continued to rule it with considerable oppression. Britain received Palestine, Iraq, and Trans-Jordan, and she also controlled the emirates of the Persian Gulf. In 1932, Britain largely withdrew from Iraq, but the Palestinian mandate turned out to be something of a poisoned chalice.

The Founding of Israel – The objective of founding a Jewish national home in Palestine was first put forward in a Zionism Congress as early as 1897. It was to be a refuge for Jewish people who were persecuted in the pogroms of eastern Europe, and it also attracted many from minority Jewish communities within the Arab world. In 1917, the British government gave support to the project, with the contradictory provision that it should not interfere with the rights of the indigenous people. The movement was given further impetus by German persecution of the Jews under Hitler. In the post war years, large numbers of European

Jews sought entry, and the British authorities had the impossible task of reconciling the opposing interests. In 1947 the United Nations voted for the partition of Palestine in the face of opposition from the Arab states and in 1948 the British withdrew. In the ensuing war, large numbers of Arabs left their homes for refugee camps in the neighbouring countries. The Arab states refused to accept the existence of a Jewish state in the Islamic heartland. The refugees remained, unsettled, waiting to return to their homeland as Israel and her neighbours continued in a state of war.

North African Independence – After World War Two the British presence in Egypt was restricted to a defensive force in the canal zone and, by 1956, Libya, Tunisia and Morocco had shaken off foreign ties. Armed conflict centred on Algeria, where over one million French settlers resisted any move towards independence. The country was declared an integral part of metropolitan France and a bitterly fought dispute continued from 1954-62. When General de Gaulle finally decided to give independence, colonists allied with army generals and France itself was taken to the brink of civil war.

Nasser and Pan-Arabism – In 1952 a group of Egyptian army officers overthrew the monarchy. Two years later, Gamal Abdel Nasser became president of the country. His objective was to establish Egypt as the unquestioned leader of a new and more coherent Arab people. Lacking oil resources, however, Egypt remained a poor country and Nasser planned a development programme based on the construction of the Aswan High Dam on the Nile. When the Americans and British withdrew offers of funding, Nasser turned to the communist bloc for support, so introducing cold war politics into the Middle East.

In 1956 he nationalized the company which administered the Suez Canal. In October the Israelis invaded Egyptian territory, ostensibly to destroy guerilla bases and this was followed by a joint attack by the British and French on the Suez Canal zone. World opinion was outraged, and the American government applied pressure which forced the invaders to withdraw.

The Suez fiasco left Nasser as the leading figure within the Arab world, but his attempts to take this towards political union were unsuccessful. In 1967 he closed the Straits of Tiran to Israeli shipping and the Israeli army launched a 'first strike' in what has become known as the Six Day War. After a successful campaign, Israel controlled new territory, including, from Jordan, the whole West Bank of the River Jordan, and, from Syria, the tactically important Golan Heights. Jerusalem, a city of great symbolic importance to all three Semitic religions, now passed under full Israeli control. Successive Israeli governments, in time reinforced by the possession of nuclear weapons, have failed to comply with United Nations resolutions demanding withdrawal from the occupied territories. Indeed, increasing numbers of Jewish immigrants have been established in West Bank settlements. As Israel's neighbour, the Lebanon, collapsed into civil war, many Arabs resorted to international terrorism.

The Oil Crisis – In 1961 Britain withdrew from her interests 'east of Suez'. Much of the, now increasingly vital, oil production of the region, however, remained under the control of western companies. A further outbreak of hostilities between Israel and her neighbours in 1973 led the Arab countries to 'play the oilcard' by taking more direct control over their own reserves and withholding supplies from Israel's allies in the developed world. This led to an increase in price, which had a sharp effect on the world economy. The Arab nations, and other oil-producing nations, led by Saudi Arabia now organized themselves into O.P.E.C., with a view to controlling world prices. This was less successful than had been anticipated because the depression caused by the price rise restricted world demand, and Britain and Norway, opening new North Sea reserves, stood outside the cartel.

In 1978 Nasser's successor, President Sadat, made peace with Israel under American sponsorship at Camp David. This did not end the conflict within the region, but rather took Egypt out of the mainstream of Arab politics.

Iran and Islamic Fundamentalism – With Egypt returned to the American sphere of influence after Camp David, the Soviet Union turned increasingly to the radical, though mutually hostile, governments of Syria and Iraq. The United States, looking for a buffer between the Soviet Union and the oil-rich Middle East, put heavy backing behind the conservative and corrupt administration of the Shah of Iran. In 1979 discontent erupted into revolution, and the Shah was replaced by a fundamentalist regime, dominated by the Ayatollah Khomeni. This sparked a wave of Islamic fundamentalism which gave expression to pent up Arab anger at the imposition of alien values by aggressive western societies. Equally hostile to capitalist and to communist ideologies,